PULPIT FICTION

AN OBJECTIVE INVESTIGATION OF FAITH

Andrew A. Bufalo

ISBN 978-0-9845957-9-2

First Printing – February 2016
Printed in the United States of America

For Allen "Max" Woodside

Thank you for inspiring me to complete what at times seemed like an insurmountable task…

&

To Denise

Thank you for your help and patience.

"If he is infinitely good, what reason should we have to fear him? If he is infinitely wise, why should we have doubts concerning our future? If he knows all, why warn him of our needs and fatigue him with our prayers? If he is everywhere, why erect temples to him? If he is just, why fear that he will punish the creatures that he has filled with weaknesses? If grace does everything for them, what reason would he have for recompensing them? If he is all-powerful, how offend him, how resist him? If he is reasonable, how can he be angry at the blind, to whom he has given the liberty of being unreasonable? If he is immovable, by what right do we pretend to make him change his decrees? If he is inconceivable, why occupy ourselves with him? IF HE HAS SPOKEN, WHY IS THE UNIVERSE NOT CONVINCED? If the knowledge of a God is the most necessary, why is it not the most evident and the clearest?"

~ Percy Bysshe Shelley
Romantic Poet and Philosopher

Table of Contents

PULPIT FICTION

Foreword

"Every (religious) sect supposes itself in possession of all truth, and that those who differ are so far in the wrong." ~ Benjamin Franklin

This book was inspired several years ago by a simple act of credulity which demonstrated how most if not all myths and beliefs begin with an iota of truth and grow from there. The title is of course drawn from the popular 1994 Quentin Tarantino film *Pulp Fiction*, in large part because a friend of mine once confidently claimed Samuel L. Jackson's famous execution ritual in that movie incorporated a verbatim Bible verse, and while it does indeed pull something from Ezekiel 25:17 the part about the righteous man and the shepherd are not part of the biblical passage and were added by Jackson and Quentin Tarantino. In fact the only part which is similar to the actual Ezekiel passage is the end of the line "and I will strike down upon thee with great vengeance and furious anger and you will know my name is the Lord when I lay my vengeance upon thee." The rest is, well… pulpit fiction.

Do you care if your beliefs are true? I would hope so, but the word "truth" itself has been hijacked by so many belief systems it has become virtually meaningless. When someone defends their religious beliefs by saying, "there is only one truth and it happens to be mine" they obviously don't understand what the word means. Think about it. While some think salvation comes through works others think it comes through belief and still other believe it is universal. The Westboro Baptist Church thinks "God loves IEDs" and hates homosexuals while others are tolerant. In fact the Gay Christian Network believes King David and possibly even Jesus himself were gay. Catholics believe the Eucharist is the actual body of Christ in accordance with the doctrine of transubstantiation but most Protestants don't believe that or take communion. Some believe in the Prosperity Gospel and send their social security checks to charlatans like Creflo Dollar and Joyce Meyer so they can purchase private jets, while others like Mother Teresa take a vow of poverty and consider being poor to be a blessing. Young Earth Creationists believe the earth is only six thousand years old and people once walked with dinosaurs while ignoring the geological and cosmological evidence to the contrary, while more progressive Christians accept scientific proof showing our planet is 4.5 billion years old. My point? All believe they are privy to the "truth," all think everyone else is wrong and all should heed the advice of Mahatma Mohandas Gandhi who wisely observed, "There is no God higher than truth."

Egyptian, Greek, Norse and Roman mythology predated the Abrahamic religions and were once as widely believed as what is now accepted, but today are considered nothing more than myths. The Jews follow the Torah, or Pentateuch, but deny the divinity of Jesus. At the same time Christians talk about how they believe in the New Testament while for the most part trying to ignore the Old and the majority of them have read neither. Muslims consider Mohammad to be the one true prophet, believe he rode a winged horse up to Heaven and think their holy Quran, which was in part allegedly dictated to him by the Angel Gabriel in a cave, is the perfect word of Allah. In fact they believe that so strongly many of them become martyrs in order to receive seventy-two virgins in Paradise. Even so Sunnis and Shiites, the two main branches of Islam, can't agree on doctrine and routinely slaughter one another just as Catholics and Protestants have done from the Reformation to Northern Ireland.

Let's look more closely at Islam for a bit to highlight this point since its history is probably a bit unfamiliar to most readers. It was created by Muhammed in the 7th Century when he founded the first Islamic state as a theocracy in Medina, which is a city in western Saudi Arabia located north of Mecca. The Sunni branch believes after his death the first four caliphs - Muhammed's successors - rightfully took his place as leaders of Islam and recognizes their heirs as legitimate religious leaders. These heirs ruled continuously in the Arab world until the break-up of the Ottoman Empire following the end of the First World War. Shiites, in contrast, believe only the heirs of the fourth caliph, Ali (Mohammad's cousin and son-in-law) are legitimate successors of Muhammed. In a nutshell, Muhammed's followers could not agree on whether to choose bloodline successors or the leaders most likely to follow the tenets of the faith… and they slaughter each other as a result.

In 931 the Twelfth Imam disappeared, and this was a seminal event in the history of Shiite Muslims. According to R. Scott Appleby, a professor of history at the University of Notre Dame, "Shiite Muslims, who are concentrated in Iran, Iraq and Lebanon (believe they) had suffered the loss of divinely guided political leadership at the time of the Imam's disappearance and not until the ascendancy of Ayatollah Ruhollah

Khomeini in 1978 did they believe they had once again begun to live under the authority of a legitimate religious figure." Another difference between Sunnis and Shiites has to do with the Mahdi, "the rightly-guided one" whose role is to bring a just global caliphate into being. As historian Timothy Furnish has written, "The major difference is that for Shiites he has already been here and will return from hiding, while for Sunnis he has yet to emerge into history - a comeback vs. a coming out, if you will." In a special 9-11 edition of the *Journal of American History* Appleby explained the Shiite outlook is far different from the Sunnis', a difference which is highly significant. For Sunni Muslims, who comprise approximately ninety percent of the Muslim world, the loss of the caliphate after World War I was devastating in light of the hitherto continuous historic presence of the caliph, the guardian of Islamic law and the Islamic state. Sunni fundamentalist leaders thereafter emerged in nations such as Egypt and India, where contact with Western political structures provided them with a model to imitate as they struggled after 1924 to provide a viable alternative to the caliphate. In 1928, four years after the abolishment of the caliphate, Egyptian schoolteacher Hasan Al-Banna founded the first Islamic fundamentalist movement in the Sunni world, the Muslim Brotherhood (al-Ikhwan al-Muslimun). Al-Banna was appalled by "the wave of atheism and lewdness (that) engulfed Egypt" following World War I. The victorious Europeans had "imported their half-naked women into these regions together with their liquors, their theatres, their dance halls, their amusements, their stories, their newspapers, their novels, their whims, their silly games and their vices." Suddenly the very heart of the Islamic world was penetrated by European "schools and scientific and cultural institutes that cast doubt and heresy into the souls of its sons and taught them how to demean themselves, disparage their religion and their fatherland, divest themselves of their traditions and beliefs and to regard as sacred anything Western." Most distressing to Al-Banna and his followers was what they saw as the rapid moral decline of the religious establishment including the leading sheikhs or religious scholars at Al-Azhar, the grand mosque and center of Islamic learning in Cairo. The clerical leaders had become compromised and corrupted by their alliance with the indigenous ruling elites who had succeeded the European colonial masters.

Osama bin Laden was a Sunni Muslim and to him the end of the reign of the caliphs in the 1920s was catastrophic as he made clear in a videotape made after 9-11. On the tape broadcast by Al-Jazeera on October 7, 2001 he proclaimed, "What America is tasting now is only a copy of what we have tasted... our Islamic nation has been tasting the same for more (than) eighty years of humiliation and disgrace, its sons killed and their blood spilled, its sanctities desecrated."

Juan Cole, a well-known historian of the Middle East, has pointed out on his blog *Informed Comment* that the split between Sunni and Shiites in Iraq is of relatively recent origin, writing, "I see a lot of pundits and politicians saying Sunnis and Shiites in Iraq have been fighting for a millennium (but) we need better history than that. The Shiite tribes of the south probably only converted to Shiism in the past two hundred years, and Sunni-Shiite riots per se were rare in 20th Century Iraq."

After the eleventh Imam died in 874 and his young son was said to have disappeared from the funeral Shiites in particular came to see the child as a Messiah who had been hidden from the public by Allah and ever since the largest sect of Shiites, known as "twelvers," have been preparing for his return. So how did the violence start? In 656 Ali's supporters killed the third caliph and soon after the Sunnis killed Ali's son Husain. Fighting continued, but Sunnis emerged victorious over the Shiites and came to revere the caliphate for its strength and piety while Shiites focused on developing their religious beliefs through their imams. The question here is who is correct, if anyone, and why? As you can see Islam is far from the "revealed truth" which Muslims claim it to be.

Contrast all that with Hinduism, which is the predominant religion of the Indian subcontinent and widely considered the "oldest living religion." A good case has been made for its Vedas (Hindu sacred writings) as being the source document for much of the Bible, but if you are a Christian you will most likely deny the Bible has anything to do with them. The question is how do you know? Have you ever read them? Almost certainly not. And what do you know about the religion itself? Probably not much. What about other religions? For instance Mormons believe Jesus once walked in America and prophet Joseph Smith was given the *Book of Mormon* by the Angel Moroni via some golden plates (which were conveniently taken back to Heaven) and some magical seer stones. Africa is filled with a variety of animist religions and Native Americans have their own. Scientologists believe humans are immortal extraterrestrials called 'thetans' who were brought here by an alien named Xenu a trillion years ago and are now trapped on earth. Zoroastrianism, founded by Zarathustra in Persia and still practiced by over two hundred thousand people, may have been the world's first monotheistic faith and most religious historians believe Jewish, Christian and Muslim beliefs were derived from it.

Now take a minute to read back over some of the beliefs just cited, and keep in mind due to space limitations I have only scratched the surface. I'm betting, if you are religious, you don't agree with or believe in 99% of those things. We can agree they are wrong, and in some cases crazy. Yet all are labeled as "truth" by someone. In the end the only real difference between a believer and an atheist is the latter doesn't believe in 100% of them, and if a religious person stops to think about why they don't believe in the other 99% they should understand why others don't believe what they do. Put simply, what makes so many people think they have somehow found the "one truth" amongst thousands of religions and sects while billions and billions of other people either believe in different things or interpret the same scriptures in a totally different way?

If there really is one true God it stands to reason everyone would believe in the same one, doesn't it? Yet even the Bible speaks of "other gods" on a number of occasions. If it was simply a matter of being either a believer or a non-believer theist arguments would be much more credible, but the reality through the ages has been this - before a discussion about belief (let alone truth) can begin it is necessary to determine which god someone is referring to because at one time or another humans beings have worshipped deities named Aditya, Aesir, Agni, Airmid, Allah, Amon, Anat, Andhrimnir, Angrboda, Antariksha, Anubis, Aphrodite, Apollo, Ares, Artemis, Artio, Asherah, Ashwinis, Astarte, Astrild, Athena, Atla, Atum, Audhumla, Ba'al Hadad, Baalat, Baal-Hammon, Bacchus, Balder, Balor, Bellona, Bes, Beyla, Borghild, Bragi, Brahma, Branwen, Brihaspati, Brono, Bylgia, Camalus, Ceres, Cerunnos, Ch'eng-Huang, Chu Jung, Cupid, Cyhiraeth, Dagon, Dagur, Demeter, Diana, Dionysus, Disen, Dishas, Druantia, Duamutef, Dyaus, Eir, El Elyon, Elli, Erh-Lang, Eshumn, Faunus, Fenrir, Flora, Forseti, Freya, Freyr, Frigg, Fu-Hsing, Ganesha, Gefion, Gep, Gerd, Giobhniu, Hades, Hapi, Hapy, Heimdall, Hel, Helios, Hephaestus, Hera, Hermes, Hermod, Hestia, Hod, Holler, Horus, Hou-chi, Hsuan-T'ien-Shang-Ti, Idun, Imsety, Indra, I-ti, Janus, Jord, Jormungand, Juno, Jupiter, Kalki, Kari, Kathirat, Khensu, Khnum, Kothar, Krishna, Kuan Ti, Kue'i-Hsing, Kurma, Kvasir, Laga, Lao-Tien-Yeh, Lares, Lei-Kung, Libintia, Llyr, Lofn, Loki, Lotan, Lugh, Lu-Hsing, Lu-Pan, Maeve, Magni, Maia, Manannan, Mani, Marduk, Margawse, Mars, Marutas, Matsya, Mebd, Melqart, Mercury, Mider, Miming, Mimir, Min, Minerva, Mithras, Modi, Moloch, Moordha, Morrigan, Mot, Narasimha, Nemain, Neptune, Njord, Norns, Nott, Odin, Ops, Osiris, Pales, Parashurama, Persephone, Pluto, Pomona, Poseidon, Prajapati, Prithvi, Proserpine, Ptah, Pusha, Qadeshtu,

Qebehsenuef, Ra, Rama, Ran, Resheph, Rudra, Saga, Saturn, Savitr, Selene, Seth, Shachar, Shalim, Shamayim, Shemesh, Shiva, Shu, Sif, Sjofn, Skadi, Sleipnir, Sobek, Sobek-Ra, Sol, Soma, Syn, Tehwom, Thor, Thoth, Tu-Ti, Tyr, Ull, Vali, Vamuna, Vanir, Var, Varuna, Vayu, Venus, Vertumnus, Vesta, Vidar, Vishnu, Vishvedavas, Vulcan, Yam-Nahar, Yarikh, Zedek and Zeus - and this list just scratches the surface.

The point here is if you happen to be a follower of one of the current major or even minor religions how do you explain the "existence" of all of those gods which presumably you do not believe in? Where did they come from? I think we can agree they were and/or are inventions of the human imagination, which begs the question what makes your god any different? Try to answer that question objectively… if you can.

What about Paganism, and how is it different from "regular" religions? The definition of what it is can be quite broad or progressively narrow with the broadest definition including all religions but the three Abrahamic faiths - Christianity, Islam and Judaism. To a member of those religions a Pagan can be anyone who is not a member of their particular church, but as you tighten the definition you must eliminate the Dharmic religions of Hinduism, Buddhism, Jainism and Sikhism as well. Whittled down to just those who call themselves Pagans you have the Wiccans, Celtic Druids, witches, Goddess worshippers and recreations of other ancient polytheistic religions such as those from ancient Egypt, Greece, Rome and the Norse and for this reason the term "Neopaganism" is a more accurate way to describe modern Pagans.

It should be pointed out that Neopaganism typically does not include Satan worshippers, which is a common misconception. It is generally polytheistic, with gods ranging from divine beings to things in nature. Spiritualism and divinity are crucial aspects because despite its separation from the world's major religions Neopagan faith is very much dependent upon supernatural beings or paranormal forces and energies, although in some cases Neopagans have advertised their faith as a way designed to reject the inconsistencies and suspensions of science required by the major religions and yet still remain spiritual. Despite that, the spiritual aspects of Paganism are equally at odds with science because the mystical forces they claim exist are still unmeasurable, undetectable paranormal entities and you can't have it both ways.

One popular allure of Paganism is the embracing of free sex and public nudity and Wiccans have even institutionalized nudity, calling it "skyclad." That makes one wonder if there is an obligation for those who are into skyclad self-expression and disestablishmentarianism to embrace the paranormal by joining a Pagan religion? To put it another way, does the average modern Celtic Druid truly and profoundly believe in the fundamental doctrines of his religion such as occult magic and reincarnation, or does he just enjoy the company of naked people with an interesting philosophy?

Human beings are credulous by nature. For instance many automatically accept as true internet rumors about chariot remains being found in the Red Sea because it reinforces their desires, but that has been proven to be a hoax. The same is the case with rumors of Noah's Ark, the Tower of Babel and the Ark of the Covenant being "found." They weren't found, any more than Bigfoot, the Loch Ness Monster and Elvis have been located. There are so many credulous people in the world who desperately want to believe these things it is easy to dupe them. As a case in point consider the example of the "giant" whose "discovery" back in the 1800s supposedly validated Bible passages such as Genesis 6:4 which tells of the Nephilim, which are said to be the giant offspring of fallen angels and human women, as well as the more well-known Goliath who was slain by David - although it is interesting to note Goliath's stature grew at the hand of scribes with the oldest manuscripts, the Dead Sea Scrolls and 4th Century Septuagint manuscripts, giving his height as "four cubits and a span" (6 feet 9 inches) while later manuscripts increase this to "six cubits and a span" (9 feet 9 inches). This is yet another example of the evolving "unchanged word."

As for the aforementioned giant hoax, George Hull of Binghamton, New York studied archeology and paleontology in the 1800s and over a period of time contemplated how to pull off a ruse. Many evangelists at that time had been preaching there were once giants on the earth (and some still do), so in June of 1868 Hull traveled to Fort Dodge, Iowa where there was a gypsum quarry he had recalled seeing two years earlier. He had noticed dark blue streaks running through the soft lime rock which resembled human veins and, realizing this appearance was tailor-made for his hoax and such rock was easy to carve, hired a group of quarry workers to cut off a slab measuring twelve feet long, four feet wide and two feet thick.

He then had the slab of gypsum shipped by rail to Chicago where he hired a stone cutter named Edward Burghardt to carve a giant and he, along with his two assistants, was sworn to secrecy. The instructions were to carve the figure as if it had died in great pain and the final result was an eerie figure, slightly twisted in apparent agony with his right hand clutching his stomach. All of the details were there - toenails, fingernails, nostrils, sex organs and so forth and a needlepoint mallet was even used to add authentic-looking skin pores. When the carving was done sulfuric acid and ink were used, possibly smudged like printer's ink, to make the figure look aged.

Once the giant was finished Hull had it shipped by rail to the farm of his cousin William Newell which was located near the town of Cardiff, New York. In the dead of night Hull, Newell and his oldest son buried the figure between the barn and house and Hull said he would let them know in about a year what the next stage would be, and as luck would have it about six months later on a nearby farm some million-year-old fossil bones were dug up. When newspapers around the country reported the finding Hull was filled with glee, and one year after burying the giant he sent word to his cousin to start the next stage of the hoax. Newell then hired two laborers to dig a new well near his home and directed them to the exact spot he wanted the well dug. He then went back into the house to wait and sure enough later that day the laborers rushed in to announce they had discovered a giant turned to stone, after which they joined both Newells in carefully excavating the area surrounding the giant.

News of this amazing discovery spread throughout the valley, soon wagon loads of neighbors streamed into the farm to see the giant and by mid-afternoon Newell had erected a tent around the "grave" and started charging twenty-five cents admission. Two days later the *Syracuse Journal* printed an article about the discovery, the greedy Newell raised the price to fifty cents and soon a stage coach company began to make four round trips a day from Syracuse to the Newell farm. Thousands came every day and among the visitors were clergymen, college professors and distinguished scientists... and before long the experts' opinions split into two theories with one side, comprised primarily of the clergy, claiming it was a true fossilized human giant and the other side pronouncing it an authentic ancient statue - but no one asserted that it was a fake.

About ten days after the discovery and around the time the "Cardiff Giant" (as the papers had named it) started receiving national attention Hull sold two-thirds interest in the giant for $30,000 to a five-man syndicate in Syracuse headed by a banker named David Hannum who moved the giant to an exhibition hall in Syracuse and raised the admission price to a dollar a head. Unbeknownst to them, famed showman P. T. Barnum had sent an agent to see the giant and make an assessment and the day the representative saw the figure the crowds were abnormally large with about three thousand people attending. The agent wired the news back to Barnum who instructed him to make an offer of $50,000 to buy it, but Hannum turned it down.

The Cardiff Giant became the most talked about exhibit in the nation and Barnum wanted to display it himself while the attraction was still a hot topic of the day, but rather than upping his offer he hired a crew of workers to carve a giant of his own. Within a short time Barnum unveiled his giant and claimed Hannum had sold him the original and was now displaying a fake. Thousands of people flocked to see Barnum's giant and many newspapers carried the version of the story he had given them. It was at this point Hannum (not Barnum, as many think today), still under the impression his giant was authentic, was ironically quoted as saying, "There's a sucker born every minute" in referring to the thousands of fools who had paid money to see Barnum's fake and not his "authentic" one. Hannum brought a lawsuit against Barnum for calling his giant a fake, but when it came to trial Hull stepped forward and confessed the Cardiff Giant was a hoax so the judge ruled Barnum could not be sued for calling Hannum's giant a fake since it was after all - and thereafter Hannum's name was all but lost to history.

The same sort of people who bought into the Cardiff Giant because it "proved" Scripture also make rationalizations about other uncomfortable realities or simply turn a blind eye to things which might undermine their beliefs, such as contradictions in the Bible. They insist there are none, when all one need do is read the four Gospels side by side to see that is not the case because even though they supposedly describe the same events each is different - and that includes the synoptic Gospels which were largely copied from one another. That's not surprising, since none of the writers were eyewitnesses as is often claimed (more on that later) and in actual fact the first Gospel wasn't written until decades after the events supposedly took place. One example of a contradiction - did Joseph and Mary flee with baby Jesus to Egypt to avoid the Slaughter of the Innocents by King Herod as one Gospel says, or simply go back to Nazareth as another claims? That is one of hundreds, and yet many Christians who have probably never read the Bible for themselves are absolutely certain the Gospels contain nothing but "the gospel truth."

The bottom line is the word "truth" has been coopted to mean your particular set of beliefs as opposed to what all other people believe or don't believe. I'm not telling anyone not to believe what they do if it makes them feel comfortable, helps them deal with life and tragedy through a placebo effect and/or mitigates their natural fear of death by promising a great beyond for which there is zero evidence - what I'm faith is true while the beliefs of others are false... without any investigation at all. Their opinions about religion are obviously based more upon feelings engendered by their culture than upon critical thinking based upon knowledge. This is why it is important for truth-seeking people to step back from their conditioning and look at issues objectively or, as Mark Twain put it, "I must studiously and faithfully unlearn a great many things I have somehow absorbed."

Let's now take a look at the nature of delusion so we can better understand why it happens. Since there is not a single piece of empirical evidence showing God is real and a mountain of evidence showing he is imaginary, God falls into the same category as Leprechauns - he is a mythological being which has sprung from human imagination. In other words religion, in all its forms, is a delusion. I understand the word "delusion" is a bit too direct for some people and may perhaps even be interpreted as being a bit insulting, however it is the correct word to use. The dictionary defines delusion in the following way: "A false belief strongly held in spite of invalidating evidence."

The invalidating evidence is all around us and chances are you have known it for many years but have been unable to face it. That's understandable. It can be terrifying to face reality. Think back to your childhood and the story of *The Emperor's New Clothes*. The Emperor had been convinced he was wearing a beautiful suit of new clothes in much the same way people have been convinced to believe in invisible gods and mythological stories throughout the ages, and it took someone speaking up and stating the obvious for him to face the reality that he was actually naked. To illustrate this point let's consider a few examples of fanatical religious delusion from the past which you, as a modern and intelligent person, would probably never have accepted but which were widely accepted by believers of the time.

A good example is the case of Cotton Mather, who was one of the most influential men in the early American colonies and had much to do with the witchcraft persecutions of his day. In 1692, when the magistrates appealed to the Boston clergy for advice in regard to the witchcraft cases in Salem, he drafted the reply upon which their prosecutions were based and in 1689 wrote *Memorable Providences Relating to Witchcraft and Possessions* - and even his earlier diaries have many entries showing his belief in diabolical possession and his fear and hatred of it. Keep in mind at that time witches were considered to be real and not just something seen in costume on Halloween, and next to the Bible the most influential and venerated book in Christian history was the *Malleus Maleficarum* or "Hammer of Witches" which was a step-by-step tutorial in how to torture "witches" and "sorcerers."

Mather believed the New World had been the undisturbed realm of Satan long before the settlements were made in Massachusetts and considered it natural that the Devil should make a peculiar effort to bring moral destruction on Godly invaders. He used prayer and fasting to deliver himself from evil enchantment, and when he saw ecstatic and mystical visions promising him the Lord's help and great usefulness in the Lord's work he feared these revelations might be of diabolic origin so he used his great influence to bring the suspected persons to trial and punishment. He attended the witch trials, investigated many of the cases himself and wrote sermons on witchcraft, notably *Memorable Providences* and *The Wonders of the Invisible World*, which increased the excitement of the people and contributed to a mass delusion. Accordingly, when the persecutions had ceased and the reaction set in much of the blame was rightly laid upon Mather and in 1700 the liberal leaders of Congregationalism in Boston assisted Robert Calef in the preparation of *More Wonders of the Invisible World,* which was a powerful criticism of Cotton Mather's part in the delusion at Salem - but the damage had been done. Just ask the falsely accused witches who had been executed in accordance with biblical instructions.

Mather himself believed strongly in God and the power of prayer and was sure his prayers were heard, but once his teachings were discredited his grief and depression grew and his later years were filled with many sorrows. Despite being a true believer he lost much of his prestige in the Church as his congregation dwindled, his son Increase turned out to be a ne'er-do-well, four of his children and his second wife died in November of 1713, his favorite daughter Katherine died in 1716 and his third wife went mad in 1719.

If you think such things are confined to the distant past you would be wrong. Kevani Kanda was just six years old when her family accused her of being a witch in 1994. She was in actuality being molested by a relative and the trauma made her wet the bed and sleepwalk, but instead of trying to find out what was wrong Kanda's Christian family was convinced she was possessed by an evil spirit - so for the next five years she was starved, forced to eat her own vomit, beaten repeatedly and given suppositories containing spices to "get rid of the evil spirits." The torture occurred in a London suburb, and she wasn't alone. London's Metropolitan Police announced that reports of abuse where the child is accused of being a witch or possessed by an evil spirit are on the rise, and fourteen years after the force recorded its first allegation of such an incident there were at least twenty-seven cases during 2014 alone - and that is scratching the surface. Most involve pastors or religious leaders in African communities who have incorporated elements of witchcraft or spirit possession into their version of fundamentalist Christianity as these beliefs are widely held in countries such as the Democratic Republic of Congo where Kanda was born, and these pastors often tell families a period of bad luck or even an illness has been caused by a child being possessed. Kanda returned to the Congo for a BBC documentary in 2013 and was shocked by what was considered acceptable in mainstream society. Asked how far the abuse went she said, "How far can your imagination go? I witnessed a four-year-old old boy brought to the church by his mother because he was playing too rough with his brother. The pastor told her the behavior was the result of him being possessed and that he was a witch." The boy endured a four-day "deliverance" in which he was starved, forced to drink hot palm oil and prevented from using the bathroom, with the adults stepping on his little body while saying they were "stepping on the spirits."

In the past decade and a half London's most high-profile cases have been linked to Christian groups with roots in Western and Sub-Saharan Africa, but cases involving other faiths such as Islam and Hinduism have emerged more recently as authorities have delved deeper. Detective Superintendent Terry Sharpe stated, "To most people accusations of witchcraft may seem so bizarre that they say, 'It can't possibly be happening,' but the more you come to learn about the cultures and beliefs of other communities, particularly now that they are moving all around the world, the more people learn about it and have the confidence to report it." Sadly that did not help eight-year-old Victoria Climbié, after whom the Victoria Climbié Foundation is named. Her guardians tortured and killed her in 2010 after claiming she was possessed by a demon. The Ivory Coast-born girl was burned with cigarettes and forced to sleep in a sealed garbage bag in the bath until she eventually died. Another high-profile case in London was that of fifteen-year-old Kristy Bamu, who was drowned in the bath on Christmas Day 2010 by his Congo-born sister and her boyfriend who claimed he was possessed.

If you've seen the 1973 movie *The Exorcist* you at least have some idea of what exorcism is all about. It has to do with ridding a human being of diabolic possession, is typically associated with Roman Catholic beliefs and if the movie is any indication it's very, very scary. You may remember with a shudder the teenage girl whose head spun around, her body in convulsions, and her voice that of a demon spewing curses and obscenities while the battered priest fought the devil to save her soul. Believe it or not this Hollywood version of an exorcism is based on a real-life exorcism performed on a Maryland boy in 1949, and priests are still performing exorcisms today.

Is exorcism real, are the subject and the exorcist unconsciously acting out roles from the movie, or are there other explanations for what some people call "possession"? The *Catholic Encyclopedia* defines exorcism as "the act of driving out, or warding off, demons or evil spirits from persons, places or things which are believed to be possessed or infested by them or are liable to become victims or instruments of their malice." There are several types in the Roman Catholic Church - Baptismal, Simple and Real - with the "Real Exorcism" being what most of us envision of when we think of the practice. In this case the priest-exorcist is dealing with a human being who is thought to be possessed by Satan. According to the Church, telltale signs of demonic possession include speaking or understanding languages which the person has never learned (different from speaking in tongues, which is considered a sign of religious ecstasy rather than possession), knowing and revealing things the person has no earthly way of knowing, demonstrating physical strength beyond the person's natural physical makeup and having a violent aversion to God, the Virgin Mary, the cross and other images of Catholic faith.

If you do a Google search for the word "exorcism" you'll find ads for exorcists such as Wanda Pratnicka, who claims "thirty years' experience with 25,000 successfully performed exorcisms." This makes demonic possession seem like a pretty common occurrence, but to the Roman Catholic Church it's rare since it only finds "true" demonic possession in about one out of every five thousand reported cases. Official numbers are hard to come by, but the journal *American Exorcism* reports that in 1996 the Catholic Church appointed ten priests to the position of exorcist in the United States, bringing the total number to eleven, with the worldwide number at somewhere between one and three hundred - while other reports claim there are three to four hundred official exorcists in Italy alone. There are also priests who are not official exorcists but claim to have permission from their local bishop to perform exorcisms at their discretion. Clearly the exorcism ritual has made a big comeback after being nearly extinct throughout most of the 20th Century.

Traditionally, Catholic exorcists undergo very little specific training to aid them in their job. While they learn a great deal about the devil and the risks and manifestations of evil, exorcism itself is not a specialized area of study in seminary school. What they do know they know from their experience in the role of priest and from the Roman Catholic Rite of Exorcism, which is the official document detailing the prayers and steps to be employed, however things are starting to change. Official exorcists of the Catholic Church formed their own organization in 1992 and the International Association of Exorcists holds biannual meetings in Rome and even sends out a quarterly newsletter to its members in which exorcists tell of particularly difficult or interesting cases and swap tricks of the trade. In 2005 Rome's Regina Apostolorum Pontifical Academy (a university connected to the Vatican) even began offering a class on exorcism.

The controversy surrounding exorcisms exists mainly on two related fronts - the huge "exorcism for profit" ministries which have sprung up in the last couple of decades, and the "psychology vs. religion" debate which sprang up with the advent of psychiatry in the 1800s. In the first, the rise of money-making "exorcism ministries" around the world leads many people who might otherwise reserve judgment to outright reject the validity of the Catholic view of possession and exorcism even though the exorcisms performed by these unofficial exorcists are not connected to the Church. A particularly popular ministry in the United States, Bob Larson Ministries, televises its weekly conferences and in these mass exorcisms - for which large groups can receive a "family rate" on tickets (donations on top of the ticket price are not required, but are welcome) - Larson exorcises the demons of an auditorium full of people.

Where one person sees possession and pulls out his rite of exorcism, another sees mental illness and pulls out the DSM IV (Diagnostic and Statistical Manual of Mental Disorders). This is probably the greatest debate surrounding the practice, because there may be earthly explanations for behavior the Church considers evidence of diabolical possession as several psychological disorders including Tourette Syndrome and schizophrenia can produce the types of behavior seen in "possessed" people. People with epilepsy can suddenly go into convulsions when having a seizure, Tourette Syndrome causes involuntary movements and vocal outbursts and schizophrenia involves auditory and visual hallucinations, paranoia, delusions and sometimes violent behavior. Psychological issues such as low self-esteem and narcissism can also cause a person to act out the role of "possessed person" in order to gain attention. In a case where the subject is in fact suffering from mental illness, the Church is doing harm by labeling the person possessed if it prevents them from seeking the medical treatment he or she requires. Even Cardinal Jorge Arturo Medina Estevez, introducing the *New Rite for Exorcisms* to the press in 1999, responded to the conflict by saying, "...It often happens that simple people confuse somatic problems with diabolical influence, but not everything can be attributed to the devil."

There is considerable documentation of the harm done by exorcisms. One widely reported incident took place in June of 2005 in Tanacu, Romania in which a priest and several nuns in a Romanian Orthodox convent believed Maricia Irina Cornici, a twenty-three-year-old nun who lived in the convent, to be possessed. Their solution was to carry out an exorcism ritual where they tied her to a cross, pushed a towel into her mouth and left her alone without food and water with the intent of driving out the demon inhabiting her body. Cornici died after three days, and subsequent investigation revealed the young woman had schizophrenia. Similarly, Pentecostal ministers in San Francisco pummeled a woman to death in 1995 as they tried to drive out her demons, and then there is the well-known case of Anneliese Michel. She was a twenty-three-year-old who had her first psychiatric episode at the age of sixteen and suffered from depression, epileptic seizures and various hallucinations. In 1973 her zealous Catholic family, who believed she was possessed by Satan, recruited two priests who performed the exorcism ritual sixty-seven times on the mentally ill woman. She weighed just sixty-nine pounds at the time of her death, and the 2005 film *The Exorcism of Emily Rose* is said to be based on her life. In 1997 a Korean Christian woman was stomped to death in Glendale, California, and in the Bronx section of New York City a five-year-old girl died after being forced to swallow a mixture containing ammonia and vinegar and having her mouth taped shut. In 1998 a seventeen-year-old girl in Sayville, New York was suffocated by her mother with a plastic bag in an effort to destroy a demon inside her, and in 2001 a thirty-seven-year old woman named Joanna Lee was strangled to death in an exorcism by a Korean church minister working in New Zealand. The minister, Luke Lee, was found guilty of manslaughter. More recently, in May of 2015 Zakieya Latrice Avery was charged with two counts of first degree murder and two counts of the attempted first degree murder of her own children in Germantown, Maryland after an exorcism gone wrong in which one-year-old Norell Harris and two-year-old Zyana Harris were found dead with multiple stab wounds and Avery's two other children, five-year-old Taniya and eight-year-old Martello Harris, were severely injured. Delusion driven by superstition is clearly harmful.

Since the Salem Witch Trials, as well as the more recent examples cited, may be considered just "small delusions" by some, let's look at a similar persecution which was much larger in scope. Tomás de Torquemada was a 15th Century Spanish Dominican friar, first Inquisitor General of Spain, confessor to Isabella I of Castile and was described by Spanish chronicler Sebastián de Olmedo as "the hammer of heretics, the light of Spain, the saviour of his country and the honour of his order." He is best known for his campaign against the crypto-Jews and crypto-Muslims of Spain and as a chief supporter of the Alhambra Decree which expelled the Jews from Spain in 1492. Concerning the number of "autos-de-fé" - which translates to "act of faith," the ritual of public penance and execution for condemned heretics and apostates which took place once the Spanish or Portuguese Inquisition decided their punishment - during Torquemada's tenure as Inquisitor General, the consensus among scholars is about two thousand people were burned at the stake by the Inquisition in Spain between 1480 and 1530. That is forty persons per year, or one person approximately every nine days.

Every Spanish Christian over the age of twelve (for girls) and fourteen (for boys) was accountable to the Inquisition and those who had converted from Judaism or Islam but were suspected of secretly practicing their old rites, as well as others holding or acting on religious views contrary to Catholicism, were targeted. In fact anyone who spoke against the Inquisition could fall under suspicion as did Saints Teresa of Avila and John of the Cross, but since secrecy was one of the keys to the workings of the Inquisition Torquemada's manual of instructions *Copilacion de las Instruciones del Offico de la Sancta Inquisicion* did not appear publicly in print until 1576 when it was published in Madrid.

So hated did Torquemada become that at one point he traveled with a bodyguard of fifty mounted guards and two-hundred-fifty armed men, and after fifteen years as Spain's Grand Inquisitor he died in 1498. Due to his role in the Spanish Inquisition Torquemada's name has become a byword for fanaticism in the service of the Catholic religion, and in 1832 his tomb was ransacked and his bones were stolen and burnt to ashes - but the damage of his delusion had already been done.

To give a broad perspective on the struggle between science and religious dogma consider the case of Galileo Galilei. In 1610 Galileo looked at Jupiter through his telescope, discovered he could see four moons and concluded if moons orbited Jupiter then not everything orbited the Earth as the Catholic Church taught. The motions of the planets in our skies now made sense to him, but only if the theories of Copernicus were true and the Earth and other planets orbited the sun. This was what Galileo taught, and in 1616 he was a subject of the Inquisition. They banned him from teaching this idea which was opposed to the "true faith" and contrary to Holy Scripture, but instead Galileo wrote a book. He was called to Rome in 1632 by the Catholic Church's Inquisition and told to recant his heretical ideas, and keep in mind this was no simple request by the Church as the Inquisition had already executed Giordano Bruno, a freethinking Italian Dominican friar, philosopher, mathematician and astronomer for espousing similar theories. In 1600 Christian authorities in Rome had taken Bruno out of the dungeon where he had been held for eight years, drove a nail through his tongue as punishment for his "lies," tied him to a metal post, put wood and some of his books under his feet and burned him to death. Bruno's "crime" was writing ideas which Catholic leaders didn't like - specifically that the Earth revolves around the sun, the sun is a star, there might be other worlds with intelligent beings on them and other "crazy" ideas. For these heretical notions the Catholic Church punished this brilliant man with an agonizingly slow death, but of course Bruno was not the only man executed by Christians for such ideas as at least seventy-seven others were either burned alive or hanged by the Inquisition in Rome between 1553 and 1600.

Over the centuries millions have been killed in religious wars or executed for heresy, which often simply meant being the "wrong" type of Christian, although sometimes it was a more explicit heresy which threatened the church's monopoly on "truth." For example Italian freethinker Lucilio Vanini suggested the pre-Darwinian idea that humans were related to (*not* "descended from") apes, and in 1618 he was tried in France and found guilty of atheism and witchcraft. He had his tongue cut out, was hanged and his body was burned as was customary with all heretics.

Not to be outdone, in Spain the Inquisition killed over 340,000 during a period of four centuries. Galileo, for his part, knew what he was up against. For the crime of heresy the Inquisition could put him in a dungeon and torture or even execute him, so after a long trial during which Cardinal Bellarmine ironically stated, "To assert that the earth revolves around the sun is as erroneous as to claim that Jesus was not born of a virgin" (more on that other claim later) he obediently got down on his knees and recanted - but even after recanting he was still sentenced to house arrest for the rest of his life. The Catholic Church officially condemned helio-centrism, the theory which says the Earth revolves around the sun, thirty-one years later when Pope Alexander VII banned all books which affirmed the Earth's motion, but even as powerful as the Church was it could not hold back the tidal wave of scientific discovery forever. The Church eventually lost its battle over their view of the universe but it took them over three hundred years to admit it and in 1992, after twelve years of deliberations mind you, they grudgingly noted Galileo had been right in supporting the Copernican theories. I suppose it took that long since the Church's official decision against Galileo had embarrassingly stated, "The doctrine that the earth is neither the center of the universe nor immovable, but moves even with a daily rotation, is absurd, and both philosophically and theologically false, and at the least an error of faith." However no such reprieve has been given for Bruno and his writings, which have since been proven correct as I'm sure you will agree, are amazingly still on the Vatican's list of forbidden texts. In fact Pope John Paul II even refused to apologize for the Catholic Church torturing and killing the poor man.

A more recent and obvious example of group delusion is the Westboro Baptist Church, an independent Baptist Church known for its extreme stance against homosexuality and protest activities which include picketing military and celebrity funerals and the desecration of the American flag. The church is widely described as a hate group and is monitored as such by organizations such as the Anti-Defamation League and Southern Poverty Law Center. Active since 1955, headquartered in a residential neighborhood on the west side of Topeka not far from the Kansas State Capitol and until his recent death headed by Pastor Fred Phelps, WBC consists mostly of members of his large family which numbered seventy-one members as of 2007.

The church describes itself as following Primitive Baptist and Calvinist principles, although mainstream Primitive Baptists have rejected both the WBC and Phelps. Phelps' followers picket approximately six locations every day, including many in Topeka and some events farther afield (on Sundays up to fifteen churches may receive pickets) and by their own count WBC has conducted a total of over 30,000 pickets in all fifty states.

Westboro Baptist Church considers membership in most religious groups such as the Roman Catholic Church or Islam as being akin to devil worship and claims those other churches are "Satanic frauds preaching Arminian lies." In addition all non-Christian entities, non-

Protestant Christian churches and all Protestant Christian churches which do not strongly condemn homosexuality are said to be sending their members to Hell. The Church bases its work around the belief expressed by its best known slogan (which is also the address of its primary website) "God Hates Fags," asserting every tragedy in the world is linked to homosexuality and more specifically to society's increasing tolerance and acceptance of the so-called homosexual agenda. The group maintains God hates gays above all other kinds of sinners and that homosexuality should be a capital crime punishable by death. Their views on homosexuality are partially based on teachings found in the Old Testament, specifically Leviticus 18:22 and 20:13, which they interpret to mean homosexual behavior is detestable and homosexuals should be put to death, respectively.

Westboro Baptist refers to Catholic priests as vampires and talks of them sucking semen out of male children's genitals much like vampires suck blood from their victims. It also called Pope Benedict XVI such epithets as "The Godfather of Pedophiles." In relation to the war in Iraq a WBC flier said, "In His retaliatory rage God is killing Americans with Muslim IEDs: 'Saying, touch not my anointed, and do my prophets no harm.' 1 Chron 16:22." They also believe Barack Obama is the Antichrist and formed an Unholy Trinity with Satan and Pope Benedict XVI, whom they believed was the False Prophet.

So, you may ask, what is the purpose of mentioning such a deluded group? The point is the members of WBC are convinced they are privy to the "truth" (there's that word again) and the rest of us are the deluded ones, and for evidence cite their own interpretation of Scripture. This is an example of what Archbishop Tutu is talking about in his story (related in a subsequent chapter) of the drunk who crossed the street. Also keep in mind Westboro Baptist, as extreme as it may be, is not the only fringe religious group which thinks it and it alone has found the "truth" - far from it.

Take for example the "Community of Divine Innocence," which has followers in nearly fifty countries. That order puts up posters near churches of other denominations and its members have bumper stickers on their cars which read, "Aborted children are in Heaven, martyrs to the Truth!" Not to beat a dead horse, but there's that pesky word "truth" again. The order was established in 1984 when a freelance jewelry designer named Patricia de Menezes claimed she saw the Virgin Mary appear in a pine tree. She has since been campaigning for the Catholic Church to proclaim aborted babies as martyrs and her group's website publishes a dialogue between de Menezes and Jesus where the latter calls abortion a "wholesale slaughter." According to the order Jesus spoke to de Menezes and said children are "put to death because their presence is inconvenient," and in another "conversation" de Menezes was supposedly visited by "Infant Jesus," but despite these "visitations" she was dismissed as a fraud by the Vatican in 2007 - although how they made that determination is unclear. It seems to me this woman's testimony is just as creditable and is based upon just as much evidence as one which might be made by me, you, a person claiming alien abduction or for that matter any of the biblical prophets... so the Church should have to accept it on faith.

A more newsworthy example of delusion occurred when a Texas jury convicted polygamist sect leader Warren Jeffs of child sexual assault in a case involving two young followers he had taken as brides in what his church called "spiritual marriages." Jeffs, the then fifty-five-year-old head of the Fundamentalist Church of Jesus Christ of Latter Day Saints - which has at least ten thousand members nationwide, is a radical offshoot of mainstream Mormonism, believes polygamy brings exaltation in Heaven and Jeffs is God's spokesman on Earth - fathered a child with a fifteen-year-old girl and also sexually assaulted a twelve-year-old girl. Naturally he claimed to be the victim of religious persecution since his actions were based upon his version of "divine truth" - a belief which is apparently shared by at least ten thousand others, including those who are willing to allow their children to be defiled in the name of God.

Another contemporary example is the condemned Pentecostal practice of handling poisonous snakes. The practice began in 1910 when an illiterate preacher tried to literally apply Mark 16:18: "And these signs shall follow them that believe; In my name shall they cast out devils; they shall speak with new tongues; They shall take up serpents; and if they drink any deadly thing it shall not hurt them; they shall lay hands on the sick, and they shall recover." These were Jesus' last words on earth according to Mark's Gospel (though only in the later manuscripts) however scholars debate the authenticity of that passage. Another key Scripture used to support their belief is Acts 28:1-6, which claims Paul was bitten by a venomous viper and suffered no harm.

Pentecostals believe in exorcisms, speaking in new tongues and laying hands on the sick, so why not take up serpents as well? To an illiterate Tennessee preacher named George W. "Little George" Hensley it seemed inconsistent, so when he preached on the Mark passage one Sunday in 1910 he concluded by taking a large rattlesnake out of a box with his bare hands, handled it for several minutes and then ordered his congregation to handle it too or else be "doomed to eternal Hell."

Hensley's fame spread throughout the Appalachian region and soon caught the attention of A. J. Tomlinson, then General Overseer of the Church of God. He ordained Hensley into the denomination and although there is no record of Tomlinson handling snakes, his daughter did. At first most of the snakes were brought to the church by unbelievers looking for a good show, and at one early meeting hecklers threw a box full of cottonmouths, copperheads and rattlesnakes in front of the former moonshiner while Hensley was preaching.

Today, as in the early days, worshipers are still encouraged to lay hands on the sick and perform faith healing, speak in tongues, provide testimony of miracles and occasionally even consume poisons such as strychnine. Gathering mainly in homes and converted buildings, they generally adhere to strict dress codes such as uncut hair, ankle-length dresses and no cosmetics for women and short hair and long-sleeved shirts for men. Most snake handlers also preach against any use of tobacco or alcohol.

Most religious snake handlers are still found in the Appalachian Mountains and other parts of the southeastern United States, especially in Alabama, Georgia, Kentucky, Tennessee, West Virginia and Ohio - however they are gaining greater recognition due to news broadcasts, movies and books about the non-denominational movement. In 2001 there were about forty small churches which practiced snake handling, most of them considered to be holiness-Pentecostals or charismatics, and in 2004 there were four snake handling congregations in the provinces of Alberta and British Columbia, Canada. Like their predecessors they believe in a strict and literal interpretation of the Bible, and most "Church of God with Signs" following churches are non-denominational because they believe denominations are manmade and carry the Mark of the Beast. Worshippers attend services several nights a week, and if the Holy Spirit "intervenes" they can last up to five hours.

Some of the leaders in these churches have been bitten numerous times as indicated by their distorted extremities. Hensley himself, the founder of modern snake handling in the Appalachian Mountains, died from a fatal snakebite in 1955 and in 1998 snake-handling evangelist John Wayne "Punkin" Brown died after being bitten by a timber rattler at the Rock House Holiness Church in rural northeastern Alabama. Members of his family contend his death was probably due to a heart attack, however his wife had died three years previously after being bitten while in Kentucky. Another snake handler died in 2006 at a church in Kentucky and in 2012 Pentecostal pastor and snake handler Mack Wolford died from a rattlesnake bite he had received while performing an outdoor service in West Virginia, as did his father in 1983. So much for the "truth" claimed to be found in Mark 16:18.

Christianity, in all of its permutations, is of course not the only worldview which suffers from delusion. As everyone knows (except for the "9-11 Truthers" who believe the U.S. government was behind the attacks and therefore suffer from their own type of delusion) the September 11, 2001 attacks were a series of coordinated suicide assaults upon the United States by al-Qaeda terrorists who hijacked four commercial airliners. Believing themselves to be martyrs of Islam conducting a jihad and destined for the Muslim version of Heaven for their efforts, the hijackers intentionally crashed two of the airliners into the Twin Towers of the World Trade Center in New York City, a third into the Pentagon and tried to target either the Capitol Building or White House with the fourth. Nearly three thousand victims died along with the nineteen hijackers, with the overwhelming majority being civilians including the nationals of over seventy countries. I don't think too many non-Muslims will dispute the assertion that the hijackers were suffering from religious delusion. Monsignor Lorenzo Albacete, who is a professor of theology at St. Joseph's Seminary in New York, expressed it best when he said, "From the first moment I looked into that horror on September 11, into that fireball, into that explosion of horror, I knew it. I knew it before anything was said about those who did it or why. I recognized an old companion. I recognized religion."

Several years later on September 30, 2005 the Danish newspaper *Jyllands-Posten* ran twelve cartoons of Islam's Prophet Muhammad. Some associated the prophet with terrorism, some did not, and while the cartoons offended Muslim sensibilities over Islamic prohibitions on depicting their prophet the real scandal emerged when it was learned that imams in Denmark, in a dossier provided to members of the Organization of the Islamic Conference (OIC), falsely asserted the newspaper was government-owned and even circulated offensive images of the Prophet which were not among the original twelve cartoons. To many observers this seemed a conscious effort to inflame tensions, but nevertheless the OIC and other Muslim officials demanded that Denmark apologize. In early 2006 several other European newspapers reran the cartoons and in response many Muslim leaders called for peaceful protests, while others issued death threats. Riots then erupted in several Islamic countries which killed more than one hundred people, mostly Muslims, in Afghanistan, Pakistan, Libya and Nigeria. Two of the Danish imams were filmed in separate instances actually discussing the *need* for violence, while many American Muslims criticized the cartoons but acknowledged the right to freedom of expression and lamented the reaction of their co-religionists as being "un-Islamic." The obvious response is to condemn the teachings of Islam and reject any comparison to Christianity or other world religions, but keep in mind this discussion is about the nature of delusion and not the relative merits of different belief systems - but with that said this might be a good time to mention a holy war of a different stripe in which the Catholic Church used delusion for its own purposes.

The Crusades were a series of religiously sanctioned military campaigns waged by much of Roman Catholic Europe, particularly the Franks of France and the Holy Roman Empire. The specific Crusades to restore Christian control of the Holy Land were fought over a period of nearly two hundred years between 1095 and 1291, although other campaigns in Spain and Eastern Europe continued into the 15th Century. They were fought mainly by Roman Catholic forces since they took place after the East-West Schism and mostly before the Protestant Reformation, against Muslims who had occupied the Near East since the time of the Rashidun Caliphate, although campaigns were also waged against pagan Slavs, pagan Balts, Jews, Russian and Greek Orthodox Christians, Mongols, Cathars, Hussites, Waldensians, Old Prussians and political enemies of the various Popes. Orthodox Christians also took part in fighting against Islamic forces in some Crusades.

The Crusades originally had the goal of recapturing Jerusalem and the Holy Land from Muslim rule and their campaigns were launched in response to a call from the Christian Byzantine Empire for help against the expansion of the Muslim Seljuk Turks into Anatolia. The Byzantine Empire was the most powerful Christian state of the Middle Ages but was not prepared to deal with the Muslim onslaught from the south and east, and as the Byzantines began to lose territory to the Muslims Alexius I, emperor at the time, wrote to Pope Urban II to ask for help - however when the disorganized and bloodthirsty feudal lords of Western Europe arrived in Constantinople Alexius realized he may have made a mistake because unlike the Western Europeans the Byzantines followed Greek Orthodoxy rather than Roman Catholicism and the two sides did not trust each other because of their religious differences.

Going forward, the term Crusades was also used to describe contemporaneous and subsequent campaigns conducted through to the 16th Century in territories outside the Levant, usually against pagans, heretics and peoples under the bane of excommunication for a mixture of religious, economic and political reasons and rivalries among both Christian and Muslim powers led to strange alliances between religious factions against their opponents such as the Christian alliance with the Sultanate of Rûm during the Fifth Crusade.

The Crusades had far-reaching political, economic and social impacts, some of which have lasted into contemporary times. Because of internal conflicts among Christian kingdoms and other political powers some of the Crusade expeditions were diverted from their original aim, such as the Fourth Crusade which resulted in the sack of Christian Constantinople and the partition of the Byzantine Empire between Venice and the Crusaders. The Sixth Crusade was the first to set sail without the official blessing of the Pope while the Seventh, Eighth and Ninth Crusades resulted in Mamluk and Hafsid victories with the Ninth Crusade marking the end of the Crusades in the Middle East. By the late 13th Century the idealism surrounding the Crusades was wavering, however King Louis IX of France was one of the few remaining monarchs who truly believed in the cause and in 1248 he initiated the Seventh Crusade - yet another attempt to retake Jerusalem. Louis decided to attack Egypt, then the center of Muslim power, but the campaign was disastrous with Louis being captured, ransomed and forced to return to Europe. Despite the setback he decided to fight for Christendom yet again in 1270 and this time the target was Tunisia with the idea being if they could take the ports of Tunisia the fighting in Egypt would be easier, but things did not go well as a large portion of his army contracted dysentery and Louis died in August with his Crusades being utter disasters despite his devotion and faith.

Notable was the siege of Jerusalem in 1099 during which Jews and Muslims fought together to defend Jerusalem against the invading Franks, something which is hard to imagine in today's world. They were unsuccessful, and on 15 July 1099 the Crusaders entered the city and proceeded to massacre the remaining Jewish and Muslim civilians and pillage or destroy mosques and the city itself. One historian wrote the isolation, alienation and fear felt by the Franks so far from home helps explain the atrocities they committed, including the cannibalism which was recorded after the Siege of Ma'arra in 1098. After a month the Muslim inhabitants had surrendered under the condition the Crusaders leave the residents unharmed, but they lied and slaughtered the people of Ma'arra. The Christians then discovered the Muslims' food stores were empty because they had been besieged and on the brink of starvation, so they began to eat the dead with Crusaders cutting pieces from the buttocks of dead Muslims and cooking them, with adults being boiled in pots, children roasted on spits and some eating the flesh uncooked.

The papal-sanctioned targets of the Crusades were the Muslims of the Middle East and the pagans of Europe, but the Crusades also initiated violent waves of anti-Semitism. Crusaders rationalized the Jews were also enemies of Christianity because they had rejected Jesus and were responsible for his death, and despite papal admonitions of restraint some veered way off course and attacked Jewish communities in Europe and the Middle East. In 1096 Crusaders attacked three prosperous and peaceful Jewish towns in the Rhineland where the inhabitants were forced to convert to Christianity or die, with some killing their own families rather than do so. Jews continued to be slaughtered each time a new Crusade was decreed and in 1320 French citizens created one called the Shepherd's Crusade which targeted Jews specifically. The popular uprising against the Jews of France included forty thousand peasants who were on average only sixteen years old, with the Crusade being responsible for the destruction of over one hundred communities and thousands of Jewish deaths.

From an individual standpoint each Crusader swore a vow or "votus" to be fulfilled upon successfully reaching Jerusalem, was granted an indulgence (full or partial remission of temporal punishment due for sins which had already been forgiven) by the Pope and received a cloth cross or "crux" to be sewn on their clothes. This "taking of the cross" eventually became associated with the entire journey and the word "crusade," which is derived from the Medieval French "croisade" and Spanish "cruzada," developed from this. Interestingly, the Crusader cry of "Deus vult," which means "God wills it," is not all that different from the phrase "Gott mit uns" (God is with us) which was inscribed on the belt buckles of Nazi troops during World War II - yet another example of perspective and the perception of truth, I suppose.

In the end estimates of the death toll range from one to three million, and naturally each side considered itself to be in possession of truth while thinking the other believed in lies and suffered from delusion, but it isn't just a case of Christians fighting Muslims and their "false religion" - far from it.

The Catholic Church was itself corrupt throughout the Middle Ages, this corruption resulted in regular calls for reform and that eventually led to the wholesale slaughter of Christians by Christians. By way of example, in the 1100s Arnold of Brescia, an Italian canon regular from Lombardy who had foolishly called on the Church to renounce property ownership, was excommunicated, hanged and burned. In similar fashion John Wycliffe of England, who had committed the unthinkable heresy of translating the Bible into English, and his followers were hunted down and killed. John Hus of Prague was excommunicated and in 1415 captured and burned despite possessing a letter of safe passage from the Emperor. Eventually the weight of the reformers grew strong enough to survive at the cost of millions of lives as the Protestant Reformation battled the Catholic Counter Reformation in towns and fields throughout Europe and soon Martin Luther's ninety-five theses, which had been nailed to a church door, set off a firestorm of violence and blood. German princes managed to fight Catholic armies to a standstill by 1555 which resulted in the Peace of Augsburg and Protestant "heretics" thereafter were allowed to live in Germany, but unfortunately that level of tolerance was not extended to other countries.

In any case that peace didn't last and from 1618 to 1648 Europe experienced the Thirty Years' War which left Germany a virtual wasteland after millions were slaughtered. Catholic armies under the leadership of Emperor Ferdinand II kept defeating Protestant armies but then made the mistake of trying to eliminate Protestantism completely by engaging in terrible repression and persecution which caused new Protestant armies to form in foreign lands like Denmark and Sweden to oppose him. The result of all this was a victory for no one and a huge drop in Germany's population, and with too few people left to work the fields and trade for goods starvation and disease ravaged the miserable survivors. Such were the fruits of European Christianity.

In France the largest Protestant group was known as the Huguenots and they were mercilessly persecuted. King Henry created a heresy court known infamously as "The Burning Chamber" since that was the standard punishment for heretics, and on the night of August 24, 1572 (which is known as St. Bartholomew's Day) Catholic soldiers swept through the Huguenot neighborhoods of Paris in a foreshadowing of what would one day happen to Jews under Nazi rule. Thousands were slaughtered in their homes and other massacres timed for the same night occurred in cities across France. Afterward Pope Gregory XIII wrote to

France's King Charles IX saying, "We rejoice with you that with the help of God you have relieved the world of these wretched heretics."

Pope Pius, who not surprisingly was canonized as a saint, later sent Catholic troops into France to aid in the repression efforts, ordering the army commander to kill all prisoners. As a result of such treatment Huguenots fled France in large numbers and when one group reached what would later become Florida in the New World they were discovered by a Spanish expedition... and of course killed.

Meanwhile in Flanders all heretical Protestants were ordered executed and thousands were burned at the stake, but Queen Mary was merciful to Protestants who recanted - instead of death by burning the men would be killed by the sword and women were buried alive. Philip II, the Spanish king and also ruler of Holland and Belgium, was positively obsessed with eliminating Protestantism and ordered all prisoners to be killed so there would be no chance they might escape through neglect or mistake. During the Eighty Years' War the Duke of Alva was sent in and began what became known as the "Spanish Fury" in which thousands of Antwerp Protestants were killed and almost all "heretics" in Haarlem massacred.

Of course Protestants should not be imagined as innocents in all of this. In attempting to abandon several centuries of developed church tradition, Protestant theology focused instead upon stricter adherence to Scripture and the harsher laws of the Old Testament developed greater prominence in Protestant domains than they had in Catholic lands. Protestant leaders also embraced some of the nastier doctrines of a few Catholic theologians such as Augustine's ideas about free will and predestination. Martin Luther wrote in 1518, "Free will after the Fall is nothing but a word. Even doing what in him lies, man sins mortally."

In Switzerland John Calvin created a vicious theocracy in which the equivalent of morality police were employed to control people's behavior with citizens being harshly punished for a wide variety of moral infractions including dancing, drinking and generally being entertained. Theological dissidents like Michael Servetus, who was burned for doubting the Trinity, were summarily executed and with that in mind it isn't surprising some of the most judgmental and unforgiving Christians in America today are themselves unabashed Calvinists.

During the many Huguenot wars ravaging France, Huguenot soldiers hunted priests like animals and one captain is said to have worn a necklace made of priests' ears. In England, after King Henry VIII created the Anglican Church, he went after both Catholics and Protestants.

Catholic loyalists like Sir Thomas More were quickly executed and Lutherans who doubted retained doctrines like transubstantiation were also not spared. Later when King Henry's daughter Mary reached the throne in 1553 she became known as "Bloody Mary" because she attempted to reinstitute Catholicism through violence, but that only managed to make the country even more Protestant.

Unsurprisingly not all Protestants were created equal, with some wretched groups being uniformly hated by virtually all parties. One example of this is the Anabaptists who were martyred for their faith in huge numbers. Anabaptists briefly took the German city of Munster, but Catholic armies regained control and tortured to death Anabaptist leaders with red-hot pincers and had their bodies hung in cages from a church steeple where they remained for years as a visible reminder of what happens to those who dare to oppose Church authority.

Even Catholic Popes - heads of the Church and Bishops of Rome - did not escape the carnage, although one would think God would protect his personal representative on earth. Many of the first twenty-five popes were believed to have been martyred by the Romans, but even after the fall of the Roman Empire the ascendency of the Catholic Church was accompanied by new and endless papal intrigues. Most papal murders occurred during the Middle Ages, particularly between 867 and 964 CE - the so-called Iron Age of the Papacy - when the politically powerful families of Rome had pontiffs elected, deposed and killed to further their own ambitions. The first to die during that period was Pope John VIII, who was so paranoid he had several powerful bishops and cardinals excommunicated before conspirators convinced a relative to poison his drink, and when the poison failed to kill him he was clubbed to death by his own aides. As an interesting aside, according to some accounts Pope John was actually Pope Joan... a female pope who was erased from the historical record when her true identity was uncovered. Although some historians dismiss this as myth others point to an obscure Church ritual which began around that time in which a papal candidate was required to sit in an elevated chair containing a hole called "sedia stercoraria" (one is in the Vatican Museums and another at the Musée du Louvre) with his genitals exposed so the cardinals could examine them, as well as the fact there is no John XX on any list of Popes - an inference that a renumbering of the popes was done to exclude Joan from history. Whether or not the legend is true is secondary to *The Oxford Dictionary of Popes* acknowledging it as being widely believed for centuries, even among Catholic circles, but ironically declaring there is no contemporary evidence for a female Pope. It makes one wonder why the Bible itself is not held to a similar standard of evidential proof, doesn't it?

Next came Pope Stephen VI, the "Mad Pope" who believe it or not placed his rival, Pope Formosus, on trial nine months after his death near the end of the 9th Century. Once Stephen was made Pope he ordered Formosus' corpse to be disinterred, placed on a throne and provided with legal counsel after which he had it thrown from a balcony to a waiting mob and then tossed into the Tiber River. Not surprisingly in the tumult which followed amongst the Roman aristocracy Stephen was imprisoned and later strangled to death, making way for a saner pontiff.

Pope John XII, who amazingly was only eighteen years old when he was elected, was a notorious womanizer who turned the papal palace into something resembling a brothel and it is said he was murdered by an outraged husband. Pope Benedict V raped a young girl and fled to Constantinople with the papal treasury, and he too was killed by a jealous husband with his corpse bearing a hundred dagger wounds as it was dragged through the streets. There are quite a few more examples which could be cited, but you get the idea.

Officially no Pope has been murdered in the modern age, although rumors suggest Pope Clement XIV was poisoned in 1771 following his disbandment of the Jesuits. Similar allegations arose again in 1978 with the sudden death of Pope John Paul I, who had planned radical reforms such as ordaining women as priests and welcoming gays into the church. His successor, John Paul II, was nearly murdered in St. Peter's Square in 1981 by a Turkish gunman named Mehmet Ali Agca and ever since whenever popes travel in public they do so in a special armored vehicle which has been dubbed the "Popemobile" - giving rise to skeptical but quite reasonable comments about how riding in a bulletproof car demonstrates a distinct lack of faith.

There are many more examples of religious violence which could be offered but even without them reasonable people should conclude the notion one group somehow possesses the "truth" to the point where it feels justified in imposing that belief on others through violence and persecution is almost universal. In a nutshell it is clear one religion's truth is simply another religion's delusion, and author Thich Nhat Hanh summed that up quite succinctly in his book *Living Buddha, Living Christ* when he wrote, "People kill and are killed because they cling too tightly to their own beliefs and ideologies. When we believe that ours is the only faith that contains the truth, violence and suffering will surely be the result."

For a moment let's assume your religion, whatever that may be, is the one true religion. How and why, one might wonder, did the hundreds of other religions come to be throughout the ages? This is important, because once you understand why people create religions you will be a step closer to embracing theological objectivity. There are four primary reasons for the creation of belief systems:

1) To explain mysterious or frightening natural phenomena which ancient man could not yet understand such as the phases of the moon, lightning and earthquakes. As Nobel Prize winning physicist Richard Feynman put it, "God was invented to explain mystery, to explain those things you do not understand, but when you finally discover how something works you don't need him anymore." Indeed, as our knowledge and understanding of the universe continues to grow there is less and less need for religiously-based explanations. No less a figure than Thomas Jefferson pointed this out when he wrote, "They (preachers) dread the advance of science as witches do the approach of daylight and scowl on the fatal harbinger announcing the subversions of the duperies on which they live," and more recently astrophysicist Dr. Neil DeGrasse Tyson said, "'God' is an ever receding pocket of scientific ignorance that's getting smaller, smaller and smaller as time goes on." In other words the more we know the less we rely on supernatural explanations.

2) Gods, religions and the "afterlifes" which almost always accompany them are a way to cope with the inevitability of death. Most humans are naturally terrified by it and invent or accept religion as a way to deal with the terror. The strongest instinct is after all the instinct of self-preservation, and what better way is there to "survive" than to become convinced you will have eternal life? The Egyptians, Greeks, Norse and many other civilizations were just as firmly convinced they knew what lay beyond the grave as Christians, Muslims and others are today, but just as those archaic beliefs are now clearly nothing more than myths so too one day will be today's notions of life after death.

3) Gods are invented as a proxy for morality and as a way to promote "goodness" and eliminate "evil" in societies. Consider this - if you tell people to do or not do a certain thing because you say so they will most likely do as they please… but convince them a god said so

and they are far more likely to be obedient, especially if you link it to their prospects for eternal reward and punishment. This is little different from telling a child to behave because Santa Claus is watching and if he doesn't be good there will be a lump of coal in his stocking come Christmas. One problem with tying morality to religion is doing so implies only the adherents of a specific belief system can possibly be moral, but as Christians who have visited India must admit even Hindus who know nothing of Jesus understand the difference between right and wrong. The bottom line is religion is an effective tool for controlling people because as Roman philosopher Seneca the Younger put it long ago, "Religion is regarded by the common people as true, by the wise as false and by the rulers as useful."

4) Religion is a means by which power can be wielded and that goes hand-in-hand with the element of control. There is no denying the Catholic Church has been a powerful political force in Europe for centuries and many predominantly Muslim countries are Islamic theocracies governed by Sharia Law. Specific examples which come to mind are Rasputin, the Russian mystic, holy man and advisor to the Russian Imperial family (who believed him to be a psychic and faith healer) and the ruthless Cardinal Richelieu, who served as "Chief Minister" of France during the reign of King Louis XIII. There are countless other examples of religion being used as an instrument of power, but you get the idea.

If it is so obvious why religions are created and that gods are constructs why would we as a species continue to create all of this nonsense over and over and over again through the millennia and more importantly why does well over half of the American population continue to believe in various religions today? The answers are simple:

1) Family, community and familiarity. As philosopher Bertrand Russell correctly pointed out, "A man's religion, almost without exception, is the religion of his community." For instance if you are now a Christian, but had instead been born in Saudi Arabia, you would almost certainly be a Muslim. That logic is undeniable.

2) Fear. This is the most basic and primal human emotion. Fear of the unknown, fear of being ostracized by your community and most of all fear of death.

3) Comfort, which goes hand-in-hand with fear. When a believer says, "I know where I'm going when I die" they of course could not possibly know such a thing but even so the self-delusion can be quite comforting.

4) Low self-esteem. Many people feel a need to believe in something "greater than themselves" and humans are hard wired to seek father figures. Not surprisingly, the Bible was written exclusively by men and depicts God as being "The Holy Father."

5) An inflated sense of importance, which is ironically quite the opposite of low self-esteem. These are people who insist there "must be a purpose to their existence" despite having no clue what that might be and who fail to understand how insignificant our little planet and its inhabitants are in a vast universe.

6) Ignorance, be it willful or otherwise. For example, embracing ignorance is fundamental to the philosophy of Intelligent Design. They say, "We don't know what this is or where it came from, so it must be the product of a higher intelligence," and investigate no further.

7) Intellectual laziness and/or limitations. Science is much more complicated than religion, so why conduct experiments and analyze data when it is far easier to say, "God did it!" It is not an accident that the majority of elite scientists and intellectuals are not theists.

8) Mental illness. Seems cruel at first blush, but stop and think about it. If someone approached you tomorrow and told you they'd had a conversation with a donkey, were acting at the behest of a burning bush or had just ridden a winged horse up to Heaven what would your reaction be? Most likely you would call the funny farm, and yet those very stories are contained in the Bible and Quran and are accepted as true by billions.

To help illustrate the preceding point about religious identification being a result of family, community and familiarity, consider the fact that surveys designed to identify people's religious affiliation are often a bit skewed due to the existence of a large population of what are known as "Cultural Catholics" and "Cultural Jews."

The term "Cultural Catholic" has its roots in the famously liberal and Irish Catholic Kennedy family and refers to people who belong to the Roman Catholic Church but observe the religion's practices as a cultural tradition rather than a spiritual exercise. Cultural Catholics may not fully understand the theology which informs their religion's rituals and in many cases may reject part or most of the theology. A related term is "Cafeteria Catholic" (or "Cafeteria Christian"), which describes someone who adheres to the aspects of Catholicism or Christianity he or she likes but rejects the rest - in many cases abortion, premarital sex, the use of birth control or by identifying as a homosexual.

In 2011 the *St. Catherine of Siena Institute* reported that thirty-two percent of Americans raised Catholic abandon the identity altogether by their mid-twenties, an additional thirty-eight retain the identity but rarely practice their faith, thirty percent of those who identify as Catholic attend Mass only once a month and on any given Sunday only 15.6% of American Catholics show up in church.

In a similar fashion "Cultural Jews" identify with Judaism through the history, civilization, ethical values and shared experiences of the Jewish people but not the religious component and connect to their heritage through the languages, literature, art, dance, music, food and celebrations of the Jewish community. This mindset was illustrated in an episode of the television show *House* (Season 7, Episode 9, entitled *Larger Than Life*) when Candace Bergen (as Arlene Cuddy) questions House (Hugh Laurie) by asking, "Say you two got married... would you convert to Judaism?" House replies, "I'm an atheist," and Arlene fires back, "Honey, half the Jews I know are atheists. It's about *community*." The bottom line is Cultural Catholics and Jews check the box which says "Catholic" or "Jew" on surveys but for all intents and purposes they are not religious people.

Everything we associate with religion is a construct. God, Allah, Vishnu, Jesus, the resurrection, prayer, the various creation stories, your soul, everlasting life, Heaven and so on are simply the product of human imagination. As a species we have accepted religious dogma for centuries and many people believe them today to some degree because they help explain the unexplainable and give us comfort when confronting difficult issues and yet they are just as fictional as the gods of the Egyptians, Romans and Aztecs. For example how do we know for sure God, and by that I mean any god which has ever been worshipped, does not answer prayers? As described later in detail, simply pray and watch what occurs. What we find is nothing happens, something Mark Twain highlighted in *Huckleberry Finn* when Huck observes, "Miss Watson she took me in the closet and prayed, but nothing come of it. She told me to pray every day, and whatever I asked for I would get. But it warn't so. I tried it. Once I got a fish-line, but no hooks."No matter how many people pray, no matter how often they pray, no matter how sincerely they pray, no matter how worthy the prayer, nothing ever happens outside of normal statistical probability. More importantly if we pray for something which is impossible, it never happens. We all know that. Conversely if we pray for something which is possible the results of the prayer will unfold exactly in accordance with the normal laws of probability. In every situation where we statistically analyze the effects of prayers, looking at both the successes and the failures, we find prayer has zero effect and every time a Christian or Muslim says, "The Lord (or Allah) answered my prayer" what we are seeing is actually a simple coincidence or the natural effects of "self-talk." Believers never discuss *failed* prayers, but if we look at prayers which fail as well as those which "work" an objective statistical analysis proves gods do not answer them.

How do we know for sure God did not write the Bible and Allah did not write the Quran? Simply read them objectively. Another reasonable question is how do we know for sure Jesus was not just a normal human being? Simply ask yourself if a man were to proclaim himself the son of God today - and some such as Alan John Miller, David Shayler and José Luis de Jesús Miranda have done exactly that - what would we do? We would ask to see incontrovertible proof. Jesus does not get a pass because he lived two thousand years ago, and please note none of his "miracles" left any lasting evidence and not one of the supposed witnesses to his miracles left behind individual attestations. Looked at objectively rather than through the lens of blind faith all of his "miracles" are either faith healings or magic tricks if they ever occurred at all and conventional wisdom tells us faith healers and magicians are frauds. Have you ever seen illusionist Criss Angel or Steven Frayne (aka "Dynamo") "walk on water," for instance? If not, there are video clips of them doing so on YouTube. It's quite amazing to watch, but I think we can agree it is a parlor trick. If they were to claim divinity based upon such tricks, would you believe them? I certainly hope not.

There is also no evidence Jesus is resurrected. He could easily appear to each of us in the flesh to prove he is resurrected just as he supposedly did with Saul/Paul, Doubting Thomas and others and in the Bible he promises that he will, and yet he never does. If he did there would be thousands of videos on the internet showing those miraculous appearances but instead what we get are grilled cheese sandwiches and cloud formations which supposedly look like him. As I told my brother-in-law when he offered his "testimony," a revelation must necessarily be a first person experience because to everyone else it is nothing more than hearsay. If that sounds harsh, let's consider a non-religious example. Imagine someone tells you he was abducted by aliens and taken to Mars in a UFO, but later escaped. Would you accept his sworn testimony, or would you demand some proof? If you say "his word is good enough for me" give me a call because I'd like to sell you a bridge in Brooklyn. In the view of Carl Sagan and others, extraordinary claims require extraordinary evidence.

God is supposedly the creator of the universe and promises to answer prayers but for some reason his churches depend on the money of mere mortals to survive, and while he once supposedly rained "manna" down from Heaven to feed his people to date I have heard of no showers of cash. If you are having a difficult time accepting or understanding some of the foregoing, or worse yet have already employed counter arguments to dismiss them, never fear - chapters on logical fallacies and apologetics follow to help you understand why and how people fail to accept self-evident truths and the portions which cover those parts of the Bible will also be covered in detail. In the end anyone who takes the time to actually read the entire Bible and/or Quran for themselves will, if they are honest with themselves and utilize critical thinking skills, rapidly reach the conclusion they were written by primitive men rather than an all-knowing, all-loving supreme being.

It has come time for rational, intelligent people to openly discuss the subject of religion because superstition and fraud are detrimental to society. There is no doubt death and morality are important to people and touch on fundamental human emotions, but if we can separate them from the mythology of gods we can understand each in a positive way and create a rational world for ourselves focused on benefiting mankind.

Logical Fallacies

Or, Mr. Spock's Worst Nightmare

"I do not feel obliged to believe that same God who endowed us with sense, reason and intellect had intended for us to forgo their use."
~ Galileo Galilei

In philosophy and logic the "liar paradox" is making the statement "this sentence is false" and trying to assign to it a classical binary truth value, which leads to a contradiction because if the statement is true then the sentence is false, but if the statement "this sentence is false" is false then the sentence is true, and so on. Simply put, "I am lying" is a self-contradiction which can be true if and only if it is false. In an episode from the original *Star Trek* series entitled *I, Mudd* the liar paradox is used by Captain Kirk and Harry Mudd to confuse and ultimately disable an android named Norman who is holding them captive when Mudd claims he is lying and Kirk claims that everything Mudd says is a lie.

Kirk: "Everything Harry tells you is a lie. Remember that. Everything Harry tells you is a lie."

Mudd: "Now listen to this carefully, Norman. I am... lying."

Norman: "You say you are lying, but if everything you say is a lie, then you are telling the truth, but you cannot tell the truth because everything you say is a lie, but you lie... You tell the truth but you cannot, for you lie... illogical! Illogical! Please explain! You are human. Only humans can explain their behavior! Please explain!"

This paradox was once discussed by St. Jerome in a sermon which began with him quoting Psalms 116:11: "I said in my alarm, 'Every man is a liar!' Is David telling the truth or is he lying? If it is true that every man is a liar and David's statement 'Every man is a liar' is true, then David also is lying as he too is a man. But if he too is lying, his statement 'Every man is a liar' consequently is not true. Whatever way you turn the proposition, the conclusion is a contradiction. Since David himself is a man, it follows that he also is lying, but if he is lying because every man is a liar, his lying is of a different sort."

That is a key point to ponder in pursuit of the nature of "truth," but before getting into specific discussions it is important to develop a basic understanding of the concept of logic as well as the types of logical fallacies which people use during the processes of intentional deception and/or self-delusion.

An argument is considered valid if and only if the truth of the premise guarantees the truth of the conclusion and it is invalid if the conclusion does not follow from the premise. It is important to realize calling an argument "valid" is not the same as saying its conclusions are true. Logic does not concern itself with the content of an argument, only its form, so from the standpoint of logic the following is a perfectly valid argument:

Premise 1: Dinosaurs are still living;
Premise 2: If dinosaurs are still living, Elvis is living;
Conclusion: Therefore, Elvis is still living.

If the two premises are true then the conclusion must be true. You and I of course know these premises are not in fact true (in the normal sense of words that is since strictly and scientifically speaking all birds are dinosaurs, so technically premise one is true - but this does not make premise two true) but their falsity is not a matter of pure logic. Simply because someone says something which is false, it does not necessarily follow that he has committed a logical fallacy.

Valid arguments fall into two categories - sound and unsound. A sound argument is a valid argument with true premises and an unsound argument is a valid argument with false premises, therefore the above argument about dinosaurs is unsound. Invalid arguments will always be logically fallacious. By way of example, the following are invalid arguments:

Premise 1: If x is a human male, then x is a human;
Premise 2: x is not a human male;
Conclusion: Therefore, x is not human.

Premise 1: If July is before June, then George Bush is the thirty-second President of the United States;
Premise 2: July is not before June;
Conclusion: Therefore, George Bush is not the thirty-second President of the United States.

Circular arguments are valid but are still considered logical fallacies, and more to the point they are absolutely useless because they establish nothing which they do not presuppose. The following are simple examples of circular arguments:

Premise 1: San Francisco is in California;
Conclusion: Therefore, San Francisco is in California.

Premise 1: Nobody likes Cherries;
Premise 2: If anyone liked cherries, then it wouldn't be the case that nobody likes cherries;
Conclusion: Therefore, nobody likes cherries.

Premise 1: God exists;
Premise 2: God knows everything;
Premise 3: God is not a liar;
Premise 4: God wrote the Bible;
Premise 5: The Bible says God exists;
Conclusion: Therefore, God exists.

Because these arguments must assume what they are attempting to prove they are logically superfluous. In each case the argument provides absolutely no support for the conclusion. We might just as well have stated the conclusion without argument. Most often circular arguments hide their circularity by keeping one or more of their premises implicit, as in the following example:

Premise 1: God is not a liar;
Premise 2: God wrote the Bible;
Premise 3: The Bible says God exists;
Conclusion: Therefore, God exists.

Although it does not explicitly say so this argument obviously depends upon a suppressed premise, namely that God exists. More accurately, no one would accept the premises unless they had already accepted the conclusion. An example of this type of argument is often made by famous theologian and debater William Laine Craig when making his "Argument From Morality":

Major Premise: If God did not exist, objective moral values and duties would not exist.
Minor Premise: Objective moral values and duties do exist.
Conclusion: Therefore, God exists.

Now let's put that premise into perspective using an analogy. This is akin to saying:

Major Premise: If Stan is a vampire then Stan will sleep during the day.
Minor Premise: Stan sleeps during the day.
Conclusion: Therefore, Stan is a vampire.

Using Craig's methodology night shift workers are all blood sucking Transylvanian Counts, however this is clearly a fallacy (irrespective of whether Stan is *actually* a vampire) because the conclusion does not follow from the premises. Craig's framing of the argument this way has the reader feeling it is wrong somehow but they are unsure of how, where or why. The fact is the argument is a null argument for God in that even if the opponent argues successfully for the non-existence of moral values and duties that won't touch Craig's God since in the strict framing of the argument the existence of God isn't contingent on the existence of moral values and duties - only the reverse. The argument is framed purely to trick the opponent into conceding what looks like an acceptable premise. Fundamentally, the structure of this argument can be used to argue for the existence of God using anything you like. Let's use something totally meaningless as an example - in this case Kim Kardashian:

Major Premise: If God does not exist, then Kim Kardashian does not exist.
Minor Premise: Kim Kardashian does exist.
Conclusion: Therefore, God exists.

This is in fact a better argument because premise two is now less contentious since sadly very few people appear to be unaware of the existence of Kim Kardashian and those who have never heard of this person can Google her to ascertain whether she exists or not, whereas there are schools of thought which deny the existence of "objective moral values and duties" either totally or in part. Theists could hardly deny the truth of premise one and would have to agree that if there were no God then nothing would exist, including Kim Kardashian.

The only fly in the ointment is rationalists will argue that the premise is false, but since that's also the case with the original argument the claim is not made worse by the substitution of Kardashian for morality. With respect to Laine's "Argument From Morality," there is an attempt by him to confuse and distract with the double use of "not." His argument, in logical form, is:

Premise: If *not* A, then *not* B.
Assertion: B.
Conclusion: Therefore A.

This form of argument is usually employed by beginning with a general, proven statement in the premise and then making a specific statement in the assertion to make a specific conclusion. For example:

Premise: If there is not (at least) a single cloud in the sky, then it cannot be raining.
Assertion: It is raining right now.
Conclusion: Therefore, there is (at least) a single cloud in the sky right now.

Craig doesn't do this with his pseudo-logic and his argument is functionally equivalent to saying:

Premise: If not squarks, then not doosits.
Assertion: Doosits.
Conclusion: Therefore, squarks.

Or, alternatively, without the use of "not":

Premise: If doosits, then squarks.
Assertion: Doosits.
Conclusion: Therefore, squarks.

So long as you have not supported your premise adequately this is not functionally different from arguing "squarks, therefore squarks" or in theist terms, "God exists, therefore God exists." Not a particularly satisfying argument, is it?

Keep in mind certain types of argumentation may be wrong or misleading without necessarily constituting a logical fallacy. For instance it may be terrible to tell someone "agree with me or you will die," but it is not terrible because of its logical structure. Similarly we may feel certain groups are too easily convinced to believe something or too quick to adopt a political or theological position on the basis of emotion, however their doing so does not constitute a logical fallacy.

Common Types of Logical Fallacies

Ad Hominem (Personal) Attack: A fallacious attack against a claim or an argument on the basis of an irrelevant fact regarding the person presenting the claim or argument.

1) Person A makes claim X.
2) Person B disregards the claim and attacks person A.
3) Therefore A's claim is false.

It is important to realize even if the attacks on the person making the claim are true that does not invalidate the claim itself. For example if Adolph Hitler was to say "the sky is blue," calling him a genocidal megalomaniac instead of addressing the veracity of the claim is irrelevant. The introduction of ad hominem attacks by an opponent is one of the surest ways of knowing you have prevailed on the basis of fact and logic. To quote Socrates, "When the debate is lost, slander becomes the tool of the loser."

Appeal to Belief/Popularity: Presenting an argument or a claim on the basis that the majority of people believe the same thing.

1) The majority of people believe claim X to be true.
2) Therefore claim X is true.

A majority cannot "elect" the truth because it exists independently whether people believe it or not. For example the vast majority believed the Earth was flat in 1500 BCE, but we now know they were wrong. Think about that the next time someone says, "surely billions of people can't be wrong regarding the existence of God," which of course raises the question of which god they are referring to because by that logic a billion Muslims can't be wrong about the existence of Allah and a billion Hindus can't be wrong about the existence of Brahman. This fallacy is exacerbated by a phenomenon known as "communal reinforcement," which is a practice by which a claim develops into a strong belief through repeated assertion by members of a community. This process is independent of the claim being properly researched or supported by empirical data significant enough to warrant belief by reasonable people. Often mass media contributes to the process by uncritically supporting the claims, but more often the media provides tacit support for untested and unsupported claims by saying nothing skeptical about even the most outlandish of them. Communal reinforcement explains how entire nations can pass on ineffable gibberish from generation to generation and how testimonials reinforced by other testimonials within the community of therapists, sociologists, psychologists, theologians, politicians, talk show hosts, etc., can supplant and be more powerful than scientific studies or accurate gathering of data by disinterested parties. Communal reinforcement explains in part why about half of American adults deny evolution occurred and instead believe Abraham's God created the universe in six days, the first man was made out of clay and a snake talked a woman into disobeying an order from God and thereby caused all of our problems. It also explains how otherwise rational and intelligent people can be persuaded to accept such stories as true when they are provided by a comforting community in a time of great emotional need. Every cult leader knows the value of communal reinforcement combined with isolating cult members from contrary ideas. As Daniel Kahneman wrote in *Thinking, Fast and Slow*, "We know that people can maintain an unshakable faith in any proposition, however absurd, when they are sustained by a community of like-minded believers." When making an argument from popularity remember the mob has the reasonable person at a disadvantage because at one time Nazism was the most popular ideology in Germany, but it was still wrong.

Appeal to Consequences of a Belief: This argument is based on holding that what a person "wishes" to be true must be true because the alternative, while probably true, is too undesirable to consider. The obvious example is "eternal life must be possible because the idea of dying is emotionally unacceptable."

Appeal to Fear: An appeal to fear is the attempt to use fear instead of logic to support a conclusion. Classic examples are "If you don't believe in God you will burn in Hell for all eternity" and "If you don't behave Santa Claus won't bring you any presents."

Appeal to Tradition: An attempt to use tradition or "common practice" instead of logic to support a conclusion or claim. The premise and the conclusion may both be true, but the premise does not necessarily support the conclusion. This form of argument is particularly appealing to people who are opposed to change. An example is "America has always been a Christian Nation, therefore Christianity is the one true religion." Clearly that logic did not work with "we have always kept slaves" or "women have never been allowed to vote," and it is equally invalid in this instance.

Begging the Question: Also known as a circular argument and covered elsewhere, this involves making a conclusion based on something which has already been presumed in the argument.

1) God wrote the Bible;
2) God never lies;
3) The Bible tells us God exists;
4) Therefore, the Bible is true and God exists.

Biased Sample: You are biased towards a certain conclusion before making arguments or looking at the evidence. People who think this way tend to say things such as "no one can convince me" or "there's no way you can prove it to me." Anyone with this kind of closed-minded stubbornness will accept all logical fallacies without a second thought even if they are obviously fallacious to an objective observer.

Confusing Cause and Effect: The assumption here is two correlated phenomena have a causal relationship such as "Adolf Hitler and Josef Stalin wore mustaches, therefore all people who wear mustaches are immoral, genocidal dictators" and "Mao Tse Tung and Josef Stalin were atheists, therefore all atheists are immoral, genocidal dictators."

Moving the Goalposts: Also known as raising or lowering the bar. If someone successfully addresses a point an opponent will then raise the bar and say he must also address some further point (it is also possible to lower the bar to reduce the burden on an argument). For example a person might claim prayer can prevent cancer, but when they contract the disease they move the goalposts and say the cancer would have been much worse if not for the prayers. Moving the goalposts to create your own unfalsifiable belief is simple. Just follow these steps - express a belief, wait until someone proposes a way in which the belief can be tested (and in the process falsified) and then add or change an attribute of the belief to render the proposed test invalid and return to step two. An excellent example of this process is Carl Sagan's "dragon in the garage" exercise in which someone claims a fire-breathing dragon lives in their garage. When you ask why you can't see it the claimant replies it is invisible, so you suggest spreading flour on the floor to capture the dragon's footprints and the claimant then responds by saying it won't work because the dragon floats in the air, so you suggest using an infrared sensor to detect the invisible fire and the claimant responds by saying the invisible fire is heatless, and so on and so on ad nauseam. The point of such an exercise is what is the difference between an invisible floating dragon who spits heatless fire, and no dragon at all? The same question applies to gods. Perhaps the most classic example of this fallacy is the Argument for the Existence of God. Due to our ever increasing understanding of nature through science many of the arguments which were once made for the existence of gods such as "Where does the sun go at night?" have necessarily been abandoned only to be replaced with new ones which usually involve questions to which science has not yet definitively found an answer. The move from literal Creationism to Intelligent Design is a prime example. Currently the origin of life is a popular argument for God (although it is also a classic argument from ignorance) and since it is an area where we very well may have a scientific answer in the next decade the "origin of life" argument will fade away and be replaced by yet another, thus moving the figurative goalposts farther back as our understanding of the natural world increases. As previously noted, in the words of Dr. Neil DeGrasse Tyson "God is an ever-receding pocket of scientific ignorance that's getting smaller and smaller and smaller as time goes on."

Post Hoc: A logical fallacy in which one argues that because one event happened after another event, the event which happened first caused the second event. An example of this is Pat Robertson claiming Hurricane Katrina was the result of "wicked behavior" in New Orleans. Post hoc reasoning is the basis for many superstitions and erroneous beliefs, but in reality many events follow sequential patterns without being causally related. For example you have a cold so you drink fluids and two weeks later your cold goes away. You have a headache so you stand on your head and six hours later your headache goes away. You put cooking oil on a pimple and three weeks later the pimple goes away. You perform some task exceptionally well after forgetting to bathe so the next time you have to perform the same task you don't bathe. A solar eclipse occurs so you beat your drums to make the gods spit back the sun and eventually the sun returns, thereby "proving" to you the efficacy of your action. You use your dowsing stick and then find water. You imagine heads coming up on a coin toss and heads comes up. You rub your lucky charm and what you wish for comes true. You lose your lucky charm and strike out six times. You have a "vision" that a body is going to be found near water or in a field and later a body is found near water or in a field. You have a dream that an airplane crashes and an airplane crashes the next day. However, sequences don't establish a probability of causality any more than correlations do. Coincidences happen. An occurrence after an event is not sufficient to establish that the prior event caused the latter one. To establish the probability of a causal connection between two events controls must be established to rule out other factors such as chance or some unknown causal factor. Anecdotes are not sufficient because they rely on intuition and subjective interpretation, so a controlled study is necessary to reduce the chance of error from self-deception.

Red Herring: Any argument designed to change or redirect the topic, usually employed when one is on the verge of defeat in a debate. For example, "Evolution is impossible because the Big Bang is unproven…" The Big Bang has nothing at all to do with evolution, so even if it was proven wrong tomorrow that wouldn't change the fact organisms either evolve to adapt to their environment or they die.

Slippery Slope: Implies, usually without foundation, that if a particular action is taken a series of increasingly unacceptable consequences will follow, for example, "If Congress does not allow school prayer it will lead to the banning of religion."

Special Pleading: Involves referencing a rule or process and then suspending the rule when it doesn't suit your purpose. For instance the common theist "Argument From Design" claims all things need a creator, but if you ask a theist "Who or what created God?" they exempt themselves and claim "God does not need a creator."

Straw Man: This is a logical fallacy in which a person manufactures a caricature (usually a misinterpretation or oversimplification) of his opponent's argument and then sets out to attack or dismiss the exaggeration, i.e. building a straw man and then knocking it down. This is a very dishonest line of argument since a person puts words into his opponent's mouth and then ridicules them. A classic example is, "We didn't come from monkeys like evolution says we did," when in reality the Theory of Evolution makes no such claim.

Observational Selection: Involves pointing out favorable circumstances while ignoring the unfavorable. Anyone who goes to Las Vegas gambling casinos will see people winning at the tables and slots because the casino managers make sure to install bells and whistles to announce the victors, while the losers never get highlighted. This may lead one to conclude the chances of winning appear good while in actuality just the reverse holds true. The same holds true for prayers - highlight those which are "answered," and ignore those which are not.

Proving Non-Existence: When an arguer cannot provide evidence for his claims he may challenge his opponent to prove it doesn't exist (e.g., prove God doesn't exist; prove UFOs haven't visited earth, etc.). Although one may prove non-existence in certain circumstances such as showing that a box does not contain specific items one cannot prove universal or absolute non-existence or non-existence out of ignorance. Proof of existence must come from those who make the positive claims.

Circular Reasoning: Already discussed, but revisited here because it is so common and so maddening. This is a classic example of illogical thought which involves stating in one's proposition the very thing which one aims to prove. For example God exists because the Bible says so, and the Bible is correct because it is the word of God. Each conclusion is dependent upon the other unproven proposition and around and around it goes. An excellent example was depicted in an episode of the television drama *Criminal Minds*. An FBI agent asks a terrorist when the Jihad (holy war) will end and he replies, "The Jihad will end when Allah wills its end." The agent then asks how we will know when it is Allah's will and the terrorist's response is, "When the Jihad ends."

No True Scotsman: A logical fallacy in which an individual attempts to avoid being associated with an unpleasant or bizarre (to them) action by asserting that no true member of the group they belong to would do or believe such a thing. Instead of acknowledging some members of a group have undesirable characteristics (for instance the Westboro Baptist Church) or differing beliefs (literal vs. liberal interpretation of the Bible) the fallacy tries to redefine the group to exclude them. Sentences such as "All real members of X have desirable trait Y" then become tautologies, because Y becomes a requirement for membership in X. The term was coined by philosopher Antony Flew, who gave an example of a Scotsman who saw a newspaper article about a series of sex crimes taking place in Brighton and responded, "No Scotsman would do such a thing." When later confronted with evidence of another Scotsman doing even worse acts his response was, "No *true* Scotsman would do such a thing," thus disavowing membership in the group "Scotsman" to the criminal on the basis of the crime while ignoring the man's birthplace and/or citizenship. Religious apologists will repeatedly try to use this argument to distance themselves from more extreme or fundamentalist groups or simply those with different opinions, i.e. Christians who support gay marriage are not real Christians or Muslims who support women's rights are not real Muslims even though they believe in the same God and get their belief system from the same book. This defense mechanism is used so often it is not unreasonable to point out that if all of the Christians who have ever been said by other Christians to not really be Christian were to vanish, there would be no Christians left.

The Ostrich Argument: When all else fails this position requires the abandonment of all logic and the use of parroted phrases such as "I just believe because I believe" and "It's called faith for a reason" and those phrases are usually accompanied by that person sticking imaginary fingers in their ears or figuratively burying their head in the sand. Once ostrich arguments begin it means two things - the person using them is in effect admitting he has no logical basis for his beliefs, and there is no point in continuing the discussion because that individual has essentially "turned off" his mind. Former evangelical pastor Dan Barker, who once regularly employed this very tactic himself, put it quite plainly when he said "Faith is a cop-out. It is intellectual bankruptcy. If the only way you can accept an assertion is by faith, then you are conceding that it can't be taken on its own merits."

Now that we have examined the predominant logical fallacies let's take a look at the tactics which are commonly employed to disseminate such propaganda, and for the purposes of this discussion "propaganda" is defined as any attempt to influence people's actions or attitudes without causing them to think. It should also be understood that these tactics are used by both sides in virtually every debate to some degree and in fact not all are bad in and of themselves because it really depends on how they are used. Analogies, humor, visualization, quotations by authorities and statistics for instance are valid parts of rhetoric (persuasive speech), can be legitimate and helpful teaching aids and only err as fallacies or become propagandistic to the extent they dodge the issue, obscure the truth, mislead or take the lazy way out of a debate - and to avoid being fooled ourselves we must be alert to these tactics of misdirection and deception.

The first is the "big lie," which can be either a complete falsehood told with bravado or pure conjecture delivered with absolute certitude. Examples of this are "Commit suicide in a jihad by killing as many innocent civilians as you can in a shopping mall and you'll get seventy-two virgins and an eternity of bliss" and "Every word in the Bible is literally true because it is the perfect and inerrant word of God."

Next is the "half-truth," which is part truth and part lie. For example after being stopped for drunk driving an inebriated driver might proclaim "I only had a couple of beers" in slurred speech, and while that might be true he may have also consumed alcoholic drinks other than beer and/or the beers may have been large bottles as opposed to the usual contents of a normal-sized can.

"Repetition," sometimes informally referred to as "proof by repeated assertion," is an informal fallacy in which a proposition is repeatedly restated regardless of contradiction until it embeds in the listener's mind and becomes accepted as fact even though repetition does not in any way establish validity. Sometimes this is done until challenges dry up, at which point it is asserted as fact due to supposedly not being contradicted (argumentum ad nauseam). Psychologist William James summed it up best when he said, "There is nothing so absurd that it cannot be believed as truth if repeated often enough."

"Speaking in generalities" is the practice of using broad-brush oversimplifications to gloss over exceptions, problems, issues or claims. "Glittering" generalities are used in advertising, politics and religion and everyone from political candidates to religious leaders makes use of such vague phrases so frequently they seem like a natural part of discourse. An example is then Presidential candidate Barack Obama saying he wanted to "make America the greatest country in the world again" without specifying which nation was currently the greatest, quantifying what it takes to be the greatest or explaining how he planned to accomplish that goal.

Using "loaded words" is a form of semantics in which emotionally charged words, whether negative or positive (euphemisms), are used to influence people's reaction by biasing their perception of something. For example a woman could be characterized as "an expectant mother carrying a baby" or "a pregnant female carrying a fetus." Is the protestor pro-life, or anti-choice? Is the abortionist pro-choice, or a baby-killer?

Fear-mongering, hate-mongering and scare tactics are amongst the worst of all. An obvious example of arousing fear of, or animosity against, a targeted individual, group or movement was Hitler's demonizing of Jews before attempting to exterminate them and in the realm of theology claims such as "atheists are of the devil" and "you will burn forever if you do not accept Jesus" are almost as bad.

Shifting the burden of proof, touched on elsewhere, is one of the most common theistic tactics and involves forgetting it is your responsibility to prove a claim rather than your opponent's place to disprove it by somehow proving a universal negative, i.e. if someone cannot prove God doesn't exist that does not mean he must. If that is not clear enough, I challenge anyone to provide definitive proof that unicorns or leprechauns do *not* exist.

Sidestepping, i.e. dodging the issue and/or changing the subject, is something which I have encountered more times than I can count. This is especially true in online debates when a question is asked and the other party either ignores a question, goes off on a tangent, disappears from the conversation altogether or declines to answer by offering a platitude such as, "You are welcome to your opinion, and I am entitled to mine, so let's just agree to disagree."

The practice of quoting out of context, sometimes referred to as "contextomy," is the use of a false attribution in which a passage is removed from its surrounding matter in such a way as to distort its intended meaning. Arguments based on this fallacy typically take two forms. As a strawman argument it involves quoting an opponent out of context in order to misrepresent their position, typically to make it seem more simplistic or extreme with the aim of making it easier to refute, and as an appeal to authority it involves quoting an authority on a subject out of context in order to misrepresent that authority as supporting a position he does not.

A related topic is quote mining, which is not only a deceitful tactic but is in fact actually a way of lying. It is widely used by Young Earth Creationists, for example, in an attempt to discredit the Theory of Evolution (see quote mine of Charles Darwin on page 196 for an example). Such "quotes" are widely passed around and used repeatedly by creationists, who of course neither bother to check the original source nor give any indication they are taken from secondary sources. More importantly, such thoughtless iterations demonstrate an unwillingness to understand the underlying issues and an indifference to the ideas and reputations of the people whose names they are appropriating.

Occam's Razor

Or, Thinking Inside the Box

☥☯⛩ॐ☸✡✝☪☬

"There is no expedient to which a man will not go to avoid the real labor of thinking." ~ Thomas Edison

Occam's Razor, generally attributed to Franciscan monk William of Ockham but posited in a variety of forms by numerous philosophers throughout the centuries, is a useful principle of parsimony, economy or succinctness used in logic and problem-solving which will help you navigate your way through many complicated concepts as we move forward so I present it here. It states that among competing hypotheses, the hypothesis with the fewest assumptions should usually be selected.

Many scientists have adopted or reinvented Occam's Razor as in Leibniz's "identity of observables" and Isaac Newton's stated rule, "We are to admit no more causes of natural things than such as are both true and sufficient to explain their appearances."

The most useful statement of the principle for scientists is, "When you have two competing theories that make exactly the same predictions the simpler one is almost always better" or "Among competing hypotheses the one which makes the fewest assumptions should be selected," although according to the *Stanford Encyclopedia of Philosophy* what Ockham actually said was, "Nothing ought to be posited without a reason given, unless it is self-evident or known by experience or proved by the authority of Sacred Scripture." That admission may give those who use the Razor to argue in favor of reason pause, but as we shall see there is a problem with the original incarnation and as a result the more commonly used versions makes a lot more sense.

Let's apply Occam's Razor, as postulated by the man himself, to a comparison between two different hypotheses about the motion of the planets. The contemporary consensus states that they revolve around the sun according to the Copernican system, Kepler's laws of motion and Newton's model of gravity as demonstrated by complex observations and significant mathematical underpinning. Few people today will disagree with that.

An alternative hypothesis states they are moved around the sky by angels as illustrated in a painting from the *Breviari d'amor* of Matfre Ermengaud (a contemporary of Ockham and also a Franciscan friar) where a convenient gear mechanism is gracefully activated by God to regulate planetary motion.

Were we to apply Ockham's formulation of the Razor literally the choice between these two hypotheses is clear. It does not favor the first hypothesis, the standard scientific interpretation, because the Scriptures clearly state that angels do exist and their reality was re-affirmed by Pope John Paul II as recently as August of 1986. Since they manifest through their actions in the heavens the second hypothesis appears far simpler than the complicated observations and calculations employed by mathematicians and astronomers which involve unseen entities such as the acceleration of gravity, centrifugal force and mass which to this day raise issues science is yet to resolve. In other words if you seriously believe in angels then the contemporary consensus about planetary motion is a case of "plurality without necessity."

We know of course the planets do in fact revolve around the sun in accordance with the laws of physics, an idea which probably would have shocked Ockham. The point is in philosophy and science we should go on selecting the hypothesis which makes the fewest assumptions when confronted with a competing explanation. A couple of examples from Islam and Mormonism, followed by two from the Bible which were drawn from hundreds of potential examples, will illustrate what I mean by this. Compare the two possible explanations for each and use logic to decide for yourself which is most likely true.

First let's examine two possible explanations for the Muslim belief that the prophet Muhammed rode some sort of animal (usually referred to as a winged horse) up to Heaven. Which explanation is most likely?

1. Muhammed actually rode up to Heaven as described in the Quran.

2. Muhammed had a vivid dream in which that happened, he was crazy or he simply made up the entire story.

Which one did you choose, and why? Next we will look at the Mormon belief which essentially says the *Book of Mormon* was given to Joseph Smith by the Angel Moroni on a set of golden plates. Once again, which explanation is most likely?

1. Joseph Smith actually received the plates from an angel and deciphered them using seer stones as God wanted.

2. Joseph Smith had a vivid dream in which that happened, he was crazy or he simply made up the entire story.

Now let's shift to a different holy book - the Bible - and consider two possible explanations for Moses coming down from the Mount with the Ten Commandments.

1. Moses climbed the mount alone, had a conversation with a burning bush, received stone tablets carved by the finger of God himself and returned forty days later.

2. Moses climbed the mount alone with a chisel under his robe, spent forty days carving instructions he wanted the tribes to follow into a tablet he fashioned out of stone and when he returned made up a story about a burning bush and told everyone the rules came directly from God in order to give them authority.

As before the question here is which explanation is most likely. To put it into perspective, how would you feel if your leader presented you with a similar story today to explain a set of rules he wanted you to follow? Would you accept that without question, or instead think he was either crazy, drunk or trying to sell you a bill of goods? The second biblical example concerns the virginity of Mary, mother of Jesus. Again, which explanation is most likely?

1. An angel appeared, announced Mary was going to bear the child of the creator of the universe, she was then impregnated by an invisible holy spirit and subsequently gave birth while retaining her virginity.

2. Mary had sex with a man other than Joseph, got pregnant and lied to him and everyone else about it.

The answer to this question should be obvious, but here are a few additional bits of information to make it even easier. First of all women have tried using this explanation for unwanted pregnancies from time immemorial, even to this day, and not surprisingly nobody believes them. Second, the "born of a virgin" story has been used in many other religions and is not unique to Christianity. Finally, many biblical scholars have conceded that the word "virgin" was mistranslated (remember, the Bible was not written in English but rather in Aramaic, Hebrew and Greek) and should have read "young girl." The problem here is this myth has become such a part a Christianity that any revision of current dogma would likely result in the collapse of the faith.

So there you have it. It's really not so difficult to separate fact from fantasy when you are honest and put your mind to it.

Recognizing Delusion

Or, You Believe... What?

"A belief is not merely an idea the mind possesses... it is an idea that possesses the mind." ~ Robert Oxton Bolt

Leopoldo Fregoli was one of the greatest entertainers of the late 19th and early 20th Centuries and he perfected a style of performance known as "quick-change" which is pretty much exactly what it sounds like - he would switch costumes and characters during his stage shows so rapidly it was suggested he actually required several other "Fregolis" for his act to be possible. If you have ever seen such a performance I am sure you have wondered and speculated about how it is done. I know I have.

Why is this relevant? In 1927 French psychiatrists Paul Courbon and Gustave Fail described the case of a twenty-seven-year-old servant who had become convinced she was being persecuted by a pair of actresses named Sarah Bernhardt and Robine whom she had seen perform at a nearby theater. The servant believed these two quick-change artists were impersonating everyone she met and saw this as more supernatural than true quick-change trickery since she thought they possessed the ability to place other people inside the bodies of those around her and could actually get inside her mind to steal her thoughts and force her to do things. She was clearly delusional, and no amount of rational explanation could convince her otherwise.

A delusion is a false belief strongly held by a person or group of people in spite of invalidating evidence, sometimes as a symptom of mental illness but more often in the form of a comfortable self-deception. In other words it is a belief held in the face of evidence to the contrary which is resistant to all reason. Here are several examples which can help explain the nature of delusion and how it fits with religion.

In the first imagine you are told a story about a man who lives at the North Pole with a bunch of elves. During the year he and the elves build toys and on Christmas Eve he loads up a sack with the toys, puts it in his sleigh, hitches up eight or nine flying reindeer and flies from house to house, landing on the rooftops. He slides down chimneys with his sack, leaves toys for the children of the household, climbs up the chimney and flies to the next house. He does this all around the world in one night and then flies back to the North Pole.

This is of course the story of Santa Claus, but let's say I am an adult friend and reveal I believe this story with all my heart and try to get you to believe it as I do. What would you think of me? You would consider me delusional, of course. Why? Obviously because you know Santa is imaginary and the story is a fairy tale, and presumably no matter how much I talk about it you are not going to believe he and his magical flying reindeer are real.

As noted, the dictionary defines delusion as "a false belief strongly held in spite of invalidating evidence" and that definition fits this scenario perfectly, but since you are my friend you might try to help me realize my belief is delusional. The way you would probably try to shake me from it is to ask logical questions, for example you might ask, "How can the sleigh possibly carry enough toys for everyone in the world?" My answer is the sleigh is magical and has the ability to do this intrinsically. "How does Santa get into houses and apartments which don't have chimneys?" Santa can make chimneys appear as shown in the movie *The Santa Clause*. "How does Santa get down the chimney if there's a fire in the fireplace?" Santa has a special flame-resistant suit. "Why doesn't the security system detect Santa?" Santa is invisible to security systems. "How can Santa travel fast enough to visit every child in one night?" Santa is timeless. "How can Santa know whether every child has been bad or good?" Santa is omniscient. "Why are the toys distributed so unevenly, since Santa delivers more toys to rich kids, even if they are bad, than he gives to poor kids?" There is no way for us to understand the mysteries of Santa because we are mere mortals, but Santa has his reasons. For example, perhaps poor children would be unable to handle a flood of expensive electronic toys, and how would they afford the batteries? So Santa spares them these burdens.

These are all logical questions you have asked, but I have answered them for you and am wondering why you can't see what I see… and you are wondering how I can be so insane. Why didn't my answers satisfy you? Why do you still think I am delusional? It is because my answers have done nothing but confirm my delusion. In order to answer your questions I invented completely out of thin air a magical sleigh, magical suit, magical chimneys, "timelessness" and invisibility. You don't believe my answers because you know I am making this stuff up. The invalidating evidence is voluminous. Now let's try another example.

Imagine me telling you I was in my room one night when suddenly everything became exceedingly bright and the next thing I knew there was an angel in the room. The angel told me there was a set of ancient golden plates buried in the side of a hill in New York on which are inscribed the books of a lost race of Jewish people who inhabited North America. Eventually the angel led me to the plates and let me take them home and even though they were written in an unknown foreign language he helped me decipher and translate them before taking them up to Heaven never to be seen again. I have the book I translated from the plates and it tells of an entire civilization of Jewish people living in the United States two thousand years ago and how the resurrected Jesus came and visited them. I showed the golden plates to a number of real people who are my eyewitnesses and have their signed attestations saying they did in fact see and touch them before they were taken up to Heaven.

What would you say about this story? Even though there is now indeed a book written in English which tells the story of this lost Jewish civilization, and even though there are signed attestations, what would you think? This story sounds delusional, doesn't it?

You would ask some obvious questions, for example, "Where are the ruins and artifacts from this Jewish civilization in America?" The book talks about millions of Jewish people doing all sorts of things in America and they had horses and oxen and chariots and armor and large cities. What happened to all of this? I answer that it is all out there but we simply have not found it yet. "Not one city? Not one chariot wheel? Not one helmet?" you ask. I say no, we haven't found a single bit of evidence yet, but it is out there somewhere. You ask dozens of questions like this, and I have answers for them all.

Most people would consider me to be delusional if I told this story. They would assume there were no plates and no angel and I had written the book myself. Most people would ignore the attestations, since having people attest to it means nothing since I could have paid the attesters off or could have fabricated them. Most people would reject my story without question, but what is interesting is there are millions of people who actually believe it. They are members of the Mormon Church and the person who told this incredible story was a man named Joseph Smith. He lived in the United States in the early 1800s, told his story and recorded what he "translated from the plates" into the *Book of Mormon.* If you meet a Mormon and ask them about this story they can spend hours talking to you about it and can answer every question you have, and yet the 6.99 billion of us who are not Mormons can see with total clarity Mormons are delusional. The Mormon story is not much different from the story of Santa. It is as simple as that.

Now imagine hearing a story about a man who was sitting in a cave minding his own business when a bright flash of light appeared and a voice spoke the word "Read!" The man felt like he was being squeezed to death, and this happened several times. The man asked, "What should I read?" and the voice said, "Read in the name of your Lord who created humans from a clinging [zygote]. Read for your Lord is the most generous. He taught people by the pen what they didn't know before." The man ran home to his wife and while running saw the huge face of an angel in the sky. The angel identified himself as Gabriel and told the man he was to be the messenger of God. That night the angel appeared to the man in his dreams. Gabriel appeared to the man over and over again, sometimes in dreams and sometimes during the day as "revelations in his heart," sometimes preceded by a painful ringing in his ears (and then the verses would flow from Gabriel right out of the man), and sometimes Gabriel would appear in the flesh and speak as scribes wrote down everything the man said. One night about eleven years after the first encounter Gabriel appeared to the man with a magical winged horse. The man got on the horse and it took him to Jerusalem and then up to the seven layers of Heaven. The man was able to actually see Heaven and meet and talk to people there before Gabriel brought him back to earth, and proved he had actually been to Jerusalem on the winged horse by accurately answering questions about buildings and landmarks there. He continued receiving revelations from Gabriel for twenty-three years at which time they stopped, but all were recorded by the scribes in a book which we still have today.

What do you make of that story? If you have never heard it before you may find it nonsensical in the same way the stories of the golden plates and Santa were, especially once you read the book which was supposedly transcribed from Gabriel. You would probably dismiss the dreams, the horse, the angel, the ascension and the appearances of the angel in the flesh as imaginary, but this story is the foundation of the Muslim religion practiced by more than a billion people around the world. The man is of course named Muhammed, the book is the Quran and it contains the sacred story of the revelation of Allah to mankind.

Despite the fact a billion Muslims profess some level of belief in this story those outside their faith consider it to be imaginary. They don't believe this claim because it is obviously a fairy tale and consider the Quran to be a book written by a man who may have been deranged and nothing more. After all, a winged horse which can fly to Heaven is as fictional as a flying reindeer.

If you are a Christian take a moment to look back at the Mormon and Muslim stories. Why is it so easy for you to look at these stories, see they are fairy tales and be sure Mormons and Muslims are delusional? You know for the same reason you know Santa is imaginary - there is no evidence for any of it. The stories involve magical things like angels, winged horses, hallucinations and dreams. Horses can't fly, we all know that, and even if one could where would it fly to? The vacuum of space? Or did the horse somehow "dematerialize" and then "rematerialize" in Heaven? If so, those processes are clearly made up too.

An unbiased observer can see how imaginary these three stories are and in addition Muslims will consider Mormons delusional, Mormons will think Muslims delusional and Christians can see that both Mormons and Muslims are deluded. Now one final story. An invisible God inseminated a virgin named Mary in order to bring his son incarnate into our world. Mary and her fiancé Joseph had to travel to Bethlehem to register for the census, where Mary gave birth to the Son of God. God put a star in the sky to guide people to the baby, in a dream told Joseph to take his family to Egypt and then stood by and watched as King Herod killed innocent babies in Bethlehem in an attempt to kill Jesus. As a man God's son claimed he was God incarnate saying, "I am the way, the truth and the life." This man performed many miracles, healed lots of sick people, turned water into wine and these miracles prove he is God. He was eventually given a death sentence, killed by crucifixion and his body was placed in a tomb. Three days later the tomb was empty and the man, alive once again but still with his wounds - so anyone who doubted could see them - appeared to many people in many places. He then ascended into Heaven and now sits at the right hand of God the father almighty. Today you can have a personal relationship with the Lord Jesus. You can pray to him and he will answer your prayers. He will cure your diseases, rescue you from emergencies, help you make important business and family decisions and comfort you in times of worry. This man will also give you eternal life, and if you believe in him and/or are good he has a place for you in Heaven after you die. The reason we know this is long after the man died four people wrote accounts of his life and their written attestations are proof of the veracity of this story.

This is of course the story of Jesus. Do you believe it? If you are a Christian you probably do. I could ask questions for hours and you will probably have answers for every one of them in the same way I had answers for all of the Santa questions in the first example and no doubt you cannot understand how anyone could question any of it because it is so obvious to you.

Here is the thing - the five billion people who are not Christians look at this story in exactly the same way you looked at the Santa story, the Mormon story and the Muslim story. In other words those five billion people stand outside the Christian bubble and know there was no magical insemination, magical star, magical dreams, magical miracles, magical resurrection, magical ascension and so on. People outside the Christian faith look at the Christian story and note the miracles which are supposed to prove Jesus is God left behind no tangible evidence for us to examine and scientifically verify today and all involved faith healings and magic tricks. Jesus is supposedly resurrected, but does not appear to anyone. The book where Matthew, Mark, Luke and John make their attestations does indeed exist but is filled with many contradictions. And so on and so on...

In other words the Christian story is no different from the other three. I am attempting to use logic to show you this, and your rational mind can see the evidence just as the five billion non-Christians who consider the Christian story to be imaginary do… but if you are a practicing Christian you can probably feel your "religious mind" overriding both your rational mind and common sense. Why were you able to use your common sense to reject the Santa story, Mormon story and Muslim story, but when it comes to the Christian story - which is just as imaginary - you cannot?

Just for a moment try to look at Christianity with the same amount of healthy skepticism you used when approaching the stories of Santa, Joseph Smith and Muhammed and use your common sense to ask some simple questions. Is there any physical evidence that Jesus existed? No, he left no trace. His body "ascended into Heaven," he wrote nothing down and none of his "miracles" left any permanent evidence. Is there any reason to believe Jesus actually performed miracles, rose from the dead or ascended into Heaven? There is no more reason to believe this than there is to believe Joseph Smith found the golden plates hidden in New York or Muhammed rode on a magical winged horse to Heaven. Actually probably less of a reason, given that the record of Jesus' life is two thousand years old while that of Joseph Smith is less than two hundred. You mean to tell me I am supposed to believe this story of Jesus even though there is no proof or evidence to go on beyond a few attestations in the New Testament of a Bible? Yes, you are supposed to believe it based upon "faith..." just as the Mormons and Muslims do.

No one other than small children and crazy people believe in Santa Claus, no one outside the Mormon Church believes Joseph Smith's story, no one outside the Muslim faith believes the story of Muhammed and no one outside the Christian faith believes in Jesus' divinity, miracles, resurrection, etc. The question is obvious - why can human beings detect myths with complete certainty when they come from other faiths but cannot detect the ones which underpin their own? Why do they believe their chosen myth with unrelenting passion and reject the others as nonsense? For example Christians clearly know when the Egyptians built pyramids and mummified the bodies of their pharaohs to help them reach the afterlife it was a waste of time, because otherwise Christians would build pyramids and practice mummification. Christians know when the Aztecs carved the heart out of a virgin and ate it that accomplished nothing, because otherwise they too would kill virgins and eat their hearts. Christians know when Muslims face Mecca to pray it is pointless, otherwise they would also face Mecca when they pray. Christians know when Jews keep meat and dairy products separate they are wasting their time, because otherwise the cheeseburger would not be a staple of the American diet. Yet when Christians look at their own religion they are for some reason blind. Why? And no, it has nothing to do with the "fact" that the Christian story is "true." Your rational mind knows that with certainty, and so do five billion others. So what is the explanation? Simply put, wishful thinking.

Wishful thinking involves forming beliefs and making decisions according to what might be pleasing to imagine instead of by appealing to evidence, rationality or reality. In other words it is a product of resolving conflicts between belief and desire. Studies have consistently shown that with all else being equal, subjects will predict positive outcomes to be more likely than negative ones.

Author Christopher Booker described wishful thinking in terms of "the fantasy cycle... a pattern that recurs in personal lives, in politics, in history - and in storytelling. When we embark on a course of action which is unconsciously driven by wishful thinking all may seem to go well for a time in what may be called the 'dream stage,' but because this make-believe can never be reconciled with reality it leads to a 'frustration stage' as things start to go wrong, prompting a more determined effort to keep the fantasy alive. As reality presses in, it leads to a 'nightmare stage' as everything goes wrong, culminating in an 'explosion into reality' when the fantasy finally falls apart."

In addition to being a cognitive bias and poor way of making decisions, wishful thinking is commonly held to be a specific informal fallacy in an argument when it is assumed that because we *wish* something to be true or false it is *actually* true or false. This fallacy has the form, "I wish that X is true/false, therefore X is true/false." Wishful thinking, if this were true, would rely upon appeals to emotion and would also be a red herring.

A by-product of wishful thinking is wishful seeing, a phenomenon in which a person's internal state influences their visual perception. People have the tendency to think they perceive the world for what it is, but research suggests otherwise and currently there are two main types of wishful seeing which are based on where it occurs - in the categorization of objects, or in representations of an environment. This helps to explain (along with the phenomenon of pareidolia, which is covered later) why some people "see" Jesus or the Virgin Mary in cloud formations, tree bark and grilled cheese sandwiches.

Most telling of all is the fact the Bible, specifically the oft-quoted Epistle to the Hebrews (Hebrews 11:1), defines faith as, "The substance of things hoped for, the evidence of things not seen." If that is not a description of wishful thinking I don't know what is, so perhaps a better bit of advice from Scripture can be found in Proverbs 14:15 which tells us, "The naive believes anything, but the prudent man considers his steps." I could not agree more.

Rationalization

Or, I Can Explain That!

"I don't know anyone who could get through the day without two or three juicy rationalizations." ~ Jeff Goldblum as 'Michael' in *The Big Chill*

The term "sour grapes" is derived from a fable attributed to Aesop called *The Fox and the Grapes*. One hot summer day a fox was strolling through an orchard when he came upon a bunch of grapes ripening on a vine which was draped over a lofty branch. "Just the thing to quench my thirst" he thought, and drawing back a few paces he took a run and jump and just missed the branch. Turning around with a "one, two, three" he jumped up again, but with no greater success. Again and again he tried after the tempting morsel but at last had to give it up, and as he walked away with his nose in the air said, "I am sure they are sour anyway."

Let's put that fable into a modern context. Sandra, who has just been rejected by a love interest, convinces herself that he rejected her because he did not share in her ideal of happiness and what's more the rejection is actually a blessing in disguise because it has freed her to find a more suitable partner. Bill said the reason he flunked out of college was the poor quality of teaching there. Recent high school graduate Cathy fails to be accepted at a top university and tells herself one of the interviewers on the panel is sexist and therefore biased against females, and convinces herself taking the upcoming gap year to re-apply would actually give her a precious opportunity to travel and see the world. After Carla rejected him, Phil told his friends he didn't think she was very attractive and interesting and that he really wasn't all that crazy about her in the first place. Jack told his parents he got a C in his psychology course because all of the A's and B's went to students who cheated on tests and had professionals write their papers for them. What do all those people have in common? They, like the fox, are rationalizing their failures.

In psychology and logic rationalization, sometimes known as "making excuses," is an unconscious defense mechanism in which perceived controversial behaviors or feelings are logically justified and explained in a seemingly rational or logical manner in order to avoid any true explanation and are made consciously tolerable or even seemingly admirable and superior by plausible means. Rationalization encourages irrational or unacceptable behavior, motives or feelings and often involves ad hoc hypothesizing. This process ranges from fully conscious (e.g. to present an external defense against ridicule from others) to mostly subconscious (e.g. to create a block against internal feelings of guilt).

People rationalize for various reasons. According to the *Diagnostic and Statistical Manual of Mental Disorders* (DSM) published by the American Psychiatric Association rationalization occurs "when the individual deals with emotional conflict or internal or external stressors by concealing the true motivations for his or her own thoughts, actions or feelings through the elaboration of reassuring or self-serving but incorrect explanations."

A rather different but perhaps complementary approach to rationalization comes from a phenomenon called cognitive dissonance, which in 1957 researcher Leon Festinger argued occurs, "When people become aware that their attitudes, thoughts and beliefs are inconsistent with one another (and) this realization brings with it an uncomfortable state of tension called 'cognitive dissonance.' One answer to the discomfort of a situation is their minds rationalize them by inventing a 'comfortable illusion.' Thus for example people who start to smoke again after quitting for a while perceive smoking to be less dangerous to their health compared to their views when they decided to stop - thereby averting their 'post-decisional regret' through their new rationalization."

In a similar way acts of aggression will often be seen as "reasonable, well justified and even necessary." People rationalize their self-interest in these ways so that, to cite Martin Luther King, Jr., "It seems to be a fact of life that human beings cannot continue to do wrong without eventually reaching out for some rationalization to clothe their act." The same may be said of the collective. When groups commit aggression or embrace a delusion they too rationalize their acts and beliefs with high-sounding words to rationalize their own self-interested desires, for example, "Our God is the right God, and we fight in his name. The other God is the strange God."

Such collective rationalizations come close perhaps to the communal illusions which Sigmund Freud wrote of as "derived from human wishes... must not the assumptions that determine our political regulations be called illusions as well?... may not other cultural assets of which we hold a high opinion and by which we let our lives be ruled be of a similar nature?"

The message here is rationalization is a tool which can be used to justify delusions of any and every kind. At best this is intellectually dishonest and at worst it is downright dangerous. An oft-cited example is the way the Nazis rationalized the need for "racial hygiene" in order to justify the mass murder of millions of Jews, Gypsies and other "inferior peoples." The point is not the wrongness of the Nazis' actions - that should be quite evident to any objective and moral person - but it is instead that millions of otherwise decent Germans could be drawn into a huge mass delusion through the mechanism of rationalization... and if you can rationalize that, you can rationalize virtually anything.

The following is a perfect example of how Christians can and do rationalize and interpret the Bible in any way which suits their personal agenda. It is from a group comprised of gay Christians called "Would Jesus Discriminate" and shows "evidence" which supports how they have interpreted Scripture to mean gay marriage is acceptable rather than an abomination as many mainstream Christians believe:

Biblical Evidence: Can two people of the same sex live in a committed, loving relationship with the blessing of God? As we grapple with this question we will look at two sets of Scriptures: those that affirm gay and lesbian people, and those that are traditionally used to condemn gay people.

Affirmation in Scripture: We discuss five passages of Scripture that affirm gay people and their relationships. These stories, which the writers of the Bible included under inspiration of the Holy Spirit, are amazingly gay-positive. Odds are you have never heard about these passages and their meaning for sexual minorities. The truth of these texts threatens some of our society's deepest prejudices, and their positive messages are usually ignored. It is our hope they will bring comfort and refreshment to many.

Are there really only six? Given how often some Christians preach against homosexuality, you would think there must be hundreds of Scriptures on the subject. In fact there are only six traditional (negative) passages and none of them speaks to the situation of twenty-first century gay people who desire to live in loving relationships with the blessing of God. On this website, we carefully walk through each of these passages and document what they do and don't say.

Prejudice can influence how we read the Bible: An example from the recent past is *The Adventures of Huckleberry Finn*, in which young Huck's father is thought to be dead and a woman named Widow Douglas takes him in. Widow Douglas is portrayed as a kindly Christian who takes care of Huck out of goodness with no thought of reimbursement. The Widow Douglas tries to "civilize" Huck, teaching him Bible stories and urging him to live a good life and pray often. She is a loving woman who studies her Bible and wants to always do the right thing. She is also a slave owner.

Later in the story Huck runs away and happens upon Jim, a slave belonging to Widow Douglas's sister, Miss Watson. The sister had intended to sell Jim to a trader in New Orleans, so fearing he would never see his wife and children again Jim runs away. He plans to escape to freedom, make some money and buy his wife and children out of slavery. Huck and Jim's adventures as they travel together down the Mississippi make up the rest of the book.

At every turn Huck finds himself feeling guilty for "stealing" Miss Watson's "property." He believes he will go to Hell for helping Jim escape, and it is clear his Christian education under Widow Douglas is part of the reason he believes this. For all her kindness and goodness, Widow Douglas reads the Bible the same way most of her friends do. She believes slavery is an institution approved by God. She probably believes all African Americans are descended from Ham and the curse recorded in Genesis 9:25-27 demonstrates why they deserve slavery. She sees nothing wrong with buying and selling people because her interpretation of the Bible tells her this is the proper role of those of European descent. In short, she allows her prejudices to mold the way she reads the Bible.

This may seem like an extreme example. Only the most bigoted Christian would argue today that the Bible endorses slavery or that Genesis 9:25-27 is a curse against Africans. But Huck's story illustrates how thoroughly we are creatures of our culture and how that culture can create prejudices that get in the way of what God wants to teach us.

The information on this site will challenge some of the deepest prejudices of our culture, prejudices that even gay people have often internalized. We will look at Scriptures that dispute some of our most deeply held beliefs, and we must be willing to let God move. In the end, our response will decide if our prejudices mold the Bible, or if we are willing to let the Bible mold us.

PULPIT FICTION

The good news at the end of *The Adventures of Huckleberry Finn* is that Miss Watson, who always felt guilty for almost selling Jim, freed him in her will - perhaps because she was able to read the Bible with a fresh perspective, or listened to the tugging of God's Spirit on her soul. Whatever the cause, she and Jim were both finally free.

As you read the following, try to set aside any prejudices you may have about the subject. Listen to the Spirit of God speaking through these Scriptures and perhaps you, like Miss Watson and Jim, will be freed.

1) **Jesus affirmed a gay couple (Matthew 8:5-13):** The Greek word that the Roman centurion uses in this passage to describe the sick man - "pais" - is the same word used in ancient Greek to refer to a same-gender partner.

2) **Ruth loved Naomi as Adam loved Eve (Genesis 2:24, Ruth 1:14):** The same Hebrew word that is used in Genesis 2:24 to describe how Adam felt about Eve (and how spouses are supposed to feel toward each other) is used in Ruth 1:14 to describe how Ruth felt about Naomi. Her feelings are celebrated, not condemned. And throughout Christian history, Ruth's vow to Naomi has been used to illustrate the nature of the marriage covenant. These words are often read at Christian wedding ceremonies and used in sermons to illustrate the ideal love that spouses should have for one another. The fact that these words were originally spoken by one woman to another tells us a lot about how God feels about same-gender relationships.

3) **Jesus said some are born gay (Matthew 19:10-12):** Here Jesus refers to "eunuchs who have been so from birth." This terminology ("born eunuchs") was used in the ancient world to refer to homosexual men. Jesus indicates that being a "born eunuch" is a gift from God.

4) **The early church welcomed a gay man (Acts 8:26-40):** In the ancient world, eunuchs were widely associated with homosexuality. Here a self-avowed eunuch is welcomed into the early church without any concerns about his sexual orientation. He was welcomed on the same basis as other people - his faith in Jesus Christ.

5) **David loved Jonathan more than women (II Samuel 1:26):** At Jonathan's funeral, David declares that he loved Jonathan more than

any woman. This is just one of several Bible passages that describe and celebrate an intense love between these two men that went well beyond friendship.

6) **Idol Worship and Rejection of God (Romans 1:21-28):** In these verses, Paul condemns idol worshippers and God haters. According to Paul, these "God haters" experiment with gay sex only as a way of seeking new thrills or in cultic worship. Clearly he is not speaking about innately gay and lesbian people who love God and want to honor God while living with integrity as who they are.

7) **Israel's Holiness Code (Leviticus 18 and 20):** The chapters that contain these verses are clearly identified as speaking against practices involved in cultic idol worship. The entire passages are generally accepted as not applying to modern Christian life.

8) **Sodom and Gomorrah (Genesis 19 & Jude 7):** The Genesis 19 account of Sodom and Gomorrah is a story of attempted gang rape of two "outsiders." It says nothing about loving gay relationships, and actually condemns the sort of violence sometimes done to gays and lesbians. Jude 7 talks about a first century Jewish legend that the women of Sodom had sex with male angels. Since it is about heterosexual sex between angels and humans, it clearly has nothing to do with gay relationships.

9) **No Fems? No Fairies? (I Corinthians 6:9-10 and I Timothy 1:10):** The words often translated "effeminate" and "homosexual" in these passages are obscure and difficult to translate. The first word identifies someone who is morally weak, and has nothing to do with nellie gay men. The second word probably means "people who use power to obtain sex," though the word is so rare that a confident translation is impossible. Neither word refers specifically to gay men or lesbians.

Okay, now that we have taken a look at how the group "Would Jesus Discriminate" views Scripture, it would be interesting to see how the Westboro Baptist Church, the group which *hates* homosexuals and runs a website with the address "GodHatesFags.com," would interpret those same nine Bible passages. Something tells me their view would be quite different. It's also ironic that gays used the Huck Finn story in an attempt to get readers to try to "set aside any prejudices they may have about the subject" since slave owners used their interpretation of Scripture to justify keeping slaves for hundreds of years.

Christians aren't the only ones who can rationalize in order to "prove" their beliefs are true. The following is a great example of how Muslims rationalize "physical evidence" for the "truth" of Islam, the existence of Allah and even the "prophecy" of a "unified religion" (this information, which is presented by Rashad Khalifa, PhD in a book entitled *Quran: Visual Presentation of the Miracle*, can be found online at *www.mathmiracle.com*):

"There now exists physical evidence for a message from God to the world. This marks the advent of a new era in religion; an era where FAITH is no longer needed. There is no need to "believe," when one "knows." People of the past generations were required to believe in God, and uphold His commandments ON FAITH. With the advent of the physical evidence reported in this book, we no longer believe that God exists; we KNOW that God exists.

Such knowledge is ascertained through God's final Scripture, the Quran, wherein overwhelming physical evidence has been encoded. Employing the ultimate in scientific proof, namely, mathematics, the evidence comes in the form of an extremely intricate code. Thus, every word, indeed every letter in Quran is placed in accordance with a mathematical design that is clearly beyond human ability.

Not only does the evidence prove the authenticity and perfect preservation of the Quran, but it also confirms the miracles of previous messengers including Noah, Abraham, Moses, David and Jesus. None of us witnessed the parting of the Red Sea, or the virgin birth of Christ. However, upon reviewing the evidence presented here, and examining the appropriate narrations, the reader will be as positively certain as an eyewitness.

Here are a few basic facts:

- God states in Chapter 74 verse 30 that the authenticity of the Quran will be proven by the number 19.
- God informs us in chapter 83 verse 20 that the Quran is a "numerically structured book."
- The word "day" occurs throughout the entire Quran 365 times.

- The word "month" occurs throughout the entire Quran 12 times.

- The mathematical structure of the Quran is based on the number 19, which represents God as the Alpha (1) and the Omega (9).

Simple to Understand, Impossible to Imitate

God informs us in Chapter 74 that the authenticity of the Quran will be proven by the number 19. Verse 35 describes this 19-based mathematical code as "One of the great miracles":

Chapter 74 - The Hidden Secret

(over it is nineteen)

Absolutely, (I swear) by the moon.
And the night as it passes.
And the morning as it shines.

This is one of the great miracles

Basic Facts:

- The Quran consists of 114 chapters, which is 19 x 6.

- The total number of verses in the Quran is 6346, or 19 x 334. (Note that 6 + 3 + 4 + 6 = 19)

- The word "God" (Allah) occurs in the Quran 2698 times, and this number equals 19 x 142.

- The total sum of verse numbers for all verses containing the word "God" is 118123, also a multiple of 19 (118123 = 19x6217).

- "The Quran" is mentioned in the Quran 57 times, which is 19 x 3.

- The first verse, known as "Basmalah," consists of 19 letters.

- The word "proof" is written throughout the entire Quran 19 times.

- The famous first revelation (96:1-5) consists of 19 words.
- This 19-worded first revelation consists of 76 letters, or 19 x 4.
- The first chapter revealed (Sura 96) consists of 19 verses.
- This first chapter revealed is placed atop the last 19 chapters. This chapter also consists of 304 letters, or 19 x 16.
- The last revelation (Sura 110) consists of 19 words.
- The first verse of the last revelation (110:1) consists of 19 letters.
- The Quran mentions 30 different numbers: 1, 2, 3, 4, 5, 6, 7, 8, 9, 10, 11, 12, 19, 20, 30, 40, 50, 60, 70, 80, 99, 100, 200, 300, 1000, 2000, 3000, 5000, 50,000, & 100,000. The sum of these numbers is 162146, which equals 19x8534.

Superhuman Mathematical Design

Now that we have grasped a few of the basic facts, let us examine the truly miraculous design of the mysterious "Quranic Initials":

- Chapter 10: A. L. R. These (letters) are the proofs of this book of wisdom.
- Chapter 28: T. S. M. These (letters) constitute proofs of this profound book.
- Chapter 38: S., and the Quran that contains the proof.

The Quranic Initials

The Quran is characterized by a unique phenomenon never found in any other book; 29 chapters are prefixed with 14 different sets of "Quranic Initials," consisting of one to five letters per set. Fourteen letters, or half of the Arabic alphabet, participate in these initials. They collectively make up an interlocking mathematical system that is easily superhuman.

These initials occur within their respective chapters, and also in combination with other initials in other chapters, in multiples of the number 19.

This mathematical system is easily superhuman. This is especially awesome in light of the fact that (1) no person was aware of its existence until recently and (2) it was revealed during the Dark Ages of Arabia before the existence of the modern number system.

The Quranic Initial "Q" (Qaaf)

- The frequency of occurrence of "Q" in Sura "Q" (No. 50) is 57, **19x3**
- The letter "Q" occurs in the other Q-initialed sura (No. 42) exactly the same number of times, 57, **19x3**.
- The total occurrence of the letter "Q" in the two Q- initialed suras is 114, which equals the number of suras in the Quran.
- "The Quran" is mentioned in the Quran 57 times, **19x3**.
- The description of the Quran as "Majid" (Glorious) is correlated with the frequency of occurrence of the letter "Q" in each of the Q-initialed suras. The word "Majid" has a geometrical value of 57
- Sura 42 consists of 53 verses, and 42+53 is 95, or **19x5**.
- Sura 50 consists of 45 verses, and 50+45 is also 95, **19x5**.
- The number of Q's in all verses numbered "19" throughout the Quran is 76, **19x4**.

Nun (Noon)
S (Saad)
Y.S. (Ya Seen)

These two letters prefix Sura 36. The letter "Y" occurs in this sura 237 times, while the letter "S" (Seen) occurs 48 times. The total of both letters is 285, 19x15.

H.M. (Ha Mim)

Seven Suras are prefixed with letters "H ح" and "M م;" Suras 40 through 46. The total occurrence of these two letters in the seven H.M.-initialed Suras is 2147, or 19x113. Naturally, the alteration of a single letter "H" or "M" in any of the seven H.M.-initialed Suras would have destroyed this intricate phenomenon.

Proclaiming One Unified Religion For All People

All religions of the world - Judaism, Christianity, Islam, Hinduism, Buddhism and others - have been severely corrupted through innovations, traditions and the idolization of humans such as the prophets and the saints.

God's plan, as stated in the Old Testament (Malachi 3:1), the New Testament (Luke 17:22-36 & Matthew 24:27) and this Final Testament (3:81), calls for the sending of God's Messenger of the Covenant after all the Scriptures have been delivered. The main function of God's Messenger of the Covenant is to purify the Scriptures and unify them into one universal message to this world from the Creator and Sustainer of this world.

This major scriptural prophecy has now been fulfilled. God's Messenger of the Covenant has arrived, supported by overwhelming tangible proof (see Appendix Two). The purification and unification process has begun. God's plan is supported by God's invisible forces, and the enormous dimensions of this divine plan is manifest in the recent exposure of false religionists and the removal of such anti-freedom barriers as the Berlin Wall, the Iron Curtain and the Bamboo Curtain.

Henceforth, there is only one religion acceptable to God - Submission. Anyone who submits to God and devotes the worship to God ALONE is a "Submitter." Thus one may be a Jewish Submitter, a Christian Submitter, a Buddhist Submitter, a Hindu Submitter or a Muslim Submitter. The only religion acceptable to God is Submission. [3:19] Anyone who seeks other than Submission as his religion, it will not be accepted from him and, in the Hereafter, he will be with the losers. [3:85]"

I realize that was a lot to digest, but the point is do you accept such tortured mathematical "proof" for the Quran's authenticity? Do you agree with the conclusions of the gay Christian group that being born homosexual is a "gift from God? Or do you consider those claims to be huge rationalizations? After all, people who begin with a predetermined destination in mind can always manage to rationalize a way to get there. A graphic example is depicted below. The dots in each are located in exactly the same places but the people connecting them did so in entirely different ways:

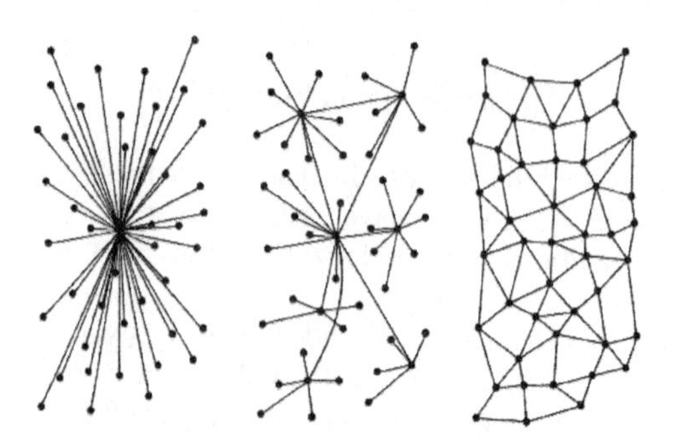

To put it all into perspective let's look at another example of how someone can use mathematics to rationalize virtually anything:

- Start with a given:

  CUTE PURPLE DINOSAUR

- Change all U's to V's (which is proper Latin):

  CVTE PVRPLE DINOSAVR

- Extract all Roman Numerals:

  C V V L D I V

- Convert into Arabic values:

  100 5 5 50 500 1 5

- Add all the numbers:

  666

- Thus, Barney is Satanic!

One final but very important point. While certainly not immune to rationalization agnostics tend not to do it, at least when it comes to the supernatural. After all, by definition agnostics are comfortable with admitting they do not know something. On the other hand rationalization is a key component of theism because the theist has already decided on the answer to a question beforehand and it is just a question of making the facts "fit" the desired outcome. As the great trial attorney Clarence Darrow put it, "I do not consider it an insult, but rather a compliment, to be called an agnostic. I do not pretend to know where many ignorant men are sure - that is all that agnosticism means."

Knowledge vs. Belief

Or, Just the Facts Ma'am

"To know that you do not know is the best. To pretend to know when you do not know is a disease." ~ Lao Tzu

In the summer of 1973 the New York Mets were mired in last place in the Eastern Division of the National League when enigmatic relief pitcher Tug McGraw uttered his now-famous rallying cry "Ya Gotta Believe!" Well they did believe and the slogan was embraced by the team and fans alike and while the Mets, only four years removed from the "miracle" of 1969, did in fact come back to win the pennant they ultimately lost the World Series to the Oakland Athletics. So much for the power of pure belief… in spite of what it may say in *The Secret*.

On a different tangent you are probably familiar with the sensational Casey Anthony trial from 2011 in which she was charged with killing her two-year-old daughter Caylee. With regard to its outcome, juror Jennifer Ford said afterward she and the other jurors cried and were "sick to their stomachs" after voting to acquit. The way she put the decision was, "I did not say she was innocent, I just said there was not enough evidence. If you cannot prove what the crime was, you cannot determine what the punishment should be."

Russell Huekler, one of five alternate jurors present for all of the testimony and sequestered along with the twelve primary jurors, said he would have delivered the same verdict and was shocked by public outrage over the trial's outcome by people who "believed in their heart" that Anthony was guilty - but gut instinct and an unquantifiable belief that you somehow "just know" something is not the road to justice… or truth. Thankfully the requirement for evidence is how the legal system works and the same criteria must also be applied to the truth claims of religion because we are the jury in this matter and since there are no modern burning bushes or parting seas believers are left with "I just know in my heart" and little else.

What about all of the archaeological and scientific proof for the Bible, you might inquire? I'm glad you asked. There is a profound contradiction rising in the world of religion because proponents of various dogmas are actually crippling their own religions by attempting to do scientific research in an effort to prove their claims and in doing so are attacking their religion's central pillar - faith.

Abraham is regarded as the father of faith among Muslims, Christians and Jews and if you believe the legend earned this title by demonstrating a willingness to sacrifice his own son, but Isaac was of course saved when God sent an angel put a stop to it at the last second because Abraham had proven his devotion. The reason this story is important is it was the supreme demonstration of faith, but for those today who claim to have faith it poses a huge question - would you have enough to plunge a dagger into your own child if you believed it was God's will? If you hedge your bets by expecting God to give you a pass by "waving you off" at the last second as he did with Abraham you clearly don't have *true* faith, plus you have either forgotten or are ignorant of the story of Jephthah found in Judges 11 in which no reprieve was granted and he had to follow through by killing his own daughter because he had made a deal with God which he could not renege on.

Let's fast forward a few thousand years and see where the faithful are today. The Associates for Biblical Research publishes a quarterly document called *Bible & Spade* which is about archaeological projects throughout the Middle East they say support the biblical record such as "evidence" showing the location of the Exodus crossing of the Red Sea. They have an exhaustive mission statement page in which they state and restate their belief the Bible is absolutely and literally a correct and true historical document which is "infallible, inerrant and authoritative." The problem with that standard should be obvious - it only takes one instance of proving something false to invalidate the entire book.

We see the same thing happening with the numerous groups seeking to find Noah's Ark on Mount Ararat in Turkey. On some of their websites you'll find tremendous amounts of information about how a wooden ark could have survived for six thousand odd years, how it could get so high on the mountain when there's not enough water on the planet to do it, exactly where it's located in the satellite photographs, exactly how two of every animal could fit on one ark, what its dimensions are, where and how it was built and so forth - but nowhere is there an explanation of why it's important that it be found.

In the early 1940s a number of religious papers in America carried a sensational story about a Russian expedition claiming to have discovered the Ark back in 1915. According to the tale, during World War I a Russian pilot flying near Mt. Ararat spotted a shiplike object protruding from a glacier and reported this to his superiors who relayed it on up the line until Czar Nicholas dispatched a large party to investigate, and after nearly a month of grueling effort the Ark was found and thoroughly explored by up to one hundred fifty men who confirmed it perfectly matched the description given in Genesis. A report was prepared and sent back to Moscow, but as luck would have it the document vanished during the Bolshevik Revolution. Somehow it reemerged a quarter of a century later and now the "truth" was out - however the ink had barely dried before serious questions and criticisms arose and the fabric of the tale quickly began unraveling. By 1945 the magazine *New Eden*, where it initially appeared, and at least two other magazines had printed retractions and the author, Floyd M. Gurley, confessed the story was ninety-five percent fiction. Subsequent examination of the remaining five percent "core of truth" has eliminated even this much and it appears the entire episode originated in the Netherlands in 1933 as an April Fool's joke.

Recantations notwithstanding modern ark fever had begun and just four years later in 1949, instructed by a "revelation from God," Reverend Aaron J. Smith of Greensboro, North Carolina set out on the first expedition specifically organized to locate the ark, thoroughly explored the region under ideal conditions… and drew a complete blank. Edwin Greenwald, a reporter who accompanied them, concluded, "The ark of Noah, if it ever landed on Mount Ararat, is lost eternally to the ages. It will never be found… The four man expedition… explored every crevice and every clue. It scouted through the villages for one hundred miles around, seeking anyone who might know anything. Nothing, absolutely nothing, was uncovered… In the villages, the old men and the young had heard the legend that a great boat once rested in the snow way up there. But no one had ever seen it, and they knew of no one who had." Smith returned home dejected, but inexplicably with his faith in the Ark's existence unshaken.

Decades later Violet M. Cummings authored several books on Noah's Ark, among them 1975's *Noah's Ark: Fable or Fact?* in which she claimed the Ark was found on Turkey's Mount Ararat, and according to the 1976 book and film *In Search of Noah's Ark* "There is now actual photographic evidence that Noah's Ark really does exist" with the claim being satellites, computers and powerful cameras have been used to pinpoint its exact location on Mt. Ararat. This is a remarkable claim because despite repeated trips to Mt. Ararat over the past thirty years the Ark remains elusive and people are *still* looking for it, but in spite of that "proof" and undeterred by the lack of evidence Cummings issued yet another book in 1982, this one published by Creation-Life Publishers and titled *Has Anybody Really Seen Noah's Ark?* The subtitle *An Affirmative Definitive Report* hints at her conclusion.

Interest in the Ark resurfaced in February of 1993 when CBS aired a two hour primetime special titled *The Incredible Discovery of Noah's Ark*, and little did they know they were using "incredible" in its accurate, proper meaning: "not credible." As Ken Feder described in his book *Frauds, Myths, and Mysteries*, the special was simply a hodgepodge of unverifiable stories and misrepresentations of the paleontological, archaeological and historical records. It included the riveting testimony of someone named George Jammal, who claimed not only to have personally seen the Ark on Ararat but to have recovered a piece of it. Jammal's story and the chunk of wood he displayed certainly impressed CBS producers and credulous viewers, yet he was later revealed to be a paid actor who had never been to Turkey and whose "piece of the Ark" was not an unknown ancient timber identified in the Bible as "gopher wood" but instead modern pine soaked in soy sauce and artificially aged in an oven. Another purported eyewitness featured in the segment was a Frenchman named Fernand Navarra who had traveled to Ararat on several occasions in the 1950's and 60's and claimed to have found wood from the Ark in 1955 and 1969. The program reported Navarra had the hand-hewn wood he found tested in three different laboratories and was told its age was around 5,000 years, clearly in line with the biblical account of the flood, but what the show did not say is one of the expedition members as well as his guides said he purchased the wood from natives in town and carried it up onto the mountain himself prior to his 1955 "discovery." The show also did not reveal the testing methods which gave an age of 5,000 years were of dubious scientific value and subsequent radiocarbon tests by six reputable labs yielded ages from 1,190 to 1,690 years old. CBS, which had obviously done little fact-checking for their much-hyped special, was naturally red-faced when all this came to light and reclassified the program as entertainment rather than a documentary.

More claims surface periodically, including in March 2006 when a team of researchers found a rock formation nearly covered in glacial ice which might resemble a huge ark. Little came of that claim, but a few months later a team of archaeologists from the Bible Archaeology Search and Exploration (BASE) Institute, a Christian organization, found yet another rock formation which they thought might be the Ark. This time it was "found" not on Ararat but at 13,000 feet in the Elburz mountains of Iran with team member Arch Bonnema remarking, "I can't imagine what it could be if it is not the Ark." The group brought back pieces of stone they claimed may be petrified wood beams as well as video footage of the rocky cliffs, and believed within the rock formation they could see evidence of hundreds of massive hand-hewn wooden beams laid out in the presumed size and shape of the Ark.

When viewed objectively they seem to have experienced something known as "pareidolia" (covered in a subsequent chapter), which simply put is someone seeing what they want to see in ambiguous patterns or images. Just as religious people will see images of Jesus or the Virgin Mary in toast, stains or cloud formations, they may also see images of Noah's Ark in stone cliffs. To offer a comparison, in New Mexico's Sandia National Forest there is a large rock formation called Battleship Rock which from a certain angle does indeed look like a battleship. One wonders what the BASE team would make of that.

Most recently former *Baywatch* star and *Playboy* centerfold Donna D'Errico, who says she first got the bug to search for Noah's Ark when she was nine or ten and in Catholic school, mounted an unsuccessful expedition of her own and produced a subsequent documentary called *The Secret of Ağrı Dağı* which contains a lot of hiking and climbing and talking… but no finding. This expedition was based largely on the claims of an Army sergeant named Ed Davis who said he had climbed Ararat in 1943, was guided to artifacts by a local guide and saw the Ark itself in the distance - but alas, it began to snow before he could get closer.

The BASE claims, as with all reports of finding the Ark, have yet to be proven but ultimately it may not matter because as BASE president Bob Cornuke stated, "I guess, as my wife says, my business is selling hope. Hope it could be true, hope there is a God." Yet the question is not about faith, hope or God, it is about if Noah's Ark is real and has been found, but like the mythical cities of Atlantis and El Dorado the ever-elusive Ark will continue to be "found" by those looking for it - whether it exists or not. To put that into perspective just imagine the Greeks mounting search after search for Jason's ship *Argo* which, if found, would presumably prove the existence of the mythical Golden Fleece. Clearly the old saying "fool me once shame on you, fool me twice shame on me" does not apply in such matters because no matter how many hoaxes are revealed there will always be plenty of credulous believers lined up and prepared to believe the next.

By definition faith needs no proof, and in the presence of proof faith becomes irrelevant. Faith means to believe without proof and indeed it means to believe in spite of evidence to the contrary. The paradox here is if Christians want to use empirical proof and science to prove their beliefs true they are admitting they no longer have sufficient faith to believe in the infallibility of the Bible. It has become nothing more than a fallback position which can be adopted when faced with difficult questions for which there are no logical or reasonable answers, i.e. "I can't answer that question (or more likely am avoiding it altogether) but still believe because I have my faith."

It has been said there are two kinds of people, those who know and those who do not know, and this knowledge is the thing which matters - however this statement does not necessarily apply when it comes to religion. As Bill Maher put it, "Religion is all about sticking fingers in your ears and humming. They don't want to hear what the reality is. They want to believe what they believe. It's not about critical thinking. I mean, faith is the purposeful suspension of critical thinking."

Knowledge is defined as "A clear perception of a truth or fact; erudition; skill from practice; to perceive with certainty; to understand clearly; to have experience of." On the other hand belief is "An assent to anything proposed or declared and its acceptance as fact by reason of the authority from whence it proceeds, apart from personal knowledge; faith; the whole body of tenets held by any faith; a creed; a conviction."

When it comes to religion a great deal could be said about the subject of belief because it is the principle on which most if not all exoteric religions are based. There is little doubt all of the various religious beliefs held by masses of people in all lands must have arisen in the beginning out of the personal experience of a few who claimed to have somehow obtained a direct perception or knowledge of certain facts. These revelations were then passed along to others, colored to a certain extent by their own personality and limited by the horizon of their own intellectual sphere. The question is to what extent should these revelations or inspirations be relied upon? In other words is it better to accept them as taught, or rely upon our own observations and experiences? In the end there are two very reasonable things we must do - separate what is true from what is false and what we know from what we do not know. In order to do that we first need to understand the meaning of the commonly misunderstood terms "agnostic" and "atheist" and how they relate to the terms "gnostic" and "theist."

First let's tackle Gnosticism. "Gnostic," from the Greek word "gnostos" meaning "known," refers to what someone knows while "theism" refers to what someone believes. In contrast the word "a-gnostic" describes a person who feels the existence of a god has not been proven while an "a-theist" does not believe in any deity. These four labels can be very useful in describing the way we feel about gods and moreover can be combined to create more precise descriptions.

An "agnostic atheist" is someone who does not believe in gods and also thinks the existence of gods cannot be known. This usually means they don't believe in gods simply because they haven't seen any evidence which supports their existence, which is a reasonable position. After all, why would someone believe in something for which there is no evidence?

A gnostic theist is someone who not only believes in a god or gods but claims to know their beliefs are true with absolute certainty. This position would be reasonable if someone has had a first-hand experience such as when Jesus supposedly appeared to Saul or Thomas, but absent such an experience it is not logical.

A gnostic atheist is someone who does not believe in gods and who thinks we can know they do not exist. This is a fairly unusual position because it is difficult if not impossible for someone to "prove a negative" and claim to have found evidence for the non-existence of gods.

Finally, an agnostic theist is someone who chooses to believe in gods but does not claim to know for certain they exist. People who fall into this category are often observing Pascal's Wager, believing in a god just in case there is one.

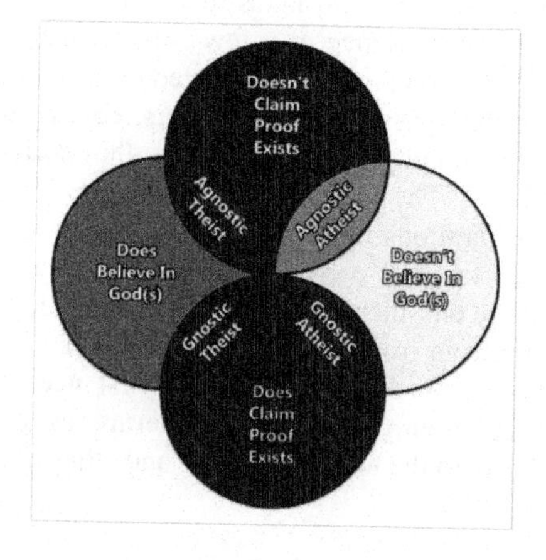

The most common positions are agnostic atheist and gnostic theist and if you look at the two of them logically the choice is clear. An agnostic atheist chooses not to believe because of the absence of evidence, while a gnostic theist claims to be certain despite a lack of empirical evidence.

It's important to remember a person's position might change depending on which god is under discussion. For example Christians will label themselves theists when it comes to Jesus but atheist when it comes to Zeus, although those who refer to themselves in casual usage as atheists usually mean they are atheists for all possible gods whilst a Muslim would be an atheist for all gods except Allah.

Here is a more detailed look at the possible choices. Think about where you fall and more importantly, why:

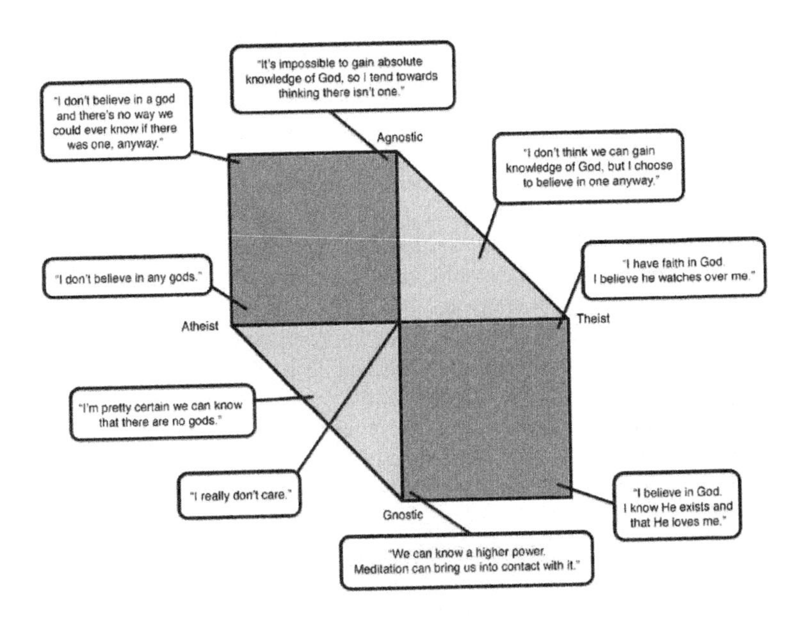

Epistemology is the investigation into the grounds and nature of knowledge itself, and the study of epistemology focuses on our means for acquiring knowledge and how we can differentiate between truth and falsehood. Modern epistemology generally involves a debate between rationalism and empiricism, or the question of whether knowledge can be acquired "a priori" (relating to or derived by reasoning from self-evident propositions) or "a posteriori" (relating to what can be known by observation rather than through an understanding of how certain things work). In other words empiricism is knowledge obtained through experience while rationalism is the belief knowledge can be acquired through the use of reason.

Epistemology is important because it is fundamental to how we think since without some means of understanding how we acquire knowledge, how we rely upon our senses and how we develop concepts in our minds we have no coherent path for our thinking. A sound epistemology is necessary for the existence of sound thinking and reasoning - this is why so much philosophical literature can involve seemingly arcane discussions about the nature of knowledge.

Epistemology matters because debates tend to revolve around fundamental issues which people don't recognize or never get around to discussing. For example many debates between atheists and theists are epistemological in nature such as whether it's reasonable to believe in the existence of God, to believe in miracles, to accept revelation and Scriptures as authoritative and so forth. They are ultimately disagreeing about basic epistemological principles and without understanding this and the various epistemological positions people will just end up talking past each other.

Atheists and theists obviously differ in what they believe since theists believe in some form of god while atheists do not. Although their reasons for believing or not believing vary, it's common for atheists and theists to also differ on what they consider to be appropriate criteria for truth and therefore the proper criteria for a reasonable belief. Theists commonly rely upon criteria such as tradition, custom, revelation, faith and intuition while atheists commonly reject these criteria in favor of empirical evidence, coherence and consistency, and without discussing these different approaches debates over what one believes are unlikely to go very far.

Some of the basic questions asked in epistemology are what can we know, how can we know it, why do we know some things but not others, how do we acquire knowledge, how can we differentiate truth from falsehood and most importantly why do we believe certain claims and not others?

There is a clear difference between empiricism and rationalism. According to empiricism we can only know things after we have had the relevant experience and this is labeled "a posteriori" knowledge because posteriori means "after," while according to rationalism it is possible to know things before we have had experiences and this is known as "a priori" knowledge because priori means "before."

Empiricism and rationalism exhaust all possibilities since either knowledge can only be acquired after experience or it is possible to acquire at least some knowledge before experience. There are no third options here except perhaps the skeptical position that no knowledge is possible at all, so everyone is either a rationalist or an empiricist when it comes to their theory of knowledge.

Atheists tend to be exclusively or at least primarily empiricists because they insist truth-claims be accompanied by clear and convincing evidence which can be studied and tested. Theists tend to be much more willing to accept rationalism, believing "truth" can be attained through revelations, mysticism, faith, etc. This is consistent with how atheists tend to place primacy on the existence of matter and argue the universe is material in nature whereas theists tend to place primacy on the existence of the mind, specifically the mind of God, and argue existence is spiritual and supernatural in nature.

Rationalism is not a uniform position as a few rationalists will argue some truths about reality can be discovered through pure reason and thought. Examples include truths of mathematics, geometry and sometimes morality, while other truths do require experience. Other rationalists will go further and argue that all truths about reality must in some way be acquired through reason, normally because our sense organs are unable to directly experience outside reality at all.

Pure empiricism on the other hand is more uniform in the sense that it denies any form of rationalism is true or even possible. Empiricists may disagree on just how we acquire knowledge through experience and in what sense our experiences give us access to outside reality, but nevertheless they all agree knowledge about reality requires experience and interaction with what can be proven.

In the end what someone chooses to believe and the type and level of proof they will accept usually comes down to what conforms to their own personal desires rather than a commitment to ascertain the truth, whatever that might be. With that in mind the conclusions of science are almost always the most correct because they tend to be arrived at dispassionately while belief systems necessarily rely on hope, faith, desire and other nebulous, emotionally driven criteria.

To summarize, science is skeptical of unsupported claims, employs critical thinking, seeks out falsifying data which might disprove a hypothesis, uses descriptive language, is self-correcting, relies on empirical evidence and reason, makes no claim of absolute knowledge and produces useful information. This is evident in everything from modern medicine to consumer electronics - tangible things which impact our lives many times each day. Conversely, pseudoscience and religion have a generally negative attitude toward skepticism, no requirement for critical thinking, routinely reject data which might potentially disprove a belief, use vague language, rely on anecdotal evidence and emotion, do not self-correct, make claims of absolute knowledge and produce no practical knowledge.

Apologetics

Or, Don't Believe Your Lying Eyes

"Doubt is not a very pleasant condition, but certainty is absurd."
~ Voltaire

During the baseball-themed movie *Bull Durham* character Crash Davis (played by Kevin Costner) was preparing young "phenom" pitcher Nuke Laloosh (Tim Robbins) for handling interviews and told him, "You're gonna have to learn your clichés. You're gonna have to study them, you're gonna have to know them." In a similar vein "apologetics" is a field of Christian theology which aims to present a rational basis for the Christian faith and defend it against objections using canned and endlessly regurgitated explanations. Apologists variously base their defense of Christianity on historical evidence, philosophical arguments, scientific investigation and arguments from other disciplines, but upon close examination most have little basis in fact and the apologist, faced with an incontrovertible piece of information which refutes his argument, will generally retreat to one of many well-rehearsed, canned "non-explanations" for how and why things happen. In a nutshell religious apologetics are essentially nothing more than non-answers to difficult or troubling questions recited by rote and the fact they are necessary illustrates that, for a God who is supposed to be perfect, people have to make an awful lot of excuses for him. If you are a religious person you will no doubt use these frequently as you proceed through this book, so you may find it an interesting exercise to keep track of how many times you find yourself parroting them. Non-religious readers are also encouraged to play along to see where these empty arguments would most likely apply. The following is a compilation of common apologetics and platitudes along with their "translated" meanings:

Apologetic: The Lord works in mysterious ways.

Translation: A coincidence, chance occurrence or events which can be somehow tied together through rationalization and/or mental gymnastics took place. This is an ad hoc statement thrown out when someone is confronted with an intractable contradiction in their belief system and is nothing more than a veiled confession of ignorance from someone who will say anything rather than question or confront their beliefs.

Example: "Yes, I realize your father died an unnecessarily horrible death at a very young age, but God works in mysterious ways. If he hadn't died of brain cancer, you and I might never have met at the hospital!"

Apologetic: It will happen in God's time.

Translation: It's taking a really, really long time and/or may never happen.

Examples: The second coming of Jesus and your job promotion.

Apologetic: It's all part of God's plan.

Translation: Everything has been decided for us ahead of time and therefore we have no free will (see "God gives us free will to choose").

Example: "It's not your fault because it was preordained and you had no choice but to marry the abusive man who beats you. I know you are upset, but it is a small part of God's grand plan for the universe which is beyond our understanding."

Apologetic: God gives us free will to choose.

Translation: There is no grand plan unfolding and we are responsible for our own actions (see "It's all part of God's plan").

Example: If you chose to marry an abusive man don't blame God because it was your choice and your own bad judgment.

Apologetic: The Lord helps those who help themselves.

Translation: If you don't choose to do something nothing will happen, which is pointless because this would also be the case if there were no outside help.

Example: Working to achieve a college degree, acquiring requisite experience, writing a resume, applying for a job, getting the job and then thanking God for it rather than giving yourself credit. This mindset makes one wonder how atheists (or Hindus, Wiccans, etc.) ever manage to become employed or achieve anything for that matter.

Apologetic: He's going to a better place.

Translation: "I hope he's not decomposing in the ground, because that means the same thing will happen to me when my time comes!"

Example: Uncle Joe, whom you knew to be a mean, drunken derelict has died and you automatically console your widowed aunt with these words without giving thought to where he might actually be. After all, even if your theology is true how can you know what he really believed?

Apologetic: It's in the Bible.

Translation: I read it (although most Christians have never read it and base this apologetic upon cherry picked verses provided by others) in an ancient book filled with absurdities and contradictions which was written by a bunch of unknown authors and later assembled and edited by a group of men, and therefore I believe it in spite of any evidence which may be offered to the contrary.

Example: The earth is flat, the earth is the center of the universe, homosexuals should be put to death, rabbits chew their cud, shellfish are forbidden, etc. Naturally, as science has proven these biblically based beliefs to be false and/or societal views of morality have changed apologists have reinterpreted the passages containing them to conform to modern science and society.

Apologetic: We can't know the mind of God.

Translation: How can we know what goes on in the mind of a perfect, omniscient invisible being when we can't really know what the person sitting next to us is thinking? Even so, people routinely claim to know what God wants when it falls in line with their own personal beliefs or desires.

Example: When asked questions such as "Why would an all-powerful God require animal sacrifice" or "How can it be moral for God to slaughter innocent infants" believers will deflect it by saying "We can't know the mind of God."

Apologetic: That was in the OLD Testament!

Translation: That may be in the Bible but it is really horrible and/or ridiculous so I am going to rationalize that none of those passages count anymore. This of course ignores the fact that the creation story, Ten Commandments and many other things Christians want and/or need to believe are also in the Old Testament.

Example: Pretty much the entire Old Testament!

Apologetic: It was God's will.

Translation: Something really bad just happened and since I can make no sense of it will assume God had a reason to do it no matter how big of a stretch it may be.

Example: An infant contracts brain cancer and dies a horrible and agonizing death.

Apologetic: I just feel God (or Jesus) in my heart.

Translation: You get a warm feeling when you pray or think about God, just as you do when you think about anything which brings comfort or joy because those thoughts release chemicals such as serotonin and dopamine in your brain. I know it sounds clinical, but that is what is actually happening.

Example: Compare how you feel when you pray to how you feel when you meditate, exercise, think about a loved one or pet, receive a gift or a compliment, watch your team win or experience any other positive event.

Apologetic: That (Bible verse) was taken out of context.

Translation: You failed to use rationalization and circular logic while interpreting that straightforward and very uncomfortable and/or patently ridiculous Bible passage. The same applies to verses which do not conform to an individual's personal desires. Even 2 Peter 3:16-17 says people will be guilty of taking Scripture out of context and make it say what they want it to say, and if the writers themselves knew the text would be ambiguous and open to manipulation how is anyone today to know what any of it is truly supposed to mean?

Example: "Prosperity Gospel" evangelists (and other pastors as well) use Ezekiel 44:30 as well as other verses to argue that members of their congregation need to tithe their earnings and that by giving money to them you are actually giving to God. This is obviously a self-serving interpretation removed from its original "context" and other Christians will argue the verses, when places into proper context, say nothing of the kind. To quote one Christian blog (Nairaland.com): "It is really sad that our pastors today are fond of picking Old Testament Scriptures and quoting them out of context for their own selfish desire."

Apologetic: You are not interpreting that (Bible verse) properly.

Translation: The way you interpret that does not correlate with the way I see it and does not support my beliefs, so therefore you do not possess my gift of insight. The Bible is a book made of rubber and can be made to say whatever the reader wants it to say.

Example: Mormon theologian James Talmadge interprets the prophecy in Isaiah 29:4 ("and thou shalt be brought down, and shalt speak out of the ground, and thy speech shall be low out of the dust, and thy voice shall be, as of one that hath a familiar spirit, out of the ground, and thy speech shall whisper out of the dust") to mean God's Word would come to people from the *Book of Mormon* which was taken out of the ground at the hill of Cumorah. Naturally mainstream Christians object to this interpretation and claim he is mistaking figurative language for literal language.

Apologetic: You can't take the Bible literally. The stories are allegorical.

Translation: Progressive Christians explain away many stories in the Bible by pointing out they are ridiculous when taken literally and are obviously allegorical parables meant to teach a lesson or convey a truth. This of course is dismissed by literalists who believe everything in the Bible happened exactly as written. The big question is how does one differentiate between the allegorical and the literal?

Examples: Adam and Eve in the Garden of Eden, Noah's Ark and the Great Flood, Sodom and Gomorrah and many others.

Apologetic: God never gives us more than we can handle.

Translation: This platitude is drawn from 1 Corinthians 10:13 and some theologians will point out the verse "really" means Paul was talking about temptation rather than suffering. This is just one more example of how Scripture can be taken out of context and/or can be made to say whatever someone wants it to say.

Example: The most obvious example of the folly of this belief is suicide, although there are less extreme examples where people go into catatonic states, suffer nervous breakdowns or simply give up on life.

Apologetic: Who would die for a lie?

Translation: The fact some Christian martyrs died rather than renounce their beliefs is claimed to be evidence of the truth of Christianity. The problem here is twofold. First of all people have died while certain of the "truth" of many other belief systems, and second what is the big deal about death if you think you are on your way to Heaven?

Example: The examples of those who have died rather than renounce other beliefs are legion. Buddhist monks set themselves on fire, Islamic terrorists routinely blow themselves up and as mentioned elsewhere people like Giordano Bruno have refused to recant scientific ideas which contradict religious teachings. Are those examples in and of themselves evidence for the truth of Buddhism, Islam and science?

Apologetic: "I believe it because I believe it," sometimes phrased as, "God said it, I believe it, that settles it."

Translation: Religion is much easier than scientific thought. That stuff requires study and experimentation and will give you a headache. Therefore I believe it… just because I do! This is the apologetic most often cited once all supposed empirical proofs for a belief have been shown to be nothing more than rationalizations based upon assumptions.

Example: A person who has read little or no Scripture for themselves (i.e. the overwhelming majority of Christians), let alone science books, blindly proclaiming the Bible is the perfect and inerrant word of God which explains everything.

Clearly a great deal of energy gets expended making these excuses, but the Bible itself ridicules this effort as unnecessary. In the book of Judges the Israelites repeatedly went astray and wound up defeated and enslaved by their enemies until they cried out to God and he raised up a hero to deliver them. Judges chapter 6 repeated this pattern with Gideon of the tribe of Manasseh who was visited by an angel and instructed to destroy his father's altar to the pagan Canaanite god Baal. He did it secretly by night but got found out anyway: "When the men of the town rose early in the morning, behold, the altar of Baal was broken down… And after they had made search and inquired, they said, 'Gideon the son of Joash has done this thing.' Then the men of the town said to Joash, 'Bring out your son, that he may die, for he has pulled down the altar of Baal and cut down the Asherah beside it.' But Joash said to all who were arrayed against him, 'Will you contend for Baal? Or will you defend his cause? Whoever contends for him shall be put to death by morning. *If he is a god, let him contend for himself,* because his altar has been pulled down.'"

That passage actually makes a very persuasive and well-reasoned argument, which is rare for the Bible. It tells us if Baal is really a god, especially the kind who is performing miracles and answering the prayers of his followers, he should be able to defend his own interests. He shouldn't need humans to serve as his agents, enforcing what they believe to be his will and punishing people who go against his decrees. And if Baal never intervenes directly and it's only his believers who are ever seen to act on his behalf, wouldn't we be justified in concluding that Baal probably doesn't exist?

The point is shouldn't that logic apply every bit as much to all gods, including Yahweh? Why do Christians rise up in outrage when church-state defenders cause Christian crosses or Ten Commandments monuments to be removed from public land and react with fury when store greeters say "Happy Holidays" or museums display blasphemous artwork? If God is real and if he cares about these things, surely he'll "contend for himself." Instead what we get is *men* claiming to speak on his behalf.

Common Arguments

Or, Who Needs Evidence?

"Sometimes people hold a core belief that is very strong. When they are presented with evidence that works against that belief, the new evidence cannot be accepted... and because it is so important to protect the core belief, they will rationalize, ignore and even deny anything that doesn't fit in with the core belief." ~ Frantz Fanon, *Black Skin, White Masks*

I bring this up now so readers will understand I am quite familiar with these arguments and promise to address each in detail in the following chapters. Keep in mind most of them can and have been made by the followers of *every* religion to justify their beliefs and "prove" their gods - not just Christians. Some rightly call many of these "zombie apologetics" because no matter how many times they are killed (i.e. debunked) they keep coming back over and over again *ad nauseum*. The following are summaries of the top arguments - as opposed to "proofs" - for the existence of gods, along with their explanations.

Teleological Argument: Also known as the "Argument From Design" or "Watchmaker Argument," this is now the most common argument theists present to "prove" God exists and they use a wide variety of props from pocket watches to cola cans to bananas to make their case. It claims every creation requires a creator and according to theists the more dramatic or complex something is the more likely this is evidence of some supernatural designer. The problem with this argument is it is basically "God of the gaps" reasoning which says if we don't understand how complicated things form then God must have done it and since we see some complex designs which we know were created by man other complex designs must also have a creator. The argument from design has been used for millennia and is probably one of the main origins of religion. It was eventually formulated into the Watchmaker Argument and later hilariously reached the internet as the "Argument from Bananas." The following is a shortened version of the classic Watchmaker Argument by William Paley: "Imagine you are walking along the beach and find a watch. You know there was a watchmaker.

Something so beautiful and complex and functional must have been designed by someone. Look around at our world, and how exquisite and symbiotic it is. Surely this is the work of God!" The problem with this argument is the notion every creation needs a creator does not reconcile with reality. For instance, is there a rainbow factory? Our improved knowledge of science continues to explain what was previously unknown and we have natural explanations for things previously attributed to the supernatural. Life reproduces and mutates by itself and the same cannot be said of an inanimate object like a watch - so this is a classic case of apples and oranges. For example if you put two watches next to one another nothing will happen, but do the same with two people of the opposite sex and there is a chance there will be a new person in nine months. Similarly if you break or scratch a watch it cannot repair itself, while living organisms are capable of healing and some varieties of lizards can even regenerate lost tails. This introduces an uneasy complexity to any discussion about creation and can lead a theist to put forward the Deist position that the universe was set in motion by a creator and left to run without further interference. Another obvious question is supposing every creation needed a creator, then who created God? You can't have it both ways. If complexity is a sign of intelligent design - and surely God must be the most complex entity of them all - he would require a designer himself. Introducing God as a cause merely creates more questions, is not an acceptable solution and usually leads to special pleading where the theist attempts to exempt God from this "rule." Who created the creator? Nobody. What was before the "Big Bang?" Nothing. This double standard negates any logic the theist may employ to claim God exists. When pressed on this issue many theists turn into amateur theoretical physicists or cosmologists and start picking and choosing little pieces of scientific gobbledygook to justify their contention that God is the beginning. A favorite argument involves referencing parts of Big Bang or Quantum Theory containing some concept of the creation of the universe by something "outside of time." The problem here is theists have no idea what they're talking about and cannot explain how such concepts work so they take snippets of scientific theory out of context and try to shoehorn them into their preconceived notion that "God did it." For issues where we know there is a creator even though we haven't seen the item created (such as a watch) there exists empirical evidence to recognize a creator existed. Theists often argue, "How do you know Shakespeare or Socrates was real if they supposedly died centuries before you were born?" The answer is we know because we have hard evidence of their existence and contemporaneous reports of each of them and their accomplishments, but even if that were not the case and some unknown person actually wrote the works attributed to them it doesn't matter because nobody is claiming they are supernatural beings. The evidence for God is not nearly as convincing. The scientific method also helps explain how this argument is false. During our lifetime we observe that paintings come from painters and we can in fact paint a painting (or build a watch) ourselves, therefore we know all paintings come from painters. If we grew up never having seen one or having been told paintings come from painters we might assume otherwise but we do not observe any evidence of a higher power creating life, earth, etc. - however by examining our world and environment we can find evidence to indicate how life, the earth, etc. could have come about.

Argument From Improbability: This is the second most common argument used to "prove" the existence of God. Theists say "look at the world" or "look at the human body," etc. with the idea being something so "perfectly tuned" surely indicates the presence of a supernatural creator. Yes the universe certainly is amazing, but this argument is a clear example of the Argument From Assumption logical fallacy and like the preceding argument it in no way addresses who or what made it all. In fact we could not be here pondering how great it is that the universe seems to be so finely tuned for life if it weren't at least sufficiently well-tuned for us to exist. The fine-tuning of the universe (such as it is - at least our little part of it) is a prerequisite for us to be here pondering. Even if there might be staggeringly huge odds against us being here, assessed well before life began to develop, those odds no longer apply once we *are* here. The probability of someone winning the lottery once they have won the lottery is 100%. Similarly, the probability of the universe having been sufficiently well-tuned to produce us given that I am sitting here typing these words and you are sitting there reading them is also 100%.

Argument From Irreducible Complexity: A variation of the argument from improbability, the irreducible complexity argument says there are structures of life which defy the laws of evolution and natural selection and "must have" been intelligently designed. The eye is most often cited in these arguments due to its complexity, however a possible evolutionary course for the eye has been produced which refutes this argument. The steps through which the eye evolved began with a simple photosensitive nerve followed by a concave depression which allowed for directional sensitivity, a spherical enclosed area with a pinhole input point which allowed for more precise directional sensitivity, a transparent humor developed inside the enclosed area, a lens formed allowing for the focusing of input light and tertiary structures form including irises which greatly increased the capability of the eye - but even if that explanation is inaccurate and it formed some other way saying something "must have" occurred absent evidence is yet another argument from ignorance.

Argument from Consciousness: Postulates that a person's personality is based on the existence of his "soul," in other words what the person feels, thinks, etc. is stored in the soul and it is the existence of this soul which is the basis of that person's life. Studies of the biology of human beings show the movement of various parts of the body are controlled by nerves which ultimately lead from the brain via electrical impulses, thus if the soul exists and is the driving force of a person it should be the ultimate cause of these signals rather than the brain, but in reality if a person suffers a stroke which causes brain damage that person's personality will be damaged or altered - something which would not happen if it were contained in or controlled by a "soul."

Ontological Argument: Ontological arguments are confusing arguments for the existence of God using premises which are supposed to derive from some source other than observation of the world - i.e. from "reason" alone. The first and best-known proposes that God is a being greater than any which can be conceived. The reasoning is if such a being fails to exist then a greater being, namely a being than which no greater can be conceived and which exists, can be conceived. But this would be absurd, since nothing can be greater than a being than which no greater can be conceived. So a being than which no greater can be conceived - i.e., God - exists. Perhaps the best known criticisms of ontological arguments were put forward by Immanuel Kant in his *Critique of Pure Reason.* He claimed ontological arguments are vitiated by their reliance upon the implicit assumption that "existence" is a predicate, however as Bertrand Russell observed it is much easier to be persuaded ontological arguments are no good than it is to say exactly what is wrong with them. In other words they are pointless.

Argument from Authority: This involves using the words of an expert or authority as the basis of an argument instead of using logic or evidence which supports that argument, i.e. "Professor so-and-so believes in creation-science" or "the Bible says donkeys have spoken," therefore it must be true. Simply because an authority makes a claim does not necessarily mean it is correct. If an arguer presents testimony from an expert, look to see if it's accompanied by reason and empirical evidence.

Argument from Scripture: The Argument from Scripture essentially says something is true because it is written in Scripture, for example God exists simply because the Bible says God exists. It assumes Scripture and its interpretation are reliable. This argument is often justified with a related - and circular - argument that Scripture is to be believed because God inspired it even though a similar argument can be made for passages in other holy books. In order for this argument to be sound one must demonstrate that Scripture is reliable, i.e. one must demonstrate if the Bible says something that statement is always true, but unfortunately for believers the Bible has been shown to be scientifically wrong over and over. For example geological evidence shows no trace of Noah's flood, and both the human race and the earth itself are far older than the 6,000-10,000 years determined by adding up the ages of people in biblical genealogies as New Earth Creationists like to do. Astronomical evidence shows the sun does not revolve around the Earth and that the Earth is not and never has been flat, which is contradictory to Scripture. The Bible has also been shown to be historically wrong. Exodus finds no historical backing and there is no archeological evidence Jews were enslaved in Egypt or millions of people wandered the desert. The Bible contains contradictions between the four Gospels as well as many other books which cast doubt on biblical reliability. The Bible also contains forgeries. Many of the letters of Paul are pseudepigrapha - fake writing - and were clearly not written by him. Apologists sometimes claim archeological research has confirmed many of the Bible's claims, including the existence of cities and kings mentioned in the Bible. For instance tablets discovered in Ebla (in Syria) allegedly contain references to cities mentioned in Genesis including Sodom and Gomorrah. While such discoveries do confirm parts of the Bible, we must be careful not to commit what might be called the "Spiderman Fallacy." Suppose a few thousand years from now an archeologist who knows nothing of our civilization discovers a cache of Spider-Man comic books. Judging by the backgrounds and dialogue the stories are clearly set in New York and of course New York is a real place as confirmed by archeology, but that does not prove Spiderman really ever existed. Similarly, the fact that Bible stories are set in real places does not mean the stories themselves are real. The Red Sea is indeed a real sea but that does not mean Moses parted it, and don't forget the pantheon of Greek Gods were said to have lived atop Mount Olympus which is also a real place. There is also reason to believe many of the stories in the Bible are simply not true. As previously mentioned there is no archeological evidence Hebrews were ever enslaved in Egypt in significant numbers as recounted in the book of Exodus. The Bible's track record as a historical book is certainly imperfect, and therefore its claims must be considered skeptically and one at a time. Another apologist argument is the Scriptures are honest depictions of the originals, i.e. the Bible was copied very meticulously and as a result we can be confident what we now have is not substantively different from the originals. Some apologists argue the *Dead Sea Scrolls* confirm that biblical manuscripts vary very little, and others include stories of multiple independent translations which differed by only a few words. They generally argue the texts we have today are very similar to the originals, were not changed much by editing or translation and therefore we can accept what they say as true but of course that is impossible to determine since we have no original "signatures" to compare them to. In the end the conclusion and argument itself are red herrings since even a perfect copy of a work of fiction is still a work of fiction. As Robgene put it, "Trying to prove God exists with the Bible is like trying to prove Superman exists with a comic book."

Argument From Ignorance: Involves appealing to ignorance as evidence for something, for example "We have no evidence God doesn't exist therefore he must exist," or "Because we have no knowledge of alien visitors that means they do not exist." Ignorance about something says nothing about its existence or non-existence. A component of the Appeal to Ignorance is known as "God of the Gaps," which is a bit of theological reasoning which invokes divine intervention as a way to understand natural phenomena which science is as yet unable to explain, i.e. since we don't know how X happens it is assumed God did it. Keep in mind that argument was once used to explain the sunrise, planetary motion, tides and thousands of phenomena we now fully understand and as those gaps were filled with naturalistic answers god(s) or the supernatural were no longer needed as an explanation. Hippocrates, the "father of western medicine," understood this 2500 years ago when he observed, "Men think epilepsy divine, merely because they do not understand it... we will one day understand what causes it, and then cease to call it divine. And so it is with everything in the universe." He was exactly right.

Appeal to Tradition: This says because people have always practiced a tradition such as astrology, religion or slavery they should continue to be embraced but it says nothing at all about their viability. Similarly, the "Bandwagon" or "Appeal to Popularity" fallacy concludes an idea has merit simply because many people believe it or practice it - i.e. most people believe in a god, therefore it must be true. Simply because many people believe something says nothing about the facts surrounding that something. For example during the Black Plague many people believed demons caused disease, but the number of believers had nothing to do with the cause of disease and we now know conclusively they were wrong and demons had nothing to do with it. Similarly slave owners in the 1800s argued that they had always kept slaves as justification for continuing the practice, but it was still wrong.

Appeal to Consequences: An argument which concludes that a premise, usually a belief, is either true or false based entirely on whether the premise might lead to desirable or undesirable consequences. For example some religious people believe knowledge of evolution leads to immorality and therefore evolution is "proven" false, but even if teaching evolution did lead to immorality it still would not imply a falsehood of the theory. The Appeal to Consequences is a cornerstone of Pascal's Wager (covered in detail in a separate chapter), i.e. believe or take a chance on burning. Albert Einstein disputed that with the observation, "Man would indeed be in a poor way if he had to be restrained by fear of punishment and hope of reward after death."

Appeal to Faith: Argues that if you have no faith you cannot learn. This is a poor argument because if you do not believe in something you cannot have faith in it and it makes no sense to require faith before being shown proof. This can also be construed as "putting the cart before the horse." If an arguer relies on faith as the basis of his argument little can be gained from further discussion because faith, by definition, relies on a belief which is not based on logic or evidence and instead depends on irrational thought which produces intransigence. Similar arguments can and have been made for the existence of UFOs, and Irish folklore tells us we can't find the pot of gold at the end of a rainbow without first believing in leprechauns. An even more illogical and disingenuous offshoot of this is the argument that atheists do not believe because they "enjoy sin too much." This is patently ridiculous because who in their right mind would trade an eternity of bliss for a few moments of pleasure and run the risk of eternal torment if they actually thought there was any truth to the claims of religion?

Argument From Miracles: This argument arises when hundreds or thousands are claimed to have witnessed the same "miracle." First of all it is important to agree on the definition of a miracle. That is covered in detail later in this section as well as in a subsequent chapter. The Argument From Miracles itself is an argument for the existence of God relying on eyewitness testimony (but rarely if ever empirical evidence) of the occurrence of miracles, usually defined as physically impossible or extremely improbable events, to establish the active intervention of a supernatural being or supernatural agents such as angels acting on behalf of that being. One example is the claim of some Christians that historical evidence proves Jesus rose from the dead and this can only be explained if God exists. This is also known as the "Christological Argument for the Existence of God." The obvious flaw is this is pure hearsay since there are no testimonials or attestations given by any of the people who supposedly witnessed this event, let alone tangible physical evidence. Another example is the claim of some Muslims that the Quran has many fulfilled prophecies and this can only be explained if Allah exists, but this is a claim I suspect most Christians will reject out of hand for lack of evidence just as was the case with the alleged resurrection of Jesus. Getting back to the definition of "miracle," definitions vary but two common ones are "something which is not naturally possible and could only have occurred because of supernatural intervention" or "anything believed to have been caused by supernatural intervention even if it is naturally possible." Both definitions are problematic, the first because it is practically impossible to demonstrate something in particular cannot occur because of natural means and the second because it is impossible to distinguish between a natural and a supernatural event when both look identical. As astronomer Johannes Kepler, a Christian who is best known for postulating the laws of planetary motion once said, "When miracles are admitted, every scientific explanation is out of the question."

Argument from Personal Experience: The argument from personal experience is an argument for God's existence based upon a personal religious experience. This argument is particularly common among certain branches of Christianity where things like possession and levitating have been claimed. An example is, "Jesus appeared to me in a vision, thus I know the doctrine of Christianity is true." Counter-arguments to the argument from personal experience express concerns over the legitimacy of personal experience as evidence and challenge the standing of its use as evidence in a few different ways. Comparing the personal experiences of the one making the argument to the personal experiences of another is a popular move. Personal experiences are used by believers of all religions as well as believers in other phenomena such as the paranormal, ghosts and UFOs and must necessarily be treated as a very weak form of evidence as so often it tends to produce contradictory conclusions when treated seriously (i.e. Christians and Muslims and Hindus and Buddhists all claiming their religion is true). The fact members of all religions have experiences which are tailored to legitimizing their own religion gives sufficient reason to be skeptical of this form of data. A Christian apologist might say, "I had a vision of Jesus, and so I know the doctrines of Protestant Christianity are true and justified." The counter-apologist could answer, "Well, that guy over there said he had a vision of Krishna, and as a result he knows the doctrines of Swami Prabhupada are true and justified. Why should I prefer your experience to his?" This is usually followed with a deferral to the subjectivity of experience as a form of evidence. As a third party, the evidence the two apologists (the Christian and the Hare Krishna) are of equal value as none of us have privileged access to either experience. It should also be noted that individuals in a particular society only ever have visions of the deities and prophets associated with the societies and religions they have been exposed to. A person in sub-Saharan Africa who has never been exposed to Hinduism will never have a vision of Krishna or Vishnu and a person in Saudi Arabia who has never been exposed to Christianity will never have a vision of Jesus, however this move towards the evidence is somewhat controversial as apologists may be liable to assert the possibility of exceptions to this rule. Such exceptions are plausible in the form of figures resembling, for example, the Virgin Mary, but these rely on vague descriptions of the religious figure in question since no one knows for sure what she or any of the others actually looked like. Personal experiences are subjective and as such cannot be directly shared, but only anecdotally related. The issue here is an individual can only offer an account of their own "vision" and the vision itself isn't available to others for evaluation. All others just have to take that individual's word for what they claim to have "seen." This can lead to challenges as to the legitimacy of the evidence. As before an apologist might say, "I had a vision of Jesus Christ, and he confirmed my belief in the doctrines of my church are justified and true." Naturally a counter-apologist responds by asking, "How can I be sure that you actually had this vision? Isn't it in your interest as an apologist to tell me this is the case?" Daniel Dennett has argued one key to the success of arguments from personal experience is they are and must remain personal. One could easily invent a story and present it as a factual account of personal experience (for example Joseph Smith's "First Vision") and others must necessarily decide whether the teller of this personal experience is delusional or a liar before allowing the story to stand as evidence, and since calling somebody a delusional liar is generally considered bad form the stories are often accepted as true.

Recently there has been a great deal of work done on the subject of temporal lobe epilepsy and its relationship to religious visions. Neuroscientist V.S. Ramachandran has written a great deal on the subject, asserting that the cause of many visions religious leaders have had over the years may have been caused by neurological function. The pervasiveness of simulated religious experiences during temporal lobe seizures offers sufficient reason to be skeptical of the claim that a vision of Jesus might actually be caused by the presence of Jesus and not by an incidental error in the wiring of the brain. So an apologist might offer, "I had an experience of the world such that I knew that there is a God. Everything felt vivid and I understood the Universe and knew God was trying to communicate his love for me," while the counter-apologist could easily dismiss the claim by suggesting, "Perhaps there was a seizure in the limbic region of your brain which caused you to have those feelings and not some sort of divine providence." One final possibility is the influence of hallucinogens. How can you be certain the person giving you his personal testimony of revelation was not under the influence at the time? Before you dismiss that out of hand consider that the drug peyote is a key component of religious ceremonies performed by American Plains Indians during which they see visions inspired by their Creator Spirit (not the God of the Bible in case you were wondering). Similarly, the Rastafarian religion encompasses themes such as the spiritual use of marijuana and as an interesting side note its adherents worship deceased Emperor Haile Selassie I of Ethiopia as either Jesus in his Second Advent or as God the Father himself. I realize these examples are on the fringe but there are plenty of instances where Christian leaders have admitted to using hallucinogens to "promote clarity," and when you consider the widespread use of recreational drugs today and throughout history how can you be sure the person making a "revelation" wasn't simply tripping? Also keep in mind the brain releases naturally occurring drugs such as serotonin and dopamine so there is room to question a visionary's state of mind. To reinforce that point, there is no way of knowing if Moses actually had an unlikely conversation with a burning bush or simply got hungry during his forty day excursion on the mount and ate a handful of the wrong mushrooms.

Argument From Martyrdom: This argument claims a religion is determined to be genuine based on the number of people who have been willing to die for it. Concerning this martyrdom argument, which is often used by Christians and commonly invoked using the phrase, "Who would die for a lie," Walter Cassels remarked, "Every religion has had its martyrs, every error its devoted victims. Does the marvelous endurance of the Hindu, whose limbs wither after years of painful persistence in vows to his Deity, prove the truth of Brahmanism? Or do the fanatical believers who cast themselves under the wheels of the car of Jagganath establish the soundness of their creed? Do the Jews, who for centuries bore the fiercest contumelies [insults] of the world and were persecuted, hunted and done to death by every conceivable torture for persisting in their denial of the 'truth' of the Incarnation, Resurrection and Ascension and in their rejection of Jesus Christ, do they thus furnish a convincing argument for the truth of their belief and the falsity of Christianity? History is full of the records of men who have honestly believed every kind of error and heresy and have been steadfast to the death, through persecution and torture, in their mistaken belief. There is nothing so inflexible as superstitious fanaticism and persecution, instead of extinguishing it, has invariably been the most certain means of its propagation. The sufferings of the Apostles, therefore, cannot prove anything beyond their own belief, and the question of what it was they really did believe and suffered for is by no means as simple as it sounds." Moreover, Muslims have regularly martyred themselves, so would a Christian then agree Islam is the "truth faith?" And since millions of so-called Pagans have been willing to die for their faith, by this faulty martyrdom logic Paganism must be the "true faith." In the final analysis, martyrdom proves nothing except the fervor of the believer.

Anecdotal (Testimonial) Evidence: This is derived primarily from claims of personal experience and is one of the most popular forms of evidence presented for beliefs in the supernatural, paranormal and pseudoscientific. Despite that, testimonials and anecdotes in such matters are of little value in establishing the probability of the claims they are put forth to support. Sincere and vivid accounts of one's encounter with an angel or the Virgin Mary, an alien, a ghost, Bigfoot, a child claiming to have lived before, purple auras around dying patients, a miraculous dowser, a levitating guru or a psychic surgeon are virtually useless in establishing the reasonableness of believing in such matters. Anecdotes are unreliable for various reasons. Stories are prone to contamination by prior beliefs, later experiences, feedback, selective attention to details and so on. Most stories get distorted in the telling and retelling. Events get exaggerated. Time sequences get confused. Details get muddled. Memories are imperfect and selective and are often filled in after the fact. People misinterpret their experiences. Experiences are conditioned by biases, memories and beliefs, so people's perceptions might not be accurate. Most people aren't expecting to be deceived, so they may not be aware of deceptions others might engage in. Some people make up stories. Some stories are delusions. Sometimes events are inappropriately deemed psychic simply because they seem improbable when they might not be improbable after all. In short, anecdotes are inherently problematic and are usually impossible to test for accuracy. Thus, stories of personal experience with paranormal or supernatural events have little scientific value. If others cannot experience the same thing under the same conditions there is no way to verify the experience. If there is no way to test the claim there is no way to tell if the experience was interpreted correctly, but if others can experience the same thing it is possible to conduct an investigation of the testimonial and determine whether the claim based on it is worthy of belief. As parapsychologist Charles Tart once said after reporting an anecdote of a possibly paranormal event, "Let's take this into the laboratory, where we can know exactly what conditions were. We don't have to hear a story told years later and hope that it was accurate." Dean Radin, Chief Scientist at the Institute of Noetic Sciences, also noted that anecdotes aren't good proof of the paranormal because memory "is much more fallible than most people think" and eyewitness testimony "is easily distorted." Testimonials regarding paranormal experiences are of little use to science because selective thinking and self-deception must be controlled for in scientific observations. Most psychics and dowsers, for example, do not even realize they need to do controlled tests of their "powers" to rule out the possibility they are deceiving themselves and are instead satisfied their experiences provide enough positive feedback to justify belief in their paranormal "abilities." Controlled tests of psychics and dowsers would prove once and for all they are not being selective in their evidence gathering. It is common for such people to remember their apparent successes and ignore or underplay their failures. Controlled tests can also determine whether other factors such as cheating might be involved. So if such testimonials are scientifically worthless, why are they so popular and convincing? There are several reasons. Testimonials are often vivid and detailed, making them appear credible. They are often made by enthusiastic people who seem trustworthy and honest and who lack any reason to deceive us. They are often made by people with some semblance of authority, such as those who hold a Ph.D. in psychology or physics. To some extent, testimonials are believable simply because people want to believe them. Often one anticipates with hope some new treatment or instruction and testimonials are usually given soon after the experience while someone's mood is still elevated from the desire for a positive outcome, so in the end the experience and the testimonial it elicits tend to be given more significance than they deserve. Finally it should be noted that testimonials are often used in many areas of life including medical science, and giving due consideration to such testimonials is considered wise rather than foolish. A physician will use the testimonies of his or her patients to draw conclusions about certain medications or procedures, for example they will take anecdotal evidence from a patient about a reaction to a new medication and use that information in deciding to adjust the prescribed dosage or to change the medication. This is quite reasonable, but the physician cannot be selective in listening to testimony by listening only to those claims which fit his or her own prejudices because to do so is to risk harming patients. Nor should the average person be selective when listening to testimonials regarding some paranormal or occult experience. This is all quite significant, given that the Bible is comprised of virtually nothing but anecdotal evidence with much of it derived from oral tradition.

Argument from Morality: The argument from morality, also known as the Axiological Argument (axios = value), is one of many arguments for the existence of God. The contention here is only God can provide moral standards for humans to live by, but it begs the question… where does God get his morals from? This is also a rephrase of the Euthyphro

Dilemma (are moral acts willed by God because they are good or are they good because they are willed by God?), so why not simply state this comes via Humanism as Occam's Razor would prefer? After all there have been many civilizations which didn't get their morality from the Bible and yet concluded the Golden Rule long before Jesus. The Akkadian Councils of Wisdom from the ancient Babylonian civilization which existed two millennia before Jesus was born stated, "Do not return evil to your adversary; Requite with kindness the one who does evil to you, Maintain justice for your enemy, Be friendly to your enemy." Buddhist wisdom written centuries before Jesus was born says, "Shame on him who strikes, greater shame on him who strikes back. Let us live happily, not hating those who hate us. Let us therefore overcome anger by kindness, evil by good, falsehood by truth. Do not hurt others in ways that would be hurtful to yourself." Taoist wisdom written centuries before Jesus was born tells us, "Return love for hatred. Otherwise, when a great hatred is reconciled, some of it will surely remain. How can this end in goodness? Therefore the sage holds to the left hand of an agreement but does not expect what the other holder ought to do. Regard your neighbor's gain as your own and your neighbor's loss as your own loss. Whoever is self-centered cannot have the love of others." The point is good and evil are psychological constructs which vary across time and societies and no particular worldview has a monopoly on morality or wisdom. This proves morality is subjective and not absolute. For example, do you agree that stealing is bad? According to the Ten Commandments it is, but what if you were a poor mother with five starving children and found an apple tree with nobody guarding it and despite knowing it belonged to someone else you stole in order to feed your children? A mother going through such a dilemma might have been correct in her action even though stealing is considered to be generally bad. George Bernard Shaw made an interesting point when he said, "The word morality, if we met it in the Bible, would surprise us as much as the word telephone or motor car." Today there are many laws which Christians are unwilling to accept such as stoning unruly children (Deuteronomy 21:18-21) as well as other Old Testament laws although many would claim such laws are no longer valid (which is quite debatable), and yet a lot of them would be quite willing to execute homosexuals while citing Old Testament laws such as Leviticus 20:13 as justification. A perplexing question is if God endowed us with an innate sense of morality as some claim how do we explain the existence of sociopaths who have no conscience or sense of guilt? One final bit of irony is that statistically speaking atheists are actually more moral than theists. After all, the population of America's jails and prisons overwhelmingly identify as Christians, don't they?

Argument from Benefit: This is similar to the Appeal to Consequences, but focuses on being rewarded rather than punished. Every time we see an infomercial on television we are experiencing this since huge promises are made, but when we view them rationally and objectively it becomes clear they will most likely never be fulfilled. Have you ever heard of Enzyte, which promises "natural male enhancement and erectile support?" It doesn't work, and in 2008 company founder Steve Warshak was sentenced to twenty-five years in prison and ordered to pay hefty fines for bilking customers, yet millions of men still continue to buy the product because of its perceived benefits. It's all about marketing and preying on human weakness and insecurities. In a similar fashion religion preys on people's fear of death, promising them eternal life and other wonderful perks - in some cases mansions, streets paved with gold, virgins, etc. - if they will just believe (and tithe). The big difference between this and the Enzyte case is nobody ever complains or sues the church when those promises are not fulfilled because it requires them to be dead in order to find out they were scammed, and by then it is too late.

There are also some patently silly anecdotal arguments and/or claims, for lack of a better term, which are generally offered by apologists *ipse dixit*, i.e. "without proof":

Atheists Convert to Theism: Many religious people claim they used to be atheists and then "found" God, and while some have indeed done that in many cases this is a bald faced lie designed to add weight to their beliefs. Well-known apologist Lee Strobel is a perfect example. He claims to have been an atheist who used his skills as an investigative journalist to determine the existence of God but that calculated assertion is designed to make his flawed arguments seem more factual and genuine than they really are. Likewise former child star Kirk Cameron claims to have been a "devout atheist" (whatever that means) although ironically, given the childlike nature of his arguments, that is irrelevant. He may have been confused and/or may have had some agnostic-like moments of weakness where his life was disappointing and he temporarily abandoned his delusional theistic rituals and beliefs, but that is not the definition of an atheist. It's like saying you're a vegetarian because at the end of one day you realized you hadn't eaten any meat. When you truly become an atheist what happens is you understand that believing in a fictional supernatural being for which there is no empirical evidence is not rational and raise the bar on your skepticism to require actual evidence of supernatural claims. Nothing short of that will convince a true atheist to believe. Likewise, once you realize the myth of Santa Claus makes more sense as a fictitious folk tale you can't honestly go back to thinking he's real unless you've suffered some sort of brain damage or actually see a bearded fat man in a red suit flying through the air on a sleigh pulled by eight reindeer. If you decide to believe in lieu of any real evidence, you're exhibiting pathology indicative of paranoid delusion. Granted it's easy to see why people continue to hold onto theist dogma when there are so many institutions and influences in society which promote it as being real, but the bottom line is there still isn't any empirical evidence. It makes you wonder, if more people talked about how Santa was a real person and flying sleighs do exist whether people would continue to believe that? It says less about what's real and true and more about the power of propaganda and peer-pressure. One of the prize "conversions" was that of philosopher Antony Flew, and while Flew did indeed state an allegiance to Deism, more specifically a belief in the Aristotelian God, apologists conveniently ignore the fact he did not become a Christian and continued to reject the ideas of an afterlife, God as the source of good and the resurrection of Jesus (despite being the son of a Methodist minister/theologian). It should also be noted that Flew's change of heart came at the age of eighty-one when he was in mental decline (his dementia was even the subject of a *New York Times Magazine* article) and the book published under his name on the subject was actually written by a man named Roy Abraham Varghese. Some also claim legal scholar Simon Greenleaf, the founder of Harvard Law School who wrote the book on how to examine evidence and conduct investigations, was an atheist who was challenged by some of his Christian students to use his methods to debunk the resurrection of Jesus Christ and "after a thorough investigation of the evidence came to the conclusion the resurrection of Jesus Christ is the most verifiable event in antiquity and converted to Christianity." Was Simon Greenleaf in fact an atheist? No. Some apologist once leapt to this conclusion and the next one copied him/her, and the next copied him/her and so on until each was copying the other with nobody attempting to verify it in any way. If 40,000 Google hits say it is true it must be, right? First of all we should note Mr. Greenleaf's own words about the subject. There are none. Nowhere does he claim to be an atheist and nowhere does he claim to have attempted to disprove the resurrection. Nothing indicates he ever was an atheist, agnostic or even a theist who disbelieved the resurrection. All evidence instead demonstrates Simon Greenleaf was a lifelong Episcopalian. He was on the Standing Committee for the Episcopalian diocese of Maine as of 1827 and at the Maine Episcopalian Conventions of 1831 and 1832, and remember this was all before he became a professor let alone having written his treatise on evidence. The fact is Greenleaf was an early 19th Century lawyer who wrote a book on evidence and used information which is now outdated to substantiate his own belief rather than an atheist "convinced by the evidence." He already believed and looked for support for those beliefs, and even if that were not the case an assertion such as "the resurrection of Jesus Christ is the most verifiable event in antiquity" is a massive overreach on the part of the apologist who concocted this tale. Really? More verifiable than the Punic Wars? Another incarnation of this tactic is the alleged deathbed conversions of prominent atheists and skeptics such as Darwin (which has since been rejected by even the most militant of Creationists such as *Answers in Genesis* because it is so easily disproven and thereby embarrassing) and because of this practice well-known skeptics such as Richard Dawkins have stated they plan to have their last days recorded in order to forestall such claims.

Atheism is a Belief/Religion: Theists like to say, "It takes as much (or more) faith to be an atheist," which is of course ridiculous. Atheism is simply a lack of belief in god(s) and it takes no faith to not believe in something. The very definition of faith is believing in something in the absence of evidence, in other words it's the opposite of coming to a conclusion based on something real and tangible. The non-existence of something is not a belief, but merely the default position one naturally comes to in the absence of evidence. Is there a large pink elephant sitting on the toilet in your bathroom? No? Why not? Do you take it on faith there isn't one? Do you think your lack of belief in this concept requires faith, or maybe it's the other way around? You only require faith to believe in something which defies the laws of logic. Is bald a hair color? Is not collecting stamps a hobby? If you no longer believe in Santa Claus do you call yourself an "A-Santa-Clausian?" Is there some doctrine you follow pursuant with your non-belief in the existence of the tooth fairy? Of course not.

Atheists "Hate" or are "Mad At" God: This is one of the most illogical premises of all. Theists often mischaracterize non-believers as people who "hate Jesus" or "hate God." When you hear someone use these terms ask yourself what it says about them. Do they hate everything they disagree with? More importantly, do they hate anything which they do not believe exists like the evil Darth Vader and Freddie Krueger? Or perhaps a non-existent (at least to a Christian) deity such as Allah? Isn't that a bit harsh? What does this say about the mental and emotional stability of someone making such a claim? To hate someone means to have intense malice towards them. Atheists cannot possibly have any hatred whatsoever against whatever deity a theist may believe in because it's not rational nor logical to have contempt for something which they don't believe exists. In the words of French Existentialist Philosopher Simone de Beauvoir, "I cannot be angry at God, in whom I do not believe." So what we have here are theists projecting their own fertile contempt and intolerance upon others. In fact I'd venture to say most atheists don't hate anybody merely because of their beliefs because that is a construct typically promoted by religious doctrine and one of the many reasons atheists dismiss religion as being counterproductive, oppressive, irrational and unethical. The next time you hear someone suggest a non-believer hates this or that ask them, "Do you hate Santa Claus for not bringing you enough gifts? Do you hate the tooth fairy for not leaving a fifty dollar bill under your pillow?" No? Why not? Oh, you don't believe in them? So is not believing in something analogous to hating it? If someone is critical of Christian doctrine or Scripture is that hate speech? By the same token, aren't Christians routinely critical of Islam? It's a shame some closed-minded people can't distinguish between criticism and hatred. Are atheists suggesting Christians should be rounded up and persecuted? Not at all. Ironically though, if you read the Bible and historical Christian doctrine as well as the Quran and other religious edicts there are many passages which support the notion non-believers should be persecuted and/or killed. So the irony here is freethinking critiques and information are not hate speech, but in fact are often an exposé of the hate speech perpetrated by religion.

Pascal's Wager: In the 17th Century mathematician Blaise Pascal formulated his infamous pragmatic argument for belief in God in Pensées. The argument suggests if you erroneously believe in God you lose nothing (assuming death is the absolute end) whereas if you correctly believe in God you gain everything (eternal bliss), but if you correctly disbelieve in God you gain nothing (death ends all) whereas if you erroneously disbelieve in God you lose everything (eternal damnation). The Wager essentially postulates it is a better bet to believe God exists than not to believe because the expected value of believing which Pascal assessed as infinite is always greater than the expected value of not believing. In other words what do you have to lose by believing? Pascal's Wager in practice is summed in the question, "What if you're wrong?," and the whole point is an attempt to bootstrap someone from unbelief to belief without any other axioms coming into play. Truly starting from zero knowledge would mean starting with no assumptions about what sorts of beliefs God is likely to reward, so just to be safe one would have to truly believe in every religion. After all, what if you are wrong about Allah and the Muslim version of Heaven and Hell? Or wrong about the Hindu gods? Or the Greek pantheon? You might end up in the Underworld facing King Hades and Queen Persephone simply because you made the wrong choice. Thus there is just as much reason to believe in a God who punishes people for believing in him as there is to believe in one who rewards people for believing in him, so the Wager's argument that belief is preferable because its rewards are infinite is bogus because it is equally likely the punishments would be infinite. In that case one might wish to maximize the sincerity of one's unbelief rather than the sincerity of one's belief. This is the opposite of the conclusion Pascal was trying to reach, but no less convincing. Religious organizations have used fear as a tactic to keep members from analyzing why they believe what they believe since the beginning. Keep in mind almost all Christian beliefs claim God to be omniscient, i.e. infinitely knowledgeable, and this means - assuming God exists - he has exact knowledge of all the beliefs, thought patterns and prejudices you have ever had. We can conclude from this God knows whether or not you actually believe or simply accept Pascal's Wager based on the prospect of not wanting to go to Hell *if* he exists. An omniscient God can surely tell if you are deceiving yourself and don't truly believe. In summary, logical faults with the Wager are a person cannot simply will himself to believe something which is evidently false to him and it would apply as much to belief in the wrong God as it would to disbelief in all gods, leaving the believer in any particular god in the same situation as the atheist or agnostic. Simply put, God would not logically reward belief if it is based solely on hedging one's bets. Philosopher Anthony Flew summed it up best when he pointed out, "Pascal tries to justify as prudent a policy of systematic self-persuasion, rather than to provide grounds for thinking the beliefs recommended are actually true." And of course the very foundation of this argument hasn't even been addressed, namely if God does indeed exist why is it so important for people to believe in him in order to be loved?

If you don't respect peoples' faith you are worse than those you criticize: Theists say atheists should at least respect their personal faith. Okay, let's examine this. Many religious people suggest criticism of their belief is offensive and tantamount to persecution but this seems quite odd since a person's beliefs, world-view and lifestyle are a conscious choice which any reasonable person should be allowed to examine and even scrutinize. Do Christian respect Islam, Wicca and other beliefs, or do they mock them as false and "of Satan"? How are atheists treated? In fact, how have religions treated those who disagree with their beliefs and doctrines throughout history? In many cases, quite brutally. This is the height of hypocrisy. Even George H. W. Bush, one of our most respected presidents, demonstrated this when he said, "I don't know that atheists should be considered as citizens, nor should they be considered patriots. This is one nation under God." That doesn't sound like someone respecting the beliefs of others, and such rhetoric is especially heinous coming from someone who was elected to represent all Americans.

America is a Christian nation: This is covered in detail in another chapter but in short theists put a different spin on the Constitution, confuse the language in that document with what the Declaration of Independence says, forget Jesus is mentioned nowhere in any founding document, are ignorant about why, how and when religious slogans were put on U.S. currency and demonstrate their "Christian tolerance" by frequently suggesting atheists and even citizens of other faiths should get out of the country because in their view those people aren't "real Americans." As a career U.S. Marine who served honorably for many years I have always taken particular umbrage to that last part.

Atheists don't follow their own laws of logic: Theists use selective interpretation of the laws of nature to try to turn them around on non-believers. An obvious example is their misunderstanding of the Second Law of Thermodynamics, which demonstrates more of a misconception about thermodynamics than about evolution. The Second Law of Thermodynamics states, "No process is possible in which the sole result is the transfer of energy from a cooler to a hotter body." Now, you may be scratching your head wondering what this has to do with evolution.

The confusion arises when the Law is phrased in another equivalent way, "The entropy of a closed system cannot decrease." Entropy is an indication of unusable energy and often but not always corresponds to intuitive notions of disorder or randomness. Creationists thus misinterpret the Law as saying things invariably progress from order to disorder, however neglect to take into account the fact life on Earth does not take place in a closed system since the sun provides more than enough energy to drive things. For example if a mature tomato plant can have more usable energy than the seed it grew from, why should anyone expect the next generation of tomatoes not to have more usable energy still? Creationists sometimes try to get around this by claiming the information carried by living things lets them create order, however not only is life irrelevant to the Second Law but order from disorder is actually common in nonliving systems as well. Snowflakes, sand dunes, tornadoes, stalactites, graded river beds and lightning are just a few examples of order coming from disorder in nature and none require an intelligent program to achieve that order. In any nontrivial system with lots of energy flowing through it you are almost certain to find order arising somewhere in that system. If order from disorder is supposed to violate the Second Law of Thermodynamics, why then is it ubiquitous in nature? The thermodynamics argument against evolution displays a misconception about evolution as well as thermodynamics since a clear understanding of how evolution works should reveal the major flaws in that argument - but that would require independent study and the average person won't take the time to find out for himself. Evolution says organisms reproduce with only infinitesimal changes between generations (after their own kind, so to speak). For example animals might have appendages which are slightly longer or shorter, thicker or flatter, lighter or darker than their parents. Once the differences appear evolution calls for differential reproductive success, for example maybe the animals with longer appendages survive to have more offspring than the short-appendaged ones. All of these processes can be observed today, and they obviously don't violate any physical laws.

You can't prove God doesn't exist! This defies logic but even so it is commonly used, usually after all of the other arguments have been debunked and there is nowhere else to turn. The response to this is usually "you can't prove a negative" and indeed the burden of proof falls upon the person making the positive claim, i.e. God exists, but more importantly such logic would necessarily have to apply to anything else which has not been proven NOT to exist such as Bigfoot, mermaids, the Loch Ness Monster, leprechauns and most notably other deities. For instance a Christian using this logic would have to accept the existence of the Hindu god Brahman unless he could prove Brahman's non-existence, which of course he cannot, and as a result this argument is pointless. This bit of common sense was made clear by J. K. Rowling in *Harry Potter and the Deathly Hallows* when the character Hermione says, "I mean, you could claim that *anything's* real if the only basis for believing in it is that nobody's proved it *doesn't* exist!"

Really Silly Arguments

These are arguments made out of a sense of a desperation which is so powerful it can only be described as self-delusion on steroids and these "proofs" are so amusing or erroneous they are fast becoming apocryphal.

The Banana Is the Atheist's Nightmare: This argument was offered in the form of a video clip by apologist Christian author Ray Comfort with former child star Kirk Cameron nodding in agreement in the background. He opens the clip with an appraisal of the design aspects of a soda can, pointing out the outer casing to contain the liquid, the size which is designed to fit the hand and the ring-pull which gives you easy access. This is to set up a comparison to the "intelligent design" aspects of the banana. He then points out the banana is shaped to fit the human hand, comes with a protective, non-slip surface to hold, is curved towards the face for ease of consumption, there is a "pull tab" at the top for easy access and it has a simple color code to show ripeness - green means too early, yellow is just right and black is too late. Ironically these features do in fact point to an intelligent designer, but it isn't God. The fallacy of the argument is it ignores the fact that while the banana has indeed been intelligently designed, it was by humans through the process of artificial selection. This is incredibly common for most if not all fruits, vegetables and even the animals we use for food in order to improve their utility. The banana was first domesticated eight or nine thousand years ago, probably in Papua New Guinea, and to say they are naturally designed by God to be the perfect food for humans is at best wishful thinking. When it became clear Comfort was ignorant of the evolutionary history of the banana he was so taken aback by people laughing at this video he claimed it was a hoax by atheists and later reversed course when that didn't gain traction and later issued an additional "apology" video to complete his self-humiliation.

Peanut Butter Disproves Evolution: The peanut butter argument for Intelligent Design, a claim made by someone named Chuck Missler, states that because life does not evolve spontaneously in sealed jars of peanut butter it is absurd to assume it evolved spontaneously on the primordial Earth. This is an example of a logical fallacy known as "denying the antecedent" and most people with half a brain don't need to go into the details of why this premise is profoundly ludicrous, yet there are Creationists out there who are willing to blindly embrace this nonsense without a second thought. Keep in mind the circumstances under which scientists posit life spontaneously happened are far different from the example of a peanut butter jar. For one the Earth had millions of years of trial and error to produce the conditions to create life, and second how can it be conclusively determined, even presupposing the idea that peanut butter is an ideal medium for spontaneously creating life, that this has *not* happened? Besides, Missler's methodology is terribly flawed because he failed to factor in the possible involvement of a jar of jelly. The bottom line is there is a huge difference between evolution and abiogenesis and what was supposedly disproved has nothing at all to do with evolution.

The "Crocoduck" Disproves Evolution: The "crocoduck, part crocodile and part duck, is a transitional fossil conceptualized by former child-star turned evangelist Kirk Cameron and his associate Ray Comfort. They argued that because we cannot see obvious inter-species evolution today that is evidence against evolution. The primary issue with this argument is no academic with a post-doctorate degree in any relevant life science has ever claimed evolution takes place in such an immediately obvious manner. In fact all evolutionary biologists agree evolution in such a manner is so monumentally improbable that for all intents and purposes it is considered impossible and any person with an adequate understanding of evolution will know it does not occur in leaps and bounds as the crocoduck implies. The above issues are compounded by the fact the crocoduck is only accepted as a logical attempt to debunk evolution by Ray Comfort, Kirk Cameron and their associates and brings up the logical question of having to find similar examples such as "dolphigiraffes." It is clear the crocoduck is simply an irrelevant, never-ending strawman since there is no reason evolution would require a crocoduck or similar organism for the theory to be valid and even if something of this magnitude did occur the fact ducks did not descend from crocodiles and vice versa make such a union between the two species completely illogical. In fact if a crocoduck were to actually be found it would be evidence against evolution as we understand it rather than in support of it.

Christian Clichés

Or, Stop Me If You've Heard This One

"It is a cliché that most clichés are true, but then like most clichés, that cliché is untrue." ~ Stephen Fry

"Everything happens for a reason." I've heard this said more times than I can count. I'm not sure where it came from, but it's definitely not in the Bible. The closest thing I can come up with is "to everything there is a season" but that's not exactly the same. When asked for the reason *why* something happened almost invariably the response will be yet another cliché such as "We can't know God's purposes" or "We can't comprehend the mind of God." The fact is faith, by definition, is not reasonable. If it could be empirically verified with facts or by using the scientific method it wouldn't be faith, it would be a theory. Also consider how such a pithy phrase sounds to someone who was raped. Do you really mean to tell them there's a reason that happened? Better to be quiet, listen and if appropriate mourn alongside them but don't dismiss grief or tragedy with such a meaningless phrase, especially when you cannot fathom what that "reason" could possibly be and must resort to using yet another cliché such as "We can't comprehend God's purposes."

"If you died today, do you know where you'd spend the rest of eternity?" No I don't, and neither do you. Asking such a presumptuous question implies you have some insider knowledge the rest of us don't. You can say you hope for it or choose to believe it all you want, but nobody knows. If your faith is entirely founded upon the notion of "eternal fire insurance" you're not sharing testimony, you're peddling propaganda.

"He (or she) is in a better place." This may or may not be true. Again, we have no way of knowing. You may believe it or hope it is true, but to speak with such authority about something we don't actually know for a fact is arrogant, plus focusing on the passing of a loved one minimizes the grief of the people they have left behind. And do you ever consider the possibility they may have gone to the *other* place?

"This could be the end of days." Many Christians love to look for signs of the end of the world. It is practically an apocalyptic fetish, as if they can't wait until everything comes to a smoldering halt so they can wave their fingers with that "I told you so" look on their faces while they levitate to Heaven and nonbelievers beg for mercy. And by the way, people have been saying this for centuries.

"Jesus died for your sins." This is an all-time Christian favorite, but even if you buy into the concept of substitutionary atonement (the idea that God set Jesus up as a sacrifice to make good for all the bad stuff mankind has done) this is an abysmal way to introduce faith to someone. Nobody asked Jesus to die for them, and if someone isn't a Christian they will have no concept of how that could possibly be a good thing. Besides, if you stop to think about the notion that God required a human sacrifice in order to dispense forgiveness it makes even less sense, not to mention the fact Jesus didn't really die if he is now sitting at the right hand of God as Christians believe.

Love the sinner, hate the sin. This is at best a backhanded way to tell someone you love them and at worst it is an outright insult. It is usually accompanied by the phrase, "I'm not judging you, but…"

The Bible clearly says… Unless you are a biblical scholar who knows the historical and cultural contexts of Scripture and can read them in their original languages the Bible isn't clear about much. Sure we can pick and choose verses which seem to say one thing or another, but by whom was it originally said and to whom? Cherry-picking Scripture to make a point is called proof-texting, and it's a theological no-no. The Bible can be used to make nearly any point you care to including the justification of slavery, and in any case spouting Bible verses is pointless unless the person you are speaking to already believes it to be the word of God.

God needed another angel in Heaven, so he called him (or her) home. Another well-meaning but insensitive thing to say. This assumes a lot about what the person you're speaking to believes and ignores the grief they're going through. God needed another angel? Right now? For what? This statement is almost childlike. At Michael Jackson's memorial Stevie Wonder got up and said, "We needed Michael here on Earth, but God needed him more," but as Bill Maher pointed out, "Really?" God needs people? God needs singers? God's up there going, 'Oh, f*ck. There is nothing on. There is never anything on. I'm tired of Sinatra and Elvis and Andy Williams. Get that Michael Jackson up here! I used to love that moonwalk thing he did. Get that mother**cker up here! He's going to entertain me."

Are you saved? Regardless of whether or not someone believes in Hell, this is a very unattractive thing to say. First of all it implies a power vs. privilege imbalance (i.e., "I'm saved, but I'm guessing you're not based on some assumptions I'm making about you) and it also leaps over the hurdle of personal investment relationship straight into the deep waters of personal faith. Plus you must define from who or what you are saved. After all, isn't it the benevolent and loving God you believe in who will torture and torment the unsaved for eternity? This concept is akin to someone holding a gun to your head saying, "Love me, or I will blow your brains out."

The Lord never gives someone more than they can handle. What about people with mental illness? What about people in war-torn countries who are tortured to death? What about the millions of Jews murdered during the Holocaust? This also implies if really horrible things are happening to you, God "gave" it to you. Is this a test? Am I being punished? Is God just arbitrarily cruel? And finally, if this cliché is true how does one explain suicide?

America was founded as a Christian nation. I find it hard to believe we are still having this conversation, dishonest historical revisionists such as David Barton notwithstanding, but here we are. Anyone with a cursory understanding of history understands the United States was founded on the principle of religious liberty for all and not just the liberty to be a Christian. Plus our Constitution is secular and many of the founding fathers were explicitly not Christian. Thomas Jefferson, anyone?

The Bible says it; I believe it; that settles it. If ever there was a top-shelf conversation killer this is it. People who say this are not inviting any opinion, response, thought or the like. They are simply making a claim and telling others to shut up. How many people actually take every word of the Bible literally? Everyone qualifies something in it like the parts about keeping kosher, wearing blended fibers, stoning adulterers, tossing your virgin daughters into the hands of an angry mob, working on the Sabbath… you get the point.

It was Adam and Eve, not Adam and Steve. This is a little "joke" some Christians use to assert the superiority of opposite-sex unions over same-sex ones but if you really believe the first and only two people on the planet at one point were Adam and Eve, who did their kids marry and have babies with? Each other. This is called incest (and it happened again if you believe Noah's family members were the only survivors of the great flood). This demonstrates selective moral blindness.

Christianity is the only way to God/Heaven. Many believe this with their whole heart and I'm sure they have Scriptures at the ready to support it, but if those they're speaking with think differently about this or haven't put much thought into it this sounds like an ultimatum or threat. Think about how such a statement might sound to someone who has lost a loved one who was not a Christian, and theologically speaking it opens up a whole Pandora's Box in answering for the fate of all those who lived before Christ, have never heard about him and so on.

When God closes a door, he opens a window. Like some other clichés, this implies when something unexpected (and usually bad) happens to you, God did it. What about someone who feels like the door has closed on them and there is no hope in sight? Perhaps they view the "open window" as an invitation to jump. That person may benefit more from a compassionate ear, loving heart and simple "What can I do to help?" than some pithy phrase which may or may not have any basis in reality.

God helps those who help themselves. Let me be clear - this is not in Scripture. People treat it like it is and many think it is, but it's not. Benjamin Franklin penned this in the *Farmers' Almanac* in 1757. The fact of the matter is people who help themselves, help themselves. How else do we explain all of the successful non-Christians out there?

God is in control. This raises a very fundamental problem of "theodicy" which most Christians are not prepared to address. Theodicy is the dilemma between belief in an all-knowing, all-loving, all-powerful God and the existence of evil and/or suffering in the world (see "the Riddle of Epicurus"). The other problem is if you believe human beings have free will, which is a central tenet of most Christian thought, it needs to be recognized as a concession of control by God and makes this cliché untrue. Telling someone who was raped, abused, tortured, neglected, etc. that God was in control during that experience is not exactly a good endorsement.

I'm praying for you: Although sometimes people mean well when they say this often it's the religious equivalent of the middle finger, i.e. "I don't like you and wish you would change so I'm going to pray you become more like me." There are those times when people say it with truly benevolent intent, but it's still a very personal thing. Instead consider asking someone if they would like for you to pray for them and ask what they would like you to pray for instead of making assumptions. More to the point if you truly believe prayers are effective and are not trying to make a point why bother telling them? Just do it.

The Bible is proven by hundreds of 100% fulfilled prophecies. This claim is made all the time but most people who say it can't even name one and if they can it is usually the return of Jews to Israel - a self-fulfilling "prophecy" which is discussed in a subsequent chapter. One Christian website smugly proclaims, "Bible prophecies are almost always specific and detailed. Fulfillment of Bible prophecies are usually obvious and are always 100% accurate..." when the truth of the matter is they are rarely specific or obvious. With regard to the claim of accuracy, the failure of prophecies concerning the destruction of Tyre, desolation of Egypt, Nile drying up, triumph of Judah, Egyptians adopting the dead language of Canaan, Israel living in peace with its neighbors and the Davidic line enduring forever falsify this claim.

The Bible is a collection of sixty-six harmonious books written by forty authors from a variety of backgrounds over a period of fifteen hundred years in three different languages on three continents and therefore must be true. This parroted claim can be found verbatim pretty much everywhere you look and is usually made by people who have never read the sixty-six books they refer to, so let's break it down. How those sixty-six books were chosen and assembled, along with those which were omitted, is discussed in detail in a subsequent chapter but the brief answer is it is a matter of politics, foreshadowing and editing. As for the forty authors, most are anonymous with the exception of Paul - the names were later assigned by tradition because why would anyone believe something as being "gospel" if the author is unknown? Plus how can their backgrounds possibly be known if the authors themselves are anonymous? What the quite true claim of three languages on three continents demonstrates is the four *other* continents made no contribution to the narrative and in fact the people on them never heard any of these stories until centuries later.

Look at the manuscript evidence. There are far more copies of the biblical manuscripts, with remarkable consistency between them, than there are for any of the classics like Plato, Aristotle and Socrates. The point being made here is, "There is no body of ancient literature in the world which enjoys such a wealth of good textual attestation as the New Testament." Using that standard we must also give similar consideration to the *Quotations of Chairman Mao* and *Quran*, which are the second and third most prolific titles. As for consistency, there are over fifty different versions of the Bible.

There is overwhelming archaeological evidence for the Bible. The claim is, "Again and again archaeological discoveries have verified the accuracy of the historical and cultural references in the Bible. The more they dig, the more it confirms the Bible." The fact Bible stories are set in real settings is not evidence for the truth of the stories themselves, especially the miracles and supernatural events. Novels are routinely set in actual locations, and we can all agree they are fiction.

The Bible is corroborated by non-biblical sources. The most common example for this one is, "Many contemporary historian such as Josephus were eyewitnesses and wrote about biblical events." The truth is there are absolutely no such contemporaneous extra-biblical corroborations, something which is covered in detail later in this book.

The Bible is true because it received expert scrutiny. A common contention is, "The early church had extremely high standards for what books were judged to be authentic and therefore included in the Bible." Obviously nobody today can possibly know what standards were used because they were not there and it is a historical fact that the men who assembled the Bible were biased. This is discussed in the chapter *Author, Author!*

The Bible is proven through leader acceptance since a majority of the greatest leaders and thinkers in history have affirmed the truth and impact of the Bible. Aside from being a blatant appeal to authority, this claim is fatally flawed for two reasons. First many great leaders and thinkers identify with different faiths or no religion at all, and second the fact that Hitler and other such leaders were professing Christians is hardly an endorsement for belief.

Name That Dogma

Or, All Those Other People Are Nuts

"Accidents of birth and geography determine to a very large extent to what faith we belong." ~ Archbishop Desmond Tutu

The following is excerpted from Archbishop Desmond Tutu's book *God is Not a Christian and Other Provocations* and was drawn from a forum in Britain where Tutu addressed leaders of different faiths during a mission to the city of Birmingham in 1989: "They tell the story of a drunk who crossed the street and accosted a pedestrian, asking him 'I *shay*, which *ish* the other *shide* of the *shtreet*?' The pedestrian, somewhat nonplussed, replied 'That side, of course!' The drunk slurred '*Shtrange*. When I *wash* on that *shide*, they *shaid* it wash *thish shide*.' Where the other side of the street is depends on where we are. Our perspective differs with our context, the things that have helped to form us; and religion is one of the most potent of these formative influences, helping to determine how and what we apprehend of reality and how we operate in our own specific context. My first point seems overwhelmingly simple: that the accidents of birth and geography determine to a very large extent to what faith we belong. The chances are very great that if you were born in Pakistan you are a Muslim, or a Hindu if you happened to be born in India, or a Shintoist if it is Japan and a Christian if you were born in Italy. I don't know what significant fact can be drawn from this - perhaps that we should not succumb too easily to the temptation to exclusiveness and dogmatic claims to a monopoly of the truth of our particular faith. You could so easily have been an adherent of the faith that you are now denigrating, but for the fact that you were born here rather than there."

Archbishop Tutu makes a very important point and destroys the argument for believing in a particular religion due to "knowledge" of the "truth." Whenever someone asks if I believe in God I usually respond by first asking, "Which one?" That may sound like a flippant remark at first blush, but there is a very good reason for the question because while the exact number of religions in the world is unknown best estimates place the total at around four thousand two hundred. Of these nearly two dozen have been classified as major world religions, but even if it were obvious the questioner were a Christian it would still beg the question which brand of Christianity do you follow because there are approximately thirty-eight thousand Christian denominations in the world, taking into consideration cultural distinctions of denominations in different countries. As others before me have said they can't all be right, in fact no two can be correct at the same time, but they certainly can all be wrong. Here is a breakdown of what the world considers to be "true":

- Christianity (including Mormons): 2 billion
- Islam: 1.3 billion
- Hinduism: 900 million
- Buddhism: 360 million
- Chinese Traditional Religion: 225 million
- Primal-Indigenous: 150 million
- African Traditional and Diasporic: 95 million
- Sikhism: 23 million
- Juche: 19 million
- Spiritism: 14 million
- Judaism: 14 million
- Baha'i: 6 million
- Jainism: 4 million
- Shinto: 4 million
- Cao Dai: 3 million
- Tenrikyo: 2.4 million
- Neo-Paganism: 1 million
- Unitarian-Universalism: 800 thousand
- Rastafarianism: 700 thousand
- Scientology: 600 thousand
- Zoroastrianism: 200 thousand

It should be readily apparent which if any is true and more to the point if there were only one religion - and it was simply a choice between believing or not believing claims for God - it would be far more compelling. And speaking of not believing, the fourth largest and fastest growing worldview includes the Secular, Nonreligious, Agnostic and/or Atheists amongst us, conservatively estimated at nearly a billion, which were omitted from the list because by definition they are not religions despite the assertions of various religious apologists to the contrary.

This wide variety of belief systems poses a serious problem for the philosophical treatise known as Pascal's Wager which suggests it is safer to believe than not and run the risk of eternal damnation. Believe in what? The one *true* religion, of course! I suppose the safest course of all, impractical as it may be, would be to take no chances and believe in all of the world's religions simultaneously. Of course doing that would require the inclusion of Scientology, but that shouldn't be so hard. After all Tom Cruise, John Travolta and more than a half million other people worldwide are on board, but accepting the teachings of unfamiliar faiths such as Baha'i, Jainism, Shinto, Cao Dai and Tenrikyo might prove to be a bit more difficult. What of the ancient religions practiced by the Greeks, Norse, Romans and others which have since been relegated to myth status? If nothing else they will provide some insight into the origins of Christianity, Judaism, Islam and other modern religions.

Religious Mythology was at the heart of everyday life in ancient Greece. In fact the Greeks regarded it as a part of their history. They used myth to explain natural phenomena, cultural variations, traditional enmities, friendships and it was a source of pride to be able to trace one's descent from a mythological hero or even a god. Few ever doubted the truth behind the account of the Trojan War contained in the *Iliad* and *Odyssey* and according to historian and former classics professor Victor Davis Hanson and John Heath, associate professor of classics at Santa Clara University, the profound knowledge of the Homeric epics was deemed by the Greeks the basis of their acculturation. Homer was the "Education of Greece" and his poetry was "The Book." In short, Prometheus and Epimetheus were spared imprisonment in Tartarus because they had not fought with their fellow Titans during the war with the Olympians and were instead given the task of creating man. The first mortal man was Deucalion, son of the Titan Prometheus, and the first woman Pandora, who was made by all the gods together. Prometheus shaped man out of mud and Athena breathed life into his clay figure - a scenario not unfamiliar to readers of Genesis. Prometheus had assigned Epimetheus the task of giving the creatures of the earth their various qualities such as swiftness, cunning, strength, fur and wings but unfortunately by the time he got to man had given all the good qualities out and there were none left - so Prometheus decided to make man stand upright as the Gods did and give them fire.

Zeus became angry at Prometheus for three things - being tricked on sacrifices, stealing fire for man and for refusing to tell Zeus which of Zeus' children would dethrone him, so Zeus had his servants Force and

Violence seize Prometheus, take him to the Caucasus Mountains and chain him to a rock with unbreakable adamanite chains where he was tormented day and night by a giant eagle tearing at his liver. Zeus gave Prometheus two ways out of this torment. He could name the mother of the child who would dethrone Zeus or he could meet two conditions - first an immortal must volunteer to die for Prometheus "sins" much like Jesus is said to have done, and second a mortal must kill the eagle and unchain him. Eventually Chiron the Centaur agreed to die, and Heracles killed the eagle and unbound him.

Lycaon, King of Arcadia, had sacrificed a boy to Zeus much as Abraham had offered to do in the Bible, but Zeus was appalled by this cannibal offering and loosed a deluge so the rivers ran in torrents and the sea flooded the coastal plain, engulfed the foothills with spray and washed everything clean - just like the great flood in Genesis. Deucalion, with the aid of his father Prometheus, was saved from this deluge by building a chest or "ark" and like his biblical equivalent Noah and Mesopotamian counterpart Utnapishtim used his chest to save himself and his wife, Pyrrah. Plutarch speaks of the pigeons by which he sought to find out whether the waters had retired and Lucian wrote of the animals of every kind which he had taken with him, details which should sound familiar to most Jews and Christians.

Since we are on the subject of floods now would be a good time to discuss the Babylonian *Epic of Gilgamesh*, dating from approximately 2700 BCE. In that story a man named Utnapishtim tells Gilgamesh a secret story about a flood of the old city Shuruppak on the banks of the Euphrates River. The god Ea commanded Utnapishtim to demolish a house and build a boat, regardless of the cost, to keep living beings alive. The boat must have equal dimensions with corresponding width and breadth and the sides of the superstructure were required to be equal widths of 120 cubits and covered over like Apsu boats. Utnapishtim promised to do what Ea commanded and made a drawing of the interior structure. The boat had six decks divided into seven and nine compartments. Once it was ready he loaded aboard all the living beings that he had along with his friends and relatives and on the seventh day released a dove which flew away but came back to him. He then released a swallow, but it also came back to him. Finally he released a raven which was able to eat and scratch and did not circle back to the boat, after which he sent his livestock out and sacrificed a sheep. Interestingly, the discovery of artifacts associated with Aga and Enmebaragesi of Kish, two other kings named in the stories, has lent some tiny bit of credibility to the historical existence of Gilgamesh - unlike Noah. Keep in mind even this ancient story was not original, having been adapted from the Sumerians' 18th Century BCE Akkadian epic of *Atra-Hasis* in which Enki warns the hero Atrahasis of Shuruppak to build a boat to escape the flood planned by the god Enlil to destroy humankind.

Various accounts of the creation of the world and human beings also appear in Norse mythology. All begin in Ginnungagap, a deep empty space between realms of heat and ice where frost formed and became a giant named Ymir. A cosmic cow named Audhumla also appeared and while licking the cliffs of ice revealed a man who had three grandsons, one of which was Odin. With his two brothers Odin killed the frost giant Ymir and formed the earth from his body, the seas and rivers from his blood and the sky from his skull which was held suspended above the earth by four strong dwarfs.

The *Voluspa* says Odin and his brothers made the first man and woman out of an ash tree and elm tree respectively and gave the humans life, intelligence and beauty. A poem called *The Lay of Vafthrudnir*, however, says the first man and first woman grew out of Ymir's armpits before he was killed so, much like the Bible, Norse mythology had its contradictions.

There was still the small matter of creating a universe to attend to. Once they had killed Ymir, Odin and the other gods created an orderly universe in three levels and while journeys between them were possible, they were difficult and dangerous even for the gods. The top or heavenly level contained Asgard, the home of the Aesir Vanaheim, the Vanir and Alfheim - the place where the light or good elves lived. Valhalla, the hall where Odin gathered the souls of warriors who had died in battle, was also located on this level. Connected to the upper level by the rainbow bridge was Bifrost, the middle or earthly level. It contained Midgard, the world of men, Jotunheim, the land of the giants, Svartalfaheim, the land of the dark elves and Nidavellir or land of the dwarfs. A huge serpent called Jormungand encircled the middle world. The bottom level consisted of the underworld of Niflheim, also known as Hel after Loki's daughter Hel who ruled there. The similarity to Hades, Hell and other versions of purgatory is interesting if nothing else.

While the preceding are examples of polytheistic religions there were also many versions of monotheism. One of the earliest, Zoroastrianism, is a religion and philosophy based on the teachings of the prophet Zoroaster, also known as Zarathustra, in Persia. Zoroaster was born in Medea, which is now modern day Iran, around 660 BCE and believed life was a constant struggle between the forces of good and evil. The spirit of good was Ahura Mazda with its helper Mithras, or "The Light." The evil spirit was Angra Mainyu, also known as Ahriman or the "Lie Demon." Man could not be neutral in the struggle and had to fight for right and live a righteous life. Those who lived righteously went to paradise, which was a state of immortal holiness in thought, word and deed, while the impious were condemned to an eternal Hell of evil thoughts, deeds and physical torment. By 500 BCE Zoroastrianism had become the leading faith in Persia and Medea and it is plain there are many parallels between it and Christianity. In fact there is little doubt many of the beliefs of the former were almost certainly copied by early Christians. For instance there is one universal and transcendental god, Ahura Mazda, the one uncreated Creator to whom all worship is ultimately directed. Ahura Mazda's creation - evident as "asha" (truth and order) - is the antithesis of chaos, evident as "druj" (falsehood and disorder). The resulting conflict involves the entire universe including humanity, which has an active role to play in the conflict. Active participation in life through good thoughts, good words and good deeds is necessary to ensure happiness and keep the chaos at bay. This active participation is a central element in Zoroaster's concept of free will. Ahura Mazda will ultimately prevail over evil Angra Mainyu, in other words Satan, at which point the universe will undergo a cosmic renovation and time will end in an apocalypse. In the final chapter all of creation, including the souls of the dead which were initially banished to darkness, will be reunited in Ahura Mazda and return to life in an undead form and at the end of time a savior-figure not dissimilar from Jesus will bring about a final renovation of the world in which the dead will be revived.

Taking all of that into consideration it would appear there are no truly original religions but instead any number of amalgamations, facsimiles and outright plagiarisms. It makes one wonder how anyone can possibly know what is true and what is not, especially since in addition to the so-called "mainstream" religions there are any number of unique and bizarre belief systems out there as well - and people believe in the "truth" of them too. Let's look at just a few.

The first one on the list is Scientology, which claims more than half a million adherents worldwide including high profile members such as Tom Cruise, Kirstie Alley and John Travolta and teaches that people are immortal beings who have forgotten their true nature. The Church of Scientology was created by science fiction author L. Ron Hubbard in

1952 as an outgrowth of his earlier self-help system called *Dianetics* and holds that at the higher levels of initiation (OT levels) mystical teachings are imparted which may be harmful to unprepared readers and as a result these teachings are kept secret from members who have not reached these levels. Hubbard explained how to reverse the effects of past-life trauma patterns which supposedly extend millions of years into the past, and then there is the story of Xenu, alien ruler of the "Galactic Confederacy." According to this story seventy-five million years ago Xenu brought billions of aliens to Earth in spacecraft, stacked them around volcanoes and detonated hydrogen bombs in the craters. The thetans (similar in concept to the spirit or soul found in other belief systems) then clustered together, stuck to the bodies of the living and continue to do so today. Scientologists at advanced levels place considerable emphasis on isolating body thetans and neutralizing their ill effects.

Similarly, Eckankar is the invention of small-time newspaper and pulp science fiction writer John Paul Twitchell and presents itself as an ancient secret teaching which has been passed down from master to student over millions of years when in fact it was hastily cobbled together by Twitchell in 1965 and is a close relative of Scientology. Clearly Twitchell took L. Ron Hubbard's advice, "If you want to make a little money write a book, but if you want to get rich start a religion," to heart. Eckankar is merely another new age religion which in its secretive, members only discourse states emphatically that it is the only way to reach "God Realization" and all other paths, philosophies and religions are misguided and decidedly inferior. Its professed end goal is for each member to achieve total God Realization in one lifetime and there is only one way to accomplish this - through Eckankar's "Living Eck Master."

Twitchell claims the ancient and most secret teachings were taught to him by a five-hundred-year-old Tibetan lama named Rebezar Tarzs who would appear to him in his apartment each night to dictate the "truths," and his most important book was based upon a purported journey he took deep into the inner planes escorted by Rebezar Tarzs where he was taken to meet God directly. Plus Eckankar's holy "bible," the *Shariyat ki Sugmad*, claims Eckankar was brought to earth by an Eck Master named Gakko six million years ago from the planet Venus. The problem is nobody had heard of this until 1965.

The Church of All Worlds is a neo-pagan religion founded in 1962 by Oberon Zell-Ravenheart and his wife Morning Glory Zell-Ravenheart. The religion evolved from a group of friends and lovers who were in part inspired by a fictional religion of the same name in the science fiction novel *Stranger in a Strange Land* by Robert A. Heinlein and the church's mythology includes science fiction to this day. They recognize "Gaea," the Earth Mother Goddess and Father God as well as the realm of Faeries as well as the deities of many other pantheons - for instance many of their ritual celebrations are centered on the gods and goddesses of ancient Greece. Following the tradition of using fiction as a basis for his ideas, Zell-Ravenheart recently founded The Grey School of Wizardry inspired in part by Hogwarts School of Witchcraft and Wizardry, the school in the Harry Potter novels.

The Nation of Yahweh is a predominantly African-American religious group which is the most controversial offshoot of the Black Hebrew Israelites line of thought. They were founded in 1979 in Miami by Hulon Mitchell, Jr., who went by the name Yahweh ben Yahweh. Their goal is to return African Americans, whom they see as the original Israelites, to Israel. The group departs from mainstream Christianity and Judaism by accepting Hulon Mitchell, Jr., er… I mean Yahweh ben Yahweh, as the Son of God. In this way their beliefs are unique and distinct from that of other known Black Hebrew Israelite groups. The group has engendered controversy due to legal issues of its founder and has also faced accusations of being a black supremacist cult by the Southern Poverty Law Center and *Miami Herald.* The SPLC has criticized the beliefs of the Nation of Yahweh as racist, stating the group believes blacks are "the true Jews" and whites are "white devils." They also claim the group believes Yahweh ben Yahweh had a Messianic mission to vanquish whites and holds views similar to the Christian Identity movement.

Universe People, aka Cosmic People of Light Powers, is a Czech religious movement centered around Ivo A. Benda. Its belief system is based upon the existence of extraterrestrial civilizations communicating with Benda and other "contactors" since October 1997 telepathically and later by direct personal contact. According to Benda those civilizations operate a fleet of spaceships led by Ashtar Sheran (a being of Nordic/Angelic appearance from Alpha Centauri) which are orbiting the Earth. They closely watch, help the good and are waiting to transport their followers into another dimension. The Universe People's teachings incorporate various elements from UFOology (some foreign "contactors" are credited, though often also renounced, after a time as misguided or deceptive), Christianity (Jesus was a "fine-vibrations" being) and conspiracy theories (forces of evil are supposed to plan compulsory chipping of the population).

The Prince Philip Movement is a "cargo cult "of the Yaohnanen tribe on the southern island of Tanna in Vanuatu with offshoots in other parts of the South Pacific. The Yaohnanen believe Prince Philip, the Duke of Edinburgh and consort to Queen Elizabeth II, is a divine being - namely the pale-skinned son of a mountain spirit and brother of "John Frum." According to ancient tales the son traveled over the seas to a distant land, married a powerful lady and would in time return. The villagers had observed the respect accorded to Queen Elizabeth II by colonial officials and came to the conclusion her husband, Prince Philip, must be the son from their legends. Exactly when the cult formed is unclear but it was likely sometime in the 1950s. Cargo cults, in a form of sympathetic magic, have built life-size replicas of airplanes out of straw and cut new military-style landing strips out of the jungle hoping to attract more airplanes similar to the ones which brought supplies during World War II because cult members thought the foreigners had some special connection to deities and ancestors of the natives - which are to them the only beings powerful enough to produce such riches.

Nuwaubianism is an umbrella term used to refer to the doctrines and teachings of the followers of Dwight York. The Nuwaubians originated as a Black Muslim group in New York in the 1970s and have gone through many changes since. Eventually the group established a headquarters in Putnam County, Georgia in 1993 which they have since abandoned. York is now in prison after having been convicted on money laundering and child molestation charges, but Nuwaubianism still endures. York developed Nuwaubianism by drawing on a wide range of sources which include Theosophy-derived New Age movements such as Astara as well as the Rosicrucians, Freemasonry, the Shriners, the Moorish Science Temple of America, revisionist Christianity and Islam and the Qadiani cult of Mirza Ghulam Ahmad, the numerology of Rashad Khalifa and the ancient astronaut theories of Zecharia Sitchin. White people are said in one Nuwaubian myth to have been originally created as a race of killers to serve blacks as a slave army, but this plan went awry. Some of the more unusual Nuwaubian beliefs include the importance of burying afterbirth so Satan does not use it to make a duplicate of the recently-born child, that some aborted fetuses survive and live in the sewers where they are being gathered and organized to take over the world, that people were once perfectly symmetrical and ambidextrous but then a meteorite struck Earth and tilted its axis causing "handedness" and shifting the heart off-center in the chest, that each of us has seven clones living in different parts of the world, that women existed for many generations before they invented men through genetic manipulation, that the species Homo sapiens is the result of cloning experiments which were conducted on Mars using Homo erectus, that Nikola Tesla came from the planet Venus and best of all that the Illuminati have nurtured a child (Satan's son) who was born on 6 June 1966 at the Dakota House on 72nd Street in New York to Jacqueline Kennedy Onassis of the Rothschild/Kennedy families. As if that were not enough they claim the Pope was present at the birth and performed necromantic ceremonies, the child was raised by former U.S. President Richard Nixon and it now lives in Belgium where it is hooked up bodily to a computer called "The Beast 3M" or "3666."

The Hare Krishnas, formally known as the International Society for Krishna Consciousness (ISKCON), was founded in 1966 by A.C. Bhaktivedanta Swami Prabhupada and is based on the teachings of 15th Century philosopher Caitanya Mahaprabhu. Scholars say it represents an orthodox version of Hinduism, and the movement became largely known for proselytizing in airports and bus stations as well as for its influence on Beatle George Harrison. As is the case with many other faiths its followers believe in simple living and are prohibited from eating meat, gambling, intoxication and sex outside marriage. They worship by repeatedly chanting God's name, and much like Christian churches ISKCON communities provide premarital counseling, participate in interfaith activities, run social service programs and offer babysitting. Another less savory similarity is the fact that during the 1970s and '80s several teachers and spiritual leaders were accused of sexually and physically molesting students in ISKCON boarding schools while superiors looked the other way. In response to the scandal and resulting lawsuit ISKCON declared bankruptcy to avoid being shut down by litigation and agreed to pay $9.5 million to several hundred victims, though litigation - and criticism of ISKCON's handling of the scandal - continues. Shades of the Catholic Church.

Then there are the Raëlians, who are naked and worship space aliens. Many people have heard of them but few know much beyond some vague references to extraterrestrials and cloning. The Raëlians were founded in 1973 by a young French street musician, race car driver and automotive journalist named Claude Vorilhon. In December of that year he was hiking around in the crater of an extinct volcano in France and claims to have been greeted by the sight of a flying saucer coming down and landing after which a little alien came out and approached him. The alien looked Japanese, fortuitously spoke French and for an hour each day over six consecutive days the alien - whose name was Yahweh, no less - met with Vorilhon and explained the true history of the Earth.

Yahweh's race were called the Elohim, which also happens to be a Hebrew word with a variety of vague meanings pertaining to holiness or divine beings, and Raëlians interpret the word as referring to the alien creators of humanity who came from the sky. Over the course of the six days Yahweh explained all of the events of the Old Testament as being actual happenings with purely natural explanations which were usually assisted by the Elohim. Adam and Eve, for example, were a literal man and woman who came from DNA custom designed by the Elohim, and like the Christian second coming Yahweh promised Vorilhon the Elohim would return to Earth once enough people have learned the true history of their race and become peaceful and prosperous. For this purpose Vorilhon was instructed to build an embassy at which the Elohim can be received when they show up. As you might imagine Vorilhon was amazed by this startling experience, so much so that he adopted the name "Raël" with a dieresis over the "e" to make it look more exotic, and went on to found the organization specified by Yahweh. In time this became the International Raëlian Movement.

Two years later Yahweh came back and this time picked up Raël, took him for a ride in his flying saucer and stopped at an orbiting spa in the outer reaches of our solar system where Raël received a massage and aromatherapy treatment. They then proceeded to the Elohim's home world, a warm jungle planet called the Planet of the Eternals, where Raël was introduced to Jesus, Buddha, Mohammad and Moses after which the group went out for dinner. Raël was then shown their facilities for creating immortal biological robots - they created one of his mother and a whole group of attractive young females - and then they all went back to Raël's apartment and had a party. Raël has written extensively about his climax at the party and all of his books are freely available on the internet, so please read these accounts for yourself if you think I am in any way exaggerating this.

The next morning Raël was taken to yet another facility where they used a helmet machine to "maximize his faculties," presumably making him as intelligent as possible. Yahweh then explained this procedure was to prepare Raël for geniocracy, a form of government where intelligence determines who should lead, before Yahweh flew Raël back to Earth. The total time between Raël's first encounter and his return was 666 days, by this time there were a few hundred members of the Raëlian movement and over the last thirty years or so this number has grown to somewhere in the tens of thousands though estimates vary. Japan and Korea in particular have taken to the Raëlian movement, and you'll find some of their largest chapters there.

Let's look at these tens of thousands of people a little more closely to find out who they are and what they believe. Significantly, they embrace technological advances to improve the human condition. They support genetically modified crops to best feed the growing population. They love advanced materials, science and nanotechnology. They support nuclear power and fusion research for cheap, clean energy. They support genetic research and manipulation to produce people who are as healthy and long-lived as genetically possible. They support terraforming of other planets as the technology becomes available. Much has been made of the company Clonaid, which is owned and operated by Raëliens and claims to have already created at least one human clone amid great scientific and ethical controversy. The child is said to be a girl named Eve living in Israel. Clonaid's mission is to create human clones which grow rapidly to serve as spare parts and new bodies for aging humans. The idea is to transfer your intelligence into your newly cloned body according to procedures detailed by Yahweh which involve advanced computer backups… and suddenly you're twenty-five again.

Philosophically Raëlians oppose war and violence in all its forms and frequently appear at anti-war rallies dressed as aliens, which seems incongruous since they say aliens look like humans. They also embrace free love and nudity and consider love to be the answer to virtually all of the world's problems. If you just focus on the true Raëlian philosophy many atheists and skeptics will find a lot they can get on board with since science as a solution to the problems of the world is a great strategy. Advanced technology to improve health and longevity is a great thing too. Love instead of war, who can argue with that? Moreover the Raëlian movement is probably less harmful than many other religions since they don't teach that your child can be cured of cancer by telepathically appealing to a paranormal superbeing, and so far nobody has fought a war or perpetrated a terrorist attack over Raëlian religious differences. So if it's that great why don't we all rush right out and become Raëlians today? There might be a lot to recommend many aspects of their philosophy, but the problem comes when you examine the underlying dogma. The truth is we can be happy and support science and technology and love without the fiction of Raël's ridiculous alternative creation myth and bizarre alien stories such as his spaceship rides and the twenty million dollar alien embassy outside Jerusalem. The Raëlian story of creation cannot be reconciled with what we know of evolutionary biology and our planet's geological development, but true Raëlians do what they do and believe what they believe because they see Raël as a prophet who brought back an alternative creation myth from outer space and in doing so are setting aside reason and rationality - but as crazy as all the foregoing sounds is it really that much more bizarre, when viewed objectively, than the claims made by mainstream religions?

Those are just a few of many, many possible examples which could be offered of different belief systems. So what, you may ask, was the point of including those strange cults? After all, those aren't *your* beliefs. It's simple. They demonstrate the credulity of human beings and our propensity for engaging in pack mentality, which is essentially the tendency to believe things as part of a group which we would never believe on our own. This is the reason churches exist, to reinforce beliefs which are not based upon reality, and it is not the only place it happens. Consider the modern internet phenomenon known as social media. How many times have you seen a Facebook post, usually a meme, about prayer or God which ends with, "If you agree, say 'Amen!" Some people post that sort of thing every single day and in many cases several times a day and what it reveals is not the depth of their belief but instead the need to have their beliefs reinforced by others. This is no different from someone who is insecure about their looks constantly posting new "selfie" photos or continuously changing profile pictures in an effort to troll for compliments. Think about it.

Isn't it interesting how people can see the folly and flaws in all of those other belief systems but for some reason cannot manage to apply that very same logic and reasoning to their own - whatever it might be? The rest is just a matter of popularity, because as they say the only difference between a religion and a cult is the number of adherents it has. If you object to your religious belief system, assuming you have one, being compared to a cult consider this ironic quote from the website *clarifyingchristianity.com*. "You cannot confirm whether a belief system is actually a cult using your common sense. If common sense was enough to recognize a cult or false religion, nobody would ever be involved in one! Further, you cannot expect a cult to admit they are one. Otherwise, why would anyone remain a member, or be interested in joining? Remember, cults will always have some sort of support for their beliefs, and the people involved sincerely believe what they are doing is right." I could not agree more since this is a clear case of the pot calling the kettle black, because in the words of Sir Arthur C. Clarke, "There's never been anything, however absurd, that myriads of people weren't prepared to believe, often so passionately that they'd fight to the death rather than abandon their illusions. To me, that's a good operational definition of insanity."

Superstition

Or, the Origins of Unfounded Fears

"The religious superstition is encouraged by means of the institution of churches, processions, monuments, festivities... the so-called clergy stupefy the masses... they befog the people and keep them in an eternal condition of stupefaction." ~ Leo Nikolaevich Tolstoy

If you are a baseball fan you might not be surprised to learn former Atlanta Braves utility man Elliot Johnson always placed a piece of Super Bubble grape-flavored bubble gum in his mouth when he ran onto the field to play defense, and when his team was batting he discarded the grape and replaced it with Super Bubble watermelon-flavored bubble gum because as he said with absolute certainty, "The hits are in the watermelon gum." It was of course preposterous but Johnson seemed to believe it, which in the world of baseball is all that matters. The belief stems from the day when he got a couple of hits in a minor league game a few years ago while chewing watermelon gum, so he began to believe it was his best chance to get two hits every night. In fact when Johnson was traded to Atlanta by the Royals the Braves didn't have the flavor of gum he needed and he was pretty upset, but one of the clubhouse kids found some at a store and that first night he got a hit - because of the gum, naturally. Of course no mention is made of the days when he chews his watermelon gum and goes hitless.

Superstition in baseball remain as alive today as it was twenty years ago when Turk Wendell pitched without wearing socks and chewed black licorice every inning on the mound and brushed his teeth after every inning. Did he ever give up runs or lose games while doing that? Of course. Despite his antics he gave up over three hundred runs and lost thirty-three games during his career as a reliever, but it is taboo to talk about such things because players are even superstitious about *being* superstitious. Instead of calling it a superstition they now call what they do a "routine," but it's semantics because the fact remains they do these weird things day after day because they feel they have to or else it will bring them bad luck.

Superstition is defined as the irrational belief an object, action or circumstance not logically related to a course of events influences its outcome; a belief, practice or rite irrationally maintained by ignorance of the laws of nature or by faith in magic or chance; an irrational belief usually founded on ignorance or fear and characterized by obsessive reverence for omens, charms, etc.

A good example is keeping one's fingers crossed to hope for good luck or success - literally, to hook one finger over another. The expression, which dates from the first half of the last century, may be connected with the old superstition which said making the sign of the cross kept bad luck away. The question is, do you think it works?

Have you ever wondered why people almost always follow a sneeze with the phrase "God bless you?" There are several explanations of where this phrase came from and why we say it. "God bless you" is not only a common English expression, it is also a socially obligated (i.e. automatic) response and something we think of as polite to say after someone sneezes, even if we don't know them. The practice or tradition of blessing a sneeze dates back to 77 CE, and the custom itself originally began as an actual blessing by Pope Gregory in 590 CE. An outbreak of bubonic plague was closing in on Rome and sneezing was thought to be an early symptom, so in hopes of fighting off the disease he ordered unending prayer and parades of chanters through the streets. Since sneezing was thought to be a symptom of the plague, saying "God bless you" was considered a defense against the disease. People also used to believe a person's soul could be thrown from their body when they sneezed, sneezing otherwise opened the body to invasion by the Devil or evil spirits or it was the body's way of forcing out an invading evil presence. In these cases, "God bless you" was used as a sort of shield against evil. The Irish folk story *Master and Man* by Thomas Crofton Croker, collected by William Butler Yeats, describes this belief. Lastly, many people used to believe sneezing was a sign God would answer their prayers or that it was an omen of good fortune or good luck and the phrase "God bless you" was recognition of that luck. The bottom line is this tradition is based upon pure superstition, so the next time someone sneezes think about why you are saying it and ask yourself why we say absolutely nothing when someone coughs.

Another commonly held superstition concerns the number thirteen in general and the date Friday the 13th in particular. The sixth day of the week and the number thirteen both have foreboding reputations said to date from ancient times, so it seems their inevitable conjunction from one to three times a year (there were three such occurrences in 2012, exactly thirteen weeks apart) portends more misfortune than some credulous minds can bear. According to some sources it's the most widespread superstition in the United States today and in fact some people refuse to go to work on Friday the 13th, some won't eat in restaurants and many would never consider setting a wedding on that date. Are you one of those people and if so, why? If you are you are not alone because many Americans, at the beginning of the 21st Century mind you, still adhere to this superstition. According to Dr. Donald Dossey, a psychotherapist specializing in the treatment of phobias, the figure may be as high as twenty-one million. If he's correct that means no fewer than eight percent of Americans remain in the grips of a very old superstition. Doesn't make much sense in this day and age, does it?

Although no one can say for sure when and why human beings first associated the number thirteen with misfortune the superstition is assumed to be quite old and there exist any number of theories, most of which deserve to be treated with healthy skepticism, purporting to trace its origins to antiquity and beyond. Ancient civilizations weren't unanimous in their dread of thirteen, however. For instance the Chinese regarded the number as lucky, as did the Egyptians in the time of the pharaohs. To the ancient Egyptians life was a quest for spiritual ascension which unfolded in stages - twelve in this life and a thirteenth beyond, thought to be the eternal afterlife. The number thirteen therefore symbolized death not in terms of dust and decay but as a glorious and desirable transformation. Though Egyptian civilization perished the symbolism conferred on the number thirteen by its priesthood survived, it has been speculated, only to be corrupted by subsequent cultures which came to associate thirteen with a fear of death instead of a reverence for the afterlife.

The number thirteen may have been purposely vilified by the founders of patriarchal religions in the early days of western civilization because it represented femininity. You see thirteen had been revered in prehistoric goddess-worshiping cultures because it corresponded to the number of lunar (menstrual) cycles in a year (13 x 28 = 364 days). The "Earth Mother of Laussel," for example - a twenty-seven-thousand-year-old carving found near the Lascaux caves in France often cited as an icon of matriarchal spirituality - depicts a female figure holding a crescent-shaped horn bearing thirteen notches. As the solar calendar triumphed over the lunar with the rise of male-dominated civilization, it is surmised, so did the "perfect" number twelve over the "imperfect" number thirteen, thereafter considered anathema.

On the other hand one of the earliest concrete taboos associated with the number thirteen, a taboo still observed by some superstitious folks today apparently, is said to have originated in the East with the Hindus who for some reason believed it was always unlucky for thirteen people to gather in one place - say, at dinner. Interestingly enough, precisely the same superstition has been attributed to the ancient Vikings.

In their mythology twelve gods were invited to a banquet at Valhalla but Loki, the Evil One and God of Mischief (every religion seems to have one) had been left off the guest list - but he crashed the party, bringing the total number of attendees to thirteen. True to character Loki raised hell by inciting Hod, the blind god of winter, to attack Balder the Good, who was a favorite of the gods. Hod took a spear of mistletoe offered by Loki and obediently hurled it at Balder, killing him instantly, and all Valhalla grieved. Although one might think the moral of this story to be "beware of uninvited guests bearing mistletoe" the Norse themselves apparently concluded that thirteen people at a dinner party is just plain bad luck, and as if to second the motion the Bible tells us there were exactly thirteen present at the Last Supper and one of the dinner guests, or should I say disciples, is said to have betrayed Jesus and set the stage for the Crucifixion. It also bears mention that the Crucifixion is supposed to have taken place on a Friday.

Some say Friday's bad reputation goes all the way back to the Garden of Eden. It was supposedly on a Friday - although how anyone knew that is an open question since there were no calendars - that Eve tempted Adam with the forbidden fruit. Tradition also holds that the Great Flood began on a Friday, God tongue-tied the builders of the Tower of Babel on a Friday and the Temple of Solomon was destroyed on a Friday. So much for TGIF! In pagan Rome Friday was execution day (later known as Hangman's Day in Britain) but in other pre-Christian cultures it was the Sabbath or a day of worship so those who indulged in secular or self-interested activities on that day could not expect to receive blessings from the gods which may explain the lingering taboo regarding embarking on journeys or starting important projects on Fridays.

To complicate matters these pagan associations were not lost on the early Church, which went to great lengths to suppress them. If Friday was a holy day for heathens, the Church fathers felt, it must not be so for Christians - thus it became known in the Middle Ages as the "Witches' Sabbath," and thereby hangs another tale.

The name "Friday" was itself derived from a Norse deity worshipped on the sixth day known either as Frigg (goddess of marriage and fertility) or Freya (goddess of sex and fertility) or both, as the two figures became intertwined in the handing down of myths over time (the etymology of "Friday" has been given both ways). The goddess Frigg/Freya corresponded to Venus, the goddess of love of the Romans who named the sixth day of the week in her honor, "dies Veneris."

Friday was actually considered quite lucky by pre-Christian Teutonic peoples, especially as a day to get married because of its traditional association with love and fertility, but all that changed once Christianity came along. The goddess of the sixth day, most likely Freya in this context given that the cat was her sacred animal, was recast in post-pagan folklore as a witch and her day suddenly became associated with evil doings.

Various legends developed in that vein, but one is of particular interest. As the story goes the witches of the north used to observe their Sabbath by gathering in a cemetery in the dark of the moon and on one such occasion the Friday goddess, Freya herself, supposedly came down from her sanctuary in the mountaintops and appeared before the group - who numbered only twelve at the time - and gave them one of her cats, after which the witches' coven numbered thirteen, and ever since by tradition every properly formed coven has been comprised of exactly thirteen.

While I have thus far insinuated any number of intriguing connections between events, practices and beliefs attributed to ancient cultures and the superstitious fear of both Friday and the number thirteen we have yet to happen upon an explanation of how, why or when these separate strands of folklore converged to mark Friday the 13th as the unluckiest day of all. The most prominent theory holds that the stigma came about not as the result of a convergence but because of a single historical event which happened nearly seven hundred years ago. That event was the decimation of the Knights Templar, the legendary order of "warrior monks" formed during the Christian Crusades to combat Islam. Renowned as a fighting force for two hundred years, by the 1300s the order had grown so pervasive and powerful it was perceived as a political threat by kings and popes alike and was brought down by a church-state conspiracy, as recounted by Katharine Kurtz in *Tales of the Knights Templar*: "On October 13, 1307, a day so infamous that Friday the 13th would become a synonym for ill fortune, officers of King Philip IV of France carried out mass arrests in a well-coordinated dawn raid that left several thousand Templars - knights, sergeants, priests and serving brethren - in chains charged with heresy, blasphemy, various obscenities and homosexual practices. None of these charges was ever proven, even in France - and the Order was found innocent elsewhere - but in the seven years following the arrests hundreds of Templars suffered excruciating tortures intended to force 'confessions' and more than a hundred died under torture or were executed by burning at the stake."

As fascinating as all of that is you may by now be wondering what is the point of discussing superstition in a book about religion? Some people become upset when confronted with that word, but the fact is the two subjects are undeniably and inexorably connected and intertwined. As Thomas Jefferson put it when writing about religion in general and Christianity in particular, "I have recently been examining all the known *superstitions* of the world, and do not find in our particular *superstition* one redeeming feature. They are all alike, founded upon fables and mythologies." The point is understanding how superstitions come to be believed by otherwise rational people may help you gain a better understanding of how many of those same people come to accept religious dogma as fact without investigating their origins for themselves.

Did you notice how virtually every component of the legend of Friday the 13th has been in some way been driven by or connected to a religious group, belief or practice? That is no accident. If you read the holy Scriptures of any religion you will find they abound with superstitions, and that is putting it mildly. After all superstition, like religion, is largely based on a fear of the unknown and astrologers, priests and various con men make great use of this fact.

No doubt you'd like specific examples, especially from Christianity and Judaism. To begin with many people think keeping a cross in the house or around their necks can ward off evil. This notion has been popularized by movies where evil spirits and vampires are scared away by simply showing the cross, but if devils or vampires were real do you really think they would be frightened away by a piece of wood or metal no matter how it happens to be shaped? Another common superstition is sleeping with a Bible under one's pillow in order to keep away bad dreams. No one seems to know where this practice began or how or why it is supposed to work and yet people do it anyway... and naturally, it doesn't work.

From a scriptural perspective Jews and Christians believe thousands of years ago in Egypt the angel of death passed over the houses of the people of Israel when he saw the blood of a lamb sprinkled over the doorposts. Ask yourself why would that be necessary if the God directing the slaughter was omniscient and privy to the very thoughts of everyone on earth - let alone knowing their identities. Another example appears in Leviticus 16:8-28 where Moses' brother Aaron is directed to get two goats, kill one, wipe, smear and sprinkle its blood on the "mercy seat" seven times and then take the other goat, place upon it the sins of all the people and send it off into the wilderness as a "scapegoat." In the event of leprosy Leviticus 14:2-52 instructs priests to get two birds, kill one, dip the live bird in the blood of the dead one, sprinkle the blood on the leper seven times and then let the blood-soaked bird fly off. Next he must kill a lamb, wipe some of its blood on the leper's right ear, thumb and big toe, sprinkle him seven times with oil and then wipe some of the oil on his right ear, thumb and big toe. I think, at least I hope, we can agree these things clearly fall into the realm of superstition.

Holy Oil, Prayer Shawls, Yarmulkes and so many of the trappings of religion have their roots in superstition. There is no special power or magic which can be obtained from oils, handkerchiefs, prayer shawls, water from the River Jordan, soil from Israel, models of the tabernacle or lamp stands with seven spouts, and yet people routinely attach mystical power to such things. Turn on the television on Sunday morning and watch Ernest Angley or some similar faith healing televangelist send special "prayer cloths" which supposedly have the power to cure diseases, cancer included, to sick people - in exchange for a donation, naturally. That is superstition plain and simple, just as thinking walking under ladders, having a black cat cross your path or lighting three cigarettes on a match are bad luck. When you think about it human beings can be incredibly credulous and will believe most anything.

Now let's look at a different but familiar sort of superstition - wishes. Whether you still make them every year when you blow out your birthday candles or scoff at the idea of throwing pennies into a fountain, the truth is we've all done it. We've all closed our eyes, looked deep inside ourselves and wished for something, and let's face it there are plenty of different ways to wish. Let's look at a few.

A star is a magical thing, but a shooting star? Well, those are practically revered. Wishing on a shooting star is believed to have been originated around 127-151 CE by Greek astronomer Ptolemy when he wrote that the gods will, out of both curiosity and boredom, occasionally peer down at the earth from between the spheres where stars could sometimes slip out of this gap and become visible as shooting or falling stars. It was believed the gods tended to be more receptive to wishes made during these times, but many other cultures also revered the shooting star such as the Jews and Christians who believed them to be fallen angels or demons while the Greeks thought of them as the rising or falling of human souls. Even now when a shooting star is seen in Chile it's believed one must pick up a stone, and when someone sees one in the Philippines they must tie a knot in a handkerchief before the star's light is extinguished. There is also the legend of wishing on the first star you see at night which we all know if from nothing else the childhood rhyme, "Star light, star bright, the first star I see tonight, I wish I may, I wish I might, have the wish I wish tonight."

Then there are wishing wells. While we may not see a lot of them today it's still a common belief that if you speak a wish over a wishing well it will be granted. This belief can be traced back to the Germanic and Celtic peoples who considered wells and springs sacred places due to the belief water housed deities and had been placed there as a gift from the gods. Germanic people would also throw the armor and trinkets of defeated enemies into these waters as well as coins to show appreciation to the deity. When coins were traditionally made of copper or silver it was discovered they had certain properties which would keep the water from going sour, and thus they were believed to be lucky - this is where the tradition of dropping pennies into fountains comes from. Wishing wells, which are most common in Europe, are known to garner millions of dollars every year just from people throwing in coins and if you look in virtually any fountain in America you'll likely find a nice sum in those as well.

Next comes the wishbone. Some people will only use this method on Thanksgiving while others may find it fair game every time you cook a chicken or turkey, but there is the belief that if you make a wish while (or after) pulling at a dried wishbone with another person and end up with the longer half your wish will come true. Even the name plays on this concept of wishing, but why? One theory says it stemmed from the ancient Italians who would remove a bird's entrails and read the future in them. They would lay the collarbone out to dry in the sun and people seeking special knowledge from the gods could then make a wish upon this bone. The Etruscans also believed fowl were fortune tellers because the hen would announce the laying of an egg with a squawk and the rooster could tell the coming of a new day with an early morning crow. With this in mind people would draw a circle in the dirt, split it in wedges to represent different letters of their alphabet and have the hen peck at grain within the circle while listing the letters in the order of the pecking so the high priests could interpret answers to questions. The Romans later adopted many Etruscan rituals and the English in turn took on many of the Roman customs so when the Christian Pilgrims arrived in the New World they brought along the wishbone and changed it from a chicken bone to a turkey bone when they discovered a plethora of turkey in the woods.

Those various forms of wishing are particularly germane because they are entreaties to gods or other mystical powers and are little different from something religious people today do with some regularity, and that is pray. As Albert Einstein put it, "A prayer is a wish addressed to a supernatural being," so wish and prayer are clearly synonyms and it is just a matter of semantics. The difference is despite the obvious connection modern religious people view one as superstition and the other as a real and effective way of getting things done, but as is demonstrated elsewhere in this book the "success rate" for each is exactly the same once you understand the concept of confirmation bias.

One last thought on the subject concerns old wives' tales, which are defined as "foolish or nonsensical stories and/or a traditional but inaccurate concept or superstition." This expression is derived from fanciful yarns often related by elderly women through the ages and not surprisingly most religious beliefs were passed down in this manner using oral tradition for centuries before finally being recorded on paper. This practice amounted in effect to a game of "Chinese whispers," a game in which one person whispers a message to another and it is passed through a line of people until the last player announces the message to the entire group. Errors typically accumulate in the retellings, so the statement announced at the end differs significantly from the one uttered by the first. Reasons for changes include anxiousness or impatience, erroneous corrections and often someone will deliberately alter what is being said in order to guarantee a changed message by the end. Do you think perhaps some of the details in religious stories may have changed or were embellished from telling to telling through the centuries? Is it possible? The nonsensical stories contained in the Bible and other holy Scriptures make a lot more sense when viewed in that light because as Thomas Paine commented in *The Age of Reason,* "Brought up in habits of superstition, people in general know not how much wickedness there is in this pretended word of God."

Science vs. Religion

Or, Fact vs. Fiction

☥☯⛩ॐ☸✡✝☪☬

"If every trace of every single religion were wiped out and nothing were passed on, they would never be created exactly that way again. There might be some other nonsense in their place, but not that exact nonsense. If all of science were wiped out it would still be true, and someone would find a way to figure it all out again." ~ Penn Jillette

Penn Jillette is exactly right. If we were to wipe the slate clean of all human knowledge and start from scratch in a few thousand years all religions would be different from the ones we know today but science would be exactly the same. An atom would still be an atom, DNA would still be DNA, the electromagnetic spectrum and periodic tables of the elements will not have changed and so on and so on. That's because facts and truths are not subject to the fickle whims of human beings.

In the past several hundred years our knowledge of the physical world has grown enormously, we are in the midst of an information explosion and as a result mankind has developed an increased reliance on the scientific method to understand the universe. The scientific method relies primarily on systematic observation of the world using formal procedures for testing cause-and-effect relationships between variables in many fields of study including social sciences, biology, chemistry and physics. Galileo, for example, used it when he studied the effect of gravity on falling objects. He observed that bodies appeared to fall faster the longer they fell, formed a hypothesis that falling bodies increase their speed at a steady rate, conducted experiments to determine the validity of his hypothesis, evaluated his data and verified the results.

It all begins with a hypothesis, which is a tentative statement in the form of a prediction about the relationship between variables. The testing of a hypothesis is done through a process of research and experimentation, and verification is the analysis of experimental results to see if they support or deny the hypothesis. If the hypothesis is unproven it is then time to make new observations and look for other cause-and-effect relationships which might explain those observations, and once something is proven it is important for other researchers to be able to replicate the results.

The scientific method is largely ignored by those making theological claims and arguments because it is a logical way of asking and answering questions by making observations, doing experiments and basing conclusions on empirical and measurable evidence subject to specific principles of reasoning. The chief characteristic which distinguishes it from other methods of acquiring knowledge is scientists let reality speak for itself, support theories when their predictions are confirmed and challenge them when their predictions prove to be false. In summary, the steps of the scientific method are to first ask a question and then do background research, construct a hypothesis, test your hypothesis by doing an experiment, analyze your data to draw a conclusion and communicate your results.

It is important for your experiment to be a "fair test," which means you may change only one factor or variable while keeping all other conditions the same. This process distinguishes it from other ways of "knowing" such as philosophy and appeal to authority. Philosophy differs in that it places a greater emphasis on reason for solving problems as opposed to observation. The domain of science is the empirical world, while philosophy makes inquiries into such nebulous things as values, meaning, existence and such.

The scientific method can also be clearly distinguished from an appeal to authority. Many people seek knowledge by appealing to an authority figure such as a doctor, teacher or religious book and when they do so believe something is true simply because that figure or book said so rather than requiring a set of systematic observations to support it. For example during the Middle Ages the Christian Church taught that all heavenly bodies revolved around the earth. Most people of the time accepted this teaching because it came from the Church's interpretation of an authoritative source, i.e. the Bible, and casual observation supported it. The heavenly bodies did in fact appear to go around the earth, but from the scientific point of view this observation led only to a hypothesis which was not tested. There were as we now know other explanations but the hypothesis was assumed to be true simply because it came from an authoritative source, and when those teachings were challenged by Copernicus and Galileo they were deemed heretical not because they were at odds with observation, but because they did not agree with an accepted authority.

In the 16th Century Copernicus argued that the earth moved around the sun rather than the reverse and needless to say his theory brought the fury of many Christians including Martin Luther, who considered him a fool who wanted to "turn the whole of astronomy upside down." Sixty years after Copernicus' death the Catholic Church, fearing a great scandal and dissent if his views were taken seriously, added his text outlining a heliocentric theory of the solar system to the *Index of Prohibited Books*.

Although Copernicus was credited with introducing the heliocentric solar system it was Galileo who was prosecuted for supporting such a view. Relying on observation of the sun, planets and stars instead of the authority contained in religious doctrine Galileo found strong empirical support for Copernicus' theory, was not afraid to go public with his views and even though forbidden by the Church published a book in 1632 which supported Copernicus' ideas. As previously discussed he was put on trial for heresy, convicted, ordered to recant his positions, sentenced to house arrest for the rest of his life and it was not until 1992 - three hundred sixty years later and after fourteen years of "study" mind you - that the Pope finally admitted Galileo was correct about the earth revolving around the sun.

Galileo's story demonstrates appealing to authority, especially when it comes from a place such as the Bible, does not always yield a valid picture of reality. It also demonstrates the power of world views to inhibit our consideration of opposing beliefs, especially when they are uncomfortable and no matter what the evidence. In this case Christians had a world view which included earth and man as center of the universe and that view prevented them from thinking objectively about alternate views even when the evidence was substantial. It also demonstrates the necessity for having the courage to engage in critical thinking and abandon unfounded beliefs which make us feel safe and secure.

True scientific inquiry uses careful, well controlled and objective methods in an attempt to determine truths while at the same time being open to the possibility of errors in its conclusions and considering alternate explanations. In other words true science develops hypotheses and theories which are testable and falsifiable, while subjects of inquiry which pretend to be scientific but lack these characteristics are called pseudosciences. Their fault is not that their beliefs are false but that those beliefs are accepted as true without careful scientific testing, or even worse in spite of it. Some common pseudosciences are astrology, parapsychology and creationism. One common characteristic of all is the tendency to give a *post hoc* (after the fact) explanation for an unfulfilled prediction without testing that explanation or intentionally presenting it in a manner which is untestable. For example many religious groups have prophesized that the world was going to end and when it did not explained their apparent mistake as a change of heart by God or mathematical error. Such explanations are untestable and designed to save face, just as so-called psychics have offered face saving reasons to explain their failure to perform psychic feats by blaming it on such things as "bad timing," an "uncooperative spirit" or "negative energy." Sadly, beliefs such as creationism, astrology and parapsychology which involve themes of power, religion, spirits and mystery seem to grasp people quickly and tenaciously and make it difficult for them to open their belief systems up to scientific scrutiny.

Experimental failures in the various pseudosciences may sometimes be attributed to sampling error or poor research design, but more often than not they are the result of what is known as "experimenter bias." This is the tendency of researchers to make errors in perception or judgment because of their expectations or desire for a particular result. In other words it is part of a general tendency to see what we would like or expect to see. Scientists go where evidence takes them, while a theist starts with the end in mind and tries to prove it. As quantum physicist David Bohm put it, "Science is about finding the truth… whether we like it or not." Conversely, Proverbs 3:5 tells the faithful, "Trust in the LORD with all your heart, on your own intelligence rely not." That is not exactly an endorsement of critical thinking.

Take for instance the newest speculations on how gold first came to be in our universe. The force proposed for this auspicious birthing is the collision of two neutron stars. Neutron stars are the remnants of stars massive enough to go supernova which then undergo a gravitational collapse so intense that (simplistically) it crushes the constituent atoms to create a mass largely composed of neutrons - hence the name. They are small in size with a radius of approximately twelve kilometers but with a mass 1.4 to 3.2 times greater than our sun, and if they emit beams of electromagnetic radiation rotating neutron stars are known as pulsars. When these were first detected it was thought by some they could be evidence of intelligent life due to their emission regularity, sort of like lighthouses in space, since typically neutron stars rotate several times a second with the fastest at over seven hundred times per second. They are a part of a universe undreamt of by our distant ancestors, a marvelous combination of understanding emerging from both particle physics and astrophysics. Truly they represent a wonder of the universe and their identification and comprehension is a notable accomplishment of the human intellect.

What does religion have to compare with this? If you are a literalist believer in any of the three major monotheistic religions this sort of scientific report must be regarded as untrue. For the literal believer the question of where gold came from is answered by "God made it." How satisfying is that? It's like eating a stale hot dog at a barbeque while everyone else is eating prime cuts of steak, or swimming in a mud puddle while everyone else is in an Olympic-sized pool. Of course the only place to run in the face of such discoveries is the apologetic, "That is the way God set it up," but that is not the way Genesis describes it. For people who actually believe what their holy books say it must be hard to accept the constant stream of scientific accomplishments which continue to define and describe our universe from the smallest discovery like the recent sighting of the Higgs Boson particle to the unimaginably large such as the Hubble Ultra-Deep Field image of more than ten thousand galaxies reaching back in time more than thirteen billion years. It's amazing, but if you are stuck believing some god, any god, magically created all of this a couple of thousand years ago you miss the majesty of these discoveries. In fact I am not sure how you can reconcile your worldview with it. So are scientists producing these results at the behest of Satan? Or perhaps it's a case of God testing human faith?

For the religious there appear to be three ways to face the progress of science in our world. In the first they deny the scientific finding as false because its proponents are corrupt or agents of evil who are trying to tempt the devout away from the path of righteousness. In this case, they dispute the findings of scientists when they conflict with the teachings in the holy book and perhaps look to reports from religious pseudoscientists who pronounce "discoveries" which support their religious view of the natural world. We commonly see this in the populist concepts known as Creationism and Intelligent Design which try to masquerade as science, and in this way the believer may think they believe in science, but the problem is it is not coherent scholarship. It also means those who tempt believers away from the "truth" as revealed in the holy books are either corrupt, themselves evil or the willing agents of evil. This is dangerous as it appears to give believers an excuse to harm or at least ostracize scientists by placing them in the same category as human-tempting demons, devils and djinns, and at the least science is a temptation akin to intellectual lust designed to lure away the unwary faithful.

In the second rationale they don't deny scientists are discovering things which contradict religion nor dispute their conclusions but instead believe God put the "false" information there to be discovered by scientists as a test of the true believers' faith. The evidence is there, the geology and fossils and galaxies - that is indisputable - but God is testing us to see if we choose our powers of reason over the words written in the holy books. This interpretation makes God a pretty odd character considering all of the terrible things we humans have had to deal with which God in his/her/its holy books didn't warn us about such as microbial and viral diseases as well as dangers from radiation and naturally occurring poisons and toxins like asbestos, tobacco smoke, etc., not to mention our having to discover useful things such as writing and agriculture. Why did we deserve this sort of a trick? What is the point of telling us the world is on pillars (Job 9:6) and the firmament is a solid dome separating the waters of the earth from the waters in the sky (Genesis 1:6-8) and that there are seven heavens (Quran 71:15 and 65:12)? Why give humans the mental capacity to understand the world if we are supposed to believe in things like a flat earth, an idea which seemed erroneous to Greek thinkers such as Pythagoras thousands of years ago? If God wants us to be dumb, why not make us that way? Why give humans the ability to reason if we are supposed to willingly suspend disbelief of stories and explanations which have proven to be false? As Galileo, a devout Catholic, argued, "I do not feel obliged to believe that the same God who has endowed us with sense, reason and intellect has intended us to forgo their use."

The third and seemingly most popular tactic is to deny or rationalize away the literal meaning of the holy books. Casting aside hundreds of years of consistent interpretation, the modern believer considers the text in the holy books to be selectively allegorical, figurative, temporally symbolic or merely a story to be viewed in context with the knowledge people possessed at the time. The mental gymnastics some people are willing to undergo to accept what they know to be true in science and still not jettison their obviously incorrect holy books is amazing. Much of what is in these holy books posturing as cosmology are the obviously ignorant (not stupid, just lacking knowledge we have today) musings of a primitive people trying to make sense of a world they little understood at the time. No harm in that, since every religion is a product of its time as is all science, and in hindsight science too has spurred some amazingly stupid beliefs over the years and has lost from time to time some of its understandings only to regain them later. Some knowledge which was developed by the Classical Greeks, much of which was wrong, at least got people thinking in the right direction and promoted an element of critical thinking which had to be relearned by Renaissance Europeans. They had largely forgotten Euclid and Archimedes, but instead remembered Ecclesiastes and Daniel. The Greeks around the end of the Bronze Age even lost the art of writing and had to relearn it.

So when faced with scientific advances, especially those dealing with the origin of the universe, evolution or historical artifacts we hear three responses from the faithful - that it is a lie and/or a conspiracy, that they (meaning scientists and those who believe in science) are deceived and need to be shown the "truth" as revealed in the holy book or that it's all part of God's beautiful creation even if he didn't tell you truthfully about it in a particular holy book. What kind of choice is that? Either all scientists are purposefully evil deceivers, men are stupid for believing in science instead of the holy books or the holy books are not literally true... but we should believe them anyway. Why not instead accept the preponderance of evidence which is now so easily accessible and admit the holy books were written by people with limited knowledge of their world who were trying to explain things they didn't have reasonable answers for at the time?

Perhaps religion can be charitably thought of as an early scientific hypothesis. For example it posed the simple question, "What is above us?" Having thought about it and lacking a telescope or access to consistently recorded observations some group of people decided the best answer was, "A solid firmament separating the waters above us from the earth below." Water is blue and the sky is blue, so it follows there is water in the sky... it does have a sort of logic to it... and there needs to be some way of keeping it up there so it doesn't fall down here so you need a firmament, but like any scientific hypothesis if it's proven to be wrong it should be discarded. Likewise at first glance it certainly looks like the sun goes around the earth. We see it "move" in the sky every day, but once we were able to study it discovered it doesn't move at all. We all know that now. It's time to accept the gift of modern science and discard the bad speculative "science" of religions so it may follow the path of other incorrect sciences.

One of the ways science maintains its honesty and objectivity is through the use of peer review, which is the impartial evaluation of work by one or more people of similar competence (peers) to the producers of the work and constitutes a form of self-regulation by qualified members of a profession within the relevant field. Peer review methods are employed to maintain standards of quality, improve performance and provide credibility and in academia is often used to determine an academic paper's suitability for publication. What that means is scientists lay out their theories and essentially ask the brightest minds in their area of expertise to try to poke holes in or even falsify them. Can you imagine a theologian doing such a thing?

When trying to understand how the universe began scientists use cosmology and astrophysics and quantum mechanics to learn as much as possible and subsequently build on (and sometimes correct and/or contradict) the work of those who came before them. They ask questions, conduct experiments, record data and develop theories. In contrast the theological explanation is, "God did it… it says so right here. Period."

When trying to understand the origins and development of life scientists use chemistry and geology and evolution to learn as much as possible and build on (and sometimes contradict) the work of those who came before them. They ask questions, conduct experiments, record data and develop theories. In contrast the theological explanation is again, "God did it… it says so right here. Period."

There are between five and six thousand languages spoken in the world depending on the criteria used to differentiate a language from a dialect with about a third of them being spoken by no more than a thousand people while two hundred are used by more than a million native speakers each. Linguists study how those languages have evolved and diversified over time and have reconstructed the history of their evolution by comparing modern languages to determine which traits their ancestral languages must have had in order for the later stages to have occurred. In contrast the theological explanation is the fanciful story of the Tower of Babel, i.e. "God did it. Period."

The same methodology, or in the case of theism lack of methodology, applies to virtually every area of study. For example Henry Morris, President of the Institute for Creation Research, said, "The only way we can determine the true age of the earth is for God to tell us what it is. And since He has told us, very plainly, in the Holy Scriptures that it is several thousand years in age, and no more, that ought to settle all basic questions of terrestrial chronology."

That is no way to discover the truth of anything. Simply put, faith does not give you the answers but rather it stops you from asking the questions. As Joseph Lewis has asked, "Is it not better to place a question mark upon a problem while seeking an answer, than to put the label 'God' there and consider the matter closed?" The Buddhists clearly agree with that. Tenzin Gyatso, the 14th Dalai Lama, said, "We must conduct research and then accept the results. If they don't stand up to experimentation, Buddha's own words must be rejected." In fact Hindu Prince Gautama Siddhartha - the Buddha himself - said, "Do not believe in anything simply because you have heard it. Do not believe in anything simply because it is spoken and rumored by many. Do not believe in anything simply because it is found written in your religious books. Do not believe in anything merely on the authority of your teachers and elders. Do not believe in traditions because they have been handed down for many generations. But after observation and analysis, when you find that anything agrees with reason and is conducive to the good and benefit of one and all, then accept it and live up to it." Why can't the dogmatic Abrahamic faiths do the same? What are they afraid of?

An extremely important point is sciences such as physics, chemistry and botany are exactly the same for people of all religions as well as those of no religion. They are totally consistent and self-evident to anyone who takes the time to objectively examine the evidence. They are demonstrable, measurable, testable and repeatable. There are no special pleadings. No rationalizations. The Periodic Table of Elements is the same in Berlin as it is in Tokyo and the stars look the same through a telescope in Seoul as they do in Albuquerque. Entire books have been written about the incompatibilities of science and religion so I am only going to touch on one more small, simple thing to demonstrate how far apart the two camps are - the subject of rainbows.

A rainbow is an optical and meteorological phenomenon which causes a spectrum of light to appear in the sky when the sun shines on droplets of moisture suspended in the Earth's atmosphere. Rainbows caused by sunlight always appear in the section of sky directly opposite the sun, take the form of a multicolored arc and in accordance with the scientific method are consistently observable, measurable, repeatable, testable and demonstrable.

Naturally people did not always know what caused rainbows and they have a place in legend owing to their beauty and the historical difficulty in explaining the phenomenon. In Greco-Roman mythology, for example, the rainbow was considered to be a path made by a messenger named Iris between Earth and Heaven. In Chinese mythology the rainbow was a slit in the sky sealed by goddess Nüwa using stones of five different colors. In the Hindu religion the rainbow is called Indradhanush, meaning "the bow of Indra, the god of lightning, thunder and rain." Another Indian mythology says the rainbow is the bow of

Rama, the incarnation of Vishnu, and it is called Rangdhonu in Bengali, meaning bow. Likewise in the mythology of Arabian Peninsula the rainbow, called Qaus Quzaḣ in Arabic, is the war bow of the god Quzaḣ. In Armenian mythology the rainbow is the belt of Tir, who was a Sun god, and in Norse Mythology a rainbow called the Bifröst Bridge connects the realms of Ásgard and Midgard, homes of the gods and humans, respectively.

The end of a rainbow is also reputed to be the Irish leprechaun's secret hiding place for his pot of gold, which is of course impossible to reach because a rainbow is an optical effect which depends on the location of the viewer. When walking towards the end of a rainbow it will appear to "move" further away and two people who simultaneously observe one from different locations will disagree about where it is.

Some folk traditions hold that leprechauns are descended from the Tuatha de Danann. According to the *Book of Invasions* when the Milesians came to Ireland they conquered the Tuatha de Danann - the "peoples of the goddess Danu," a race of people in Irish mythology who are thought to derive from the pre-Christian deities of Ireland - and forced them to live underground. When the surviving stories were written Ireland had been Christian for centuries and the Tuatha Dé were represented as mortal kings, queens and heroes of the distant past, however there are many clues to their former divine status and naturally when Christianity took religious precedence the importance (and thus the size) of the leprechauns decreased.

Another ancient portrayal of the rainbow is given in the *Epic of Gilgamesh* where the rainbow is the "jeweled necklace of the Great Mother Ishtar" that she lifts into the sky as a promise that she "will never forget these days of the great flood" that destroyed her children. Then Ishtar arrived. She lifted up the necklace of great jewels that her father Anu had created to please her and said, "Heavenly gods, as surely as this jeweled necklace hangs upon my neck, I will never forget these days of the great flood. Let all of the gods except Enlil come to the offering. Enlil may not come, for without reason he brought forth the flood that destroyed my people." That should sound familiar to Christians and Jews, because according to Genesis after Noah's flood God put the rainbow in the sky as the sign of his promise that he would never again destroy the earth with flood (Genesis 9:13–17): "I do set my bow in the cloud, and it shall be for a token of a covenant between me and the earth. And it shall come to pass, when I bring a cloud over the earth, that the bow shall be seen in the cloud: And I will remember my covenant, which is between me and you and every living creature of all flesh; and the waters shall no more become a flood to destroy all flesh. And the bow shall be in the cloud; and I will look upon it, that I may remember the everlasting covenant between God and every living creature of all flesh that is upon the earth. And God said unto Noah, 'This is the token of the covenant, which I have established between me and all flesh that is upon the earth.'"

The question is which explanation for rainbows do you believe, and more importantly why? Do any of them, aside from the scientific explanation, really make any sense? Carl Sagan summed it up perfectly when he asked, "Who is more humble? The scientist who looks at the universe with an open mind and accepts whatever the universe has to teach us, or somebody who says everything in this book must be considered the literal truth and can never be questioned - and never mind the fallibility of all the human beings involved?"

Even worse than those professing blind faith are pseudoscientists who masquerade as credible researchers. A perfect example is "Doctor" Kent Hovind, a Young Earth Creationist and conspiracy theorist famous for creation science seminars which aim to convince listeners to reject modern theories of evolution, geophysics and cosmology in favor of the Genesis creation narrative. He claims to hold three degrees from unaccredited institutions - a Bachelor of Religious Education from Midwestern Baptist College and a Master's and Doctorate in Christian Education through correspondence from non-accredited diploma mill Patriot University (now Patriot Bible University), whose policies allow students to attain PhDs in months rather than years for as little as $25 per month. The obviously unqualified Hovind summarizes his version of the creation story in the eponymous "Hovind Theory" which says in part that after Noah's family and two of every animal (including young dinosaurs) boarded the Ark a giant ice meteor hit the earth, caused the flood and that explains fossils, plate tectonics, the Grand Canyon (which was formed in a couple of weeks) and the shortening of human lifespans. Chemist Karen Bartelt commented, "Hovind's message appeals to those who are unaware his 'evidence' is without merit," and the plausibility of his theory has even been criticized by other Young Earth Creationists who believe many of his arguments are invalid and consequently undermine their cause - and yet he has still managed to attract a following, including my pastor brother-in-law, with his phony credentials.

Change and progress are slow processes. James Randi has said, "Religion is based upon blind faith supported by no evidence. Science is based upon confidence that results from evidence - and that confidence can be modified and/or reversed by further observations and experimentation. Science approaches truth, closer and closer, by hard dedicated work. Religion already has it all decided, and it's all 'in the book.' It's dogma, unchangeable, and unaffected by reality and whatever facts we come upon in the real world." While that is still largely true there is a glimmer of hope in the form of something called the "Clergy Letter Project," which as of this writing is an initiative boasting thirteen thousand clergy signers.

The letter states, "Within the community of Christian believers there are areas of dispute and disagreement, including the proper way to interpret Holy Scripture. While virtually all Christians take the Bible seriously and hold it to be authoritative in matters of faith and practice, the overwhelming majority do not read the Bible literally, as they would a science textbook. Many of the beloved stories found in the Bible - the Creation, Adam and Eve, Noah and the Ark - convey timeless truths about God, human beings and the proper relationship between Creator and creation expressed in the only form capable of transmitting these truths from generation to generation. Religious truth is of a different order from scientific truth. Its purpose is not to convey scientific information but to transform hearts. We the undersigned, Christian clergy from many different traditions, believe that the timeless truths of the Bible and the discoveries of modern science may comfortably coexist. We believe that the theory of evolution is a foundational scientific truth, one that has stood up to rigorous scrutiny and upon which much of human knowledge and achievement rests. To reject this truth or to treat it as 'one theory among others' is to deliberately embrace scientific ignorance and transmit such ignorance to our children. We believe that among God's good gifts are human minds capable of critical thought and that the failure to fully employ this gift is a rejection of the will of our Creator. To argue that God's loving plan of salvation for humanity precludes the full employment of the God-given faculty of reason is to attempt to limit God, an act of hubris. We urge school board members to preserve the integrity of the science curriculum by affirming the teaching of the theory of evolution as a core component of human knowledge. We ask that science remain science and that religion remain religion, two very different, but complementary, forms of truth."

That's a good start, but there is still a long, long way to go.

Creation

Or, Where Did It All Come From?

"We ought to recognize that religious strife is not the consequence of differences among people. It's about conflicts between creation stories." ~ E. O. Wilson

During my time in the Marine Corps I spent two years at the American Embassy in Canberra, Australia, and while there took a trip up north to Queensland where I visited an Aboriginal cultural center called Dreamland. It was there I first heard the Aboriginal creation story. It begins with what they call "The Dreaming," a time when the world was bare and cold and the Rainbow Serpent slept underground with all the animal tribes in her belly. When the time was right, she emerged and spewed forth the animals along with the features of the natural world. The Rainbow Serpent was the maker of laws which all creatures must obey and in some variations of the myth she swallowed wrongdoers and spat out their bones to form rocks and hills and in others she rewarded those who obeyed the law by giving them human form and turned the lawbreakers into stone. The Rainbow Serpent is sometimes called the "Old Woman," and it was she who taught humans how to get food. In tribes which believe they are descended from animals she was said to have given each a totem and ruled that no man could eat the animal it represented and in this way ensured there would be enough food for all. Who is to say that is not how it happened?

Who are we and where did we come from? It's a question as old as humankind, and everyone seems to have a different answer. Determining the origin of the universe is beyond the scope of this book and in any case has little bearing on the practice of religious dogma but it still must be addressed to some extent because a couple of simple but pertinent questions must be asked and answered before we can proceed. The first question is why select a particular creation story of the many which have been put forward to explain our origins? The second is why would an omnipotent superbeing create a universe, and for that matter humans, in the first place? Did he wake up one morning, decide he was bored and get creative? Or did he feel the need to create insignificant little creatures to worship and fear him due to a monumental inferiority complex?

A creation myth is a symbolic narrative of how the world began and how people first came to inhabit it. While in popular usage the term "myth" often refers to false or fanciful stories, cultures regard their creation myths as true to varying degrees. In the society in which it is told a creation myth is usually regarded as conveying profound truths metaphorically, symbolically and sometimes in a historical or literal sense and are commonly, although not always, considered cosmological myths - that is, they describe the ordering of the cosmos from a state of chaos or amorphousness.

Creation myths often share a number of features, usually are considered sacred accounts and can be found in nearly all known religious traditions. They are all stories with a plot and characters who are either deities, human-like figures or animals who speak and transform easily and are often set in a dim and nonspecific past - what historian of religion Mircea Eliade termed "in illo tempore" (at that time). Creation myths address questions deeply meaningful to the society which shares them, revealing their central worldview and the framework for the self-identity of the culture and individual in a universal context. They develop in oral traditions and therefore typically have multiple versions, are the most common form of myth and are found throughout human culture.

Creation *ex nihilo* (Latin for "out of nothing"), also known as "creation de novo," is a common type of mythical creation which is found in creation stories from ancient Egypt, the Rig Veda, the Bible, the Quran and many animistic cultures in Africa, Asia, Oceania and North America. One interesting paradox from a theological standpoint is people who accept these stories as true also reject scientific theories such as the Big Bang and others by derisively claiming something *cannot* come from nothing.

For instance the *Popol Vuh* is the creation story of the Maya. I chose this example because of recent claims about the apocalyptic prophecy thought to be contained in the Mayan calendar by many people. The following part of this story recounts the first attempts of the creator, Heart of Sky, to make humans. The story goes on to explain that the final attempt which resulted in the "true people" was accomplished by constructing people with maize (corn). This is a very reasonable explanation since in essence it was the cultivation of maize which gave the early Mayan culture the means to change from hunter-gatherers to their highly advanced civilization.

"Here is the story of the beginning, when there was not one bird, not one fish, not one mountain. Here is the sky, all alone. Here is the sea, all alone. There is nothing more - no sound, no movement. Only the sky and the sea. Only Heart-of-Sky, alone. And these are his names: Maker and Modeler, Kukulkan, and Hurricane. But there is no one to speak his names. There is no one to praise his glory. There is no one to nurture his greatness. And so Heart-of-Sky thinks, 'Who is there to speak my name? Who is there to praise me? How shall I make it dawn?' Heart-of-Sky only says the word, 'Earth,' and the earth rises, like a mist from the sea. He only thinks of it, and there it is. He thinks of mountains, and great mountains come. He thinks of trees, and trees grow on the land. And so Heart-of-Sky says, 'Our work is going well.' Now Heart-of-Sky plans the creatures of the forest - birds, deer, jaguars and snakes. And each is given his home. 'You the deer, sleep here along the rivers. You the birds, your nests are in the trees. Multiply and scatter,' he tells them. Then Heart-of-Sky says to the animals, 'Speak, pray to us.' But the creatures can only squawk. The creatures only howl. They do not speak like humans. They do not praise Heart-of-Sky and so the animals are humbled. They will serve those who will worship Heart-of-Sky. And Heart-of-Sky tries again. Tries to make a giver of respect. Tries to make a giver of praise. Here is the new creation, made of mud and earth. It doesn't look very good. It keeps crumbing and softening. It looks lopsided and twisted. It only speaks nonsense. It cannot multiply. So Heart-of-Sky lets it dissolve away. Now Heart-of-Sky plans again. Our Grandfather and Our Grandmother are summoned. They are the most wise spirits. 'Determine if we should carve people from wood,' commands Heart-of-Sky. They run their hands over the kernels of corn. They run their hands over the coral seeds. 'What can we make that will speak and pray?' asks Our Grandfather. 'What can we make that will nurture and provide?' asks Our Grandmother. They count the days, the lots of four, seeking an answer for Heart-of-Sky. Now they give the answer, it is good to make your people with wood. They will speak your name. They will walk about and multiply. 'So it is,' replies Heart-of-Sky. And as the words are spoken, it is done. The doll-people are made with faces carved from wood. But they have no blood, no sweat. They have nothing in their minds. They have no respect for Heart-of-Sky. They are just walking about, but they accomplish nothing. 'This is not what I had in mind,' says Heart-of-Sky. And so it is decided to destroy these wooden people. Hurricane makes a great rain. It rains all day and rains all night. There is a terrible flood and the earth is blackened. The creatures of the forest come into the homes of the doll-people. 'You have chased us from our homes so now we will take yours,' they growl. And their dogs and turkeys cry out, 'You have abused us so now we shall eat you!' Even their pots and grinding stones speak, 'We will burn you and pound on you just as you have done to us!' The wooden people scatter into the forest. Their faces are crushed, and they are turned into monkeys. And this is why monkeys look like humans. They are what is left of what came before, an experiment in human design."

As I am sure you will agree there are some interesting parallels between that myth and the Abrahamic creation story. Let's look at another. One of the many creation myths of the African animist religions tells of Mbombo, also called Bumba, who is the creator god in the religion and mythology of the Kuba people of Central Africa. In this creation myth Mbombo, who was a giant in form and white in color, tells that in the beginning he was alone and darkness and water covered all the earth. It happened that Mbombo came to feel an intense pain in his stomach and then vomited out the sun, moon and stars. The heat and light from the sun evaporated the water covering the earth creating clouds, and after time the dry hills emerged from the water. Then Mbombo vomited once more bringing forth nine animals - the leopard called Koy Bumba, the eagle Ponga Bumba, the crocodile Ganda Bumba, the fish Yo Bumba, the tortoise Kono Bumba, a black leopard-like animal called Tsetse Bumba, a white heron called Nyanyi Bumba, a scarab and a goat named Budi. Mbombo also vomited many men, and one of them was called Loko Yima. These nine animals went on to create all the world's creatures. The heron created all flying birds but one, the kite, and the crocodile created snakes and the iguana. The goat Budi brought forth all the horned animals, the scarab all insects and Yo Bumba all fish.

Three of Mbombo's sons then said they would finish creating the world. The first to try, Nyonye Ngana, vomited white ants but died after. To honor him the ants went deep in the earth for dark soil to bury him and transformed the barren sands at the earth's surface. The second, Chonganda, created the first plant which in turn gave rise to all trees, grasses and flowers. And Chedi Bumba, the third son, made the last bird, the kite.

Tsetse Bumba caused trouble on the earth so Mbombo chased him into the sky where he became the thunderbolt. This left people without fire, so Mbombo showed them how to make it from trees. Once the creation was complete and peaceful Mbombo delivered it to mankind and retreated into the heavens, leaving Loko Yima to serve as "god upon the earth." The woman of the waters, Nchienge, lived in the East, and her son, Woto, became the first king of the Kuba.

That is what many have long believed on the continent of Africa, but the Americas have myths of their own. According to the account recorded in 1900 by the Bureau of American Ethnology in North America the Cherokee creation belief, also one of many, describes the earth as a great floating island surrounded by seawater which hangs from the sky by cords attached at the four cardinal points. The story tells that the first earth came to be when Dâyuni'sï (Beaver's Grandchild) the little Water beetle came from Gälûñ'lätï, the sky realm, to see what was below the water. He scurried over the surface of the water but found no solid place to rest so he dove to the bottom and brought up some soft mud which expanded in every direction and became the earth.

The other animals in Gälûñ'lätï were eager to come down to the new earth and first birds were sent to see if the mud was dry. Buzzard was sent ahead to make preparations for the others but the earth was still soft, and when he grew tired his wings dipped very low and brushed the soft mud, gouging mountains and valleys in the smooth surface and the animals were forced to wait again but when it was finally dry they all came down. It was dark so they took the sun and set it in a track to run east to west, at first setting it too low and the red crawfish was scorched so they elevated the sun several times in order to reduce its heat.

The story also tells how plants and animals acquired certain characteristics and this is related in one of their medicine rituals. They all were told to stay awake for seven nights, but only a few animals such as owl and panther succeeded and they were given the power to see and prey upon the others at night. Only a few trees succeeded as well, the cedar, pine, spruce and laurel, so the rest were forced to shed their leaves in the winter. The first people were a brother and sister. Once the brother hit his sister with a fish and told her to multiply. Following this she gave birth to a child every seven days and soon there were too many people so women were then forced to have just one child every year.

Now let's look at another myth from a different part of the world. In the Indian sub-continent the *Purusha Sukta* of the earliest Hindu text *Rig Veda* mentions Purusha, the primeval cosmic being who is described as all that has ever existed and will ever exist. Viraj, variously interpreted as the mundane egg (Hiranyagarbha) or the twofold male-female energy, was born from Purusha and the Purusha was born again from Viraj. The gods then performed a sacrifice with the Purusha, leading to the creation of the other things in the manifested world from his various body parts and his mind. These things included the animals, the *Vedas*, the *Varnas*, the celestial bodies, the air, the sky, the heavens, the earth, the directions and even Indra (leader of the Devas or demi-gods and the lord of Svargaloka or heaven) and Agni (one of the most important of the Vedic gods - the god of fire and acceptor of sacrifices). This myth is similar to other myths found in the Indo-European cultures in which the creation arises out of the dismemberment of a divine being, for example Ymir of Norse mythology.

The *Enûma Eliš* (also spelled "Enuma Elish") is the Babylonian creation myth and is centered on the supremacy of Marduk and the creation of humankind. The composition of the text dates to the Bronze Age, the time of Hammurabi or perhaps the early Kassite era (roughly 18th to 16th Centuries BCE) although some scholars favor a later date of c. 1100 BCE. The first tablet begins, "When the sky above was not named, and the earth beneath did not yet bear a name, and the primeval Apsû, who begat them, and chaos, Tiamat, the mother of them both, their waters were mingled together, and no field was formed, no marsh was to be seen; when of the gods none had been called into being."

The epic names two primeval gods, with Apsû (or Abzu) representing fresh water and Tiamat the oceanic waters. Marduk is appointed as their leader, becomes very powerful, challenges Tiamat to combat and destroys her. He then rips her corpse into two halves (remember, she represents oceanic waters) with which he fashions the earth and the skies. Marduk then creates the calendar, organizes the planets and stars and regulates the moon, sun and weather. Marduk then destroys Tiamat's husband Kingu and uses his blood to create humankind. This myth is old, but not the oldest.

The Sumerian conception of the creation of the universe, which predates all others, says once upon a time there was a huluppu-tree (perhaps a willow) planted on the banks of the Euphrates which was nurtured by the waters of that river, but the South Wind tore at it, root and crown, while the Euphrates flooded it with its waters. Inanna, queen of Heaven, while walking by took the tree in her hand and brought it to Erech, the seat of her main sanctuary, and planted it in her holy garden. There she tended it most carefully for when the tree grew big she planned to make of its wood a chair for herself as well as a couch.

Years passed and the tree matured and grew big, but Inanna found herself unable to cut it down for at its base the snake "who knows no charm" had built its nest, in its crown the Zu-bird (a mythological creature which at times wrought mischief) had placed its young and in the middle Lilith (the maid of desolation) had built her house - and so poor Inanna, the light-hearted and ever joyful maid, shed bitter tears. As the dawn broke and her brother the sun-god Utu arose from his sleeping chamber she repeated to him tearfully all that had befallen her huluppu-tree.

Now Gilgamesh, the great Sumerian hero (forerunner of the Greek Heracles) who lived in Erech, overheard Inanna's weeping complaint and chivalrously came to her rescue. He donned his armour and slew the snake who knows no charm at the base of the tree, seeing which the Zu-Bird fled with his young to the mountain and Lilith tore down her house and fled to the desolate places which she was accustomed to haunt. The men of Erech who had accompanied Gilgamesh now cut down the tree and presented it to Inanna for her chair and couch.

What did Inanna do? Of the base of the huluppu-tree she made an object called the pukku (probably a drum) and of its crown she made another related object called the mikku (probably a drumstick) and gave them both to Gilgamesh, evidently as a reward for his gallantry. The story continues with the statement "because of the cry of the young maidens" the pukku and the mikku fell into the nether world, evidently through a hole in the ground. Gilgamesh put in his hand to retrieve them but was unable to reach them. He put in his foot but was just as unsuccessful. And so he seated himself at the gate of the nether world and cried with fallen face.

His servant Enkidu, his constant follower and companion, heard his master's cries and planned to descend to the nether world. Thereupon Gilgamesh warned him of the dangers involved. But Enkidu heeded not the advice of his master and he did the very things against which Gilgamesh had warned him. And so he was seized by the nether world and was unable to reascend to the earth. Thereupon Gilgamesh, greatly troubled, proceeded to the city of Nippur and wept before the great air-god Enlil, the god who in the third millennium BCE was the leading deity of the Sumerian pantheon. But Enlil refused to stand by Gilgamesh, who then proceeded to Eridu and repeated his plea before the water-god Enki, the god of wisdom. Enki ordered the sun-god Utu to open a hole in the nether world and to allow the shade of Enkidu to ascend to earth. The sun-god Utu did as bidden and the shade of Enkidu appeared to Gilgamesh. Master and servant embraced and Gilgamesh questioned Enkidu about what he saw in the nether world.

Heaven and earth, originally united, were separated and moved away from each other and thereupon the creation of man was ordained. An, the

Heaven-god, then carried off Heaven while Enlil, the air-god, carried off earth. All this seems to be according to plan but then the goddess Ereshkigal (counterpart of the Greek Persephone, whom we know as queen of the nether world but who originally was probably a sky-goddess) was carried off into the nether world, perhaps by Kur. No doubt to avenge this deed the water-god Enki set sail to attack Kur. The latter, evidently to be conceived as a monster or dragon, did not stand idly by but hurled stones large and small against the keel of Enki's boat while the primeval waters attacked it front and rear. The poem does not give the result of this struggle between Enki and Kur since the entire cosmogonic or creation introduction has nothing to do with the basic contents of the Gilgamesh composition, and it was placed at the head of the poem only because Sumerian scribes were accustomed to beginning their stories with several introductory lines dealing with creation.

Some pretty crazy myths, aren't they? Virtually every culture and religion has one, from Bumba to the Hindus to well… you name it. So where did they all come from, and why did people believe them? The one they choose is of course largely due to enculturation, but no matter which is believed the one undeniable truth is nobody was there to record it.

Let's look at just one more creation story, a more familiar one this time, and if you can manage to do so try to read it as if you are hearing it for the very first time: "In the beginning God created the heavens and the earth. Now the earth was formless and empty. Darkness was on the surface of the deep. God's Spirit was hovering over the surface of the waters. God said, 'Let there be light,' and there was light. God saw the light, and saw that it was good. God divided the light from the darkness. God called the light Day, and the darkness he called Night. There was evening and there was morning, one day.

God said, 'Let there be an expanse in the midst of the waters, and let it divide the waters from the waters. God made the expanse, and divided the waters which were under the expanse from the waters which were above the expanse, and it was so. God called the expanse sky. There was evening and there was morning, a second day.

God said, 'Let the waters under the sky be gathered together to one place, and let the dry land appear,' and it was so. God called the dry land Earth, and the gathering together of the waters he called Seas. God saw that it was good. God said, 'Let the earth put forth grass, herbs yielding seed, and fruit trees bearing fruit after their kind, with its seed in it, on the earth,' and it was so. The earth brought forth grass, herbs yielding seed after their kind, and trees bearing fruit, with its seed in it, after their kind: and God saw that it was good. There was evening and there was morning, a third day.

God said, 'Let there be lights in the expanse of sky to divide the day from the night; and let them be for signs, and for seasons, and for days and years; and let them be for lights in the expanse of sky to give light on the earth,' and it was so. God made the two great lights: the greater light to rule the day, and the lesser light to rule the night. He also made the stars. God set them in the expanse of sky to give light to the earth, and to rule over the day and over the night, and to divide the light from the darkness. God saw that it was good. There was evening and there was morning, a fourth day.

God said, 'Let the waters swarm with swarms of living creatures, and let birds fly above the earth in the open expanse of sky.' God created the large sea creatures, and every living creature that moves, with which the waters swarmed, after their kind, and every winged bird after its kind. God saw that it was good. God blessed them, saying, 'Be fruitful, and multiply, and fill the waters in the seas, and let birds multiply on the earth.' There was evening and there was morning, a fifth day.

God said, 'Let the earth bring forth living creatures after their kind, cattle, creeping things, and animals of the earth after their kind,' and it was so. God made the animals of the earth after their kind, and the cattle after their kind, and everything that creeps on the ground after its kind. God saw that it was good.

God said, 'Let us make man in our image, after our likeness: and let them have dominion over the fish of the sea, and over the birds of the sky, and over the cattle, and over all the earth, and over every creeping thing that creeps on the earth.' God created man in his own image. In God's image he created him; male and female he created them. God blessed them. God said to them, 'Be fruitful, multiply, fill the earth, and subdue it. Have dominion over the fish of the sea, over the birds of the sky, and over every living thing that moves on the earth.' God said, 'Behold, I have given you every herb yielding seed, which is on the surface of all the earth, and every tree, which bears fruit yielding seed. It will be your food. To every animal of the earth, and to every bird of the sky, and to everything that creeps on the earth, in which there is life, I have given every green herb for food.' And it was so. God saw everything that he had made, and, behold, it was very good. There was evening and there was morning, the sixth day.

The heavens and the earth were finished, and all the host of them. On the seventh day God finished his work which he had made; and he rested on the seventh day from all his work which he had made. God blessed the seventh day, and made it holy, because he rested in it from all his work which he had created and made.

This is the history of the generations of the heavens and of the earth when they were created, in the day that Yahweh God made earth and the heavens. No plant of the field was yet in the earth, and no herb of the field had yet sprung up; for Yahweh God had not caused it to rain on the earth. There was not a man to till the ground, but a mist went up from the earth, and watered the whole surface of the ground. Yahweh God formed man from the dust of the ground, and breathed into his nostrils the breath of life; and man became a living soul. Yahweh God planted a garden eastward, in Eden, and there he put the man whom he had formed. Out of the ground Yahweh God made every tree to grow that is pleasant to the sight, and good for food; the tree of life also in the midst of the garden, and the tree of the knowledge of good and evil. A river went out of Eden to water the garden; and from there it was parted, and became four heads. The name of the first is Pishon: this is the one which flows through the whole land of Havilah, where there is gold; and the gold of that land is good. There is aromatic resin and the onyx stone. The name of the second river is Gihon: the same river that flows through the whole land of Cush. The name of the third river is Hiddekel: this is the one which flows in front of Assyria. The fourth river is the Euphrates. Yahweh God took the man, and put him into the Garden of Eden to dress it and to keep it. Yahweh God commanded the man, saying, 'Of every tree of the garden you may freely eat: but of the tree of the knowledge of good and evil, you shall not eat of it: for in the day that you eat of it you will surely die.'

Yahweh God said, 'It is not good that the man should be alone; I will make him a helper suitable for him.' Out of the ground Yahweh God formed every animal of the field, and every bird of the sky, and brought them to the man to see what he would call them. Whatever the man called every living creature, that was its name. The man gave names to all cattle, and to the birds of the sky, and to every animal of the field; but for man there was not found a helper suitable for him. Yahweh God caused a deep sleep to fall on the man, and he slept; and he took one of his ribs, and closed up the flesh in its place. He made the rib, which Yahweh God had taken from the man, into a woman, and brought her to the man. The man said, 'This is now bone of my bones, and flesh of my flesh. She will be called Woman, because she was taken out of Man.' Therefore a man will leave his father and his mother, and will join with his wife, and they will be one flesh. They were both naked, the man and his wife, and were not ashamed.

Now the serpent was more subtle than any animal of the field which Yahweh God had made. He said to the woman, 'Yes, has God said, 'You shall not eat of any tree of the garden?'' The woman said to the serpent, 'Of the fruit of the trees of the garden we may eat, but of the fruit of the tree which is in the midst of the garden, God has said, 'You shall not eat of it, neither shall you touch it, lest you die.'' The serpent said to the woman, 'You won't surely die, for God knows that in the day you eat it, your eyes will be opened, and you will be like God, knowing good and evil.'

When the woman saw that the tree was good for food, and that it was a delight to the eyes, and that the tree was to be desired to make one wise, she took of the fruit of it, and ate; and she gave some to her husband with her, and he ate. Both of their eyes were opened, and they knew that they were naked. They sewed fig leaves together, and made themselves aprons. They heard the voice of Yahweh God walking in the garden in the cool of the day, and the man and his wife hid themselves from the presence of Yahweh God among the trees of the garden.

Yahweh God called to the man, and said to him, 'Where are you?'

The man said, 'I heard your voice in the garden, and I was afraid, because I was naked; and I hid myself.'

God said, 'Who told you that you were naked? Have you eaten from the tree that I commanded you not to eat from?'

The man said, 'The woman whom you gave to be with me, she gave me of the tree, and I ate.'

Yahweh God said to the woman, 'What is this you have done?'

The woman said, 'The serpent deceived me, and I ate.'

Yahweh God said to the serpent, 'Because you have done this, cursed are you above all cattle, and above every animal of the field. On your belly shall you go, and you shall eat dust all the days of your life. I will put enmity between you and the woman, and between your offspring and her offspring. He will bruise your head, and you will bruise his heel.'

To the woman he said, 'I will greatly multiply your pain in childbirth. In pain you will bring forth children. Your desire will be for your husband, and he will rule over you.'

To Adam he said, 'Because you have listened to your wife's voice, and have eaten of the tree, of which I commanded you, saying, 'You shall not eat of it,' cursed is the ground for your sake. In toil you will eat of it all the days of your life. Thorns also and thistles will it bring forth to you; and you will eat the herb of the field. By the sweat of your face will you eat bread until you return to the ground, for out of it you were taken. For you are dust, and to dust you shall return.'

The man called his wife Eve, because she was the mother of all living. Yahweh God made coats of skins for Adam and for his wife, and clothed them.

Yahweh God said, 'Behold, the man has become like one of us, knowing good and evil. Now, lest he put forth his hand, and also take of the tree of life, and eat, and live forever...' Therefore Yahweh God sent him forth from the Garden of Eden, to till the ground from whence he was taken. So he drove out the man; and he placed Cherubs at the east of the Garden of Eden, and the flame of a sword which turned every way, to guard the way to the tree of life."

That is of course the creation story in Genesis, the first book of the Bible, which is considered to be an allegorical or mythological account by most rational people although some biblical literalists believe these events actually happened exactly as written when in fact most biblical scholars consider it to be a confused melding of three distinct sources plus an editor, making it highly self-contradictory - but if you are a biblical literalist those contradictions magically disappear.

Traditionally, Genesis and the other four Mosaic books were considered to have been written by Moses himself and although a minority among conservative Christians still hold to this view the greater part of modern scholarship believes they were collected in the middle of the first millennium BCE from a number of older sources. Literary criticism and analysis suggests three sources for the original material which was then edited by a redactor, however the fact Moses' death is described in Deuteronomy 34 has amazingly changed few fundamentalist opinions even though nowhere in Scripture is he identified as the author.

It is worth noting the Jewish and Christian versions of Genesis have quite a few differences (as do much of the Hebrew Scriptures in general) including the order of sentences and passages, the structure of passages, emphasis on the importance of particular stories and in fact word choice when translating into non-Hebrew languages which can drastically alter meanings of particular verses so it would be inaccurate for someone who is schooled only in one version of Genesis to suggest he or she understands the other point of view.

Genesis is typical of the contemporary Mesopotamian worldview and likely had been strongly influenced by non-Abrahamic religions or myths. Based on similarities in both the story itself as well as shared cultural worldviews many scholars argue the story of creation week in Genesis is strongly influenced by, if not based on, the previously mentioned Babylonian creation myth *Enuma Elish.* Similarities with *Enuma Elish* include the order of creation, the sixth day creation of man, the concept that man is created in God's image and the idea of light being created before the sun.

The Sumerian myth and Eden story also share some similar aspects such as the setting of a garden paradise surrounded by desert, forbidden fruits, expulsion from paradise and punishment for eating the fruit, using a rib from a male to create womankind and even the meaning of the female names. There are also not surprisingly similarities with Greek mythology, for example in Genesis Eve's curiosity triggers chaos and in Greek myth Pandora's curiosity does the same thing plus both Deucalion and Noah are commissioned to build boats and fill them with animals.

As mentioned previously most biblical scholars believe the first two chapters of Genesis actually contain two creation myths spliced together along with editorial comments from the compiler since he or she adds meticulous details like lists of "begats," pages of cubit measurements for a boat and repetitive, redundant and recurring language. There are also contradictions which are the result of those multiple myths, for example in Genesis 1:6-8 the earth is covered in water and God (Elohim) commands the waters covering the earth to separate forming land and sea but in Genesis 2:5-6 the earth is dry since God had not yet caused it to rain but he then causes water to spring up from beneath the earth. In Genesis 1:27-28 God (Elohim) creates man and woman (both unnamed) together and then tells them to be fruitful and multiply and replenish the earth while in Genesis 2:7 the LORD (YHWH-Elohim) creates Adam and *then* creates Eve from Adam's rib in Genesis 2:21-22. The first myth lacks geographical references, while in the second the editors inserted names of rivers and lands near the Garden of Eden. In the first myth the animals of the sea and air were created on Thursday while the animals of the land, including man, were created on Friday and in the second man is created before any plants are created let alone animals to eat them. And so on… plus there are many more examples of contradiction in the subsequent Genesis story of Noah's flood.

Naturally apologetics abound which claim the accounts in Genesis are literal history, in this case from the *Christian Courier* (my comments are in parenthesis): "There are several lines of evidence which may be employed to show that the Genesis record of the creation is not a myth, nor is it symbolic. First, though, we must emphasize that in approaching this matter one must recognize that the student will have to possess sufficiently developed study skills to be able to evaluate evidence. Many of our nation's youngsters today readily believe anything they hear - whether at school or via television (or in church). Frequently they array this sort of public propaganda against the Bible school teacher, whom they feel is a nice person and well-meaning, but not nearly as informed as the 'experts.' We must train them to think, to analyze, to logically scrutinize, and then to draw sound conclusions (yes, please do!).

Consider then the following: The language in the opening portion of Genesis is in the same literary style as the balance of the book (as is the case with the Quran and for that matter Harry Potter). It is historical prose. For example it considers Adam and Eve to be actual people, just as Abraham and Sarah were (however there is no extra-biblical evidence for their existence either). Eden was as real as Ur of the Chaldees (which is also only found in Genesis). There is no change in style as the narrative progresses. One must have a valid reason, therefore, for dismissing Genesis 1 as being myth. A mere assertion by some TV personality will not accomplish that (who is 'some TV personality,' and how does that differ from 'a mere assertion from some theologian' as is the case here?).

There is a vast contrast in the dignity and tone of Genesis 1 and the creation myths that are common to the ancient world. For example, the Babylonian creation account is fraught with ridiculous absurdities that are light years removed from the stately manner of the Genesis account. In that story, Enuma Elish has two 'gods' at war; one kills the other and cuts her body into two pieces. From one of these the earth is fashioned, and from the other the heavens are formed (but speaking the universe into existence, making a man out of dirt and a woman out of a rib, a talking serpent and dividing the waters into the ocean and sky is *not* ridiculously absurd?).

There is no basis for suggesting that Genesis 1 is symbolic. Some liberal critics have argued that the 'days' of the creation week are mere figures of speech, representing millions of years. Others contend that the 'days' are simply poetic devices that outline the author's main theological points. These baseless theories clearly contradict Exodus 20:11, which views the creation days in the same literal sense as the Sabbath. The only rationale for this novel interpretative approach is an attempt to harmonize Genesis with the chronology required by the evolutionary scheme of history - which is without scientific substance. (Based upon what? Is the author of this apologetic an evolutionary scientist?).

Though penned many centuries ago, the Mosaic narrative is still brilliantly relevant. There is not a factual scientific error to be found within it (there are actually many which will be addressed shortly). In fact, famed archaeologist W. F. Albright (so famous I have never heard of him) once said that 'modern scientific cosmogonies show such a disconcerting tendency to be short-lived that it may be seriously doubted whether science has yet caught up with the biblical story' (cosmogonies is the branch of science which deals with the origin of the universe, especially the solar system, and Albright is an *archaeologist*... plus this statement was made way back in 1948 so what was considered "modern" then is now comparatively ancient).

Jesus Christ accepted the literal historicity of the Genesis account. He affirmed that the first human beings: (a) were made by God; (b) were made male and female; and, (c) had a history extending back to the 'beginning of the creation' (but since the character known as Jesus only exists in the Bible words attributed to him cannot constitute proof of anything, therefore this is a prime example of trying to use the Bible to prove the Bible true). The conclusion, therefore, must be this: Genesis 1 is not myth; it is not symbolic or poetic; it is straight-forward, literal history. That is the fact of the situation."

It should go without saying that asserting, "Many... youngsters today readily believe anything they hear" and "We must train them to think, to analyze, to logically scrutinize, and then to draw sound conclusions," followed by such baseless theories (to use their own term) and tortured rationalizations is incredibly ironic. A literal interpretation of Genesis is inconceivable because of the vagueness of the language used in the first few chapters, for example, "God created the heavens and the earth" is scientifically meaningless and can only be interpreted as a metaphor. The entire Bible, especially Genesis, leaves far too many things up to the imagination of the reader.

Clearly there are some, such as whoever penned that *Christian Courier* editorial, who claim they take the entire Bible word for word despite the necessary mental acrobatics and the absurdity of the claim itself, however many other believers claim to take the Bible word for word... but only in certain places. One would think that kind of interpretation would raise questions and suspicions in the mind of the semi-literalist, but enter the patented Christian defense mechanism, "God works in mysterious ways" - a brilliantly crafted auto-response system which suppresses any further desire to question or reason. A similar form of the defense mechanism is, "You just have to believe." In the mind of the believer mysteries, at least religious ones, are meant to remain unsolved and the believer is left to bask in their insolubility and in fact the greater the mystery the better it is not to solve it - and the more absurd the verse, the more of a virtue it is to believe it.

An obvious question which arises against semi-literal interpretations is on whose authority does one decide which verses to take literally and which to take as metaphor or allegory? There are of course also an infinite number of degrees of semi-literal interpretation of the Bible where some people may adhere literally to more verses than others, which makes that question all the more important.

There are Christians who believe the Earth is older than six thousand years as well as those who go so far as saying Genesis was not written by or even inspired by God. These kinds of interpretations require blocking out entire chapters of the Bible and treating them as nothing but metaphor and bits of ancient wisdom, so what then becomes left of the Bible? Why not simply take the next step and consider "God" a metaphor for the universe as well? In any case it seems that a strictly literal interpretation of Genesis would be fitting for this kind of analysis. This would minimize discrimination against anybody's personal interpretation and at the same time invite believers to examine such a literal interpretation and demonstrate how each verse falls apart at the slightest application of reason.

Genesis 1:1 of course says, "In the beginning God created the heavens and the earth," but to what "Heaven" is this referring? It could be referring to our atmosphere, but if the Earth was "without form" it wouldn't be able to hold an atmosphere gravitationally. Of course "Heaven" might also refer to the empty space which fills up the rest of the universe outside of our planet, but if that is the case where did God exist before he created space itself? For that matter, where does God exist now? Literalist responses might be, "God exists outside of normal space" or "God exists in the spiritual realm" or God exists "outside of creation," but all those do is raise more questions instead of providing answers. Until someone defines the meaning of "outside creation" or "spiritual realm" and provides a basis in fact for those definitions this kind of response is vacuous.

The next question is in the beginning… of what? What did God do *before* the beginning? The response usually consists of the Cosmological Argument which is covered elsewhere but it essentially says, "Everything requires a cause, by induction into the past there must exist a 'first cause' that initiated all future events and this first cause is God." Several objections can be made against this argument, with the most obvious being if everything requires a cause then what created God? And if you claim everything but God requires a cause then you are engaging in what is known as a "special pleading" and in doing so invalidating your own first cause argument.

Why doesn't the author of Genesis provide a rudimentary explanation of how God creates anything? Simply saying he created something is meaningless. It's like asking someone how a microwave oven works and receiving the answer, "It's magic." The Bible makes no mention of the actual physical processes which take place when God does his creating, and because of that glaring shortcoming any child or primitive man could have been the author.

Genesis 1:3 says, "And God said, let there be light: and there was light." The problem here is for light to exist there needs to be a light source and of course the light source in our solar system is the sun, but it had not yet been created. From where was this light emanating? A typical response is, "God is all-powerful. Surely he can create light without a light source. It can emanate from empty space if he so wills it." God may be all-powerful, but overlooking the fallacious appeal to authority in this argument, if there was already light why bother to create the sun at all? And if he is doing all of the creating by himself why does he need to say anything, and to whom was he speaking?

Genesis 1:4 tells us, "And God saw the light, that it was good: and God divided the light from the darkness." This suggests there was a chance the light may have been bad instead of good, but how could a perfect being create anything bad? Wouldn't it be good by default? And why does he need to divide light from darkness? If light was created then doesn't this automatically define light as separate from darkness? Verse 1:5 follows with, "And God called the light day, and the darkness he called night. And the evening and the morning were the first day." Why assign them names if he doesn't have anybody to tell about it?

Morning and evening are defined by the apparent rising and setting of our sun, however the sun did not exist yet so what is the definition of morning and evening in this case? This is also the first reference to God as "He." Why does God require a gender, and if this is absolutely necessary why is it male? This is a perfect example of how humans tend to personify their deities, and that it was a men rather than women who wrote Genesis.

Genesis 1:6-7 says, "And God said, let there be a firmament in the midst of the waters, and let it divide the waters from the waters. And God made the firmament, and divided the waters which were under the firmament from the waters which were above the firmament: and it was so." It goes without saying there is no reservoir of water above the sky. The idea of a firmament which holds up a layer of water might have presumably been used by ancient people to explain rain, i.e. the firmament opens up and lets rainwater through, however today we know water evaporates, forms clouds and comes back down as rain droplets.

Genesis 1:8 says, "And God called the firmament Heaven. And the evening and the morning were the second day," but didn't God already create a "Heaven" in Verse 1? What's the difference between the two? As for it being the second day, the sun still does not exist to account for evening and morning so how can there be days?

Genesis 1:9 says, "And God said, let the waters under the heaven be gathered together unto one place, and let the dry land appear: and it was so," which implies there was a single continent and single ocean on the planet and yet anyone with a map knows there are multiple continents and multiple bodies of water. Naturally the apologetic here is God changed things after the great flood. Okay, why?

Genesis 1:14 states, "And God said, let there be lights in the firmament of the heaven to divide the day from the night; and let them be for signs, and for seasons, and for days, and years." Finally we have some clue as to the meaning of evening and morning. The verse even says so itself with the phrase "and for days." So what was the author talking about when he spoke of days in earlier verses? And didn't God already divide the day from the night in verse 4?

Genesis 1:15 says, "And let them be for lights in the firmament of the heaven to give light upon the earth: and it was so." This verse makes it sound as if the stars were created with the sole purpose of giving light to the earth when in reality the light which shines on the earth from any star in the sky is less than a billionth of a percent of the star's total output. Plus there are millions of galaxies which are so far away they can only be seen with the most powerful telescopes and entire galaxies which only radiate in the infrared or radio portions of the electromagnetic spectrum. Why were all these distant and super-massive objects created if they serve no practical purpose as far as the Earth is concerned? Naturally the men who wrote those lines could not have known about such celestial objects because they could not detect them.

Genesis 1:16 tells us, "And God made two great lights; the greater light to rule the day, and the lesser light to rule the night: he made the stars also." The sun is hardly a great star, being at best of average size and brightness. An example of a great star would be the Pistol Star which is one hundred times more massive than the sun and ten million times as bright, but of course whoever wrote Genesis did not realize the sun was simply one star among billions and it only seemed great because it is the closest. For its part the moon is by no means a light, but instead a satellite of the Earth which reflects light from the sun. It also does not rule the night since it is visible during the day and night an equal amount of time and during a new moon phase is not visible at all. As wait... didn't God already create the stars back in verse 14?

Genesis 1:17 says, "And God set them in the firmament of the heaven to give light upon the earth." This suggests the stars are small dots which hang somewhere above the ground and although I am sure they appeared that way to the naked eye thousands of years ago we now know they are celestial bodies millions of times larger than the Earth and many billions of miles away. These verses also suggest the sun is somehow different from the stars since it was created separately when in fact it is just another star.

God also created several extra planets in our solar system which are completely uninhabitable as well as thousands of asteroids of various sizes, pulsars, quasars and black holes. Why are they there? In addition we are now discovering numerous planets in orbit around other stars. What possible use could those be to God's earthly creation and to a universe which is "finely tuned" for life? Genesis 1:18 then says, "And to rule over the day and over the night, and to divide the light from the darkness: and God saw that it was good." Once again didn't God divide the light from the darkness back in verse 4?

Genesis 1:26-27 states, "And God said, let us make man in our image, after our likeness: and let them have dominion over the fish of the sea, and over the fowl of the air, and over the cattle, and over all the earth, and over every creeping thing that creepeth upon the earth. So God created man in his own image, in the image of God created he him; male and female created he them." *Our* image? Isn't Christianity a monotheistic religion which believes in only one God? Male and female? Is there a Mrs. God? And what does "in his own image" mean? Does it mean the physical attributes depicted by Michelangelo on the ceiling of the Sistine Chapel? Perfect? Omniscient? Also notice this particular creation story suggests God created multiple humans, not necessarily two, and allowed them to multiply with no mention of Adam, Eve or anybody else from other biblical stories as is the case in Chapter 2.

Genesis 1:28 says, "And God blessed them, and God said unto them, be fruitful, and multiply, and replenish the earth, and subdue it: and have dominion over the fish of the sea, and over the fowl of the air, and over every living thing that moveth upon the earth." Replenish what? The Earth was just made. And the command to be fruitful and multiply does not account for humans at that time being immortal, so if they were to keep multiplying but nobody died it would be an overpopulation nightmare. Plus if God wanted the world to be filled with people why not simply create lots of them as was the case with all of the other species?

Next Genesis 2:7 tells us the Yahweh God formed man from the dust of the ground and later Eve is fashioned from his rib, and yet up to that point everything else in the universe including the stars and planets had been spoken into existence *ex nihilo* (out of nothing). Why the sudden need for raw materials? Could this simply be a literary plot device to highlight humans as being special? In fact, more special than the entire universe?

In Genesis 2:18-20 the Yahweh God said, "It is not good that the man should be alone; I will make him a helper suitable for him. Out of the ground Yahweh God formed every animal of the field, and every bird of the sky, and brought them to the man to see what he would call them. Whatever the man called every living creature, that was its name. The man gave names to all cattle, and to the birds of the sky, and to every animal of the field; but for man there was not found a helper suitable for him." If one actually takes the time to think about that passage rather than simply glossing over it the absurdity is palpable. First of all the notion of one man with no education and presumably no language (since no mention had been made of such things) sitting there naming creature after creature is ludicrous given that there are today an estimated 8.7 million species and the number is actually much higher since of all species which have ever existed on Earth 99.9 percent are now extinct. Can you just picture God lining them all up so they can parade by Adam to get a name? And one must wonder how those names were recorded for posterity so that future humans would know them. In reality the classification of species, i.e. the assignment of species to phylum, class, order, family and genus, is a bit more complicated especially when you consider that of the 8.7 million species at least 2.2 million are marine life… so how did Adam manage to name the fish? Plus all of the non-marine species would have had to have been transported on the ark to survive. This passage also makes it sound as if God is auditioning all of the animals to be Adam's "helper," and the notion that a suitable helper had not been found is laughable given that God presumably knew what he had created.

Genesis 2:24-25 says, "Therefore a man will leave his father and his mother, and will join with his wife, and they will be one flesh. They were both naked, the man and his wife, and were not ashamed." Where did the concept of father and mother come from? No one had yet given birth, and there were no children at all. As for them not being ashamed of being naked, why would or should they be since they had never heard of clothes and the concept of nudity was unknown.

Things then get really interesting in Genesis 3:1 with, "Now the serpent was more subtle than any animal of the field which Yahweh God had made. He said to the woman, 'Yes, has God said, 'You shall not eat of any tree of the garden?'" Setting aside the obvious problem of a *talking serpent* it is noteworthy that the serpent and/or snake is one of the oldest and most widespread mythological symbols, has been associated with some of the oldest rituals known to humankind and represents dual expressions of good and evil. Due to that last bit people often assume the serpent is actually Satan, but the Bible never says that is the case so it is just an assumption.

Following that in 3:2-3, "The woman said to the serpent, 'Of the fruit of the trees of the garden we may eat, but of the fruit of the tree which is in the midst of the garden, God has said, 'You shall not eat of it, neither shall you touch it, lest you die,'" but that surely meant nothing to her since she could not possibly have any concept of death as they were immortal and no one had ever died.

In verse 3:9, "Yahweh God called to the man, and said to him, 'Where are you?'" and in 3:11 God asked, "Who told you that you were naked? Have you eaten from the tree that I commanded you not to eat from?" These are very strange questions for an omniscient being to ask. He didn't know? Yoo-hoo, Adam… where *are* you?

Now God is mad. In 3:14, "Yahweh God said to the serpent, 'Because you have done this, cursed are you above all cattle, and above every animal of the field. On your belly shall you go, and you shall eat dust all the days of your life.'" What kind of punishment is that for a serpent? I mean, how could it have been a serpent if it did not already crawl on its belly? Then in 3:16, "To the woman he said, 'I will greatly multiply your pain in childbirth. In pain you will bring forth children. Your desire will be for your husband, and he will rule over you.'" That's pretty vindictive to say the least, and also punishes all women who follow including those who don't even like fruit. Plus it is misogynistic. And what about the animals? They too give birth in pain just as humans do. What did they do to deserve that? Now it is the man's turn. In 3:19 God says to him, "By the sweat of your face will you eat bread until you return to the ground, for out of it you were taken. For you are dust, and to dust you shall return." What did Adam and Eve know of bread? Was there a bakery in Eden? As for returning to dust that was one of the few accurate things said since no mention is made of Heaven, Hell or an afterlife, things which an omniscient being surely would have known he would create.

In verses 3:22-24 Yahweh God said, "Behold, the man has become like one of us, knowing good and evil. Now, lest he put forth his hand, and also take of the tree of life, and eat, and live forever... therefore Yahweh God sent him forth from the Garden of Eden, to till the ground from whence he was taken. So he drove out the man; and he placed Cherubs at the east of the Garden of Eden, and the flame of a sword which turned every way, to guard the way to the tree of life." First of all there is that "one of *us*" reference again. And if the tree of life was in the midst of the garden, but God is omnipotent, I fail to see how eating a piece of fruit from it would make someone immortal if that is not what God wanted to happen. Was it irreversible? And for that matter weren't they already immortal? As for knowledge of good and evil that would require evil to have already existed, and since God made everything that means it too was created by him (as is later confirmed in Isaiah 45:7). That is troubling in itself. Why not create a universe free from evil if you are truly omnibenevolent? I know I would. Wouldn't you? And one must wonder why the tree of life is not still there to this day, guarded by the Cherubs and a flaming sword, since Scripture makes no mention of its removal.

Okay… if I had lived three thousand years ago and had the desire to write a creation story it would probably have been something similar. The Genesis story simply embodies the sum of human knowledge at the time of its conception and the conclusions the authors arrived at are based upon that limited knowledge. Believing the Earth to be the center of the solar system or for that matter the entire universe and thinking the sky is enveloped by a solid canopy from which stars are suspended is perfectly understandable for an ancient culture, however it is absurd to continue to hold such beliefs in our modern age. In the words of Dr. Francis Crick, co-discoverer of the structure of the DNA molecule, "A belief, at the time it was formulated, may not only have appealed to the imagination but also fit well with all that was then known. It can nevertheless be made to appear ridiculous because of facts uncovered later by science. What could be more foolish than to base one's entire view of life on ideas that, however plausible at that time, now appear to be quite erroneous?"

The bottom line is the universe began somehow. We know that because it's here. Life began somehow. We know that because we're here. While unlikely, it could be that a higher power of some sort did initiate life on earth and moved on. That would satisfy proponents of Intelligent Design, wouldn't it? But it would not prove any particular dogma, so any god ever worshipped could have been the creator. It would also satisfy Deists who think of God as a nomadic farmer who plants seeds and moves on but does not involve himself in the day to day workings of the universe. Roman Philosopher Gaius Plinius Secundus, better known as Pliny the Elder, spoke of this two thousand years ago when he remarked, "It is ridiculous to think that a Supreme Being, whatever it is, cares about human affairs."

And there is always the possibility the higher power was not immortal as people seem to think. Nietzsche may have been correct when he famously said "God is dead." After all, how could we possibly confirm such a thing? The point is this book is not about the origins of the universe or the formation of life, although as stated earlier it necessarily must touch on those things in order to create a baseline for a conversation about whether or not there is any "truth" to the claims made by religion with regard to the effectiveness of prayer, nature of sin, accuracy of Scripture and anything else which suggests religion has it all figured out.

The Universe

Or, Is It All Here Just For Us?

"Only two things are infinite, the universe and human stupidity, and I'm not sure about the former." ~ Albert Einstein

In the very last lines of the 1997 film *Contact* astrophysicist Dr. Ellie Arroway, played by Jodie Foster, told a group of children, "I'll tell you one thing about the universe, though. The universe is a pretty big place. It's bigger than anything anyone has ever dreamed of before. So if it's just us... seems like an awful waste of space. Right?" She was absolutely correct about that.

In the 19th Century there were many books and articles about the possible inhabitants of other planets and many people believed intelligent beings might live on the Moon, Mars and Venus, but since travel to other planets was not yet possible some people suggested ways to signal extraterrestrials even before radio was discovered. Carl Friedrich Gauss suggested a giant triangle and three squares, the Pythagoras, could be drawn on the Siberian tundra with the outlines of the shapes being ten-mile-wide strips of pine forest and the interiors rye or wheat. Joseph Johann Littrow proposed using the Sahara as a blackboard where giant trenches several hundred yards wide could delineate twenty-mile-wide shapes. Then the trenches would be filled with water, enough kerosene could be poured on top of the water to burn for six hours and by using this method a different signal could be sent every night. Meanwhile astronomers were looking for signs of life on other planets and in 1822 Franz von Gruithuisen thought he saw a giant city and evidence of agriculture on the moon, but astronomers using more powerful instruments refuted his claims. Von Gruithuisen also believed he saw evidence of life on Venus. "Ashen light" (a hypothesized subtle glow) had been observed there, and he postulated it was caused by a great fire festival put on by the inhabitants to celebrate their new emperor but later revised his position and stated the Venusians could be burning their rainforest to make more farmland.

By the late 1800s astronomers had put forward the Kant-Laplace Hypothesis, which stated the farthest planets from the sun are the oldest and therefore Mars was more likely to have advanced civilizations than Venus, and since Venus was perpetually shrouded in clouds it was reasoned the Venusians probably would not be very good astronomers. Subsequent investigations focused on contacting Martians, and in 1877 Giovanni Schiaparelli announced he had discovered "canali" on Mars with this claim being followed by thirty years of Mars enthusiasm.

Inventor Charles Cros was convinced pinpoints of light observed on Mars and Venus were the lights of large cities and spent years trying to get funding for a giant mirror with which to signal the Martians. The idea was to focus on the Martian desert, where intense reflected sunlight could be used to burn figures into the Martian sand. Inventor Nikola Tesla mentioned many times during his career that he thought inventions such as his Tesla coil, used in the role of a "resonant receiver," could communicate with other planets and even observed repetitive signals of what he believed were extraterrestrial radio communications coming from Venus or Mars in 1899 - however these signals turned out to be nothing more than terrestrial radiation. Then around 1900 the Guzman Prize was created and the first person to establish interplanetary communication was to be awarded 100,000 francs under one stipulation - Mars was excluded because Madame Guzman thought communicating with Mars would be too easy to deserve a prize, but when the Martian canals proved illusory it seemed we humans were alone in the solar system but not necessarily the galaxy… or the universe.

Michael Shermer, in *Why Darwin Matters: The Case Against Intelligent Design*, makes an obvious but often overlooked (or ignored) point when he writes, "Finally, from what we now know about the cosmos, to think that all this was created for just one species among the tens of millions of species who live on one planet circling one of a couple of hundred billion stars that are located in one galaxy among hundreds of billions of galaxies, all of which are in one universe among perhaps an infinite number of universes all nestled within a grand cosmic multiverse, is provincially insular and anthropocentrically blinkered. Which is more likely? That the universe was designed just for us, or that we see the universe as having been designed just for us?"

In 1990 the *Voyager 1* space probe took a photograph of planet Earth from a record distance of about 3.7 billion miles which became known as the "Pale Blue Dot" and in the image Earth is shown as a fraction of one pixel (0.12 pixel in size) against the vastness of space. When the spacecraft passed Saturn in 1981 astronomer Carl Sagan had promoted the idea of taking one last picture of Earth, and although he conceded the photo would not be mainly scientific since the Earth would appear too small for the Voyager's cameras to make out any detail he suggested it might be useful as a perspective on our place in the cosmos.

In his book *Pale Blue Dot: A Vision of the Human Future in Space,* Sagan related his thoughts on a deeper meaning of the photograph: "From this distant vantage point, the Earth might not seem of any particular interest. But for us, it's different. Consider again that dot. That's here. That's home. That's us. On it everyone you love, everyone you know, everyone you ever heard of, every human being who ever was, lived out their lives. The aggregate of our joy and suffering, thousands of confident religions, ideologies and economic doctrines, every hunter and forager, every hero and coward, every creator and destroyer of civilization, every king and peasant, every young couple in love, every mother and father, hopeful child, inventor and explorer, every teacher of morals, every corrupt politician, every 'superstar,' every 'supreme leader,' every saint and sinner in the history of our species lived there - on a mote of dust suspended in a sunbeam. The Earth is a very small stage in a vast cosmic arena. Think of the rivers of blood spilled by all those generals and emperors so that in glory and triumph they could become the momentary masters of a fraction of a dot. Think of the endless cruelties visited by the inhabitants of one corner of this pixel on the scarcely distinguishable inhabitants of some other corner. How frequent their misunderstandings, how eager they are to kill one another, how fervent their hatreds. Our posturings, our imagined self-importance, the delusion that we have some privileged position in the universe are challenged by this point of pale light. Our planet is a lonely speck in the great enveloping cosmic dark. In our obscurity - in all this vastness - there is no hint that help will come from elsewhere to save us from ourselves. The Earth is the only world known, so far, to harbor life. There is nowhere else, at least in the near future, to which our species could migrate. Visit, yes. Settle, not yet. Like it or not, for the moment, the Earth is where we make our stand. It has been said that astronomy is a humbling and character-building experience. There is perhaps no better demonstration of the folly of human conceits than this distant image of our tiny world. To me, it underscores our responsibility to deal more kindly with one another and to preserve and cherish the pale blue dot, the only home we've ever known."

That was quite compelling and insightful to say the least. World renowned physicist Stephen Hawking put a similar sentiment into layman's terms when he said, "The human race is just chemical scum on a moderate sized planet orbiting around an average sized star in the outer suburb of one among a hundred billion galaxies (and) we are so insignificant I can't believe the whole universe exists just for our benefit."

In *A Brief History of Time* Hawking asked, "If the universe is really completely self-contained, having no boundary or edge, it would have neither beginning nor end: it would simply be. What place, then, for a creator?" Indeed, the more humanity learns about the universe in which we are just a very miniscule part the less need we have for a higher power. The Theory of Evolution cogently describes how we as a species came into being and the Big Bang elegantly enumerates how the universe itself came into existence. As our scientific understanding expands purely religious answers for life's big questions seem to contract, but what would it mean for belief or non-belief if we discovered the existence of extraterrestrial life?

This question is central to the premise of a new book called *Religions and Extraterrestrial Life: How Will We Deal with It?* by an astronomy professor at Vanderbilt University named David Weintraub. The book examines the stances, if any, of the world's major religions in regard to the possibility of life beyond our own planet. Wintraub reports that one-fifth to one-third of Americans believe alien life probably exists and with the exponential increase in the discovery of new planets finding one which would harbor living beings seems more and more likely, however not all Americans are quick to embrace the idea of extraterrestrials. While Weintraub found that fifty-five percent of atheists felt the existence of aliens was possible or even probable, he also states that evangelical and fundamentalist Christians are the least likely of any religious group in the United States to embrace the thought life may exist beyond Earth. This reticence of fundamentalist Christians to believe in aliens in terms of salvation stems from Christian concepts of original sin, since the need for atonement through Christ's sacrifice on the cross would be complicated by the existence of otherworldly beings who may not require the same redemption or for that matter know anything at all about earthly religions.

While theological debates over the implications of alien life may be theoretically interesting, one factor often not taken into account is the distrust of science among fundamentalists since worldviews such as creationism and intelligent design present a purely human-centric view of the universe. From this perspective the universe was created in six twenty-four-hour days, never mind the universal perspective, since the concept of a "day" is relative to what planet one might inhabit. Also inherent in the fundamentalist Christian perspective is the idea God gave humanity dominion over all of creation, meaning humans have free reign to do with the Earth's natural resources - and presumably the resources of every other planet - as they please. The existence of extraterrestrials would clearly muddy these straightforward concepts found in fundamentalist Christianity. Alien life, especially intelligent alien life, would mean our perspective of the universe is relative and we as a species are not specially appointed to control the cosmos. In other words if there is life on other planets, and there probably is from a statistical standpoint, it stands to reason that if there is a God we have the same creator. That is significant, because what if the day comes when we make contact and the aliens have never heard of him? Or for that matter what if they have completely different beliefs?

Weintraub also points out not all religions would be troubled by the discovery of aliens. Hinduism and Buddhism have speculated that humans could be reincarnated as extraterrestrials, while Judaism and Islam see their tenets as only applicable to humans on Earth regardless of life on other planets. Even some Catholics and Protestants have managed, somewhat ambiguously, to incorporate extraterrestrials into their understanding of God's plan. So while the discovery of life on other planets might strike a blow to the worldviews of fundamentalists, the existence of aliens would not necessarily mean the end of all religion.

On the other hand Humanism, with its emphasis on science and logical reasoning, would have no qualms about accepting the presence of extraterrestrials if such beings could be scientifically demonstrated to exist. Instead of looking to ancient texts or dogma to determine the possibility of alien life on other planets, humanists simply wait for the evidence. Do *you* believe there are likely to be aliens in other parts of the universe? Why, or why not?

There are many theories about where the universe may have come from including Conformal Cyclic Cosmology, Eternal Inflation, Steady State and a host of others, and given the nature and immensity of the subject we may never know for sure, but the Big Bang is currently the most comprehensive theory of how the universe as we know it came to be. It says the visible portion of the universe was smaller than an atom when, in a split second, it exploded, cooled and expanded rapidly, much faster than the speed of light. New results from a look into the split second after the Big Bang indicate the universe is millions of years older than previously thought but the core concepts of the cosmos - how it began, what it's made of and where it's going - seem to be on the right track. The European Space Agency's *Planck* space probe recently looked back at the afterglow of the Big Bang and those results have now added about eighty million years to the universe's age, putting it at 13.81 billion years old.

Those findings bolster a key theory called "inflation," which says the universe burst from subatomic size to its now-observable expanse in a fraction of a second. The probe also found the cosmos are expanding a bit slower than originally thought, has a little less of that mysterious dark energy than astronomers figured and a tad more normal matter - but scientists say those are small changes in calculations about the cosmos and are nothing dramatic when dealing with numbers so massive.

George Efstathiou, director of the Kavli Institute for Cosmology at the University of Cambridge who announced the *Planck* satellite mapping said, "We've uncovered a fundamental truth of the universe. There's less stuff that we don't understand by a tiny amount." The $900 million *Planck* space telescope was launched in 2009 and mapped the sky, examining light fossils and sound echoes from the Big Bang by looking at the background radiation in the cosmos until late 2013 when it ran out of cooling fluid. Officials at NASA, which also was part of the experiment, said this provided a deeper understanding of the intricate history of the universe and its complex composition. Outside scientists said the result confirmed on a universal scale what an announcement by a different European group confirmed on a subatomic scale - that they had found the Higgs boson particle which explains mass in the universe. "What a wonderful triumph of the mathematical approach to describing nature," said Brian Greene, a Columbia University physicist who was not part of the new research. "It's an amazing story of discovery."

In his 2012 book *A Universe from Nothing* Lawrence Krauss, a theoretical physicist and cosmologist who is Foundation Professor of the School of Earth and Space Exploration at Arizona State University and director of its Origins Project, formulated a model in which the universe could have potentially come from "nothing" and since his model appears to agree with experimental observations of the universe with regard to its shape and energy density, it is referred to as a "plausible hypothesis." Does that mean he has it all figured out? Absolutely not, but what is does mean, as it does in every other area of scientific discovery, is we have to keep searching and learning and pursuing every possible explanation for the way things are with an open mind. We don't have all of the answers.

So what, you may be asking, does this have to do with the subject of religion? Quite a lot. For one thing it illustrates the difference between innovating, exploring and seeking answers and simply accepting fanciful explanations from antiquity for which there is no evidence. It also bears out the biblical axiom which tells us that in order to find we must first seek, but in a different and more logical way. We could be content to just sit here and act as if we know all the answers, which is the lazy man's way, or take a look at things for ourselves and fill in the blanks bit by bit with each new discovery.

Some people claim the universe is finely tuned for life and that points to the existence of a creator, but if you take a look at the universe in its entirety and not just our tiny little corner it becomes clear that is not the case. First let's look at one of the "empirical proofs" creationists offer to make their case for fine tuning. They say, "It just so happens that the sun gives off the perfect amount of heat during the day and allows living things time of essential rest at night. It always keeps appropriate distance from the earth throughout each year. If that distance were closer, we would burn to death. If that distance were farther, we would all freeze to death. In either circumstance life on earth would come to an end."

That reasoning presupposes we came first and our environment was designed to support us, but it really is just a case of the chicken and the egg. Life took root here because the environment was suitable and adapted to it rather than the other way around. Ask yourself a question. Aside from deflecting a few asteroids, what is the purpose of the other planets in our solar system? Why is there no life on them? The answer is they have no purpose and in fact the writers of the Bible never even suspected their existence. Each of them were formed randomly as a result of natural causes just as the Earth was, but since they do not reside in the "Goldilocks Zone" of our solar system they are either too hot or too cold and their atmospheres and gravitational fields are inhospitable as well. Our planet is just one of eight circling our sun and that sun is just one amongst approximately 100 octillion stars - that is a mind boggling 100,000,000,000,000,000,000,000,000,000 stars - in the observable universe. That means we occupy such as small part of what exists that it is incredibly arrogant to believe all of it was made just for us or that it is finely tuned when most of it is anything but. In the words of French Astronomer Camille Flammarion, "Men have had the vanity to pretend that the whole creation was made for them, while in reality the whole creation does not suspect their existence." The universe was not made to fit us, but instead we evolved to fit this little corner of it. Douglas Adams made a great point about that with the analogy, "Imagine a puddle waking up one morning and thinking, 'This is an interesting world I find myself in - an interesting hole I find myself in - fits me rather neatly, doesn't it? In fact it fits me staggeringly well, must have been made to have me in it!' This is such a powerful idea because as the sun rises in the sky the air heats up and the puddle gets gradually smaller and smaller, but it's still frantically hanging onto the notion that everything's going to be alright because this world was meant to have him in it, was built to have him in it; so the moment he disappears it catches him rather by surprise. I think this may be something we need to be on the watch out for."

This chapter began with a quote from Ellie Arroway in *Contact* so I shall close with another. "So what's more likely? That an all-powerful, mysterious God created the Universe and decided not to give any proof of his existence? Or that he simply doesn't exist at all and we created him so that we wouldn't have to feel so small and alone?"

Abiogenesis

Or, In the Beginning…

"One has only to contemplate the magnitude of this task to concede that the spontaneous generation of a living organism is impossible. Yet here we are - as a result, I believe, of spontaneous generation."
~ George Wald, Harvard University biochemist and Nobel Laureate

Many years ago in Mr. Majerle's high school biology class I first learned about the Miller-Urey experiment conducted in 1953 by Stanley Miller and Harold Urey at the University of Chicago (and later the University of California in San Diego) which simulated the conditions thought to exist on the early Earth with the objective of duplicating the occurrence of chemical origins of life. Specifically, the experiment tested Alexander Oparin and J.B.S. Haldane's hypothesis that conditions on the primitive Earth favored chemical reactions which synthesized more complex organic compounds from simpler organic precursors.

After Miller's death in 2007 scientists examining sealed vials preserved from the original experiments were able to show there were actually well over twenty different amino acids, which are the building blocks of life, produced in Miller's original experiments. That is considerably more than what Miller originally reported and more than the twenty which naturally occur in life. Moreover, some evidence suggests Earth's original atmosphere might have had a different composition from the gas used in the Miller-Urey experiment because there is abundant evidence of major volcanic eruptions four billion years ago which would have released carbon dioxide, nitrogen, hydrogen sulfide and sulfur dioxide into the atmosphere. That is significant because subsequent experiments using these gases in addition to the ones in the original Miller-Urey experiment have produced more diverse molecules. Do these experiments prove abiogenesis? Of course not, but what they do prove is we have much to learn and must keep searching for the truth as we have in every other area of science rather than accepting the easy answers offered by religion.

Many Creationists ask, "If God didn't create life, then where did it come from?" A reasonable question, but one which is also the ultimate invocation of the "God of the Gaps." The honest answer is we don't know for sure but that doesn't mean we should just say "Goddunnit!" and stop trying to find out what happened because as has been shown time and again in disciplines from biology to astrophysics we usually figure things out given enough time and research. In fact there are a number of creditable theories being discussed which could explain the rise of life from non-living molecules. Abiogenesis is the scientific term referring to the origin of life from nonliving molecules, and such an event is obviously possible because it has happened.

Do "evolutionists" only separate the origin of life from evolution - and keep in mind they are in fact *very* different things - in order to dodge the fact there is little experimental support showing how life could have arisen from non-living molecules? Not at all. In fact the allegation doesn't make sense from the standpoint of those who understand and accept evolution. We need to be able to clearly distinguish and define what we are talking about, because even the most avid Young Earth Creationists believe life arose from nonliving molecules. Think about it. They believe God fashioned man and animals from dirt, thus the question is not whether life originated from non-life but how that could happen.

The Young Earth Creationist "theory" (it is actually a claim) is life arose by the command of God when in in Genesis 1:20 he said, "Let the waters bring forth in abundance moving creatures that have life." Never mind that there was no one around to hear him say it… but yet there it is, written in the Bible, so they believe it must be true and no further thought or investigation is necessary.

Scientists, of course, have very different ideas and we will discuss two leading hypotheses here - although there are a number of others. One of the more popular ones postulates that life may have begun with self-replicating RNA (ribonucleic acid) since these have been produced in laboratories and there is evidence the early earth had the conditions to produce them. In 1996 biochemist Leslie Orgel demonstrated when "activated" nucleotides, those with an extra bit tacked onto the phosphate, were added to a kind of volcanic clay and RNA molecules up to fifty-five nucleotides long formed. While that certainly is exciting, it is not proof. I point this out to highlight the higher standard of evidence required by science because abiogenesis, as a field of scientific inquiry, is still in its infancy.

The other leading hypothesis says life may have formed at hydrothermal vents in the deep sea since the heat and chemicals which would have been available there include naturally forming molecules which are heavily featured in biology. There are a number of books and websites which delve much more deeply into the idea abiogenesis may have first occurred at deep sea thermal vents, but since this is not a science text it would be pointless to expound upon the specifics here.

As a final note on theories about the beginning of life there is also the possibility DNA evolved elsewhere - perhaps on Mars, one of the moons or asteroids further out in our solar system or even in some other solar system - and then came to earth in the form of a meteorite, although it is more likely to have begun on earth from self-replicating RNA whether formed in thermal vents or somewhere else in the primordial oceans.

As was noted earlier those who argue against evolution tend to object strongly to abiogenesis, the arising of life from non-living molecules, being considered a different science than evolution, which is the descent of all later organisms from the first living cells, but it most certainly is as surely as apples are different from oranges. That is because to a creationist who opposes evolution, and remember not all do, any shortcoming in that theory appears to be an open door to assert there must be a God who created life. Thus when an evolutionist tells such a creationist the lack of evidence for the origin of life from non-living molecules does not take away from the abundant evidence for evolution, the creationist is miffed because he sees his open door being closed.

No “evolutionist” sees it that way, however. The reason science separates biological evolution from abiogenesis is because the evidence for one is unrelated to the evidence for the other and proving natural processes can produce life from non-living molecules does not prove or disprove the Theory of Evolution, just as proving or disproving the Theory of Evolution is irrelevant to how life originated in the first place.

One other key point is even if abiogenesis were to be totally ruled out as the possible origin of life and science concluded there was indeed some sort of creator that would in no way indicate which if any of the gods now worshipped would have been responsible or validate as true any of the dogmas and beliefs associated with those gods. Instead it would point to the sort of creator which a Deist might believe in.

Evolution

Or, Why Are There Still Monkeys?

"...Evolution is not a religious tenet to which one swears allegiance or belief as a matter of faith. It is a factual reality of the empirical world. Just as one would not say 'I believe in gravity,' one should not proclaim 'I believe in evolution.'" ~ Michael Shermer

According to disgraced televangelist Jimmy Swaggart, who was obviously drawing on his vast experience in the realm of scientific inquiry (just kidding), "Evolution is a bankrupt speculative philosophy, not a scientific fact. Only a spiritually bankrupt society could ever believe it... only atheists could accept this Satanic theory." Hmmm... I guess someone needs to tell the Pope, who has proclaimed the Theory of Evolution true, that he is an atheist. Even more disturbing, in the March 1981 issue of *Time* magazine Judge Braswell Deen opined, "This monkey mythology of Darwin is the cause of permissiveness, promiscuity, prophylactics, perversions, pregnancies, abortions, pornotherapy, pollution, poisoning and proliferation of crimes of all types." Really? Try as I might I fail to see a connection to any of those things and even if you are a dedicated Creationist that's just a bit overstated, don't you think? Sadly that's the sort of hysterical rhetoric which comes from people who would rather vilify something than try to understand it because it conflicts with their desires. As author David Mills has pointed out, "In reality geology shows that fossils are of different ages. Paleontology shows a fossil sequence, the list of species representing changes through time. Taxonomy shows biological relationships among species. Evolution is the explanation that threads it all together. Creationism is the practice of squeezing one's eyes shut and wailing, 'Does not!' The reason Christians view evolution as such an absurdity is because their only exposure to evolutionary theory is through absurd caricatures and the harebrained misrepresentations offered by pulpit-pounding evangelists." In other words in most cases they have not bothered to learn about it themselves.

Mention the word "evolution" and you are certain to generate conversation and controversy. What causes such continued resistance to a central scientific principle which is overwhelmingly supported by consistent evidence from biology and other sciences? Surely people have not been getting worked up about the evolution of mollusks over the years? No, it has always been and will continue to be human evolution which many people outside the scientific community find difficult to accept. Humans are special, aren't we, and immune from the mechanical processes of other species? We could not possibly share common ancestors with apes, for then how could we be in league with the angels?

Charles Darwin knew human evolution would pose the greatest obstacle to the acceptance of his theories and devoted his second book, *The Descent of Man*, to this topic. He argued that humans could claim no past exemption from the inexorable forces of natural selection and boldly predicted that, given our obvious affinity with apes, our remote ancestors probably came out of Africa.

He was right. In 1924 Raymond Dart examined the fossil skull of an apelike creature excavated from a quarry in Taung, South Africa and announced the discovery of a pre-human species, "Australopithecus Africanus" (southern ape of Africa). Subsequent evidence showed this skull of an immature primate to be more than two million years old and the "Taung child" became just the first in a cascading series of discoveries of pre-human fossils from Africa, particularly in the Rift Valley of central East Africa where rips in the Earth's crust revealed long-buried bones. Louis Leakey and his remarkable family subsequently uncovered evidence of a variety of pre-human species, termed "missing links" by the press and "hominids" by scientists, all pointing to the evolution of humans stretching over three million years in Africa.

By far one of the most dramatic discoveries in the field of Paleoanthropology was made by Donald Johanson in 1974 in the Afar region of Ethiopia where he discovered the relatively complete skeleton of a female hominid. Named "Lucy" after a Beatles song, she turned out to be slightly over three million years old. Although ape-like in appearance with a small brain and protruding face, she once walked upright on her legs and immediately distinguished herself from other primates and as a result earned a separate species designation, "Australopithecus Afarensis." Despite all that and so much more, evolutionary science is still called false and impossible by the uninformed and afraid.

From Darwin's *On the Origin of Species* to the contemporary works of Richard Dawkins and others there are many references out there which do a fine job of explaining the science of evolution and I have no intention of trying to duplicate them here. Instead I would like to clarify a few key points, dispel a couple of commonly held misconceptions and dispense a bit of common sense. I do this because the vast majority of people who scornfully reject the concept of evolution out of hand have never bothered to learn a thing about it and instead parrot the talking points of those who feel threatened by advances in scientific knowledge because accepting anything other than the story of Adam and Eve in the Garden doesn't fit with the Bible. This is especially important because so many people intentionally distort or misrepresent the facts. Believers are always telling skeptics to have an open mind where God is concerned but so rarely take their own advice and learn about the other side of the issue. What are they so afraid of and why do they feel compelled to lie about the science of evolution and create strawman arguments? The only answers which make sense are they are either incapable of understanding a complex subject, realize their limitations and refuse to try, are intellectually lazy and prefer to accept an easy answer which requires little or no thought or are willfully dishonest because they suspect they may come to question their current beliefs and as a result refuse to learn. Simply put, an easily-understood, workable falsehood is often more useful than a complex, incomprehensible truth.

Those traits and attitudes were borne out for all to see in the infamous "Scopes Monkey Trial" of 1925 in which high school science teacher John Scopes was accused of violating Tennessee's Butler Act, which made it unlawful to teach human evolution in any state-funded school. The trial publicized the Fundamentalist-Modernist Controversy which set Modernists who said evolution was not inconsistent with religion against Fundamentalists who said the word of God as revealed in the Bible took priority over all human knowledge. The case was thus seen as both a theological contest and a trial on whether modern science regarding the Creation-Evolution controversy should be taught in schools.

The Butler Act had been passed at the behest of State Representative John W. Butler, a Tennessee farmer and head of the World Christian Fundamentals Association who later admitted, "I didn't know anything about evolution... I'd read in the papers that boys and girls were coming home from school and telling their fathers and mothers that the Bible was all nonsense."

It goes without saying that is hardly a solid foundation for the introduction of legislation. Not surprisingly during the course of the trial the lead council for the prosecution, famed three-time Democratic presidential nominee, former Secretary of State and lifelong Presbyterian

William Jennings Bryan, demonstrated his own ignorance of the subject when he chastised evolution for teaching children that humans were but one of thirty-five thousand types of mammals (which we are) and bemoaned the notion human beings were descended, "...not even from American monkeys, but from old world monkeys" - a commonly used strawman which will be covered later in this chapter.

In 1922, three years before the Scopes trial, President Woodrow Wilson wrote in a letter to a friend, "Of course, like every other man of intelligence and education I do believe in organic evolution. It surprises me that at this late date such questions should be raised," but unfortunately even today many people have persistent misconceptions about the subject. Some are simple misunderstandings, ideas which develop in the course of learning, but other misconceptions may stem from purposeful attempts to misrepresent evolution and undermine the public's understanding of this topic. To that point evangelical Christian radio host and president of the Christian Research Institute Hank Hanegraaff, aka "The Bible Answer Man," has revealingly stated, "Evolution is the most important battle that Christians have to fight today, a battle we must win by any means, fair or foul!" Clearly he is more interested in maintaining his current beliefs than pursuing truth, and he is far from alone in his efforts. The reason for that is obvious since the acceptance of evolution, not to mention advances in abiogenesis, relegate the Adam and Eve in the Garden of Eden story to the realm of myth and in doing so call into question biblical literalist claims of inerrancy and invalidates the premise of "original sin." Interestingly a growing number of progressive Christians who recognize the factual nature of evolution now claim God used it as his method of creation in an attempt to reconcile science with faith, and in doing so have incurred the wrath of fundamentalists who refuse to believe anything which does not come from the Bible. Being aware of inaccurate preconceptions can help you avoid reinforcing such mistaken beliefs and correct those ideas, and the following points address some common misconceptions regarding evolution and provide clarifications for each.

MISCONCEPTION: Evolution is just a theory.

CORRECTION: This misconception stems from a mix-up between the casual and scientific uses of the word "theory." In everyday language "theory" is often used to mean a hunch with little evidential support, similar to a scientific hypothesis. Scientific theories, on the other hand, are broad explanations for a wide range of phenomena and in order to be accepted by the scientific community must be strongly supported by many different lines of evidence. Evolution is a well-supported and broadly accepted scientific theory, and as such is not just a hunch. If you believe most biologists consider evolution to be just a theory you are behind the times because almost all of them call it a fact. When believers try to put evolution down by dismissing it as "just a theory" they're actually acknowledging its scientific validity - but to understand why, it's necessary to understand what a theory is. When people use the term to disparage evolution they really should be using the word "hypothesis," which is a provisional idea and suggested explanation which requires validation. Evolution is well beyond that stage. In order to qualify as a theory something must meet the following criteria: it must originate from and be well supported by experimental evidence. It must be supported by many strands of evidence and not just a single foundation. It must be specific enough to be falsifiable by testing and if it cannot be tested or refuted it can't qualify as a theory. It must make specific, testable predictions about things not yet observed. It must allow for changes based on the discovery of new evidence (quite unlike religious dogma) and must be dynamic, tentative and correctable. Note that last one - tentative, correctable and allowing for future changes. Creationists often point out the Theory of Evolution is (like all theories) incomplete as if this disproves it, but to be a theory something must be incomplete by definition and (no pun intended) constantly *evolving*. The strict scientific definition of a fact is both simpler and hazier. A fact is a verifiable observation, and evolution has been verified so many times throughout the entire science of biology most biologists call it a fact, however many scientists contend that every fact has some element of theory to it so in this sense it doesn't really make any difference whether evolution is called fact or theory. To put all of that into context, consider the scientific Theory of Gravity. Since we are not floating off the planet, it is clearly much more than a simple hypothesis.

MISCONCEPTION: Evolution teaches humans came from monkeys.

CORRECTION: This is the most oft-repeated evolutionary strawman of all. The Theory of Evolution in no way suggests we came from monkeys but instead explains we share a common ancestor, similar to how the horse and zebra share a common ancestor. That should be easy to visualize. Some people take exception to the notion they are in any way related to apes, and yet according to the Bible the first human was made of dirt… and they seem to have no problem with that.

MISCONCEPTION: Evolutionary theory is invalid because it is incomplete and cannot give a total explanation for the biodiversity we see around us.

CORRECTION: Once again this misconception stems from a misunderstanding of the nature of scientific theories. All scientific theories, from evolutionary theory to atomic theory, are works in progress. As new evidence is discovered and new ideas developed our understanding of how the world works changes and so do scientific theories. While we don't know everything there is to know about evolution or any other scientific discipline for that matter we do know a great deal about the history of life, the pattern of lineage-splitting through time and the mechanisms which have caused these changes - and more will be learned in the future. Evolutionary theory, like any scientific theory, does not yet explain everything we observe in the natural world, however it does help us understand a wide range of observations from the rise of antibiotic-resistant bacteria to the physical match between pollinators and their preferred flowers. It also makes accurate predictions in new situations (i.e. treating AIDS patients with a cocktail of medications slows the evolution of the virus) and has proven itself time and again in thousands of experiments and observational studies. To date, evolution is the only well-supported explanation for life's diversity.

MISCONCEPTION: Gaps in the fossil record disprove evolution.

CORRECTION: While it's true there are gaps in the fossil record this does not constitute evidence against evolutionary theory. Scientists evaluate hypotheses and theories by figuring out what we would expect to observe if a particular idea were true and then seeing if those expectations are borne out. If evolutionary theory were true then we'd expect there to have been transitional forms connecting ancient species with their ancestors and descendants. This expectation has been borne out. Paleontologists have found many fossils with transitional features and new fossils are discovered all the time, however we could not reasonably expect all of these forms to be preserved in the fossil record because many organisms don't have body parts which fossilize well, the environmental conditions for forming good fossils are rare and of course we've only discovered a small percentage of the fossils that might be preserved somewhere on Earth. As a result scientists expect that for many evolutionary transitions there will be gaps in the fossil record.

MISCONCEPTION: The theory of evolution is flawed but scientists won't admit it.

CORRECTION: Scientists have studied the supposed "flaws" anti-evolution groups claim exist in evolutionary theory and have found no support for these claims. These "flaws" are based on misunderstandings of evolutionary theory or misrepresentations of the evidence. As scientists gather new evidence and as new perspectives emerge evolutionary theory continues to be refined, but that doesn't mean the theory itself is flawed. Science is a competitive endeavor, and scientists would be eager to study and correct "flaws" in evolutionary theory if they existed.

MISCONCEPTION: Evolution is a theory in crisis and is collapsing as scientists lose confidence in it.

CORRECTION: Evolutionary theory is not in crisis. Scientists accept it as the best explanation for life's diversity because of the multiple lines of evidence supporting it, its broad power to explain biological phenomena and its ability to make accurate predictions in a wide variety of situations. Scientists do not debate whether evolution took place but do debate many details of how it occurred and occurs in different circumstances, and anti-evolutionists may hear those debates and misinterpret them as being about whether evolution takes place. Evolution is sound science and is treated accordingly by scientists and scholars worldwide.

MISCONCEPTION: Most biologists have rejected "Darwinism" and no longer agree with the ideas put forth by Darwin and Wallace.

CORRECTION: It is true that we have learned a lot about evolution since Darwin's time, just as we continue to learn and broaden our knowledge about any subject in every scientific discipline. Today we understand the genetic basis for the inheritance of traits, can date many events in the fossil record to within a few hundred thousand years and can study how evolution has shaped development at a molecular level. These advances, ones Darwin likely could not have imagined, have expanded evolutionary theory and made it much more powerful rather than overturning the basic principles of evolution by natural selection and common ancestry which Darwin and Wallace laid out. Just as our understanding of planetary motion evolved from Ptolemy to Copernicus to Galileo to Kepler to Newton, so it is with evolution. It's important to keep in mind elaboration, modification and expansion of scientific theories are normal parts of the process of science.

MISCONCEPTION: Evolution leads to immoral behavior.

CORRECTION: Evolution does not make ethical statements about right and wrong. Some people misinterpret the fact evolution has shaped animal behavior, including human behavior, as supporting the idea whatever behaviors are "natural" are the "right" ones. This is not the case. It is up to us as societies and individuals to decide what constitutes ethical and moral behavior. Evolution simply helps us understand how life has changed and continues to change over time and does not tell us whether these processes or the results of them are right or wrong. Furthermore, some people erroneously believe evolution and religious faith are incompatible and so assume accepting evolutionary theory encourages immoral behavior. That is demonstrably false.

MISCONCEPTION: Evolution supports the concept of "might makes right" and rationalizes the oppression of some people by others.

CORRECTION: In the 19th and early 20th Centuries a philosophy called Social Darwinism arose from a misguided effort to apply lessons from biological evolution to society. Social Darwinism suggests society should allow the weak and less fit to fail and die and that this is good policy and morally right - and supposedly evolution by natural selection provided support for these ideas. Pre-existing prejudices were rationalized by the notion colonized nations, poor people or disadvantaged minorities must have deserved their situations because they were less fit than those who were better off. In this case science was misapplied to promote a social and political agenda, but while Social Darwinism as a political and social orientation has been broadly rejected it has nothing at all to do with the scientific idea of biological evolution which has withstood the test of time.

MISCONCEPTION: Evolution and religion are totally incompatible.

CORRECTION: Because some individuals and groups stridently declare their beliefs it's easy to get the impression science (which includes evolution) and religion are at war, however the idea one always has to choose between science and religion is incorrect. People of many different faiths and levels of scientific expertise see no contradiction at all between the two because in many cases science and religion simply deal with different realms. Science deals with natural causes for natural phenomena, while religion deals with beliefs beyond the natural world. Of course some religious beliefs explicitly contradict science (i.e. the belief the world and all life on it was created in six literal days does conflict with evolutionary theory), however most religious groups (including the Catholic Church as of late) see no conflict with the Theory of Evolution or other scientific findings. In fact many religious people, including some theologians, feel a deeper understanding of nature actually enriches their faith and there are even a few scientists who are devoutly religious while also accepting evolution. As Charles Darwin wrote in *On the Origin of Species*, "I see no good reason why the views given in this volume should shock the religious feelings of anyone."

MISCONCEPTION: Teachers should teach both sides of the evolution issue and let students decide for themselves - i.e. give equal time to evolution and creationism.

CORRECTION: Equal time does not make sense when the two sides are not equal. Religion and science are very different endeavors and religious views do not belong in a science classroom at all. In science class students should have opportunities to discuss the merits of arguments and evidence within the scope of science. For example students might investigate and discuss exactly where birds branched off of the tree of life, i.e. before dinosaurs or from within the dinosaur clade. In contrast, a debate pitting a scientific concept against a religious belief has no place in a science class and misleadingly suggests that a choice between the two must be made, and yet the "fairness" argument has been used by groups attempting to infiltrate their religious beliefs into science curricula. Look at it from the reverse perspective. How would theologians feel about evolution being taught in churches in the interest of equal time?

MISCONCEPTION: Evolution is itself religious, so requiring teachers to teach evolution violates the First Amendment.

CORRECTION: This fallacious argument is based on the idea evolution and religion are somehow fundamentally the same since both are supposedly belief systems - a premise which is simply incorrect. Belief in religious ideas is based on faith and religion deals with topics beyond the realm of the natural world, while acceptance of scientific ideas like evolution are based on evidence from the natural world and science is limited to studying its phenomena and processes. Supreme Court and other Federal Court decisions clearly differentiate science from religion and do not permit the advocacy of religious doctrine in science (or other public school) classes and other decisions specifically uphold a school district's right to require the teaching of evolution.

MISCONCEPTION: Evolution is a theory about the origin of life.

CORRECTION: While abiogenesis specifically addresses the question of life's origin, evolutionary theory does encompass ideas and evidence regarding whether or not it happened near a deep sea vent, which organic molecules came first, etc., but this is not its focus. Most of evolutionary biology deals with how life changed after its origin. Regardless of how life started, afterwards it branched and diversified and most studies of evolution are focused on those processes.

MISCONCEPTION: Evolutionary theory implies life evolved and continues to evolve randomly or by chance.

CORRECTION: Chance and randomness do factor into evolution and the history of life in many different ways, however some important mechanisms of evolution are non-random and these make the overall process non-random. For example consider the process of natural selection, which results in adaptations - features of organisms which appear to suit the environment in which they live (i.e., the fit between a flower and its pollinator, the coordinated response of the immune system to pathogens or the ability of bats to echolocate). Such amazing adaptations clearly did not come about by chance, but instead evolved via a combination of random and non-random processes. The process of mutation which generates genetic variation is random, but selection is not because selection favored variants which were better able to survive and reproduce (i.e. to be pollinated, fend off pathogens or navigate in the dark). Over many, many generations of random mutation and non-random selection complex adaptations evolved, so to say evolution happens by chance ignores half of the picture.

MISCONCEPTION: Because evolution is a slow process humans cannot influence it.

CORRECTION: Evolution sometimes occurs quickly and since humans often cause major changes in the environment we are frequently the instigators of evolution in other organisms. A few examples of human-caused evolution are fish populations which have evolved in response to our fishing practices, insects such as bedbugs and crop pests which have evolved resistance to our pesticides, bacteria, HIV, malaria and cancers which have evolved resistance to our drugs and the several species which have evolved in response to climate change.

MISCONCEPTION: Humans are not currently evolving.

CORRECTION: Humans are now able to modify our environment with technology. We have invented medical treatments, agricultural practices and economic structures which significantly alter the challenges to reproduction and survival faced by modern humans. For example because we can now treat diabetes with insulin the gene versions which contribute to juvenile diabetes are no longer strongly selected against in developed countries. Some have argued such technological advances mean we've opted out of the evolutionary game and set ourselves beyond the reach of natural selection - essentially, that we've stopped evolving - however this is not the case. Humans still face challenges to survival and reproduction, just not the same ones we faced thousands of years ago. For example modern humans living in densely populated areas face greater risks of epidemic diseases than did our hunter-gatherer ancestors who did not come into close contact with so many people on a daily basis and this situation favors the spread of gene versions which protect against these diseases. Scientists have uncovered many such cases of recent human evolution.

MISCONCEPTION: Natural selection is about survival of the very fittest individuals in a population.

CORRECTION: Although "survival of the fittest" is the catchphrase of natural selection, "survival of the fit enough" is more accurate. In most populations organisms with many different genetic variations survive, reproduce and leave offspring carrying their genes in the next generation. It is not simply the one or two best individuals in the population which pass their genes on to the next generation. This is apparent in the populations around us. For example a plant may not have the genes to flourish in a drought or a predator may not be quite fast enough to catch her prey every time she is hungry. These individuals may not be the fittest in the population, but they are fit enough to reproduce and pass their genes on to the next generation.

MISCONCEPTION: Charles Darwin himself did not believe in his own theory.

CORRECTION: That is totally untrue and demonstrates the lengths to with anti-evolutionists will go to misrepresent both the theory and its adherents. One of the most famous, and disingenuous, examples of quote mining is the following misquotation of Charles Darwin which is often presented without including the rest of the quote. "To suppose that the eye, with all its inimitable contrivances for adjusting the focus to different distances, for admitting different amounts of light and for the correction of spherical and chromatic aberration, could have been formed by natural selection seems, I freely confess, absurd in the highest possible degree." Seems like a pretty damning indictment of Darwin's theory by the man himself, doesn't it? At least until you read the part that came next which was conveniently, i.e. intentionally, left out: "Yet reason tells me that if numerous gradations from a perfect and complex eye to one very imperfect and simple, each grade being useful to its possessor, can be shown to exist; if further, the eye does vary ever so slightly, and the variations be inherited, which is certainly the case; and if any variation or modification in the organ be ever useful to an animal under changing conditions of life, then the difficulty of believing that a perfect and complex eye could be formed by natural selection, though insuperable by our imagination, can hardly be considered real. How a nerve comes to be sensitive to light hardly concerns us more than how life itself first originated; but I may remark that several facts make me suspect that any sensitive nerve may be rendered sensitive to light, and likewise to those coarser vibrations of the air which produce sound." Obviously the quote has been taken out of context to give it the opposite meaning, thus appearing to support a different conclusion from that in the original article, and it demonstrates how much some creationists fear the science of evolution and the lengths to which they will go to try to discredit it.

Intelligent Design

Or, We Can't Be An Accident… Can We?

☥☯⛩ॐ☸✡✝☪☬

"Another practice that isn't science is embracing ignorance. Yet it's fundamental to the philosophy of Intelligent Design. 'I don't know what this is... so it *must* be the product of a higher intelligence.'" ~ Dr. Neil DeGrasse Tyson

Not long ago a school district in rural Pennsylvania officially recognized a supposed alternative to "Darwinism" and in a one-minute statement read by an administrator ninth-grade biology students were told evolution was not a fact and they were encouraged to explore a different explanation for life called "Intelligent Design." So what is Intelligent Design? Its proponents maintain living creatures are just too intricate to have arisen by evolution and say throughout the natural world there is evidence of deliberate design, which infers the existence of an intelligent designer. To evade the charge that Intelligent Design is a religious theory - i.e. "Creationism dressed up as science" - its advocates make no explicit claims about who or what this designer might be, but students will presumably get the desired point as a result of their enculturation. As one Pennsylvania teacher observed, "The first question they will ask is, 'Well, who's the designer? Do you mean God?'"

From a scientific perspective one of the most frustrating things about Intelligent Design is unlike Darwinian Evolution it is virtually impossible to test. Old-fashioned biblical Creationism at least risked making some hard factual claims, for example the Earth was created before the sun, but Intelligent Design by contrast leaves the purposes of the designer wholly mysterious. Although any pattern of data in the natural world is presumably consistent with his/her/its existence, if we can't infer anything about the design from the designer perhaps we can go the other way.

What can we tell about the designer from the design? While there is certainly much which is marvelous in nature, there is also much which is flawed, sloppy and downright bizarre. Some nonfunctional oddities like the peacock's tail or the human male's nipples or vestigial organs such as the appendix might be attributed to a sense of whimsy on the part of the designer. In fact your coccyx, better known as your tailbone, is the very last part of your vertebrae and is actually the remnant of a lost tail. Even today between stages fourteen and twenty-two of human embryogenesis one can observe a tail-like structure which is usually later absorbed, and occasionally a child is born with a "soft tail" which contains no vertebrae but only blood vessels, muscles and nerves - although there have been several documented cases of vestigial tails containing cartilage and up to five vertebrae.

Others design flaws just seem grossly inefficient. In mammals, for instance, the recurrent laryngeal nerve does not go directly from the cranium to the larynx the way any competent engineer would have arranged it, but instead extends down the neck to the chest, loops around a lung ligament and then runs back up the neck to the larynx. In a giraffe that means a twenty-foot length of nerve where one foot would have been sufficient. Then there is the dual function of the human reproductive organs, which are also tasked with eliminating bodily waste. This is akin to building an entertainment center in a sewer. If those are evidence of design, it would seem to be of the unintelligent variety. Such disregard for economy can be found throughout the natural order, or as Joseph Heller put it in *Catch 22*, "How much reverence can you have for a supreme being who finds it necessary to include such phenomena as phlegm and tooth decay in his divine system of creation?"

Perhaps ninety-nine percent of the species which ever existed have died out and evolution has no problem with that because random variation will inevitably produce both fit and unfit varieties, but what sort of designer would fashion creatures so out of sync with their environments that they are doomed to extinction? The gravest imperfections in nature are moral ones, however. Consider how humans and other animals are intermittently tortured by pain throughout their lives, especially near the end. Our pain mechanism may have been designed to serve as a warning signal to protect our bodies from damage but in the majority of diseases, for instance cancer or coronary thrombosis, the signal comes too late to do much good and the horrible suffering which ensues is completely useless. Plus the entire ecosystem has one major flaw which Darwin hinted at when he commented, "I cannot persuade myself that a beneficent and omnipotent God would have designedly created parasitic wasps with the express intention of their feeding within the living bodies of caterpillars," and Dr. Nel Noddings put it even more succinctly when she observed, "What sort of

God would deliberately create a world in which his creatures must eat one another in order to live?"

On a smaller scale why should the human reproductive system be so shoddily designed, as fewer than one-third of conceptions culminate in live births while the rest end prematurely either in early gestation or by miscarriage. Nature appears to be an avid abortionist, which ought to trouble Christians who believe in both original sin and the doctrine that a human being equipped with a soul comes into existence at conception. Souls bearing the stain of original sin, we are told, do not merit salvation and that is why according to traditional theology unbaptized babies have to languish in limbo for all eternity. Owing to faulty reproductive design, it would seem the population of limbo must be at least twice that of Heaven and Hell combined... but wait, the church has recently reexamined the concept and now concedes limbo is merely a "theory" with no foundation in Scripture so such a place may not exist.

It is hard to avoid the inference that a designer responsible for such imperfections must have been lacking some divine trait, be it benevolence, omnipotence, omniscience or perhaps all three, but what if the designer did not style each species individually? What if he/she/it merely fashioned the primal cell and then let evolution determine the rest, kinks and all? That would let him off the hook.

That is what biologist and Intelligent Design proponent Michael J. Behe has suggested. He says the little protein machines in the cell are too sophisticated to have arisen by mutation, an opinion his scientific peers overwhelmingly do not share by the way, but whether or not he is correct his version of Intelligent Design implies a curious sort of designer who seeded the Earth with elaborately contrived protein structures and then absconded while leaving the rest to blind chance.

One beauty of evolution is the intellectual freedom it allows. That is why Pope John Paul II was comfortable declaring that evolution has been "proven true" and "truth cannot contradict truth." If God created the universe wholesale rather than retail by endowing it from the start with an evolutionary algorithm which progressively teased complexity out of chaos, then imperfections in nature would be a necessary part of a beautiful process.

Of course proponents of Intelligent Design are careful not to use the "G-word" because they claim theirs is not a religiously based theory, so biology students can be forgiven for wondering whether the mysterious designer they're told about might not be the biblical God after all but instead some advanced yet mischievous or blundering intelligence -

extraterrestrial scientists, for instance. The important thing, as the Pennsylvania school administrator reminded them, is for everyone to keep an open mind.

By the way, several parents won a lawsuit against that school district in 2005 by arguing that unlike the Theory of Evolution which is taught at most schools as a fact-based science, Intelligent Design is nothing more than a philosophy predicated on Judeo-Christian beliefs which says the logical sequences found in nature are not random happenings or surprising mutations but deftly managed events created by a greater omniscient and omnipresent intelligence with a specific plan - in short, the work of God. A federal judge thought otherwise, but therein lies the rub - which god? Naturally, the one you happen to believe in.

There is no more notorious enemy of Darwinian Evolution today than Intelligent Design "theory" and no one is taken to represent the gist of ID so much as 18th Century theologian William Paley, who compared the complexity of natural flora and fauna to finding a fully functional mechanical watch lying on the beach. Surely, he argued, we are forced to deduce the watch is so complicated it must have been made by some intelligent designer, and the same could be said of living things.

Paley died decades before *On the Origin of Species* was published, and ever since that time his views have been so repeatedly set in opposition to Darwin's that Richard Dawkins titled one of his books on evolution *The Blind Watchmaker*. A closer look at Paley's own thinking reveals, however, a God who works through the laws of nature rather than beyond them like the modern ID theorists' designer. Paley had no objection to species changing over time, and it's only in today's highly polarized culture-war climate that we don't bother to notice one of the forefathers of Intelligent Design might have been perfectly comfortable with evolution.

Despite all that, in 2010 Texas Governor and Republican presidential candidate Rick Perry said, "I am a firm believer in Intelligent Design as a matter of faith and intellect and believe it should be presented in schools alongside the Theory of Evolution," and in 2011 Congresswoman Michele Bachmann proclaimed, "I support Intelligent Design. What I support is putting all science on the table and then letting students decide. I don't think it's a good idea for government to come down on one side of scientific issue or another, when there is reasonable doubt on both sides." Apparently Bachmann thinks Intelligent Design is science and not what it really is - a proposition based on biblical stories. And the notion children should decide for themselves what is true and what is not is ludicrous. In what other subjects do we allow them such discretionary latitude? None that I can think of. Author Judith Hayes put that notion into perspective when she wrote, "If we are going to teach 'Creation Science...' as an alternative to evolution, then we should also teach the 'Stork Theory' as an alternative to biological reproduction." In other words if the theory of sexual reproduction is taught in schools it must only be taught as a theory and not as the truth, and alternative theories such as the theory of the stork must also be taught.

Free Will vs. God's Plan

Or, Not Having Your Cake and Not Eating It Too

"We must believe in free will. We have no choice." ~ Isaac Bashevis Singer

George Carlin once observed, "Pray for anything you want... but what about the Divine Plan? Remember that? The Divine Plan. Long time ago God made a Divine Plan. Gave it a lot of thought. Decided it was a good plan. Put it into practice. And for billion and billions of years the Divine Plan has been doing just fine. Now you come along and pray for something. Well, suppose the thing you want isn't in God's Divine Plan? What do you want him to do? Change his plan? Just for you? Doesn't it seem a little arrogant? It's a Divine Plan. What's the use of being God if every run-down schmuck with a two dollar prayer book can come along and f*ck up your plan? And here's something else, another problem you might have. Suppose your prayers aren't answered. What do you say? 'Well, it's God's will. God's will be done.' Fine, but if it's Gods will and he's going to do whatever he wants to anyway, why the f*ck bother praying in the first place? Seems like a big waste of time to me. Couldn't you just skip the praying part and get right to his will?"

He makes a valid point. One of the more fascinating conundrums faced by religious apologists is the question of Free Will versus God's Plan. On the one hand they say we have the free will to make our own choices and will have to suffer the consequences of our actions if we don't repent, and on the other they claim everything which happens is part of a predetermined grand and perfect plan which is unfolding. Both cannot possibly be true at the same time, and yet many apologists somehow manage to reconcile the two schools of thought.

The debate about free will and causal determinism parallels in many ways another debate about free will, this one stemming from what is often called "theological determinism." Some religious traditions hold that God is ultimately responsible for everything which happens and according to these traditions God's willing 'X' is necessary and sufficient for 'X,' but if he is ultimately responsible for everything by virtue of what he wills he is also ultimately responsible for all actions and volitions performed by each of us. God willing someone to take their dog for a walk, for instance, is thus necessary and sufficient for taking the dog for a walk, but if this is true it is hard to see how that person could have free will. Consider how many times you have heard it said everything happens for a reason or God has sent a person into someone's life to do a thing or he has caused a particular action to occur for some higher purpose. In such a world free will simply is not possible.

The problem becomes especially acute when considering doctrines of eternal punishment. For example the traditional Christian doctrine of Hell says is it is a place of eternal punishment for non-repentant sinners, but if theological determinism is true whether or not people repent is ultimately up to God, not the people themselves. This worry over free will thus gives rise to a particular version of the problem of evil, namely why does God not will all people to come to faith when his having such a will is sufficient for their salvation? The common apologetic here, which is also frequently used to explain why God does not directly reveal himself to us, is "God doesn't want robots," but in neither case does that make sense if you take the time to consider a key point about the concept of free will.

Imagine a gunman is holding a revolver to your head and tells you if you don't love him he is going to pull the trigger. It's not enough that you say you do, but you must *actually* love him. Assuming the gunman is somehow capable of telling whether or not you are sincere, would you be able to do it? Now imagine the gunman tells you if you do not comply with his demand it will be your choice and your fault when your brains get blown out, not his. It will in effect be you who is actually pulling the trigger. Would you accept the logic that you have the free will to choose, and then blame yourself?

Ridiculous, isn't it? But that is one of the central tenets of Christianity where people are told, "God doesn't pull the trigger. We are pulling it on ourselves and God has done nothing but tried to show us his love so that we won't do it. God is willing to step in between and take that bullet for us. If we push Him away, the consequences are on us."

An added dynamic concerning faith stems from how you would feel about the prospect of the gunman pulling the trigger in the first place. If you are truly a person of faith and believe you will be going to Heaven you should have no problem with it but if there are doubts in your mind, or if you are the sort of person who simply claims to believe because it is expected of you without giving it much thought, you will do anything you can to prevent your demise. At this point many people are no doubt rationalizing and forming "logical" reasons why they would not be ready to die such as they need to care for their families, but if you really believe in God wouldn't he take care of them for you? Besides, what is a short lifetime together on this dirty little planet compared to the eternity you will spend with your loved ones in paradise? It shouldn't matter, and after all they will be joining you soon, won't they? Perhaps if you are lucky the gunman will shoot them too so the whole family can travel to eternal bliss together. How you would react speaks volumes about what you really believe, as opposed to what you want or hope for or claim. As English author John Ruskin once observed, "I know few Christians so convinced of the splendor of the rooms in their Father's house, as to be happier when their friends are called to those mansions... Nor has the Church's ardent 'desire to depart and be with Christ' ever cured it of the singular habit of putting on mourning for every person summoned to such departure."

This leads us to the question of what constitutes just punishment, and for that matter what constitutes a "crime" (or if you prefer, "sin"). If you are a believer, ask yourself why God created mankind in the first place? What possible reason could there be other than he felt a need to be worshipped and there was nobody around to do it. So he made us. After all if that isn't the reason, why is so much importance placed on the need to believe in and love God in order to receive salvation?

The unpardonable crime to hear Christians tell it is not believing in and/or not loving and/or not obeying God, and the punishment for that is eternal torment and damnation with no possibility of parole. Let's take a look at that concept and put it into perspective. According to the teachings of the church we are all God's children and he is our Holy Father, a relationship not unlike the one those of us with children have with our own kids - although I doubt many, if any, of us procreated in order to create someone to love, obey and worship us. Imagine how hurtful it would be to have your offspring disobey you, not love you or even disown you by claiming they are not your child! Now imagine you punish them by locking them in a basement, dousing them with gasoline and setting them on fire. After all you brought them into this world, i.e. created them, and therefore isn't it your right to dole out what you consider to be just punishment?

How would such an act be viewed by others? I think that is pretty obvious. It is an unspeakably cruel action born of your own insecurities and paranoia and you would deserve to be punished for what you did. Yet God is considered to be righteous when he casts someone into a lake of fire to suffer for all eternity, which is in effect an infinite punishment for the finite "crime" of simply not believing (probably due to a lack of evidence... and isn't that God's fault?). At least your children only would have suffered for a short time before dying in flames. Whatever happened to unconditional love? Are we not supposed to love and protect our children no matter what, with no expectation or requirement for reciprocation? Isn't that what love is all about?

So why is not believing in God a crime which is punishable in such a final and heinous fashion? If you were to burn your children alive it would most likely be because you'd had your feelings hurt and gotten your nose out of joint, which are very human traits, but it begs the question... is God that petty? Why give humans free will at all when the only two options are do what I want you to do or burn? William C. Easttom II hit the nail on the head when he pointed out, "God says, 'Do what you wish, but make the wrong choice and you will be tortured for eternity in Hell.' That sir, is not free will. It would be akin to a man telling his girlfriend, 'Do what you wish, but if you choose to leave me I will track you down and blow your brains out.' When a man says this we call him a psychopath and cry out for his imprisonment and/or execution. When God says the same we call him 'loving' and build churches in his honor."

No doubt Christian apologists will be ready with rationalizations to explain away those questions such as, "Only God has the right to do such things" and "You can't compare humans to God" and "We can't understand the mind of God" and on and on, but the question remains. If "God is love" and love is unconditional, why attach such a seemingly minor condition? Aren't Christians expected to forgive? Then why not their God?

That raises another question. Does God even have free will himself? You are probably thinking, "Of course he does, because he's God!"... but stop and think about the paradox for a moment. If he is omniscient and knows what is going to happen in the future how can he possibly deviate from what he knows is going to happen? For example if God knows your Grandmother is going to die of cancer on a certain date and you pray for her to get better, how can he possibly answer your prayer when he already knows the outcome? If he were to grant your wish and change the course of the future that would create a paradox because it would mean he actually did not know what was going to happen in the future and is therefore not omniscient. This obviously presents a big problem for people who use "fulfilled prophecy" as evidence of the Bible's authorship and authenticity. So which is it? Is God omniscient, or does he have the free will to answer prayers? It can't be both.

So if not free will, then what? Well if you believe in God you are probably familiar with "God's Plan." This is the way many believers traditionally explain things like amputations, cancer, hurricanes and car accidents with the idea being even if something bad happens it is actually good because it is part of God's perfect plan, and naturally we imperfect humans can't possibly comprehend his purposes - which is of course another of the primary apologetics.

If you have ever read the *New York Times* number one best-selling book *A Purpose Driven Life* you know how pervasive the concept of God's Plan is. This book, written by mega-church Pastor Rick Warren, has sold more than twenty million copies so it is a reasonable assumption many people subscribe to the views contained therein. There is a paragraph in Chapter 2 which says, "Because God made you for a reason, he also decided when you would be born and how long you would live. He planned the days of your life in advance, choosing the exact time of your birth and death. The Bible says, 'You saw me before I was born and scheduled each day of my life before I began to breathe. Every day was recorded in your book!' [Psalm 139:16]" There are also parts which read "Regardless of the circumstances of your birth or who your parents are, God had a plan in creating you" and "God never does anything accidentally, and he never makes mistakes. He has a reason for everything he creates. Every plant and every animal was planned by God, and every person was designed with a purpose in mind."

Under this view of the universe God plans everything, but if you think about it for more than thirty seconds it becomes obvious God's Plan is an impossibility. Let's look at a few of the specific implications. First we must accept that God plans all abortions. Remember, "He planned the days of your life in advance, choosing the exact time of your birth and death." What this means is God pre-planned every abortion which has ever taken place and both the mothers who requested them and doctors who performed them are blameless because they were simply puppets carrying out his plan.

Next we must accept that God plans all murders and rapes. As in the case of abortion if God chooses the exact time of death then all murders are planned by him and murderers are simply his puppets, and since God decided when you would be born and knew who your parents would be it stands to reason every rape resulting in a conception must be part of the grand plan. For that matter if God had a plan in creating everyone that would necessarily have to apply to monsters such as Jeffrey Dahmer and

Adolph Hitler, and everything which happened to the people who suffered at their hands was predestined.

Finally, if Pastor Warren and his millions of followers are correct you have no free will and prayer is meaningless. For instance, who will you marry? You have no choice. Your spouse(s) (keep in mind many people have more than one in their lifetime) was/were pre-chosen by God for you so you would create the children who are a part of his plan (including those with birth defects and pediatric cancer). You also have no choice in the number of children you will have since God has also pre-planned their births. Where will you live? What will your profession be? Don't worry about it, since God plans all of that too.

If you are a Christian right about now you are probably thinking to yourself that Pastor Rick Warren doesn't speak for God, so let's take a look at what Scripture has to say. Romans 8:29-33 says, "For whom [God] did foreknow, he also did predestinate to be conformed to the image of his Son, that he might be the firstborn among many brethren. Moreover whom he did predestinate, them he also called: and whom he called, them he also justified: and whom he justified, them he also glorified. What shall we then say to these things? …. Who shall lay any thing to the charge of God's elect? It is God that justifieth," Romans 9:14-21 adds, "Is there unrighteousness with God? God forbid. For he saith to Moses, I will have mercy on whom I will have mercy, and I will have compassion on whom I will have compassion. So then *it is not of him that willeth, nor of him that runneth, but of God that sheweth mercy*. For the Scripture saith unto Pharaoh, Even for this same purpose have I raised thee up, that I might shew my power in thee, and that my name might be declared throughout all the earth. Therefore hath he mercy on whom he will have mercy, and *whom he will he hardeneth*. Thou wilt say then unto me, Why doth he yet find fault? For who hath resisted his will? Nay but, O man, who art thou that repliest against God? Shall the thing formed say to him that formed it, Why hast thou made me thus? *Hath not the potter power over the clay, of the same lump to make one vessel unto honour, and another unto dishonour?*"

Those verses make it clear what God's views on free will are. Salvation is "not of him that willeth" but the choice of God, who selects some people and shows mercy to them. The rest, like Pharaoh, he "hardens" so they will reject him and be condemned, but the most incontrovertible proof that this passage teaches predestination is Paul anticipates the obvious counterargument that it would be unjust for God to punish people for being as he made them to be and responds to it by saying since God is the maker he can do whatever he wants with us - just as a potter shapes clay into different vessels to suit his purposes - and we have no right to lay a charge of injustice against him.

Verses like these may disturb Christians who've always believed God gave us free will but the truth is that concept finds little support in the Bible. By contrast, the predestination verses are numerous and specific in their wording: God makes us as he chooses, rewards the people whom he made to be good and punishes the ones whom he made to be evil, even though neither group had any choice in how they would turn out. Many influential historical Christian thinkers including Augustine, Martin Luther and John Calvin accepted these verses for what they say but today this view is much less popular, probably because of its unsettling moral implications for God's goodness.

If you don't think people today are prepared to surrender their free will "willingly" look no farther than the online dating site *Christian Mingle* whose tagline is "Find God's Match For You." The implication is the Almighty is a cosmic matchmaker who will steer that special someone in your direction. Naturally their commercials feature success stories, but not surprisingly never mention all of the Christians who try the site and never meet Mr. or Ms. Right never mind relationships which devolve into acrimony, stalking and violence. This is just another example of selective observation - count the hits and ignore the misses.

Now ask yourself if you believe God plans all abortions and that murderers and rapists have no choice with regard to their actions, because if those things are true it means you are in fact a robot. If on the other hand you believe we all have free will and are responsible for our actions you cannot possibly believe in God's Plan.

The notion of "God's Plan" is impossible to reconcile with what actually happens in the real world. There is no plan and therefore the apologetic statement, "It is part of God's plan" is meaningless, which leaves us with free will. Do we as sentient individuals really need to have that given to us? Of course not. That is why atheists embrace the concept of free will as an intrinsic trait. Think about that.

So how do you feel about God's Plan? On the macro level German philosopher Johann Wolfgang von Goethe observed, "If God created this world, then he should review his plan" and he certainly had a point. Just take a look around. On the micro level, Stephen Hawking has pointed out, "I have noticed even people who claim everything is predestined, and that we can do nothing to change it, still look before they cross the road."

Our Eternal Spirit

Or, I'm a Soul Man

The life and death of blues musician Robert Leroy Johnson, whose landmark recordings in 1936 and 1937 display an uncommon combination of singing, guitar skills and songwriting talent which has influenced later generations of musicians, have given rise to much legend - including the Faustian myth he sold his soul at a crossroads to achieve success. According to one legend, as a young man living on a plantation in rural Mississippi Johnson was branded with a burning desire to become a great blues musician and was instructed to take his guitar to a crossroad near Dockery Plantation at midnight. There he was met by a large black man - the Devil - who took the guitar, tuned it, played a few songs and returned the guitar to Johnson, thereby giving him mastery of the instrument. This was in effect a deal with the Devil mirroring the legend of *Faust*, because in exchange for his soul Johnson was able to create the blues for which he became famous.

Most people of a religious bent believe in life everlasting for the faithful, i.e. a continuation of the life force which reaches far beyond the limitations of mortal flesh. In such belief systems death is not an end but a transformation in which people shed their corporeal selves at the moment of demise and the things which made them unique such as personality and memories live on as they join their Creator. We call this intrinsic personness "the soul," an entity described in the dictionary as "the immaterial essence, animating principle or actuating cause of an individual life." Yet as much as we believe in the concept of "soul" this remains strictly an article of faith because as central as it is to our perception of ourselves it can't be seen or heard or smelled or touched or tasted - a state of affairs which leaves some of us uneasy. Without the soul dead is dead, period, but if it could be proven to exist a great deal of anxiety over what happens to us when we die would be vanquished.

Many religious and philosophical traditions support the view that the soul is the ethereal substance, in other words a spirit or non-material spark, particular to a unique living being. Such traditions often consider the soul to be both immortal and innately aware of its immortal nature, as well as the true basis for sentience in each living being. This concept has strong links with notions of an afterlife, but opinions may vary wildly even within a given religion as to what happens to the soul after death. Many within these religions and philosophies see the soul as immaterial, while others consider it possibly material.

One person holding the latter position was Dr. Duncan MacDougall of Haverhill, Massachusetts. The doctor postulated the soul was material and therefore had mass, so a measurable drop in the weight of the deceased would be noted at the moment it parted ways with the physical remains. With the goal of seeking to determine "if the psychic functions continue to exist as a separate individuality or personality after the death of brain and body," MacDougall constructed a special bed in his office "arranged on a light framework built upon very delicately balanced platform beam scales" which were sensitive to what he claimed to be two-tenths of an ounce. He installed upon this bed a succession of six patients in the end stages of terminal illnesses (four from tuberculosis, one from diabetes and one from unspecified causes), observed them before, during and after the process of death and measured any corresponding changes in weight. He then attempted to eliminate as many physiological explanations for the observed results as possible.

MacDougall repeated his experiment with fifteen dogs and observed "the results were uniformly negative, no loss of weight at death" which seemingly corroborated MacDougall's hypothesis that the loss in weight recorded as humans expired was due to the soul's departure from the body since according to his religious doctrine animals have no souls. MacDougall's explanation that "the ideal tests on dogs would be obtained in those dying from some disease that rendered them much exhausted and incapable of struggle" but "it was not my fortune to get dogs dying from such sickness" led author Mary Roach to observe, "Barring a local outbreak of distemper, one is forced to conjecture that the good doctor calmly poisoned fifteen healthy canines for his little exercise in biological theology."

In March of 1907 accounts of MacDougall's experiments were published in *The New York Times* and the medical journal *American Medicine*, but it would take a great deal of credulity to conclude his experiments demonstrated anything about post-mortem weight loss much less the quantifiable existence of the human soul. For one thing his results were far from consistent, varying widely across his half-dozen test cases. Out of six tests two had to be discarded altogether, one showed an immediate drop in weight and nothing more, two showed an immediate drop in weight which then increased with the passage of time and one showed an immediate drop in weight which reversed itself but later recurred - and even these results cannot be accepted at face value as the potential for experimental error was extremely high since MacDougall had difficulty determining the precise moment of death, one of the key factors in the experiments. MacDougall later attempted to explain away the timing discrepancies by asserting, "The soul's weight is removed from the body virtually at the instant of last breath, though in persons of sluggish temperament it may remain in the body for a full minute," but how he arrived at that conclusion is anyone's guess.

Dr. MacDougall admitted in his journal article that his experiments would have to be repeated many times with similar results before any conclusions could be drawn from them but nonetheless believed he was onto something, and four years later the *New York Times* reported in a front-page story he had moved on to experiments which he hoped would allow him to take pictures of the soul, writing, "Dr. Duncan MacDougall of Haverhill, who has experimented much in the observation of death, in an interview published here today expressed doubt that the experiments with X-rays about to be made at the University of Pennsylvania will be successful in picturing the human soul, because the X-ray is in reality a shadow picture. He admits, however, that at the moment of death the soul substance might become so agitated as to reduce the obstruction that the bone of the skull offers ordinarily to the Roentgen ray and might therefore be shown on the plate as a lighter spot on the dark shadow of the bone. Dr. McDougall is convinced from a dozen experiments with dying people that the soul substance gives off a light resembling that of the interstellar ether."

MacDougall seems not to have made any more experimental "breakthroughs" regarding the measurement of the human soul after 1911, at least none considered remarkable enough to have been reported in the pages of the *New York Times*, and passed away himself in 1920. Nonetheless his legacy lives on in the oft-expressed maxim that the human soul weighs 21 grams and the term has since been memorialized in a 2003 film by the same name starring rapper Eminem.

What to make of all this? MacDougall's results were fatally flawed because the methodology used to harvest them was suspect, the sample size far too small and the ability to measure changes in weight imprecise. For this reason credence should not be given to the idea his experiments proved something, let alone measured the weight of the soul as 21 grams, and his postulations on this topic are a curiosity and nothing more. An interesting counterpoint to this item is another widespread belief of those long-ago times which held that the human body *gained* weight after death, hence the term "dead weight," which is the exact opposite of what MacDougall was attempting to prove. This was highlighted in 2000 when a sheep rancher in Bend, Oregon named Lewis E. Hollander, Jr. became the second man in history to set up a soul-weighing operation when he rigged a seven-by-three-foot platform to a Toledo model 8132 electronic digital indicator, a quartet of load cells and a computer in his barn. His subjects were eight sheep, three lambs and a goat, all of which were sedated and then euthanized. According to Hollander, the animals actually gained weight upon death instead of losing it as expected.

In many religious, philosophical and mythological traditions the soul is the incorporeal, and in many conceptions immortal, essence of a living thing and according to most but not all Abrahamic religions souls, at least immortal souls, belong only to human beings. For example Catholic theologian Thomas Aquinas attributed "soul" to all organisms but taught only human souls are immortal while other religions, most notably Jainism and Hinduism, teach that all biological organisms have souls and for their part Animists claim even non-biological entities such as rivers and mountains possess them.

The concept of soul is hardly new or unique. For instance there are at least two currently known interpretations from accounts of ancient Norse belief in which the last breath a person took was understood to be an evaporation of the life principle into a source of life which was primeval and in the world of the gods, nature and the universe. There was also a "free soul" or "dream soul" which could only leave the body during moments of unconsciousness, ecstasy, trance and sleep. The conscious soul which comprised emotions and will was located in the body and could only be released when the body was destroyed through decay or immolation, i.e. when the body had been broken down the conscious soul could then start its journey to the realm of the dead, possibly by using the free soul as an intermediary.

The deceased's "grave goods," or objects to be used in eternity, had to be subjected to the same treatment as the body if they were to accompany the dead person to the afterlife. If a person was immolated the grave goods had to be burnt as well, and if the deceased was to be interred the objects were interred together with him. A free man was usually given weapons and equipment for riding, while an artisan such as a blacksmith could receive his entire set of tools. Women were provided with their jewelry and often tools for female and household activities, however the usual grave for a thrall (slave) was probably not much more than a hole in the ground and he was probably buried in such a way as to ensure he did not return to haunt his masters and but could be of use to them in the afterlife after they died. In fact slaves were sometimes sacrificed for this purpose.

It was common to burn the corpse and grave offerings on a pyre which was constructed so the pillar of smoke would be as massive as possible in order to elevate the deceased to the afterlife. On the seventh day after the person had died people celebrated the "sjaund," or "funeral ale" as the feast was called, since it involved ritual drinking. This was a way of socially demarcating the death and it was only after the funeral ale that the heirs could rightfully claim their inheritance.

The grave was often described as an abode for the dead and was also the location of cultic rites, with the tradition of putting out food and beer on the tumulus surviving even into modern times in some parts of Scandinavia. This tradition is a remainder of the ancestor worship common during early Norse culture with the idea being if the dead were taken care of they would in return protect the homestead and its people and provide for its fertility.

Similarly in the ancient Egyptian religion an individual was believed to be made up of various elements, some physical and some spiritual. The Egyptians believed a human soul was made up of five parts - the Ren, Ba, Ka, Sheut, and Ib - and in addition to these components of the soul there was the human body, called the "Ha."

An important part of the Egyptian soul was thought to be the Ib, or heart, because the metaphysical heart was believed to be formed from one drop of blood from the child's mother's heart at conception. It was thought to be the seat of emotion, thought, will and intention and was also the key to the afterlife since it was envisioned as surviving death in the nether world where it gave evidence for or against its possessor. Specifically, it was thought the heart was examined by the god Anubis and other deities during the "Weighing of the Heart" ceremony and if it weighed more than the "feather of Maat" it was immediately consumed by the monster Ammit.

As a part of the soul a person's "Ren" was given to them at birth and the Egyptians believed it would live for as long as that name was spoken, which explains the practice of placing it in numerous writings with the idea being the greater the number of places a name was used the greater the possibility it would survive to be read and spoken. For example part of the *Book of Breathings*, a derivative of the *Book of the Dead*, was a means of ensuring the survival of the name and a cartouche (magical rope) was often used to surround the name and protect it. Conversely, the names of deceased enemies were hacked out of monuments in a form of "damnatio memoriae" - a Latin phrase literally meaning "damnation of memory" in the sense that a person must not be remembered.

The "Ba" was everything which makes an individual unique, similar to the notion of personality, and was an aspect of a person the Egyptians believed would live after the body died. It was sometimes depicted as a human-headed bird flying out of the tomb to join with the "Ka" in the afterlife. In the *Coffin Texts* one form of the Ba which comes into existence after death is corporeal - eating, drinking and copulating - and Egyptologist Louis Žabkar argued the Ba is not part of the person but *is* the person himself unlike the soul in Greek or later Judaic, Christian or Muslim thought. The idea of a purely immaterial existence was so foreign to Egyptian thought that when Christianity spread in Egypt they borrowed the Greek word "psyche" to describe the concept of soul and not the term Ba. In another mode of existence the Ba of the deceased is depicted in the *Book of Going Forth by Day* as returning to the mummy and participating in life outside the tomb in non-corporeal form, echoing the solar theology of Re (or Ra) uniting with Osiris each night.

Depending on the region, Egyptians believed Heket or Meskhenet was the creator of each person's Ka, breathing it into them at the instant of their birth as the part of their soul which made them come alive - something which resembles the concept of spirit in other religions.

The "Akh" was a concept of the dead which varied over the long history of ancient Egyptian belief. It was associated with thought not as an action of the mind, but instead intellect seen as a living entity. The Akh also played a role in the afterlife. Following the death of the Khat (physical body) the Ba and Ka were reunited to reanimate the Akh, but the reanimation of the Akh was only possible if the proper funeral rites were executed and followed with constant offerings.

Similar ideas were found in ancient Assyrian and Babylonian religions. Kuttamuwa, an 8th Century BCE royal official from Sam'al, ordered an inscribed stele - a stone slab erected as a monument, very often for funerary or commemorative purposes - raised upon his death. The inscription requested that his mourners commemorate his life and afterlife with feasts "for my soul that is in this stele" and it is one of the earliest references to a soul as a separate entity from the body.

The Bahá'í Faith affirms that, "The soul is a sign of God, a heavenly gem whose reality the most learned of men hath failed to grasp, and whose mystery no mind, however acute, can ever hope to unravel."

Bahá'u'lláh, founder of Bahá'í, stated the soul not only continues to live after the physical death of the human body, but is in fact immortal. Heaven can be seen partly as the soul's state of nearness to God, and Hell as a state of remoteness from God. Each state follows as a natural consequence of individual efforts, or lack thereof, to develop spiritually. Bahá'u'lláh taught that individuals have no existence prior to their life here on earth and the soul's evolution is always towards God and away from the material world.

Buddhism teaches all things are in a constant state of flux, all is changing and no permanent state exists by itself. This applies to human beings as much as to anything else in the cosmos, thus a human being has no permanent self. According to this doctrine of "anatta" ("no-self" or "no soul") the words "I" or "me" do not refer to any fixed thing but are simply convenient terms which allow us to refer to an ever-changing entity. To be clear the anatta doctrine is not a kind of materialism. Buddhism does not deny the existence of immaterial entities and at least traditionally distinguishes bodily states from mental states and thus the conventional translation of anatta as "no-soul" can be confusing. If the word soul simply refers to an incorporeal component in living things which can continue after death then Buddhism does not deny the existence of the soul but instead denies the existence of a permanent corporeal entity. When the body dies the incorporeal mental processes continue and are reborn in a new body, and because the mental processes are constantly changing the entity being reborn is neither entirely different from nor exactly the same as the being that died. In other words Buddhist teaching holds that the notion of a permanent, abiding self is a delusion which is one of the causes of human conflict on emotional, social and political levels. They add that an understanding of anatta provides an accurate description of the human condition and this understanding allows us to pacify our mundane desires.

Various schools of Buddhism have differing ideas about what continues after death. The Yogacara school in Mahayana Buddhism says there are "store consciousness'" which continue to exist after death and in some schools, particularly Tibetan Buddhism, the view is there are three minds - very subtle (which does not disintegrate in death), subtle (which disintegrates in death and is the "dreaming" or "unconscious mind") and gross (which does not exist when one is sleeping). Therefore gross mind is less permanent than subtle mind which does not exist in death, however very subtle mind does continue and when it coincides again with phenomena a new subtle mind emerges with its own personality/assumptions/habits and that entity experiences karma in the current continuum. Simple, right?

In Hinduism the Sanskrit words most closely corresponding to soul are jiva, Ātman and "purusha" (meaning the individual self). The term "soul" is misleading as it implies an object possessed, whereas self signifies the subject which perceives all objects. This self is held to be distinct from the various mental faculties such as desires, thinking, understanding, reasoning and self-image or ego, all of which are considered to be part of nature.

The three major schools of Hindu philosophy agree the atman (individual self) is related to Brahman or the Paramatman, i.e. the Absolute Atman or Supreme Self, but differ in the nature of this relationship. In Advaita Vedanta (a sub-school of the Vedanta school of Vedic or Hindu philosophy) the individual self and Supreme Self are one and the same. Dvaita rejects this concept of identity, instead identifying self as a separate but similar part of Supreme Self (god) which never loses its individual identity. Visishtadvaita takes a middle path and accepts the atman as a "mode" (prakara) or attribute of the Brahman. The atman becomes involved in the process of becoming and transmigrating through cycles of birth and death because of ignorance of its own true nature with the spiritual path consisting of self-realization. This is a process in which one acquires knowledge of self and through this knowledge, applied through meditation and realization, then returns to the source which is Brahman. In the *Bhagavad Gita* Lord Krishna describes the atman in the following way: "For the atman there is neither birth nor death at any time. He has not come into being, does not come into being, and will not come into being. He is unborn, eternal, ever - existing and primeval. He is not slain when the body is slain."

Islam teaches the soul is immortal and eternal and what a person does is recorded and will be judged at the final court of Allah. The Quran mentions the soul, saying "...and they ask you, [O Muhammad], about the soul (Rûh). Say, 'The soul (Rûh) is of the affair of my Lord. And mankind have not been given of knowledge except a little'" and "it is Allah that takes the souls at death: and those that die not (He takes their souls) during their sleep: those on whom He has passed the Decree of death He keeps back (their souls from returning to their bodies); but the rest He sends (their souls back to their bodies) for a term appointed. Verily in this are Signs for those who contemplate."

In Jainism every living being, from a plant or bacterium to a human, has a soul and that concept forms the very basis of Jainism. The soul is basically categorized in two forms based on its liberation state with liberated souls being those which have attained "Moksha" (meaning emancipation, liberation or release) and never become part of the life cycle again, while non-liberated souls are those of any living being stuck in the life cycle of four forms - Manushya Gati (human being), Tiryanch Gati (any other living being), Dev Gati (Heaven) and Narak Gati (Hell). Until the time the soul is not liberated from the innumerable birth and death cycles it gets attached to different types of the above bodies based on the karma of the individual soul, and according to Jainism there is no beginning or end to the existence of soul as it is eternal in nature and changes its form until it attains Moksha. Concerning this view of the soul Jain scholar Virchand Gandhi said, "The soul lives its own life, not for the purpose of the body, but the body lives for the purpose of the soul. If we believe that the soul is to be controlled by the body then soul misses its power."

In Judaism the Hebrew terms "Nephesh" (living being), "Ruach" (wind), "Neshama" (breath), "Chaya" (life) and "Yechidah" (singularity) are used to describe the soul or spirit. The soul is believed to be given by God to a person by his/her first breath as mentioned in Genesis, "And the LORD God formed man [of] the dust of the ground, and breathed into his nostrils the breath of life; and man became a living being." Judaism relates the quality of one's soul to one's performance of mitzvot (commandment) and reaching higher levels of understanding and thus closeness to God. A person with such closeness is called a tzadik, therefore Judaism embraces nahala (heritage) and not someone's birthday as a festive of remembrance for only toward the end of life's struggles, tests and challenges can human souls be judged and credited via b'ezrat hashem (with the help of heaven) for righteousness and holiness.

Kabbalah (famously practiced by pop star Madonna among others) and other mystic traditions go into greater detail regarding the nature of the soul. Kabbalah separates the soul into five elements corresponding to the five worlds - Nephesh (related to natural instinct), Ruach (related to emotion and morality), Neshamah (related to intellect and the awareness of God), Chayah (considered a part of God) and Yechidah (the essential [inner] Jew). This aspect is essentially one with God. Kabbalah has also proposed a concept of reincarnation, the "Gilgul."

Sikhism considers the soul (atma) to be part of God, aka "Waheguru" and various hymns are cited from the holy book *Sri Guru Granth Sahib* which suggest this belief. They believe, "God is in the soul and the soul is in the God." The same concept is repeated, for example, "The soul is divine; divine is the soul. Worship Him with love" and "The soul is the Lord, and the Lord is the soul; contemplating the Shabad, the Lord is found." According to Sikhism the soul is an entity or "spiritual spark" or "light" in our bodies which enables them to sustain life and on the departure of this entity from the body it becomes lifeless.

According to Chinese traditions every person has two types of soul called "hún" and "pò" which are respectively "yang" and "yin," while Taoism believes in ten souls known as sanhunqipo - "three hún and seven pò." The pò is linked to the dead body and the grave whereas the hún is linked to the ancestral tablet, and a living being that loses any of them is said to have mental illness or unconsciousness while a dead soul may reincarnate to a disability, lower desire realms or may even be unable to reincarnate.

In yet another perspective "Brahma Kumaris," a millenarian new religious movement (NRM) linked to the Hindu tradition which "provides teaching and education in spiritual and moral values," teaches that human souls are believed to be incorporeal and eternal with God being considered to be the Supreme Soul with maximum degrees of spiritual qualities such as peace, love and purity.

Shamanism, a belief system which involves a practitioner reaching altered states of consciousness in order to encounter and interact with the spirit world and channel these transcendental energies into this world, has a unique view of the soul because according to Nadya Yuguseva, a shaman from the Altai mountains in East-Central Asia, "a woman has forty souls (while) men have just one."

In Russian occultist Helena Blavatsky's "Theosophy," which she defined as "the archaic Wisdom-Religion and esoteric doctrine once known in every ancient country having claims to civilization," the soul is both the field of our psychological activity (thinking, emotions, memory, etc.) and so-called paranormal or psychic phenomena (extrasensory perception, etc.) - however it is not the highest, but instead a middle dimension of human beings. Higher than the soul is the spirit, which is considered to be the real self and source of everything we call good such as happiness, wisdom, love, etc., and while the spirit is eternal and incorruptible the soul, which acts as a link between the material body and the spiritual self and therefore shares some characteristics of both, is not. Here the soul can be attracted either towards the spiritual or towards the material realm, being thus the battlefield of good and evil, and it is only when it is attracted towards the spiritual and merges with the self that it becomes eternal and divine.

Austrian philosopher and esotericist Rudolf Steiner, who founded a spiritual movement called Anthroposophy which had its roots in Theosophy and German idealist philosophy, differentiated by postulating three stages of soul development which interpenetrate one another in consciousness - the "sentient soul" (centering on sensations, drives, and passions with emotional components), the "intellectual" or "mind soul" (internalizing and reflecting on outer experience with strong feeling and cognitive components) and the "consciousness soul" (in search of universal objective truths).

So where do all of these differing ideas come from? The Modern English word soul is itself derived from an Old English word first attested to in the 8th Century poem *Beowulf* and a more recent suggestion connects it with a root for "binding," a Germanic notion of being "bound" in death and the practice of ritually binding or restraining the corpse of the deceased in the grave to prevent his or her return as a ghost. The Greek word is derived from a verb "to cool, to blow" and hence refers to the vital breath, the animating principle in humans and other animals which is also alluded to in the Genesis passage, "...and (God) breathed into his nostrils the breath of life; and man became a living soul." It could refer to a ghost or spirit of the dead in Homer as well as a more philosophical notion of an immortal and immaterial essence left over at death since the time of the Greek lyric poet Pindar.

The Ancient Greeks used the same word for "alive" as for "ensouled," indicating the earliest surviving western philosophical view believed the soul was that which gave the body life, i.e. it was considered the incorporeal or spiritual breath which animates the living organism. English classical scholar Francis M. Cornford quotes Pindar as saying, "The soul sleeps while the limbs are active, but when one is sleeping, the soul is active and reveals in many a dream 'an award of joy or sorrow drawing near,'" while German scholar Erwin Rohde writes, "The early pre-Pythagorean belief was the soul had no life when it departed from the body and retired into Hades with no hope of returning to another body."

Drawing on the words of his teacher Socrates, Plato considered the psyche to be the essence of a person, i.e. that which decides how we behave. He considered this essence to be an incorporeal, eternal occupant of our being. Socrates said even after death the soul exists and is able to think and also believed as bodies die the soul is continually reborn in subsequent bodies. Plato believed this as well, however he thought only one part of the soul was immortal (the "logos"). The Platonic soul comprises three parts: The "logos" (mind or reason), "thymos" (emotion) and "eros" (desire). He further believed those parts are located in different regions of the body with the logos being located in the head, thymos near the chest region and eros residing in the stomach. Each of these has a function in a balanced, level and peaceful soul, however the logos governs the others in order for the "psyche" or soul to function optimally. Plato also compared the three parts of the soul or psyche to the caste system of a society, postulating that the three-part soul is essentially the same thing because in order to function well each part has to make a contribution in order for the whole to function well.

Aristotle defined the soul as the "first actuality" of a naturally organized body but argued against it having a separate existence from the physical body, i.e. in his view the primary activity of a living thing constitutes its soul. For example the purpose or "final cause" of the soul of an eye, if it were an independent organism, would be seeing. Put another way, for Aristotle the soul was the form of a living creature. The various faculties of the soul constitute the "second actuality," or fulfillment, of the capacity to be alive. A good example is someone who falls asleep as opposed to someone who falls dead. While the former can wake up and go about their life, the latter can no longer do so. Aristotle further identified the three hierarchical levels of living things as plants, animals and people, for which groups he identified three corresponding levels of soul or biological activity. They are the nutritive activity of growth, sustenance and reproduction which all life share, the self-willed motive activity and sensory faculties which only animals and people have in common, and finally reason - of which people alone are capable.

Persian Muslim philosophers Avicenna (Ibn Sina) and Ibn al-Nafis further elaborated on Aristotle's understanding of the soul and developed their own theories about it with both making a distinction between the soul and spirit and in particular the Persian Avicennian doctrine on the nature of the soul. Avicenna, regarded both in Europe and the Middle East as one of the most significant thinkers and writers of the Islamic Golden Age, put forward views on the soul which included the idea the immortality of the soul is a consequence of its nature rather than a purpose for it to fulfill, and in his theory of "The Ten Intellects" he viewed the human soul as the tenth and final intellect.

While imprisoned he wrote his famous "Floating Man" thought experiment to demonstrate human self-awareness and the substantiality of the soul in which he told readers to imagine themselves suspended in the air and isolated from all sensations including no sensory contact with their own bodies. He argued that in this scenario one would still have self-consciousness and thus concluded the idea of the self is not logically dependent on any physical thing and the soul should not be seen in relative terms but instead as a primary given, i.e. a substance. This argument was later refined and simplified by French philosopher and father of modern philosophy René Descartes in epistemic terms when he stated, "I can abstract from the supposition of all external things, but not from the supposition of my own consciousness."

Following Aristotle and Avicenna was St. Thomas Aquinas, who claimed the soul to be the first actuality of the living body. Consequent to this he distinguished three orders of life - plants (which feed and grow), animals (which add sensation to the operations of plants) and humans (which add intellect to the operations of animals). With regard to the human soul his epistemological theory required that since "the knower becomes what he knows" the soul was definitely not corporeal for if it were, when it knew what some corporeal thing was, that thing would come to be within it and therefore the soul had an operation which did not rely on a bodily organ - and as a result could subsist without the body. Furthermore, he said since the rational soul of human beings was a subsistent form and not something made up of matter it could not be destroyed in any natural process.

Several hundred years later rational psychologist Immanuel Kant identified the soul as the "I" in the strictest sense and claimed the existence of inner experience can neither be proved nor disproved, saying, "We cannot prove *a priori* the immateriality of the soul, but rather only so much: that all properties and actions of the soul cannot be cognized from materiality." It is from the "I" (or soul) that Kant proposed transcendental rationalization, but he cautioned that such rationalization can only determine the limits of knowledge if it is to remain practical.

As far as Christianity is concerned most Christians believe the soul is an ontological reality distinct from and yet integrally connected with the body and its characteristics can be described in moral, spiritual and philosophical terms. According to a common Christian eschatology when people die their souls will be judged by God and determined to spend eternity in either Heaven or Hell. Though all branches of Christianity - Catholics, Eastern Orthodox, Oriental Orthodox, Evangelical and mainline Protestants - teach that Jesus Christ plays a decisive role in the Christian salvation process the specifics of that role and the part played by individual persons or ecclesiastical rituals and relationships is a matter of wide diversity in official church teaching, theological speculation and popular practice. Some Christians believe if one has not repented of their sins and trusted in Jesus Christ as Lord and Savior they will go to Hell and suffer eternal damnation or eternal separation from God although variations also exist on this theme, i.e. some claim the unrighteous soul will be destroyed instead of suffering eternally - something known as Annihilationism. There is also a belief that babies, including the unborn, as well as those with cognitive or mental impairments who have died, will be received into Heaven on the basis of God's grace through the sacrifice of Jesus although other Christians say there is uncertainty regarding whether human embryos have souls and at what point between conception and birth the fetus acquires a soul, consciousness and/or personhood. In addition there are also those who believe in universal salvation, the doctrine that all sinful and alienated human souls will ultimately be reconciled to God because of divine love and mercy, as well as Christian Conditionalism, which is the concept of special salvation in which the gift of immortality is simply attached to and conditional upon belief in Jesus Christ.

St. Augustine, one of western Christianity's most influential early thinkers, described the soul as "a special substance, endowed with reason, adapted to rule the body" and some Christians espouse a trichotomic (three-way classificatory division) view of humans which consists of a body, soul and spirit, however the majority of modern Bible scholars point out how spirit and soul are used interchangeably in many biblical passages and so hold to dichotomy, i.e. the view that each of us is body and soul. Paul said the "body wars against" the soul and "I buffet my body" to keep it under control, while philosopher Anthony Quinton hypothesized the soul is a "series of mental states connected by continuity of character and memory, [and] is the essential constituent of personality. The soul, therefore, is not only logically distinct from any particular human body with which it is associated; it is also what a person is." Christian philosopher of religion at Oxford University Richard Swinburne wrote, "It is a frequent criticism of substance dualism that dualists cannot say what souls are... souls are immaterial subjects of mental properties. They have sensations and thoughts, desires and beliefs and perform intentional actions. Souls are essential parts of human beings."

The origin of the soul has provided a vexing question in Christianity with the major theories put forward including soul creationism, traducianism and pre-existence. According to creationism each individual soul is created directly by God either at the moment of conception or at some later time, according to traducianism the soul comes from the parents by natural generation and according to the pre-existence theory the soul exists before the moment of conception.

The present Catechism of the Catholic Church defines the soul as, "The innermost aspect of humans, that which is of greatest value in them, that by which they are most especially in God's image: 'soul' signifies the spiritual principle in man. All souls living and dead will be judged by Jesus Christ when he comes back to earth. The souls of those who die unrepentant of serious sins, or in conscious rejection of God, will at judgment day be forever in a state called Hell. The Catholic Church teaches that the existence of each individual soul is dependent wholly upon God: 'The doctrine of the faith affirms that the spiritual and immortal soul is created immediately by God.'"

Eastern Orthodox and Oriental Orthodox views are essentially similar to Roman Catholic views although they differ on the specifics. Orthodox Christians believe after death the soul is judged individually by God and then sent to either "Abraham's Bosom" (temporary paradise) or Hades/Hell (temporary torture) and at the Last Judgment God judges all people who have ever lived all at once at which time those who "know the spirit of God because of the sacrifice of Jesus" go to Heaven (permanent paradise) whilst the damned experience the Lake of Fire (permanent torture).

Protestants generally believe in the soul's existence but fall into two major camps about what this means in terms of an afterlife. Some following John Calvin believe in the immortality of the soul and conscious existence after death, while others following Martin Luther believe in the mortality of the soul and unconscious "sleep" until the resurrection of the dead.

Other Christians reject the idea of the immortality of the soul, citing the Apostles' Creed's reference to the "resurrection of the body" which implies it involves the whole person, and consider the soul to be the life force which ends in death and will be restored in the resurrection. Theologian Frederick Buechner summed up this position in his 1973 book *Whistling in the Dark* when he wrote, "We go to our graves as dead as a doornail and are given our lives back again by God (i.e. resurrected) just as we were given them by God in the first place."

Christadelphians believe we are all created out of the dust of the earth and became living souls once we received the breath of life based on the Genesis 2 account of humanity's creation where Adam was said to have become a living soul. His body (made from dust) did not contain a soul, but rather his body plus the breath of life together were called a soul - in other words a living being. They believe we are mortal, when we die our breath leaves our body, our bodies return to the soil and we remain mortal until the resurrection from the dead when Christ returns to this earth and grants immortality to the faithful. In the meantime the dead lie in the earth in the sleep of death until Jesus comes.

Seventh-day Adventists believe the main definition of the term "soul" is a combination of spirit (breath of life) and body, disagreeing with the view that the soul has a consciousness or sentient existence of its own. They affirm this through Genesis 2:7, claiming when God united his breath (or spirit) with man, man became a living soul composed of body and spirit. Adventists believe at death the body returns to dust and life returns to the God who bestowed it with this belief being expressed in a quotation from their fundamental beliefs, "The wages of sin is death. But God, who alone is immortal, will grant eternal life to His redeemed. Until that day death is an unconscious state for all people..."

Jehovah's Witnesses take the Hebrew word "Nephesh," which is commonly translated as "soul," as meaning a person, an animal or the life a person or animal enjoys. They also believe the Hebrew word "Ruach" ("pneuma" in Greek) which is commonly translated as "spirit" but literally means "wind," refers to the life force or the power which animates living things. A person is a breathing creature, a body animated by the "spirit of God," not an invisible being contained in a body and able to survive apart from that body after death. According to their beliefs Jesus spoke of himself having life and a soul and when he surrendered his life he surrendered his soul because John 10:15 reads, "Just as the Father knows me and I know the father, and I surrender my soul in behalf of the sheep." This belief that man is a soul, rather than has a soul, is also in line with the belief Hell represents the common grave with the hope of resurrection rather than eternal torment in hellfire.

The Church of Jesus Christ of Latter-day Saints teaches the spirit and body together constitute the Soul of Man, i.e. mankind, saying "the spirit and the body are the soul of man." Latter-Day Saints believe the soul is the union of a pre-existing, God-made spirit and a temporal body which is formed by physical conception on earth and after death the spirit continues to live and progress in the spirit world until the resurrection when it is reunited with the body which once housed it. This reuniting of body and spirit results in a perfect soul which is immortal and eternally young and healthy and capable of receiving a fullness of joy. Latter-Day Saint cosmology also describes "intelligences" as the essence of consciousness or agency which are co-eternal with God and animate the spirits, and the union of a newly created spirit body with an eternally-existing intelligence constitutes a "spirit birth" and justifies God's title "Father of our spirits."

In theological reference to the soul the terms "life" and "death" are viewed as emphatically more definitive than the common concepts of "biological life" and "biological death." Because the soul is said to be transcendent of the material existence and to have (potentially) eternal life the death of the soul is likewise said to be an eternal death, thus in the concept of divine judgment God is commonly said to have options with regard to the dispensation of souls ranging from Heaven (i.e., angels) to Hell (i.e., demons) with various concepts in between. Typically both Heaven and Hell are said to be eternal, or at least far beyond a typical human concept of lifespan and time.

In contrast to all of these philosophical and theological hypotheses and assertions, science and medicine seek naturalistic accounts of the observable natural world. This stance is known as "methodological naturalism." Much of the scientific study relating to the soul has involved investigating it as an object of human belief or as a concept which shapes cognition and an understanding of the world rather than as an entity in and of itself. When modern scientists speak of the "soul" outside of this cultural context they generally treat it as a poetic synonym for "mind." Nobel Laureate Francis Crick's book *The Astonishing Hypothesis*, for example, has the subtitle *The Scientific Search For the Soul.* Crick held the position that one can learn everything knowable about the human soul by studying the workings of the human brain and depending on one's belief regarding the relationship between the soul and the mind the findings of neuroscience may be relevant to one's understanding of the soul. Furthermore, skeptic Robert T. Carroll points out the concept of a "non-substantial" substance is an oxymoron, and the scholarship done by philosophers based on the assumption of a non-physical entity has not furthered scientific understanding of the workings of the mind.

Daniel Dennett has championed the idea that human survival strategy depends heavily on adoption of the intentional stance, a behavioral strategy which predicts the actions of others based on the expectation they have a mind like one's own. Mirror neurons in brain regions such as Broca's area, a region in the frontal lobe of one hemisphere of the hominid brain, may facilitate this behavioral strategy. The intentional stance, Dennett suggests, can be so successful that people tend to apply it to all aspects of human experience, thus leading to animism or other conceptualizations of soul.

Some parapsychologists have attempted to establish by scientific experiment whether a soul separate from the brain exists as more commonly defined in religion rather than as a synonym of psyche or mind, but in his 1979 book *Search for the Soul* prominent illusionist Milbourne Christopher explained that none of the attempts by parapsychologists have yet succeeded. Not surprisingly, most credible scientists regard parapsychology as pseudoscience and it has been criticized for continuing investigation despite being unable to provide convincing evidence for the existence of any psychic phenomena after more than a century of research.

Contemporary psychology is defined as the study of mental processes and behavior, however the word "psychology" literally means "study of the soul" and psychologist James Hillman, the founder of archetypal psychology, has been credited with "restoring 'soul' to its psychological sense." Although the words soul and spirit are often viewed as synonyms Hillman argues they can refer to antagonistic components of a person. Summarizing Hillman's views, psychotherapist Thomas Moore associates spirit with "afterlife, cosmic issues, idealistic values and hopes and universal truths," while placing soul "in the thick of things: in the repressed, in the shadow, in the messes of life, in illness and in the pain and confusion of love." Hillman believes religion, especially monotheism and monastic faiths, and humanistic psychology have tended to the spirit, often at the unfortunate expense of soul. This happens, Moore says, because to transcend the "lowly conditions of the soul... is to lose touch with the soul, and a split-off spirituality, with no influence from the soul, readily falls into extremes of literalism and destructive fanaticism."

Hillman's archetypal psychology is in many ways an attempt to tend to the oft-neglected soul which he views as the "self-sustaining and imagining substrate" upon which consciousness rests. Hillman described the soul as that "which makes meaning possible, [deepens] events into experiences, is communicated in love, and has a religious concern," as well as "a special relation with death." Departing from the Cartesian dualism "between outer tangible reality and inner states of mind," Hillman takes the Neoplatonic stance that there is a third, middle position in which soul resides. Archetypal psychology acknowledges this third position by attuning to, and often accepting, the archetypes, dreams, myths and even psychopathologies through which, in Hillman's view, soul expresses itself.

For a contemporary understanding of the soul/mind and the problem concerning its connection to the brain/body consider the rejection of

Descartes' mind-body dualism by Gilbert Ryle's "ghost-in-the-machine" argument (the perceived absurdity of dualist systems like Descartes' where mental activity carries on in parallel to physical action, but where their means of interaction are unknown or at best speculative), the tenuous unassailability of Richard Swinburne's argument for the soul and the advances that have been made in neuroscience which are steadily undermining the validity of the concept of an independent soul/mind. The philosophies of mind and of personal identity also contribute to a contemporary understanding of the mind. The contemporary approach does not so much attack the existence of an independent soul as render the concept less relevant. The advances in neuroscience mainly serve to support the mind/brain identity hypothesis, showing the extent of the correlation between mental states and physical-brain states. The notion of soul has less explanatory power in a western worldview which prefers the empirical explanations involving observable and locatable elements of the brain. Even so there remain considerable objections to simple-identity theory, notably by philosophers such as Thomas Nagel and David Chalmers who have argued the correlation between physical-brain states and mental states is not strong enough to support identity theory. Nagel argued that no amount of physical data is sufficient to provide the "what it is like" of first-person experience and Chalmers argued for an "explanatory gap" between functions of the brain and phenomenal experience. On the whole brain/mind identity theory does poorly in accounting for mental phenomena of qualia, which are individual instances of subjective, conscious experiences, and intentionality, which is a philosophical concept defined as the power of minds to be about, to represent or to stand for things, properties and states of affairs. The bottom line is while neuroscience has done much to illuminate the functioning of the brain, much of subjective experience remains mysterious.

As you can see there has been a lot of conjecture about the nature of the soul, but no definitive answer - although as usual each belief system thinks its beliefs are the true ones. The bottom line to all of the foregoing, as stated by Thomas Edison, is, "I cannot believe in the immortality of the soul… no, all this talk of an existence for us, as individuals, beyond the grave is wrong. It is born of our tenacity of life - our desire to go on living… our dread of coming to an end."

Poly-Monotheism

Or, Some of These Gods Are Just Like the Others

"The great unmentionable evil at the center of our culture is monotheism. From a barbaric Bronze Age text known as the Old Testament, three anti-human religions have evolved - Judaism, Christianity, and Islam. These are sky-god religions. They are, literally, patriarchal - God is the Omnipotent Father - hence the loathing of women for 2,000 years in those countries afflicted by the sky-god and his earthly male delegates." ~ Gore Vidal

The purpose of this chapter is threefold. First, to give the reader some background on and a better understanding of some religions which they probably have heard of in passing but probably never investigated in any depth, second to explain the true nature of some supposedly monotheistic doctrines and third to question why did/do millions of people accept such things as being true. Hopefully by better understanding the beliefs of others readers will be better equipped to understand the origin, doctrine and practice of their own beliefs.

Julia Sweeney, in her one woman show *Letting Go of God*, described what it was like for her to hear Mormon beliefs for the very first time when she was visited by two elders of the LDS church. At the time she was a practicing Catholic and after a bit of reflection realized how strange her own beliefs - the virgin birth, crucifixion and resurrection for example - would sound to someone hearing about them for the very first time. The way she put it was, "Well, I was just used to *that* story!"

Some non-believers humorously describe the Christian narrative as the belief a walking dead Jewish deity who was his own father (although he had always existed) committed suicide by cop (although he didn't stay dead) in order to give himself permission not to send you to an eternal place of torture he created for you, but instead will let you live forever if you symbolically eat his flesh, drink his blood and telepathically promise him you accept him as your master so he can cleanse you of an evil force he created which is present in mankind because a rib-woman and a mud-man were convinced by a talking snake to eat from a magical tree (which he knew they would do to begin with).

Admittedly that is a bit snarky, but it does capture the gist of the story Christians are taught from birth. Be that as it may this chapter is about polytheism, which is defined as the worship of or belief in multiple gods and/or demi-gods which are usually assembled into a pantheon of gods and goddesses. Polytheists do not always worship all of those gods equally but can be henotheists who specialize in the worship of one particular deity, while other polytheists can be kathenotheists who worship different deities at different times.

The term itself comes from the Greek "poly" (many) and "theoi" (gods) and was first invented by Jewish writer Philo of Alexandria because he wanted to argue with the Greeks. When Christianity spread throughout Europe and the Mediterranean non-Christians were called Gentiles (a term originally used by Jews to refer to non-Jews), "pagans" (locals) or in a clear pejorative "idolaters" (those worshiping "false" gods). Monotheism, in contrast, is the worship of one and only one god - but as we shall see that is often more of a perception than a reality.

Polytheism was the typical form of religion during the Bronze and Iron Ages up until the Axial Age. The subsequent gradual development of monotheism, pantheism and atheism is well documented in the historical religions of Classical antiquity - particularly Greek and Roman polytheism - especially after the decline of Greco-Roman polytheism in tribal religions such as Germanic paganism or Slavic mythology. There are various polytheistic religions practiced today, for example Shintoism, Ásatrú, Chinese folk religion, Druidry, Taoism, Thelema, Wicca and Candomble. Hinduism is sometimes included in this listing, but despite the presence of polytheistic elements it contains pantheistic and monotheistic ones as well and has been classified by some as "pantheism with polytheistic elements."

The first one we will discuss, Greek mythology, is the body of myths and teachings of the ancient Greeks concerning their gods and heroes, the nature of the world and the origins and significance of their own cult and ritual practices. It was in effect the religion of ancient Greece and modern scholars refer to and study their myths in an attempt to throw light on the religious and political institutions of Ancient Greece and its civilization as well as to gain an understanding of the nature of myth-making itself.

Greek mythology is explicitly embodied in a large collection of narratives and implicitly in Greek representational art such as vase-paintings and votive gifts. Greek myth attempted to explain the origins of the world and details the lives and adventures of a wide variety of gods, goddesses, heroes, heroines and mythological creatures - many of which are similar to those contained in the Bible such as unicorns, sea monsters and dragons. These accounts initially were disseminated in an oral-poetic tradition much as the stories contained in the Bible were passed down from generation to generation before being committed to written form, but today Greek myths are known primarily from Greek literature.

The oldest known Greek literary sources, Homer's epic poems *Iliad* and *Odyssey*, focus on the Trojan War and its aftermath while two poems by his near contemporary Hesiod, *Theogony* and *Works and Days*, contain accounts of the genesis of the world, the succession of divine rulers, the succession of human ages, the origin of human woes and the origin of sacrificial practices. In short it was not all that different from the Bible in scope and theme. Myths are also preserved in the *Homeric Hymns*, in fragments of epic poems of the Epic Cycle, in lyric poems, in the works of the tragedians of the 5th Century BCE, in writings of scholars and poets of the Hellenistic Age and in texts from the time of the Roman Empire by writers such as Plutarch and Pausanias. The obvious question is where did these myths and stories come from in the first place? Could they have possibly been divinely inspired by the Greek gods in the same way the contents of the Bible, Quran and Torah were "dictated" by the gods of the Abrahamic religions… and if not, why not? It seems to be just as plausible an explanation for all of them, if for any.

Archaeological findings provide a principal source of detail about Greek mythology with gods and heroes featured prominently in the decoration of many artifacts. Geometric designs on pottery from the 8th Century BCE depict scenes from the Trojan cycle as well as the adventures of Heracles. In the succeeding Archaic, Classical and Hellenistic periods Homeric and various other mythological scenes appear, supplementing the existing literary evidence. Greek mythology has had an extensive influence on the culture, arts and literature of Western civilization and remains part of Western heritage and language as poets and artists from ancient times to the present have derived inspiration from it and have discovered contemporary significance and relevance in the themes. In many cases the existence of this corpus of data is a strong indication that many elements of Greek mythology have strong factual and historical roots.

Mythical narration plays an important role in nearly every genre of Greek literature but nevertheless the only general mythographical handbook to survive from Greek antiquity was the *Library* of Pseudo-Apollodorus of Athens who lived circa 180-125 BCE and wrote on many of these topics. This work attempts to reconcile the contradictory tales of the poets and provides a grand summary of traditional Greek mythology and heroic legends. His writings may have formed the basis for the collection, however the "library" discusses events which occurred long after his death - hence the name Pseudo-Apollodorus.

As previously noted, among the earliest literary sources are Homer's two epic poems the *Iliad* and the *Odyssey*. Other poets completed the "epic cycle," but these later and lesser poems are now lost almost entirely and despite their traditional name the "Homeric Hymns" have no direct connection with Homer but are instead choral hymns from the earlier part of the so-called Lyric Age. Hesiod, a possible contemporary with Homer, offers in his *Theogony* (*Origin of the Gods*) the fullest account of the earliest Greek myths dealing with the creation of the world, Titans, giants and elaborate genealogies, folktales and etiological myths. Hesiod's *Works and Days*, a didactic poem about farming life, also includes the myths of Prometheus, Pandora and the Five Ages in which the poet gives advice on the best way to succeed in a dangerous world rendered yet more dangerous by its gods.

Lyrical poets often took their subjects from myth but their treatment became gradually less narrative and more allusive with Greek lyric poets including Pindar, Bacchylides, Simonides and bucolic poets such as Theocritus and Bion relating individual mythological incidents. Additionally, myth was central to classical Athenian drama. The tragic playwrights Aeschylus, Sophocles and Euripides took most of their plots from myths of the Age of Heroes and the Trojan War and many of the great tragic stories (i.e. Agamemnon and his children Oedipus, Jason, Medea, etc.) took on their classic form in these tragedies. The comic playwright Aristophanes also used myths in *The Birds* and *The Frogs*.

Historians Herodotus and Diodorus Siculus, as well as geographers Pausanias and Strabo, traveled throughout the Greek world and noted the stories they heard, supplied numerous local myths and legends and often gave little-known alternative versions. Herodotus in particular searched the various traditions presented to him and found the historical or mythological roots in the confrontation between Greece and the East and in the process attempted to reconcile the origins and blending of differing cultural concepts.

The discovery of the Mycenaean civilization by German amateur archaeologist Heinrich Schliemann in the 19th Century and the discovery of the Minoan civilization in Crete by British archaeologist Sir Arthur Evans in the 20th Century helped to explain many existing questions about Homer's epics and provided archaeological evidence for many of the mythological details about gods and heroes. The significance of that is an archaeological foundation for Greek myths had been found in much the same way an "archaeological foundation" for stories found in the Bible is claimed due to the existence of places like Jerusalem and Bethlehem. The ramifications should be obvious - in neither case does the existence of geographical locations validate the truth of the fantastic and magical stories which are claimed to have taken place there.

Geometric designs on pottery of the 8th Century BCE depict scenes from the Trojan cycle as well as the adventures of Heracles. These visual representations of myths are important for two reasons. For one, many Greek myths are attested on vases earlier than in literary sources, for instance of the twelve labors of Heracles only the Cerberus adventure occurs in a contemporary literary text. In addition visual sources sometimes represent myths or mythical scenes which are not attested to in any extant literary source. In some cases the first known representation of a myth in geometric art predates its first known representation in late archaic poetry by several centuries.

Greek mythology changed over time to accommodate the evolution of their culture of which mythology, both overtly and in its unspoken assumptions, is an index of the changes. The earlier inhabitants of the Balkan Peninsula were an agricultural people who, using Animism, had assigned a spirit to every aspect of nature and eventually these vague spirits assumed human forms and entered the local mythology as gods. When tribes from the north of the Balkan Peninsula invaded they brought with them a new pantheon of gods based on conquest, force, prowess in battle and violent heroism and the old gods of the agricultural world fused with those of the more powerful invaders or else faded into insignificance.

After the middle of the Archaic Period myths about relationships between male gods and male heroes became more and more frequent, indicating the parallel development of "pedagogic pederasty" which is thought to have been introduced around 630 BCE. By the end of the 5th Century BCE poets had assigned at least one "eromenos" (an adolescent boy who was their sexual companion) to every important god except Ares as well as many legendary figures. Previously existing myths, such as those of Achilles and Patroclus, also were cast in a pederastic light. Alexandrian poets at first, then more generally literary mythographers in the early Roman Empire, often readapted stories of Greek mythological characters in this fashion.

The achievement of epic poetry was to create story-cycles and as a result develop a new sense of mythological chronology, and thus Greek mythology unfolds as a phase in the development of the world and of humans. While self-contradictions in these stories make an absolute timeline impossible, an approximate chronology may be discerned.

"Myths of origin" or "creation myths" represent an attempt to explain the beginnings of the universe in human language. The most widely accepted version at the time, although only a philosophical account of the beginning of things, is reported by Hesiod in his *Theogony*. He begins with Chaos, a yawning nothingness, and out of the void emerged Gaia (the Earth) and some other primary divine beings: Eros (Love), the Abyss (the Tartarus) and the Erebus. Without male assistance (shades of the Virgin Mary and many other immaculate conception myths) Gaia gave birth to Uranus (the Sky) who then fertilized her. From that union were born first the Titans - six males named Coeus, Crius, Cronus, Hyperion, Iapetus and Oceanus, and six females named Mnemosyne, Phoebe, Rhea, Theia, Themis and Tethys. After Cronus was born Gaia and Uranus decreed no more Titans were to be produced. They were followed by the one-eyed Cyclopes and the Hecatonchires (Hundred-Handed Ones) who were both thrown into Tartarus by Uranus. This made Gaia furious and Cronus, "the wily, youngest and most terrible of Gaia's children," was convinced by Gaia to castrate his father. He did this, and became the ruler of the Titans with his sister-wife Rhea as his consort while the other Titans became his court.

The motif of father-against-son conflict was repeated when Cronus was confronted by his son Zeus. Because Cronus had betrayed his father he feared his offspring would do the same, so each time Rhea gave birth he snatched up the child and ate it. Rhea hated this and tricked him by hiding Zeus and wrapping a stone in a baby's blanket which Cronus ate, and when Zeus was full grown he fed Cronus a drugged drink which caused him to vomit and throw up Rhea's other children and the stone which had been sitting in Cronus' stomach all along. Zeus then challenged Cronus to war for the kingship of the gods and at last, with the help of the Cyclopes (whom Zeus freed from Tartarus) Zeus and his siblings were victorious while Cronus and the Titans were hurled down to imprisonment in Tartarus.

Zeus was himself plagued by the same concern, and after a prophecy that the offspring of his first wife Metis would give birth to a god "greater than he" Zeus swallowed her but she was already pregnant with Athena, who burst forth from his head fully-grown and dressed for war.

According to Classical-era mythology after the overthrow of the Titans the new pantheon of gods and goddesses was confirmed. Among the principal Greek gods were the Olympians residing on Mount Olympus under the eye of Zeus, and the limitation of their number to twelve seems to have been a comparatively modern idea similar to the disciples of Jesus. Besides the Olympians the Greeks worshipped various gods of the countryside, the satyr-god Pan, Nymphs (spirits of rivers), Naiads (who dwelled in springs), Dryads (who were spirits of the trees), Nereids (who inhabited the sea), river gods, Satyrs and others. In addition there were the dark powers of the underworld such as the Erinyes (Furies) who were said to pursue those guilty of crimes against blood-relatives, and in order to honor the Ancient Greek pantheon poets composed the Homeric Hymns (a group of thirty-three songs).

In the wide variety of myths and legends Greek mythology consists of gods which were native to the Greek peoples being described as having essentially corporeal but ideal bodies and the defining characteristic of Greek anthropomorphism is they are persons rather than abstractions, ideas or concepts. Regardless of their underlying forms the ancient Greek gods have many fantastic abilities, most significantly they are not affected by disease and can be wounded only under highly unusual circumstances. The Greeks considered immortality as the distinctive characteristic of their gods and this immortality, as well as unfading youth, was ensured by the constant use of nectar and ambrosia by which the divine blood was renewed in their veins.

Each god descended from his or her own genealogy, pursued differing interests, had a certain area of expertise and was governed by a unique personality, however these descriptions arose from a multiplicity of archaic local variants which do not always agree with one another. When these gods are called upon in poetry, prayer or cult they are referred to by a combination of their names and epithets which identify them by these distinctions from other manifestations of themselves. Alternatively the epithet may identify a particular and localized aspect of the god, sometimes thought to be already ancient during the classical epoch of Greece.

Most gods were associated with specific aspects of life, for example Aphrodite was the goddess of love and beauty, Ares the god of war, Hades ruler of the underworld and Athena goddess of wisdom and courage. Some gods such as Apollo and Dionysus revealed complex personalities and mixtures of functions while others such as Hestia (literally "hearth") and Helios (literally "sun") were little more than personifications. The most impressive temples tended to be dedicated to a limited number of gods who were the focus of large Pan-Hellenic cults, but it was also common for individual regions and villages to devote their own cults to minor gods. Many cities also honored the more well-known gods with unusual local rites and associated strange myths with them which were unknown elsewhere, and during the Heroic Age the cult of heroes (or demi-gods) supplemented that of the gods.

Bridging the time when gods lived alone and the time when divine interference in human affairs was limited was a transitional age in which gods and mortals moved together. These were the early days of the world when the groups mingled more freely than they did later and most of these tales were later told by Ovid's *Metamorphoses* and are often divided into two thematic groups - tales of love and tales of punishment.

Tales of love often involve incest or the seduction or rape of a mortal woman by a male god (reminiscent of the Nephilim in Genesis who came down to earth and took mortal women as wives) resulting in heroic offspring. In a few cases a female deity mates with a mortal man as in the *Homeric Hymn to Aphrodite* where the goddess lies with Anchises to produce Aeneas. The stories generally suggest relationships between gods and mortals are something to avoid, since even consenting relationships rarely had happy endings.

The second type, tales of punishment, involve appropriation or invention of important cultural artifacts such as when Prometheus steals fire from the gods or when Tantalus steals nectar and ambrosia from Zeus' table and gives them to his own subjects and in the process reveals to them the secrets of the gods. In that vein Stanford professor of classics Ian Morris considers Prometheus' adventures, "A place between the history of the gods and that of man." An anonymous papyrus fragment dated to the 3rd Century BCE vividly portrays Dionysus' punishment of the King of Thrace, Lycurgus (whose recognition of the new god came too late) and the horrific penalties which extended into the afterlife. The story of the arrival of Dionysus to establish his cult in Thrace was also the subject of an Aeschylean trilogy. In another tragedy, Euripides' *The Bacchae*, Pentheus (King of Thebes) is punished by Dionysus because he disrespected the god and spied on his Maenads, who were the female worshippers of the god. How, I must wonder, are such artifacts any different from the famous *Dead Sea Scrolls?*

The age in which the heroes "lived" is known as the Heroic Age and its epic and genealogical poetry created cycles of stories clustered around particular heroes or events and established the family relationships between the heroes of different stories - and thus they arranged the stories in sequence. According to Ken Dowden, professor of classics and head of the School of Philosophy, Theology and Religion at the University of Birmingham, "There is even a saga effect: we can follow the fates of some families in successive generations."

After the rise of the hero cult, gods and heroes constituted the sacral sphere and were invoked together in oaths and prayers addressed to them. In contrast to the Age of Gods, during the Heroic Age the roster of heroes is never given fixed and final form. Great gods were no longer born, but new heroes could always be raised up from the army of the dead. After all, if such a thing was possible for Lazarus, why not for Hippolytus as well? In case you are not familiar with the story Asclepius, who was the son of Apollo, the god of medicine and healing and the father of Hygieia ("Hygiene," who is the goddess/personification of health, cleanliness and sanitation), was struck dead by Zeus with a thunderbolt because he had raised Hippolytus (among others) from the dead. Apparently Hades thought no more dead spirits would come to the underworld due to the meddling Asclepius, so he asked his brother Zeus to stop him.

Keep in mind during the 1st Century when Christianity began, gods were expected to be able to raise people bodily from the dead and physical resurrections were actually in vogue. Doctors associated themselves with Asclepius and many legends were circulating of physicians becoming famous by restoring the dead to life as recounted by Pliny the Elder, Apuleius and others. Asclepius was also called SOTER, or "The Saviour," as many gods were in that day. He was especially so-named for being able to cure the sick and bring back the dead and since "Jesus" (or more properly Joshua) means "The Saviour" in Hebrew it may have been expected that his resurrection would be physical in nature also. After all so was Lazarus and the boy raised by Elijah in 1 Kings - a prophet with whom Jesus was often equated. Jesus' association with many healing miracles may also have implied a deliberate rivalry with Asclepius and indeed Jesus was actually called SOTER and still is today as we now see Christian fishes on the backs of cars containing the Greek word ICHTHUS, the last letter of which stands for SOTER. Not to be outdone by a pagan god, Christians may have simply expected that their god could also raise himself physically from the grave.

But the pagans had Asclepius, their own healing saviour, centuries before and after the ministry of Christ and surviving testimonies to his influence and healing power throughout the Classical Age are common enough to fill a two-volume book. Of greatest interest are the inscriptions set up for those healed at his temples because they give us almost first hand testimony - more reliable evidence than anything we have for the miracles of Jesus - of the blind, lame, mute and even the victims of kidney stones, paralytics and one fellow with a spearhead stuck in his jaw all being cured by this pagan "saviour." These testimonies go on for centuries with inscriptions spanning from the 4th Century BCE to the 3rd Century CE and later all over the Roman Empire. Clearly the people of this time were quite ready to believe such tales and they were not considered unusual or remarkable at all.

In honor of Asclepius a particular type of non-venomous snake was often used in healing rituals and these snakes, known as the Aesculapian Snakes, slithered around freely on the floors of dormitories where the sick and injured slept. These snakes were introduced at the founding of each new temple of Asclepius throughout the classical world and from about 300 BCE onwards the cult of Asclepius grew very popular and pilgrims flocked to his healing temples or "Asclepieia" to be cured of their ills in much the same way the Catholic faithful today make pilgrimages to Lourdes to become magically healed. It is also interesting to note the original Hippocratic Oath began with the invocation, "I swear by Apollo the Physician and by Asclepius and by Hygieia and Panacea and by all the gods..." and that the Rod of Asclepius (a snake-entwined staff) remains a symbol of medicine to this day.

Another important difference between the hero cult and the cult of gods is the hero became the center of local group identity, with the monumental actions of Heracles being regarded as the dawn of the Age of Heroes. To the Heroic Age are also ascribed three great events - the Argonautic expedition, the Theban Cycle and the Trojan War.

The only surviving Hellenistic epic, the *Argonautica* of the epic poet, scholar and director of the Library of Alexandria known as Apollonius of Rhodes, tells the myth of the voyage of Jason and the Argonauts to retrieve the Golden Fleece from the land of Colchis. Jason is impelled on his quest by King Pelias, who receives a prophecy that a man with one sandal would be his nemesis. Naturally Jason loses a sandal in a river, arrives at the court of Pelias and the epic is set in motion. Nearly every member of the next generation of heroes, including Heracles, went with Jason aboard the ship *Argo* to fetch the famous Golden Fleece.

Although Apollonius wrote his poem in the 3rd Century BCE the composition of the story of the Argonauts is actually earlier than *Odyssey* which shows familiarity with the exploits of Jason, and the wandering of Odysseus may have been partly founded on it. In ancient times the expedition was regarded as a historical *fact* and was an incident thought to be connected to the opening up of the Black Sea to Greek commerce and colonization.

Greek mythology culminated in the Trojan War fought between Greece and Troy and its aftermath. In Homer's works such as the *Iliad* the chief stories had already taken shape and substance and individual themes were elaborated later. The Trojan War also elicited great interest in the Roman culture because of the story of Aeneas, a Trojan hero whose journey from Troy led to the founding of the city which would one day become Rome as recounted in Virgil's *Aeneid.*

Anyone who has seen the Brad Pitt movie *Troy* knows the story of the Trojan War and to this day the concepts of the Trojan Horse, Achilles Heel and beauty of Helen - with "a face that could launch a thousand ships" - remain a part of our lexicon. Troy is of course a real historical place located in northwest Anatolia in what is now Turkey, south of the southwest end of the Dardanelles and northwest of Mount Ida. As for the historicity of the *Iliad* and the Trojan War itself this has been a topic of scholarly debate for centuries. While researchers of the 18th Century had largely rejected the story of the Trojan War as fable, discoveries made by Heinrich Schliemann reopened the question in modern terms and the subsequent excavation of Troy has as made it plausible that the Trojan War cycle was at least remotely based on a historical conflict of the 12th Century BCE even if the poems of Homer are removed from the event by more than four centuries of oral tradition. To put that into perspective, there is just as much evidence for the events and personages depicted in the *Iliad* as there are for Abraham, Moses, Sodom and Gomorrah and a host of other biblical myths and yet no one today is touting the "truth" of the Homeric stories based upon "archaeological evidence" as is the case with Judeo-Christian stories.

After the rise of philosophy, history, prose and rationalism in the late 5th Century BCE the fate of myth became uncertain and mythological genealogies gave place to a conception of history which tried to exclude the supernatural (such as the Thucydidean history). While poets and dramatists were reworking the myths, Greek historians and philosophers were beginning to criticize them with a few radical philosophers like Xenophanes of Colophon already beginning to label the poets' tales as blasphemous lies as early as the 6th Century BCE. He complained that Homer and Hesiod attributed to the gods, "All that is shameful and disgraceful among men; they steal, commit adultery and deceive one another." It is important to note that he never questioned the existence of the gods, just the way in which they had been portrayed. This line of thought found its most sweeping expression in Plato's *Republic* and *Laws*. Plato created his own allegorical myths such as the vision of Er in the *Republic*, attacked the traditional tales of the gods' tricks, thefts and adulteries as immoral and objected to their central role in literature. That criticism was the first serious challenge to the Homeric mythological tradition, particularly where he referred to the myths as "old wives' chatter." For his part Aristotle criticized the Pre-Socratic quasi-mythical philosophical approach and underscored that "Hesiod and the theological writers were concerned only with what seemed plausible to themselves, and had no respect for us... but it is not worth taking seriously writers who show off in the mythical style; as for those who do proceed by proving their assertions, we must cross-examine them." Nevertheless even Plato did not manage to wean himself and his society from the influence of myth as his own characterization for Socrates is based on the traditional Homeric and tragic patterns and was used by the philosopher to praise the righteous life of his teacher. Plato's rejection of the Homeric tradition was not favorably received by the grassroots Greek civilization and the old myths were kept alive in local cults, continued to influence poetry and were the main subject of painting and sculpture.

More sportingly, 5th Century BCE tragedian Euripides often played with the old traditions, mocked them and through the voice of his characters injected notes of doubt, yet the subjects of his plays were taken without exception from myth. Many of these plays were written in answer to a predecessor's version of the same or similar myth and Euripides mainly impugns the myths about the gods and begins his critique with an objection similar to the one previously expressed by Xenocrates that the gods, as traditionally represented, were far too crassly anthropomorphic.

During the Hellenistic period mythology took on the prestige of elite knowledge which marked its possessors as belonging to a certain class and at the same time the skeptical turn of the Classical Age became even more pronounced. Greek mythographer Euhemerus established the tradition of seeking an actual historical basis for mythical beings and events and although his original work *Sacred Scriptures* is lost much is known about it from what is recorded by Diodorus and Lactantius. How honest and refreshing.

Rationalizing hermeneutics of myth became even more popular under the Roman Empire thanks to the physicalist theories of Stoic and Epicurean philosophy. Stoics presented explanations of the gods and heroes as physical phenomena while the Euhemerists rationalized them as historical figures. At the same time the Stoics and Neoplatonists promoted the moral significations of the mythological tradition, often based on Greek etymologies. Through his Epicurean message Lucretius sought to expel superstitious fears from the minds of his fellow citizens, and Livy too was skeptical about the mythological tradition and claimed he did not intend to pass judgment on such legends. The challenge for Romans with a strong and apologetic sense of religious tradition was to somehow defend that tradition while conceding it was often a breeding-ground for superstition, and in a similar fashion "progressive" or "liberal" Christian apologists today are doing the same thing when they reject literal interpretations of the Bible. The antiquarian Varro, who regarded religion as a human institution with great importance for the preservation of good in society, devoted rigorous study to the origins of religious cults. In his *Antiquitates Rerum Divinarum* (which has not survived, but Augustine's *City of God* indicates its general approach) Varro argued that whereas the superstitious man fears the gods, the truly religious person venerates them as parents. In this work he distinguished three kinds of deities - gods of nature who were personifications of phenomena such as rain and fire, gods of the poets who were invented by unscrupulous bards to stir the passions and gods of the city who were invented by wise legislators to soothe and enlighten the populace.

The Roman academic Cotta ridiculed both literal and allegorical acceptance of myth, declaring roundly that myths have no place in philosophy. Cicero was also generally disdainful of myth but like Varro was emphatic in his support for the state religion and its institutions, however it is difficult to know how far down the social scale this rationalism extended. Cicero asserted that no one, "not even old women and boys," were so foolish as to believe in the terrors of Hades or the existence of Scyllas, centaurs and other composite creatures, but on the other hand the great orator elsewhere complains of the superstitious and credulous character of the people, and clearly not much has changed in that regard during the intervening centuries.

In Ancient Roman times a new Roman mythology was born through the syncretization of numerous Greek and other foreign gods. This occurred because the Romans had little mythology of their own and inheritance of the Greek mythological tradition caused the major Roman gods to adopt the characteristics of their Greek equivalents. The gods Zeus and Jupiter are an example of this mythological overlap. In addition to the combination of the two mythological traditions the association of the Romans with eastern religions led to further syncretizations. For instance the cult of Sun was introduced in Rome after Aurelian's successful campaigns in Syria and the Asiatic divinities Mithras (that is to say "the Sun," who was essentially a forerunner of Jesus of Nazareth, aka "the Son") and Ba'al were combined with Apollo and Helios into one Sol Invictus with conglomerated rites and compound attributes. Apollo might be increasingly identified in religion with Helios or even Dionysus, but texts retelling his myths seldom reflect such developments. The traditional literary mythology was increasingly dissociated from actual religious practice and the worship of Sol as special protector of the emperors and the empire remained the chief imperial religion until it was replaced by Christianity.

The surviving 2nd Century CE collection of *Orphic Hymns* and the *Saturnalia* of Macrobius Ambrosius Theodosius (5th Century CE) are influenced by the theories of rationalism and the syncretizing trends as well. The *Orphic Hymns* are a set of pre-classical poetic compositions attributed to Orpheus who was himself the subject of a renowned myth. In reality these poems were probably composed by several different poets and contain a rich set of clues about prehistoric European mythology. The stated purpose of the *Saturnalia* was to transmit the Hellenic culture Macrobius had derived from his readings even though much of his treatment of gods is colored by Egyptian and North African mythology and theology, something which also affected the interpretation of Virgil.

The genesis of modern understanding of Greek mythology is regarded by some scholars as a double reaction at the end of the 18th Century against "the traditional attitude of Christian animosity" in which the Christian reinterpretation of myth as a "lie" or fable had been retained. The development of comparative philology in the 19th Century together with ethnological discoveries in the 20th Century established the science of myth, and since the time of the Romantics all study of myth has been comparative. Folklore scholars Wilhelm Mannhardt, James Frazer and Stith Thompson employed the comparative approach to collect and classify the themes of folklore and mythology and in 1871 Edward Burnett Tylor published his *Primitive Culture* in which he applied the comparative method and tried to explain the origin and evolution of religion. Tylor's procedure of drawing together the material cultures, rituals and myths of widely separated cultures influenced both Carl Jung and Joseph Campbell, while philologist Max Müller applied the new science of comparative mythology to the study of myth in which he detected the distorted remains of Aryan nature worship.

Of course the Greco-Roman versions of polytheism were not the only ones practiced in antiquity, which brings us to the Egyptian religious traditions which are fascinating in their own right but are particularly interesting in light of Egypt's purported involvement in the Judeo-Christian Exodus story.

Setting aside the concept of "truth" for a moment, without the ancient Egyptian religion there would probably be little reason for one to visit Egypt today. The great Pyramids would not exist, nor the fabulous temples and tombs on the West Bank of Thebes (modern Luxor) with their mummies or the colorful decorations which adorn these structures and have lured travelers to Egypt over the past three thousand years or so. Come to think of it the same would also hold true for the adjacent Holy Land of the Abrahamic religions. After all, who would travel there if not for the Dome of the Rock, Wailing Wall, Cavalry and Bethlehem?

Behind every aspect of Egyptian life including the art, political structure and cultural achievements one cannot help but see the religious forces which shaped the fabric of ancient Egypt. The spiritual world which was created by the Egyptians was a richly fascinating one which remains unique in the history of human religion but at the same time is somehow familiar in many ways. The character of that spiritual world was both mysterious and manifest, at once accessible and hidden, for although Egyptian religion was often shrouded in layers of myth and ritual it nevertheless permeated the ancient civilization of the Nile and ultimately shaped, sustained and directed Egyptian culture in almost every way - whether it was true or not.

One thing which does seem familiar about their ancient religion was the Egyptian people were extremely concerned about the afterlife. Furthermore, in order to avoid being counted among the damned of the afterlife they had to not only venerate the Egyptian gods but also live by a code of standards which would be judged after death. Sound familiar?

In his masterpiece *The Histories* Herodotus, known as "The Father of History," tells us the Egyptians "are religious to a higher degree than any other people" and some six centuries later in his *Perfect Discourse* Hermes Trismegistos summed up the spirit of Egyptian religious beliefs for his disciple Asclepius in a striking metaphor: "(Egypt) has become the image of Heaven, and what is more, the resting place of Heaven and all the forces that are in it. If we should tell the truth; our land has become the temple of the world."

Like the members of any other human culture the ancient Egyptians were driven to find meaning in existence but there were also other influences on their religion such as the need to justify kingship, among others. Religion has been defined as a belief in and reverence for a supernatural power or powers regarded as creator and governor of the universe but this is somewhat of an over simplification because religions usually include a system of values as well as various practices. Egyptian religion can be said to encompass their ancient gods, the mythology or accounts of those gods and other aspects of the religion such as creation, death and the afterlife and the cults who worshipped the gods, however there are certainly more complexities to the religion such as how the king played into this structure of religion and moral dogma concerning what the gods expected of humans (i.e. a system of values).

We cannot say with any certainty exactly when the foundations of Egyptian religion were laid, although it was certainly prior to recorded history. In fact some of the important mythology such as the *Contendings of Horus and Seth* could have possibly been rooted in real events prior to Egypt's unification. The story is also significant because it puts forth the idea of the god Horus as the living king on earth which was arguably and in fact quite likely a model for the later incarnation of Jesus in Christian tradition.

We must be careful when examining the ancient Egyptian religion because even though there was a considerable amount of consistency between various areas of Egypt over the religion's long existence there were also significant variations, and over time those changes were included in the theology. For example while some 1,500 gods and goddesses are known by name, many were not worshipped at any one time or in any one place.

Over time many changes took place with some coming to pass in dramatic fashion and the telltale signs often being quite obvious. For example the burial practices of the Egyptians, which were certainly affected by their religious ideologies, went from simple "mastabas" (eternal houses) in the very early periods and during the Pre-Dynastic Period to monumental pyramids during the Old and Middle Kingdoms, but then after the first ruler of Egypt's New Kingdom built a Pyramid at Abydos subsequent kings suddenly did away with superstructures altogether in favor of hidden tombs with no superstructures at all. Perhaps part of the reason was the security of the tomb and its content of valuables although it did not do much to stop tomb robbers, but it also had much to do with the Egyptian religion's movement towards Osiris. The god Osiris also seems responsible for another major change in Egyptian religion through its long history, that being it's popularization, since Osiris was a democratic god who doubtless became popular because the theology surrounding him allowed even common Egyptians the opportunity for immortality after their death.

Of course some things did stay the same to an extent. There seems to have always been a sun god from the earliest of times, with the god Ra being worshipped at Egypt's earliest shrines and his veneration probably reaching a high point during the late Old Kingdom when kings not only built their pyramids but also erected specialized temples to worship him - but his worship also changed, sometimes dramatically.

Perhaps one of the most consistent aspects of ancient Egyptian religion was the role of the King, which seems to always have been central to the ancient Egyptian religion. What did change was the perception of his role, though even this remained somewhat consistent particularly after the Early Dynastic Period.

While Egyptologists may sometimes address the reasons for changes within the ancient Egyptian religion this may be one of its most unknown aspects. Did priests have heated debates over theology which culminated in change? If they did it must have been mostly narrative in nature for we have little if any record of it, and if such discussions did take place the King must have been involved because it is through his actions that most new religious foundations were created and it was his funerary monuments which seem to have changed the most over time. That theological discussion (and probably discourse) took place is almost certain, because over time the mythology of the religion evolved and became more complete. This is particularly obvious from funerary texts, beginning with the *Pyramid Texts* and moving on to numerous texts particularly during the New Kingdom. On the other hand it is likely changes also took place because of shifts in regional power. This certainly seems the case because during the New Kingdom the center of religious activity shifted to Thebes, where the state god Amun rose to acclaim. Furthermore, the need of the common populous to be included also effected changes, particularly towards Osiris.

Consistently from the beginning of Egyptian religion to its final stand at the Temple of Philae (with the possible exception of one brief period) most scholars agree the religion was polytheistic, although a number of attempts have been made to explain Egyptian religion in terms of monotheism and certainly scholars of the 19th Century who were steeped in Christian tradition tended to find traces of monotheism in Egyptian beliefs in an effort to bolster the believability of their own narrative. The main evidence they cited was the anonymous "god" the Egyptians referred to in literary and wisdom texts, but now that anonymous god is understood to represent a way of invoking any divine power emanating from any gods or sometimes a specific, assumed god worshipped by an individual or someone in a specific region.

Even during the 18th Dynasty reign of Amenhotep IV, who apparently tried to introduce and promote a single god (the Aten), Egyptian religion cannot be said to have been monotheistic for even while the king himself may have worshipped a single god (and even that is uncertain) his religion never caught on and for the most part Egyptians in general continued to worship their traditional gods.

Several researchers have applied the concept of henotheism to Egyptian religion, a practice which focuses on one god addressed in a particular time of worship. Essentially henotheism is the belief in one god without denying the existence of others, i.e. the believer simply unites all known divine powers in his favorite god.

The situation with gods was further complicated by syncretism and other forms of combining them. The term "syncretism" has a special meaning in Egyptology, referring to the combination or merging of aspects of one god in another. This feature first appeared in the 4th Dynasty with Atum-Re of Heliopolis, and by Middle Kingdom there were many such combinations. It has been shown that this was probably a temporary fusion of gods, with each keeping their own characteristics.

Then there is the matter of manifestation, a concept which is frequently misunderstood as Egyptians almost certainly did not worship statues and paintings of gods or animals. These objects were simply believed to be the manifestation, or temporary habitats, of the gods who they worshipped. It should also be noted that the Egyptians created personified conceptions such as Ma'at (truth, balance) and Hapi (the inundation), although these were always joined with a god or used as decorations.

Cults, a term with a far different meaning in today's world, were the official structures used to worship the Egyptian gods. These structures included the priests who carried out rituals associated with the gods (who were frequently manifest in the form of statues) within the cult temples. The center of the Egyptian cult was the temple, a sacred area enclosed by a wall which excluded the profane. Temples could be called a "house," "chapel" or "chapel of the god," and included a section devoted to worldly needs. Inside the sanctuary of the temple was the cult statue which served as the dwelling for the god worshipped in the cult center, although there could be and usually were more than one in many temples.

Cult rituals were actually a dialogue between the gods and the king (or a priestly substitute for the king) acted in the divine performance as a god. Until the Middle Kingdom the spheres of administration and cult were not separated, but in the 18th Dynasty a special priesthood was established. Rituals centered around offerings much like the Old Testament animal sacrifices of the Israelites, but there were certainly numerous other rituals including daily functions such as washing and clothing the gods (or at least their statues). Other rituals took the form of celebrations when for example one god might be taken to visit the cult center of another, and it was during these festivals that common Egyptians probably came closest to their gods for at other times they were prohibited from the sanctuaries which housed the cult statues.

At first the cult and for that matter the benefits of religion and the gods which it served was limited to the king for the most part, although many functions and rituals were performed by his substitutes (i.e. priests). Common Egyptians could only hope the king took his religious duties seriously or otherwise they might expect to suffer famine or other disasters and for that matter any chance of an afterlife. As time passed religion became much more popularized and as a result later in Egyptian history common Egyptians demanded their own means of worshipping and being accepted by their gods. More and more, common Egyptians built shrines within their homes for their personal worship or small public shrines where they could worship and pray together, however throughout Egyptian history they were limited as to the scope of their participation in state cult centers.

So how much of Egyptian religion was based in fact, and why did it flourish the way it did? Strictly speaking a myth may be defined as a traditional, typically ancient story dealing with supernatural beings, ancestors or heroes which serves as a fundamental "truth" in the worldview of a people by explaining aspects of the natural world or delineating the psychology, customs or ideals of society, but unlike many modern religions there was no single textual source which bound up the religious ideology of the ancient Egyptians. There was no Bible as such nor could there have been, because the beliefs sometimes varied from region to region and the mythology evolved over time as well.

Texts are known from as early as the 3rd Dynasty which make reference to the activities of the gods, usually within accounts of relations between nobles and the king and in fact most of the known Egyptian myths concern the origins and nature of kingship as the central topic of interest. Narrative literature did not appear before the Middle Kingdom, but myths certainly existed in oral tradition long before and allusions to the deeds of gods are inserted in early ritual texts such as the *Pyramid Texts* and *Book of the Dead.*

The *Book of the Dead* is an ancient Egyptian funerary text which was used from the beginning of the New Kingdom around 1550 BCE to about 50 BCE. The original Egyptian name for the text is translated as *Book of Coming Forth by Day*, and another translation would be *Book of Emerging Forth Into the Light*. The text itself consists of a number of magic spells intended to assist a dead person's journey through the *Duat*, or underworld, and into the afterlife.

The *Book of the Dead* was part of a tradition of funerary texts which includes the earlier *Pyramid Texts* and *Coffin Texts* which were painted onto objects rather than papyrus and some of the spells included were drawn from these older works and actually date to the 3rd millennium BCE. Other spells were composed later in Egyptian history and date to the Third Intermediate Period (11th to 7th Centuries BCE) and a number of the spells which made up the Book continued to be inscribed on tomb walls and sarcophagi as had always been the spells from which they originated. The *Book of the Dead* itself was also placed in the coffin or burial chamber of the deceased for his personal use.

It should be noted there was no single or canonical *Book of the Dead* as the surviving papyri contain a varying selection of religious and magical texts and vary considerably in their illustration and some people even commissioned their own copies, perhaps choosing the spells they thought most vital for their own progression to the afterlife, however they were commonly written in hieroglyphic or hieratic script on papyrus scrolls and illustrated with vignettes depicting the deceased and their journey into the afterlife.

As previously stated the *Book of the Dead* developed from a tradition of funerary manuscripts dating back to the Egyptian Old Kingdom. The first of them were the *Pyramid Texts*, which were first used in the pyramid of King Unas of the 5th Dynasty around 2400 BCE. These texts were written on the walls of the burial chambers within pyramids and were exclusively for the use of the Pharaoh (and from the 6th Dynasty on, the Queen). The *Pyramid Texts* were written in an unusual hieroglyphic style, with many of the hieroglyphs representing humans or animals left incomplete or drawn mutilated - most likely to prevent them from causing any harm to the dead pharaoh. The purpose of the *Pyramid Texts* was to help the dead king take his place amongst the gods, in particular to reunite him with his divine father Ra, since during this period the afterlife was seen as being in the sky rather than the underworld described in the *Book of the Dead*. Towards the end of the Old Kingdom the *Pyramid Texts* ceased to be an exclusively royal privilege and were adopted by regional governors and other high-ranking officials.

In the Middle Kingdom a new funerary text eventually emerged which were known as the *Coffin Texts*. They used a newer version of the language, new spells and included illustrations for the first time. The *Coffin Texts* were most commonly written on the inner surfaces of coffins, although they are occasionally found on tomb walls or papyri. They were available to wealthy private individuals, vastly increasing the number of people who could expect to participate in the afterlife - a process which has been described as the "democratization of the afterlife."

The earliest known occurrence of the spells included in the *Book of the Dead* is from the coffin of Queen Mentuhotep of the 13th Dynasty although some of the spells introduced at this time claim an older provenance, for instance the rubric (title or heading) to spell number 30B states it was discovered by Prince Hordjedef in the reign of King Menkaure, many hundreds of years before it is attested to in the archaeological record. By the 19th Dynasty the *Book of the Dead* had become widespread not only for members of the royal family, but courtiers and other officials as well. At this stage the spells were typically inscribed on linen shrouds wrapped around the dead, though occasionally they were still written on coffins or papyrus.

The New Kingdom saw the *Book of the Dead* develop and spread further still, and the famous Spell 125 - the "Weighing of the Heart" - is first known from the reign of Hatshepsut and Tuthmose III (c.1475 BCE). From this period onward the book was typically written on a papyrus scroll and the text was illustrated with vignettes, and during the 19th Dynasty in particular those vignettes tended to be lavish, sometimes at the expense of the surrounding text.

The last use of the *Book of the Dead* was in the 1st Century BCE, although some artistic motifs drawn from it were still in use in Roman times. At present some 192 spells are known, although no single manuscript contains them all and the texts and images were magical as well as religious. Magic was as legitimate an activity as praying to the gods, even when the magic was aimed at controlling the gods themselves. Indeed, there was little distinction for the ancient Egyptians between magical and religious practice.

The spells of the *Book of the Dead* made use of several magical techniques which can also be seen in other areas of Egyptian life. A number are for magical amulets which would protect the deceased from harm, sort of the "rosary beads" of their time. In addition to being represented on a *Book of the Dead* papyrus, these spells appeared on amulets wound into the wrappings of a mummy. Everyday magic made use of amulets in huge numbers and other items in direct contact with the body in the tomb such as headrests were also considered to have amuletic value. A number of spells also refer to Egyptian beliefs concerning the magical healing power of saliva.

One aspect of death was the perceived disintegration of the various *kheperu*, or modes of existence, and funerary rituals served to re-integrate these different aspects of being. Mummification served to preserve and transform the physical body into *sah*, an idealized form with divine aspects, and the *Book of the Dead* contained spells aimed at preserving the body of the deceased which may have been recited during the process of mummification. The heart, which was regarded as the aspect of being which included intelligence and memory, was also protected with spells, and in case anything happened to the physical heart it was common to bury jeweled heart scarabs with a body to provide a replacement. The *ka*, or life-force, remained in the tomb with the dead body and required sustenance from offerings of food, water and incense, and in the event priests or relatives failed to provide these offerings Spell 105 ensured the *ka* was satisfied. The name of the dead person, which constituted their individuality and was required for their continued existence, was written in many places throughout the *Book* and spell 25 ensured the deceased would remember their own name. The *ba* was a free-ranging spirit aspect of the deceased and it was the *ba*, depicted as a human-headed bird, which could "go forth by day" from the tomb into the world - spells 61 and 89 acted to preserve it. Finally the *shut*, or shadow of the deceased, was preserved by spells 91, 92 and 188, and if all these aspects of the person could be variously preserved, remembered and satiated the dead person would live on in the form of an *akh* - a blessed spirit with magical powers who would dwell among the gods.

The nature of the afterlife which the dead person enjoyed is difficult to define because of the differing traditions within ancient Egyptian religion, but then again no two modern Christians can seem to agree on the nature of their version either. In the *Book of the Dead* the departed were taken into the presence of the god Osiris, who was confined to the subterranean *Duat* and also depicts the dead living on in the "Field of

Reeds" - a paradisiacal likeness of the real world depicted as a lush, plentiful version of the Egypt of the living where the deceased person is shown encountering the Great Ennead, a group of gods, as well as his or her own parents... which seems to be a common thread throughout many belief systems.

If all the obstacles of the *Duat* could be negotiated the deceased would be judged in the "Weighing of the Heart" ritual mentioned earlier. The decedent was led by the god Anubis into the presence of Osiris where the dead person swore he had not committed any sin from a list of forty-two sins, demonstrating that the concept of "sin" is not unique to Christianity or any other religion, and recited a text known as the "Negative Confession." Then the dead person's heart was weighed on a pair of scales against that of the goddess Ma'at, who embodied truth and justice and was often represented by an ostrich feather (the hieroglyphic sign for her name). At this point there was a risk the deceased's heart would bear witness and own up to sins committed in life, but Spell 30B guarded against this eventuality. If the scales balanced this meant the deceased had led a good life and Anubis would take them to Osiris at which time they would find their place in the afterlife, becoming *maa-kheru* (meaning "vindicated" or "true of voice"). If however the heart was out of balance with Ma'at a fearsome beast called *Ammit* (the Devourer) stood ready to eat it and put the dead person's afterlife to an early and unpleasant end. This same idea is reflected by the Bible in Proverbs 21:2 which says, "Every way of a man is right in his own eyes, but the LORD weighs the hearts."

The foregoing scene is remarkable not only for its vividness but because it is one of the few parts of the *Book of the Dead* with explicit moral content, with the judgment of the dead and Negative Confession being a representation of the conventional moral code which governed Egyptian society. For every "I have not" in the Negative Confession it is possible to read an unexpressed "Thou shalt not," although while the Ten Commandments of Judeo-Christian ethics are rules of conduct laid down by a perceived divine revelation the Negative Confession is more a divine enforcement of everyday morality. Views differ among Egyptologists about how far the Negative Confession represents a moral absolute, with ethical purity being necessary for progress to the afterlife. John Taylor of the Department of Ancient Egypt at the British Museum points out the wording of Spells 30B and 125 suggests a pragmatic approach to morality in that by preventing the heart from contradicting him with any inconvenient truths, it seems the deceased could enter the afterlife even if their life had not been entirely pure. Much like the confession of a Catholic, the Egyptians were offered a "way out" in recognition of the fact humans are imperfect.

Because Egypt had many gods they also had many myths. Some of them, such as those surrounding the sun god Ra (particularly during the earlier periods) and later ones such as the contention of Horus and Seth, became central to the Egyptian religion, perhaps mainly due to their relevance to kingship, however other myths involving for example Hathor as a healer were very important to more common Egyptians as were myths concerning Bes, a goddess of childbirth and the home. There were certainly other myths which explained creation, dealt with the afterlife and even spoke about the "end of times"... long before the *Book of Revelation* was written.

A value system, not unlike the Commandments and Mosiac Laws of the Bible, was important to the ancient Egyptians in much the same way it is today. In fact many of the values of modern society were present in the Egyptian system. What is perhaps different is the exact relevance the ancient Egyptians gave their value system although it certainly had both a secular and religious side. On the religious side, as in many religions today, one was judged upon death for his or her actions during life and either condemned to be a member of the damned or the blessed, demonstrating the "fear and reward" or "carrot and stick" approach is not unique to Christianity, Islam or any other belief system. On the secular side a system of values was also important for social order just as it is today, and then as now a criminal system was available to punish offenders during their lifetime for certain offenses.

Somewhat different was the matter of Ma'at, a personified concept of truth, balance and order. An individual could violate Ma'at by his actions, but so too could the nation as a whole. To put that into perspective, think about the "America is losing its moral foundations" argument which is frequently put forward today to explain things such as the devastation of Hurricane Katrina and the 9-11 terrorist attacks. Similarly the ancient Egyptians believed failure to maintain the morality of Ma'at as a country could result in divine intervention when the Egyptian gods provided only low Nile floods and thus famine, enemy incursions or even complete chaos within the country. This is an important point so I will say it again. This notion of a national Ma'at is not lost to us today, since many people of religion continue to believe a nation's fortunes are dictated by their adherence to both good deeds and a general belief in a particular god, and biblically speaking there are more than a few stories about states suffering the wrath of God due to a lack of perceived values as well.

The king's divine status was discussed earlier and so important was the king to ancient Egyptian religion that he was theoretically required to be the head of all ceremonies and rites throughout the country at the same time, not unlike the way Saul, Solomon and David were viewed in Abrahamic dogma. The practical answer to this was for the king to elevate members of the royal family during the Old Kingdom, and nobles of his court later on, so they could represent him. This became the Egyptian priesthood, which eventually developed its own independence and titles during the New Kingdom.

It is not unreasonable for our concept of how the Egyptians worshiped their many gods to change extensively as we discover more and more new information, and indeed over the years there have been shifts in how Egyptology views the religion. One might consider the amount of material available on our modern religions, which are still mysterious to a large extent, and compare it to what we have on the Egyptian religion to have an understanding of just how little we actually know about this complex and ancient belief system.

Which brings us to Hinduism, the dominant religion of the Indian subcontinent which is comprised of the three major traditions of Shaivism, Vaishnavism and Shaktism and whose followers consider Shiva, Vishnu and Shakti (also called Devi) to be the supreme deity respectively with most other deities being either related to them or different forms (incarnations) of these deities. Hinduism has been called the oldest religion in the world, and many practitioners refer to it as the *Sanātana Dharma* (eternal law).

Many of the names of the Indo-Aryan deities such as Agni, Indra and Varuna are almost synonymous with deities in the Persian, Greek and Roman religions and it has been speculated this is due to the several waves of Aryan immigration which are believed to have taken place in northwest India around 1500 BCE. Through a slow process of hybridization the Indo-Aryan deities are believed to have merged into the many local cults, a process which spread from the northwest to the east and south of the subcontinent through the movement of "fortune-seekers, traders or teachers" and still continues today in some parts of India.

In most Hindu philosophies there is only one ultimate reality. Also known as Brahman - the infinite manifestation of the universe, not to be confused with Atman which is the manifestation of god within a body and somewhat comparable to a soul - all others are considered his aspects or "avatars." Vishnu the protector or preserver and Shiva the destroyer are the main examples of this due to them being more popular aspects of the Ultimate Reality, although in their personal religious practices Hindus may worship primarily one or another of the aspects known as their "Ishta Devata" or "Ishvara" (chosen deity). The particular gods worshipped are a matter of individual preference, although regional and family traditions can play a large part in influencing this choice. Vaishnavism, Shaivism, Shaktism and the Ganapatya sects of Hinduism state that Vishnu, Shiva, Devi and Ganesh respectively equate to Brahman and that all other deities are aspects of their chosen deity. Some popular deities and avatars include Vishnu and his form as Jagannath, Vithoba, Venkateshwara and his Avatars Narasimha, Krishna, Rama (and others), Shiva (Hanuman the monkey god is worshipped as his aspect), Shakti the feminine principle (her aspects Durga, Kali, Saraswati, Lakshmi and others) as well as Ganesh and Murugan - and to the uninitiated that no doubt sounds pretty darn confusing.

Within Hinduism a large number of personal gods (Ishvaras) are worshipped as murtis (divine spirits). These beings are significantly powerful entities known as devas, and the exact nature of belief in regards to each deity varies between differing Hindu denominations and philosophies. Often these beings are depicted in humanoid or partially humanoid forms, complete with a set of unique and complex iconography in each case. The devas are expansions of Brahman into various forms, each with a certain quality. In the *Rigveda* thirty-three devas are described which are personifications of phenomena in nature.

Hindu philosopher Adi Shankara has said that there is only one Supreme Para-Brahman and all the other deities are the forms and expansions of this Para-Brahman. It is believed all Vaishnava and other schools attribute "personhood" to this concept as in Svayam Bhagavan (a Sanskrit theological term for Lord Krishna), and under terms of some schools of Vedanta it has three modal aspects with the highest as Para Brahman or Lord Vishnu. Para-Brahman means Supreme Brahman, Supreme Cosmic Spirit or Godhead, and although an ineffable entity it could be said to be that which contains and pervades the universe. Para-Brahman "from beyond" encompasses the transcendent and immanent ultimate reality Brahman, and since the Absolute Truth (a term which demonstrates a claim to "truth" is not the exclusive domain of *any* worldview) is both subject and object there is no qualitative difference so terms like Parameshvara, Ishvara, Bhagavan, Brahman and Paramatma are held to be synonymous with Para-Brahman.

Adi Shakti is the concept, or personification, of divine feminine creative power which is sometimes referred to as "The Great Divine Mother" in Hinduism and she is regarded as the one who remote controls trinity, Devas, planets and other heavenly bodies. In fact Scriptures refer to her as "the originator of all." Adi (first) Para (beyond) Shakti (energy) is Divine Energy beyond universe, and she took many forms. Srimad Bhagwat Purana and Shiva Purana associate Shakti as "ChinMai" and there is a concept of only Shakti (energy to destroy and preserve), but Srimad Devi Bhagwat Purana is talking about energy beyond universes, hence associating herself as Para Brahman or "ultimate god."

Popular goddesses worshiped in Hinduism are Lakshmi, Saraswati, Parvati, Durga and Kali, and Shaktism recognizes Shakti as the supreme goddess. The concept of supreme goddess emerged in historical religious literature as a term used to define the powerful and influential nature of female deities in India. Throughout history goddesses have been portrayed as the mother of the universe through whose powers the universe is created and destroyed, and the gradual changes in belief through time shaped the concept of Mahadevi and express how the different goddesses, though very different in personality, all carry the power of the universe on their shoulders. Jagaddhatri and Mariamman are other significant female deities and Aagneya or Agneya (also known as Agnayi) is the Hindu goddess of fire who is worshiped throughout different parts of India as the daughter or consort of Agni the fire god.

Shiva and Vishnu are of course regarded as Mahādevas (great gods) due to their central positions in worship and Scriptures and these two along with Brahman are considered the Trimurti, or three aspects of the universal supreme God. These three aspects symbolize the entire circle of samsara in Hinduism with Brahman as creator, Vishnu as preserver or protector and Shiva as destroyer or judge - a "Hindu trinity" reminiscent of the Christian "Father, Son and Holy Spirit."

The Tridevi or triplet goddesses of Hinduism have equal importance as the Trimurti. Brahman is the creator so he needs the knowledge of goddess Saraswati (Vaak) to create, Vishnu is the preserver so he needs the goddess of wealth and prosperity Lakshmi (Shri) and finally Shiva is the destroyer and re-creator so he needs the goddess Parvati, Durga or Kali (various manifestations of goddess Shakti) for power.

Many denominations of Hinduism such as Vaishnavism and some schools of Saivism teach that occasionally a god comes to Earth as a human being to help humans in their struggle toward enlightenment and salvation (moksha), not unlike the incarnation of God as Jesus in

Christianity. Such an incarnation of a god is called an avatar, and Hinduism teaches there have been multiple avatars throughout history and will be more. The most famous of the divine incarnations are Rama, whose life is depicted in the *Ramayana*, and Krishna, whose life is depicted in the *Mahābhārata* and the *Bhagavata Purana* - and the *Bhagavad Gita*, which contains the spiritual teachings of Krishna, is one of the most widely read Scriptures in Hinduism.

Now that we have examined the polytheistic religions of the Greeks, Romans, Egyptians and Hindus, and keeping in mind there are many more which cannot be reviewed due to space limitations, it is time to look at the Godhead which denotes the Divine Nature or Substance (*Ousia*) of the Christian God. Within some traditions such as Mormonism the term is used as a non-trinitarian substitute for the term "Trinity" and denotes the Father, Son and Holy Spirit not as a Trinity but as a unified council of separate beings in full harmony. More specifically in the Mormon theology adhered to by most Mormon communities including The Church of Jesus Christ of Latter-day Saints "God" means Elohim (the Father) whereas "Godhead" means a council of three distinct divine beings - Elohim, Jehovah (the Son) and the Holy Spirit. The Father and Son have perfected, glorified, material bodies while the Holy Spirit is a spirit and does not have a body, a conception which differs from the traditional Christian Trinity.

Keep in mind most early Latter Day Saints came from a Protestant background and believed in the doctrine of Trinity which had been developed during the early centuries of Christianity. Until about 1835 Mormon theological teachings were similar to that established view, however Joseph Smith's teachings regarding the nature of the Godhead developed during his lifetime and became almost fully elaborated in the years prior to his murder in 1844. Beginning as an unelaborated description of the Father, Son and Holy Spirit as being "one," Smith taught the Father and Son were distinct personal members of the Godhead as early as 1832. His public teachings later described the Father and Son as possessing distinct physical bodies and being one together with the Holy Ghost not in material substance, but instead united in spirit, glory and purpose - a view often called "social trinitarianism."

The Book of Mormon describes God the Father, his Son Jesus Christ and the Holy Ghost as being "one" with Jesus appearing with a body of spirit before his birth and a tangible body after his resurrection, and the book also describes the "Spirit of the Lord" as capable of appearing in the form of a man and speaking as a man would speak. After Jesus' resurrection and ascension into Heaven *The Book of Mormon* also states he visited a small group of people in the Americas who saw that he had a resurrected, tangible body and during his visit he was announced by the voice of God the Father and those present felt the Holy Spirit - but only the Son was actually seen. The LDS Church interprets this "oneness" as a metaphorical oneness in spirit, purpose and glory rather than a physical or bodily unity, but on the other hand some Latter Day Saint sects such as the Community of Christ consider the *Book of Mormon* to be consistent with trinitarianism. Some scholars have also suggested the view of Jesus in *The Book of Mormon* is also consistent, or perhaps most consistent, with monotheistic Modalism.

In 1835 Smith and former Baptist minister Sidney Rigdon publicly taught the idea Jesus Christ and God the Father were two separate beings, and although never part of the official Mormon canon the *Lectures on Faith* were included as part of the 1835 *Doctrine and Covenants*. Having never been accepted as binding doctrine they were eventually removed from the *Doctrine and Covenants* by the LDS Church and Community of Christ, and most modern Latter Day Saints do not accept the idea of a two-personage Godhead with the Father as a spirit and the Holy Spirit as the "shared mind" of the Father and the Son. Moreover many Latter Day Saint apologists propose a reading of *Lectures on Faith* which is consistent with Smith's earlier or later doctrines by putting various shadings on the meaning of "personage" as used in the *Lectures*. This serves as just one more example of different factions within a religion having a different interpretation of a key tenet of the faith.

During the latter part of his life Smith also introduced a theology which could support the existence of a Heavenly Mother with the primary source for this theology being the sermon he delivered at the funeral of King Follett which today is commonly called the King Follett Discourse. The LDS Church believes a Heavenly Mother exists, but very little is acknowledged or known beyond her "existence."

Mainstream Christians might scoff at those Mormon beliefs and even distance themselves from the concept of the Godhead but many of them actually worship or at least acknowledge a pantheon of what amount to demi-gods themselves - the saints. This is because humans have always wanted spiritual assistance nearer to their heart and something or someone to identify with and approach, and as God's "go-betweens" the saints are reassuringly human because they are full of flaws and foibles.

In the simplest of terms a saint is someone who has been recognized for having an exceptional degree of holiness, sanctity and virtue. While the English term "saint" originated in Christianity historians of religion now use the term in a more general way to refer to the state of special holiness which many religions attribute to certain people with the Jewish Tzadik, Islamic Mu'min, Hindu Rishi or Guru and the Buddhist Arhat or Bodhisattva also referred to as saints. Depending on the religion, saints are recognized either through official church recognition or by popular acclaim, i.e. "folk saints."

In Christianity "saint" has a wide variety of meanings depending on its usage and the denomination. The original Christian usage referred to any believer who is "in Christ" and in whom Christ dwells, whether in Heaven or on earth. In Orthodox and Catholic teachings all Christians in Heaven are considered to be saints, but some are considered to be worthy of higher honor, emulation or veneration with official church recognition given to some saints through canonization or glorification.

The English word saint is from the Latin "sanctus," in origin a term in indigenous tradition connected to the name of the god Sancus, but in Christian context used to translate the Greek "hagios" which is derived from the verb "hagiazo" which means "to set apart," "to sanctify" or "to make holy," and the word appears two hundred twenty-nine times in the Greek New Testament and sixty times in the corresponding text of the King James Version. As used by the apostolic authors of Scripture "saint" did not refer to deceased persons who have been granted sainthood, but rather to living persons who had dedicated themselves to God.

The word was originally a technical term in ancient Roman religion but due to its globalized use in Christianity the modern term (in English or Romance languages) is now also seen as translation of comparable terms for people "worthy of veneration for their holiness or sanctity" in other religions. As previously mentioned many religions use similar concepts but different terminology to venerate individuals worthy of honor in some way, i.e. Hindu saints.

The Catholic Church teaches that it does not make or create saints but rather recognizes them and in the Church the title refers to a person who has been formally canonized (officially recognized) by the Catholic Church and is therefore believed to be in Heaven. By this definition there are many people the church believes to be in Heaven who have not been formally declared saints but who are otherwise referred to as such since they are believed to be completely perfect in holiness, and unofficial devotions to uncanonized individuals routinely take place in certain regions of the world.

In Church tradition a person who is seen as exceptionally holy can be declared a saint through a formal process called "canonization." Formal canonization is a lengthy process which often takes many years, and sometimes even centuries, to complete. The first step in this process is an investigation of the candidate's life which is undertaken by an "expert." After this is done the report on the candidate is given to the bishop of the area and more study is conducted, after which it is sent to the Congregation for the Causes of Saints in Rome.

If the application is approved the person may be granted the title of "Venerable" and further investigations may lead to the candidate's beatification whereupon he or she is given the title of "Blessed." At a minimum two important miracles are required in order to be formally declared a saint, and these miracles must be posthumous. Finally, when all of this is done to his satisfaction, the Pope canonizes the saint.

In 993 Pope John XV was the first to officially proclaim a saint when at the request of the German ruler he canonized Bishop Ulrich of Augsburg. This was an important decision by the Church because up until that time saint cults had only been local and spontaneous. Pope John XVIII next declared a cult of five Polish martyrs and Pope Benedict VIII followed suit by making the Armenian hermit Symeon a saint, but it was not until the time of Pope Innocent III that popes claimed an exclusive monopoly on canonization. In 1153 Walter of Pontoise was the last person in Western Europe to be canonized by an authority other than the pope when he was elevated by Archbishop of Rouen Hugh de Boves, because in 1170 a decree of Pope Alexander III officially gave the prerogative exclusively to the pope so far as the Western Church was concerned.

In his book *Making Saints* author Kenneth L. Woodward notes the following: "A saint is always someone through whom we catch a glimpse of what God is like - and of what we are called to be. Only God 'makes' saints, of course. The church merely identifies from time to time a few of these for emulation. The church then tells the story. But the author is the source of the grace by which saints live. And there we have it: A saint is someone whose story God tells." An interesting perspective to be sure, but one which raises some questions from the objective observer such as where in Scripture did God make such a declaration and if he did why did the Church wait over a thousand years to start doing it?

The veneration of saints, in Latin "cultus" (cult of the saints), describes a particular popular devotion or abandonment to a particular saint or saints. Although the term "worship" is sometimes used it is intended in the old sense meaning to honor or give respect, because according to the Catholic Church divine worship is reserved only for God and never to the saints, although they can be asked to intercede for those still on earth just as one can ask someone on earth to pray for them - and as it happens even popes pray to them or at least to the remains of what they think is a saint.

Consider that in November of 2013 the Vatican publicly unveiled a handful of bone fragments purportedly belonging to none other than St. Peter himself, reviving the scientific debate and tantalizing mystery over whether relics found in a shoe box truly belong to the first pope. The nine pieces of bone sat nestled like rings in a jewel box inside a bronze display case on the side of the altar during a Mass commemorating the end of the Vatican's yearlong celebration of the Christian faith, and it was the first time they had ever been exhibited in public. Pope Francis prayed before the remains at the start of the service and then clutched the case in his arms for several minutes after his homily. No pope has ever definitively declared the fragments to belong to Peter, but in 1968 Pope Paul VI said fragments found in the necropolis under St. Peter's Basilica were "identified in a way that we can consider convincing" - whatever the heck that means.

Naturally some archaeologists dispute the finding but top Vatican official Archbishop Rino Fisichella said it almost doesn't matter if archaeologists one day definitively determine the bones aren't Peter's, saying Christians have prayed at Peter's tomb for two millennia and will continue to do so regardless. "It's not as if pilgrims who go to the altar (of Peter's tomb) think that in that moment in which they profess their faith that below them are the relics of Peter, or of another or another still," he told reporters. "They go there to profess the faith." It does raise the question, however, of whether or not popes would continue to display and pray to the bones were such a determination to be made.

The relics were first discovered during excavations begun under St. Peter's Basilica in the years following the 1939 death of Pope Pius XI, who had asked to be buried in the grottoes where dozens of popes are buried, according to the 2012 book by veteran Vatican correspondent Bruno Bartoloni, *The Ears of the Vatican.* During the excavations archaeologists reportedly discovered a funerary monument with a casket built in honor of Peter and an engraving in Greek that read "Petros eni" (Peter is here), but as the "burial box of James" hoax demonstrated such claims must be taken with a grain of salt. Scholar of Greek antiquities Margherita Guarducci, who had deciphered the engraving, continued to investigate and learned one of the basilica workers had been given the remains found inside the casket and had stored them in a shoe box kept in a cupboard of all places. She reported her findings to Paul VI who later proclaimed there was a "convincing argument" the bones belonged to Peter, but how he could have possibly arrived at that conclusion given the circumstances and lack of a chain of custody is anyone's guess. Even so top Vatican Jesuits and other archaeologists strongly denied the claim but had little recourse and were forced to rationalize that, according to Bartoloni, "No pope had ever permitted an exhaustive study, partly because a thousand-year-old curse attested to by (naturally) secret and apocalyptic documents threatened anyone who disturbed the peace of Peter's tomb with the worst possible misfortune" - a claim not dissimilar from the one made in 1923 regarding the dire consequences which awaited anyone who entered the sealed tomb of King Tutankhamun of Egypt.

Once a person has been declared a saint his or her body is considered holy and the remains are called "holy relics" and usually housed in churches. In fact even the saints' personal belongings may be used as relics, some have a symbol which represents their life and it is believed one of the ways the holiness of a person is revealed is through the condition of their relics. In some Orthodox countries such as Greece graves are often reused after three to five years because of limited space and when that occurs the bones of the displaced "occupant" are washed and placed in an ossuary, often with the person's name written on the skull. Occasionally when a body is exhumed for this purpose something miraculous is reported as having occurred, for instance exhumed bones are claimed to have given off a fragrance like flowers or a body is reported as having remained free of decay despite not having been embalmed (traditionally the Orthodox do not embalm the dead) after having been buried for some years in the earth. An example of this is the case of St. Anthony of Padua, who is buried in a chapel within the large basilica built to honor him where his tongue is displayed for veneration. The story goes that when his body was exhumed thirty years after his death it was found to have turned to dust, but the tongue was claimed to have glistened and looked as if it was still alive and moist and a further claim was made that this was due to his gift of preaching.

According to the Catholic faith a body which is incorruptible by decay is a miracle and a person who dies and proves incorruptible can thus qualify as a saint. There are quite a few alleged examples of this, so let's take a look at some of the best known - but first we should examine exactly what the church's criteria are for incorruptibility. In essence it means the body does not decompose after death in a miraculous manner not explainable by natural processes. The body must remain flexible and is supposed to be indistinguishable from sleep, i.e. it can't dry out like an Egyptian mummy and be stiff. The body also must not have been embalmed or otherwise preserved.

The most famous of the Catholic incorruptibles is Saint Bernadette who is currently on display at the Chapel of St. Bernadette in France. She died in 1879 and was exhumed thirty years later, so the story goes, and was discovered to be incorrupt and free of odor... however two doctors swore a statement after their examination of the body clearly describing a partially mummified corpse and the body as "shriveled" while saying the lower parts of the body had turned black, the nose was "dilated and shrunken" and the whole body was rigid and "sounded like cardboard when struck." The body was then prepared and reburied in a sealed casket, and when it was dug up again in 1919 another doctor filed the following report: "The body is practically mummified, covered with patches of mildew and quite a notable layer of salts which appear to be calcium salts... the skin has disappeared in some places, but it is still present on most parts of the body."

At her third and final exhumation in 1925 it was noted that the blackish tinge to the face and the sunken eyes and nose would make an unpleasant impression on the public so the decision was made to display the corpse with a wax mask. That's right, the "miraculous" photos you see on the internet of St. Bernadette's beautiful, incorrupt corpse are of a wax mask placed on an obviously mummified body. The descriptions of her condition openly violate all the requirements of incorruptibility and yet St. Bernadette is the most often cited example of same, and when you think about it if a saint dies and God decides the body should be incorruptible you'd think it would remain absolutely perfect like Sleeping Beauty and shouldn't be only slightly less decomposed than the average body.

St. Catherine of Bologna is another nun whose supposedly incorrupt body is on display. She died in 1463 and the story goes that she was buried without a coffin and exhumed only eighteen days later due to a strong sweet scent coming from her grave. Her body is displayed at the chapel of Poor Clares in Bologna, Italy in a seated position inside a glass case and as you can see from the many photos on the Internet it is completely mummified, black and shriveled and can by no definition be called incorrupt… and yet she is called just that anyway in spite of the blatantly obvious evidence to the contrary.

Saint Silvan was a young man thought to have been killed for a his faith in the year 350 and his body is on display in Dubrovnik, Croatia replete with a fresh-looking gash on his throat said to have been the cause of death, and in this case the body appears to be perfect. The only problem is it is a sculpted effigy and St. Silvan's actual remains are contained within the box below the effigy, but of course there is no signage to explain this to the faithful and many come away with photographs of what they think is the actual body. If he is incorrupt as the church claims why display the effigy instead of the body?

Padre Pio, the 20th Century priest famous for his stigmata, is also on the church's list of incorruptibles however according to the church's own records his body was embalmed with formaldehyde upon death, but even so at his exhumation forty years later the remains were described as "partially skeletal" and morticians were unable to restore the face to a viewable condition so he is displayed today with a lifelike silicone mask.

When exhumed, incorruptible bodies are often said to be accompanied by a sweet odor which Catholics called the "Odor of Sanctity," and this odor is also said to come from stigmata on living saints and some are said to have exuded this odor after death. Of course the obvious explanation for such a smell would be embalming fluid, however modern embalming fluids (basically formaldehyde mixtures) have a strong, unpleasant smell like gasoline and as a result most manufacturers mask the smell with perfume additives. Historically, sweet-smelling ointments were used on corpses to counter the smell of decomposition and many such ointments are now known to have contained guaiacol which is an effective preservative made from beechwood tar (similar to creosote).

The best examples of natural incorruptibility come from the peat bogs of northern Europe where about a thousand individuals have been exhumed and a unique combination of cold conditions and chemical processes preserved the soft tissues. Most come from the Celtic Iron Age but some are far older, with the oldest being Koelbjerg Woman who is 5,500 years old. In "bog bodies," peat acid actually dissolves the bones but leaves the soft tissues pliable like rubber, though stained brown and actually tanned into leather. Technically these bodies meet the Catholic criteria of incorruptibility far better than any of the dried mummified corpses which the church claims, so why are the bog people not considered saints? At least their bodies remain flexible. The church probably says the natural chemical process counts as embalming, which of course it does, but at least this is a natural process and not deliberate human embalming as has happened with so many of the so-called "miraculous" Catholic incorruptibles.

Then there is the case of Hambo Lama Itigelov, a Buddhist monk who died in the Russian Mongol territory of Buryatia in 1927 and was exhumed seventy-five years later in 2002 in accordance with his last request. His condition was described by monks and a pathologist in attendance as that of someone who had died only thirty-six hours before, and while video shows what looks to be a well-preserved mummy it is hardly that of someone who died only hours before. His body is on display in the open air and is claimed to remain pliable, a claim which is untested, and despite a Russian documentary movie finding no explanation and the monks' claims to the contrary the pathologist's own report found the body to have been preserved with bromide salts. Itigelov had also instructed that his body be packed in salt, which is another way to help prevent decomposition by absorbing moisture away from the body, but the point is this Buddhist monk can hardly be called a Christian saint.

Buddhist monks have long practiced self-mummification and some Japanese monks used to prepare themselves for self-mummification through a technique called "sokushinbutsu" in which they ate a subsistence diet of nuts and seeds for one thousand days to get rid of all their fat and then spent the next thousand days eating only bark, roots and drinking the tea of a poisonous tree called the urushi in an effort to make their body both dehydrated and toxic to parasites. They would then place themselves inside a stone tomb, ringing a bell once each day, and when the bell failed to ring the other monks would seal the tomb, wait another thousand days and then open it to find out whether the monk had mummified. Only about twenty such monks were successfully mummified in this manner and the rest decomposed normally, but even this number is impressive given that the internal organs, which are a prime source of bacteria and contribute to decomposition, remained. Tests of the mummies have revealed toxic levels of arsenic, which is another embalming agent. Together with the lack of body fat and pre-existing dehydration monks practicing sokushinbutsu actually had a reasonable chance of mummification if their tomb was well sealed and conditions were dry, and Hambo Lama Itigelov's technique of using bromide salts and salt packing appears to be a scientifically updated form of sokushinbutsu.

You could not call these monks incorruptible any more than you can use the term to describe Catholic saints who are obviously mummified since mummification is the natural, expected process which happens to a body under the right conditions and there's nothing miraculous about a natural, expected process. Some people might claim in a few of these cases decomposition should have taken place instead of mummification, and thus the miracle, but is leaving a few strands of decomposed flesh stretched over bones the best a miracle-creating superbeing can muster? Incorruptible should mean incorruptible, and we've never seen anything remotely like that anywhere on the planet.

Be that as it may, the reason relics are considered sacred is because for the Orthodox the separation of body and soul is unnatural. Body and soul both comprise the person and in the end they believe body and soul will be reunited, therefore the body of a saint shares in the holiness of the soul of that saint. As a general rule only clergy will touch relics in order to move them or carry them in procession, however in veneration the faithful will kiss the relic to show love and respect toward the saint. Not surprisingly every altar in every Orthodox church contains relics, usually of martyrs, and church interiors are covered with the Icons of saints.

In contrast to the Western Church, in the Eastern Orthodox Church a saint is defined as anyone who is in Heaven whether recognized here on earth or not. By this definition Adam and Eve, Moses and the various prophets are given the "honorary" (for lack of a better term) title of "Saint." Sainthood in the Orthodox Church does not necessarily reflect a moral model, but communion with God. There are countless examples of people who lived in "great sin" and became saints by humility and repentance such as Mary of Egypt, Moses the Ethiopian and of course Dysmas, the repentant thief who was crucified.

Orthodox belief says God reveals his saints through answered prayers and other miracles although saints are usually recognized by a local community and often by people who directly knew them, and as their popularity grows they are eventually recognized by the church. Since there is no pope as in the Western Church the formal process of recognition involves deliberation by a synod of bishops and if successful this is followed by a service of glorification in which the saint is given a day on the church calendar to be celebrated by the entire church. This does not however make the person a saint, since according the Orthodox beliefs the person already was a saint and the Church was simply recognizing it.

In many Protestant churches the word “saint” is used more generally to refer to anyone who is a Christian and is similar in usage to Paul’s numerous references in the New Testament of the Bible. In this sense, anyone who is “within the body of Christ” (i.e., a professing Christian) is a saint because of their relationship with Jesus. Many Protestants consider prayers to the saints to be idolatry, since in their eyes an application of divine worship which should be given only to God himself must not be offered to other believers, whether dead or alive. Many Protestant sects also consider the practice to be similar to necromancy, as the dead are believed to be awaiting resurrection and unable to do anything for the living.

In the Lutheran Church all Christians whether in Heaven or on earth are regarded as saints, however the church still recognizes and honors specific saints including some of those recognized by the Catholic Church, but in a qualified way. According to the Augsburg Confession, which is the primary confession of faith of the Lutheran Church and one of the most important documents of the Lutheran Reformation, the term “saint” is used in the manner of the Roman Catholic Church only insofar as to denote a person who received exceptional grace, was sustained by faith and whose good works are to be an example to any Christian. Traditional Lutheran belief proclaims prayers to the saints are prohibited as they are not mediators of redemption, but Lutherans do believe the saints themselves pray for the Christian Church in general. Philip Melancthon, author of the *Apology of the Augsburg Confession*, approved honoring the saints by saying they are honored in three ways - by thanking God for examples of his mercy, by using the saints as examples for strengthening faith and by imitating their faith and other virtues. The Lutheran Church also has liturgical calendars in which they honor individuals as saints.

While Methodists as a whole do not practice the patronage or veneration of saints they do honor and admire them. Methodists believe all Christians are saints but mainly use the term to refer to biblical characters, Christian leaders and martyrs of the faith. Many Methodist churches are in fact named after saints such as the Twelve Apostles, John Wesley, etc., although most of them are instead named after geographical places associated with an early circuit or prominent location. Some Methodist congregations observe All Saints Day if they follow the liturgical calendar and many encourage the study of saints, i.e. the biographies of holy people. The 14th Article of Religion in the United Methodist Discipline states, “The Romish doctrine concerning purgatory, pardon, worshiping and adoration, as well of images as of relics, and also invocation of saints, is a fond thing, vainly invented and grounded upon no warrant of Scripture, but repugnant to the Word of God."

John Wesley, the theological father of world Methodism, did not practice or permit Roman Catholic practices associated with the veneration of the Virgin Mary or prayers to saints but despite that particular scriptural interpretation there is little difference between the way many Christians act towards saints and how the ancient Greeks acted toward their gods. They each pray to their respective saints/gods, believe them to have power, choose a different one to venerate depending upon their circumstances or the nature of their request, have physical statues of them and even name buildings and places after them - but don't take my word for it. According to the Catholic Church itself, "Certain Catholic saints are associated with certain life situations. These patron saints intercede to God for us. We can take our special needs to them and know they will listen to our prayers, and pray to God with us."

So how many saints are there? One Roman Catholic website states, "There are over ten thousand named saints and beatified people from history, the Roman Martyrology and Orthodox sources, but no definitive head count." Reverend Alban Butler published *Lives of the Saints* in 1756 containing 1,486 saints and the latest edition of this work edited by Father Herbert Thurston and British author Donald Attwater contains narratives of 2,565 of them however Monsignor Robert Sarno, an official of Vatican's Congregation for the Causes of Saints, has said it is impossible to say the exact number.

There is for all intents and purposes a saint for every location and occasion. You can even have your own patron saint. To put it another way saints have holy wells and work miracles as they become, to the untrained eye, demi-deities in their own right. In fact it was the saints, angels and holy artifacts which in large part helped draw polytheistic pagans to Christianity in the first place.

A saint may be designated as a patron saint of a particular cause or profession or invoked against specific illnesses or disasters, sometimes by popular custom and sometimes by official statements of the Magisterium - the authority which dictates what is an authentic teaching of the Church. Saints are generally not thought to have power of their own but only that which is granted by God, and relics of saints are respected in a manner similar to holy images and icons with the practices of past centuries in venerating relics of saints for healing being taken from the early Church. For example in the year 2000 an American deacon claimed that "Blessed John Henry Newman" interceded with God to cure him. The American, Jack Sullivan, asserted that after addressing Newman he was cured of spinal stenosis in a matter of hours and in 2009 a panel of theologians (rather than physicians) concluded Sullivan's recovery was the result of his prayer to Newman since according to the Catholic Church to be deemed a miracle a medical recovery must be instantaneous, not attributable to treatment and disappear for good.

Another more specific tradition is the "patron saint" who in some Christian denominations is regarded as the tutelary spirit or heavenly advocate of a nation, place, craft, activity, class, clan, family or person. Patron saints, having already transcended to the metaphysical, are believed to be able to intercede effectively for the needs of their special charges. Professions sometimes get a patron owing to that individual saint being involved with it somehow, but lacking such a saint an occupation would have a patron whose acts or miracles in some way recall the profession. For example when the hitherto unknown profession of photography appeared in the 19th Century, Saint Veronica was made its patron owing to how her veil is alleged to have miraculously received the imprint of Christ's face after she wiped the blood and sweat off of him (even though there is no evidence such a thing ever occurred). Quite ironically, it would have been nice to have had a photographer present to record the event if it did happen.

There are in fact saints who can be invoked against toothaches (St. Apollonia), colic (St. Agapitus of Palestrina), procrastination (St. Expeditus), hemorrhoids (St. Fiacre), gout (St. Apollinaris), snakebites (St. Peregrine of Auxerre) and pretty much anything you can think of, although it must be pointed out there are multiple saints assigned to many areas so it can get a bit confusing. There are yet other saints who advocate for professions such as bartenders (St. Amand), gamblers (St. Cajetan), comedians (St. Lawrence) and even thieves (St. Dismas) and of course there are also those who "keep an eye" on places from the continent of Africa (St. Moses the Black) to the Islamic country of Iran (St. Maruthas) right on down to the city of Detroit (St. Anne) - and judging by the condition of bankrupt, impoverished and violent Detroit, Saint Anne has been asleep at the wheel for some time now.

In a similar fashion the Olympian gods of ancient Greece presided over every facet of life and were often grouped according to their common functions. For example Athena was the goddess of wise counsel, Hermes the god of commerce and Hephaestus the patron god of artisans such as weavers, potters, metalworkers, sculptors, etc. The god of the sea was of course Poseidon although several of the other Olympian gods had minor maritime roles including Apollo, Artemis, Aphrodite and the Dioscuri who presided over embarkations, harbors, safe voyages and salvation from storms. Much like Christian patron saints, the list of gods and their specific "area of expertise" is virtually endless.

Let's take it one step further and compare specific Christian saints with corresponding Greek gods. In ancient Greece Akeso, for example, was the goddess of curing illness and today St. Arthelais is (one of) the patron saints of illness. Aphrodite was the goddess of love, beauty and procreation while now St. Valentine and St. Raphel are considered to be the patron saints of love. Apollo (a real multi-tasker) was the god of music, prophecy and healing and in a similar fashion St. Agabus is patron saint of prophets, St. Cecilia of musicians and St. Theresa of Avila, St. Catherine of Sweden and St. Bernadette (Our Lady of Lourdes) share the duties for healing. Artemis, in addition to being the goddess of hunting, was also responsible for childbirth and children and in the Christian world St. Gerard Majella is responsible for pregnancy and St. Juliana of Nicomedia for childbirth. Demeter was the goddess of agriculture and today St. Bernard of Vienne and St. Botulph are the patron saints of farmers, farmhands and husbandry. In a nutshell there is now a patron saint (and sometimes several) which corresponds with virtually every Greek (and for that matter, Roman) god.

Not only are saints and Greek/Roman gods similar in many ways, many Christian saints are actually based on pagan gods and goddesses. That is not surprising when you consider many Christian traditions are derived from pagan practices, something which is covered elsewhere in this book. Often information about Christianity is a major source of information about Pagan religions and conversely an understanding of Pagan religions is quite revealing when it comes to the later monotheistic faiths.

With the advent of Christianity the Egyptian god Osiris was transmogrified into St. Onuphrius and the Greek god Dionysus/Roman god Bacchus variously became St. Dionysius, St. Bacchus and several other saints. Venus initially became St. Venere, Artemis became St. Artemidos and Helios became St. Elias, all of whom now tend to be mysteriously omitted from modern lists while others have suffered "downsizing." St. Charity for example does much the same job as the Greek goddesses known as the "three Charities." Sometimes there was cross-borrowing, for instance St. Mercourios took over from the god Mercury and St. Michael took over the warlike functions of Mars, but St.

Michael also took over some of the responsibilities of Mercury such as the weighing of souls.

Clearly many of the saints recognized by mainstream Western Christian Churches are ancient gods who have been forcibly recruited into the ranks of the saints, although some were merely heroes in their previous incarnation. Hippolytus, the son of Theseus who died while being dragged by horses, became St. Hippolytus since he had supposedly been martyred in a similar way. The Irish St. Bridget is the ancient Celtic goddess Brigid who has slowly been losing her divinity over the centuries, and St. Vitus was a central European god as was at least one of the saints called Valentine.

This phenomenon was neither restricted to Europe nor early Christianity since modern depictions of Mexican saints are often indistinguishable from those of Aztec gods. For instance at least one of the Virgin Mary's multiple personalities is Aztec. In her persona as Our Lady of Guadeloupe she looks like a Central American native and in this guise is a Christianized version of the "Little Mother," the Aztec earth goddess Tonantzín. In fact believers still leave her votive offerings of corn just as they did before the coming of Christianity.

Abrahamic religions have long been considered to be misogynistic in nature as borne out in the Bible and Quran and as a result it is interesting to note that while many pagan goddesses did indeed become Christian saints, if they were considered to be powerful in the pagan religion they were either reduced to rape victims or repentant prostitutes or had to change gender entirely and become male warrior saints. For example Demeter was the goddess of many festivals, most importantly the Thesmophoria which fell in late October, and became St. Demetrios, a masculine warrior saint whose feast day is October 26th. The goddess Aphrodite became St. Aphrodite (and/or St. Catherine) of which there are several, all with tales which tell of how she became a "repentant whore." The Greek goddess Nike was transmogrified and picked up as St. Nicholas, who became extremely popular wherever shipping was important and is now the patron saint of Russia, Holland and Germany.

Many Catholic Saints are in fact "votive saints," that is their names were copied off votive offerings for pagan gods and especially from the altars and statues which were still standing in Rome in the 4th Century CE. The Roman god Mars was originally a deity who guarded wheat fields and became St. Martin (St. Martin-in-the-fields). Although March is the month associated with Mars because it was the beginning of the military campaigning season in Roman times, the major festival for him in Christian times now usually falls in February. The Roman god Quirinus became St. Cyrinus and there are various derivative "equestrian warrior saints" such as St. Cyr in France and St. Quirina, mother of St. Lawrence. These saints were very popular and widely worshiped during the Middle-Ages in France, Holland and eastern Christian countries. The Roman gods known as the Lares became St. Lawrence (St. Lawrence beyond-the-wall) as the Lares were field gods who protected the grain growing in the fields. In Italy he became St. Lorenzo Beyond the Walls (meaning outside of the walls of the city) and there is still a church in Rome as well as many "daughter" churches which developed from it. The Roman gods known as the Gemini who were protectors of sailors in Roman Pagan times became the Sanctos Geminos, with a number of forms in the various Christian traditions. Santiago de Compostela, (St. James in English) became the protector of pilgrims during the Middle Ages, with forms of St. James all seeming to be Christianized from various forms of the Proto-Indo-European god Yama.

Of course not all Christian saints came from Roman and Greek Pagan deities. Ahura Mazda, a major god in the Zoroastrian religion, became Ador Ormazd (Saint Ahura Mazda) in the early Syriac Christian church. And not all pagan saints are even based on pagan gods. Some are based on pagan holidays. For example the Roman festival of Caro Patri or "Dear Parents" (a festival to remember one's ancestors) in the Roman Pagan calendar of Philocalus became the festival of St. Peter's Chair in the Roman Catholic Martyrology (saints' calendar). This was one of the sources which contributed to the character of Saint Peter, who became one of the most important saints in the Roman Catholic Church since he is the source of their theological claim for apostolic succession.

Other saints are "archaeological" saints, that is they are based on archaeological monuments or finds. St. George is of this type, and the famous image of him killing a dragon is based on sculptures erected by the Romans to threaten barbarians in Eastern Europe. The iconography then spawned stories of him killing a dragon rather than the reverse as many people seem to think.

Naturally not all saints are connected to other mythologies, but even so Christianity has managed to come up with a few bizarre incarnations on its own. If your only knowledge of Christian saints is that certain holidays and cities are named after them you are grossly misinformed. Some supposedly could fly, slay dragons and function without heads.

A good example to begin with is St. Denis of Paris. Life as a missionary can admittedly be tough especially if it was in 3rd Century

Paris under Roman rule, but undeterred by government death threats a missionary named Denis continued to convert Parisians to Christianity and it resulted in him being beheaded - and he was *still* undeterred! The story goes that after his execution Denis picked up his own severed head, washed it by a spring and walked two Gallic miles (about six statute miles) while continuing to preach through the mouth on the severed head he was carrying until he reached a spot he thought would make a good burial site where he eventually dropped dead.

Today he's naturally the patron saint of people suffering from headaches and apart from several paintings depicting him with head in hands the motif was extended to the world of sculpture where St. Denis is permanently remembered not for his good deeds but for being someone who could evangelize while headless. One interesting aspect of the tale, aside from its obvious impossibility, is if he was preaching the whole time while walking around headless someone was presumably listening. Can you imagine anyone then or now who upon seeing a headless man walking toward them with blood spurting from a ragged neck stump and carrying a head which is offering them an inspirational message of salvation being able to actually listen to and absorb what the head was saying?

As you can see from the previous story the Romans often served as the villains in the old tales of the saints. For instance when St. Margaret of Antioch resisted the advances of a local Roman prefect he purportedly had her arrested, tortured and then thrown into the dungeon. As if that were not bad enough, things took a turn for the worse when Satan himself appeared before her in the form of a massive dragon and swallowed Margaret whole. What happened next varies depending on which account you read but one version involves Margaret cutting her way out of the dragon's stomach, which I suppose is not so difficult to accept if you already believe a dragon who was actually Satan had swallowed her in the first place. The next day the Romans tried to execute her by drowning and then by lighting her on fire, but apparently bathing in the blood of a dragon made her immune to most ordinary causes of death because neither the drowning nor flames harmed her so the Romans eventually had to resort to chopping her head off.

Then there is the popular story of St. Christopher. Before becoming a saint he had tried going a different direction and was a follower of Satan, but figuring this was probably not the best move in the long run chose to change sides and converted to a follower of Christ. This was deemed to be significant in part because he was three times taller than the average person. According to the tale written in the saints compendium called *The Golden Legend* Christopher was eighteen feet tall, or as the writing of the time put it he was twelve cubits in height (with a cubit being eighteen inches). As it turns out the most important event in his life was putting the then three-year-old Jesus Christ on his shoulders and wading across a river, hence the name Christopher ("Christ bearer"). Of course one would think Christ would be the last person who would need someone to carry him across a river given that the Bible tells us he was capable of walking on water, but in such stories accuracy was obviously a secondary consideration and naturally St. Christopher became the patron saint of traveling. On top of all that, when it came time to fold the story of St. Christopher into Eastern Orthodox doctrine an error transmogrified him because he was a Canaanite and this was mis-translated as "canine" - and as a result artists and iconographers ended up depicting him as something resembling a werewolf.

Next we will look at the story of St. Columbanus, who is said to have roamed the forests with birds flying around his head and landing on his shoulders while squirrels ran up and down his robes and nested in his cowl. As the Catholic Church tells it, while walking through the forest one day Columbanus was confronted by a dozen hungry wolves and walked right through them unmolested. Later he decided to retire into a mountain cave for prayer and meditation, but the only problem was this particular cave was the home of a very large sleeping she-bear. According to the legend Columbanus then woke the giant sleeping animal and ordered it to leave the cave and never return, and the bear ran away with its tail between its legs. Sometime later Columbanus came upon yet another bear feasting on the carcass of a deer in the middle of the woods and decided he could use a new pair of shoes, so the saint ordered the bear not to harm the skin of the deer so that he could use it to make some. Yet another story tells us the monastery where Columbanus lived was having trouble planting its crops one year, so he solved this problem by making a bear which he summoned from a nearby forest hook up to a plow like a mule. Shades of the Beastmaster.

According to medieval historians Thomas of Cantimpre and Jacques de Vitry a nice girl named Christina was in her early twenties when she suffered a seizure and apparently died. Since it was the 13th Century and medicine was not very advanced it was understandingly surprising when she woke up during her funeral and "disagreed" with the prospect of being buried by flying up to the rafters of the chapel while complaining about the sinful stench of the unwashed masses below. The story goes on to say the young woman declared she had seen purgatory and decided that her suffering in their stead would help guide souls out of the cleansing fire and straight into Heaven, and witnesses supposedly testified she had been seen crawling into hot ovens, handling fire, standing in freezing water for hours, getting mauled by dogs and being dragged around and around by a mill wheel without sustaining so much as a single scratch… and when she wasn't doing such things she would sleep in tombs and caves, climb trees and buildings or simply levitate to avoid contact with the people she identified as sinners by their smell alone.

While most saints purportedly used their miraculous powers to help their fellow man by healing the sick, feeding the hungry or something equally altruistic St. Joseph of Cupertino was an Italian friar who could, according to legend, fly. In fact he's said to have been capable of soaring into the sky and flying over crowds of people. The first reported instance of this was during a procession on the feast day for St. Francis of Assisi. Joseph was walking along like everyone else when suddenly he became "overwhelmed by the spirit" and soared into the air over the crowd, where he remained until one of his superiors ordered him to come down. This wasn't a one-time event, however. Joseph's flights reportedly became so frequent that the friars had to forbid him from doing it because he was causing a distraction. Evidently the friars had better things to do with their time than watch someone defy the laws of physics. This ban may have been for Joseph's own safety however, since aside from his aerial acrobatics he was known for being incredibly simple - he couldn't read or write, for example - and his lack of intelligence was supposedly so pronounced it led to him becoming among other things the patron saint of the mentally handicapped.

For a more modern look at the process of canonization let's look at the case of Mother Teresa. It used to be that a person could not even be nominated for beatification until five years after his or her death in order to guard against local or popular enthusiasm in the promotion of dubious characters, however Pope John Paul II nominated Mother Teresa just a year after her death in 1997. It also used to be that there was an apparatus of inquiry, including the scrutiny of an advocatus diaboli or "devil's advocate," to test any extraordinary claims, but the pope abolished that office and created more instant saints than all of his predecessors combined going as far back as the 16th Century.

As for the "miracle" that had to be attested to (two are required for sainthood) surely any respectable Catholic cringes with shame at the obvious fakery. A Bengali woman named Monica Besra claimed a beam of light emerged from a picture of Mother Teresa and relieved her of a cancerous tumor, however her physician, Dr. Ranjan Mustafi, said she didn't have a cancerous tumor in the first place and the tubercular cyst she did have was cured by a course of prescription medicine, saying, "It was not a miracle... she took medicines for nine months to one year." Was he interviewed by the Vatican's investigators? Of course not. Even Besra's own husband said, "My wife was cured by the doctors and not by any miracle." In addition, according to an uncontradicted report in the Italian paper *L'Eco di Bergamo*, the Vatican's secretary of state sent a letter to senior cardinals that June asking on behalf of the pope whether they favored making Mother Teresa a saint right away since the pope's clear intention had been to speed the process up in order to perform the ceremony in his own lifetime. According to Father Brian Kolodiejchuk, the Canadian priest who acted as postulator or advocate for the canonization, the response was in the negative, but the damage to the "integrity" of the process (such that it was) had already been done. As an interesting and unrelated aside which demonstrates how religious superstition can overshadow medical diagnoses, Archbishop of Calcutta Henry Sebastian D'Souza ordered a priest to perform an exorcism on Mother Teresa with her permission when she was first hospitalized with cardiac problems because he thought she might have been under attack by the Devil.

I realize that was a lot of information, although in reality it barely scratched the surface of what could have been presented, but hopefully it has accomplished the stated purpose of giving the reader a better understanding of other religions and how they are connected to modern beliefs and practices. More importantly, hopefully the foregoing has prompted you to not only question why did/do millions of people accept such things as being true but to seek a better understanding of the origin, doctrine, practice and very "truth" of your own beliefs.

Baptism

Or, A Uniquely Christian Rite… Not

"With soap, baptism is a good thing." ~ Robert G. Ingersoll

During a 2002 episode of the popular television series *Sex and the City* entitled *Unoriginal Sin* Miranda's Catholic husband Steve suddenly says, "I was thinking… maybe we'd want to get Brady (their baby) baptized…"

Miranda, who is an atheist, is surprised by that and replies, "Neither of us ever go to church."

He responds, "Yeah, I know that, but it's tradition you know… you know, I was baptized, my father was baptized, my father's father, everybody in my family gets baptized… it's not about religion, it's not about God, it's just something you do in case… so the baby don't end up in… limbo…"

Miranda says, "You don't even know what that means!"

Steve answers, "I do so… it's a place where babies fly around without bodies, just wings under their necks…"

Miranda rolls her eyes and says, "Yeah, that sounds like something we should worry about!"

I should just laugh at that but in the interest of full disclosure must admit I participated in the baptism of my own two daughters. Why? Because it was almost automatic in our Italian-American family. It was simply a reflex, and in retrospect one I regret being a party to.

Christians seem to think the practice of baptism is unique to Christianity, but that is just not the case. There have been many versions of this rite through history in a variety of belief systems, but like most things few people bother to learn about history or facts.

When John the Baptist came to the deserts of Judea "preaching a baptism of repentance for the forgiveness of sins" he apparently met with great success. Matthew 3:5 says, "People went out to him from Jerusalem and all Judea and the whole region of the Jordan. Confessing their sins, they were baptized by him in the Jordan River." Luke 3:7, 21 adds that crowds were coming out to be baptized by him and "when all the people were being baptized, Jesus was baptized too."

The Jewish people to whom John's ministry was directed were familiar with the concepts of repentance and forgiveness of sins even though complete forgiveness was for some reason not possible apart from the shed blood of Christ, but what familiarity did the Jews of the first century have with the practice of baptism?

The New Testament points out the baptism of John was from God, came from Heaven and was administered for the spiritual purpose of proclaiming repentance and receiving forgiveness of sins, but the act of baptism itself has a history beyond the Scriptures.

The Greek word "baptizo" as used in Mark 1:4 ("and so John came, baptizing in the desert region...") was very common among Greek-speaking people, was used in every period of Greek literature and was applied to a great variety of matters including the most familiar acts of everyday life. Greek speakers understood the word at the time John was preaching and it had no doubtful meaning. It meant what we express by the Latin word "immerse" and similar terms, so no one could possibly have attributed to it a different meaning such as "sprinkle" or "pour." *The Encyclopedia of Religion* points out that the word baptism means to plunge, to immerse or to wash and also signifies from the Homeric period onward any rite of immersion in water, and goes on to say the baptismal rite is similar to rituals found in a number of religions.

The practice of baptism in pagan religions seems to have been based on a belief in the purifying properties of water. According to the *Tablets of Maklu* in ancient Babylon water was important as a spiritual cleansing agent in the cult of Enke, lord of Eridu. In Egypt, the *Book of Going Forth by Day* contains a treatise on the baptism of newborn children which was performed to purify them of blemishes acquired in the womb. Water, especially the Nile's cold water which was believed to have regenerative powers, was used to baptize the dead in a ritual based on the Osiris myth. Egyptian cults also developed the idea of regeneration through water. The bath preceding initiation into the cult of Isis seems to have been more than a simple ritual purification. It was probably intended to symbolically represent the initiate's death to the life of this world by recalling Osiris' drowning in the Nile.

In the cult of Cybele a baptism of blood was practiced in the rite of the Taurobolium where one was covered with the blood of a bull. At first this ritual seems to have been to provide the initiate with greater physical vitality, but later it acquired more of a spiritual importance. A well-known inscription attests that he who has received baptism of blood has received a new birth in eternity, however the fact that this baptism was repeated periodically shows the idea of complete spiritual regeneration was not associated with it.

The properties of immortality were also associated with baptism in the ancient Greek world. A bath in the sanctuary of Trophonion procured for the initiate a blessed immortality even while in this world, and the mystery religions of that period often included ablution rites of either immersion or a washing of the body for the purposes of purification or initiation. Other concepts said to have been associated with these forms of cultic baptisms included the transformation of one's life, the removal of sins, symbolic representation, the attainment of greater physical vitality, a new beginning and/or spiritual regeneration. It is believed all ancient religions recognized some form of spiritual cleansing, renewal or initiation accomplished through a washing or immersion in water.

The liturgical use of water was also common in the Jewish world. The Law of Moses required ablutions (washings) on the part of priests following certain sacrifices and on certain individuals who were unclean because of an infectious disease. In fact the natural method of cleansing the body by washing and bathing in water was always customary in Israel, and the washing of their clothes was an important means of sanctification imposed on the Israelites even before the law was given at Mt. Sinai. The use of water for cleansing was used symbolically as well in such passages as Ezekiel 36:25 where God says, "I will sprinkle clean water on you, and you will be clean; I will cleanse you from all your impurities..." It is not believed the practice of baptism for the remission of sins as taught in the New Testament was based on anything in the Old Testament, however the Old Testament washings with or in water which were for the purpose of physical cleansing can be seen as a type of New Testament baptism which is for the purpose of spiritual cleansing.

Toward the beginning of the Christian era the Jews adopted, as a custom unrelated to divine guidance, the custom of baptizing proselytes seven days after their circumcision. A series of specific interrogations made it possible to judge the real intentions of the candidate who wished to adopt the Jewish religion, and after submitting to these interrogations he was circumcised and later baptized before witnesses. In the baptism he was immersed naked in a pool of flowing water, and when he rose from the pool he was a true son of Israel. After their baptism, new converts were then allowed access to the sacrifices in the Temple.

Mormons, for their part, practice a ritual known as the "Baptism of the Dead." Also known as vicarious baptism or proxy baptism, this is the religious practice of baptizing a living person on behalf of an individual who is dead with the living person acting as the deceased person's proxy. It has been practiced since 1840 in the Church of Jesus Christ of Latter-day Saints and is also called temple baptism because it is performed only in dedicated temples.

In practice a proxy is baptized by immersion on behalf of a deceased person of the same gender. During the ritual the person performing the baptism says, "Having been commissioned of Jesus Christ, I baptize you for and in behalf of (full name of deceased person) who is dead, in the name of the Father, and of the Son and of the Holy Ghost. Amen." The proxy is then immersed briefly in water. Baptism for the dead is a distinctive ordinance of the Church and is based on the belief baptism is a required ordinance for entry into the Kingdom of God.

The Church of Jesus Christ of Latter-day Saints vicariously baptizes people regardless of race, sex or creed, including both victims and perpetrators of genocide, and as a result some Jewish survivors of the Holocaust and their supporters have objected to this practice.

In some denominations of the Latter Day Saint movement the "temple garment" (or the Garment of the Holy Priesthood) is a set of sacred underclothing worn by adult adherents who have taken part in a ritual ceremony known as the washing and anointing ordinance, usually in a temple as part of the Endowment ceremony. Adherents consider them to be sacred and may be offended by public discussion of the garments, and not surprisingly anti-Mormon activists have publicly displayed or defaced temple garments to show their opposition to the LDS Church.

According to generally accepted Mormon doctrine the marks in the garments are sacred symbols. One proposed element of the symbolism, according to early Mormon leaders, was a link to the "Compass and the Square," the symbols of freemasonry, to which Mormon founder Joseph Smith had been initiated about seven weeks prior to his introduction of the Endowment ceremony.

Another rite is Kaparot, a traditional Jewish religious ritual which takes place around the time of the High Holidays. Classically, it is performed by grasping a live chicken by the shoulder blades and moving it around one's head three times, symbolically transferring one's sins to the chicken. The chicken is then slaughtered and donated to the poor, preferably to be eaten at the pre-Yom Kippur feast. In modern times Kapparos is performed in the traditional form mostly in Haredi communities, preceded by the reading of Psalms 107:17-20 and Job 33:23-24.

To give this a contemporary perspective, on the eve of Yom Kippur in 2005 more than two hundred caged chickens were abandoned in rainy weather as part of a Kaparot operation in Brooklyn, New York and subsequently some of the starving and dehydrated fowl were rescued by the American Society for the Prevention of Cruelty to Animals. Jacob Kalish, an Orthodox Jew from Williamsburg, was charged with animal cruelty for the drowning deaths of thirty-five of these chickens. In response to such reports of the mistreatment animal rights organizations have begun to picket public observances of Kaparot, particularly in Israel. Sound crazy? Maybe, but certainly not to the practitioners of this particular religious order.

The Golden Rule

Or, What Goes Around Comes Around

"This is the sum of duty. Do not unto others that which would cause you pain if done to you." ~ Mahabharata 5 1517 from the Vedic tradition of India (circa 3000 BCE)

If you want to know what true Christianity is in a moral sense it is not a belief in some sort of mystical creator god but rather adherence to the teachings of Jesus - the good ones, anyway. Thomas Jefferson recognized this when he rejected the superstitions and mysticism of Christianity and went so far as to edit the Gospels by removing the miracles and magic of Jesus in his "Jefferson Bible" and leaving only what he deemed to be his correct moral philosophy. In a similar fashion if you view Jesus as a philosopher and teacher rather than as the "Son of God" who walks on water and rose from the dead a case can be made for the positive nature of Christianity in today's world. Such a view would be like that found in Confucianism, which is an ethical and philosophical system developed from the teachings of the Chinese philosopher Confucius, because while no one has ever claimed him to be a god the wisdom of his teachings remain valid just the same.

The core of Confucianism is Humanism or what philosopher Herbert Fingarette calls "the secular as sacred." Confucianism focuses on the practical, especially the importance of the family rather than a belief in gods or the afterlife, and broadly speaking does not exalt faithfulness to divine will or higher law. This stance rests on the belief that human beings are teachable, improvable and perfectible through personal and communal endeavor, especially self-cultivation and self-creation. In other words Confucian thought focuses on the cultivation of virtue and maintenance of ethics. Some of the basic Confucian ethical concepts and practices include *ren*, *yi*, and *li*. *Ren* is an obligation of altruism and humaneness for other individuals, y*i* is the upholding of righteousness and the moral disposition to do good and *li* is a system of norms and propriety which determines how a person should properly act in everyday life. In short Confucianism is about morality, not divinity, which flies in the face of the Christian apologetic which asks how morality can possibly exist without the guidance of a divine lawgiver.

The ethic of reciprocity or the "Golden Rule" is a fundamental moral value which simply means "treat others as you would like to be treated" and is arguably the most essential basis for the concept of human rights. As Michael Shermer said in *The Science of Good & Evil* "(no one should) find the Golden Rule surprising in any way because at its base lies the foundation of most human interactions and exchanges and it can be found in countless texts throughout recorded history and from around the world - a testimony to its universality."

Do you think Jesus, assuming he existed, was the first to put forth this concept? Think again. One of the earliest examples of the Golden Rule is found in book 15, chapter 23 of the *Analects of Confucius* which were written around 500 BCE, five hundred years before the purported birth of Christ. In it a disciple named Tsze-kung asked, "Is there one word which may serve as a rule of practice for all one's life?" and the Master (Confucius) replied by saying, "Is not 'reciprocity' such a word? What you do not want done to yourself, do not do to others."

This precept is of course similar to the Golden Rule of the Christian Bible as later enunciated in the Sermon on the Mount and reported in Matthew, chapter 7, verse 12, "All things therefore whatsoever you would that men should do to you, do you also to them" and Luke, chapter 6, verse 31, "And as you would that men should do to you, do you also to them in like manner." The concept certainly is not unique to the Bible or even original as many Christians seem to believe. Not by a longshot.

Even before Confucius the Hindu Mahabharata (c. 800 BCE), which is one of the two major Sanskrit epics of ancient India (with the other being the *Ramayana*) and contains the *Bhagavad Gita*, said, "Deal with others as thou wouldst thyself be dealt by. Do nothing to thy neighbor which thou wouldst not have him to thee hereafter." About a hundred years later a Zoroastrian known as Dadistan-I dinik, Zend-Avesta (c. 700 BCE) echoed that sentiment when he opined, "That nature only is good when it shall not do unto another whatever is not good for its own self." Similarly Pittacus of Mytilene (650-570 BCE) said, "Do not that to thy neighbor that thou wouldst not suffer from him," the Buddhist Undana Varga (c. 500 BCE) said, "Hurt not others with that which pains yourself," Aristotle (384-322 BCE) offered, "We should behave to our friends as we would wish our friends to behave to us," the Indian Panchatantra (c. 200 BCE) tells us, "Ponder well the maxim: Never do to other persons what would pain thyself" and Hillel Ha-Babli (c. 200 BCE) in the thirty-first book of *The Sabbath* raised the Golden Rule to the ultimate moral principle when he wrote, "Whatsoever thou wouldst that men should not do to thee, do not that to them. This is the whole law. The rest is only explanation." There are of course more examples, but you get the idea.

Even if the foregoing had not been true other belief systems have adopted similar views and in doing so have diluted the Christian claim to absolute morality vis-à-vis the Golden Rule. For example in Islam number thirteen of Imam Al-Nawawi's Forty Hadiths says, "None of you [truly] believes until he wishes for his brother what he wishes for himself," and even the Wiccan Creed states, "Do what thou will, but harm none."

In an interesting and thought provoking contrast to "the Rule," George Bernard Shaw once commented, "Do not do unto others as you expect they should do unto you, since their tastes may not be the same," which makes sense when placed into the context of, for instance, how one might deal with a masochist who would like to be whipped. Another angle which might be called "mutual altruism" is presented in a scene from the classic Jackie Gleason television show *The Honeymooners* (as quoted in Michael Shermer's *The Science of Good and Evil*) and concerns a couple of baked potatoes:

Ralph: "When she put two potatoes on the table, one big one and one small one, you immediately took the big one without asking me what I wanted."
Norton: "What would you have done?"
Ralph: "I would have taken the small one, of course."
Norton: "You would?"
Ralph: "Yes, I would."
Norton: "So, what are you complaining about? You *got* the small one!"

Clearly the Golden Rule is not unique to Judeo-Christian beliefs, but wait… what about the Ten Commandments? Aren't they the foundation of morality?

Morality

Or, The Ten Suggestions

"The greatest tragedy in mankind's entire history may be the hijacking of morality by religion." ~ Arthur C. Clarke

Bob and Carol only went to church a couple of times per year and as they were leaving their pew the Priest said, "Bob, it sure would be nice to see you and Carol here more than once a year."

"I know Father," replied Bob, "but at least we make it a point to keep the Ten Commandments."

"That's great," the Pastor said. "I'm glad to hear that you keep the Commandments."

"Yep," Bob said proudly, "Carol keeps six of them, and I keep the other four!"

Presumably that means Bob is guilty of six sins and Carol of four. So what exactly is a sin, anyway? It is defined as something you're not supposed to do according to a given set of religious restrictions. They are not necessarily illegal, not necessarily wrong, don't necessarily harm anyone and in fact many can be completely harmless like the thinking of impure thoughts. So why are sins bad? I guess that all depends on whose definition of "bad" you use. For example if you are a Muslim it's sinful to get urine on yourself while the rest of us would not worry about it too much, Buddhists consider skeptical doubt to be a sin and most Christians consider polygamy to be sinful - but not all of them do, because it's common in most of Africa and the East as well as some Mormon sects - so there's no clear yardstick for determining what's sinful and what's not. In other words it depends completely upon the religious context, and outside of that the word "sin" is for all practical purposes meaningless.

Christians in particular consider everyone to be sinful regardless of their performance. They call this "original sin" and it begins at birth because according to the story, Adam and Eve had the gall to eat some fruit and as a result we are all considered guilty by association and are thus fundamentally sinful people.

Some Christians also have to deal with "mortal sins" which, if left unrepented, will send them to Hell when they die. There is no list of which sins guarantee a date with the devil but there are some general rules, and the big ones such as murder and adultery put you on the fast track. It is also important to note that mortal sins must be done deliberately.

Next there are venial sins. If you "forget" to go to church, "accidentally" put on a condom or "unintentionally" ogle an attractive person out of the corner of your eye for a moment you can get away with those, but if you do them deliberately they are mortal sins.

Worst of all is eternal sin, i.e. to deny God, which cannot be forgiven. The punishment is the same as for a mortal sin with the difference being there's no opportunity to be forgiven. In other words according to many Christian doctrines you can murder someone, or even millions of people, repent and be forgiven, but simply deny that for which there is no evidence and you burn forever. Makes perfect sense.

When you eliminate activities which injure others there are still items on the sin list which are essentially victimless "crimes" such as plural marriages, same sex marriages and anyone living together or having sex outside of wedlock. Straight sex between married partners is all right so long as it never extends to include masturbation, fetishism, lust or impure thoughts, and keep in mind the list is not static and has even been updated to include cybersex. None hurt anyone mind you, and if you take them out of a religious context suddenly there's nothing wrong with any of it. Essentially what happened here is a very long time ago someone was personally offended by such things, put it into writing and claimed it came from a "higher power" in order to gain compliance. The point is who is being hurt? Nobody.

A perfect example of a "sin" which harms no one is masturbation. This particular affront to God is based upon the story in Genesis 38 in which Onan "spills his seed," but how does it relate to reality? There is an old joke about a gym teacher asking the one hundred boys in his class to raise their hands if they had ever masturbated, and after a few uncomfortable moments one hand slowly went up. When asked for the results of his survey later that day the teacher replied, "Basically there was one masturbator… and ninety-nine goddam liars." *The Mormon Guide to Self-Control* (yes, they actually have a book for this) instructs, "When the temptation to masturbate is strong, yell 'Stop!' to those thoughts as loudly as you can in your mind. Then recite a portion of the Bible or sing a hymn." The Catholic teaching on masturbation says that "Masturbation is a grave (i.e. mortal) sin, by which we reject God's offer of life." As previously mentioned the biblical story of Onan is traditionally linked to masturbation and condemnation thereof, but the act described is actually coitus interruptus, not masturbation. There is no explicit claim in the Bible that masturbation would be sinful, although Leviticus 15 states that any male having a "flow" is ceremonially defiled, must cleanse himself with water and then in the evening begin to count a period of seven days after which he must wash in water again and then bring two pigeons or doves to the priests on the 8th day who will make the sacrifice for him. This "flow" refers to ejaculation of semen, whether through masturbation or nocturnal emission, however verse 3 states he is rendered unclean even if the flow is "blocked," i.e. even if he stops short of ejaculation. Like any of that ever happens. It is clear there is nothing to be gained by heaping guilt on little boys for a purely natural act, but a case certainly can be made for the harm it causes. Perhaps if the practice were encouraged rather than condemned child molestation by priests seeking to satisfy their biological urges would not be quite so common. And what about women? As usual females are all but forgotten by the Bible, almost as if they do not exist. A 2008 *Gossard* Big M Survey which interviewed one thousand women ages eighteen to thirty revealed that ninety-two percent of those women masturbate regularly, but the Bible is silent about how God views that.

Idolatry is yet another sin, and it doesn't necessarily relate to graven images or statues of other gods. It is the practice of loving anything or anyone more than you love God, and that includes your kids. In fact in Luke 14:26 Jesus says, "If any man come to me, and hate not his father, and mother, and wife, and children, and brethren, and sisters, yea, and his own life also, he cannot be my disciple" and in Matthew 10:37 he proclaims, "Anyone who loves their father or mother more than me is not worthy of me; anyone who loves their son or daughter more than me is not worthy of me." Talk about an inferiority complex.

Then there is lying, aka "bearing false witness," and I don't know how anyone can claim they don't practice this sin every day no matter how pious they are. Have you ever told someone you could not go somewhere or do something when the truth was you simply didn't want to? Have you ever stopped talking about someone when they entered the room to deceive them into thinking you weren't doing so? Have you ever given someone you do not particularly like a fake smile when you pass them in the hall as if seeing them makes you happy? And what response will you give to the question "do I look fat in this dress" when it is asked by a corpulent loved one? All of those things make you a liar. You see lies don't have to be spoken and are usually not malicious, but they are lies nonetheless.

Not content with the definitions of sin found in the Bible, the church developed a list which became known as the "Seven Deadly Sins." In the Book of Proverbs 6:16-19, among the verses traditionally associated with King Solomon, it states the Lord specifically regards "six things the Lord hateth, and seven that are an abomination unto Him" and another list, given this time in the Epistle to the Galatians (Galatians 5:19-21) which includes more of the traditional seven sins although it is substantially longer: adultery, fornication, uncleanness, lasciviousness, idolatry, sorcery, hatred, variance, emulations, wrath, strife, seditions, heresies, envyings, murders, drunkenness, revelings "and such like" - which can be interpreted to mean whatever you'd like it to - and Paul goes on to say persons who practice these sins "shall not inherit the Kingdom of God," so they are usually listed as possible mortal sins rather than capital vices.

The modern concept of the seven deadly sins is linked to the works of 4th Century monk Evagrius Ponticus who listed eight evil thoughts in Greek: gluttony, prostitution/fornication, avarice, hubris (rendered as self-esteem), sadness (rendered as envy, i.e. sadness at another's good fortune), wrath, boasting and acedia (rendered as dejection). These were translated into the Latin of Western Christianity largely due to the writings of John Cassian and thus became part of the Western traditions' spiritual pietas (Catholic devotions) as follows: gluttony, fornication/ lust, avarice/greed, hubris/pride, sorrow/despair/despondency, wrath, vainglory (vanity) and sloth.

In 590 CE, a little over two centuries after Evagrius wrote his list, Pope Gregory I revised it to form the more commonly known "Seven Deadly Sins" by folding sorrow/despair/despondency into acedia, vainglory into pride and adding envy. In the order used by the Pope and repeated by Dante Alighieri centuries later in his epic poem *The Divine Comedy* the seven deadly sins are as follows: lechery/lust, gluttony, avarice/greed, sloth/discouragement, wrath, envy and pride. The identification and definition of the seven sins over their history has been a fluid process and the idea of what each of the seven actually encompasses has evolved over time, which is not what you would expect if these were directives emanating from a perfect, divine being.

The modern Catholic Catechism now lists the sins as pride, avarice, envy, wrath, lust, gluttony and sloth and each of them now also has an opposite among the corresponding seven holy virtues - sometimes also referred to as the "contrary virtues." The seven virtues are actually the union of two sets of virtues with the four cardinal virtues coming from ancient Greek philosophy and including prudence, justice, temperance (or restraint) and courage (or fortitude) and the three theological virtues of faith, hope and charity (or love) from the letters of St. Paul of Tarsus. These were adopted by the Church as the Seven Virtues.

The first virtues were identified not by Christians but by the Greek philosophers Aristotle and Plato who regarded temperance, wisdom, justice and courage as the four most desirable character traits, but after the New Testament was written these four virtues were assimilated and became known as the cardinal virtues. As is so often the case we find a Christian tradition with its roots in Pagan beliefs.

Let's look at that core set of behaviors and ethics which governs the way we conduct ourselves and live our lives, what is known as our "moral center" or "moral compass." A common generalization made by some religious people is the non-religious among us lack a moral center and faith is necessary to develop one. The implication is religious beliefs play an important role in the development of a normal, healthy system of ethics and personal conduct and without it one cannot be a moral person. Put another way, they say without belief in a higher power there is nothing to stop someone from committing all manner of atrocities.

With that in mind, how would you view someone who lived their life according to a set of tenets which says they should strive to act with compassion and empathy towards all creatures in accordance with reason, the freedoms of others should be respected (and) to willfully and unjustly encroach upon the freedoms of another is to forgo their own, and if they make a mistake they should do their best to rectify it and resolve any harm that may have been caused? Sounds pretty reasonable, don't you think? Absolutely, at least until you find out those principles are tenets of the Satanic Temple.

Is religion necessary to develop a good moral center? Before we can answer that we must as usual define which religion we are talking about because everyone tends to think strictly in terms of their own beliefs. Let's begin by comparing moral centers to see where these supposed differences lie. First of all you probably find most non-believers you know personally to be upstanding people like yourself, and in fact you probably don't even realize who some of them are. Like most people they are generally honest, don't cheat people in business, steal or commit crimes worse than speeding on the freeway. They do lie all the time however, but only when it is helpful such as telling the wife, "Yes dear, you look *great* in that dress." They also have a clear sense of right and wrong, i.e. they understand behavior which injures someone else is wrong and most avoid doing that whenever possible, and if for example they see a complete stranger drop his wallet they will probably return it.

When a non-believer sees an elderly woman they don't run over, punch her in the face and steal her purse and neither do most religious people, and it should be noted no religious person ever says, "I would love to punch out that old woman but the only thing stopping me is my belief in God." No sane person is going to do something like that because it is so obviously wrong to us all. The lesson here is rarely if ever does a generally good person, and remember that's most of us, need religious commandments to stop them from doing something which is considered wrong by society at large. In summary, the moral center of a religious person is essentially the same as that of a non-religious person and is derived from the basic goodness of human nature, societal norms and the sense of right and wrong which is universally shared by all people. It does not stem from having read any particular set of religious commandments or from fear of punishment by a deity.

A common retort from religious people is God gave us all those things intrinsically, i.e. he "wrote a sense of right and wrong on our hearts." If that is so and everyone, atheists included, have been gifted with all the fundamentals needed to develop a moral center then religious faith is superfluous when it comes to the question of morality. It also makes it difficult to explain the existence of people like Hitler and Jeffrey Dahmer. Did God neglect to write on their hearts? Or perhaps his handwriting was just illegible.

In the previous chapter the fallacy of believing the Golden Rule to be a moral tenet unique to Christianity, let alone the notion it was an original idea attributable to Jesus, was demonstrated to be incorrect so let's now go down a different path. Many Christians claim their morality is derived from the Ten Commandments and in fact often protest outside of courthouses to object to the removal of monuments containing them, but there are a few problems with this school of thought.

According to the story in Exodus Moses smashed the first set of tablets in a fit of anger because the Israelites chose to worship the golden calf and as a result God said he'd make a new set containing "the words that were on the first" (Exodus 34:1), however the second set of Commandments in no way resembles the first so when someone says they want to place the Commandments in a school or courthouse they need to specify which ones they are referring to - although of course most people, having never read the Bible, are unaware of the other set.

Let's have a look at that second set. I wonder how many people are familiar with Commandments such as, "The feast of unleavened bread shalt thou keep in the month when the ear is on the corn?" How about, "All the first-born are mine?" Does "Thou shalt not offer the blood of my sacrifice with leavened bread" ring a bell, and what exactly is the point of "The fat of my feast shall not remain all night until the morning?" And what about that cornerstone of morality, "Thou shalt not seethe (boil) a kid in its mother's milk?" It seems to be one of the most effective since I have never once heard of someone doing that, unlike the prohibitions against theft and murder which are ignored every day. Is it any wonder nobody ever mentions these Commandments? But they are there.

As we have seen there are multiple sets of Commandments in Scripture, and even those are listed and interpreted differently by different religions. Although the Protestant, Catholic and Hebrew Bibles vary but slightly and then only textually, not all religions which accept the Commandments as the revealed words of God condense them in the same manner or interpret them the same way. They are arranged to suit the exigencies of the particular creed and to fit the ritual of the particular form of worship. We are told by religious leaders the Bible is the inspired word of God and man must not presume to pit his finite intelligence against it, yet that is exactly what religionists have done with so important a part of the Bible as the Commandments - God's supposed words, written with his own finger. If there is any place where perfect accord should exist in biblical matters among the sects it should be in the Decalogue because if they do not agree about the only message God is supposed to have delivered himself how can we expect to find them in agreement on matters about which they admit there exists much doubt and speculation?

As an example of how they differ, in the First Commandment the words "I am the Lord thy God, who brought thee out of the land of Egypt, out of the house of bondage" is left out of the Protestant account completely, is partially omitted from the Catholic version and forms the First Commandment according to the Hebrews. In the Catholic and Protestant versions the reference to being "brought out of the land of Egypt, out of the house of bondage" was left out because that part of the Commandment has absolutely nothing to do with Protestants or Catholics because when the Commandments were written they were not yet in existence. They were never in Egypt, the Lord had no occasion to free them from the yoke of bondage and by this very omission the Ten Commandments are stamped as a purely provincial code applicable, if at all, only to the Children of Israel. In this respect both Catholics and Protestants have judiciously, yet deceitfully, refrained from using it despite the fact it is part of the Decalogue. In wording this Commandment, however, the Catholics were more clever than the Protestants as they used the first five words of the Commandment but left out the succeeding damaging phrase and added, though in a corrupted form, the first part of the Second Commandment while the Protestants, unable to use the First Commandment as biblically recorded, have daringly taken the first sentence of the Second Commandment as the first one in their arrangement of the Decalogue. So much for the perfect and immutable word of God.

Now that you get the idea of how this works let's look at some other abbreviated and sanitized examples such as the familiar "Thou shalt not covet." What it actually says is, "Thou shalt not covet thy neighbor's house, thou shalt not covet thy neighbor's wife, nor his manservant, nor his maidservant, nor his ox, nor his ass, nor any thing that is thy neighbor's." There are three problems here. First of all the abbreviated version leaves out things like manservant, maidservant, ox and ass because they sound ridiculous in the modern age and open the Commandments up to ridicule and dismissal. Second, why bother to list specific things like ox and ass when "any thing that is thy neighbor's" covers it all? And finally why would coveting, which is essentially nothing more than a thought crime, be considered a sin at all let alone make it into the top ten? It makes no sense.

It must also be pointed out the first four Commandments have absolutely nothing to do with morality and everything to do with the insecurity of the deity. What exactly do "I am the Lord your God… you shall have no other gods before me, you shall not make for yourself a graven image, you shall not take the name of the Lord your God in vain and remember the Sabbath day to keep it holy" have to do with morality? Not a thing, but they do make one wonder why the creator of the universe would be so insecure. If the Commandments are indeed the foundation of our secular laws as fundamentalists claim should working on Sunday or being a Hindu or muttering "goddamit!" when you accidentally hit your thumb with a hammer be written into our penal code and punishable with jail time? I certainly hope not. This is just one more example of cherry picking. Even an evangelical Christian such as columnist Cal Thomas understands this saying, "Christians claim American law is based on the Ten Commandments. All of them? There are only two that relate to secular law (not counting the one about adultery). One prohibits murder, the other outlaws stealing. The rest are about relationships between God and man and between humans. Do the protesters want laws that force people to honor their mothers and fathers or not 'covet' their neighbor's property or 'honor the Sabbath day and keep it holy' or worship only their God?"

We have already discussed how coveting is a thought crime so let's move on to the one which tells you to honor your father and your mother, something which opens up a whole can of worms. It goes without saying many parents abandon and abuse their children every single day and yet here is the creator of the universe issuing a Commandment - meaning it is not optional - which requires battered, abandoned and sexually abused children to honor those who do not deserve it. Again, it makes no sense.

Another obvious shortcoming of the so-called bedrock of Christian morality is not what the Commandments say but what they don't. If you were tasked with creating a law of moral conduct and had to limit yourself to ten for some reason would you waste space with "no graven images" and "keep the Sabbath" or replace them with "do not rape" and "do not molest children"? If your answer is to point out there are many other biblical laws to cover such things you have painted yourself into a corner, something covered in detail in the following chapter.

So what did Jesus have to say on the subject in the New Testament? In Matthew 19:18-19 he says in response to the Pharisees' question about which laws to obey after he instructed them to keep the Commandments, "Thou shalt do no murder, thou shalt not commit adultery, thou shalt not steal, thou shalt not bear false witness, honour thy father and thy mother and thou shalt love thy neighbour as thyself." That's right, Jesus' list has only six and the sixth is not even one of the original ten. Plus the Commandments recited by Jesus are all secular rather than religious in nature.

In his book *Letter to a Christian Nation* Sam Harris wrote, "If you think it would be impossible to improve upon the Ten Commandments as a statement of morality you really owe it to yourself to read some other Scriptures. Once again, we need look no further than the Jains. Mahavira, the Jain patriarch, surpassed the morality of the Bible with a single sentence: 'Do not injure, abuse, oppress, enslave, insult, torment, torture, or kill any creature or living being.' Imagine how different our world might be if the Bible contained this as its central precept. Christians have abused, oppressed, enslaved, insulted, tormented, tortured, and killed people in the name of God for centuries, on the basis of a theologically defensible reading of the Bible."

He makes an excellent point. Ironically, the first thing Moses did after coming down from the mount and finding his people dancing around a golden statue of Ba'al was order brother to kill brother, thus violating the Commandment not to kill. In Exodus we find, "Then Moses stood in the gate of the camp and said, 'Whoever is for the LORD, come to me!' And all the sons of Levi gathered together to him. He said to them, 'Thus says the LORD, the God of Israel, every man of you put his sword upon his thigh, and go back and forth from gate to gate in the camp, and kill every man his brother, and every man his friend, and every man his neighbor.' So the sons of Levi did as Moses instructed, and about three thousand men of the people fell that day."

Modern Christian apologists will explain the Commandments actually say not to murder (a fairly recent interpolation) and will point out any act directed by God, even one which contradicts his own directive, would be correct, but the paradox remains nevertheless. It is basically a case of God saying (through Moses, naturally), "Never mind what I told you… I'm telling you!" Talk about rationalization.

The Ten Commandments are not even unique. Hammurabi was the ruler who chiefly established the greatness of Babylon, the world's first metropolis. Many relics of his reign (1795-1750 BCE) have been preserved, and today we can study this remarkable king as a wise law-giver through the celebrated code known as *The Code of Hammurabi.*

By far the most remarkable of the Hammurabi records is his code of laws, the earliest-known example of a ruler proclaiming publicly to his people an entire body of laws arranged in orderly groups so that all men might read and know what was required of them. The Code was carved upon a black stone monument which was eight feet high and clearly intended to be read in public view and unlike the mythical tablets of the Ten Commandments this stone was actually found in the year 1901, although not in Babylon but a city in the Persian mountains to which some later conqueror must have carried it in triumph. It begins and ends with addresses to the gods since in those days even a law code was regarded as a subject for prayer, although the prayers here are chiefly cursings of whoever shall neglect or destroy the law.

The Code then regulates in clear and definite strokes the organization of society. The judge who blunders in a law case is to be expelled from his judgeship forever and heavily fined. The witness who testifies falsely (i.e. bears false witness) is to be slain. Indeed, all of the heavier crimes are made punishable by death. Even if a man builds a house badly and it falls and kills the owner the builder is to be slain. If the owner's son was killed then the builder's son is slain. We can certainly see where the Hebrews learned their practice of "an eye for an eye." These grim retaliatory punishments take no note of excuses or explanations but only of fact, with one striking exception. An accused person was allowed to "cast himself into the river," i.e. the Euphrates. Apparently the art of swimming was then unknown, for if the current bore him to the shore alive he was declared innocent but if he drowned he was guilty. So we learn from this that faith in the justice of the ruling gods was already firmly, although somewhat childishly, established in the minds of men.

The actual Code begins, "When Anu the Sublime, King of the Anunaki, and Bel, the lord of Heaven and earth, who decreed the fate of the land, assigned to Marduk, the over-ruling son of Ea, God of righteousness, dominion over earthly man, and made him great among the Igigi, they called Babylon by his illustrious name, made it great on earth, and founded an everlasting kingdom in it, whose foundations are laid so solidly as those of Heaven and Earth; then Anu and Bel called by name me, Hammurabi, the exalted prince, who feared God, to bring about the rule of righteousness in the land, to destroy the wicked and the evil-doers; so that the strong should not harm the weak; so that I should rule over the black-headed people like Shamash, and enlighten the land, to further the well-being of mankind." 282 laws follow, many of which are not unlike the 613 Mosaic Laws contained in the Bible, so as you can see the concept of divine laws given by a god are not unique to the Abrahamic faiths.

Many religious people will use the logic that God must exist because without him a man cannot know for himself what is good and what is evil. They believe without God there can be no good or evil and any behavior is just as good as any other. That logic is of course demonstrably false, since people of all cultures and religions have been deciding what is good and what is evil for thousands of years. It also ignores the fact that the overwhelming majority of our prison population is comprised of Christian inmates. And while we are on the subject, it must be pointed out that according to Isaiah 45:7 and Proverbs 16:4, God intentionally invented evil. Why?

Getting back to the Ten Commandments, once we have discarded those which concern God's self-esteem, the thought crime of coveting and the nonsensical admonition to honor parents regardless of how they act, what are we left with? Next comes the prohibition against bearing false witness, i.e. lying, and it comes with its own set of paradoxes. First of all as was mentioned earlier lying in some form is a part of life, everyone does it and in fact it is not against the law with the exception of perjury while under oath and in certain transactions. What if you were hiding a Jewish family from the Nazis during the 1940s and were questioned by the Gestapo? Would you tell the truth or lie to protect them, and in doing so violate God's directive? Keep in mind there is no caveat such as, "Thou shalt not bear false witness, unless it is for a noble purpose." Finally there is the prohibition against committing adultery. According to the Bible that one is virtually impossible to keep because in Matthew 5:27-28 Jesus states, "You have heard that it was said, 'Do not commit adultery.' But I tell you that anyone who looks at a woman lustfully has already committed adultery with her in his heart." Once again what we have here is a thought crime, and it should also be pointed out that not a word is said about someone looking at a man lustfully. Why the omission and double standard?

So now we get down to the only Commandments which have any bearing on or resemblance to secular laws, killing and stealing. Let's start with a question everyone understands: is murder good or evil? Forget about God and answer using your own common sense. Is it right or wrong? Obviously it is wrong. We all know that, including the murderers amongst us, with the exception of the insane. So how and why do we know it is wrong? We simply look inside ourselves and ask, "Do I want to be murdered?" The answer is, "Of course not." It is so obvious. Life is the most precious thing each of us possesses because we understand without it we do not exist.

We live in a society, are all in this together and by protecting the right of others to live their lives free from the threat of murder you protect yourself as well. By working together to protect everyone we improve our own lives. "Thou shalt not murder other human beings" is a Commandment *we* effectively created to project this universal truth and we enforce it with laws, police departments and courts of our peers which we have created to protect ourselves and each other. In the words of the Dalai Lama, "I am convinced that everyone can develop a good heart and a sense of universal responsibility, with or without religion."

It is interesting to note, "Thou shalt not murder other human beings" is not what the Bible says. The Sixth Commandment is actually, "Thou shalt not kill/murder," so strictly speaking it is much broader. When we eat meat we are killing. When people sacrificed animals as God prescribed in the Old Testament those animals were killed. Cutting down a tree for lumber kills the tree. In fact spraying Lysol kills millions of germs. Nevertheless the vast majority of us understand the universal truth that murder of another human being is wrong.

We also understand there are valid exceptions to the Commandment. We can see situations involving a greater good and reason them out, for example if someone attacks you and tries to kill you it is okay to kill that person in self-defense if necessary because we have the right to defend our own lives. We understand it at the societal level as well. If a person has been in a car wreck and is brain dead but still technically "alive" we could keep that person alive indefinitely with a ventilator and feeding tube, but knowing the person will never recover we can decide the higher good is to turn off the ventilator and donate the person's organs to others. Technically we have murdered the person as defined in the Bible, but most people understand it is okay.

What about stealing? It works in exactly the same way. You don't need God to know stealing is wrong. You simply ask yourself, "Do I want to have my possessions stolen from me?" Obviously not, therefore you do not steal from others because you don't want to be stolen from either. Stealing is wrong, but once again there is a paradox which in not addressed in this Commandment. What if a mother steals an apple from someone else's tree to feed her starving child? Consider Victor Hugo's masterwork *Les Miserables* in which peasant Jean Valjean is imprisoned for five years for the crime of stealing a loaf of bread for his starving sister and her family. Shouldn't Scripture be just a bit more explicit about such things?

Even when the Bible tells us something is okay our minds and humanity tell us objectively and with moral authority it is wrong. For example it says slavery is acceptable, something which is discussed in another chapter. Even so, do we allow slavery today? Of course not. Any decent human being should agree slavery is morally wrong because we only need ask ourselves, "Would I like to be a slave?" The answer is no, and we extrapolate that obvious conclusion to apply to others so therefore slavery is wrong. "Thou shalt not enslave others" should in fact be a Commandment, but it's not. In the United States and other developed nations we override the Bible, the "perfect word" of the Lord, without hesitation because we know slavery is wrong. Clearly human beings define goodness, not God. We do not need God to act as a moral authority. It is simple for human beings to figure out right and wrong. We do it all the time, and that is where our legal system comes from.

Ninety-nine percent of the people in this country can agree murder and slavery are wrong including Hindus, Buddhists and atheists for the obvious reason no one wants to be murdered or enslaved themselves. Consider the *Wiccan Rede* (the word "Rede" derives from Middle English meaning "advice" or "counsel"), the statement which provides the key moral system in the Neopagan religion of Wicca and certain other related witchcraft-based faiths. A common form of the *Rede* simply says, "An it harm none, do what ye will." While I am certainly not endorsing the underlying mystical beliefs of such a system, that makes far more sense than the guilt-ridden victimless crimes and thought crimes associated with the Abrahamic faiths.

These concepts are important because they allow good people to live their lives in peace and happiness. We understand that when evil people kill, enslave or steal they adversely affect everyone else. These common sense concepts are the foundation of our legal system, and from that foundation we derive thousands of specific legal concepts such as first and second degree murder, manslaughter, vehicular homicide, armed robbery, medical malpractice, product safety laws and so on. These manmade concepts are far more sophisticated that what is detailed in any religious Scripture.

What makes Christian beliefs about morality even more bizarre is many denominations, most notably Catholics (although Protestants, Mormons, Jews and even Muslims have a variation on the practice) have built a loophole known as "confession" into their system of divine judgment. If someone sins all they need do is privately confess to the wrongdoing in order to, for the most part, be let off the hook. In the movie *The Godfather* Michael Corleone's thugs are out murdering the heads of the five families on his orders while he is in church attending the baptism of his godchild and all he must do to remove that hypocrisy from the books and have a clear conscience is make a quick visit to the confessional. Remember when evangelist Jimmy Swaggart famously and tearfully confessed his sins publicly? Now he is back in the televangelism business and feels he is "square with God." That is exactly how it works. Can you imagine if secular laws and courts operated the same way and all that was required to have the charges against you dismissed was to admit you had committed the crime? Wouldn't make much sense, would it? And yet some fundamentalists still think the Bible and Christian dogma are the keys to moral behavior.

Former Vice-Presidential candidate Sarah Palin once said we must "Go back to what our Founders and our founding documents meant - they're quite clear - that we would create law based on the God of the Bible and the Ten Commandments…" but if you contrast that with what

Founding Father Thomas Jefferson himself actually wrote in a letter to Major John Cartwright, "...the common law existed while the Anglo-Saxons were yet pagans, at a time when they had never yet heard the name of Christ pronounced or knew that such a character existed," it tells a much different story. In fact Jefferson had earlier stated in a letter to Thomas Law, "If we did a good act merely from the love of God and a belief that it is pleasing to Him, whence arises the morality of the Atheist? It is idle to say, as some do, that no such thing exists. We have the same evidence of the fact as of most of those we act on, to wit: their own affirmations, and their reasonings in support of them. I have observed, indeed, generally, that while in Protestant countries the defections from the Platonic Christianity of the priests is to Deism, in Catholic countries they are to Atheism. Diderot, D'Alembert, D'Holbach, Condorcet are known to have been among the most virtuous of men. Their virtue, then, must have had some other foundation than love of God." That same rationale was expressed again much later by Albert Einstein when he observed, "A man's ethical behavior should be based effectually on sympathy, education, and social ties; no religious basis is necessary. Man would indeed be in a poor way if he had to be restrained by fear of punishment and hope of reward after death."

So what do Christians think happens to virtuous non-Christians when they die? Consider the case of Mahatma (meaning "high-souled") Mohandas Gandhi, who was the preeminent leader of the Indian independence movement in British-ruled India. He employed nonviolent civil disobedience to lead India to independence and inspired civil rights movements and freedom across the world, but given that Gandhi didn't accept Christ and everyone who doesn't do so is said to go to Hell after they die, did he go there? It's almost universally accepted Gandhi was a good person because he advocated non-violent pacifist protests. He lived what he believed. Thus, God must have welcomed him into Heaven upon the shedding of his mortal coil because he was so Christ-like, even if he wasn't Christian. He even said he liked and admired Christ, in spite of all the un-Christlike Christians he knew. An all-loving God wouldn't condemn such a good and holy person to Hell, would he? That just seems so unfair, since according to most Christian doctrine even Hitler is in Heaven provided he accepted Jesus and confessed his sins.

This is known as the paradox of the virtuous pagan and it forces many Christians to become so uncomfortable they have no choice but to equivocate. Different denominations have dealt with the paradox in different ways, and while some certainly will and do say Gandhi is burning in Hell as punishment for his disbelief a common "solution" is to invent some sort of limbo from which the virtuous pagan can be eventually saved. The idea is they do enter Heaven, but a lesser version or at a later time. Christian universalists will say Christ died for the salvation of everyone in the world, regardless of any voluntary or symbolic acceptance of Christian doctrine, and therefore a virtuous pagan goes directly to Heaven like everyone else. Catholics will say, based on an idea of Thomas Aquinas, virtuous pagans go to limbo until Christ intervenes to liberate them. Methodists, Anglicans, Episcopalians and Lutherans will say human beings are justified by faith, Jesus acts as judge, he judges with compassion and so people who reject him are only at risk of being "separated from God." Baptists and non-denominational evangelicals don't even bother to try to answer the question and will say the fate of virtuous pagans is not just unknown, but also unknowable. Mormons will say a virtuous pagan like Gandhi can be posthumously baptized and accept Christianity in the spirit world. As usual, there is a lack of agreement amongst Christians.

The truth is the concept of sin has no place in the lives of intelligent adults in modern society. As Sigmund Freud observed in *Civilization and Its Discontents,* "The different religions have never overlooked the part played by the sense of guilt in civilization. What is more, they come forward with a claim... to save mankind from this sense of guilt, which they call sin." Author and Recipient of the Presidential Medal of Freedom Eric Hoffer phrased the same sentiment a bit differently when he remarked, "The aim of a religious movement is to inflict a malady in society (sin), and then offer religion as a cure."

God's Laws

Or, That's in the OLD Testament

"Do not think that I have come to abolish the Law or the Prophets; I have not come to abolish them but to fulfill them." ~ Jesus (Matt 5:17-18)

In September of 2014 a thirty-seven-year-old man named Mohsen Amir-Aslani was executed in Iran after being found guilty of heresy and insulting the prophet Jonah. He was hanged for making "innovations in the religion" and "spreading corruption on earth" by providing his own interpretations of the Islamic holy book the Quran and interpreting Jonah's story as a symbolic tale. Clearly, Iranian authorities are sensitive towards those practicing Islam in ways not conforming to the official line and in recent years several members of Iran's Gonabadi "dervishes" religious minority have been arrested and are currently serving lengthy prison terms. Such is the nature of Sharia.

Sharia law (meaning "way" or "path") is the law of Islam which is cast from the actions and words of Muhammad known as "Sunnah" and the Quran which he authored. Sharia *literally* means "religious code of life" and it is used to refer both to the Islamic system of law and the totality of the Islamic way of life. Traditional Muslims, meaning mullahs, Mawlanas, Muftis and Islamic scholars who understand the Quran and Hadith, believe Sharia expresses the highest and best goals for all societies on Earth because it is the "Law of Allah." Because of this ardent belief, devout Muslims all over the world are in a constant struggle known as Jihad with their governments to establish Islamic Sharia as the country's only rule by replacing modern secular democracy - i.e. laws made by humans.

"Sharia" in all four Madhabs (schools of thought) is essentially the same with the principal sources being the Quran, Hadiths and Sunnah (the sayings, practices and teachings of the Prophet Muhammed) and the secondary sources consisting of Ijma (consensus), Kiyas (analogy), Ijtihad (responsible individual opinion) and Istihsan (Juristic references).

There are four main schools of Sharia. "Hanbali" is the most conservative and is used in Saudi Arabia and some states in Northern Nigeria, "Maliki" is based on the practices of the people of Medina during Muhammad's lifetime, "Shafi'i" is a conservative school which emphasizes the opinions of the companions of the Prophet Muhammad and "Hanifi" is the most liberal school and relatively open to some limited modern ideas since the interpretation of the Sharia, called "figh," gives imams some leeway - however Sharia itself cannot be altered because God's laws are immutable and hence can never be altered or amended by any means. Sharia law has been adopted in various forms by many countries ranging from a strict interpretation in Saudi Arabia, Iran, northern states of Nigeria, Sudan and al-Qaeda occupied Somalia to a relatively liberal interpretation in much of Malaysia, Pakistan, Bahrain, Yemen and the United Arab Emirates.

As a legal system Sharia covers a very wide range of topics. While other legal codes deal primarily with public behavior, Sharia covers not only public and private behavior but private beliefs as well. For example while theft is punishable by amputation of the right hand, criticizing or denying any part of the Quran or denying Muhammad as the one true prophet is punishable by death. A man can marry an infant girl and consummate the marriage when she is nine years old. A woman can have one husband, but a man can have up to four wives. A man can beat his wife for insubordination. The testimonies of four male witnesses are required to prove the rape of a woman, and a woman who has been raped cannot testify in court against her rapist(s). A woman cannot drive a car, as it leads to fitnah (upheaval). Meat must come from animals which have been sacrificed to Allah - i.e., be "Halal."

Muslims are taught they should engage in "Taqiyya" (Islamic deception) and lie to non-Muslims to advance Islam because the faith permits the devout to lie, cheat and deliberately bluff non-Muslims to protect or promote the religion of Islam anytime and anywhere. That is not all that dissimilar from a statement made by Martin Luther in which he rationalized, "What harm would it do, if a man told a good strong lie for the sake of the good and for the Christian church... a lie out of necessity, a useful lie, a helpful lie, such lies would not be against God, he would accept them." Some people question the accuracy of that quote, but there is little doubt Emperor Constantine's Bishop Eusebius of Caesarea said, "How it may be lawful and fitting to use falsehood as a medicine, and for the benefit of those who want to be deceived." It seems Islam and Christianity are not so different after all.

So how does Sharia compare to the Mosiac Laws found in the Bible? Jewish tradition holds that there are 613 laws in the Torah (a word which literally means Law), and they are not all that different from what we find in Islam. For example which holy book do you think says if anyone, even your own family, suggests worshipping another God, kill them, if you find out a city worships a different god destroy the city and kill all of its inhabitants including the animals, and you are required to kill anyone of a different religion? If you said those directives are from the Quran you would be wrong, because they are actually found in the Bible in Deuteronomy 13:6-10, 13:12-15 and 17:2-7 respectively.

Leviticus 19:19 says don't plant a variety of crops in the same field or wear clothes made of more than one fabric and Leviticus 19:27 says don't cut your hair nor shave, all under penalty of death. In addition, according to Leviticus 20:9 any person who curses his mother or father must be killed. If a man cheats on his wife or vice versa, both the man and the woman must die per Leviticus 20:10. Leviticus 20:11 tells us if a man sleeps with his father's wife both he and his father's wife are to be put to death, although for some reason there is no such prohibition against a woman sleeping with her mother's husband. Leviticus 20:14 explains if a man sleeps with his wife and her mother they are all to be burnt to death. Leviticus 20:15-16 directs if a man or woman has sex with an animal both human and animal must be killed, even though the innocent animal obviously had no say in the matter. If a man has sex with a woman on her period they are both to be "cut off from their people" according to Leviticus 20:18, and if a priest's daughter is a whore she is to be burnt at the stake in accordance with Leviticus 21:9. Even the natural process of menstruation is considered to be "unclean" since Leviticus 15:19-20 explains, "When a woman has a discharge of blood, which is her regular discharge from her body, she shall be in her impurity for seven days, and whoever touches her shall be unclean until evening." In case the Bible's language is a too coy for you, whenever a woman has her period she becomes impure and whatever she sits or lies on during those seven days is also impure therefore anyone who sits where she has sat becomes impure by association. Leviticus 20:27 directs psychics, wizards and so on are to be stoned to death, but provides no guidance on how to identify who they are. Leviticus 21:17-18 bans people who have flat noses or are blind or lame from approaching an altar of God, even though he was presumably the one who made them that way in the first place. Anyone who curses or blasphemes God should be stoned to death by the community as Leviticus 24:14-16 says, and Leviticus 19:19 prohibits the heinous crime of letting cattle graze with other kinds of cattle. What about Deuteronomy 25:11-12 which says, "When men fight with one another, and the wife of the one draws near to rescue her husband from the hand of him who is beating him, and puts out her hand and seizes him by the private parts, then you shall cut off her hand." Yes, you read that right. If you're getting your butt kicked by another guy and your wife grabs your opponent's testicles to help you out she gets her hand cut off. Then there is Deuteronomy 13:5 which says anyone who dreams or prophesizes anything which is against God or anyone who tries to turn you from God is to be put to death. The dream police? Really? Not exactly an endorsement of the concept of free will, is it?

The killing of homosexuals is condoned and encouraged in Leviticus 20:13 which clearly states, "If a man also lie with mankind, as he lieth with a woman, both of them have committed an abomination: they shall surely be put to death; their blood shall be upon them," a directive which has been embraced not only by the almost universally reviled Westboro Baptist Church but also by mainstream stalwarts of the Religious Right such as Jerry Falwell who said, "AIDS is not just God's punishment for homosexuals, it is God's punishment for the society that tolerates homosexuals" and Mother Teresa who claimed, "It (AIDS) is a just retribution for improper sexual misconduct." As misguided as those statements are, far worse words were spoken by fundamentalist segregationist J. B. Stoner when he uttered the words, "We had lost the fight for the preservation of the white race until God himself intervened in earthly affairs with AIDS to rescue and preserve the white race that he had created... I praise God all the time for AIDS." While those words are clearly hateful and despicable they are also rendered nonsensical when you consider not everyone who gets AIDS is gay, not all gays get the disease and innocent babies are born with it.

There are obviously some big problems with the Mosiac laws and there are several ways Christians deal with them. Many fundamentalists actually still follow them as best they can today, taking Jesus at his word when he purportedly said, "For truly I tell you, until Heaven and Earth disappear, not the smallest letter, not the least stroke of a pen, will by any means disappear from the Law until everything is accomplished." In the second view they ignore what Jesus said in Matthew 5:18 and Luke 6:17 and rationalize that the sacrifice of Jesus created a "new covenant" which negated Old Testament Law while conveniently forgetting that is precisely where the Ten Commandments are found, and in fact many of those same Christians cherry pick which OT laws to obey (a popular one is the aforementioned prohibition against homosexuality) and which to ignore. The third view involves excusing them as being okay "in the context of the times they were handed down" but that begs the question, did these things really *ever* make sense? That is a question which must be answered, but rarely is. Why was it ever a sin to wear clothes made of more than one fabric or acceptable to stone a child to death? It makes no sense, and I think most of the pious Christians of today would have ignored those laws had they lived during the time of the Old Testament. Even so many of those laws were used as justification for what occurred during the Inquisition and even today are the cause of many hate crimes.

You might be thinking by this point it is a good thing the Old Testament has been "discarded," at least in the minds of some, and you do not have to be subjected to the arcane laws of the Quran, but how then does one explain 1 Timothy 2:12-14, part of the New Testament, which tells us women must not have authority over men by saying, "I do not permit a woman to teach or to have authority over a man." One can only assume Margaret Thatcher, Condoleezza Rice and Hillary Clinton have never read those words. And what about 1 Corinthians 11:6, also in the New Testament, which says women must cut their hair off if they don't cover it? Is that one followed? Doesn't make a whole lot of sense, does it?

Good vs. Evil

Or, the Dark Side of the Force

"Mankind is not likely to salvage civilization unless he can evolve a system of good and evil which is independent of Heaven and Hell."
~ George Orwell

Bad things happen every day, we all know that, and some occurrences are worse than others. Take for instance the infamous school massacres in Columbine, Colorado and Newtown, Connecticut. How can such things happen? More to the point, why does God allow such things to happen? Let's look at an example to see if we can better understand.

One such massacre took place on March 21, 2005 on the Ojibwe Red Lake Reservation in Red Lake, Minnesota. That morning sixteen-year-old Jeffrey Weise killed his sleeping grandfather, who was a tribal police officer, and his grandfather's girlfriend at their home and after taking his grandfather's police weapons and ballistic vest drove to Red Lake Senior High School where he had been a student some months before. Weise shot and killed seven people at the school beginning with an unarmed security guard at the entrance and wounded five others, with the dead including a teacher and five students. Once the police arrived he exchanged gunfire with them and after being wounded committed suicide in a vacant classroom.

Imagine being a high school English teacher working through the day's lesson when the sound of gunshots and screaming fill the classroom. The gunman has entered the school and is shooting people as he makes his way down the hallway toward your classroom. What would you do? Sixty-two-year-old Neva Jane Winnecoup-Rogers took immediate action by shutting off the lights in the classroom, closing and locked the door and telling her students to crouch in a corner to get out of harm's way. She then stood in the middle of the room and began praying. According to student witnesses Rogers prayed, "God be with us. God help us."

The gunman walked to the classroom door and found it locked so he shot out the glass panel next to it and it exploded in a shower of fragments. He then reached through the hole, unlocked the door, entered the classroom and looked at Ms. Rogers as she prayed. Armed with a 12-gauge shotgun, he raised the weapon with both hands so that it was pointing straight at the teacher's head.

What do you think God should or would do in a situation like that? Try to look at it from his perspective. He is all-knowing, so he certainly was watching as events unfolded. He no doubt heard the prayers of Neva Rogers and others and saw Weise pointing the shotgun at her head, and of course Jesus promises in the Bible that God will help when asked in prayer. Now think of all of the options an omnipotent God would have had at his disposal. Perhaps the easiest thing would have been to strike the gunman dead with a heart attack, aneurism or stroke right then and there since hundreds of people die of such things in the United States every day. Non-believers would chalk it up to coincidence, but God's followers would understand what had really happened. If God had a desire to be a bit more spectacular there were other possibilities, for example he could have caused an earthquake, sent an angel to stand between the gunman and the teacher to deflect the bullets or perhaps a meteorite could have crashed through the ceiling and struck him dead. Or since God "uses people" he could have caused a police officer to burst into the classroom at that moment and kill the gunman on the spot. There were a million things an all-powerful, all-knowing, all-loving God could have done to answer Neva Rogers' prayers, but he did none of them.

What actually happened was Weise pulled the trigger, but nothing happened. There was a click, but the gun did not fire. It seemed like a miracle. Surely it was the hand of God. Unfortunately the gunman had a backup weapon and did not hesitate to use it. He pulled out a pistol, pointed it at Rogers' head as she prayed and squeezed the trigger. The pistol did not misfire and he shot her three times in the head and then once in the face for good measure. She died instantly and fell into a pool of her own blood on the floor right in front of her stunned students.

According to *Time* magazine the gunman next aimed his gun at one of the students and asked, "Do you believe in God?" This recreated a scene from the shootings at Columbine where the student answered yes and was shot to death, but at Red Lake the student answered no so the gunman spared that student's life and started shooting other students instead. A situation like that is paradoxical. Why did an all-powerful God ignore prayers and allow ten people to die, but save the student who denied his existence? Why didn't he strike the gunman dead at the scene or help him earlier in life so as to prevent the situation before it happened? How could a loving God allow such needless suffering when he clearly has the power and authority to prevent it? Why would Jesus promise to answer prayers in the Bible and then renege? How can God answer millions of mundane prayers around the world such as "help me find my car keys" while at the same time ignoring this tragedy? It is hard for us to know what to think because Neva Rogers' death was senseless and we have no easy way to penetrate "the mysteries of the Lord," but what we do know is these deeply paradoxical situations happen all the time and there must be a reason for that... right?

In the philosophy of religion the "problem of evil" is the question of how to reconcile the existence of evil with a deity who is supposed to be omnipotent, omniscient and most importantly *omnibenevolent* - and an argument from evil attempts to show the co-existence of evil and such a deity is unlikely or impossible. Greek philosopher Epicurus summed up this paradox when he posed his famous riddle in which he asked, "Is God willing to prevent evil, but not able? Then he is not omnipotent. Is he able, but not willing? Then he is malevolent. Is he both able and willing? Then whence cometh evil? Is he neither able nor willing? Then why call him God?" Read that again, think about it and try to reconcile your answer with the world as it is. I have personally posed that question to believers innumerable times, have yet to receive a coherent answer and in most cases get no answer at all. People usually change the subject, ignore the question altogether or "answer" by countering with another question. I wonder why? There are four clear choices, and if people choose they will be forced to think about the paradox and face it.

Now let's look at a different sort of tragedy - the Prescott Arizona wildfire of 2013 which was ignited by lightning on June 28, 2013 and killed nineteen firefighters of the Granite Mountain Hotshots. Strong winds of more than twenty-two miles per hour quickly spread the fire from three hundred to over two thousand acres and a long-term drought in the area contributed to the fire's rapid spread and erratic behavior. The lone survivor from the twenty-man crew was twenty-one-year-old Brendan McDonough, who had been serving as a lookout when the fire threatened to overtake his position. He was about to deploy his safety shelter when he was rescued by Brian Frisby, Superintendent of the Blue Ridge Hotshots, and Frisby and other members of his group then attempted to rescue the entrapped firefighters but were forced back by the intense flames and heat.

The question is simple and once again there are four possible answers. Did God kill those men on purpose? If you believe he is in control of everything and the cause of all things then the answer would have to be yes. Did he see this happening, whether it was caused by the devil, nature or some other force, hear the prayers of the suffering and choose to do nothing? If so, he is indifferent. Did he see this happening, whether it was caused by the devil, nature or some other force, hear the prayers of the suffering and want do help, but lacked the ability to do so? In that case as Epicurus once asked why call him "God" since he is not omnipotent? There is of course the fourth possibility that there is no God, natural causes were at work and there was no one to intervene. It is a simple question with four possible answers. Which seems most likely? There is one more thing to consider. Should McDonough surviving be considered a miracle attributable to God, or was it due to the quick thinking and heroism of Brian Frisby? If you are tempted to suggest he was "sent by God" that raises two more questions. Was Frisby's free will usurped, and why was no one sent to help the other nineteen men?

Let's look at one more example. During the time I lived in Tampa, Florida I was witness to another tragedy which dominated the news in the area. Nine-year-old Jessica Marie Lunsford was a girl who was abducted from her home in Homosassa, Florida on the morning of February 24, 2005 and held captive, raped and later murdered by forty-six-year-old John Couey in a trailer just a hundred yards away from her home. As soon as news of Jessica's disappearance began to spread in the community members of her church began to pray and search parties were organized, and at one point police canvassed the very trailer in which she was being held.

In his confession Couey said he entered Lunsford's house through an unlocked door at about three o'clock in the morning, awakened her, said "Don't yell or nothing" and told her to follow him out of the house. He admitted raping Lunsford in his bedroom and keeping her in his bed that evening and raping her again in the morning. Couey then put her in his closet and ordered her to remain there while he reported for work, and three days later tricked Jessica into getting into two garbage bags by saying he was going to take her home. He instead buried her alive, as he had decided he could do nothing else with the girl and "didn't want people seeing him and Lunsford across the street." On March 19, 2005 police found Jessica, along with her favorite plush dolphin toy, buried in a hole approximately two and a half feet deep and covered with leaves. Her body had undergone moderate to severe decomposition and according to autopsy reports two fingers which she had desperately poked through the bags had become skeletonized before she suffocated to death. I can't begin to image the terror she must have felt as the life drained from her little body, and the fact Couey said he would apologize to Jessica in Heaven rings hollow.

How do we explain the Hotshots, Jessica Lunsford and Neva Rogers? When Christians are trying to reconcile why such bad things happen to good people they commonly quote Matthew 5:45 which says, "God sends rain on the just and the unjust," but it is almost always being quoted out of context and completely misinterpreted because this verse is being used to explain why good people must face trials since many people think of rain as bad because it interferes with picnics and outdoor activities, but in fact those words were meant for farmers living in a land with low rainfall who relied on rain to make their crops yield a harvest. Their food supply depended on rain, so to them it was a blessing and the context of the verse makes it clear rain is an example of how blessings are bestowed on everyone, both good and bad, and not the reverse. A simple way of putting it is, "God waters the weeds along with the flowers" and in any case Proverbs 12:21 clearly states, "There shall no evil happen to the just: but the wicked shall be filled with mischief," which pretty much invalidates the entire premise.

That raises another possibility. Is God, if he exists, actually a demon? After all, who said he was good? He did, in his own book! A demon would have no problem telling a little fib to gain our adulation and obedience, would he? Perhaps we have been hoodwinked. In 2009 philosopher Stephen Law proposed a response to the problem of evil he called "The Evil-God Challenge." Law concluded the strength of the case for an all-powerful, all-good God is neck-and-neck with that for an all-powerful, all-evil God. He reasoned this evil God hides from us on purpose and tries to confuse us in all sorts of ways, including getting people to believe in various opposing religions so we'll do more evil to one another - i.e. all the world is rigged to ensure freely acting human beings will commit lots of evil acts. The evidence for this is, unfortunately, stronger than we might like. There is one other possibility however, one which says there is no God, evil or otherwise, and things simply occur due to cause and effect. The universe actually makes a lot more sense when you look at it that way.

A Mysterious God

Or, Why So Shy Big Guy?

"The invisible and the non-existent often look very much alike."
~ Delos B. McKown

Everyone knows the story of the *Wizard of Oz* and over the decades L. Frank Baum's tale has been seen by many Christians as an allegory of faith. They equate the Yellow Brick Road with the path to enlightenment, with the characters encountering a variety of sin and temptation on the way to the Emerald City (which represents a kind of a heaven) and the evil Wicked Witch being killed with water, suggesting baptism. That's quite a stretch, to put it mildly. The real message is the Wizard, i.e. God, isn't real since there is actually a mortal behind the curtain and all of the spiritual mumbo jumbo is illusory smoke and mirrors. In fact Dorothy and her friends are told to ignore the man behind the curtain even after he has been exposed, so soon after the book was published Christian Fundamentalists who presumably had not yet rationalized the Yellow Brick Road angle tried to get it banned for suggesting humanity's gifts came from within rather than being God given.

Let's get back to the case of Neva Rogers. She prayed, but God ignored her. Why? Could it be she was actually praying to the man behind the curtain? You may have noticed this in your own life. It is quite common for God to ignore prayers and that is odd because the Bible is clear about how prayer is supposed to work. In Mark 11:24 Jesus promises, "Therefore I tell you, whatever you ask for in prayer, believe that you have received it, and it will be yours," and in John chapter 14, verses 12 through 14, Jesus tells us how easy prayer can be when he says, "Truly, truly, I say to you, he who believes in me will also do the works that I do; and greater works than these will he do, because I go to the Father. Whatever you ask in my name, I will do it, that the Father may be glorified in the Son; if you ask anything in my name, I will do it." In Matthew 18:19 Jesus says it again with, "Again I say to you, if two of you agree on earth about anything they ask, it will be done for them by my Father in Heaven. For where two or three are gathered in my name, there am I in the midst of them." Given these verses and the fact Neva Rogers was a faithful believer, shouldn't her prayers have worked?

We have no way to know what God is thinking, his actions can at times be mysterious and even when prayer does seem to work it is often shrouded in mystery. For example in the May, 2004 issue of *Guideposts* magazine there is a story about a huge wildfire which swept through San Diego, California. A man named Steve Homel lived in a subdivision engulfed by that fire, he prayed and God answered his prayer. He had seen the fire approaching, was understandably terrified and described "an eighty-foot wall of flames rolling down the ridge that overlooks our street." Steve and his wife evacuated to the home of his grown daughter about fifteen miles away and as they watched the news on TV saw the flames reaching his neighborhood.

What is the thing to do in such a situation? As with Neva Rogers the answer was prayer, but Steve decided to take an innovative approach. According to the newspaper article, "Suddenly Steve grabbed a piece of paper, scrawled 'God bless this house and the firemen who protect it' and faxed it to the fax machine in his home, and days later when Steve and his neighbors were allowed to return to their subdivision what he found was amazing. In spite of the raging inferno Steve's house stood completely unscathed and even the trees in the yard were untouched. It was as though there had never been a fire. They then found Steve's prayer in the tray of his fax machine. It had received the message, and obviously God had too.

Since Steve had prayed and his house survived believers are sure God had reached down and worked a miracle. When God acts in such an obvious fashion it is a source of hope, a testimony to God's grace, a shining example of the power of prayer… and such stories get written up in magazines and sent to millions of believers. God had saved Steve's house. Hallelujah! Steve's story certainly sounds miraculous but if we probe below the surface we discover another paradox not unlike that of Neva Rogers. Every other house on Steve's street had burned to the ground since according to the article, "The only things standing were a few brick chimneys. The rest had been reduced to ash." The other thirty-nine houses on the street had been completely destroyed so the question is if God had reached down to bless Steve by saving his house did he choose to curse Steve's neighbors, some of whom had no doubt been praying themselves, by letting their homes burn to the ground? Why would a loving, all-powerful God save only one house when it would have been just as easy to save all forty? Could it have been because none of the others owned fax machines?

This is where the "mystery of God" comes in. There is no way to understand why God would protect one house while destroying the other thirty-nine so we are forced to consider scenarios which are less appealing. Was God specifically cursing the other homeowners because of sins they had committed? If you believe we are all sinners that means God may curse us at any moment so he might burn our houses to the ground or shoot us in the head as punishment for our transgressions. It is hard to reconcile that kind of behavior with the traditional all-loving God many believe in. Did the other homeowners not pray properly or hard enough? What if God was only accepting fax prayers that day? This implies there may be some sort of "magic incantation" or "secret code" which unlocks God's blessing and it would appear thirty-nine out of forty homeowners didn't know the secret. Could this all be part of God's plan? Perhaps the other homeowners were all supposed to learn something from seeing Steve's house survive or perhaps all of their lives were somehow improved by losing everything and having to start over. This feels better but is hard to apply in other scenarios. For example when the 2005 tsunami killed 200,000 people how did it make their lives better? Also, it demonstrates that prayer is meaningless. If God's plan is to burn your house down your prayers are irrelevant, so why bother? Or maybe it happened because Steve prayed too selfishly and God wanted to teach him a lesson at the expense of his neighbors.

This "selfish" theory is actually something to consider. Think about it. Steve's prayer was incredibly selfish. What if he had changed just one word so it had said, "God bless this subdivision and the firemen who protect it?" Would all forty homes have been saved? What if Steve had prayed, "God bless this nation and the firemen who protect it?" Would every fire in the entire country immediately extinguish itself? If so we could save billions of dollars per year by closing every fire station in the nation and relying on Steve and his fax machine to take care of us. Most of us understand closing every fire station in America would be irresponsible, but why? That raises an interesting question. If you actually believe God answered Steve's prayer why don't you believe God would answer a nationwide prayer as well?

What is God thinking when he allows things like this to happen to some people but not others, even if both are fervently and faithfully praying? What was God's purpose when he let Neva Rogers die? We can say, "It is all part of God's plan," but what sort of plan is that? What greater purpose could possibly be served by allowing the grotesque murder of Jessica Lunsford? Some might rationalize her death prompted her father to push for legislation which became "Jessica's Law," but it makes no sense that an omnipotent God would need to leverage such a tragedy to influence lawmakers when he is powerful enough to protect children himself.

One way to remove the selfishness aspect of intercessory prayer is by having others do the praying. In a March 2006 article entitled *Long-Awaited Medical Study Questions the Power of Prayer* the *New York Times* reported on a major study which did just that. The conclusion it reached was prayers offered by strangers had no effect on the recovery of people who were undergoing heart surgery and patients who knew they were being prayed for actually had a higher rate of post-operative complications such as abnormal heart rhythms, perhaps because of the expectations the prayers created.

This study, which took almost a decade to complete, was the most scientifically rigorous investigation to date into the question of whether prayer can heal illness and at a cost $2.4 million dollars and with the involvement of more than 1,800 patients it was by no means cursory. The study was the subject of a great deal of speculation because while at least ten other studies of the effects of prayer had been carried out in the previous six years this new study, which appeared in *The American Heart Journal*, was crafted to overcome flaws in the methodology of the earlier investigations.

In the study the researchers monitored 1,802 patients at six hospitals who received coronary bypass surgery in which doctors rerouted circulation around a clogged vein or artery. The patients were broken into three groups, with two being prayed for and the third not. In addition half the patients who received the prayers were told they were being prayed for and the other half that they might or might not receive prayers. The researchers asked the members of three congregations - St. Paul's Monastery in St. Paul, Minnesota, the Community of Teresian Carmelites in Worcester, Massachusetts and Silent Unity, which is a Missouri prayer ministry near Kansas City - to deliver the prayers using the patients' first names and the first initials of their last names. This diversity was designed to counter inevitable claims the "right kind of Christians" were not used, although with thirty-three thousand different denominations worldwide it would have been impossible to represent them all. The congregations were told they could pray in their own ways, but were instructed to include the phrase "for a successful surgery with a quick, healthy recovery and no complications."

After analyzing complications in the thirty days after the operations researchers found no difference between those patients who were prayed for and those who were not. In another of the study's findings a significantly higher number of the patients who knew they were being prayed for (fifty-nine percent) suffered complications, compared with fifty-one percent of those who were uncertain. The authors left open the possibility this was a chance finding, but said being aware of the strangers' prayers also may have caused some of the patients a kind of performance anxiety. The study also found more patients in the uninformed prayer group (eighteen percent) suffered major complications like heart attack or stroke compared with thirteen percent in the group which did not receive prayers. The researchers suggested this finding might also have been a result of chance.

One reason the study was so widely anticipated was it was led by Dr. Herbert Benson, a cardiologist and director of the Mind/Body Medical Institute near Boston, who in his work has emphasized the soothing power of personal prayer and meditation. His participating was a clear indication this study was objective and not a hatchet job designed to disprove religious claims.

Before we can further discuss the concept God we need to have a clear idea of who or what God is. If you consult the dictionary you will find the definition "a being conceived as the perfect, omnipotent, omniscient originator and ruler of the universe, the principal object of faith and worship in monotheistic religions." Most believers would agree with this broad definition, although there are many quibbles about the details and believers express their differences in dozens of denominations including Presbyterians, Lutherans, Catholics, Baptists, Methodists Episcopalians and so on… but there are a set of core ideas which most accept. If you were to make a list of the fundamental beliefs it would say people believe God is the almighty ruler of the universe, all-powerful, all-knowing, eternal, timeless, omnipresent, perfect and the creator of everything including life and the universe itself. They believe God instills in each of us a unique and everlasting soul, he wrote or at least inspired the Bible and it is his word (while some claim the Bible is infallible, inspired and inerrant others are not that literal). People believe God is a benevolent and loving ruler saying, "God is good" and "God is love" and that he loves each of us and we can speak to and have a personal relationship with him through prayer. Many also believe God has a plan for each of us and we each have a distinct purpose in his universe. If you ask any believer about any of these core concepts there might be a quibble about some of the details since for example some do not believe in a literal Adam and Eve, are not certain God wrote everything in the Bible, etc. but these core beliefs are found across most denominations.

Many people believe they can pray to God or Jesus or even Mary and certain saints depending upon their denomination, they will be heard and God will reach down and use his infinite power to answer our prayers, cure diseases, save lives, protect us, solve personal problems and make our lives better. No doubt there is something comforting about the thought of an all-loving, all-knowing, all-powerful being watching over us and welcoming us into Heaven for eternity when we die. We would all like to believe in and put our faith in such an amazing being, yet you have to wonder once you see the paradox. Given this definition of God the murders of Neva Rogers and Jessica Lunsford make no sense. It would seem he is so mysterious as to be irrelevant.

No Legs To Stand On

Or, Why Doesn't God Heal Amputees?

"Mysteries are not necessarily miracles." ~ Johann Wolfgang von Goethe

I have a good friend who lost one of his legs in combat during the Vietnam War. There is nothing I would like to do more than help him get his limb back and if there were even the slightest chance that could be accomplished through prayer I would be down on my knees beseeching the Lord right at this very moment, but sadly that is not the case.

Does God answer prayers? According to believers the answer is certainly yes. In any Christian bookstore you will find hundreds of books about the power of prayer, on the Internet you can find thousands of testimonials celebrating the many ways God works in our lives and even newspapers and magazines run stories about answered prayers. God seems to be interacting with our world and answering millions of prayers on planet Earth every day, and his power can often be quite dramatic. Take for example this story from Marilyn Hickey Ministries, which is similar to many others which can be found all over the internet: "Prayer is a communication system we have available to fellowship with our heavenly Father and which activates His promises in our lives. No one can beat this system. It's quick. It's efficient. And it's available to you right now! Prayer reaches our heavenly Father instantly. Years ago my mother's doctors found a tumor in her brain. When I heard the news, I was out of town so I could not lay my hands on her. That night as fear swept over me, the Lord quickened Psalms 107:20 to my spirit: 'He sent his word and healed them, and delivered them from their destructions.' I sent God's Word long distance to my mother's brain. When she was X-rayed again by her doctors there was no evidence that any tumor had ever existed! Hallelujah! Our prayers are swifter than any medical technique. Only born again believers who have accepted Jesus Christ as Lord can have a relationship with the Father and prayer is the communication method you must use to develop that relationship."

For believers it is obvious why prayers are answered because in the Bible Jesus says, "For truly, I say to you, if you have faith as a grain of mustard seed, you will say to this mountain, 'Move from here to there,' and it will move; and nothing will be impossible to you." Since a mustard seed is a tiny inanimate object about the size of a grain of salt it is easy to imagine the faith of a mustard seed is fairly small. To paraphrase what Jesus was saying, if you have the tiniest bit of faith you can move mountains. He said something similar in Matthew 21:21. "I tell you the truth, if you have faith and do not doubt, not only can you do what was done to the fig tree, but also you can say to this mountain 'go, throw yourself into the sea' and it will be done. If you believe, you will receive whatever you ask for in prayer." This message is reiterated in Mark 11:24, and in John chapter 14, verses 12 through 14 Jesus tells us just how easy prayer can be. In Matthew 18:19 he says it again with the words, "Again I say to you, if two of you agree on earth about anything they ask, it will be done for them by my Father in Heaven. For where two or three are gathered in my name, there am I in the midst of them." According to these statements Jesus is in our midst and answers our prayers, but will those claims stand up to objective examination?

There are so many examples of the power of prayer but one in particular deserves special consideration because it is so well documented - the December 2004 case of a girl named Jeanna Giese, who survived a bite from a rabid bat through prayer. Hundreds of newspapers ran stories about the miracle of her recovery with headlines such as *Rabies Girl in Miracle Recovery*. In the December 17, 2004 edition of the *Raleigh News and Observer* the headline was *Web Weaves Global Prayer Circle - Petitions Circle the World as Girl Beats Rare Case of Rabies*. Jeanna had been in a church service in Wisconsin when a brown bat fell into the aisle so she picked it up, carried it outside and no one gave it a second thought until a month later when she developed a full case of rabies. Keep in mind no human has ever survived this disease without being vaccinated and up until 2004 full-blown rabies had always been fatal.

According to the article a global prayer circle helped Jeanna survive. Once she got sick Jeanna's father called friends and asked them to pray for her and soon people around the world heard about her story through the press and word of mouth. They prayed, sent emails and passed the word along. Millions of people heard about Jeanna's plight, said prayers for her and it worked. Through the power of God Jeanna recovered and became the first human to survive rabies without the vaccine. Dr. Charles Rupprecht of the Center for Disease Control in Atlanta called Jeanna's case a miracle and the family and everyone else in her global prayer circle are sure God heard their prayers and answered them.

Did a loving God hear the prayers of Jeanna's worldwide prayer circle and reach down from Heaven to help her through a divine miracle? Or could there be a different explanation? We can answer that question with a simple experiment. Find a deserving person who has had one of his legs amputated, for example a sincere, devout Christian veteran of the Iraq War or someone who was involved in an automobile accident. In my case this is easy, namely the aforementioned Vietnam veteran. Now start a prayer circle like the one created for Jeanna Giese and pray for God to restore the amputated leg of this deserving person. I do not mean pray for a team of surgeons to somehow graft the leg of a cadaver onto the person or scientists to craft a mechanical leg. Pray for God to spontaneously and miraculously restore the leg overnight in the same way he spontaneously and miraculously cured Jeanna Giese and Marilyn Hickey's mother. Use the power of the internet to get millions of people all over the planet to join the prayer circle and pray their most fervent prayers. Get millions praying in unison for a single miracle for this one deserving amputee and then stand back and watch what does or does not happen.

Jesus said not once but many times and in many ways if you believe you will receive whatever you ask for in prayer and yet even with millions of people praying nothing will happen. No matter how many people pray, how sincere they are, how much they believe or how devout and deserving the recipient, nothing will happen. The legs will not regenerate because prayer will not restore the severed limbs of amputees. You can read all of the medical journals ever written and will find no documented case of an amputated leg ever being restored spontaneously, even though there are parallels in nature such as lizards regenerating severed tails.

It is clear God ignores the prayers of amputees because otherwise we would be seeing amputated legs growing back every day. Isn't that odd? It is even stranger when you consider God is so powerful he can do anything and regenerating a leg is trivial compared to creating an entire universe. God is perfect and in his inerrant book Jesus makes very specific statements about the power of prayer, and since Jesus is God and both God and the Bible are perfect those statements should be true. God certainly knows about the plight of the amputee, loves him very much, is ready and willing to answer your prayers no matter how big or small and has no discernable reason to discriminate against amputees. If he is answering millions of prayers every day he should be answering the prayers of amputees too.

Nonetheless, amputated legs are not going to regenerate. Why? It is not that God sometimes answers the prayers of amputees and sometimes does not as he seems to do with others types of prayers. It would appear to an unbiased observer God is singling out amputees and purposefully ignoring them. This fact reframes our conversation because no longer are we talking about faith, but instead something far more fundamental.

The question is simple. Are Jesus' statements in the Bible true or false? For example in John 3:16 Jesus says, "For God so loved the world that he gave his one and only Son, that whoever believes in him shall not perish but have eternal life." People take that at face value as meaning if you believe in Jesus you will have eternal life so when he says, "Believe that you have received it, and it will be yours," isn't it the same thing? Can't we take that statement at face value as well?

At this stage there are a dozen apologetic rationalizations which might be employed. You may for instance say "God cannot be tested" but that only excludes our one little experiment. What about the many thousands of amputees who have earnestly prayed to get their leg back with no intention of testing the power of prayer? It didn't work for them either. By looking at those amputees we can see God never answers prayers to spontaneously restore lost limbs despite Jesus' statements in the Bible. Accepting this piece of logic, rather than denying it, is the first step in understanding how prayer really works.

If you take a liberal rather than literal stance on the Bible you may not believe "nothing will be impossible for you" nor that "faith can move mountains" but it is an irrefutable fact that God, and this applies to every god ever worshipped, never regenerates lost limbs through prayer even though people believe he is answering millions of other prayers every day. How do you explain this?

Let's examine some possible explanations. An explanation you may have heard or even used is, "The reason God cures thousands of cancers, infections, etc. each day but never intervenes with amputees is because it is not God's will to do so and/or is not part of his plan." This explanation is empty and devoid of reason. In other words it is a classic apologetic. If God answers prayers as promised in the Bible and is performing all of the medical miracles we read about in inspirational literature he should also be restoring amputated limbs. Why would he help cancer victims like Marilyn Hickey's mother and people bitten by rabid bats but discriminate against amputees? The likely apologetic for that will be "we can't know the mind of God," but it is important to remember Jesus did not say if you believe you will receive whatever you ask for in prayer unless it does not conform with my plan, if you ask anything in my name I will do it unless I don't feel like doing it, ask and it will be given you unless it involves helping amputees grow back a leg, nothing will be impossible to you as long as it is not visible or verifiable like a relocated mountain or regenerated limb and believe that you have received it and it will be yours… while keeping in mind belief and reality are not necessarily the same thing.

In a similar vein many believers will say "God always answers prayers but sometimes his answer is 'no,' so if your prayer does not fit with God's will then he will say no to you." The problem with that is God's answer to *every* amputee is *always* no when it comes to regenerating lost limbs, unlike his answer to other prayers. Another explanation you might have heard is "God needs to remain hidden and restoring an amputated limb would be too obvious." We discuss this idea in more detail in other chapters, but let's touch on it here.

Does God need to remain hidden? That does not seem to be the case since he seemed to have no problem doing things which are obvious throughout history. Think about the Bible. Writing the Bible and having billions of copies published all over the world is obvious. So is parting the Red Sea, carving the Ten Commandments on stone tablets, sending his son to earth and having him perform dozens of miracles and so on. It makes no sense for a God which is in hiding to incarnate himself or do these other things. Why send your son to earth and then write a book which talks about his exploits if you are trying to hide? Another example is seen in Jeanne's rabies case discussed earlier. Tens of millions of people are aware of the Jeanna's rabies "miracle" because they read about it in the newspaper. What is hidden about her recovery? So why then does God ignore the prayers of amputees?

Some people might say, "Everyone's life serves God in different ways. Perhaps God uses amputees to teach us something. God must have a higher purpose for amputees." That may be the case and God may very well be trying to send a message but once again it seems odd he would single out this one group of people to handle the delivery. To quote Marilyn Hickey once again, "No matter what has happened in your past, no matter what is happening in your present, seek out your Heavenly Father in prayer as often as you can. Take my word for it - He loves you and wants to answer your prayers." You see this logic all the time in inspirational literature and hear every Sunday at thousands of churches, "God loves you, hears your prayers and will answer them for you," and yet for some reason miracles never happen when it comes to regenerating lost limbs.

Some people ascribe the problems amputees face to free will. They will say, "If you go into a war zone and get your legs blown off that is your own free will. God gives us free will. You made a free choice to be a soldier. It is not God's fault and therefore he has no obligation to repair the damage." Okay then, what about people who are born with missing limbs or those who lose limbs to diseases and accidents through no fault or choice of their own? How are these people any different from cancer victims who are supposedly being constantly healed? God ignores all amputees, regardless of the cause of the missing limb. Why doesn't he heal thalidomide babies who are by definition completely innocent? Or children who lose their limbs in mine fields? Why would God heal millions of other diseases but completely ignore anything which results in a lost or missing limb?

Some believers will say, "God does help amputees. He inspires scientists and engineers to create artificial limbs for them." Fine, except many people do not have access to that technology, plus this logic makes little sense if we look at other examples such as smallpox. Millions upon millions died of smallpox until a vaccine was invented in the 20th Century and if God inspired the scientists who developed it why did he wait until so long to do it? Why would God want to allow all of the suffering smallpox caused prior to that time and why do we pay scientists if their work is simply God's inspiration?

Someone might say, "Thou shalt not test the Lord. It says so in the Bible." This is hard to swallow because every prayer is a test. Either God answers the prayer or he does not and there is no difference between praying for an amputee and praying for Jeanna Giese and her rabies. Note also that many believers track their prayers with prayer journals (for an example visit *prayer-journal.com*). Why not pray to God to heal an amputee and track the results of that prayer in a prayer journal?

Some people might say, "Jesus never says when he will answer your prayers so maybe it will be answered in the afterlife," but that seems ridiculous since he is supposedly answering millions of prayers for everyone else in the here and now. Why single out amputees for treatment in the afterlife, and for that matter will people even have physical limbs there? Marilyn and Jeanna seem to have gotten their prayers answered almost instantaneously.

Someone might say, "God will answer your prayers but not immediately, so you must be patient." In other words it will happen "in

God's time." They will then point to a situation like that found in Mark 6:47-51 which says, "And when evening came, the boat was out on the sea, and he was alone on the land. And he saw that they were making headway painfully, for the wind was against them. And about the fourth watch of the night he came to them, walking on the sea. He meant to pass by them, but when they saw him walking on the sea they thought it was a ghost, and cried out; for they all saw him, and were terrified. But immediately he spoke to them and said, 'Take heart, it is I; have no fear.' And he got into the boat with them and the wind ceased." A person might say, "See, he came in the fourth watch (generally understood to be 3 AM to 6 AM), not in the first or second or third. You must be patient and wait for the Lord to answer your prayers." This is just as silly as the previous explanation since God does not answer the prayers of any amputee to restore lost limbs no matter how long they wait.

A believer, or at least some of them, might say, "You are taking the Bible too literally." How else are we supposed to take it? Jesus clearly says, "If you ask anything in my name, I will do it." Presumably that means if you ask for anything, he will do it. What else could it possibly mean? Believers often respond by saying, "Jesus was employing poetic embellishment when he said nothing will be impossible for you and faith can move mountains," which begs the question which prayers does God answer and how can we know which of his statements are embellished and which are literal? The response to that inevitably is "God is omnipotent so he can do anything," which leads us right back to the question of why won't God heal amputees if he can.

Then there is the oft-used all-purpose apologetic, "There is no way to understand the mysteries of the Lord. There must be a good reason for it." On one side of the conversation is someone defending the all-powerful, all-knowing, all-loving creator of the universe so his position should be unassailable, and yet if God exists and answers prayers there is no explanation for what actually happens except to say, "We cannot understand the mysteries of the Lord." In other words God exists and answers prayers but for some reason chooses to ignore the prayers of amputees.

Now look at it from another point of view. For just a moment assume God does not exist because this explanation fits the facts perfectly and in the case of amputees explains reality. If God is imaginary he does not answer prayers at all, therefore the prayers of amputees would of course go unanswered. There is no hand waving or rationalization necessary, no contradictions and no paradox because this explanation makes complete sense. This explanation also covers the cases of Neva Rogers and Jessica Lunsford. Why did Neva and Jessica die? Because there was no God to save them. On a larger scale why did two hundred thousand people die in the tsunami? For the same reason. It explains amputees as well.

Some will still claim, "Just because God never answers the prayers of amputees does not mean he does not answer other prayers. Sure it is unfair to amputees and contradicts what Jesus teaches in the Bible, but God has his purposes and for some reason it is not part of his plan. There is no way to understand the mysteries of our Lord, but he does have his reasons and they will become clear to us when we die and go to Heaven." Yet the paradox remains. The possible explanations for this paradox are God can't do it, won't do it or doesn't exist. Which is most likely correct? If you employ Occam's Razor the answer should be obvious.

At the global level we see the evidence every day in many different ways. For example millions of children die every year as a result of the effects of poverty, malnutrition, unsafe water and inadequate sanitation. According to UNICEF more than ten million children die totally preventable deaths each year due to pneumonia, diarrhea, measles, HIV/AIDS as well as indirect causes such as war. Jesus is supposed to love all the children of the world. As the ditty says, "Red and yellow, black and white, they are precious in his sight." If children are indeed precious to him why is he allowing ten million of them to die every year in such a manner? That's twenty-seven thousand dead children every day, more than a thousand each hour, and yet many people believe God is helping them find a mate or locate their car keys.

The question of why won't God heal amputees illustrates an aspect of prayer having to do with ambiguity and coincidence. Imagine you pray for something, it does not really matter what. Let's imagine you have cancer, you pray to God to cure you and the cancer goes away. There is ambiguity in your cure. God might have miraculously cured the disease as many people believe but on the other hand the chemotherapy drugs and surgery might be the things which cured it. Or your body might have cured the cancer itself, since the human body has a powerful immune system and the ability to eliminate cancer in some cases. When your tumor disappeared it might have been a coincidence that you happened to pray.

How can we determine whether it was God or coincidence? One way is to eliminate the ambiguity. In a non-ambiguous situation there is no potential for coincidence and as a result we can determine whether or not God is answering the prayer. That is what we are doing when we look at amputees. When we pray to restore an amputated limb there is only one way for the limb to regenerate, God must exist and must answer prayers, but in a non-ambiguous situation like this he never does.

When confronted with this dilemma believers sometimes claim God has indeed restored lost limbs and cite the cases of St. Anthony of Padua (1195-1231) the patron saint of amputees no less (among other things) who is said to have restored an amputated foot, John Damascene, who they claim miraculously restored his own amputated hand in 726 and the "The Miracle of Calanda" which is said to have taken place in Spain in 1640 when a young man's injured leg was amputated and two and a half years later miraculously restored.

According to a website devoted to the veneration of St. Anthony, "A great miracle was caused by a confession. A man from Padua called Leonardo once told the man of God (Anthony) that among his other sins he'd kicked his mother, and with such violence that she fell heavily to the ground. The blessed Father Anthony, who strongly detested all wrong-doing, in the fervor of the spirit said deploringly, 'the foot which kicks a mother or father should be cut off straight away.' This simpleton, having misunderstood the sense of this phrase and out of remorse for his ill deed and the cruel words of the Saint, rushed home and cut off his foot. The news of such a cruel punishment spread through the city and reached God's servant. He went to the man's house straight away after an apprehensive, devout prayer, joined the cut off foot to the leg, making the sign of the cross. A miracle! As soon as the Saint had attached the foot to the leg, tracing out the sign of the Crucifix, passing his sacred hands gently over the leg, the foot became attached to the leg so quickly that the man stood up happily and began to run and jump, praising God and giving infinite thanks to the blessed Anthony who had made him sound again in such a miraculous way." The question is, do you believe that?

Next we have Saint John of Damascus, also known as John Damascene, who was a Syrian monk and priest. His biography was written by an Arab monk named Michael who explained he decided to write it more than three hundred years after John's death in 1084 because none was available in his day, but not surprisingly it was written from a hagiographical (worshipful or idealizing, rather than factual) point of view and prone to exaggeration and some legendary details, therefore it is obviously not the best historical source. It recounts one episode which is understandably deemed to be improbable or legendary when it reports that Pope Leo III sent forged documents to the caliph which implicated John in a plot to attack Damascus, and as a result the caliph ordered

John's right hand cut off and hung up in public view. Some days afterwards John purportedly asked for the restitution of his hand, prayed fervently to the Theotokos (the Greek title of Mary, mother of Jesus) before her icon and thereupon his hand is said to have been miraculously restored. In gratitude for this miraculous healing he attached a silver hand to the icon which thereafter became known as "Three-handed" or "Tricheirousa." Do you believe *that* one?

Finally there is what has become known as the Miracle of Calanda, which is one of the best documented of all "miracles" and in fact is one for which the faithful claim to have hard evidence. Was the event truly miraculous and unexplainable? In 1637 Miguel Juan Pellicer, a strapping young fellow of about twenty years old, was working at his uncle's farm in the village of Castellón when a mule-drawn cart ran over his right leg and fractured the tibia. His uncle quickly drove him to the hospital at Valencia, and according to the story Pellicer stayed there for five days until it was decided he needed better help than they could provide so he was sent on foot (with a broken leg, no less) to the larger hospital in Zaragoza. The journey is said to have taken fifty days.

Once he arrived in Zaragoza doctors found his leg to be gangrenous so it was amputated "four fingers below the knee" and was buried in a "special plot," after which he stayed in the hospital for several months and was provided with a wooden leg and crutch. He applied to the church authorities at the Basilica of Our Lady of the Pillar in Zaragoza for authorization to make a living as a beggar which was granted, and then lived in Zaragoza for two years during which time he attended mass daily at the Basilica and accepted alms from the citizenry.

When at last he decided to return home he rode a donkey all the way to his parent's home in Calanda where he'd grown up and his family was overjoyed to see him, but since he couldn't work he spent a couple of weeks riding his donkey to neighboring villages and begging… and then one night it happened. A traveling soldier was spending the night in Pellicer's room so he took a bedroll on the floor in his parents' bedroom, and in the morning his parents saw not one but two feet protruding from the end of the short blanket. They excitedly woke their son, who was as surprised as anyone, and the news quickly spread throughout the village of the young amputee who had been miraculously healed.

An examination of the leg revealed it was the same one he'd always had because it bore a scar from where a cyst had been excised when he was a child, two scars made by thorns and another from a dog bite on his calf and of course a scar where the cart wheel had crushed his tibia. The leg was said to appear thin and atrophied, but within a few days he was using it normally.

As the story spread it drew in the curious and a few days after the "miraculous restoration" a delegation consisting of a priest, a vicar and the local royal notary came to Calanda to see for themselves and prepare an official record of the event for which they took statements from witnesses and carefully documented Pellicer's story. Two months later a trial was opened in Zaragoza where more than one hundred people testified they had known Pellicer with only one leg, whereas now he had two. Ten months later the archbishop rendered a verdict that the restoration of the leg was to be canonized as a true miracle and ever since that date skeptics have no longer been able to charge that God does not heal amputees - or so it would seem.

The most authoritative work on the Miracle of Calanda is the 1998 book *Il Miracolo* by Catholic scholar Vittorio Messori which identifies and records the pieces of written evidence collected by the delegation which survive today which include documentation of Miguel Juan Pellicer's baptism to confirm he was a real person, registration of his admittance to the hospital at Valencia, the delegation's original notarized report of the statements collected in Calanda including statements by people who saw him come to town with one leg and a certified and notarized copy of the original minutes of the trial at Zaragoza. If we accept that these documents are indeed legitimate, and I think we can, do they prove a miraculous restoration of an amputated limb occurred?

To the religious person the foregoing is no doubt enough to seal the deal but when viewed by the objective person a giant, gaping hole appears in the story. There is no documentation or witness account confirming his leg was ever gone in the first place in spite of all those witnesses who "knew him with one leg." A more plausible alternative version of what might have happened which requires no miraculous intervention and is still consistent with all of the documentary evidence is Pellicer's leg was indeed broken in the accident as witnessed and reported, but like most broken legs it did not develop gangrene. His uncle then took him to the hospital at Valencia as documented where he spent five days, during which time his uncle presumably went back to his farm and the broken leg was set.

The next fifty days were spent convalescing as his leg mended and unable to work during this time he was forced to earn a living as a beggar… and found that the broken leg did wonders for the collection of alms. Once his leg was sound, he reasoned, if a broken leg was good a missing leg would be even better so he bound his right foreleg up behind his thigh, got ahold of a wooden leg and traveled to Zaragoza which was the home of the great Basilica. It was also a place where he wasn't known. For two years young Pellicer enjoyed the relative financial success of panhandling among the Basilica's devotees as an amputee with a sad story, but once he made it back home to Calanda his plans were accidentally foiled when the existence of his complete, sound leg was revealed. When his parents saw his feet sticking out from under his blanket he had little choice but to lie, and at that point the miracle story was a perfect cover because by now many people knew him as the man with one leg but could quite plainly see he now had two. There was no way he could lose.

It should be mentioned that faking blindness, infirmity, poverty and all manner of ailments is hardly unheard of among beggars as anyone who has seen Eddie Murphy as "Agent Orange" in the movie *Trading Places* knows. It is now, and has been for millennia, a pillar of the profession. Note that no evidence exists his leg was ever amputated or that he was even treated at all at the hospital in Zaragoza aside from his own word. He named three doctors there, but for some reason there is no record of them having been interviewed by either the delegation or the trial. The trial did find that no leg was buried where he said it was at the hospital but this is exactly what we'd expect to find if it had never been amputated and although this lack of a buried leg is often put forth as evidence the story is true it is actually the opposite. This is where Occam's Razor comes into play - the most likely explanation is the one which requires the fewest assumptions.

Clearly there is absolutely no real evidence or documentation which supports the veracity of those three fantastic and archaic stories and yet people continue to use them as examples of limb restoration without knowing a thing about the underlying stories or where these legends came from. Surely there must be a more recent example, complete with witnesses and scientific documentation?

According to Bernard Ruffin, a pastor at Holy Comforter Lutheran Church in Washington, D.C., more astounding still may be the "thoroughly-documented" cure of a construction worker named Giovanni Savino who was severely injured on February 15, 1949 in a dynamite mishap. Ruffin writes in his book *Padre Pio: The True Story* (note the use of the ever present word "true" in the title) that when Dr. Guglielmo San-guinetti, a physician, and Padre Raffaele, another Capuchin, and Father Dominic Meyer rushed to the injured man's side, "All three men noted that among Savino's numerous injuries his right eye was gone entirely. They agreed that 'the socket was empty.'" He added that other (unnamed, naturally) doctors confirmed the eye was completely annihilated and the other one badly damaged.

It looked like Savino was going to be totally blind and for three days he lay on a hospital bed with his head and face bandaged. When a surgeon entered the room three days later, Savino reported that Padre Pio of Pietrelcina (who has since been canonized) had visited him - something Savino recognized because he had detected the "beautiful aroma" so often reported around the priest. A week later at about 1 AM on February 25, 1949 Savino felt a slap on the right side of his face, which was the side where the eye was completely gone. "I asked, 'who touched me?'" testified Savino. "There was nobody. Again I smelled the aroma of Padre Pio. It was beautiful."

When later the (naturally anonymous) ophthalmologist, who was not surprisingly characterized as an atheist to lend weight to the story, came to examine the remaining eye there was a shock. "To their amazement," writes Ruffin, "the doctors found that his shattered face was fully healed and covered with new skin. Savino, however, was most delighted at the fact that he could see. 'I can see you!' he said excitedly to the eye specialist."

"And indeed, as is 'medically documented,'" claims Ruffin, "the doctor saw to his 'utter astonishment' that Savino had his right eye back. Somehow, the eye had materialized. 'Now I believe too,' exclaimed the (anonymous atheist) doctor, 'because of what my own hands have touched!'" Ruffin notes, "It's one thing when diseases disappear; this is exciting. It's tremendous to hear of diabetes or arthritis or even cancer leaving a person. For a missing part of the body to be restored, however, is another matter."

Yes indeed, it *would* be.

Heavenly Insurance

Or, Who Needs the Gecko?

"I still say a church steeple with a lightning rod on top shows a lack of confidence." ~ Doug McLeod

Peaceful Valley Cemetery sits on a windswept hill thirty miles east of Boise, Idaho and some of the Followers of Christ faith healers bury their dead there. The same last names appear over and over again going back decades and some such as Beagley are the same as those you will see in a similar cemetery in Oregon City. In 2010 jurors in Clackamas County convicted Jeff and Marci Beagley of letting their son Neal die of an untreated urinary tract infection, a reporter named Dan Tilkin covered the story, and afterwards he traveled to Idaho to trace the connections between Followers members in both states and a trail of dead children.

A former member of the Followers of Christ advised him to go to Peaceful Valley and look for two specific names. He found them and many more, such as Garrett Dean Eells. The coroner's report says Garrett was a six-day-old baby who died of interstitial pneumonitis, which is untreated pneumonia. Jackson Scott Porter was a baby girl who lived for only twenty minutes because according to the coroner's report she received no pre-natal care and her grandfather, Mark Jerome, said she died in his house after his daughter went into labor. The coroner used the words "extreme prematurity" to describe the labor and Jerome said he doesn't regret the lack of pre-natal care, something which gets to the heart of faith-healing. "That's the way we believe," he said. "We believe in God and the way God handles the situation, the way we do things."

Then there are the cases of Preston Bowers and Rockwell Sevy. Two-year-old Preston had Down's Syndrome, died of pneumonia and his death was reported in 2011 along with that of fourteen-year-old Rocky. Rocky isn't buried in the cemetery but lived nearby with parents Sally and Dan, who didn't want to talk about not getting him treatment. Instead Dan said, "What I will talk to you about is the law. I would like to remind you this country was founded on religious freedom, and on freedom in general. I would like to say, I picture freedom as a full object. It's not like you take 'a' freedom away. It's that you chip at the entire thing. Freedom is freedom. Whenever you try to restrict any one person, then you're chipping away at freedom. Yours and mine." That was that and Sevy didn't want to talk any more about it. "I told you I'm not going to do that," he said. "You don't understand the full story… all I see is an aggressive campaign against Christianity in general, it's amazing to me in this day and age where Muslims get soft pedaled and Christians are under attack. It just blows my mind."

Unfortunately those weren't the only names in the cemetery and there are many more new graves belonging to children which have appeared since that report in 2011. Arrian Jade Granden was fifteen years old and ran track at Parma Middle School, but in June of 2012 she got food poisoning and vomited so badly she ruptured her esophagus after which she slipped into unconsciousness, went into cardiac arrest and died. The autopsy of Micah Taylor Eells says he died of "likely an intestinal blockage." He was four days old. Of the 553 marked graves at Peaceful Valley Cemetery, 144 appear to be children under eighteen. That's more than twenty-five percent, but none of the parents of the children who are buried there will be prosecuted because while Oregon wiped out its laws protecting faith-healers, Idaho did not.

Doctor Charles Garrison performed the autopsy on sixteen-year-old Pamela Jade Eells after she died of pneumonia and stated, "If you've ever been in a situation where you can't breathe, it's pretty desperate. You're drowning in your own fluids." The coroner's report says Pamela died after a long chronic battle with an infection in her pelvic bone, and Garrison hasn't forgotten. "It's inexplicable to me to comprehend how anyone can watch a child die and do nothing," he said.

Linda Martin has seen it before. She's a former Followers of Christ member who grew up near Boise, left when she was a teenager and now lives in Oregon. She contacted authorities when she realized more children were dying, said she is related to many of them and even keeps their obituaries in an album. "Everybody hears about the Oregon City trials and the Oregon City churches," she said. "What they don't understand is the Idaho churches are more rigid, they are unbending and they are more ruthless than the Oregon churches are. It happens one at a time, and the church is so good at covering up that most people don't even know what's going on next door to them." She knows from personal experience, as her cousin Jerry Gardener died from diabetes at the age of eleven in 1980. Both Linda and Dr. Garrison are frustrated Idaho hasn't followed Oregon's lead because in Idaho you can amazingly still use faith-healing as a defense when it comes to children while in Oregon you can't.

As a case in point Syble Rossiter was twelve when she died in Albany, Oregon and her parents Travis and Wenona Rossiter faced manslaughter charges. They belong to a congregation called Church of the First Born in Brownsville, Oregon and according to Linda Martin's family tree and other historical sources that church is related to the Followers of Christ. The only significant difference between the churches is when a child dies in Idaho due to lack of medical care the parents aren't breaking any laws.

"The state of Idaho has the religious shield laws to where you can just about murder your child in cold blood and claim religious exemptions and get away with it," Martin said. There are four such churches in Idaho, and as it turns out they don't get along. "Difference of opinions, difference of religion, different ideas - we follow the word for what it is, what the Bible says," said Mark Jerome, who attends the Followers of Christ Church in Marsing, Idaho.

Followers' members use at least two more cemeteries. The caretaker at Star Cemetery in Star, Idaho said a Followers member showed up saying he needed to bury a baby which was in the back seat of his car. The caretaker said he made the church member get a death certificate before he buried the child, and while the state recently put together a child death review team which will likely be looking at faith-healing deaths soon no significant move to change the law is underway. How many more children must die unnecessarily before we move out of the Dark Ages?

If you think the situation in Idaho is unusual you would be wrong. It is pervasive. For example families who attend Faith Tabernacle Congregation in North Philadelphia and First Century Gospel Church in Juniata Park, Pennsylvania have unnecessarily lost more than two dozen children to illness since 1971 because both churches believe in the power of prayer over modern medicine. As a result each of the faith-healing churches has a long history of the youngest members of their congregations dying because their parents refused medical care. For example Herbert and Catherine Schaible were charged with third-degree murder and other crimes after their seven-month-old son Brandon died from bacterial pneumonia, dehydration and a group B streptococcus infection. Philadelphia District Attorney Seth Williams said at the time the boy's death could have been prevented, but the couple instead turned to prayer. That was the second time the couple had lost a child to illness, having been previously sentenced to ten years' probation after their two-year-old son Kent died in 2009 after contracting pneumonia, an illness prosecutors said could have been prevented with basic medical care. With Brandon's death, prosecutors alleged the couple violated their probation by not taking the baby to the doctor. One would think the first tragedy would have taught them something, but sadly it did not.

In 1991 Faith Tabernacle lost five children to the measles after an outbreak and one child from First Century Gospel named Dean Heilman also died at twenty-two months old when he bled to death as a result of his hemophilia. His parents, Dean and Susan, were charged with involuntary manslaughter and sentenced to probation in 1997. Annemarie and Daniel Foster were also charged in 1997 with endangering the welfare of their son Patrick because the two-year-old went months without treatment for a tumor. The Fosters were given probation and finally got Patrick treatment, but it was too late and he died in 2007.

Lu Ann Cahn of Philadelphia television station NBC10 spoke to one member of First Tabernacle who refused to give his last name during the interview about the church's beliefs. "The church believes that people get sick because they're not doing the right thing," the man named John said. "God promised us that if we do his will, that there's no infection; all these diseases that you name, would not come to you." He added that he believes the congregation is being persecuted for their beliefs.

Dr. Paul Offit, Chief of the Division of Infectious Diseases at Children's Hospital of Philadelphia, said a parent's faith does not trump their child's healthcare and made the point, "Although you are allowed to martyr yourself, in the State of Pennsylvania there are religious exemptions to child abuse and neglect laws. We are backward in that sense." Contrast the foregoing with how you view healthcare when it comes to yourself and your loved ones. Do you consistently adhere to what the Bible says, or do you opt for modern medicine?

Most people are familiar with the cute little GEICO Gecko on those television commercial who promises to get everyone a better deal on car insurance, but if you believe in the truth of Scripture why would you need insurance at all? When people are sick they often pray for a cure, and this is especially true in the case of life-threatening illnesses and chronic diseases. We've all heard the stories of amazing cures and medical miracles which come through prayer, for example the testimony of a housewife in Santa Monica who said, "I went to the doctor and he told me I had cancer of the uterus. One solution was a radical hysterectomy, but he wanted to try chemotherapy first just in case. My goal in life was to have children and I could not let the doctor make me sterile with a hysterectomy, so that very day I got down on my knees and prayed to God for a miracle. I read every passage of the Bible having anything to do with healing and wrote them all down on index cards which I carried with me everywhere. I recited the verses and prayed whenever I had a spare minute, whether I was waiting at a stop light or for my husband to come home for dinner. And you know what? The good Lord cured me. I started on chemotherapy and at the very next visit my doctor noticed a change. At my next visit he said, 'Let's postpone the surgery and see what happens.' A year later he could no longer detect the tumor and declared me cured. I knew in my heart it was the power of those Scripture verses. God answered my prayers and cured me." Apparently the year of chemotherapy had *nothing* to do with it.

If you subscribe to *Guideposts* magazine you can read a new story like that just about every month. Even major newspapers and national magazines report on such stories now and then and the story of Jeanna Giese is a perfect example. But there are two obvious questions which must be asked. Why did the housewife from Santa Monica need chemotherapy if God was going to cure her anyway? God is all-powerful so his cure should be instantaneous and free of side-effects. And what if she had received the exact same chemo without praying? On the flip side if God's Plan were for her to have a hysterectomy what point would there be in praying, since it would run its course no matter what she did?

There is another way this sort of belief is harmful to children, but it is psychological rather than physical in nature. Not long ago the *Seattle Times* ran a generally heartbreaking series called *You Know I've Been Down... Forgive Me* about a young girl with terminal cancer, with the title being derived from a quote of the girl herself. It was read by a general surgeon named Sid Schwab and one installment put him, as he put it, "over the edge." He said he understood and even supported the decision to stop drug therapy and turn in another direction after conventional treatment had failed but railed against the use of prayer, at least in the way it was being done, and called it child abuse.

Dr. Schwab had previously mentioned in his blog how as a surgeon he had seen faith, at least for some people, make facing deadly illness easier, although he also indicated he had seen it accomplish just the opposite. Patients' faith clearly can make it easier for the doctor who must give bad news and care for the dying, but he pointed out the prayer circles discussed in the article and the continuing belief healing will happen if enough people pray - and implicitly, if the girl herself is godly enough - sets up the poor child for a death bathed in self-recrimination.

Dr. Schwab noted there is absolutely nothing worse than the death of a child and said he has attended to dying children and their families and in fact lived with it in his own family, and he has nothing but sympathy and sorrow for the family and the little girl in the article. He would say to them pray if you need to - pray for comfort, for understanding, for strength - but get off this miracle healing thing because you are ruining what life your child has left. Keep up hope? Sure, as long as it's reasonable. But give her an out, a way to accept what's happening to her if such a thing is possible, without blaming herself.

There is something perverse to the point of revulsion in the idea of a God who will heal a girl if enough people pray for her. What sort of God is that? To believe that, you must also believe he deliberately made her ill and is putting her through enormous pain and suffering with the express plan to make it all better only if enough people tell him how great he is, and to keep it up unto her death if they don't. If that sort of God is out there we are in big, big, trouble. If people survive an illness because of prayer, does that mean God has rejected those who didn't pray? If you pray for a cure and don't get it, and if you believe praying can lead to a cure, then mustn't you accept that God heard your prayers and said no? If so, are you going to Hell? But if you say either outcome is God's will, what is the value of prayer in the first place? In this case it seems it's only to make the girl feel guilty and unworthy.

Does this family's God need reminders or is he waiting for them to hit a magic number of people praying, a certain quantum of prayer-units which must be achieved? Does he give credit for getting close, maybe knock off a little pain when they hit eighty percent, or is it an all or nothing proposition? In praying to him - and if, as the article says, people around the child see God at work in all his glory - shouldn't they be thanking him for their daughter's misery rather than asking for a change of plans? Shouldn't they be delighted? If he is perfect how can you add to that by praying or expect a change? What of children who have no one to pray for them? If prayer works, what happens to those kids? Does this prayer-tabulating yet perfect God not care about them? Or isn't he paying attention? Has he deliberately set them up in a situation where they're screwed?

Dr. Schwab closed by saying, "If a child is sick like this one and is old enough to comprehend what's going on, people need to think it over carefully. If they need to pray they shouldn't just pray for a cure and lay it at her feet, as it's virtually certain to be a losing proposition. Help her come to grips, but don't put the whole burden for survival on her because it's a horrible thing to do. She's asking God's forgiveness? He should be asking for hers."

He was quite right and I saw the truth about medical prayer firsthand when my Mother was stricken with kidney cancer. She had surgery, it was removed and naturally the entire family had prayed - myself included. Our prayers seemed to be answered when the doctors said she was cancer-free, and naturally more credit was given to God than to medical science as is often the case in such matters, but soon the cancer returned and this time it had metastasized to my Mom's bones and elsewhere. My devout older half-sister took her into her home, prayed regularly and even organized a prayer circle at her church, but over the coming months our Mother withered away to virtually nothing as the cancer ate her up. I could have picked her up with one hand by the end, and even worse she was in constant and total agony until the moment she died. I wondered why God had once again not answered our prayers, as had been the case with my Father's fatal heart attack. If he was so adamant about taking this good woman, why couldn't he at least mitigate her pain? I thought about it and began to think about the possible answers. I had at this point in my life never heard the Riddle of Epicurus, but on my own arrived at similar conclusions. Was God not powerful enough to do anything? But I was taught he is omnipotent. Did God not hear our prayers or know about my Mother's suffering? But I was taught he is omniscient. Was God evil and does he enjoy watching people suffer? But I was taught he was the embodiment of all that is good. Was God indifferent to suffering? But if all the other qualities of God were true how could he know about suffering, be good and loving, have the power to do something about it and not do it? That left just one more possibility - there was no God. In a way that made me feel much better. I could accept that death and disease are a part of life which have natural causes we can understand. Conversely, believing in a God who either doesn't care or lacks the power to help us is pointless and worshipping one who is evil is just wrong. I did leave open the door to faith, don't get me wrong, but at this point I would no longer accept it blindly and without question.

The next events which influenced my beliefs concerned my middle sister. She had always been the sibling to which I was closest and for as long as I could remember she had dreamt of having a big family, so it came as a shock when I learned she had suffered a late term miscarriage.

Upon receipt of the Red Cross message I was flown off a Navy ship by helicopter and back to New York to provide comfort, and when I got there couldn't help but notice the nursery had already been decorated in anticipation of the blessed event. In fact a name had already been chosen for her son and that is not something you take back, so he was buried as any adult would be without having ever seen the light of day or knowing the loving touch of his mother. My sister was devastated. The priest's graveside platitudes provided no comfort whatsoever, and once again I had someone I loved crying on my shoulder and asking "why?" Determined to put the episode behind her and start anew my sister eventually became pregnant once again with a son, but this time it turned out even worse. The baby stopped moving, and for medical reasons she was required to carry a stillborn child to term and deliver him as if he were alive. Once again I attended a funeral for someone who never had a chance to get started in life, and the image which will always stay with me is of the tiny little coffin. It was the size of a small cooler. Once again the question "why" was asked, and this time it got me thinking. If God did not want a child to be born to my sister for some cosmically unfathomable reason fine, but if that was so why did he allow her to get pregnant in the first place? Why not just intervene between the sperm and egg and spare her all that grief? The same questions which I had asked upon my Mother's death came to mind once again, as well as one other thought. If God is in control and causes these things to happen that makes him for all intents and purposes an abortionist, which didn't make any sense considering the Church's position on abortion. The obvious rationalization here is anything God does is by definition automatically correct, but once again why allow the pregnancy and cause so much heartache later on?

Fast forward a couple of years. Now it was my older half-sister's turn to contract cancer. This was the same woman who had prayed so hard and cared for our Mother so lovingly in her last days. At the time I learned of the situation I was stationed in Africa, and while I wasn't able to be there in person I offered as much moral support and advice as I possibly could. Eventually I found out the doctors felt her cancer was treatable and the course of treatment would include aggressive transfusions. That gave me hope, but what I was told next made me angry. My sister's church was one which did not believe in transfusions because they believed it was a violation of biblical Scripture, specifically Genesis 9:4, Leviticus 17:10 and Acts 15:29 among others. I told her to get the treatments but her faith was strong, and besides her church had set up a prayer circle. Naturally my thoughts went back to the one which had been organized for our Mom, but my sister put her life in the hands of God. It was quite sad when she passed away so unnecessarily and so young - she was only fifty-three - and when that happened I went from someone who questioned the existence of God to someone who saw the harm religious beliefs and practices can cause.

Once again, if God answers prayers why do you need health insurance? Think it through. If what Jesus says about prayer in the Bible is true and stories about medical miracles in inspirational literature are true and the cure of Jeanna Giese is true and your belief in God and the power of prayer is correct and God has a plan for you, why do you ever need to visit a doctor or go to the hospital? Why don't you simply pray for a cure whenever you get sick? In fact, why not pray preemptively every day and go through your life completely healthy? The reason I ask is because of the statement in Psalms Chapter 41, "Blessed is he who has regard for the weak; the Lord delivers him in times of trouble. The Lord will protect him and preserve his life; he will bless him in the land and not surrender him to the desire of his foes. The Lord will sustain him on his sickbed and restore him from his bed of illness." Then in Mark 16 Jesus talks about the laying on of hands saying, "He who believes and is baptized will be saved; but he who does not believe will be condemned. And these signs will accompany those who believe: in my name they will cast out demons; they will speak in new tongues; they will pick up serpents, and if they drink any deadly thing, it will not hurt them; they will lay their hands on the sick, and they will recover." Even more to the point is James 5:15 where the Bible says, "And the prayer offered in faith will make the sick person well; the Lord will raise him up." That is completely unambiguous, and if these words are true it seems a faithful person should have no need for doctors or health insurance.

What reason would a perfect God have for making false statements in the Bible? Yet by visiting a doctor and/or owning health insurance you demonstrate that something in these verses is amiss, assuming you have read the Bible you profess to believe in. Obviously you don't trust God with your healthcare because he is so random when it comes to answering prayers. This is why people need doctors and health insurance. If God exists, answers prayers and has a plan for each of us there is no point in ever visiting a doctor and owning health insurance is a waste of money because either God will or will not answer any prayer for healing. If he does answer the prayer there is no need for a doctor and if he does not God's plan is for you to be sick and since God is omnipotent no amount of doctoring can change the outcome.

If you are a believer look at your healthcare policy from another angle. Turn to Matthew 6:25-34 where Jesus says, "Therefore I tell you, do not worry about your life, what you will eat or drink; or about your body, what you will wear. Is not life more important than food, and the body more important than clothes? Look at the birds of the air; they do not sow or reap or store away in barns, and yet your Heavenly Father feeds them. Are you not much more valuable than they? Who of you by worrying can add a single hour to his life? And why do you worry about clothes? See how the lilies of the field grow. They do not labor or spin. Yet I tell you that not even Solomon in all his splendor was dressed like one of these. If that is how God clothes the grass of the field, which is here today and tomorrow is thrown into the fire, will he not much more clothe you, O you of little faith? So do not worry, saying 'What shall we eat?' or 'What shall we drink?' or 'What shall we wear?' For the pagans run after all these things, and your Heavenly Father knows that you need them. But seek first his kingdom and his righteousness, and all these things will be given to you as well. Therefore do not worry about tomorrow, for tomorrow will worry about itself."

Jesus' is clear when he says, "Do not worry about tomorrow, for tomorrow will worry about itself," and yet health insurance is a physical manifestation of worry and you buy it because you are worried about how your health will be tomorrow. The question is obvious. If you are a believer why would you need health or for that matter car, life or home owner's insurance? Why are you worrying when Jesus has told you specifically not to worry and promised to cure any illness which arises? In addition why are you worrying about money, which is what health insurance is all about, when in Matthew 6:19 Jesus specifically says, "Do not lay up for yourselves treasures on earth, where moth and rust destroy and where thieves break in and steal; but lay up for yourselves treasures in Heaven, where neither moth nor rust destroys and where thieves do not break in and steal. For where your treasure is, there your heart will be also." And then there is Proverbs 3:5-8 which says, "Trust in the Lord with all your heart and lean not on your own understanding; in all your ways acknowledge him, and he will make your paths straight. Do not be wise in your own eyes; fear the Lord and shun evil. This will bring health to your body and nourishment to your bones."

So why do you own a health insurance policy when you are supposed to be putting your trust in the Lord, who will bring health to your body?

Why are you ignoring what it tells you to do? Is it possible you are ignoring the Bible because in your heart you know God isn't real? What other reason could there be for a believer to ignore him?

You may be thinking, "You do not understand God. He must remain hidden. If he answered medical prayers it would destroy faith. That is why we need doctors." There are several problems with that. As previously noted there is no evidence God wants to remain hidden since he supposedly parted the Red Sea, carved his Commandments into stone tablets with his own finger and incarnated himself in the form of Jesus who performed miracles on earth to prove he is God. Second, if by answering prayers God would destroy faith, the aforementioned Santa Monica housewife should have had hers destroyed. Third, any medical miracle God performs today is obvious because we have advanced technology. The removal of a cancerous tumor, for example, is obvious because it is measurable. One month the tumor is visible to everyone on the X-ray and the next month it is not so if God eliminated the tumor it is obvious to everyone who sees it. There is nothing hidden about that. Another example is Jeanna's rabies case. Millions of people are aware of the rabies "miracle." What is hidden about her recovery? If you believe such "miracles" are evidence for God's existence on the one hand, you cannot claim he wants to remain hidden on the other.

Another common explanation is, "God is under no obligation to answer prayers. He helps those who help themselves. Therefore when you get sick you go to a doctor because he works through them." And yet almost without exception if that doctor cures them God and prayer will get the lion's share of the credit, but if the treatment or operation fails incompetent doctors will shoulder the blame and no mention will be made of God and those unanswered prayers will be all but forgotten because nobody ever files a malpractice suit against God.

Let's look at an example. Imagine the rate of remission for a particularly nasty type of cancer such as the pancreatic variety is five percent. That means if twenty people get this type of cancer it is almost always fatal and only one of the twenty will survive. All of them have read James 5:15, so all pray. Nineteen die, and the one who lives proclaims, "I prayed to the Lord and He answered my prayers. My disease is cured. It is a miracle!" But you will never hear about the nineteen who died. No one ever writes about them in a magazine because *Person Prays, Then Dies* is not a great headline, and since they are dead you will never hear from any of the people who had their prayers fail. As a result you only hear about the one out of twenty which succeeded so it appears prayer is successful. You can pick any disease and if you analyze both the successes and failures of prayer you will discover the same thing. It does not matter how many people pray, how often they pray, how sincere they are or how devout and worthy the patient is. Based upon statistics God ignores all medical prayers, and plenty of scientific studies confirm it. In the largest study of its kind (detailed elsewhere) researchers found having people pray for heart bypass surgery patients had no effect on their recovery and in fact patients who knew they were being prayed for had a slightly higher rate of complications.

Yes there are people who do pray and live and their stories sound convincing, but only because the millions who pray and die never get to tell their stories and those left behind rarely if ever mention them. Consider the miracle of Jeanna Giese. Had she died the story of her prayer circle never would have appeared in the paper. People assemble prayer circles which fail all the time but you never hear about them, so to the casual observer it appears they always work. Do you remember what happened when popular former New York Mets catcher Gary Carter was diagnosed with inoperable brain cancer in 2011? Probably not, and I will tell you why. His devoutly Christian daughter Kim began writing a blog in which she tracked the progress of his treatment and asked people to pray for her father. They did so by the thousands. In response to that she wrote confidently, "Team Carter believes that dad will hit one out of the park. We are pouring the 'unknown' and fearful thoughts to Jesus and not allowing Satan to get the best of us," adding, "the Lord is my strength and shield. I trust him with my heart." Sadly that trust turned out to be misplaced when Carter died less than a year later at the age of fifty-seven and Kim was forced to rationalize, "I am deeply saddened to tell you all that my precious dad went to be with Jesus today at 4:10 p.m… he is in heaven and has reunited with his mom and dad. I believe with all my heart that dad had a STANDING OVATION as he walked through the gates of heaven to be with Jesus." Of course that was the last we heard of those prayers and naturally his parents were believed to be in Heaven waiting to greet him rather than the other place, but more to the point can you imagine the clamor from the devout if he had miraculously recovered? But he didn't.

That closely parallels the story of Andrew Smith, a former star basketball player at Butler University who had played his high school ball at a school called Covenant Christian. On January 12, 2013 the former Bulldogs star, who had played in two national championship games, died at the age of twenty-five after a two-year battle with cancer.

His deep religious convictions gave him and his family hope he could win his fight and after he was diagnosed with an aggressive form of non-Hodgkin lymphoma early in 2014 his wife Samantha started documenting her husband's battle by providing updates and inspirational messages on a blog called "Kicking Cancer with the Smiths." The week before his death she, along with his parents and former college teammates, began pleading for more prayers on social media. They got them, but apparently God wasn't listening. Samantha wrote, "I can't wrap my head around the fact that there is nothing left to do for Andrew except tell him how much I love him, hold his hand and be with him for every second we have left together. The doctors tell me death is imminent and that Andrew is going to die from this disease. There are no treatments, no clinical trials. There is nothing left to do. I struggle to grasp what they've told me and I spend my nights crying and moaning in pain as I think about losing the one I hold most dear and close to my heart - my husband." What sort of God causes or allows such a thing to happen to a devout young man and his family? This tragedy is easy to understand if there is no God because disease is a natural and explainable part of life, but if he does exist his failure to answer these heartfelt prayers is troubling. What sort of excuses come to mind? The faithful will have many.

A better known story is that of Chicago Bears running back Brian Piccolo which was the subject of the 1971 movie *Brian's Song*. Piccolo was diagnosed with embryonal cell carcinoma and soon after an initial surgery at Sloan-Kettering Cancer Center in New York City to remove the tumor he underwent a second procedure in April 1970 to remove his left lung and pectoral muscle, only to be re-admitted in early June at which time doctors determined the cancer had spread to other organs including his liver. He died in the early morning of June 16 at the age of twenty-six. The month before Piccolo's death teammate Gale Sayers was accepting the George S. Halas Award for Most Courageous Player and told the crowd they had selected the wrong person for the award. He said, "I love Brian Piccolo and I'd like all of you to love him too. Tonight, when you hit your knees to pray, please ask God to love him, too." No doubt many did so, but it didn't help. God was nowhere to be found.

Another thing to consider is the claims of those who pray to other gods. They truly believe their prayers are being answered by a deity which people of your faith, whatever that happens to be, do not believe exists. How is that possible if they do not worship the one "true" God?

The final apologetic in the face of all of the foregoing is, "God can't answer my prayers because if he did it would take away my free will to believe in him" which is virtually the same thing as saying he does not answer prayers at all. This is the "robot argument," which is covered elsewhere in this book. What sort of plan did God have for Gary Carter, Andrew Smith, Brian Piccolo and their loved ones? In cases like these faith is little more than a tool to console those who have been left behind. The bottom line is even if God does exist suffice it to say, as author Bret Harte once observed, "The Creator who could put a cancer in a believer's stomach is above being interfered with by prayers."

Think about that for a moment. In order for medical prayers to be necessary there first must be disease, and if God created everything that means in addition to making trees and sunrises and puppies he must also necessarily have created malaria, measles, the Black Plague, cancer, diabetes, Ebola, gastric reflux, Alzheimer's, arthritis, tuberculosis, epilepsy, gallstones, herpes, hemorrhoids, pneumonia, influenza and the other *thirty thousand* diseases known to modern medicine. Why? One possible explanation is design flaw, which suggests God is not as perfect as he claims to be. Can you imagine an automobile manufacturer rolling out a model with that many flaws? They would be sued and go out of business overnight. Another possibility is those maladies are inflicted on purpose, which is not something an omnibenevolent deity would do, with the idea being to make people ill in order to cause dependence and generate prayers. This is akin to someone stabbing you with a knife so you will beg him to stitch up the wound, and when he does so you praise him for being merciful. This suggests a God who suffers from "hero complex" in much the same way some firefighters and police officers do. For example in July of 2004 transit police officer Joseph Rodriguez placed a bomb in the Times Square subway station and then warned commuters of an impending explosion, and in 2009 volunteer firefighter Caleb Lacey set fire to a neighbor's apartment building in North Lawrence, New York and then waited at the fire station for the alert so he could help put it out. In a similar fashion God creates the problem to generate a need for his "cure."

Once again we must make a choice. Did God make mistakes which led to your little niece's pediatric cancer and favorite aunt's Alzheimer's Disease? Did he do those things to them on purpose? Or is it possible he does not exist and those disorders are simply the unfortunate but natural consequences of being living organisms?

Supernatural Claims

Or, Faith Can't Move Mountains

"Pray, v: To ask that the laws of the universe be annulled in behalf of a single petitioner, confessedly unworthy." ~ Ambrose Bierce, *The Devil's Dictionary*

A man once bought a lamp at an auction, took it home and had begun to polish it when suddenly a genie appeared and said, "I'll grant you three wishes, Master." The man said, "I wish I could believe in you," so the genie snapped his fingers and suddenly the man believed in him. The man then said, "Wow… I wish everyone in the world would also believe in you," so the genie snapped his fingers again and suddenly people all over the world begin to believe in genies. "What about your third wish?" asked the genie. "Well," said the man, "I wish for a billion dollars." The genie snapped his fingers for a third time, but nothing happened. "What's wrong?" asked the man. The genie shrugged and answered, "Just because you believe in me doesn't necessarily mean I *really* exist."

Many people believe God, much like a magic genie, reaches down to earth on a regular basis to answer prayers. People talk about their "answered prayers" all the time and inspirational books and magazines document thousands of them, however as we have learned there is a specific group of people who represent those whom God never helps through prayer. No matter how much they pray, no matter how many people gather in prayer groups, no matter how much they believe, as we have previously discussed no matter how deserving and holy they are, what we have found is God never reaches down to earth to regenerate the legs of amputees - and amputees aren't the only group he completely ignores. For example God never cures those who suffer from Down's Syndrome, and for that matter there are hundreds of diseases which are impossible to "cure" with prayer.

In the previous chapter we discovered God does not answer medical prayers in general, but even so it is easy to create the illusion prayer works. The way you do it is by reporting only on the "successes" of prayer, but as soon as you start tracking both the successes and the failures and apply some statistical analysis to the data it is easy for an objective person to see prayer has no effect.

The amputation experiment discussed earlier falls into a class of prayers which could be called "impossible prayers" because it is impossible in the natural course of events for a human leg to regenerate. It is easy to think of hundreds of other impossible prayers and they can each teach us something about how prayer works. For example, "I pray that you completely eliminate all of the diseases in the world tomorrow. Amen." If you were to say that prayer it will never be answered. We all know that.

What if the impossible prayer is incredibly worthy but less grandiose? After all, the elimination of all disease is a big deal. What if for example you pray for God to levitate a car because a drunk driver has run over a small child and she is pinned under one of the wheels? Or if you pray for the ability to fly like Superman so you can soar up to a tenth story window and save two children from their burning apartment? None of it matters, because God never answers impossible prayers. Why is that?

We can use Mount Everest as a simple example. It should be easy to move it to Newark since in Matthew 17:20 Jesus specifically talks about mountains and says quite clearly, "For truly, I say to you, if you have faith as a grain of mustard seed, you will say to this mountain, 'Move from here to there,' and it will move; and nothing will be impossible to you." There are no caveats. A devoted person with a little faith should be able to move Mt. Everest to Newark. What could be clearer than "nothing will be impossible to you?" And yet we have never seen a mountain move, although Marco Polo once wrote in his diary about how in the late 900s a caliph required Christians to move a mountain in three days under pain of death. The Coptic Pope of Egypt supposedly then asked everyone to pray and in a vision the Virgin Mary told the pope to get intercession from a one-eyed man carrying water through the market. This was St. Simon the Tanner, who directed the prayers of the Christians and as a result the Mokattam Mountain was allegedly lifted and set back down in its proper place several times before the caliph. All I can say about this is if you believe this one, perhaps I could interest you in a bridge in Brooklyn?

Next come rationalizations such as, "Coal miners move mountains, scientists create artificial limbs for amputees and a crane can make a car levitate. These human accomplishments are divinely inspired and God acts on this world through men." There are three problems with this argument. First of all in Matthew 21:21 Jesus says, "I tell you the truth, if you have faith and do not doubt, not only can you do what was done to the fig tree, but also you can say to this mountain, 'Go, throw yourself into the sea,' and it will be done. If you believe, you will receive whatever you ask for in prayer." Jesus does not say, "You will have to hire thousands of people, spend a billion dollars on heavy equipment and work twenty-four hours a day for twenty years to move this mountain into the sea, and it will be done." The mountain actually moves itself in Jesus' statement. The second problem is the vast majority of people do not have the resources to move a mountain even if that had been what Jesus meant, therefore Jesus' statement is false even if he did have earth-moving machinery which had not yet been invented in mind. The third is if human accomplishments are indeed "divinely inspired" there should be no reason why God did not divinely inspire them thousands of years ago. For example why didn't God inspire a smallpox vaccine in 2000 BCE rather than waiting until 1950? Why would he want tens of millions of people to suffer and die from smallpox over thousands of years but then suddenly decide to divinely inspire a cure in the 20th Century?

The reason we call them human accomplishments is because they are exactly that and God had nothing to do with them. If he is divinely inspiring them the headline in the paper should never be *Scientist Discovers Cure for Polio* but instead should always read *God Divinely Inspires Scientist to Discover Cure for Polio.* In that case you have to wonder why he is so unfair in his distribution of inspirations and for that matter why we pay scientists since clearly they are unable to do anything on their own.

Let's imagine a person prays for something impossible, no matter what it is, for example the instant elimination of cancer worldwide. Obviously this is not going to happen despite all of Jesus' promises, so the religious person prays and nothing happens. So how does he rationalize the prayer's failure? Probably by employing a meaningless apologetic such as, "It is not part of God's plan." Ask them to explain what that plan is. The response will be yet another apologetic such as, "We can't understand God's purposes." Now consider a different situation in which a person prays for something which is possible, for example to win a church raffle, and he actually does win. What happened is nothing more than a coincidence, but in his mind that coincidence is now an "answered prayer." How can we prove this so-called answered prayer is a coincidence? Simply look at all of the losers. If there were a million people entered in the raffle that means 999,999 of them lost, and since it was a church raffle they all must be believers and all probably prayed. That's 999,999 unanswered prayers vs. one answered prayer. That is a terrible ratio.

An excellent example of what faith really entails can be found in the classic 1947 Christmas movie *Miracle on 34th Street.* Doris (Maureen O'Hara) has raised her young daughter Susan (Natalie Wood) to not believe in fairy tales, but Susan's lack of faith is shaken when she sees department store Santa Kris Kringle conversing in Dutch with an adopted girl who does not know English. Doris asks Kris to tell Susan he is not really Santa Claus, but Kris insists he is. Lawyer Fred Gailey, who is defending Kris in court, tells Doris, "Faith is believing, when common sense tells you not to. Don't you see? It's not just Kris that's on trial, it's everything he stands for. It's kindness and joy and love and all the other intangibles," and eventually she tells Susan, "Sometimes you just have to have faith." Susan is not convinced because she has observed that many Christmas wishes are not granted, so Kris tells her, "Now wait a minute, Susie. Just because every child can't get his wish that doesn't mean there isn't a Santa Claus." So little Susan sits there chanting, "I believe, I believe, I believe" over and over to see if she had been wrong and fantasy was actually reality. It is important to remember they are talking about *Santa* being real and *wishes* being granted, not God being real and prayers being answered, but it is essentially the same premise.

As an interesting aside, the movie was given a 'B' rating (signifying it was morally objectionable) by the Catholic Legion of Decency for its portrayal of the mother as being divorced, which seems rather petty considering half of all marriages end in dissolution. Times certainly have changed. The 'B' category was eventually merged into the 'O' category which caused the movie to appear on the list of films condemned by the Legion of Decency.

In a similar vein eight-year-old Virginia O'Hanlon once wrote a letter to the editor of New York's *Sun* newspaper asking if Santa Claus was real, and the quick response was printed as an unsigned editorial on September 21, 1897. It was the work of veteran newsman Francis Pharcellus Church, and has since become history's all-time most reprinted newspaper editorial. Here is the letter, followed by the reply, with one small editorial change. The words "Santa Claus" have been replaced with the word "God" throughout.

"DEAR EDITOR: I am eight years old. Some of my little friends say there is no God. Papa says, 'If you see it in the *Sun* it's so.' Please tell me the truth; is there a God? (signed) Virginia O'Hanlon, 115 West Ninety-Fifth Street."

"Virginia, your little friends are wrong. They have been affected by the skepticism of a skeptical age. They do not believe except [what] they see. They think that nothing can be which is not comprehensible by their little minds. All minds, Virginia, whether they be men's or children's, are little. In this great universe of ours man is a mere insect, an ant, in his intellect, as compared with the boundless world about him, as measured by the intelligence capable of grasping the whole of truth and knowledge. Yes, Virginia, there is a God. He exists as certainly as love and generosity and devotion exist, and you know that they abound and give to your life its highest beauty and joy. Alas! How dreary would be the world if there were no God. It would be as dreary as if there were no Virginias. There would be no childlike faith then, no poetry, no romance to make tolerable this existence. We should have no enjoyment, except in sense and sight. The eternal light with which childhood fills the world would be extinguished. Not believe in God! You might as well not believe in fairies! You might get your papa to hire men to watch in all the churches on Easter and Christmas to catch a glimpse of God, but even if they did not see God, what would that prove? Nobody sees God, but that is no sign that there is no God. The most real things in the world are those that neither children nor men can see. Did you ever see fairies dancing on the lawn? Of course not, but that's no proof that they are not there. Nobody can conceive or imagine all the wonders there are unseen and unseeable in the world. You may tear apart the baby's rattle and see what makes the noise inside, but there is a veil covering the unseen world which not the strongest man, nor even the united strength of all the strongest men that ever lived, could tear apart. Only faith, fancy, poetry, love, romance, can push aside that curtain and view and picture the supernal beauty and glory beyond. Is it all real? Ah, Virginia, in all this world there is nothing else real and abiding. No God! Thank God! He lives, and he lives forever. A thousand years from now, Virginia, nay, ten times ten thousand years from now, he will continue to make glad the heart of childhood."

Once again the difference between this letter and the original is the name "Santa Claus" was replaced with the word "God." Now think about what Mr. Church's intent was when he wrote to little Virginia. It was to convince her that Santa, or at least a belief in Santa, was real. Now, assuming you are an adult and realize Santa Claus is a fictional character, what does that tell you about belief in God? It tells us people employ this very same type of poetic rationalization to convince others, and themselves for that matter, that a God or gods actually exist.

The foregoing highlights a Bible verse which tells believers, "Except he be converted, and become as little children, ye shall not enter into the

Kingdom of Heaven," which makes blind, childlike faith out to be a virtue. Is it not better to grow up and accept responsibility rather than act like a helpless child? Far more reasonable was the position of Galileo Galilei who, though a pious man, said, "I do not feel obliged to believe that the same God who has endowed us with sense, reason and intellect has intended us to forgo their use."

Bad Things, Good People

Or, Good Things, Bad People

At age thirteen future Apple magnate Steve Jobs asked the Lutheran pastor of his parents' church if God knew about starving children. "Yes, God knows everything," the pastor replied. Jobs never returned to church, refusing to worship a God who allowed such suffering, and eventually became a Buddhist.

In 1863 Mary Virginia "Jennie" Wade was a twenty-year-old resident of Gettysburg engaged to be married to Corporal Johnston H. Skelly of the 87th Pennsylvania Regiment. She worked as a seamstress with her mother in their home and to make ends meet they also took care of a six-year-old boarder named Isaac. For safety during the first day's battle Jennie and her family moved to the home of Jennie's sister who had given birth with great difficulty one hour before the Confederates rode into Gettysburg, and Jennie was caring for her as well. There was no heavy fighting in that area but a Federal picket line did run behind the little brick house and there was intermittent skirmishing between it and Confederate outposts in the town proper. Protected by the sturdy brick walls of the house, they lived for three days in the midst of the greatest battle ever seen in this hemisphere. Jennie spent most of July 1st distributing bread to Union soldiers and filling their canteens with water and by late afternoon on July 2nd the diminishing supply of bread made it apparent more would be needed the next day. Jennie and her mother left the yeast in the kitchen to rise, and the next morning Confederate sharpshooters began firing at the north windows of the house. Meanwhile the prep work to bake biscuits was begun and while Jennie stood in the kitchen kneading dough a Confederate musket ball smashed through a door on the north side of the house, struck her in the back beneath her left shoulder blade and embedded itself in her corset - killing her instantly. In the early afternoon of July 4th Jennie's mother baked fifteen loaves of bread from the dough Jennie had kneaded. Jennie Wade was the only civilian casualty of the battle of Gettysburg and if you subscribe to the notion of a divine plan, innocent as she was, she never had a chance - and of course this is just one example amongst millions.

Now let's look at the flip side. Even the most callous person would be shocked by the crimes of Josef Mengele, Auschwitz's notorious "Angel of Death," who saved women and children from the gas chambers only to experiment on them instead - amputating limbs, removing organs without anesthetic, injecting ink directly into eyeballs, vivisecting (literally "to cut up something that's alive") pregnant women, crudely sewing two children together and dissecting babies just to see what happened. Even by the horrific standards of the 20th Century he was one of the worst butchers who ever lived, and he was never caught. At the end of World War II Mengele escaped to Argentina and for the rest of his life was sought by Germany, the Mossad and others but no one ever came close to finding him. If you subscribe to the notion of a divine plan, guilty as he was, they never had a chance.

Believers will rationalize those things happened for a purpose and console themselves by believing poor Jennie Wade went on to her just reward in Heaven and Mengele will pay for his crimes in Hell for eternity, and while I wish that were true a few questions must be asked. What if Jennie were not a Christian? What if Mengele accepted Jesus as his personal savior before he died? Of course not all Christians subscribe to that route to the hereafter and some believe your works determine your destination but as was pointed out at the beginning of this book that sort of disagreement is one of the big problems with religion, so let's look at a biblical example of bad things happening to a good person.

The book of Job is a full-length argument about whether or not the misfortunes which befall ostensibly good people come to them from the hand of God. In it Satan wagers Job will lose his faith if he loses his possessions, God takes the bet, Job's wealth is stolen, his family is killed and Satan afflicts him with disease... but Job recognizes God's power and God saves the day by giving Job "twice what he had before" including 14,000 sheep and 6,000 camels, although his family remained dead even though God could have presumably restored them as well as he would do with Lazarus one day. In the end this fable poses the question why does God inflict such misery on some people?

To answer it let's compare the God of Abraham to the Norse gods. Odin and the Norse pantheon were believed to have some influence on the world but weren't omnipresent, weren't omniscient and weren't omnipotent. They weren't omnibenevolent either, but even if they were some bad things would happen which they couldn't prevent because they either couldn't be everywhere at once, other equally powerful forces were working against them or they allowed bad things to occur through clumsiness, malice, oversight or indifference. The God of Job also doesn't seem to be omniscient, or else why would Satan bother arguing hypotheticals with him? He would have already known what Job would do just as he should have known Abraham was prepared to sacrifice his son, but he made them go through the motions anyway. God (who along with Satan was part of a polytheistic and/or henotheistic pantheon when Job was written) also let Job's family be killed and his property destroyed just to settle a wager about the nature of piety in much the same manner Mortimer and Randolph Duke ruined the life of Louis Winthorpe to settle a bet in the film *Trading Places*. It isn't so much malice as indifference to human suffering and a willingness to inflict misery for reasons which are hardly justifiable morally, since Job was "blameless" by premise and his family certainly did not deserve their fate. Of course in a world without deities there are still plenty of forces and entities which want to hurt good people or which punish altruism in other ways, so dropping the theistic component doesn't so much resolve the moral questions as make them easier to ignore. Clearly omnibenevolence is not an attribute the author of Job, whoever he was, seems inclined to attribute to the deity.

"Why do bad things happen to good people?" is an incredibly common question. In fact it is so common there is a well-known book by that title written by Melvin Tinker, another even better known book entitled *When Bad Things Happen to Good People* by Harold Kushner and an even more popular book called *When God Doesn't Make Sense* by Dr. James Dobson - and for James Dobson to weigh in, this must be an important question.

This is a paradox for any believer, and rightly so. In his book Dr. Dobson opens with the story of Chuck Frye, a gifted student who graduated from college and was accepted to medical school. Frye had decided to work as a medical missionary and Dobson says, "If permitted to live, Chuck could have treated thousands of poor and needy people who would otherwise suffer and die in utter hopelessness. Not only could he have ministered to their physical needs, but his ultimate desire was to share the gospel with those who had never heard this greatest of stories." Unfortunately, despite fervent prayers from his parents, family and friends, Frye contracted and then died of leukemia shortly after starting medical school. As Dobson puts it, "How can we make sense of this incomprehensible act of God?"

We see this kind of thing all the time. For example we read about a woman who is such a devout believer she goes to church three times a week, gives her time and money to charity, is constantly helping others and wears both a crucifix and a "WWJD" bracelet. In other words she "walks with Jesus." Then one day a carjacker forces his way into her car. There is a Bible sitting right there on the front seat next to her, but it doesn't matter. The carjacker shoots her in the head, dumps her body in a ditch and her family is left to pick up the pieces in bewilderment.

When we ask why bad things happen to good people the essence of the question is if God is answering our prayers how could he allow such horrible things to happen to true believers while ignoring their prayers? If someone lives a good and faithful life and is doing God's work why would he allow bad things to happen to that person? Why doesn't he instead protect a person who is going to church every Sunday, putting money in the offering plate, following the Commandments, praying faithfully and so on? The question is puzzling because it makes two assumptions - God exists, and he keeps score.

In other words the question assumes God is looking down on us answering our prayers and keeping track of who is good and bad on a minute-by-minute basis. We assume God keeps a record of "goodness" and "badness" for each of us much like Santa Claus and the reason he keeps score is to decide whose prayers he should answer and who should go to Heaven, but what if we were to approach the question from the opposite angle? What if we hypothesize, just for a moment, that God doesn't exist?

Once we do that the paradox evaporates because if there is no one answering prayers and keeping score it is easy to understand why bad things happen to good people. When you look at it this way everything makes sense because whether you are good or bad is irrelevant. In the real world things like cancer, hurricanes and serial killers have no way to know whether you are good or bad nor would they care, therefore bad things would happen to good people just as often as they happen to everyone else. Bad things happen to everyone.

Let's look at a simple example. In the real world what are your chances of getting cancer if you are a good person? Exactly the same as if you are a bad one. That is easy to prove statistically since believers who have the same risk factors get cancer just as often as non-believers. Why might that be? It is because any given cell in every human body has some probability of turning cancerous and that probability is the same regardless of religious background. There are many different paths to cancer, but let's focus on one and use it as an example - cosmic rays.

Every hour of every day your body is bombarded by ultraviolet rays which may alter the DNA of a cell in your body, and if a cell is altered in a certain way it can turn cancerous and a tumor begins to form. These rays have no way of knowing if you are good or bad or whether or not you believe in God, nor do they care. Everyone gets hit by the same number and therefore we all have the same probability of getting cancer.

You actually can change the probabilities in certain cases. Someone who smokes increases his probability of getting lung cancer. A person who lies on a tanning bed increases her probability of getting skin cancer. A pilot or an astronaut gets hit by more cosmic rays and increases their probability of cancer. So by not smoking, staying on the ground and remaining pale you can reduce your cancer risk, but no one can eliminate it totally - certainly not by praying.

In a similar fashion a hurricane does not care if the people in its path are good or bad. Both hardened criminals and innocent infants die in them. A deer does not care whether the driver is good or bad when it leaps out onto a highway at midnight and crashes through a windshield. Fat molecules do not care whether you are good or bad as they attach themselves to your heart's arteries and create the conditions necessary for a heart attack. The examples are virtually endless.

A hurricane causes just as much damage for believers as non-believers. God does not divert them away from devout nations. They hit the United States every year, often with devastating results, despite the fact the majority of Americans believe in God. In spite of what people like Pat Robertson say about God "lifting his protection from New Orleans" during Hurricane Katrina due to sin, he is not reaching down from Heaven and arbitrarily modifying the laws of probability on behalf of believers. Volcanoes, forest fires, tornadoes, tsunamis, car crashes and diseases do not care if you have been bad or good or whether or not you believe in God. They are equal opportunity disasters.

Take for example the 1755 disaster known as the Great Lisbon Earthquake which occurred at 9:40 AM on the morning of 1 November during the holiday of All Saints Day. Lisbon was a pious city, and since it was a major church holiday many thousands were in church worshipping when it struck. In combination with subsequent fires and a tsunami the earthquake almost totally destroyed Lisbon and adjoining areas including major churches such as the Lisbon Cathedral, the Misericórdia Church and the Basilicas of São Paulo, Santa Catarina and São Vicente de Fora. The Royal Hospital of All Saints in the Rossio square, which was the largest public hospital at the time, was consumed by fire and hundreds of patients burned to death. Estimates place the death toll in Lisbon alone between 10,000 and 100,000 people, making it one of the deadliest earthquakes in history, and because it had struck on an important church holiday and destroyed almost every important church in the city anxiety and confusion reigned amongst the citizens of a staunchly devout Roman Catholic country which had been a major patron of the Church. Theologians speculated on the religious cause and message, seeing the earthquake as a manifestation of divine judgment, however most philosophers rejected that on the grounds that the Alfama, which was Lisbon's red-light district, suffered only minor damage.

Which brings us to God's Plan, which is how many believers traditionally explain things like earthquakes, cancer, hurricanes and car accidents. For example the destruction of Lisbon and the deaths of tens of thousands of people, both good and bad, were part of that plan. When God ignored the prayers of Neva Rogers and allowed the Red Lake gunman to shoot her in the head she died as part of that plan as well. Her death somehow had a purpose and God "called her home" for a reason. In other words even if something bad happens it is rationalized as actually being good because it is part of God's master plan.

You can see how pervasive this plan is by reading inspirational books and magazines. For example in the book *The Purpose Driven Life* by Rick Warren it says, "Because God made you for a reason, he also decided when you would be born and how long you would live. He planned the days of your life in advance, choosing the exact time of your birth and death. The Bible says, 'You saw me before I was born and scheduled each day of my life before I began to breathe. Every day was recorded in your book!' [Psalm 139:16]" and "Regardless of the circumstances of your birth or who your parents are, God had a plan in creating you."

As discussed in the chapter on free will, under this view of the universe God plans everything. Take a moment and think about that. Rick Warren said, "He planned the days of your life in advance, choosing the exact time of your birth and death." Let's once again examine an implication of this statement. As previously noted this means God pre-planned every abortion which has ever taken place. If you think about that you will realize how impossible the notion of a plan is. If the concept is true God wants us to abort children and since every abortion is planned by God he must be doing it for a reason, so both the mother who requests the abortion and the doctor who performs it are blameless since it is God who planned it because, according to Rick Warren, God chose the exact time of the death so the mother and doctor are simply puppets. You may be thinking God does not intend for us to perform abortions, but if you believe Rick Warren you are obviously incorrect.

In order to better understand this concept let's look at one of the biggest global events in history, World War II. According to *Encarta* "The human cost [of WWII], not including between 5.6 million and 5.9 million Jews killed in the Holocaust who were indirect victims of the war, is estimated to have been fifty-five million dead - with twenty-five million of those military and thirty million civilian." In addition, sixty-one countries and 1.7 billion people participated, which means seventy-five percent of all human beings alive at the time participated in WWII in some way. World War II was obviously a major disaster, perhaps the most horrific event the world has ever seen, and it is safe to say the majority of human beings on planet Earth prayed to some god or another for victory and/or for the war to end.

Then there is Adolph Hitler. Consider the statement, "Hitler is part of God's plan" and think about what Rick Warren wrote. "He planned the days of your life in advance, choosing the exact time of your birth and death. The Bible says, 'You saw me before I was born and scheduled each day of my life before I began to breathe. Every day was recorded in your book!' [Psalm 139:16]" He also said, "God never does anything accidentally and he never makes mistakes. He has a reason for everything he creates. Every plant and every animal was planned by God, and every person was designed with a purpose in mind."

So if God has a divine plan for each of us then he had a divine plan for Hitler too, and when you stop to think about it the contradiction hits home. Since God is all-powerful his plan would of necessity be all-inclusive and Hitler and WWII would simply be pieces in a supreme plan of massive proportions with millions dying for specific reasons and each death having a purpose and meaning. Now let's imagine you say a prayer in this sort of universe. What difference would it make? God has his plan and it is running down its track like a freight train. If there is a plan then everyone who died in the Holocaust had to die. Holocaust victims and soldiers could pray all day and they would still die. The idea of a plan makes the notion of a prayer-answering relationship with God ridiculous, yet people attach themselves to both ideas despite the irresolvable contradiction. As Christopher Hitchens put it, "The man who prays is the one who thinks that God has arranged matters all wrong, but who also thinks that he can instruct God how to put them right."

Think about what God's plan means for you personally. If it says you will get hit by a bus tomorrow or terrorists will blow you up then that's what will happen. The same goes for disease. If you contract cancer this afternoon and die three months later that is God's plan for you and praying for a cure is a waste of time because he has pre-programmed the exact time of your death and there is nothing you can do to change it.

Hitler was clearly blameless. He was not evil because he had no free will and was simply playing out his role in the plan. God planned for millions of people to die in the Holocaust, in fact he planned their deaths in exact detail according to Rick Warren, so Hitler had no choice but to kill those people because he was God's puppet. The 2008 BBC/WGBH Boston television play *God On Trial*, which takes place in the Auschwitz concentration camp during World War II, makes a brilliant examination of the Holocaust question from a different angle. The Jewish prisoners there put God on trial *in absentia* for abandoning the Jewish people, specifically questioning whether he had broken his covenant with the Jewish people by allowing the Nazis to commit genocide. I highly recommend watching this though provoking and well received drama because as reviewer James Walton of London's *Daily Telegraph* observed, "As the fierceness of the intellectual and emotional grip tightened, it was impossible to imagine any halfway-thoughtful viewers, of whatever prior convictions, not having a disturbing sense of their own ideas coming under sustained and convincing attack."

Does God Take Sides?

Or, Pick Me! Pick Me!

☥✵☯⛩ॐ☸✡✝☪☬

"I don't believe in God. In Spain all twenty-two players cross themselves. If it works, the game is always going to be a tie."
~ Soccer star Johan Cryuff

In 1991 the late Ann Mara, wife of New York Giants owner Wellington Mara, was praying over her rosary beads when Buffalo Bills' placekicker Scott Norwood's last-second forty-seven-yard field goal attempt missed wide right and sealed the Giants' victory in Super Bowl XXV. Twenty years later the Giants were playing in Super Bowl XLVI and were trailing the New England Patriots late in the fourth quarter when she invoked her magical beads once again and quarterback Eli Manning responded by throwing a miraculous pass to Mario Manningham down the left sideline to keep the game winning drive alive. After the game Mrs. Mara exclaimed, "I asked the Blessed Mother to tell him (Manning) where to throw the ball, and she did!"

So does God, or perhaps the Virgin Mary, play a role in determining which team wins a sporting event like the Super Bowl? Does the Virgin Mary understand the mechanics of a sideline route? Does God reward athletes who publicly praise him on the field of play? After their Super Bowl win in 2012 Ray Lewis of the Baltimore Ravens made a (perhaps) well-intentioned yet theologically inept statement in response to being asked what it was like to be a Super Bowl champion saying, "When God is for you, who can be against you?" Similarly, quarterback Russell Wilson gushed, "God is great!" after his Seahawks had won the big game in January of 2014. Yes it certainly must feel that way, at least for the victor. We see it every day. Teams praying in the locker room and players pointing to the sky after hitting a homerun or scoring a touchdown. It makes you wonder if God is a Yankee fan, because that team has won more championships than any in sports. For that matter what does he have against the Chicago Cubs, who have not won the World Series in more than a century?

Is God actually concerned with sports? A survey released by the Public Religion Research Institute found nearly three in ten Americans believe God plays a role in determining which team wins a sporting event. A significantly higher number of people, fifty-three percent, believe God rewards athletes who have faith with good health and success on the field and in fact 2012 was deemed "The Year of the Outspoken Christian Athlete" by *Relevant* magazine. The article cited NFL quarterback Tim Tebow, pro golfer Bubba Watson, Houston Rockets point guard Jeremy Lin and Olympic Gold Medal winning gymnast Gabby Douglas among others as reasons for the rise of public Christianity in sports.

Getting back to the case of Super Bowl XLVI it must be pointed out that the Patriots and their fans were no doubt also praying when their team later came down the field on one last drive and a few assistant coaches joined hands with the team's priest as quarterback Tom Brady heaved the final, and ironically named, "Hail Mary" pass into the air... and it fell to the ground incomplete, leaving their prayers unanswered. So if it is so obvious God does not take sides, why do fans continue to pray?

As discussed earlier Jesus makes a clear statement about prayer in Mark 11:24 when he says, "Therefore I tell you, whatever you ask for in prayer, believe that you have received it, and it will be yours." Nothing could be simpler. All that you have to do is say a prayer, believe you have received it and your prayer will be answered, but is that true? We can test it with a thought experiment. Imagine two girls named Alicia and Kristin are attending a Catholic high school. Both are good students, devout believers, obey God's Commandments, attend church twice a week and pray to God daily. And both are beautiful, so clearly God has shown them favor. The prom is coming up, and the most eligible boy at the school is named Mark. He is a great student, star athlete and good looking, yet humble and friendly. Everyone loves him. He too is a devout believer, and he knows both Alicia and Kristin well. With the prom approaching, both Alicia and Kristin pray a simple prayer. They both ask God to be Mark's date for the prom. They do this separately, and neither knows the other is praying. Alicia believes with all her heart God will answer her prayer. Kristin believes with all her heart God will answer her prayer. As expressions of their belief both Alicia and Kristin go shopping for prom dresses, knowing Mark will invite them.

Jesus has made a promise he cannot keep. God is perfect and unerring so the Bible can contain no mistakes but clearly it has made one here since both girls believe their prayers will be answered, but one of them is going to lose. Jesus is going to end up lying to either Alicia or Kristin, or he might end up lying to them both. Maybe Mark is in love with someone named Buffy and invites her instead. Whenever two or more people pray for the same thing and only one person can have it someone is always going to lose. For every lottery winner who credits prayer there are millions who lost in spite of theirs and it does not matter if they all believe or how fervently and sincerely they pray. The same logic applies to sporting events. The fact is both cannot get the same thing and therefore Mark 11:24 is wrong, but of course Christians try to explain away this discrepancy by claiming unanswered prayers are actually being answered in ways we do not comprehend. This rationalization is even borne out in the song *Unanswered Prayers* by Garth Brooks. In addition there is nowhere in the belief structure which says people are God's puppets and much like the genie in *Aladdin* he cannot force someone to fall in or out of love because of someone else's prayer.

What if two people pray for two things which are opposites? If both believe, who is going to win? For example imagine a farmer prays for a good, soaking, daylong rain on Saturday to water his newly planted crops while a bride having her wedding nearby prays for crystal clear sunshine on the same day. One of them is going to lose. Imagine one member of a devout couple prays to become pregnant and the other prays they do not. Once again one of them is going to lose. Someone must lose, and Jesus' promise in Mark 11:24 turns into a lie. It does not matter how much you believe or how fervently you pray, if someone else is praying for the opposite of what you are praying for one of you must lose.

If prayer worked the way the Bible says it does Las Vegas could not exist because people would have prayed all of the money out of there years ago. Imagine you take thirty-eight devout, cash strapped believers to the roulette table, have them all pray and let all of them call prayer circles on their cell phones. Then have each believer bet a different single-number bet since there are thirty-eight pockets on a roulette wheel. That would mean one devout believer is betting on each of the pockets. Spin the wheel. How many of these prayerful people will win? One. That is how the real world works.

A believer might say, "Out of the thirty-eight people, God will pick the one who is most deserving." An easy way to prove that statement false is to put one devout believer and thirty-seven godless, convicted murders around the wheel. If God were to pick the most deserving person the believer should win every time, but that is not what happens. The laws of probability will make sure each of the convicted murderers win just as often as the believer and it does not matter how much anyone prays or believes. A believer might say, "God only intervenes in lotteries and casinos occasionally when it is his divine will and only for the most deserving people," but that is not what Jesus promises in the Bible. The real point is God only "intervenes" in ways which exactly follow the laws of probability.

If we look at things objectively the truth is apparent. Outcomes exactly follow the natural laws of probability, and that tells us God is not answering prayers. What we are seeing is coincidence. If God were actually answering prayers we would see a statistical aberration and the laws of probability would work differently for praying people than for others. In other words we would have two "laws of probability," one for believers and one for non-believers.

Another person might explain it all by saying, "Well of course Jesus does not answer prayers in a casino. Jesus never answers prayers for money. Prayers for money represent greed." Perhaps, but in that case Jesus should have said, "Nothing will be impossible to you except if you pray for money"… but he didn't. Besides, there are lots of believers who would disagree because they believe God has answered their monetary prayers and claim the "Prayer of Jabez" is all about money. Prosperity Gospel, anyone?

Another believer might say, "God cannot bend the laws of probability in the same way he cannot bend the laws of nature. If God was constantly bending the laws of probability, they would not be laws anymore." That makes some sense but is not what Jesus said, plus if the Bible is to be believed God has bent and even broken the laws of nature many, many times in the past from the parting of the Red Sea to the raising of Lazarus.

Atheists in Foxholes

Or, Soldiers of NO God

"In a Holy War, God is always on the side of the biggest battalion."

Lieutenant Clebe McClary is a medically retired Marine who is now one of the most recognized motivational and inspirational speakers in America. He proudly proclaims himself to be "in the service of the Lord's Army" and asserts that to him USMC means "U. S. Marine for Christ." There is much to be admired about this Marine, but at the same time he is representative of a growing problem in both the Marine Corps and the military in general.

In 1968, during his nineteenth reconnaissance mission in Vietnam, McClary was critically wounded during an enemy attack, suffered the loss of an eye and an arm and was told he would never walk again. Despite all that he never lost the determination, dedication and courage to overcome his circumstances and as a result of his bravery under fire and the concern he showed for his men was awarded Silver and Bronze Star Medals. The details of his last mission and subsequent journey are spelled out in his book *Living Proof.*

The question is, living proof of what? You see I have a great deal of admiration for Lieutenant McClary just as I do for all who have served bravely and honorably and especially so when they somehow overcome a set of circumstances which would be life shattering to a lesser person. I also fully support whatever mechanism it is they use to get through those difficult challenges whether it be family, religion or even therapeutic needlepoint. That said, I find it disappointing when a man who has served so valiantly and sacrificed so much in the name of freedom chooses to routinely and emphatically denigrate the equally loyal service of others who do not share his religious views.

The subject of religion and the military has become a touchy one in this age of Islamic jihad but the concept and practice of religious freedom in the United States Armed Forces dates back to the earliest days of this nation. The Constitution outlines the basic concept of religious freedom in the Bill of Rights, more specifically the First Amendment which specifies that "Congress shall make no law respecting an establishment of religion or prohibiting the free exercise thereof..."

All branches of the United States military are afforded the same rights to religious freedom as are American civilians, however members of the Armed Forces willingly surrender certain rights when it impinges on military discipline or the successful completion of an objective. This guarantee of religious freedom is codified for the Armed Forces in *Accommodation of Religious Practices Within the Military Services* which describes the commander's responsibility to provide for religious accommodation for everyone.

Religious freedom in the military has by and large followed the same path as American society in general, that is as the understanding of free exercise expanded outside the military so did it expand within the services. The growing embrace of religious pluralism can perhaps best be seen in the expansion of the Chaplaincy, whose role it is to provide for the free expression of religious belief by the troops. For example, not until the war with Mexico in 1846 were Roman Catholics incorporated into the Chaplain Corps. Up until that time only Protestants served as chaplains, which put the United States at a propaganda disadvantage when fighting Catholic Mexico. Then in 1862 the word "Christian" was stricken from regulations governing the appointment of chaplains in order to allow for the appointment of Jewish chaplains, and that was brought about as a result of a request made to President Abraham Lincoln by the Board of Delegates of American Israelites. Then during World War II Greek Orthodox chaplains were authorized to minister to members of the Eastern Orthodox Church and in 1987 the Department of Defense registered the Buddhist Churches of America as an ecclesiastical endorsing agency and thus opened the door for Buddhist chaplains. In 1993 the first Muslim chaplain was added, which was yet another sign of America's growing religious diversity in recognition of the Armed Forces' Constitutional responsibility to meet the free expression needs of those in its ranks who hold minority religious views.

Religious diversity takes on additional importance in the current international environment where spiritual motivations are an increasing rationale for waging conflict because at a time when the United States is encouraging greater religious freedom in Muslim nations it is imperative for us to show by example that religious pluralism is a viable and preferred option. Any sign of hypocrisy in Unites States policy, official or otherwise, toward the free exercise of religion - including freedom from religion - within the military makes it more difficult to convince others to follow our lead.

Unfortunately evangelical extremists such as Lieutenant McClary do not support the practice of other religions let alone no religion which is, as I previously demonstrated, one of the principles this nation was founded upon. In fact he is even critical of other Christians who do not practice his particular brand of faith, and when it comes to those who do not adhere to any religion at all the rhetoric becomes downright nasty.

The fact of the matter is non-theistic members of the military serve honorably around the world and always will. For example Pat Tillman, the pro football player turned Army Ranger who gave up a lucrative career in the wake of 9-11 and ended up making the ultimate sacrifice for our country, was an atheist. In the eyes of people like Clebe McClary he was a heathen who deserves to burn in Hell. In my eyes he was a patriot. How do you see him?

Now, with growing advocacy for gays and women in the military, this group has become the last unprotected minority. The non-theistic - whether they be atheist, humanist, agnostic, freethinker or other secular minority - have served with just as much valor as anyone but even so are discriminated against for not being believers. To be honest, I have always had a difficult time reconciling the phrase, "Praise the Lord and pass the ammunition" with the Sixth Commandment… you know, the one which says, "Thou Shalt Not Kill." The obvious rationalizations are to say it is okay to kill while doing the Lord's work or to reinterpret the biblical translation to read "murder" rather than "kill," but in doing so Christians are opening up a whole new can of worms because we must always remember the justification Islamo-fascist Jihadist suicide bombers cite while slaying infidels is they are doing Allah's work and/or carrying out the law of the Quran.

Many people would be surprised to learn non-theists comprise 20.7% of today's military and 27.8% of those serving in the Guard and Reserve, and the percentage is increasing with every passing year. That is significant, but even so official military functions continue to include Christian prayers to the exclusion of Jews, Muslims, Buddhists, Zoroastrians, Wiccans and atheists. It is time for Clebe McClary to realize he has no right to co-opt the acronym USMC to suit his own narrow interpretation of what is good and right in the world because in doing so he is disrespecting all of the fine men and women who have worn our uniform proudly but do not share his point of view.

In declaring that Americans are free to practice their chosen religion, the Constitution also guarantees the right to be free from religion if we so choose. Isn't that part of what we are fighting for? And yet as recently as August of 2014 an airman at Creech Air Force Base in Indian Springs, Nevada was barred from reenlisting in the Air Force after omitting the phrase "so help me God" from his contract and was told by his superiors he must swear to God or leave the Air Force. This of course violated the service member's Constitutional protections under the Establishment Clause and infringed on his right to reenlist with secular affirmations, as the government cannot compel a person to take an oath which invokes a supreme being because Article VI of the Constitution states, "No religious test shall ever be required as a qualification to any office." Air Force Public Affairs Officer Chris Hoyler told *The Huffington Post* in a statement, "Reciting 'so help me God' in the reenlistment and commissioning oaths is a statutory requirement," adding that an October 2013 amendment to the pertinent Air Force Instruction no longer authorized [airmen] to omit those words.

That same year the Air Force Academy's Colorado Springs campus moved to allow its four thousand cadets to opt out of the "so help me God" clause in the honor code during their annual oaths and as a result many observers were disturbed over allegations that officers, staff members and senior cadets at the Academy had used their positions to push their evangelical Christian beliefs on them. The controversy first surfaced in 2004 when a "Cadet Climate Survey" found that more than half of cadets polled had heard religious slurs and almost half felt ostracized if they weren't religious. The survey also found about one-third of the non-Christian cadets polled believed Christian cadets were given preferential treatment. That same year a Yale Divinity School team reported they saw proselytizing during basic training and in 2005 Captain Melinda Morton, a chaplain at the academy, said religious proselytizing was "systematic and pervasive" there. Morton was later transferred because of her public criticisms. The accusations led to an investigative commission which concluded that while there was no overt religious discrimination there was "a failure to fully accommodate all members' needs and a lack of awareness over where the line is drawn between permissible and impermissible expression of beliefs."

Is it true there are no atheists in foxholes? Two scenes from the movie *We Were Soldiers* (starring Mel Gibson as Lieutenant Colonel Hal Moore) illustrate perfectly the folly of battlefield prayers, believing God takes sides in war, the "my God is greater than your God" mentality and the unfounded assumptions which are based upon that illusion. In the first scene the devout Moore is praying in the chapel with a Lieutenant named Jack Geoghegan as their unit prepares to deploy to Vietnam. Geoghegan's wife has just given birth to their first child so Moore appeals to God, "Our Father in Heaven, before we go into battle every soldier among us will approach you each in his own way. Our enemies too, according to their own understanding, will ask for protection and for victory. And so we bow before your infinite wisdom. We offer our prayers as best we can. I pray you watch over young Jack Geoghegan. Use me as your instrument in this awful hell of war to watch over the men I lead into battle. Especially if they're men like this one beside me, deserving of a future in your blessing and goodwill. Amen... oh yes, and one more thing dear Lord about our enemies, ignore their heathen prayers and help us blow those little bastards straight to Hell. Amen."

The second scene occurs after the ensuing battle and at the end of the movie. In it Moore writes to the wife of Lieutenant Geoghegan, who has been killed in action despite the earlier heartfelt prayer in which he asked God to protect him, saying, "Dear Barbra, I have no words to express to you my sadness at the loss of Jack. The world is a lesser place without him. But I know he is with God and the angels and I know even Heaven is improved by his presence there. I know you too are sure of this and yet this knowledge can't diminish his loss and your grief. With abiding respect and affection, Hal Moore."

What is wrong with Colonel Moore's prayer? First of all when he says "every soldier among us" he assumes every soldier under his command is a believer and that sort of assumption is at the very heart of the no atheists in foxholes fallacy. Next he asks God to "watch over the young Jack Geoghegan... (who is) deserving of a future in your blessing and goodwill" as if he can determine who is deserving of what, and as it turned out God did not agree with his assessment. Finally he prays, "...ignore their heathen prayers and help us blow those little bastards straight to Hell," which is reminiscent of a scene in the movie *Kingdom of Heaven* in which the Christian army rides into battle preceded by a giant cross against the Muslim forces of Saladin who are riding under the banner of Allah with each side believing it has God on their side. Later, rather than facing the fact his prayers have failed, Moore doubles down on his faith and writes the words, "I know he is with God... I know you too are sure of this."

Now consider the following story. In August of 1914 near Mons in Belgium the German army was making its sweep into France during the opening stages of World War I and as heavily outnumbered units of the British Expeditionary Force came under vastly superior German fire their destruction seemed assured - but in perhaps the strangest tale in modern warfare the British were saved at the last moment by an inexplicable heavenly presence when a brigade of warrior angels appeared and wrought destruction upon the Germans and handed victory to the British. At least that's the legend.

The "Angel of Mons" was not only a military first, it was also fairly influential in popular culture at the time because both *Lord of the Rings* novelist J.R.R. Tolkien and Mary Norton, author of the *Bedknobs and Broomsticks* trilogy, are said to have been inspired by the story of supernatural soldiers saving outnumbered good guys from evil enemy forces. In the decades since the story had faded into history, but with the New Age resurgence of angel worship beginning in the 1980's it has found its way back into popular mythology and is usually retold without critique.

Contrary to the popular telling this was not a clear British victory and in fact those who survived barely escaped with their lives. Outnumbered approximately four to one at the start of the battle, the English did indeed stop the German advance and inflict heavy casualties because the British infantry were expert shots with their Lee-Enfield rifles and many could take a man down at a range of two hundred yards while the relatively inexperienced Germans had no answer for this. The British also used air-bursting shrapnel, which the Germans lacked. After two days of fighting during which the larger German force continuously pushed the British back the Germans finally sounded a cease-fire and the British withdrew. British casualties in the battle were sixteen hundred, while the Germans had lost five thousand.

There was no miraculous British victory explainable only by supernatural intervention and nothing suggesting such a thing appears in any military accounts, but this first clash with the Germans was big news in Britain as you can well imagine and new volunteers flooded the recruiting stations when the story broke. In such circumstances it's easy to conceive of infectious patriotism sweeping the land, the telling of heroic tales and the trumpeting of news of an early victory. Hungry for such stories a London paper called the *Evening News* engaged a Welsh writer of Gothic horror stories named Arthur Machen to publish a tale he called *The Bowmen* in which the besieged British soldiers at the Battle of Mons appealed to St. George for heavenly aid and who should appear but phantom Medieval longbowmen from the Battle of Agincourt, five hundred years past, and the heavenly longbowmen decimated the Germans while mysteriously leaving no visible wounds and carried the day for the British: "And as the soldier heard these voices he saw before him, beyond the trench, a long line of shapes, with a shining about them. They were like men who drew the bow, and with another shout their cloud of arrows flew singing and tingling through the air towards the German hosts."

When pressed by eager editors for more information about this miraculous delivery Machen was the first to stand up and remind everyone it was a work of fiction, however by some accounts the article had an effect not unlike that of Orson Welles' *War of the Worlds* when it was mistaken for an actual news report by many readers.

The Bowmen was published five weeks after the Battle of Mons on September 29, 1914 and perhaps the best evidence these stories have no factual basis is the absence of any known published accounts referencing supernatural intervention other than a book published in 1931 by Brigadier-General John Charteris based on a collection of letters he claimed to have written during the war. In one addressed to his wife dated September 5 (purportedly more than three weeks before *The Bowmen*) he wrote, "Then there is the story of the 'Angel of Mons' going strong through the II Corps, of how the angel of the Lord on the traditional white horse and clad all in white with flaming sword faced the advancing Germans at Mons and forbade their further progress."

The authenticity of Charteris' letter has come under intense scrutiny because for one thing he served as Chief of British Army Intelligence from 1915 to 1918 and was involved in numerous schemes to disseminate propaganda, and for another all of the letters written to his wife during the war were preserved and catalogued by her with microfilm copies now kept at the Liddell Hart Centre for Military Archives at King's College, University of London which show there is no letter dated September 5 and none mentioning any Angel of Mons. Since these archived letters formed the source material for Charteris' 1931 book researchers like David Clarke have concluded he falsified this letter after the fact as part of his propaganda duties, especially since he was known to have done so in other cases - notably one where he promoted a false rumor the Germans were collecting the bodies of their dead and rendering them down in a "cadaver factory" to produce oil and lubricants for their war effort which was obviously an urban myth.

For six months *The Bowmen* was reprinted not only in newspapers and magazines but also in spiritual journals and for that period of time there was yet no reference in print to angels so author David Clarke performed an extensive survey of British magazines, newspapers and journals from the period and searched for the terms "Angel of Mons" and "Angels at Mons" and found that it was not until April 3, 1915 that any mention appeared. It was in a story from the *Hereford Times* entitled *A Troop of Angels* and gave the report of a young lady named Miss Marrable who conveyed "stories she'd heard" from soldiers who were supposedly at the battle: "Last Sunday I met Miss Marrable [who] knew the officers, both of whom had themselves seen the Angels, who saved our left wing from the Germans when they came right upon them during our retreat from Mons... one of Miss Marrable's friends, who was not a religious man, told her he saw a troop of Angels between us and the enemy, and has been a changed man ever since. The other man she met in London last week [said that] while he and his company were retreating, they heard the German cavalry tearing after them... they turned around and faced the enemy expecting instant death when to their wonder they saw between them and the enemy a whole troop of Angels. And the horses of the Germans turned around, terrified out of their senses, and stampeded."

A Troop of Angels was then broadly reprinted, most influentially in May 1915 in the (Clifton) *All Saints Parish Magazine,* but when Miss Marrable was sought out for more information she said she'd been misquoted. Naturally none of the soldiers in her story were named, but some people later began coming forward saying they knew someone… who had met someone… who had heard the story from their very reliable friend - the hallmark of myth.

Author Harold Begbie published *On the Side of the Angels* in which he charged Arthur Machen with exploiting the "true story of angels" for his own financial gain and in turn Machen challenged Begbie to then produce these witnesses and Begbie countered that a government cover-up had silenced them. As is the case today, there's nothing quite like a juicy conspiracy theory to explain away a lack of evidence. Suffice it to say beyond hearsay accounts in newspapers no reliable evidence or witnesses were ever produced which could corroborate stories of anything unusual happening at Mons.

The story was exploited by the British army for propaganda purposes, but the same certainly wasn't true on the German side of the lines and there is no record of Germans reporting being chased away by angels or shot at by medieval archers and one can't plausibly credit a British government cover-up for that. In the end no reliable records exist of this ever having happened and the genesis of the story is well documented as fiction and derivative reporting based upon that fiction, but there is a more important question. Why would the angels favor the British? After all Germany, the home of Martin Luther, is predominantly Christian, and remember this all took place during World War I so there was no "Hitler factor" involved… so why were there no angels from the Order of Brothers of the German House of Saint Mary in Jerusalem (aka the Teutonic Order) helping the Germans? Isn't it funny how the good guys who are on God's side are always the ones writing the stories?

Let's look at a hypothetical example which demonstrates what is called the "Battlefield Effect," since it is a common reason many people believe in the power of prayer. Let's say a general sends ten thousand soldiers into a fierce battle. The enemy has thirty thousand troops plus artillery and close air support, is able to decimate the ten thousand soldiers in short order and once the battle is over one hundred survivors out of the original ten thousand limp and crawl back to their base.

If there truly are no atheists in foxholes we can assume every single one of the ten thousand soldiers who marched into battle prayed fervently and deeply for God to spare his life but despite those prayers the enemy proceeded to attack and all but one hundred of those who prayed wasted their breath and died. The hundred who survived the battle, however, naturally feel as though their prayers were answered. They have been through a horrific firefight and are deeply grateful to have escaped with their lives. At the time they prayed they were terrified and desperate, and to them having survived seems like a miracle.

The hundred survivors then fan out with their personal stories of answered prayers and tell their buddies how they prayed for their lives and how their prayers were answered. Then they arrive home and tell their families and friends about their harrowing experience on the battlefield and how nothing but their prayers saved them. They also give testimonials at church, give speeches in the community and write articles for magazines (or write a book as was the case with Clebe McClary) and as a result millions of people are exposed to the positive, powerful, personal testimonials of the hundred survivors.

This is statistically misleading, but it is great advertising for prayer. And it works. People hear the stories of survivors and believe. The real power of this approach however comes from the fact the 9,900 dead soldiers never get to tell their side of the story. Ninety-nine percent of the soldiers died and only one percent survived. Far more men prayed and died but never get to tell anyone about their disappointment. As one realistic soldier once put it, "You'll never find a dead Christian soldier in a foxhole who did not pray to survive." So the hundred personal testimonials for prayer are strong, loud, frequent and compelling while the 9,900 personal testimonials against prayer are silent because dead soldiers never get a chance to speak. To a casual observer it appears prayer works because every story you hear is positive, while the reality is ninety-nine percent of the praying people died.

Let's say you are listening as a survivor says, "There I was in a horrific firefight. All of my friends around me were dropping like flies, but I prayed to God and he saved me." The question an objective person would ask is obviously, "Why did God let all the others drop like flies and why are you worshipping a God who allowed ninety-nine percent of your friends to be killed instead of answering their equally fervent prayers?" The fact 9,900 praying people died while only a hundred survived should be plenty of evidence to show prayer does not work, but for some reason believers never seem to think about the casualties. They instead celebrate the "answered prayers" of the hundred and the 9,900 who died are swept under the rug. It is obvious what happened on the battlefield had nothing to do with prayer. Instead the survivors benefitted from their skill and/or random luck and their "answered prayers" are simple coincidences.

Legendary actress Marlene Dietrich recognized this when she said, "Back in my early childhood I had learned that God doesn't fight on any army's side so there was little point in praying, nonetheless before every battle prayers were read, all kinds of incantations were recited, staged by all sorts of preachers. We attended these ceremonies and I saw how the soldiers stood in place as though they couldn't believe their ears. I couldn't believe it either but I counted for nothing. Since then I've given up any belief in God, in a 'light' that leads us or anything of this sort."

There are many more examples of the same coincidental phenomenon. Imagine you hear the following stories from four survivors. First, "I was a prisoner in a concentration camp, and in the morning we were marched to the death chambers. I knew that I could not die. I had to live so that I could see my baby again, so I began praying the most intense prayers I have ever prayed as soon as we started marching. When we got to the gas chambers an amazing miracle occurred. I somehow had moved to the end of the line and there was no room for me in the chamber. I was told to join a nearby work group and survived. God heard my prayers and I was saved!"

Second, "It was the most destructive flood in the history of Colorado. An immense wall of mud cascaded down the mountain and through our city, killing twenty thousand people. I was caught in the tide of sludge and sucked deep into the bowels of the torrent. In just a few seconds I would drown and die in a sea of mud, but I prayed to the Virgin Mary and not one second later my head popped to the surface and I was able to grab a nearby branch and pull myself out. The Virgin Mary answered my prayers!"

Third, "There is no way to explain the miracle. I said a quick prayer before my car slammed into and then underneath the truck in front of me, and as if by magic the entire car crumpled like a wad of paper… except for the passenger area where I was sitting. God heard and answered my prayers by using his power to protect the interior of the car and save my life!"

Finally, "I was on a business trip, got drunk and had a one night stand with a stranger. It is totally unlike me, but it happened. In the morning I realized what I had done and was wracked with guilt. I got down on my knees and prayed, 'Dear God, please don't let me have AIDS. The embarrassment and pain would be too much for my spouse, my children and my parents. It only happened one time, I promise it will never happen again and if you will grant me this prayer I will do anything you ask. Amen.' I waited three months and was a nervous wreck, but when I went to my doctor to get tested I was clean. The relief I felt was incredible, like a huge burden being lifted from my soul. God personally answered this prayer for me!"

Believers love these stories and we hear miraculous personal testimonies like these all the time because they show the "power of prayer" and the "love of God." What needs to considered however is both sides of the story, the successes and failures of prayer. If God let millions of people die in the Holocaust but "heard the prayers" of one person and saved him, what sort of God is that? Allowing millions to die and saving one is a terrible ratio. God would have to be a monster, but believers seem to be comfortable with that sort of schizophrenia. They are happy about the one person saved from the Holocaust by a prayer, in fact they actually celebrate his story, but do not seem to care that if God saved him it must also have been he who allowed the deaths of millions of others by ignoring their prayers.

In the case of the Holocaust survivor what actually happened was luck and coincidence. In the case of the mudslide do you believe Mary heard the prayers of one person while purposely ignoring the prayers of the twenty thousand who died? Of course not. Clearly that man's survival involves luck and coincidence as well. In the case of the car it is not a miracle the passenger compartment remained intact because that is how cars are designed. It is called a passenger safety cage and God had absolutely nothing to do with it. In the United States forty thousand people die every year in car accidents so if God actually saved this driver one must also accept that he let the other forty thousand people die by ignoring their prayers. In the case of the AIDS survivor tens of millions of people have died of AIDS and to believe God answered this one prayer is to also believe he killed tens of millions of other praying people. What actually happened is random luck, plus despite all of the media attention AIDS gets less than one percent of the sexually active adult population in the United States has the virus and it is not a *fait accompli* it will be transmitted during every sexual encounter. The odds are actually excellent (in this case 99:1) that after one sexual encounter a person will not get AIDS and it does not matter whether or not they pray.

Next let's assume a powerful hurricane like Katrina hits Louisiana again and does an incredible amount of damage, destroying hundreds of thousands of homes, killing thousands of people and wiping entire towns off the map. Your sister is a devout believer who happens to live in Louisiana, and once cell phone service is restored she gives you a call and the first words out of her mouth are, "God has blessed us so much this week. We prayed all through the storm and he answered our prayers. The next town over was completely decimated, but our house is still standing. We are so blessed!"

Think about how arrogant this is. What she is saying is, "I am so special and God loves me so much that he heard my prayers and personally helped me." For a believer to talk about his or her blessings in such a way is to implicitly ignore the suffering of others. If God blessed one while completely ignoring millions of other believers in the same predicament it says nothing about blessings, but what it does suggest is he is either a demon or doesn't exist. For anyone to believe God personally helped them while at the same time wreaking havoc on millions of others is supreme arrogance and yet believers never seem to give it a second thought. What actually happened was the hurricane hit, God neither blessed nor cursed anyone, the storm did its damage according to the laws of nature and the fact one house is undamaged while thousands of others were swept into the sea is not a blessing. It is random luck.

The focus of this chapter is atheists in foxholes and a perfect example of the Christian mindset is what happens when troops die in, for example, a helicopter crash. Without exception these tragedies elicit immediate and well-meaning posts to social media proclaiming the fallen are now "guarding the streets of Heaven" - a reference to the last lines of the Marines' Hymn - but that sentiment, while it may give comfort to some, misses the mark for two reasons. First of all how can anyone possibly know the religious beliefs of strangers? What is happening here is an assumption they were not only Christians but the "right" kind as well. Second, it is always assumed they are now guarding the gates of Heaven rather than Hell despite the ironic Marine nickname of Devil Dog.

As a career Marine it is my opinion that while all Americans have a right to practice whatever religion they choose the military should not allow proselytization or evangelism. In a similar fashion troops can register and vote with a political party but are not allowed to campaign or promote a particular political ideology. If anyone is persecuted in this country it is non-believers who, while as patriotic as anyone else, are treated as lesser Americans or worse by many religious people.

So yes there most assuredly are atheists in foxholes and while most soldiers, sailors, airmen and Marines practicing a religion have chaplains advocating for them until recently all others have had to go it alone. Thankfully that is changing and today organizations such as the Military Association of Atheists and Freethinkers and Military Religious Freedom Foundation are dedicated to ensuring all members of the Armed Forces fully receive the Constitutional guarantee of religious freedom to which they and all Americans are entitled.

If anything there are actually no true *believers* in foxholes because even those who think God is looking out for them wear their helmets and body armor in combat. As Han Solo said in *Star Wars*, "Hokey religions and ancient weapons are no match for a good blaster at your side."

On Bended Knee

Or, Living On a Wing and a Prayer

"A research scientist will hardly be inclined to believe that events could be influenced by prayer, i.e. by a wish addressed to a supernatural being." ~ Albert Einstein

The Native Americans of the arid southwestern United States were dependent upon corn for their main supply of food and when they planted it counted upon the rains to come and make it grow. They realized how important precipitation was to their survival, so they danced to inform the "kachinas" (gods) the corn had been planted and needed life-giving rain. Fast forward to present day California. In January of 2014 that state, which was experiencing its third-worst drought in 106 years, entered its third straight year of dangerously dry conditions. Amid what Governor Jerry Brown proclaimed as a drought emergency, Gil "Feather" Fernandez led a traditional rain dance on a hot and sunny winter day joined by Sam Bearpaw, Windwalker and dozens of other Native Americans from multiple tribes who work to keep the traditions and rituals of their culture alive in a modern world. According to the National Weather Service the chance their rain dance would produce moisture was "zero," and most people shouldn't be surprised by that because our common sense tells us people dancing in a circle wearing feathers and turquoise (which symbolize wind and rain respectively) while chanting will have no effect on weather patterns.

As Governor Brown sought financial aid from the federal government during the state's third dry year other people were asking for help from a different "higher authority." The California Catholic Conference of Bishops issued a call for all people of faith to join in prayer for God's mercy and compassion, specifically by sending relief in the way of rainfall. So did the Catholics prevail where the Native American's had failed? Sadly no, and when California's rainfall year ended six months later the state ended up with one of its lowest totals since the 1920s, but the irony is some of the very same people who laughed at the idea of a Native American rain dance will believe the eventual rainfall (and it will rain sooner or later) would be due to *their* prayers instead.

Similarly in 2011 the state of Texas was in the throes of a terrible drought with lakes drying up, cattle dying and crops failing, so in April of that year Governor Rick Perry issued a Gubernatorial Proclamation mandating a weekend of prayer from Friday, April 22 (Good Friday) to Sunday, April 24 during which Texans were supposed to pray for God to relieve the terrible drought, saying in part "...throughout our history, both as a state and as individuals, Texans have been strengthened, assured and lifted up through prayer; it seems right and fitting that the people of Texas should join together in prayer to humbly seek an end to this devastating drought and these dangerous wildfires... under the authority vested in me by the Constitution and Statutes of the State of Texas... I urge Texans of all faiths and traditions to offer prayers on that day for the healing of our land..."

The drought continued to worsen for four months following the Days of Prayer and while only 15-17% of the state had been undergoing exceptional drought in late April the percentage actually grew to fifty percent a month later and by late June more than seventy percent of the state was experiencing exceptional drought conditions, a level which persisted until August 18, 2011. Most of the drought conditions did not subside until the end of summer and during Labor Day weekend drought-driven wildfires raged and destroyed 1600 homes with the first major rain in the state after the Days of Prayer not coming until October 9, 2011, a full six months later.

Of course none of this matters because everyone knows droughts don't last forever and eventually conditions will improve to some degree prayer or no prayer, but even if it had rained a year or even ten years later the devout would still claim a direct relationship between entreaties to the almighty and inevitable weather cycles. A good example of this mindset is the comment of fundamentalist Christian pastor Rick Scarborough who spun things by saying, "When he (Perry) led that complete day in prayer and fasting for God to break the drought, a lot of people criticized him in the press... but a few *months* (emphasis mine) later it began to rain...," but as *Tonight Show* host Steve Allen had observed many decades earlier, "If you pray for rain long enough it does eventually fall. If you pray for floodwaters to abate they eventually do. The same happens in the absence of prayers."

Prayer is of course not unique to Christianity, with most every belief system having its own version. In Islam Sujūd, or sajdah (an Arabic word meaning prostration to God), is performed in the direction of the Kaaba at Mecca, usually during the daily prayers known as salat. While in

Sujūd, it is essential for Muslims to praise and glorify Allah. The position involves having the forehead, nose, both hands, knees and all toes touching the ground together. If you don't happen to be Muslim it probably seems silly to do that five times a day every day, but that is how they "talk to God."

A somewhat similar way to genuflect is the Kowtow, a phrase borrowed from "kau tau" in Cantonese or "koutou" in Mandarin Chinese. It is the act of deep respect shown by prostration, that is kneeling and bowing so low as to have one's head touching the ground. In East Asian culture the kowtow is the highest sign of reverence. It was widely used to show reverence for one's elders, superiors and especially the Emperor, as well as for religious and cultural objects of worship. Depending on the solemnity of the situation different grades of kowtow would be used. In the most solemn of ceremonies, for example at the coronation of a new Emperor, his subjects would undertake the ceremony of the "three kneelings and nine kowtows," the so-called grand kowtow, which involves kneeling from a standing position three times and each time performing the kowtow three times while kneeling.

In the West the practice of kneeling and clasping hands originated around the 11th or 12th Century when peasants would beg for work from the feudal lord. This was a gesture of utmost humility and pleading, and you can read about it in Edward Schillebeeck's book *The Church With a Human Face* where it is briefly mentioned. According to Nathan Ausubel, "Religious historians trace the gesture back to the act of shackling a prisoner's hands with vine or rope. Joined hands came to symbolize submission. In ancient Rome a captured soldier could avoid immediate death by joining the hands together, and just as in waving a white flag today the message was clear: 'I surrender.' Centuries later subjects demonstrated their loyalty and paid homage to their rulers by joining their hands, and in time clasping the hands together communicated both an acknowledgement of another's authority and one's own submission to that authority."

In the Bible 1 Timothy 2:8 says men are to pray with holy hands lifted to God, free from anger and controversy, but I cannot find any specific reference in the Bible to bowing heads during prayer. Nowhere in the entire Bible does it mention anyone clasping their hands to pray, so where did we get the idea that we should do such a thing? The obvious answer is from paganism. Just as Christmas, Easter and Halloween are all originally pagan holidays, Christians have incorporated paganism into their worship of God in many ways. As previously noted the bowed head goes back to the days of "divine" monarchy when kings demanded an act of submission or servitude from their serfs, and early Christians followed the Jewish practice of "davening," that is swaying back and forth while praying, until reverence for the Eucharist and the "King of Kings" led to kneeling and head bowing. As an interesting side note kneeling was an integral part of Jewish ritual at the Temple in Jerusalem, but when Christians began to kneel rabbis prohibited it in Jewish worship so if you were to attend a synagogue today you would find people standing and sitting, but none kneeling.

Modern Christians of course disagree and speculate hands are placed facing each other in prayer not as a form of begging or humility, but instead to represent the joining of "who we were born to become represented in the left hand" and "who we are actually becoming represented by the right hand" and the symbolism of this act is a reminder that when communicating with God we are requesting that as Jesus Christ fulfilled his purpose on Earth we are also guided to fulfill our true purpose on Earth - but where they got this obviously made up notion is anyone's guess because it certainly did not come from Scripture. The point is there are many ways to pray but when viewed objectively all alike in one respect which was summed up quite nicely by neurologist Sam Harris when he observed, "Some people say they speak to God every day and that is accepted, but if they claimed to speak to him through a hair dryer other people would think they were mad. I fail to see how the addition of a hair dryer makes it any more absurd."

If I had a nickel for every time I have heard someone say another person is in their prayers or they are praying for someone or something I would be richer than Bill Gates. What does that really mean and who do those prayers really benefit? For example if you are a Christian or Hindu how would you feel if a Muslim told you he was going to pray for you during one of his five daily calls to prayer? No matter how well intentioned that person might be, would you expect to see a result or receive a benefit? Probably not if you don't believe in Allah, but even so the Muslim might feel better because he sincerely thinks he is doing something to help you. So the beneficiary here is actually the person doing the praying.

Earlier we looked at the Bible and found Jesus made a number of specific promises having to do with prayer. For example Matthew 7:7 says, "Ask, and it will be given you; seek, and you will find; knock, and it will be opened to you. For every one who asks receives, and he who seeks finds, and to him who knocks it will be opened. Or what man of you, if his son asks him for bread, will give him a stone? Or if he asks for a fish, will give him a serpent? If you then, who are evil, know how to give good gifts to your children, how much more will your Father who is in Heaven give good things to those who ask him!" Matthew 17:20 and 21:21, Mark 11:24 and John 14 reinforce that message. The Bible is unambiguous. God answers prayers. Ask and you will receive. It is reiterated over and over. Mark 9:23 says, "All things are possible to him who believes" and Luke 1:37 asserts, "For with God nothing will be impossible. Nothing is impossible through prayer."

The problem is when we look at the world around us we find things are not like that at all since God never answers prayers which break the laws of nature or probability. When people talk about the power of prayer what they are actually describing is the power of coincidence. There are mountains of empirical and statistical evidence which support this conclusion. So if it is so obvious, why do believers so adamantly insist God answers prayers? Why is there an entire industry built around inspirational literature? Why do believers demand prayer in public schools? Why do believers hang onto the notion of prayer so strongly? The answer is simple. It is an illusion and people who believe are ignoring reality. Even so, Christians cling to their beliefs and find themselves in awkward positions since they must believe God answers their prayers although it is obvious he does not. It seems to be the only way for them to maintain the illusion God exists and wrote the Bible.

There are murderers, rapists, robbers, child molesters, terrorists, etc. in the news every day. How can anyone believe God is all-knowing and all-loving and answers prayers if he simply watches as people murder, rape, molest and terrorize others and does nothing to help them? Imagine him saying, "Look at all of those praying people getting tortured in that death camp and begging for help. I won't do anything to stop that. Look at that little girl being raped and murdered. She is praying and so is her mother but I won't do anything to stop that either. There are three terrorists preparing to blow up a church and kill fifteen hundred people who are reciting the Lord's Prayer. I won't do anything to stop that either. A thousand prayerful people will die of starvation today in Ethiopia and I won't do anything to stop that either. But wait, there's Suzy praying for me to remove a pimple from her nose before her big date with Chad. Let me help her..." Should a rational person believe in a God who acts like that? If you believe God reaches down from Heaven to answer your trivial prayer to help you find your lost keys while at the same time allowing thousands of children to die of starvation each day by specifically ignoring those prayers that is the very definition of selective observation.

Coincidences, even remarkable ones, happen all the time. The dictionary defines the word coincidence as "a sequence of events that although accidental seems to have been planned or arranged." "Answered prayers" are always coincidences and nothing more. The easy way to see that is by counting unanswered prayers along with seemingly answered prayers and analyzing the results. You could pray for a dozen trivial things. For your car to start in the morning, for it not to rain, for the value of a particular stock to go up, for there to be an available washing machine at the laundromat, for your team to win the game on Sunday and so on. Some of your prayers will get "answered" and some will not. The next day simply watch as twenty trivial things happen *without* praying. Some will work out in a positive way, some will not. If you are a believer try going a week without praying. You will find things work and don't work in exactly the same way they do when you do pray. Good coincidences will not stop happening if you stop praying, and bad coincidences do not stop happening no matter how much you pray. The act of praying does not change the outcome. Coincidences happen every day, but believers rationalize that if something nice happens it is attributable to God because he answered your prayer and is looking out for you, but if you pray for something and it does not happen or if something bad happens it is all part of "God's Plan" and/or is "his will."

An unbiased observer looks at the same things and sees them for what they are - random events. God has nothing to do with them. It is the same with any superstition. Walking under a ladder is not bad luck and neither is breaking a mirror or seeing a black cat. They have no effect on your life. Comedian George Carlin had a humorous take on this phenomenon when he said, "You know who I pray to? Joe Pesci… I noticed that of all the prayers I used to offer to God, and all the prayers that I now offer to Joe Pesci, are being answered at about the same fifty percent rate. Half the time I get what I want. Half the time I don't."

The fact no prayers are answered has meaning on a personal level. Let's say you have a thirty-five year old friend who finds out she has breast cancer. The cancer is fairly advanced, the prognosis does not look promising and if you are a believer what is the first thing you will do? Pray. Perhaps you will even create a prayer circle to channel the Lord's healing power to your friend. But surely an omniscient God already knows about the cancer. In fact he must already know what you want him to do about it. So what point is there in telling him? And if God is omnipotent and in control he either caused it to happen in the first place as part of his master plan, or at the very least allowed it to occur. He must know what he is doing, being God and all, but when you pray you are essentially telling him that you know better and want him to change his plan just for you. Or perhaps he allows bad things to happen because he likes to hear people beg for help, or perhaps he simply does not exist. Consider this simple flow chart:

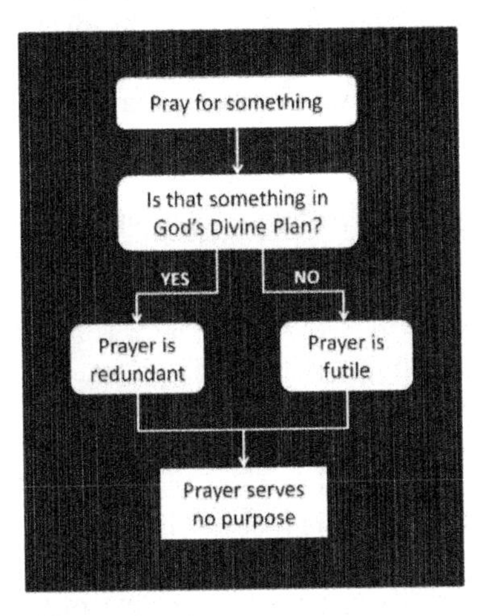

No matter how you look at it prayers are pointless. So, what should you do instead to actually help your friend? Rather than wasting time praying consider making her family dinner, offering to take care of her kids while she recovers from chemo, raising money for cancer research or sitting by her bedside and reading to her. As the saying goes, "Two hands working accomplish far more than a hundred clasped in prayer." That sort of practical approach was highlighted in 2013 when CNN's Wolf Blitzer interviewed Oklahoma tornado survivor Rebecca Vitsmun. After he asked her if she had "thanked the Lord" for helping save her family she sincerely denounced faith by stating she was an atheist and that triggered an immediate response by many atheist communities who, instead of "sending prayers," donated more than $90,000 in relief funding to help this woman rebuild her home.

Author, Author!
Or, Who Wrote the Bible?

☥☸☯⛩ॐ✋☸✡✝☪☬

"It has often been said that anything may be proved from the Bible; but before anything can be admitted as proved by the Bible, the Bible itself must be proved to be true; for if the Bible be not true, or the truth of it be doubtful, it ceases to have authority, and cannot be admitted as proof of anything." ~ Thomas Paine

One of the more "inspirational" passages in the Bible, found in 4 Kings 2:23-24, tells the story of Elijah, a wise man who was cursed with male pattern baldness. One day he was minding his own business and making the long walk to Bethel when he was accosted by a roving band of children who teased him with horrible names like "bald head." Elijah was having none of this, cursed them in the name of the Lord and instantly two female bears presumably sent by God emerged from a nearby wood and mauled all forty-two children to death. Apologists try to validate this tale by making it sound like the children were actually an early incarnation of the Crips and Bloods of South Central LA complete with switchblades and zip guns, but the text of the Scripture only says they were children who called him "bald head" and nothing more. A bit of overkill, wouldn't you say?

Judges 3:21-25 tell us Ehud, the Bible's sneakiest assassin and as it happens the only left-handed person mentioned in Scripture, was on a mission to deliver a "message from God" to King Eglon. Ehud waltzed in to meet the gluttonous king, pulled out a sword and stabbed Eglon in the stomach. At first he couldn't get it in but he pushed harder and eventually reached his intestine. Eglon was so overweight his fat covered the hilt of the sword so he pushed it further into his stomach until it was not even visible - and at this point Eglon lost control of his bowels and began to defecate all over his chamber. The King's attendants eventually came back but did not enter the bed chamber because they assumed he was relieving himself and after waiting "to the point of embarrassment" they finally burst in to find their king dead on the floor covered in his own fecal matter. As we might say today, TMI! Why couldn't it just have said Ehud killed Eglon and left the disgusting details out?

Genesis 38:8-10 is a story so eponymous it gave way to its own neologism - "Onanism" - which is an archaic term for masturbation. For some unstated reason God killed Er but in a stroke of good luck Er's father Judah had given Onan the right, nay duty, to have sex with his dead brother's wife. Onan was a bit apprehensive at first but agreed to go through with the bizarre scheme to create a true heir to Er and began to have sex with the girl, but at the last minute decided to pull out and "spill his seed upon the ground." God was so irked he decided to kill Onan too, nobody got an heir and this story essentially became the basis for the Christian condemnation of masturbation and birth control. Really.

Within the Bible one occasionally finds stories so horrible one can only wonder what their purpose is and Judges 19:22-30 is a good example of that. Not only is this tale utterly bizarre, it is absolutely sickening. A man and his concubine were wandering the streets when they decided to seek shelter for the night and found a man kind enough to let them stay, but that night a group of men turned up at the door and demanded to see the guest so that they may have sex with him, shades of Genesis 19. This seems to be one of God's favorite plot lines. The owner was unwilling to let his male lodger be raped and so he instead offered up his virgin daughter, however this was still not good enough for the men so the owner offered them his guest's concubine as well and the men accepted. The men brutally raped the woman and left her on the doorstep where she bled to death and as if that is not enough when she was found by her husband he chopped her up into twelve pieces which he then sent to each of the twelve tribes of Israel, but since Fedex and UPS did not yet exist one must wonder how he managed to do that or if he received delivery confirmation. The story ends with the words, "Consider of it, take advice, and speak your mind"... and I invite the reader to do exactly that. What could that possibly mean?

According to both Matthew 21:19 and Mark 11:13-14 Jesus was walking from Bethany one fine day and feeling a bit puckish when he encountered a fig tree, but unfortunately it was barren because figs were then out of season. Jesus was annoyed and demanded the tree bear him fruit, however it didn't respond (remember, it's a tree) so Jesus cursed it to death. This story is bizarre for many reasons but mainly for how little it means to the Jesus story, and yet both Mark and Matthew mention it while Luke wisely saw fit to omit the tale as he was furiously plagiarizing most of the rest of Mark.

Moses was finally going to meet God face to face in Exodus 33, was understandably quite excited and when the appointed time came positioned himself on a rock and prepared to see the divine creator himself - but God backed out at the last minute while claiming no man can see his face and live. Does that mean God had no choice in the matter? In any case he instead let Moses have a peek at his backside, "And I will take away mine hand, and thou shalt see my back parts: but my face shall not be seen." Moses was hoping to see God's face, not his bottom, but in any case this is an excellent example of how people tend to personify deities by giving them human attributes and foibles. Apparently God has a face, "back parts" as well and is shy to boot.

In Numbers 22:28-30 Balaam was riding his ass (donkey) when suddenly he heard a voice which turned out to be said donkey in a scene reminiscent of *Shrek* (I always imagine he sounded just like Eddie Murphy), who was asking why his owner was whipping him. Balaam didn't seem the least bit surprised that his donkey had starting speaking in the same language as he and said, "Because thou hast mocked me." The donkey then got philosophical, explained the nature of their relationship, how his feelings had been hurt and eventually they made peace. Oh yes, did I mention it was a talking donkey? When defending the literal nature of this story believers will naturally say God can do anything, but I think the real lesson according to Occam's Razor is people can only *claim* God can do anything.

One of the most bizarre tales in the Bible can be found in Genesis 30:37-39 and contains an amusing explanation of the genetic code. In it Laban was taking all of Jacob's beloved striped and spotted cattle and Jacob was left with plain-colored cattle which he didn't seem to like, so he concocted a cunning plan in which he collected some sticks and painted stripes on them. He then planted them next to his cattle, thinking if he could get his livestock to look at the striped sticks while copulating they would give birth to striped young. Naturally we'd all expect this idiotic plan to fail and Jacob to learn a lesson about genetics but no, it actually worked and the cattle gave birth to striped young. Anyone with even the most basic understanding of genetics knows this is nonsense and since this story seems to have no purpose or moral one must question why it was even included. I can't help but wonder how many Bible-believing scientists painted sticks and attempted to repeat this process before geneticist Gregor Mendel (who was ironically a monk) came along and said, "I'm pretty sure that's not how it's supposed to work."

Christians try to validate the Bible by claiming, "It is comprised of sixty-six books written over a period of about fifteen hundred years by over forty authors from all walks of life, with different kinds of personalities, and in all sorts of situations... it was written in three languages on three continents, covers hundreds of controversial subjects, and yet fits together into one cohesive story with an appropriate beginning, a logical ending, a central character and a consistent theme," and often add the claim that the "truth" of their holy book has been validated by archaeology and science. Why is this so important? Because the very existence of Christianity depends upon acceptance of the Bible as the true and perfect Word of God, just as Islam is dependent upon belief the Quran was dictated to Muhammed by Allah - but very few believers ever take the time to learn what's in it, find out who actually wrote it or understand how it was assembled. Having just read that sampling of biblical tales do they sound like something an omniscient super-intelligent being may have composed, or is it more likely they are the work of some superstitious men? Try to be honest and give your own impression rather than searching for some complex, tortured apologetic because that only demonstrates an inability to think for oneself.

Let's start from the beginning. The oldest known religious texts are the Pyramid texts of ancient Egypt which date to 2400-2300 BCE, although there are older quasi-religious texts which contain religious undertones without specifying the actual incantations performed such as the Sumerian "Locust Charm" text which is a listing of someone clearing out pests from various people's fields. The *Epic of Gilgamesh* from Sumeria, dated around 2150-2000 BCE, is also one of the earliest literary works to include various mythological figures. The *Rigveda* of Hinduism is estimated to have been composed between 1700-1100 BCE, making it possibly the world's oldest religious text still in use, while the oldest portions of the Zoroastrian *Avesta* are believed to have been transmitted orally for centuries before taking written form. Although widely differing dates for Gathic Avestan (the language of the oldest texts) have been proposed, scholarly consensus points to around 1000 BCE. The first Scripture printed for wide distribution to the masses was a Buddhist Scripture called *The Diamond Sutra* and it is the earliest recorded example of a dated printed text, bearing the Chinese calendar date of 11 May 868 CE.

The Quran is of course the holy book of Islam. According to Muslims it was revealed by the Angel Gabriel directly to the Prophet Muhammed and they claim it is unique because it is the only revealed book which exists today in the precise form and content in which it was originally revealed and furthermore it was recorded at the time the religion was being established. They say the distinctive approach of the Quran is its spiritual message includes practical injunctions aimed at the general welfare of human beings, society and the environment in which we live. They also believe the message is eternal and universal, transcends our differences in race, color, ethnicity and nationality, provides guidance on every aspect of human life from economics and the ethics of trade to marriage, divorce, gender issues, inheritance and parenting. In addition it neither condemns nor tortures the flesh nor does it neglect the soul, does not humanize God nor deify man and describes signs of Gods existence in the universe and how everything is carefully placed in the total scheme of creation.

The Quran is also said to be the only book which has been memorized in its entirety by millions. The process of memorization began during the prophet's life and continues to be emphasized by Muslims even to this day. The use of memorization in oral transmission through the generations had mitigated somewhat from the beginning the worst perils of relying solely on written records, and despite being illiterate Muhammad was very vigilant in preserving the entire Quran in written form as well. The prophet could not read or write, so as soon as a portion was revealed he called upon his scribes to record the text. Muhammed specified the part of the Quran the revelation belonged to and had the companions read back what was written to ensure it corresponded exactly with what was revealed, thus the complete Quran was not only memorized by the prophet and many of his companions but also existed in written form during his lifetime. Within a year after Muhammed's death a manuscript of the entire Quran was assembled by a committee led by the chief scribe, who followed stringent criteria to safeguard against any errors. The manuscript was unanimously approved by the hundreds who had memorized the entire Quran, with several replicates of the manuscript being prepared under the leadership of the third caliph and distributed to the main Muslim centers. One such copy is currently at the museum in Tashkent in the former Soviet Union and a facsimile of it, produced in 1905, is available in the Columbia University Library.

The Quran was "revealed" at a time when Arabs excelled in oral poetry, with poetry competitions being held in the marketplaces, and Muhammad's recitation stunned listeners with its beauty in Arabic. It is claimed many converted simply by listening to the deep acoustic rhythms, literary merit and wisdom of the Quranic verses.

The Quran is said to be a highly comprehensive book containing divine truths, metaphysics, religious beliefs and worship, prayer, law and morality. It is a book fully describing the other life, a book of psychology, sociology, epistemology and history, and a book containing scientific facts and the principles of a utopian life. A testament to the divine authenticity of the Quran is that such a comprehensive book, revealed over a period of twenty-three years, does not have any contradictory points. If it had been from other than God they would have found therein much contradiction and incongruity. [Quran, 4.82]

Muslims are asked, "Could Muhammad have been a liar or had motives for inventing the Quran?" They say no, because the early years of Muhammad's mission were punctuated by persecutions and sorrow as his followers were brutally tortured, killed and forced to migrate in much the same way Christians proclaim the "truth" of *their* beliefs are proven through the martyrdom of the apostles saying, "Who would die for a lie?" Muhammed's clan was boycotted, he was stoned and his enemies even offered him wealth and kingship if he abandoned his call to believe in Allah, but instead he lived a very austere life and never pursued any worldly gains. Furthermore, the life of Muhammad is said to be a practical embodiment of the divine message and a study of his life through the Hadith provides an appreciation of this fact. Even before he received the Prophethood he was known in his society as Al-Ameen (The Trustworthy) and As-Sadiq (The Truthful) and both Muslim and non-Muslim scholars attested to his honesty and integrity.

It is also claimed the Quran mentions things which were not known at the time. Muslims say, "How can the existence of these verses be explained? The Quran has scientific descriptions only recently discovered by modern science which could not have been known 1400 years ago. For instance it describes the expansion of the universe, saying 'And it is we who have built the universe with (our creative) power; and verily, it is we who are steadily expanding it." [Quran, 51:47]. It was not until 1925, when Edwin Hubble provided evidence of receding galaxies, that the expanding universe came to be accepted as a scientific fact. World famous geologist Professor Alfred Kroner explained, "Thinking about many of these questions and thinking where Muhammad came from, he was after all a Bedouin. I think it is almost impossible that he could have known about things like the common origin of the universe, because scientists have only found out within the last few years with very complicated and advanced technological methods that this is the case. The Quran also describes geographical concepts that were proven after its revelation. For example, it was the common dogma 1400 years ago that the earth was flat, but the Quran described it as a sphere, compressed at each end (like an ostrich egg): 'And the earth moreover, He has made egg shaped.' [Quran 79:30]. In 1597, when Sir Francis Drake sailed around the world, the earth became known to be a sphere."

It is claimed there are no contradictions in the Quran. It says, "Do they not attentively consider the Quran? If it had been from any besides Allah, they would certainly have found therein many contradictions." (Sura 4:82). The Quran confirms and explains the Bible. "This Quran could not have been composed by any except Allah; but it is a confirmation of that which was revealed before it, and an explanation of the Scripture; there is no doubt thereof; sent down from the Lord of all creatures." (Sura 10:37). It has unsurpassed literary quality. "Will they say, 'Muhammed hath forged it'? Answer: 'Bring therefore a chapter like unto it, and call whom ye may to your assistance, besides Allah, if ye speak truth.'" (Sura 10:38). The truth of the Quran can be found in its incorruptibility, because unlike the Bible it has never been changed since being given to Muhammed.

Those are the claims of Islam. Let's see how they compare to those made by Christians. The Bible is of course the sacred text of the Christian faith. It is also one of the best known books on the planet. All around the globe there are billions of copies in every language and chances are good you have at least one in your home right now. Nearly everyone does. To Christians the Bible is the error-free word of God, not the work of men. It is God's word to his creation. To reinforce this belief there are over four thousand places in the text where it says things like, "Thus says the Lord," and the Bible refers to its "author" in a number of places. For example in 2 Timothy 3:16 the Bible says, "All Scripture is God-breathed and profitable for teaching, for reproof, for correction and for training in righteousness." 1 Thessalonians 2:13 says, "And we also thank God constantly for this, that when you received the word of God which you heard from us, you accepted it not as the word of men but as what it really is, the word of God." 2 Peter 1:20-21 says, "Above all, you must understand that no prophecy of Scripture came about by the prophet's own interpretation. For prophecy never had its origin in the will of man, but men spoke from God as they were carried along by the Holy Spirit." And Psalm 19:7 says, "The law of the Lord is perfect, reviving the soul. The Bible is the law of the Lord, and it is perfect. So says the Lord."

The *Christian Courier* sums up the position of many Christians on the origin of the Bible when it says, "God, although using human writers in the composition of the Bible, is nevertheless its ultimate author. And since the perfect God cannot be the source of confusion (1 Corinthians

14:33) or contradiction (Hebrews 6:18), it must be acknowledged that the Bible is perfectly harmonious. The fact that the Bible is written by God gives the Bible ultimate authority - God's authority. Because it is the perfect, error-free word of God, the Bible is essential to Christianity. The Bible acts as the single God-given source of information for Christians."

If God exists and the Bible is his perfect word then everything Christians believe is true without exception, but what if the Bible was not written by God? What if it is simply a book of legends and stories written by human authors and God had nothing to do with it? In that case Christianity collapses, so clearly there is a lot riding on the Bible.

One problem is there are dozens of versions, hundreds of interpretations and different groups even disagree on how many books there should be. You'd think a perfect and all-powerful deity could at least manage to be consistent but no, the collection of books making up the Bible differs between the various branches of Judaism and Christianity. The smallest biblical canon is that of the Samaritans who recognize only five books, while mainstream Judaism recognizes thirty-nine as does the Protestant Old Testament, while the Roman Catholic and Orthodox Old Testaments contain further books as well as some additions to a few of the Jewish books. There are twenty-seven books in most Christian New Testaments, but some branches of Christianity have even more. While the books of the Jewish Bible and Protestant Old Testament are the same their organization is different with the Hebrew Bible grouping them in three divisions of Law (Torah), Prophets (Nebi'im) and Writings (Ketubim). The books of the Hebrew Bible/Protestant Old Testament are treated first, then come the extra books of the Catholic and Orthodox Old Testaments followed by the New Testament.

All of that doesn't even take into account the apocryphal "lost books" of the Bible and the way it was ultimately assembled smacks of politics, power and outright lies. In tracing the origin of the Bible one is led to 325 CE when Constantine the Great called the First Council of Nicaea, which was composed of three hundred religious leaders. In all eighteen hundred were invited, but due to primitive modes of travel and communication at the time most did not show up and participate. Three whole centuries after Jesus lived this council was given the task of somehow separating "divinely inspired" writings from those of questionable origin, and in the end many books were left out including one thought to have been written by Jesus' own brother James.

The actual compilation of the Bible was an incredibly complicated project which involved churchmen of many varying beliefs being thrown together in an atmosphere of dissension, jealousy, intolerance, persecution and outright bigotry. At the time the question of the divinity of Jesus had split the church into two factions and Constantine offered to make the then little known Christian sect the official state religion of Rome if they would settle their differences. He didn't particularly care what they believed as long as they agreed upon a belief, any belief, because Constantine thought compiling a book of sacred writings would give authority to the new church and help solidify his empire.

We have long known about disagreements over religious doctrine between different sects of Christianity, but most people are unaware of how deep the differences are about some fundamental topics. Take Presbyterians, for example. We usually assume they are mild-mannered Protestants, but their doctrine is surprisingly harsh They don't believe man has free will, think only those God chose before time began can make it to Heaven and there is nothing the "non-elect" can do to change that. Even babies can't make it to Heaven because they haven't had the opportunity to learn the correct doctrine through the Holy Spirit and therefore have no chance of being born again. Baptists heartily disagree but are unable to explain Matthew 13 which states Jesus purposefully taught in parables so that many people cannot understand the "word" and would be condemned to Hell. Of course this is all nonsense and since no two denominations of Christianity can agree it leads the objective observer to conclude the Bible is merely a clumsy compilation of forgeries filled with puzzling contradictions.

If you don't agree with that last statement here is a startling fact. Virtually all academic religious scholars agree the different books of the Bible weren't even written by the prophets and disciples whose names appear as the authors. For example nowhere does it actually say Moses wrote the Pentateuch, i.e. the first five books of the Bible. That is just an assumption people make which they refer to as "tradition," but more to the point he could not possibly have written Deuteronomy because it describes his own death in the past tense. In fact Deuteronomy 34:10 states, "There has never been another prophet like Moses..." which sounds like a passage written long after Moses' death because enough time would have had to pass for many other prophets to have arisen, pass from the scene and be evaluated for that to make any sense. In spite of that, conservative theologians continue to cling to the notion of Mosaic authorship despite a mountain of evidence to the contrary and so they put forward a variety of theories as to how he could have done it. Similarly, Peter certainly did not write the epistles of Peter. The real author, whoever he was, happened to admire Peter and decided to put his name as the author in his honor. In other words they're all forgeries with the exception of some of Paul's letters which many scholars agree were probably written by Paul as advertised. Evidence that the Gospels themselves weren't actually written by Matthew, Mark, Luke and John is abundant and obvious partly because the disciples were supposed to be Jewish and yet they discuss the Jews in the third person as if they were foreigners. For example John said, "And Passover, a feast of the Jews was neigh." To put that into perspective, an American would never write, "It was the fourth of July, a holiday of the Americans."

There are also thousands of contradictions in the Bible. For instance one of the Ten Commandments clearly states there is only one God, however the Old Testament refers to multiple gods over one thousand times. Some Christians try to explain this away by claiming these multiple gods are the parts of the trinity, but this is a laughable defense because the Jews who wrote the OT did not believe in the trinity and the references to multiple gods unmistakably link Judeo-Christianity with its pagan ancestry.

Then there is the "go teach all nations" forgery. Christianity was originally an obscure end-of-the-world cult within Judaism, and in numerous passages Jesus claims he will come back and the world will end within the lifetime of the disciples. Moreover he said, "I am not come but for the lost sheep of Israel." Gentiles were evidently not part of his flock and only Jews could be saved when the world ended, but later in Matthew and Mark Jesus contradicts himself and tells the disciples to "go teach all nations." What really happened? The end of the world obviously did not occur within the lifetime of the disciples as promised and the cult of Christianity was dying out so Paul and other Christian leaders were forced to include the Gentiles in order to keep the cult alive and some early priests interpolated the "go teach all nations" fiction into the texts of Matthew and Mark. All early texts were handwritten and only a few people were literate enough to spot this fraud, therefore this interpolation didn't take place until after Acts was written because in this book the disciples act as if they had never heard the teach-all-nations command. If the original texts of Matthew and Mark had included this command the author of Acts wouldn't have found it necessary to make up his story about how Cornelius had to convince the disciples to teach all nations because according to the revised Matthew and Mark they already were doing so. Furthermore the "Great Commission" of Matthew 28:19 describes Jesus sending his disciples out to preach the gospel "in the name of the Father, and of the Son and of the Holy Ghost," in other words the three persons in one God, and this is an important piece of scriptural evidence for the doctrine of the Trinity, however the rest of the New Testament refers to baptism only in the name of Jesus. For example in Acts 2:38 Peter preaches that believers should "repent and be baptized, every one of you, in the name of Jesus Christ for the forgiveness of your sins" and this has led some to suspect the Triune baptismal formula was added later in order to shore up the doctrine of the Trinity which had been rejected by the Arians and other early Christian sects. The 4th Century Church historian Eusebius quotes the text as, "Go ye into all the world and make disciples of all the Gentiles in My Name," however it is questionable whether Eusebius was quoting verbatim since he was often prone to paraphrasing, plus he had quoted the longer reading elsewhere. Additionally the Didache, a Christian text believed to have been written in the 1st Century, contains the long form as do writings by many early Church fathers. In light of this it cannot be said with any certainty the text was added later, although various Pentecostal groups continue to insist it was.

Clearly the highly nuanced doctrine of the Trinity is a bit hazy in the Bible so some scholars think scribes might have resorted to fabricating scriptural proof for it, notably by adding the famous Johannine Comma to I John 5:7 which reads, "And there are three that bear record in heaven, the Father, the Word and the Holy Ghost. And these three are one." This is one passage where the case for inauthenticity is virtually a slam dunk because only eight extant Greek manuscripts from the 10th Century onward contain the comma, four of those have the text only on the margin and all appear to be translations of the Latin Vulgate which is itself a late text. It is supposed the comma originated as a marginal note in certain Latin versions and eventually made its way into the Vulgate, and no Church Father quotes it in debates with anti-Trinitarian heretics such as the Arians. The few proponents of the comma accuse the Arians of suppressing the text and argue that Bishop Cyprian appears to reference it around 250 CE. In the late 4th Century St. Jerome was aware of copies with the comma and raged against scribes who were deleting it, calling them "unfaithful translators… who have kept just the three words water, blood and spirit in this edition, omitting mention of Father, Word and Spirit," but is it really believable the Arians could have expunged so many Greek manuscripts, even with their dominance of the Eastern

Roman Empire for half a century? Textual critics think not and modern critical versions of the Bible now usually omit the comma, for example the English Standard Version reads, "For there are three that testify: the Spirit and the water and the blood; and these three agree."

Peter and Paul are considered early Christianity's "dynamic duo," working in tandem to evangelize the Roman Empire, and in Galatians 2:7-8 Paul spells out this partnership writing, "I had been entrusted with the task of preaching the gospel to the uncircumcised, just as Peter had been to the circumcised. For God, who was at work in Peter as an apostle to the circumcised, was also at work in me as an apostle to the Gentiles." Even so Marcion of Sinope, the most reviled heretic of the 2nd Century and a close follower of Paul, hinted that Peter had betrayed the trust placed in him by Jesus and spurned the tyrannical Jewish God of the Old Testament as having nothing to do with the loving God of the New Testament. To this end he compiled a distinctive canon of Scriptures containing only Paul's epistles and a version of Luke with most of the Old Testament references omitted and as a result his opponents accused him of doctoring the texts by eliminating all the Jewish features he could find. Not surprisingly Marcion's version of Paul's epistles does not include the aforementioned Galatians 2:7-8 and naturally many scholars point to this as one of the passages which Marcion cut out for conflicting with his teachings, but even today there is considerable debate as to whether Marcion really expunged the text or whether it was later inserted by orthodox scribes attempting to refute him. Proponents of this opinion point to the oddity of Paul switching to the name Peter in verses 7-8 when he usually refers to him as Cephas, plus his other writings make no reference to the division of missionary responsibility spelled out in the disputed verses and in fact in I Corinthians he sees the "Cephas party" as just another faction he must contend with. It is also argued that Tertullian, whose five volume work *Against Marcion* constitutes the most detailed attack on him, would not have failed to use the disputed verses had they existed at the time because as New Testament scholar Adolf von Harnack put it, "How advantageous would it otherwise have been for Tertullian to be able to triumphantly hold up… the acknowledgement of the Petrine Jewish apostolate by Paul himself, with this sentence to be able to negate the entire position of Marcion."

Many scholars have also commented on the peculiarities of the salutation which opens Romans, Paul's most theologically oriented epistle. In the ancient world letters began with simple greetings such as "Apion to Epimarchus his father and lord, heartiest greetings" or

"Polycrates to his father, greeting," and Paul himself normally began with a formulaic greeting along the lines of "Paul the Apostle, unto [recipients]; Grace be unto you, and peace, from God our Father and the Lord Jesus Christ," but the greeting to the Romans departs from the norm by being extraordinarily long. Scholar J.C. O'Neill has remarked that the passage "completely overloads the salutation and makes it a grammatical monstrosity, which no one writer would have perpetrated, and it looks very like a later insertion," while those who hold that Paul wrote the passage in its entirety explain the odd opening as Paul quoting a pre-existing creed known to the Roman church in order to reassure a congregation he was apparently about to meet for the first time, however O'Neill thinks it strange Paul would cite a creed which is never brought up again and has no relevance to the rest of the epistle. His theory that it is a later insertion finds support in its omission from the *Greek Codex Boernerianus* which opens simply, "Paul, servant of Jesus Christ, called an apostle among all the Gentiles on his behalf," and in O'Neill's opinion it is "hard to imagine a scribe omitting such a long and important section, even by accident, and therefore I conclude that the long section was a marginal comment or interpolation, which was incorporated very early into the standard text of Romans."

Then there is the "Agony In the Garden" episode where a despairing Jesus raised bloody sweat and had to be strengthened by an angel. This was problematic for the early Christian sect known as the Docetists who believed Jesus was a divine phantom who did not have a physical body and there are modern textual critics who believe Luke 22:43-44, where the story is found, was a later corruption inserted to confound the Docetists while at the same time creating a fulfillment scenario for Psalm 91:11-12. Proponents of interpolation argue Luke would not have portrayed Jesus in such a feeble, terrified state and a comparison with the Gospel of Mark indicates he usually went out of his way to eliminate words which show Jesus in anguish. Manuscript evidence is inconclusive with slightly more ancient sources lacking the verses than having them, but the passage was certainly known and used by Church fathers in the 2nd Century while its omission can only be dated to the beginning of the 3rd Century, so if the passage is genuinely Lukan why is it missing in so many manuscripts from the 3rd Century onward? One shaky explanation is the period in question saw Christianity under attack from pagans such as Celsus, Porphyry and Julian the Apostate, who used the Scriptures to disparage Christ, and the episode in Gethsemane provided fodder for those who called Jesus a coward.

Christian Eucharistic celebrations repeat Christ's words over the cup of wine at the Last Supper, "This is the chalice, the new testament in my blood, which shall be shed for you," but did he actually say that? The passage where it appears, Luke 22:20, is not in the 5th or 6th Century *Codex Bezae* and since *Bezae* is notorious for adding text rather than subtracting it the omission has caused some scholars to speculate those words were not originally part of Luke. The doctrine of atonement conveyed is also alien to Luke since in his Gospel and Acts he portrays Christ's death as a horrendous miscarriage of justice and nothing more with Christ's blood being significant only in the sense that his unjust death pricked the conscience of some who called for it and led to their conversion. The rejection of a vicarious sacrifice was quite intentional on Luke's part and as Bible scholar Bart Ehrman wrote, "Luke eliminated or changed the Markan references to Jesus' atoning sacrifice; he chose not to quote Isaiah 53 to depict Jesus' death as an atonement for sins, even though he quoted the passage otherwise... it is not at all difficult to account for an interpolation of the disputed words." Moreover, the wording of the disputed passages is rather non-Lukan and in fact look closer to something Paul might have written and thus the longer version may be a scribal attempt to inject I Corinthians 11:24 into Luke's Gospel.

Did Paul consider women to be second-class citizens as I Corinthians 14:34-35, where he commands the ladies to be submissive and keep silent in church, suggests? This passage is a head-scratcher since Paul specifically gives rules for women speaking in church a few chapters earlier, so unless Paul was schizophrenic one of the two passages must have been written by someone else. Most scholars believe 14:34-35 is the false one since it echoes the misogyny of I Timothy 2, a passage which is generally considered a forgery, so presumably the verses were added by someone with an agenda against the female sex since they fit poorly with Paul's declaration "there is neither male nor female. For you are all one in Christ Jesus." Another clue is how out of place it seems between verses 33 and 36, which both discuss prophecy, and in some ancient manuscripts 33 and 36 are connected with 34-35 only appearing at the end of the chapter - so how the text ended up in two different places is inexplicable if the text is authentic. As a result in 546 CE Bishop Victor of Capua ordered 34-35 to be dropped entirely from the *Codex Fuldensis*, an indication he was aware of manuscripts, now long gone, which omit the passage entirely.

Christians who oppose the death penalty frequently quote John 8:7 in which Jesus makes a famous challenge to the accusers of a woman caught in adultery, "He that is without sin among you, let him first cast a stone at her," but most scholars now agree the story of the adulteress was not originally in John and in fact the newest versions often contain marginal notes making readers aware of its spurious nature, for example the New International Version informs readers "the earliest and most reliable manuscripts and other ancient witnesses do not include John 7:53-8:11." No surviving Greek manuscript before the 5th Century contains the story, with the first attestation being contained in the *Codex Bezae* - which, as previously noted, had a habit of adding things. Early texts also tend to move it around with it being found at the very end of the Gospel of John in some, in the margin near 7:52 in others and some even locate it after Luke 21:38, so Byzantine scribes indicated on the margin beside the text they were doubtful of its genuineness and church Fathers such as Origen and Chrysostom never referred to it in their verse-by-verse commentaries on John's Gospel. In fact at the start of the 5th Century St. Augustine was so bothered by the large number of copies without the story he offered the explanation, "Certain persons of little faith, or rather enemies of the true faith, fearing, I suppose, lest their wives should be given impunity in sinning, removed from their manuscripts the Lord's act of forgiveness toward the adulteress, as if he who had said, 'sin no more,' had granted permission to sin," and modern supporters of the story are of the same opinion, but if it was edited out why were the inoffensive verses in 7:53-8:2 deleted as well? In the end the manuscript evidence, stylistic differences between the story and the rest of John - seventeen percent of its words cannot be found elsewhere in the Gospel - as well as the break in the flow of thought it creates between 7:52 and 8:12 make an overwhelming case for inauthenticity.

There are of course many more examples, but at this point I shall cut to the heart of the matter and point out belief in a virgin birth has pagan origins. The Jews believed the messiah was supposed to be a genealogical descendent of David, and the marriage of paganism and Judaism which is Christianity conflicts here because Matthew and Luke give completely different fictional genealogies in order to prove Jesus is the biological descendent of David. They both say Joseph rather than Mary is the biological descendent of David and of course they supposedly never has sexual relations, so there is no way Jesus could have been born of a virgin and also be his descendent. What probably happened was some anonymous priest interpolated the story of the virgin birth into the Gospels to appeal to pagans, and in doing so created what is perhaps the most ridiculous contradiction of all. Or maybe he didn't, since many scholars now point to the fact "virgin" was simply a mistranslation of "young girl."

Someone once said Christianity is one woman's lie about having an affair that got out of hand, and that whimsical point of view has a great deal of merit. How could anyone possibly know whether or not a woman who lived two thousand years ago was actually a virgin? For that matter how could the Gospel authors have known this, writing decades later as they did, and even if they had been present they couldn't have known for sure. A good and far more recent example of the gullibility of the masses came in the form of a newspaper article published on May 6, 2010 entitled *Woman Says She Became Pregnant After Watching Porn in 3D* which claimed a "miraculous conception." According to the article, "A white American woman who had a black baby claims she fell pregnant whilst watching a porn movie in 3D. According to reports the child's father, who is white, was serving in the military in Iraq when she became pregnant and his wife Jennifer told him the child was conceived whilst she was watching a porn movie in 3D. 'I see it as suspicious,' he said. 'The films in 3-D are very real. With today's technology, anything is possible. Jennifer claimed she went to watch a porn film with her friends in New York, she doesn't usually watch porn movies, she went to experience the effects in 3D and the child looks like the black actor in the movie. For her part Jennifer said, 'A month after watching the movie I started feeling dizzy and the results were positive,' while admitting her marriage could be in trouble. 'Even though my husband believed in me my marriage could be at risk, but he knows I'm faithful.'"

This story of course proved to be a hoax, but the point is thousands of people believed it. Face it, human beings are gullible. In fact a *Fox News* report in December of 2013 said nearly one percent of young women in a U.S. study who have become pregnant claim to be virgins according to Britain's *BMJ* medical journal. Based on interviews with 7,870 women and girls ages fifteen to twenty-eight, forty-five of the 5,340 pregnancies in this group through the years - 0.8 percent - occurred in women who reported they had conceived independent of men. The figure does not include pregnancies which result from in-vitro fertilization or other assisted reproductive technology.

So let's move on to another apologetic fallacy. The Christian website ironically called *All About Truth* claims, "The Bible also validates its divine authorship through fulfilled prophecies. An astonishing 668 prophecies have been fulfilled and none have ever been proven false (three are unconfirmed). An honest study of biblical prophecy will compellingly show the divine authorship of the Bible. Further, archeology confirms (or in some cases supports) accounts in the biblical record. No other holy book comes close to the Bible in the amount of evidence supporting its divine authorship."

So how do they know those 688 prophecies have been fulfilled? Why, it's all right there... in the Bible. Think about that. When an author writes a mystery novel things which happen at the end are foreshadowed earlier in the book, but that doesn't mean it's not a work of fiction. Right about now believers are saying, "What about things which have actually happened and are not only in the Bible? What about the Jewish people returning to Israel just as had been prophesized?" The answer should be obvious. They went there because that's where the Bible said they were supposed to go. Imagine two people have just bought new bicycles for their children and begin to assemble them. There are dozens of parts, including many screws in several sizes. The first person carefully reads the instructions and inserts 'screw 4B' into 'slot G8.' The second person randomly reaches into the bag of parts, pulls out the same screw, and puts it into the very same hole. Are these events identical? Of course not. You may ask why this is relevant. The answer is simple. If the Jews had returned to Israel in 1948 without ever having read the Bible that would be significant and might be a legitimate prophecy, but in reality they went there because they were following the instructions in their holy book. When it comes right down to it the cryptic predictions of Nostradamus about the 9-11 attacks, French Revolution, death of King Henry II and many other world events are far more accurate and compelling than any made in the Bible, and their "fulfillment" takes place in actual events rather than later on in the very same narrative. At this juncture it is important to understand there are five types of "fulfilled" Bible prophecies:

1) **Self-Fulfilling Prophecies.** The Jews returning to Israel is a perfect example of this because they were simply doing what the Bible said they were supposed to do. If it had said Hoboken, New Jersey they would have gone there instead. Even today there are people who are actively trying to make biblical prophecies come true (i.e. self-fulfill) as is the case with efforts to breed an unblemished red heifer to help usher in the "end times" (more on that elsewhere).

2) **Tailor-Made Prophecies**. The authors of the New Testament had of course read the Old Testament and it was only natural for them to

write stories which contained events which had been "predicted" by the previous book. It should also be pointed out the only evidence any of these events ever took place is contained in - you guessed it - the Bible. A good example is Jeremiah 31:15 which says, "Thus says the LORD, 'A voice is heard in Ramah, lamentation and bitter weeping. Rachel is weeping for her children; she refuses to be comforted for her children, because they are no more.'" That "prediction" is supposedly "fulfilled" in Matthew 2:16-18 which says "...then that which was spoken through Jeremiah the prophet was fulfilled, saying, 'A voice was heard in Ramah, weeping and great mourning, Rachel weeping for her children; and she refused to be comforted, because they were no more.'"

3) **Reverse Prophecies.** These are invented by readers trying to validate Scripture and were not even intended to be prophecies by the writers of the Bible. It involves reading about an event in the NT and then combing the OT for a passage which seems to predict it. For example in Isaiah 53 there is a famous passage, discussed in detail elsewhere, which is claimed by some to be a prediction of Jesus but the entire chapter is written in the past tense and has to do with somebody who has already died rather than someone in the distant future.

4) **Ambiguous Prophecies.** These are passages which, when read objectively, bear little resemblance to the claimed prophecy. These Bible verses can be twisted to say anything and a hundred people would reach a hundred different conclusions when reading them. An example of an ambiguous, supposedly fulfilled Bible prophecy is where Daniel 2:32-33 predicts the four great kingdoms by saying, "The head of the statue was made of pure gold, its chest and arms of silver, its belly and thighs of bronze, its legs of iron, its feet partly of iron and partly of baked clay." Huh?

5) **Inevitable or Common Sense Prophecies.** These are prophecies which are almost certainly going to happen and are among the most worthless. For example one of the signs of the "end times" is "foretold" in Daniel 12:4 where he predicts "an increase in knowledge and travel" with the verse, "But as for you, Daniel, conceal these words and seal up the book until the end of time; many will go back and forth, and knowledge will increase." Apologists

then add, "Billy Graham was quoted as saying, 'ninety percent of all the engineers and scientists who have ever lived are alive today.' Air travel, space travel, DNA research and human cloning are all examples of the rapid increase in knowledge in our generation." Well no kidding. What did they expect, a decrease in knowledge? Less scientists in the world?

Be honest. Is the meaning of the two passages from Daniel crystal clear to you with no possibility of multiple, alternative interpretations? Or do you need to have it "explained" to you? Some believers rationalize it is fulfilled prophecy by claiming, "In Daniel 2:32-33, there is a prophetic passage that symbolically identified the four great kingdoms that would rise up and control much of world, beginning in Daniel's lifetime. The head of gold refers to the Babylonian Empire that ruled much of the world about 2600 years ago. Daniel then said the head-of-gold empire would be followed by an empire symbolized by arms of silver. Christian scholars have often interpreted this to refer to the Medo-Persian Empire which later conquered the Babylonian Empire. The scholars say the two arms refer to the two groups - the Medes and the Persians - who comprised the Medo-Persian Empire. The third kingdom was symbolized by the statue's belly and thighs of brass. Some scholars believe this is a reference to the Grecian Empire, which conquered the Medo-Persian Empire. The symbol of a belly and thighs of brass suggests the kingdom was to start out as a united empire but end up as a divided empire. Under the leadership of Alexander the Great the Grecian Empire was a united empire, but after Alexander's death the empire was divided up. The fourth symbol, that of iron legs and feet that were part iron and part clay, has often been suggested to be a reference to the Roman Empire, which later conquered the Grecian Empire. These four kingdoms ruled over much of the world, and each of the four ruled over the land of Israel during times in which a significant number of Jews, and perhaps a majority of Jews, were living in their homeland. Before the collapse of the Roman Empire Jerusalem was destroyed, and hundreds of thousands of Jews were forced into exile. Even today, a majority of Jews live outside of Israel."

What? Is that how you would honestly interpret those words on your own? Even when referring to the unnamed "scholars," phrases such as "have *often* interpreted this," "*some* scholars *believe*" and "has *often* been *suggested* to be" are used because no one really knows what the heck

Daniel 2:32-33 is supposed to mean. Does any of that sounds like a definitive case for fulfilled prophecy?

Here is another interesting piece of spin. There are actually apologetics which claim something *not* happening constitutes fulfillment of a prophecy. Specifically, Matthew 24:36-37 says no one will know the hour or the day of Jesus' return and since it hasn't happened (and therefore no one knows) it must be true. They then go on to tell us false predictions have been made many times by people such as William Miller (who began the Adventist movement and predicted Jesus would return sometime between March 21, 1843 and March 21, 1844), Samuel Snow (October 22, 1844) and Joseph Smith (the founder of Mormonism who claimed Jesus would return by 1891). If that makes any sense to you I would like to offer my own prophecy. I predict no man, including the reader, can know in advance the hour of his own death (suicide is cheating). I guess that makes me a prophet, since you are presumably still alive and reading.

It is important to note Christians are not the only ones to claim prophetic inspiration and scriptural inerrancy. Muslims claim the Quran is also proven by prophecy and of course refer to Muhammed as "the one *true* prophet." Let's take a look at some of their claims in the words of a Muslim apologist and see how they compare to biblical claims.

The Quran contains many prophecies which are claimed to have been fulfilled, but in this discussion we will limit ourselves to only five. The first two prophetic claims are noteworthy in that unlike any other world Scripture the Quran prophesizes its own preservation under divine care and also makes a claim no other religious text makes - that God himself (Allah) will keep its text safe from alteration. The Quran says, "Behold, it is we ourselves who have gradually revealed this reminder, and behold, it is we who shall truly guard it." Muslims also claim Allah made the Quran easy to memorize, with their holy book claiming "and in truth we have made the Quran easy to remember; who then is willing to take it to heart?" There is not a single Scripture or religious text in the world that is as easy to memorize; even non-Arabs and children commit it to memory easily. The entire Quran is memorized by almost every Islamic scholar and hundreds of thousands of ordinary Muslims, generation after generation and almost every Muslim has some portion of the Quran memorized to read in his prayers. Contrast that with the vast majority of professing Christians who have never read the Bible for themselves.

Next is the so-called "Twofold Prophecy." Before the rise of Islam the Romans and Persians were two competing superpowers. The Romans were led by Christian Emperor Heraclius (610-641 CE), whereas the Persians were Zoroastrians led by Khosrow Parviz (who reigned 590-628 CE) under whom the empire achieved its greatest expansion. In 614 the Persians conquered Syria and Palestine, took Jerusalem and destroyed the Holy Sepulcher and 'True Cross' carried to Ctesiphon, and then in 619 they occupied Egypt and Libya. Heraclius met them at Thracian Heraclea (617 or 619), but they sought to capture him and he rode madly back to Constantinople while being hotly pursued.

The Muslims were grieved by the Roman defeat as they felt spiritually closer to Christian Rome than Zoroastrian Persia, but the Meccans were naturally buoyed by the victory of pagan Persia. To Meccans the Roman humiliation was an omen of the defeat of the Muslims at pagan hands, although at the same time a prophecy comforted faithful Muslims saying, "the Romans have been defeated - in a land close by; but they, (even) after (this) defeat of theirs, will soon be victorious - within ten years. With God is the decision, in the past and in the future: on that day shall the believers rejoice with the help of God. He helps whom he will, and he is the mighty, the most-merciful."

The Quran had apparently made a prophecy of two victories - the future Roman victory within ten years over Persians, something "unimaginable at the time," and the joy of the faithful on a victory over the pagans. In 622 Heraclius left Constantinople as prayers rose from its many sanctuaries for victory over the Persian Zoroastrians and the reconquest of Jerusalem, devoted the next two years to campaigns in Armenia and in 627 met the Persians near Nineveh. There he killed three Persian generals in single combat, killed the Persian commander and scattered the Persian host. A month later Heraclius entered Dastagird with its stupendous treasure and Khosrow was overthrown by his son, who made peace with Heraclius. Returning to Constantinople in triumph, Heraclius was hailed as a hero. Also in the year 624 AH (according to the Hijri calendar which is used to date events in many Muslim countries) Muslims defeated the Meccans in the first and decisive Battle at Badr. In the words of an Indian scholar: "...a single line of prophecy was related to four nations and the fate of two great empires. All this proves the Holy Quran to be the Book of God."

The Quran appears to have predicted the defeat of unbelievers in Mecca while Prophet Muhammad and his followers were still being persecuted by them with the words "or do they (the Meccan disbelievers) say 'We are a great multitude, and we shall be victorious?' Their multitude will be defeated, and they shall turn their backs (in flight)!"

The prophecy was revealed in Mecca but was said to have been "fulfilled" at the Battle of Badr two years after the Prophet's migration to the city of Medina.

The next prophecy concerns the fate of specific individuals. Waleed bin Mugheera was a staunch enemy of Islam who openly ridiculed the Quran by saying, "This is nothing but magic, derived from of old; this is nothing but the word of a mortal!" and the Quran prophesized he would never accept Islam by predicting, "Soon will I cast him into Hell-Fire! And what will explain to thee what Hell-Fire is? It leaves naught nor does it spare aught." Muslims view the fact Waleed died in a state of disbelief as prophesized by the Quran as proof, but that is much like saying a prediction Richard Dawkins will die as an atheist will prove the Bible true. Similarly, concerning a fiery opponent of Islam named Abu Lahab, the Quran foretold he would die opposing the "religion of God" with the words, "May the hands of Abu Lahab perish, and (indeed) he has perished. His wealth and gains will not profit him. He will be plunged in flaming fire." Specifically, three prophecies were made about Abu Lahab - the conspiracies of Abu Lahab against the Prophet would not succeed, his wealth and children would not benefit him and he would die opposing "God's religion" and "enter the fire." While Abu Lahab did indeed die in a state of disbelief as prophesized by the Quran, the contention that had he or Waleed accepted Islam outwardly that would have disproved its prophecies and thus its heavenly source is laughable - with the idea being through their *belief* they would have proven the Quran and therefore Islam to be false. Plus, how exactly are we supposed to know for sure someone has fulfilled a prophecy by "entering the fire"?

According to Muslims and Christians alike a key foundation to believing Scripture is actually a revelation from God is internal truth, whether it be in regards to occurrences in the past or those to come in the future and/or in contemporary ages. As one can see, there are many "prophecies" of that which is to come, some of which were "fulfilled" in the Prophet's lifetime or have been fulfilled since his death while others are yet to appear. Is that sufficient proof of the Quran, and therefore Islam? Of course not, and the Bible is no different.

Yet the very same Christian apologists who quite rightly reject the authenticity of the Quran, in a mind-numbing bit of circular reasoning fueled by cognitive dissonance, claim the question of who wrote the Bible can be definitively answered by examining the biblical texts in light of the external evidences which support its claims. For example they say, "2 Timothy 3:16 states that 'all Scripture is inspired by God....'

and in 2 Peter 1:20-21 Peter reminds the reader to 'Know this first of all, that no prophecy of Scripture is a matter of one's own interpretation, but men moved by the Holy Spirit spoke from God.' The Bible itself tells us that it is God who is the author of His book."

Think about that for a moment. How can something possibly be external evidence for itself? This is a classic example of attempting to use the Bible to prove the Bible true. How do Christians know that Scripture (i.e. the Bible) is the inspired word of God and not the work of mere mortals? Why it says so right there... in the Bible.

Next let's examine the claim messages hidden within the Bible predict the future. In 1994 an American journalist named Michael Drosnin visited Israel and told a friend named Chaim Guri he had a letter for Prime Minister Yitzhak Rabin in which he warned that according to an obscure code embedded within the Torah - the Hebrew version of the first five books of the Old Testament - Rabin would be assassinated. Guri passed the letter along and "amazingly" Rabin was in fact assassinated... a year later.

Convinced his prediction must have been divinely inspired Drosnin wrote a book called *The Bible Code* in which he detailed his coding methodology, which was based on the work of Israeli-Latvian mathematician Eliyahu Rips, who had in turn based his work upon that of school teacher Avraham Oren.

The "codes" in the Bible are what is called "Equidistant Letter Spacing" or ELS, and a very simple example of this is the word "troops." Take every other letter and you'll get the word "top," which is said to be encoded within the word troops as an ELS with a "skip" of two. That's all there is to it. Now imagine a sentence written out in a grid without spaces or punctuation like a giant crossword puzzle with no black squares. A word encoded in this manner will appear in a line vertically, diagonally or horizontally and can even skip squares and will often be at an angle something like a knight's move in chess, i.e. four squares up and one square to the left. Using such a method and with a large enough block of text it is possible to find just about *any* word. Add a computer to the mix to crunch of all the possibilities and you'll be surprised how many words crop up. Short words are everywhere, but each time you add a letter to make your target word longer the number of hits drops dramatically and it's rare to find a word of seven or more letters.

Now that you know how to find words encoded within a text, what about sentences? Followers of the Bible Code methodology take a pretty liberal approach to this and it is not necessary to find the entire sentence as one long ELS string because that's impossible. Instead all you have to do is find words which appear on the grid near each other, usually near enough to be viewed on the same grid (you can make your grid as large as you prefer) and words can go in different directions with different skips. For context picture a word search puzzle with a whole bunch of words circled in it and this is how sentences are found using the Bible Code. There are no rules governing this process, it's completely up to the individual to decide which words to search for within a text and they then place them in the desired order. There are always many extra words, especially shorter ones, scattered through a given grid so the researcher has plenty of words to choose from to form the desired sentence.

If that seems pretty weak, that's because it is. It turns out there are now several inexpensive commercial software programs which perform these searches and include a number of source texts including the New and Old Testaments as well as *War and Peace.* Any long text will do including completely random words, and if you're patient enough, willing to try all sorts of alternate wordings and stick with as many short words as possible you can find just about any sentence you want.

There is another aspect to the Bible Code which must be mentioned and that is the Hebrew language. Remember the Indiana Jones movie where he almost steps through the wrong floor tile because of an ambiguity about the spelling of Jehovah? Hebrew has different forms and different spellings of the same words and in some cases a number of different spellings, and when Drosnin wrote *The Bible Code* he took full advantage of these ambiguities to find the maximum number of matches for a given word in constructing his sentences - and has been widely (and rightly) criticized for this. If he'd have stuck to one form of Hebrew or another many sentences would be considered misspelled but even so in order to find the name Yitzhak Rabin in Hebrew he had to use a skip value of 4,772 characters which covers a massive block of text in which it's possible to find just about any word.

Clearly it is possible to find almost anything you want in almost any text using the ELS method and the nature of entropy means there will be accidental words and sentences everywhere. When Bible Code proponents find a sentence how do they know it was placed there deliberately by some higher power and was not just another accidental hit? Proving that distinction is really the key to proving there's any substance to Bible Code claims and so far nobody has put forward any reasonable suggestion of what form such proof might take.

Bible Code proponents often point out that Eliyahu Rips co-authored an article about his discovery which was published in a legitimate peer-reviewed mathematical journal called *Statistical Science* in 1994, but what they fail to mention is that publication was in no way endorsing Bible Codes as predictors of future events let alone divine inspiration. *Statistical Science* is a mathematics journal, has nothing to do with religion or predictions and does not publish research - the ELS article was simply published as a mathematically challenging word puzzle - but Drosnin says it's more than that. In his first sequel book *The Bible Code II* he states the Bible was written by aliens, in fact the very same ones who brought DNA to Earth and caused life to develop here. Drosnin believes the aliens left the key to decoding the Bible Code inside a steel obelisk buried near the Dead Sea and claims to have gone searching for it himself, but why an elaborately buried key is necessary is unclear since cheap software "decodes" it just fine.

As for Drosnin's famous prediction of Yitzhak Rabin's assassination it does sound impressive, but consider three points. First it was only one of innumerable predictions Drosnin made, the rest of which turned out to be nonsense such as the nuclear destruction of civilization in both 2000 and 2006 as well as the devastation of Los Angeles by a meteor in 2006. This is the tool of the celebrity psychic and religious apologist, remembering only the hits and ignoring the misses.

Second, at the time Drosnin made the Rabin prediction it was a near certainty he was going to be assassinated since the hardcore right-wing Jews were as angry with Rabin as the Palestinians he was trying to make peace with and pundits said at the time it was only a question of which anti-peace group was going to get him first. Psychics all over the world also predicted his assassination, but Drosnin was lucky enough to be the one who was invited onto the *Oprah Winfrey Show* even though his prediction provided no useful information about the date or place of the assassination.

Third, the actual "prediction" Drosnin found contained simply the name "Yitzhak Rabin" and a Hebrew word which can mean "assassinate" but shortened can also mean "assassin." In a block of text that massive innumerable shorter words are found so Drosnin chose "will," selected a few words from his palette and arranged them into "assassin will assassinate Yitzhak Rabin" while using the word for assassin twice. Note that it could also have been arranged into "assassin Rabin will assassinate Yitzhak" or any of numerous other names also found within the block, so in short it's very hard for a critical thinker who understands ELS coding to conclude Drosnin had found a definitive prediction Rabin would be killed - and this foolishness remains the strongest evidence in favor of a Bible Code.

What if we were to view Scripture as something other than a literal description of actual events? It has been said the difference between a fairy tale and the Bible is one begins with "Once upon a time" and the other starts out saying "In the beginning," and that really is not as flippant a remark as it may sound. Television commentator Bill O'Reilly, who professes to be a devout Catholic, often defends his religion by making the point the Bible is not literal history as many Christians claim but is instead a collection of allegorical stories.

That actually makes sense when you compare the contents to, for example, the *Fables of Aesop*. The Greek fabulist Aesop is said to have lived c. 620-564 BCE and according to tradition was born a slave. Although known for the fables attributed to him Aesop's existence remains uncertain like that of Moses and no writings by him survive, yet numerous fables appearing under his name were gathered across the centuries and in many languages in a storytelling tradition which continues to this day. In many of these tales animals speak and have human characteristics, much like the talking snake, donkey and trees found in the Bible.

Scattered details of Aesop's life can be found in ancient sources including Aristotle, Herodotus and Plutarch. An ancient literary work called *The Aesop Romance* tells an episodic, probably highly fictional version of his life, including the traditional description of Aesop as a strikingly ugly slave who by his cleverness acquired freedom and became an adviser to kings and city-states, while a later and different tradition dating from the Middle Ages depicted Aesop as a black Ethiopian.

Imagine if the collected fables of Aesop had been found in a cave as were the *Dead Sea Scrolls* and were thought to be some sort of religious instruction. After all, many of his tales are useful parables which can serve as instructions for life and when you get right down to it wasn't that the intent of the laws and parables of the Bible? The only differences are Aesop did not advocate atrocities as the God of the Bible did and did not try to pass off his thoughts as being divinely inspired. Even if the scribes who wrote the Bible were clean and sober we are expected to accept as fact that these forty people were divinely inspired, but at the same time dismiss the claims of other prophets such as Muhammed.

While we are on the subject of prophets let's consider the case of Dena Schlosser, who killed her eleven-month-old daughter Margaret in

2004 and amputated the baby's arms with a knife while believing she was offering her to God. On November 22, 2004 the Texas Police arrived at Schlosser's apartment to find the mother of three sitting calmly in her living room listening to hymns while covered in blood and holding a knife. The officers were responding to a 911 call made by workers at a day care center who had spoken to Schlosser earlier that day. The 911 operator had subsequently telephoned Schlosser, who euphorically confessed she had cut the arms off her eleven-month-old baby daughter as the song *He Touched Me* played in the background. The child later died in the hospital.

Psychiatrist David Self later told a court Schlosser had taken a television news story about a boy being mauled by a lion as a sign of the apocalypse. Self, who assessed Schlosser in the months after her arrest, also said Schlosser had heard God commanding her to remove her baby's arms and then her own and the attack was ultimately described as a case of "religious frenzy."

Schlosser was found not guilty by reason of insanity, sent to the North Texas State Hospital until no longer deemed a threat to herself or others, and while there shared a room with Andrea Yates - who had drowned her five children in a bathtub in order to protect them from Satan. The common thread is they both had "heard voices" just as Moses and other prophets supposedly had, and the scary thing is they were not all that unusual.

Peter William Sutcliffe, for instance, was an English serial killer who was dubbed "The Yorkshire Ripper." In 1981 he was convicted of murdering thirteen women and attacking several others, and at his trial Sutcliffe pleaded not guilty to all thirteen counts of murder with the basis of his defense being the claim he was the tool of God's will. Sutcliffe claimed to have first heard voices while working as a gravedigger where he was ultimately ordered to kill prostitutes, testified the voices originated from the headstone of a deceased Polish man named Bronisław Zapolski and said it was God who was doing the talking. How can we differentiate that from the claim Moses "heard" God order him to have the Israelites slaughter one another when he returned from the mount?

During the last days of November in 1971 a jury convicted a man named John Linley Frazier of murdering the five members of the Ohta family. Apparently "voices from God" had commanded him to "seek vengeance on those who rape the environment." After first killing the father he asked each one of the remaining four if they believed in God and they said yes, so he told them they had nothing to be afraid of. He then walked behind each of his helpless victims and shot them at the base of the neck, killing the two women first and then the two boys. Prior to the murders Frasier had exhibited "extreme religiosity," as seen by his excessive underlining in a Bible he carried, plus he considered himself to be John from the Bible and author of the Book of Revelations.

Hamilton Howard "Alber" Fish was a serial killer, child rapist and cannibal who was obsessed with religion and specifically the story of Abraham and Isaac which appears in Genesis 22:1-24. Fish believed that by similarly sacrificing a boy it would be penance for his own sins, and even if the act itself was wrong angels would come to prevent it if God did not approve. Not surprisingly, they didn't.

Harvey Louis Carignan, known as the "Want-Ad Killer," beat a death sentence and continued to manipulate, rape and bludgeon women to death after using want ads to lure his young female victims. His weapon of choice was a claw hammer, earning him the nickname "Harv the Hammer." He described himself as "an instrument of God, one who was acting under His personal instructions." In his mind murder, rape and mutilation are all part of God's Grand Plan.

President James A. Garfield was shot on July 2, 1881 at the Baltimore and Potomac Railroad Station by self-styled theologian Charles J. Guiteau less than four months into his term as twentieth President of the United States and died eleven weeks later. Guiteau believed he had been commanded by God to kill the President and is quoted as saying, "I leave my justification to God." On June 11, 1880 Guiteau had been a passenger aboard the ship *SS Stonington* when it collided with *SS Narragansett* at night in heavy fog. The *Stonington* was able to return to port, but *Narragansett* burned to the waterline and sank with significant loss of life. Although none of his fellow passengers on the *Stonington* were injured the incident left Guiteau believing he had been spared for a "higher purpose." At his trial he claimed he was not guilty because Garfield's murder was the will of God and he was only an instrument of God's will. He also dictated an autobiography to the *New York Herald* which ended with a personal ad for "a nice Christian lady under thirty," and when he went to the gallows recited a poem he had written called *I Am Going to the Lordy.*

I'm sure you believe all of these people were crazy based upon their actions, and I could not agree more. The point is every one of them believed they were an instrument of God and had received divine inspiration. Who is to say they were insane for believing that, while those who act in a more benign manner, after claiming to hear the voice of God, are credible? Let's face it, we all hear voices in our heads. That's called an internal monologue. It is when we start believing those voices belong to someone or something outside of our own consciousness that we begin to cross the line, but no one notices unless you cut the arms off of a baby or shoot a President.

In the words of Elmer Homrighausen, Professor of Christian Education at Princeton Theological Seminary, "Few intelligent Christians can still hold to the idea that the Bible is an infallible book, that it contains no linguistic errors, no historical discrepancies, no antiquated scientific assumptions, not even bad ethical standards. Historical investigation and literary criticism have taken the magic out of the Bible and have made it a composite human book, written by many hands in different ages. The existence of thousands of variations of texts makes it impossible to hold the doctrine of a book verbally infallible. Some might claim for the original copies of the Bible an infallible character, but this view only begs the question and makes such Christian apologetics more ridiculous in the eyes of the sincere man." Similarly, Episcopal Bishop John Shelby Spong has said, "I could not believe anyone who has read this book would be so foolish as to proclaim the Bible in every literal word was the divinely inspired, inerrant word of God. Have these people simply not read the text? Are they hopelessly misinformed? Is there a different Bible? Are they blinded by a combination of ego needs and naïveté?" Thomas Paine explained this phenomenon when he observed, "The continually progressive change to which the meaning of words is subject, the want of a universal language which renders translation necessary, the errors to which translations are again subject, the mistakes of copyists and printers, together with the possibility of willful alteration, are themselves evidences that human language, whether in speech or in print, cannot be the vehicle of the Word of God."

Interpreting Scripture

Or, What They Are REALLY Saying…

"No man ever believes that the Bible means what it says. He is always convinced that it says what he means." ~ George Bernard Shaw

A team of archaeologists was excavating a site in Israel when they found a cave with the symbols of a woman, a donkey, a shovel, a fish and the Star of David painted on the wall. The head archaeologist pointed to the drawing of the woman and said, "This indicates these people were family oriented and held women in high esteem. The donkey shows they were smart enough to use animals to till the soil. The shovel means they were able to forge tools. Even further proof of high intelligence is the fish, because if famine hit the earth they would take to the sea for food. The last symbol is the Star of David, telling us they were Hebrews." The second archaeologist shook his head in disagreement. "Hebrew is read from right to left," he explained. "It actually says, 'Holy Mackerel, Dig the Ass on that Chick!'"

Hermeneutics is the theory of text interpretation, especially the interpretation of religious Scripture, wisdom literature and philosophical texts. Although the terms "hermeneutics" and "exegesis" are sometimes used interchangeably hermeneutics is a wider discipline which includes written, verbal and nonverbal communication while exegesis focuses primarily upon texts. It is a fancy way of saying someone is claiming to understand the true meaning of Scripture, while the person who disagrees with him is misinterpreting it.

Christian bookstores are overflowing with companion guides which attempt to enlighten the reader as to the "true" interpretation of a certain verse or the "real" reason a certain biblical event took place but why is any of this necessary if it is the Bible itself we are supposed to believe and not some biased third-party supplement? One would think an omniscient being who wants to communicate his message to the entire human race would be clear about what his book means so the average person can understand it without doing mental gymnastics or relying on the opinions of other human beings, wouldn't one?

At some point the writers of the Bible realized Scripture could be interpreted to mean anything the reader wanted it to and in response Paul warned, "...that we henceforth be no more children, tossed to and fro, and carried about with every wind of doctrine, by the sleight of men, and cunning craftiness, whereby they lie in wait to deceive..."

What does that mean? As the words of George Bernard Shaw at the top of the chapter explained he is telling us, "No man ever believes the Bible means what it says. He always is convinced it says what he means." This problem is not unique to Christianity. For example Supreme Leader of the Islamic Government Ayatollah Ruhollah Khomeini once warned, "Christian, Jewish and Baha'i missionary centers are spread in Tehran to deceive people and to lead them away from the teachings and principles of [true] religion. Isn't it a duty to destroy these centers?"

One common tool of hermeneutics is equivocation definition, which entails confusing the issue by using vague terms or shifting the definitions of words such as was the case when President Clinton famously proclaimed, "It depends on what the meaning of 'is' is." Another is the claim that a verse of Scripture has been "taken out of context" when it is interpreted as meaning something other than what the person making the charge has decided it means. This is the most powerful weapon in the hermeneutic arsenal.

2 Peter 3:16-17 says, "As also in all his epistles [Paul's], speaking in them of these things; in which are some things hard to be understood, which they that are unlearned and unstable wrest, as they do also the other Scriptures, unto their own destruction. Ye therefore, beloved, seeing ye know these things before, beware lest ye also, being led away with the error of the wicked, fall from your own steadfastness." In other words Peter is saying people will be guilty of taking Scripture out of context and making it say what they want it to say. No kidding. As Mark Twain once said, "It ain't those parts of the Bible that I can't understand that bother me, it is the parts that I *do* understand!" To gain a better understanding of the many ways this tool is employed let's look at twenty ways the Bible is supposedly taken out of context by heathens according to James Sire's book *Scripture Twisting*.

The first is the "inaccurate quotation," i.e. a biblical text is referred to but is either not quoted in the way the text appears in the Bible or is wrongly attributed. The example given by Sire is the Maharishi Mahesh Yogi saying, "Christ said, 'Be still and know that I am God.'" He then points out Psalm 46:10 actually says, "Be still, and know that I am God."

Basically he is claiming the omission of one comma changes the entire meaning. Do you agree? And if so, what is the difference?

Next comes the "twisted translation," a biblical text which is retranslated to fit the preconceived teachings of what he refers to as a cult. His example is Jehovah's Witnesses translating John 1:1 as "In (the) beginning the Word was, and the Word was with God, and the Word was a god," when in his view it actually states, "In the beginning was the Word, and the Word was with God, and the Word was God." How do those two translations differ in meaning in your mind?

Third is what he calls the "biblical hook," a text of Scripture quoted primarily as a device to grasp the attention of readers or listeners followed by a teaching which is so unbiblical it would appear far more dubious to most people had it not been preceded by a reference to Scripture. The example given is Mormon missionaries quoting James 1:5, "If any of you lack wisdom, let him ask of God, that giveth to all men liberally, and upbraideth not; and it shall be given him," prior to explaining Joseph Smith was given a revelation from which he concluded God the Father has a body. The question is how can Sire possibly know for certain Smith was wrong?

Next comes "over specification," in other words a more detailed or specific conclusion than legitimate is drawn from the text. As an example he tells us the Mormon missionary manual quotes the parable of the Virgins (Mt. 25:1-13) to document the Mormon concept mortality is a probationary period during which we prepare to meet God, but claims the parable of the virgins could and most probably does mean something far less specific, for example human beings should be prepared at any time to meet God or to witness the Second Coming of Christ. The problem here is twofold. First of all even he is not sure of the meaning since he uses the words "could" and "probably," and second drawing a more specific conclusion than is legitimate is part and parcel of most of the Bible and the practice of hermeneutics.

In "word play" he claims a word or phrase from the Bible is examined and interpreted as if the revelation had been given in a language other than the original Hebrew, Greek or Chaldean and uses the instance of Mary Baker Eddy, founder of the Christian Science movement, saying the name Adam consists of two syllables, A-"dam" which means an obstruction, in which case Adam signifies "the obstacle which the serpent, i.e. sin, would impose between man and his Creator." In this case he is correct, although it will come as a surprise to many devout Christians that Scripture was not written in English.

The "figurative fallacy" is either mistaking literal language for figurative language or mistaking figurative language for literal language. The example given is Mormon theologian James Talmadge interpreting the prophecy in Isaiah 29:4, "And thou shalt be brought down, and shalt speak out of the ground, and thy speech shall be low out of the dust, and thy voice shall be, as of one that hath a familiar spirit, out of the ground, and thy speech shall whisper out of the dust" to mean God's Word would come to people from the *Book of Mormon* which was taken out of the ground at the hill of Cumorah. The obvious question here is how can anyone possibly know what is meant to be literal or figurative anywhere in the Bible?

Next come "speculative readings of predictive prophecy" which are said to occur when a predictive prophecy is too readily explained by the occurrence of specific events despite the fact equally committed biblical scholars consider the interpretation highly dubious. For example the stick of Judah and the stick of Joseph in Ezekiel 37:15-23 are interpreted by the Mormons to mean the Bible and the Book of Mormon, something mainstream Christians heartily disagree with, but as the chapter on prophecy explains those same people are themselves to seeing prophecy where there is none.

"Saying but not citing" is when a writer claims the Bible says such and such but does not cite the specific text, which often indicates there may be no such text as all, for example claiming the Bible says, 'God helps those who help themselves'" when it was actually Benjamin Franklin. This happens all the time.

"Selective citing" attempts to substantiate a given argument but only a limited number of texts are quoted, so the total teaching of Scripture on that subject would lead to a conclusion different from what was intended by the writer. For example Jehovah's Witnesses critique the traditional Christian notion of the Trinity without considering the full set of texts scholars use to substantiate the concept, but to be fair mainstream Christians criticize Mormon teachings on the subject without bothering to learn about foundation of their beliefs.

"Inadequate evidence" is a hasty generalization drawn from too little evidence such as when Jehovah's Witnesses teach that blood transfusion is nonbiblical, but the biblical data which they cite fails either to speak directly to the issue or to adequately substantiate their teaching. The irony here is obvious because if this standard were applied to most religious claims they would crumble under the weight of their own ambiguity.

"Confused definition" occurs when a biblical term is misunderstood in such a way that an essential doctrine is distorted or rejected such as Edgar Cayce's followers confusing the Eastern doctrine of reincarnation with the biblical doctrine of being born again. Using that criteria the entire book of Revelation can be said to be confused since there is wide disagreement about its meaning.

"Ignoring alternative explanations" happens when a specific interpretation is given to a biblical text or set of texts which could well be and often have been interpreted in quite a different fashion, but these alternatives are not considered. For example Erich von Daniken, author of *Chariots of the Gods*, asks why in Genesis 1:26 God speaks in the plural ("us") and suggests this is an oblique reference to God being one of many astronauts while failing to consider alternative explanations. This is of course incredibly hypocritical since believers tend to ignore any explanation which contradicts their faith and personal beliefs.

In the "obvious fallacy" words and phrases such as "obviously, undoubtedly, certainly, all reasonable people hold that" and so forth are substituted for logical reasons, but this is a double edged sword since this very fallacy is employed by Sire himself.

"Virtue by association" occurs when a cult writer associates his teaching with those accepted as authoritative by traditional Christians, for example Rick Chapman lists "twenty-one gurus you can't go wrong with" including Jesus, St. Francis and St. Theresa, or cult writings are likened to the Bible such as was the case when the Mormon "Doctrine and Covenants 93" interwove phrases from the Gospel of John to maintain a superficial similarity.

"Esoteric interpretation" operates under the assumption the Bible contains a hidden, esoteric meaning which is open only to those who are initiated into its secrets and the interpreter declares the significance of biblical passages without giving much if any explanation for his or her interpretation. This is the very cornerstone of hermeneutics.

"Supplementing biblical authority" occurs when a new revelation from post-biblical prophets either replaces or is added to the Bible as authority, for example the Mormons supplement the Bible with the Book of Mormon, the Doctrine and Covenants and the Pearl of Great Price. This can also apply to the doctrines of the Catholic Church and well as those of many Protestant denominations.

"Rejecting biblical authority" is said to occur when either the Bible as a whole or texts from the Bible are examined and rejected because they do not square with logic, reason or other authorities such as a subsequent revelation but seriously, this is nothing more than a misguided Argument From Authority since there is nothing wrong with discarding ideas which have been proven wrong.

Finally, "worldview confusion" is said to occur when scriptural statements, stories, commands or symbols which have a particular meaning or set of meanings when taken within the intellectual and broadly cultural framework of the Bible itself are lifted out of that context, placed within the frame of reference of another system and thus given a meaning which markedly differs from their intended meaning such as Maharishi Mahesh Yogi interpreting, "Be still, and know that I am God" as meaning that each person should meditate and come to the realization that he is essentially Godhood itself. We have now come full circle in this chapter, since this is simply another way of articulating the opinion that "No man ever believes the Bible means what it says. He always is convinced it says what he means."

One thing becomes clear if nothing else - Sire is not a Jehovah's Witness, Christian Scientist, Mormon or Hindu because in his view they misinterpret everything while he gets it all right. As Ambrose Bierce explained in *The Devil's Dictionary* "Scriptures (are) the sacred books of our holy religion, as distinguished from the false and profane writings on which all other faiths are based," but it really doesn't matter because to most Christians the Bible is like a software license. Nobody actually reads it. They just scroll to the bottom and click "I agree."

Revelation

Or, That Little Voice in Our Heads

"Religion is an illusion and it derives its strength from the fact that it falls in with our instinctual desires." ~ Sigmund Freud

Saint Marie-Bernarde Soubirous, who was born Maria-Bernada Sobirós on 7 January 1844, was a miller's daughter born in Lourdes who from 11 February to 16 July 1858 reported eighteen apparitions of "a small young lady." Despite initial skepticism from the Catholic Church these claims were eventually declared to be "worthy of belief" after a canonical investigation and the apparition is now known as Our Lady of Lourdes. Let's examine the claim for ourselves.

On 11 February 1858 Bernadette, then age fourteen, was out gathering firewood and bones with her sister and a friend at the grotto of Massabielle outside Lourdes when she had her first vision. As she recounted later, while the other girls crossed the little stream in front of the grotto and walked on Bernadette stayed behind looking for a better place to cross where she wouldn't get her stockings wet. She finally sat down in the grotto to take her shoes off in order to cross the water and was lowering her first stocking when she heard the sound of rushing wind, but nothing moved. A wild rose in a natural niche in the grotto did move however, and from the niche, or rather the dark alcove behind it, "came a dazzling light and a white figure." This was the first of eighteen visions of what she referred to as "aquero" (Gascon Occitan for "that"). In later testimony she called it "a small young lady" (uo petito damizelo), but her sister and friend stated they had seen nothing.

After Sunday mass on 14 February Bernadette, along with her sister Toinette and some other girls, returned to the grotto. Bernadette knelt down immediately, saying she saw aquero again and fell into a trance. When one of the girls threw holy water at the niche (did young girls routinely make it a habit to carry holy water, one must wonder?) and another threw a rock from above that shattered on the ground the apparition disappeared. Bernadette fell into a state of shock and the girl who had thrown the rock actually thought she had killed her. After her next visit on 18 February she said "the vision" had asked her to return to the grotto every day for a fortnight.

Bernadette's story caused a sensation with the townspeople who were divided in their opinions as to whether or not she was telling the truth. Some believed her to have a mental illness and demanded she be put in an asylum, but she soon had a large number of people following her on her daily journey - some out of curiosity, and others who firmly believed they were witnessing a miracle.

The other contents of Bernadette's reported visions were simple and focused on the need for prayer and penance. On 24 February she reported that aquero had said Penitenço... Penitenço... Penitenço ("penance"). That afternoon Bernadette kissed the muddy ground of the grotto and the next day she went further - during her trance she chewed and ate grass plucked from the ground, rubbed mud over her face and actually swallowed some mud to the disgust of the many onlookers and the embarrassment of those who believed in her visions. She explained the vision had told her to "drink of the water of the spring, wash in it and eat the herb that grew there" as an act of penance.

As Bernadette later reported to her family and to church and civil investigators, during the ninth visitation the lady told Bernadette to drink from the spring which flowed under the rock and eat the plants which grew freely there. Although there was no known spring and the ground was muddy, Bernadette saw the lady pointing with her finger to the spot and said later she assumed the lady meant the spring was underground. She did as she was told by first digging a muddy patch with her bare hands and then attempting to drink the brackish drops. She tried three times, failing each time, but on the fourth try the droplets were clearer and she drank them. She then ate some of the plants. When finally she turned to the crowd her face was smeared with mud and no spring had been revealed. This understandably caused much skepticism among onlookers who shouted, "She's a fraud!" or "She's insane!" while embarrassed relatives wiped the adolescent's face clean with a handkerchief. In the next few days however a spring began to flow from the muddy patch first dug by Bernadette. Some devout people then followed her example by drinking and washing in the water, which was soon reported to have "healing properties."

Bernadette was a sickly child who had cholera in infancy and suffered most of her life from asthma. Some of the people who interviewed her following her revelation of the visions thought her simple-minded, and she eventually contracted tuberculosis of the bone in the right knee. She later followed the development of Lourdes as a pilgrimage shrine while still living there, but was not present for the consecration of the Basilica of the Immaculate Conception in 1876 and eventually died of her long-term illness at the age of thirty-five on 16 April 1879 - hardly an indication of the healing properties of the spring water.

In the one hundred fifty years since Bernadette dug up the spring sixty-seven cures have been "verified" by the Lourdes Medical Bureau as "inexplicable" after what the Church claims were "extremely rigorous scientific and medical examinations" which failed to find any other explanation. The Lourdes Commission which examined Bernadette after the visions also ran an intensive analysis on the water, at least as "intensive" as was possible given the technology available to them in the mid-1800s, and found while it had a high mineral content it contained nothing out of the ordinary which would account for the cures attributed to it. Bernadette herself of course maintained it was faith and prayer which had cured the sick.

Lourdes has since become something of a tourist attraction and the town itself is monetarily dependent upon pilgrimages of the faithful so it obviously in their best interest, not to mention the best interest of the Catholic Church, to perpetuate the myth of miraculous healing.

Not to be outdone, a small village in Bosnia-Hercegovina named Medjugorje claims the Blessed Virgin Mary has been appearing there since 1981 and giving messages to the world. According to the locals, "She tells us God has sent her to our world and these years she is spending with us are a time of Grace granted by God. In her own words she tells us, 'I have come to tell the world that God exists. He is the fullness of life, and to enjoy this fullness and peace you must return to God.' Our Lady continues to give messages to six people from the village of Medjugorje: Ivan, Jakov, Marija, Mirjana, Vicka, and Ivanka. These six people, referred to as 'visionaries,' have had apparitions of the Blessed Virgin Mary since June 24, 1981. In addition to the public messages, Our Lady is to give each of the six visionaries a total of ten 'secrets' or happenings which will occur on earth in the near future. Some of the secrets pertain to the whole world, while others concern the visionaries themselves or the local village. Only one of the secrets has so far been revealed by the visionaries. Our Lady has promised to leave a supernatural, indestructible and visible sign on the mountain where she first appeared. Our Lady said, 'This sign will be given for the atheists. You faithful already have signs and you have become the sign for the atheists. You faithful must not wait for the sign before you convert;

convert soon. This time is a time of grace for you. You can never thank God enough for his grace. The time is for deepening your faith and for your conversion. When the sign comes, it will be too late for many.'

When each of the six visionaries has received all ten 'secrets' Our Lady will stop appearing to them on a daily basis. Currently Marija, Vicka and Ivan have received nine secrets and Our Lady still appears to them every day, wherever they are, at 5:40 PM during daylight savings time and 6:40 PM the rest of the year. Mirjana, Jakov and Ivanka have received all ten secrets, and Our Lady appears to them once per year and will do so for the rest of their lives. For Ivanka, who received her tenth secret on May 7, 1985 it is on the anniversary of the apparitions, June 25 each year. For Jakov who received his tenth secret on September 12, 1998, it is on Christmas Day each year. And for Mirjana who received her tenth secret on Christmas 1982, it is on her birthday, March 18 each year. Our Lady has also been appearing to Mirjana on the 2nd of each month since August 2, 1987 for the purpose of praying for all unbelievers. Mirjana tells us it is very important that all of us pray for the unbelievers in the world, who are described as those who have not yet experienced God's love. Sometimes these appearances on the 2nd of each month are apparitions, and sometimes locutions. No one knows when Our Lady will give the tenth secret to Marija, Ivan and Vicka.

Once Our Lady stops appearing there will be three warnings given to the world. Mirjana will witness the warnings and they will occur on the earth. Ten days before each of the warnings she will advise the priest she chose for this task - Father Petar Ljubicic - who will then pray and fast with Mirjana for seven days. Then, three days before the warning is to take place, Father Petar will announce to the world what, where and when the warning is to take place. Father Petar has no choice, and must reveal each warning. Mirjana's testimony will be a confirmation of the validity of the apparitions and a further incentive for the conversion of the world. After the first warning the others will follow within a rather brief period of time. After the three warnings, the permanent visible sign will be left on the mountain where Our Lady first appeared in Medjugorje. Those who are still alive will have little time for conversion (this is reminiscent of the "act now!" call to action one finds in the infomercials we see on late night television). For that reason, the Blessed Virgin calls for urgent conversion and reconciliation. The permanent sign will lead to many healings and conversions before the messages become reality.

The ninth and tenth secrets are grave matters. They are a chastisement for the sins of the world. The punishment is inevitable because we cannot expect the conversion of the entire world. The chastisements can be lessened by prayers and penance, but they cannot be suppressed entirely. An evil which threatened the world according to the seventh secret (whatever that was) has been eliminated through prayer and fasting. For that reason the Blessed Virgin continues to ask for prayer and fasting. The invitation to prayer and penance wards off evil and war, and above all, saves souls. Our Lady says: 'You have forgotten that with prayer and fasting you can ward off wars, suspend natural laws.'"

That all sounds pretty ominous, doesn't it? At least until you get to the part of the official Medjugorje website which says, "Welcome to our Online Store! We are happy to be able to offer items from Medjugorje in our online store such as books, rosaries, medals, crucifixes, statues, videos, music, pictures and prayer cards, vestments and much more. With the purchase of these items you are helping to support our mission, the local parish of Medjugorje, as well as individual local families working and living in and around Medjugorje. Many of the books we offer are only available at the parish Franciscan Shop, located on the grounds of St. James church in Medugorje. With special permission from the parish we are able to offer books, videos, CDs and other items by Fr. Slavko, Fr. Svetozar, Fr. Jozo and other local priests of the parish. Please also visit our sister store The Catholic Gift Store with over 1500 Items!" Yes, it seems Medjugorje is just another cheesy tourist trap and the so-called "secrets" are, well, you figure it out.

Of course those stories are not unique or even original. Consider the case of Our Lady of Fátima, which is a title for the Blessed Virgin Mary due to her alleged apparitions to three shepherd children - Lúcia Santos and her cousins Jacinta and Francisco Marto - at Fátima, Portugal on the thirteenth day of six consecutive months in 1917. The events at Fátima gained fame due to their elements of secrets, prophecy and eschatology, particularly with regards to World War II and possible world wars in the future. Chief among these is also the alleged urgent need for "the Consecration of Russia to the Immaculate Heart of Mary."

The reported apparitions at Fátima have since been officially declared "worthy of belief" by the Catholic Church as was the case with Lourdes. In the spring and summer of 1916 the three children claimed to have experienced the visitation of an angel on three separate occasions as they watched their sheep who taught them specific prayers to pray, to make sacrifices and to "spend time in adoration of the Lord." These three visits were apparently to prepare the children for the visitations of the "Blessed Mother" which were to follow in 1917.

On May 13, 1917 ten-year-old Lúcia Santos and her younger cousins were herding sheep at a location known as the Cova da Iria near Fátima when Lúcia described seeing a woman "brighter than the sun, shedding rays of light clearer and stronger than a crystal goblet filled with the most sparkling water and pierced by the burning rays of the sun" - hardly typical language for a functionally illiterate ten-year-old sheep herder! Astonished, they ran back to their village and told everyone. Further appearances were later reported to have taken place on the thirteenth day of the month in June and July. In these "the woman" asked the children to do penance and acts of reparation as well as make personal sacrifices to save sinners, so the children subsequently wore tight cords around their waists to cause themselves pain, performed self-flagellation using stinging nettles, abstained from drinking water on hot days and performed other works of penance. The sins of the world were apparently being placed on the shoulders of three small children in an obscure Portuguese town by the mother of Jesus. Makes perfect sense.

According to Lúcia's account in the course of her appearances the woman confided to the children three secrets which are now known as "the Three Secrets of Fátima," which should not be confused with the ten secrets and three warnings she would later confide to the residents of Medjugorje in 1981. Thousands of people flocked to Fátima and Aljustrel in the following months drawn by reports of visions and miracles, and that month instead of the usual apparition in the Cova da Iria on the 13th the children reported they saw the Virgin Mary on 15 August at the Feast of the Assumption in nearby Valinhos.

As early as July it was claimed the Virgin Mary had promised a miracle for the last of her apparitions on October 13th so that all would believe, and what happened then became known as the "Miracle of the Sun." A crowd believed to number approximately 70,000 including newspaper reporters and photographers gathered at the Cova da Iria, and the rain which had been falling finally ceased and a thin layer of clouds cloaked the sun. Lúcia, moved by what she said was an interior impulse, called out to the crowd (of 70,000 - she must have had an awfully loud voice) to look at the sun. Witnesses later spoke of the sun appearing to change colors and rotate like a wheel, but not everyone saw the same things and they gave widely varying descriptions of the "sun's dance." For that matter not all witnesses reported seeing the sun "dance" at all. Some people only saw the radiant colors and others, including many believers, saw nothing. While the crowd was staring at the sun Lucia, Francisco and Jacinta - ages ten, nine and seven at the time - said later they were seeing lovely images of the Holy Family, Our Lady of Sorrows with Jesus Christ and then Our Lady of Mount Carmel, and they also said they saw Saint Joseph and Jesus bless the people.

Not surprisingly no movement or other phenomenon of the sun was registered by scientists at the time and since we know the sun does not deviate from its orbit - because if it did it would have massive repercussions for the entire solar system - that is a clear indication it didn't physically move but rather what people "saw" was either an optical illusion or psychosomatic in nature. As for colors changing it is important to understand color is nothing more than how light is refracted by the atmosphere.

Since no scientifically verifiable physical cause can be determined various explanations have been advanced to explain the descriptions given by witnesses. A leading conjecture is mass hallucination stimulated by the religious fervor of a crowd which was expectantly waiting for a predicted sign. Another is a possible visual artifact caused by looking at the sun for a prolonged period. As noted by Auguste Meessen, a professor at the Institute of Physics of Catholic University of Leuven, looking directly at the sun can cause phosphine, visual artifacts and temporary partial blindness. He proposed the reported observations were optical effects caused by staring at the sun and therefore retinal after-images produced after brief periods of sun gazing were a likely cause of the "dancing" effects. In addition Meessen stated the color changes witnessed were most likely caused by the bleaching of photosensitive retinal cells. Reverend Joaquim Lourenço, in describing his boyhood experience in Alburitel (eighteen kilometers from Fatima) gave an indication of that when he said, "I looked fixedly at the sun, which seemed pale and did not hurt my eyes. Looking like a ball of snow, revolving on itself, it suddenly seemed to come down in a zig-zag, menacing the earth. Terrified, I ran and hid myself among the people, who were weeping and expecting the end of the world at any moment."

It must be pointed out that similar solar "miracles" have been reported in many places where religiously charged pilgrims have gathered and been encouraged to stare at the sun such as in Lubbock, Texas in 1989, the Mother Cabrini Shrine near Denver, Colorado in 1992 and in Conyers, Georgia in the early to mid-1990s. The confounding thing about those events is no one managed to document them. In each case there were photographers present, but for some reason they seem to have only taken pictures of the crowd.

The apparitions at Heroldsbach, Germany in 1949 are one of the best examples of such phenomena because exactly the same optical effects as at Fátima were witnessed by more than ten thousand people. Numerous apparitions and visions of the "seven seer girls of Heroldsbach" began there on October 9, 1949 with the green lucent sign "JSH" above the birch trees. "J" is said to have meant "Jahwe," "H" is "Hyos" (Greek for "son") and "S" is "Spiritus Sanctus," but how and by whom that determination was made is unclear. After this the Virgin Mary purportedly appeared above the birches praying with folded hands while wearing white clothes with red roses on her feet and a black rosary, although a subsequent account says until October 31, 1952 she appeared mainly with a blue dress and a golden crown.

It is further claimed she "insistently wished prayers, penitence and expiation" and from January 13, 1950 on "the Mother of God left her place above the birches and came regularly to the seer children (yes, once again small children were the chosen ones). They were allowed to touch her body and hands. They could note her real presence combined with a fluent force. Furthermore they touched and carried the Jesus Child who later came also as boy, adult savior, sacred heart, good shepherd and redeemer on the cross."

Today the official website tells us, "The pilgrims club of Heroldsbach has been existing since 1953 and campaigns for the authenticity of the apparitions and the buildup and maintenance of the prayers' place. If you want to be a member of the club please go to 'Downloads' and fill in your data. The minimum contribution amount is EUR 10 per year." In the best Bernie Madoff fashion they then add, "The club members trust the Mother of God who said goodbye with the words: 'I'm always here, although you can't see me.'" There truly is a sucker born every minute.

In addition to the Miracle of the Sun the seers at Fátima claimed their apparition prophesied a "great sign in the night sky" which would precede a second great war. On January 25, 1938 the "bright lights" of an aurora borealis, ironically called "Dance of the Spirits" by the Cree tribe, named after Roman goddess of dawn Aurora and commonly believed to be a sign from God in Medieval Europe, appeared and Lúcia, the sole surviving seer at the time (cousins Francisco and Jacinta were both victims of the Great Spanish Flu Epidemic of 1918-20) later claimed to have indicated it was the sign foretold - and just over a month later Hitler seized Austria and eight months later (which makes one wonder what the shelf life of a prophecy is) invaded Czechoslovakia.

Sounds pretty impressive, doesn't it? The only problem is all of that was quite predictable and linking them together was nothing more than an example of the "cause and effect" logical fallacy which suggests simply because one event follows another the first event was related in some way to the second. First of all the appearance of an aurora borealis in a temperate latitude can and does occur when a magnetic storm temporarily enlarges the auroral oval and large magnetic storms are most common during the peak of the eleven-year sunspot cycle, which was the case in 1938. Similarly, if it had been 1910 or 1986 it could have just as easily been claimed Halley's Comet was the "great sign in the night sky" since it makes a predictable appearance every seventy-five years. Second, predicting a major conflict in the years leading up to WWII was no big deal since many others had already done so. Take for instance the "vision" of Ellen White, one of the founders of the Seventh-day Adventist Church and a self-proclaimed "messenger of the Lord," which allegedly "spoke of two world wars" and was originally published in the *Second Advent Review and Sabbath Herald* of August 21, 1861 - but of course like most prophecies it could have been interpreted to mean a thousand different things and nobody made a connection to the World Wars until after they had occurred. Freemason Albert Pike also supposedly received a vision which he described in a letter dated August 15, 1871 which graphically outlined plans for the three world wars he saw as necessary to bring about a One World Order. Some claim the Mayans accurately predicted both World Wars as well, presumably without the assistance of the Virgin Mary whom they had presumably never heard of, and naturally one of Nostradamus' quatrains is said to have made the prediction as well. But to anyone living in 1938 who knew about the 1932 invasion of China by the Japanese, which is viewed by many historians as the actual beginning to WWII, and who had been following the rise of Hitler and events in Europe this was not much of a prediction not to mention the fact it was not "revealed" until 1941.

As for the "three secrets" the first was a vision of Hell which Lúcia describes in her Third Memoir, which once again was not written until 1941 as follows: "Our Lady showed us a great sea of fire which seemed to be under the earth. Plunged in this fire were demons and souls in human form, like transparent burning embers, all blackened or burnished bronze, floating about in the conflagration, now raised into the air by the flames that issued from within themselves together with great clouds of smoke, now falling back on every side like sparks in a huge fire, without weight or equilibrium, and amid shrieks and groans of pain and despair, which horrified us and made us tremble with fear. The demons could be distinguished by their terrifying and repulsive likeness to frightful and unknown animals, all black and transparent. This vision lasted but an instant. How can we ever be grateful enough to our kind heavenly Mother, who had already prepared us by promising, in the first apparition, to take us to Heaven. Otherwise, I think we would have died of fear and terror." The most revealing aspect of that description of Hell is it is exactly as a ten-year-old Catholic child would imagine it to be.

The second secret included "Mary's instructions" on how to save souls from Hell and convert the world to the Christian faith and was also revealed by Lúcia in her Third Memoir in 1941: "I have seen Hell where the souls of poor sinners go. To save them, God wishes to establish in the world devotion to my Immaculate Heart. If what I say to you is done, many souls will be saved and there will be peace. The war is going to end: but if people do not cease offending God, a worse one will break out during the Pontificate of Pius XI (Pope from February 1922 to February 1939). When you see a night illuminated by an unknown light (it should be pointed out we *know* what an aurora borealis is as well as what causes them) know that this is the great sign given you by God that he is about to punish the world for its crimes by means of war, famine and persecutions of the Church and of the Holy Father. To prevent this I shall come to ask for the consecration of Russia to my Immaculate Heart, and the Communion of reparation on the First Saturdays. If my requests are heeded, Russia will be converted and there will be peace; if not, she will spread her errors throughout the world, causing wars and persecutions of the Church. The good will be martyred; the Holy Father will have much to suffer; various nations will be annihilated. In the end, my Immaculate Heart will triumph. The Holy Father will consecrate Russia to me and she shall be converted and a period of peace will be granted to the world." Wow, talk about a God with a vindictive nature!

Lúcia reported seeing the Virgin Mary yet again in 1925 at the Dorothean convent at Pontevedra, Galicia in Spain. This time she said she was asked to convey the message of the First Saturday Devotions, by her account a subsequent vision of Christ as a child reiterated this request and she reportedly saw Mary in private visions periodically throughout the rest of her life. Most significant was the apparition in Rianxo, Galicia in 1931 in which she claimed Jesus visited her, taught her two prayers and delivered a message for the church's hierarchy. One would think he would eliminate the middle man (or middle nun) and tell the Pope whatever it was directly, wouldn't one?

In 1936 and again in 1941, many years after it happened naturally, Lúcia claimed the Virgin Mary had predicted the deaths of two of the children in 1920 during the second apparition on June 13, 1917. According to the 1941 account Lúcia had asked the Virgin if the three children would go to Heaven when they died and she said she heard Mary reply, "Yes, I shall take Francisco and Jacinta soon, but you will remain a little longer (which turned out to be to the age of ninety-seven) since Jesus wishes you to make me known and loved on Earth."

The third secret, a vision of the death of the Pope and other religious figures, was transcribed by the Bishop of Leiria and reads: "After the two parts which I have already explained, at the left of Our Lady and a little above, we saw an Angel with a flaming sword in his left hand; flashing, it gave out flames that looked as though they would set the world on fire; but they died out in contact with the splendor that Our Lady radiated towards him from her right hand: pointing to the earth with his right hand, the Angel cried out in a loud voice: 'Penance, Penance, Penance!' And we saw in an immense light that is God: 'something similar to how people appear in a mirror when they pass in front of it' a Bishop dressed in White 'we had the impression that it was the Holy Father.' Other Bishops, Priests, Religious men and women going up a steep mountain, at the top of which there was a big Cross of rough-hewn trunks as of a cork-tree with the bark; before reaching there the Holy Father passed through a big city half in ruins and half trembling with halting step, afflicted with pain and sorrow, he prayed for the souls of the corpses he met on his way; having reached the top of the mountain, on his knees at the foot of the big Cross he was killed by a group of soldiers who fired bullets and arrows at him, and in the same way there died one after another the other Bishops, Priests, Religious men and women, and various lay people of different ranks and positions. Beneath the two arms of the Cross there were two Angels each with a crystal aspersorium in his hand, in which they gathered up the blood of the Martyrs and with it sprinkled the souls that were making their way to God."

Pope John Paul II credited Our Lady of Fátima with saving his life following the assassination attempt on Wednesday, May 13 1981, the Feast of Our Lady of Fátima naturally, and on that day in 2010 Pope Benedict XVI recalled the "invisible hand" that saved John Paul II and in doing so each unintentionally revealed the falsity of the prophecy since it claimed to be a vision of the *death* of the Pope.

The Vatican withheld this third secret until 26 June 2000 despite Lúcia's declaration that it could be released to the public after 1960. When 1960 arrived, rather than releasing the secret, the Vatican published an official press release stating it was "most probable the secret would remain, forever, under absolute seal." Presumably that was the Vatican's way of saying, "I could tell you, but then I'd have to kill you." After this announcement immense speculation over the content of the secret materialized and according to the *New York Times* speculation over the content of the secret ranged from worldwide nuclear annihilation to deep rifts in the Roman Catholic Church leading to rival papacies. Some sources claim the four-page, handwritten text of the third secret released by the Vatican in the year 2000 is not the real secret, or at least not the full secret. In particular it is alleged Cardinals Bertone, Ratzinger and Sodano engaged in a systematic deception to cover-up the existence of a one-page document containing the so-called words of the Blessed Virgin Mary which some believe contains information about the Apocalypse and a great apostasy. These sources contend the third secret actually comprises two texts, where one of these texts is the published four-page vision and the other is a single-page letter allegedly containing the words of the Virgin Mary which has been concealed.

Many Roman Catholics today recite prayers based on Our Lady of Fátima and Lúcia later said she and her cousins had several visions of an angel calling himself the "Angel of Portugal" and "Angel of Peace" who had taught them to bow with their heads to the ground and to say "My God, I believe, I adore, I hope, and I love you. I ask pardon for those who do not believe, do not adore, do not hope and do not love you." Lúcia later even set this prayer to music and a recording exists of her singing it. It was also said that sometime later the angel returned and taught them a Eucharistic devotion now known as the Angel Prayer. It seems some people have all the luck when it comes to meeting angels, and no doubt if I were to make similar claims people would nod their heads and say "Isn't that nice…" as they backed slowly towards the nearest door.

Not to be outdone by the neighboring Portuguese, during the Spanish Second Republic the Virgin Mary was also "seen" on Spanish soil (absent a sun miracle) at Ezquioga and a woman named Ramona Olazabal insisted Mary herself had marked the palms of her hands with a sword. The "visions" at Ezquioga were widely covered in the press, as were the sixteen other visitations of the Virgin to Spain in 1931. That Mary sure does get around… and packing a sword no less!

The widely reported Miracle of the Sun soon led to the tiny sheep herding hamlet of Fátima (population 7,000) becoming a major center of pilgrimage with two million pilgrims visiting the site in the decade following the events of 1917. A small chapel known as the Capelinha was quickly built by local people on the site of the apparitions, in 1935 the bodies of visionaries Jacinta and Francisco were reinterred in the basilica and today pilgrimage to the site goes on year round and additional chapels and other facilities have been constructed. The principal pilgrimage festivals take place on the thirteenth day of each month from May to October on the anniversaries of the original appearances and the largest crowds gather on 13 May and 13 October when up to a million pilgrims have attended to pray and witness processions of the statue of Our Lady of Fátima, both during the day and by the light of tens of thousands of candles at night. In short, this legend has become a huge cottage industry with pilgrims spending many millions of dollars annually in Fátima and the surrounding area and there is little doubt that even if the whole thing were to be proven a hoax tomorrow it would effectively become the *fourth* "secret" of Fátima. Even outside of Portugal money is being made off of people's belief in this myth, for example the Fatima Gift and Book Shop located at the National Shrine Basilica of Our Lady of Fatima in Lewiston, New York of all places is where one can find "a large selection of Nativity sets (including Fontanini), crucifixes, rosaries, Catholic jewelry and much more… plus the Book Shop has Bibles, prayer books, music, DVDs, and CDs, Children's Bibles and books, and titles on Scripture, Prayer, Our Lady, Spirituality and Theology." So there you have it. As George Carlin has said, "God needs money!"

Yet another apparition purportedly appeared to Faustina Kowalska, a Polish nun who joined the convent of Our Lady of Mercy in Warsaw in 1925. In her diary, which was later published as the book *Diary: Divine Mercy in My Soul*, she wrote about a number of visions of Jesus and conversations she had with him. It seems that in 1930 while Faustina was assigned to the convent in Płock, Poland she was in her cell on the night of 22 February when Jesus appeared to her robed in a white garment as the "King of Divine Mercy." Faustina wrote that Jesus' right hand was raised in a sign of blessing and the other was touching the garment near his breast, and that from beneath the garment emanated two large rays - one red, and the other white. Jesus told her, "Paint an image according to the pattern you see, with the signature, 'Jesus, I trust in You.' I desire that this image be venerated, first in your chapel, and then throughout the world. I promise that the soul which will venerate this image will not perish."

Not knowing how to paint (one would think Jesus, who knows everything, would have chosen a nun with artistic talent to do his portrait), Faustina approached some other nuns at her convent for help but received no assistance. She then attempted to sketch the image with charcoal on canvas but had little success and in her diary wrote that Jesus told her she would receive "visible help" with the task adding, "Not in the beauty of the color, nor of the brush lies the greatness of this image, but in my grace." Humble, isn't he?

In November of 1932 Faustina left Płock and returned to Warsaw and in May 1933 she was sent to the convent in Vilnius to work as the gardener. There she met Father Michael Sopocko, the newly appointed confessor to the nuns, who supported Faustina's efforts and arranged for the first painting of the image by artist Eugene Kazimierowski.

After the canonization of Faustina in April of 2000 (in what other profession can someone have a hallucination, have it painted by a third party and be made a saint instead of being sent to see a psychiatrist?) devotion to the "Divine Mercy image" as it came to be known increased, with the following of the image and Faustina's message stronger among Catholics at large than among better informed theologians. In 2010 it was said to be over one hundred million Catholics.

Faustina also claimed Jesus told her he wanted the Divine Mercy image to be "solemnly blessed" on the first Sunday after Easter which was to be called the Feast of Mercy and in 2000 Pope John Paul II instituted Divine Mercy Sunday and placed it on the General Roman Calendar. As a result the image is often carried in processions on that Sunday and placed in a location in the church where it can be venerated by those who attended Mass, all because one person claimed to have met and talked with Jesus with no witnesses, evidence or corroboration of any kind. Makes perfect sense.

Naturally you might expect skeptics and scientists, as unbelievers, to scoff at the claims made with regard to visions and revelation so let's take a look at what non-Catholic Christians think about these "miracles." The following is from the 'jesus-is-savior' website: "Woe unto Catholics! Our Lady of Fatima is a dirty Satanic hoax perpetrated by the Catholic religion. It is of the Devil and blatant idolatry. Roman Catholics claim that a supernatural event occurred in 1917 in which the 'Blessed Virgin Mary' appeared repeatedly to three children in Fatima, Portugal. Supposedly the Virgin Mary gave a message to the three children. The

Message of Fatima consists of an alleged number of precise predictions, requests, warnings and promises concerning the Catholic faith and the world which were conveyed by the Blessed Virgin Mary to three shepherd children - Lucia, Jacinta and Francisco - in a series of ghostly apparitions at Fatima, Portugal from May to October 1917. An 'apparition' means 'the unexpected or unusual appearance of a ghostly figure.' It's a scam, a falsehood, a lie of the Devil, unscriptural in every way. Many Catholic cultures pass a statue of Our Lady of Fatima around from house-to-house throughout the year. It's considered a good-luck charm while in their home. The heathen statue is adorned in the center of their living room, given undivided attention by the family and it is worshipped, which is the horrible sin of idolatry. Exodus 20:5 says that those who bow and pray to statues HATE God. Exodus 20:4-5, 'Thou shalt not make unto thee any graven image, or any likeness of anything that is in Heaven above, or that is in the earth beneath, or that is in the water under the earth: Thou shalt NOT BOW DOWN THYSELF TO THEM, nor serve them: for I the LORD thy God am a jealous God, visiting the iniquity of the fathers upon the children unto the third and fourth generation of THEM THAT HATE ME.' I make no apologies to rain on your parade when I speak the TRUTH... God hates the Catholic Church! God loves people, but God hates IDOLATRY. Often a photo of Lucia, Jacinta and Francisco is passed around amongst the idolatrous group as they feast on food and praise the graven image. They talk about the alleged miracle of Our Lady of Fatima. Then the photo is placed next to the statue, adorned so beautifully as the centerpiece of their living room. The graven image is alleged to bring a special blessing upon the home. One Catholic man told me that he waited for eight years, only after persistent request, to finally have the statue of Our Lady of Fatima brought to his home for one week. The man's family fried fish and praised the demonic image, praying to the image, and committing idolatry instead of worshipping God in spirit and in truth as John 4:24 commands. Our Lady of Fatima is a rotten hoax, a sinister TRADITION of men passed down from generation to generation. The hoax of Fatima allegedly happened in 1917, later turned into official Catholic dogma by the Vatican, provoking the wrath of God. If you have a statue in your home of Our Lady of Fatima, Our Lady of Guadalupe or The Image of Divine Mercy (allegedly seen by sister Faustina) then you are committing the wicked sin of IDOLATRY, spitting on the God of Israel. Catholics are arrogant, sinfully proud, and Jesus said about them: 'Full well ye reject the commandment of God, that ye may keep your own tradition'

(Mark 7:9). Catholics have been deceitfully taught by the demonic Vatican that statues are no different than a picture of one's family and loved ones and adoration of statues is similar to looking at a photo of one's family and feeling love and admiration. However, this is a fraudulent teaching by the Vatican, because no one worships God by bowing and praying to a photo of their spouse and children. Catholics chant recited Rosaries and pre-written so-called 'prayers.' It is 100% manmade tradition and idolatry. I asked a Catholic man why he recites memorized chants, instead of praying from the heart. He said it was the way he was brought up as a child. That is unacceptable to God. The Bible condemns placing family traditions above the Word of God (Mark 7:13). Catholics HATE GOD according to Exodus 20:5. Oh what wickedness in the sight of God! The statue of Our Lady of Fatima is idolized while in the possession of that family, guests are invited, a fish fry is cooked, prayers are made to the statue of Our Lady of Fatima, the Rosary is chanted... AND GOD IS ANGRY!!! (Exodus 20:4-5)."

So there you have it. If you are a Christian the camp you think is crazy will naturally depend on the tradition you have been raised in or currently follow. Is it the side which believes in the alleged visions of small children who claim to somehow know what God wants and pray to statues, is it the vitriolic side which condemns the first group as being deceived by the devil and also somehow knows what God wants… or could it be it both?

No doubt some will discount the foregoing and say they choose to believe one or more of the accounts of divine revelation based on faith alone, something they say a nonbeliever cannot understand, so let's look at an important example of revelation from outside Christianity which also relies upon faith to be believed.

Muhammad was born and raised in Mecca and when he was nearly forty he used to spend many hours alone in prayer and speculating about the aspects of creation. Modern Muslim clerics claim he was concerned with social unrest, injustice, widespread discrimination (particularly against women), fighting amongst tribes and abuse of tribal authorities prevalent in pre-Islamic Arabia - but that is another issue. They further claim the moral degeneration of his fellow people and his own quest for a "true" religion further lent fuel to this, with the result being he began to withdraw periodically to a cave named Mount Hira three miles north of Mecca for contemplation and reflection. Islamic tradition holds that Muhammad during this period began to have dreams replete with spiritual significance which were fulfilled according to their true import, this was the commencement of his divine revelation and this created his inclination to engage in solitary worshipping.

According to Islamic tradition during one such occasion while he was in contemplation the archangel Gabriel appeared before him in the year 610 CE and simply said, "Recite," to which he replied, "I am unable to recite." Thereupon the angel caught hold of him and embraced him heavily, and this happened two more time after which the angel commanded Muhammad to recite the following verses: "Proclaim! in the name of thy Lord and Cherisher, Who created - Created man, out of a clot of congealed blood: Proclaim! And thy Lord is Most Bountiful, - He Who taught the pen - Taught man that which he knew not." That verse would become sura 96 (Al-Alaq), ayat 1-5 of the Quran.

Muhammad's experience is mentioned in the Quran 53:4-9: "It is a revelation which has been revealed to him and taught to him by the great mighty one; One strong, then he stood straight and he appeared on the uppermost horizon; He then came nearer and nearer until he was as close to him as the distance of two bows, or even less."

Perplexed by this new experience, Muhammad made his way home where he was consoled by his wife Khadijah. She then took him to her Christian cousin Waraqah ibn Nawfal, who was familiar with Jewish and Christian Scriptures. Islamic tradition holds that Waraqah, upon hearing the description, testified to Muhammad's prophethood and convinced Muhammad the revelation was from God. Waraqah said, "O my nephew! What did you see?" When Muhammad told him what had happened to him, Waraqah replied, "This is Namus (meaning Gabriel) that Allah sent to Moses. I wish I were younger. I wish I could live up to the time when your people would turn you out." Muhammad asked, "Will they drive me out?" Waraqah answered in the affirmative and said, "Anyone who came with something similar to what you have brought was treated with hostility, and if I should be alive until that day then I would support you strongly." A few days later Waraqah died. The initial revelation was followed by a pause and a second encounter with Gabriel when Muhammad heard a voice from the sky and saw the same angel "sitting between the sky and the earth" and the revelations resumed with the first verses of chapter 74 of the Quran.

At-Tabari and Ibn Hisham reported that Muhammad left the cave of Hira after being surprised by the revelation but later on returned to the cave and continued his solitude, though subsequently he returned to Mecca. Tabari and Ibn Ishaq write that Muhammad told Zubayr, "When I was midway on the mountain, I heard a voice from Heaven saying 'O

Muhammad! You are the apostle of Allah and I am Gabriel.' I raised my head towards Heaven to see who was speaking, and saw Gabriel in the form of a man with feet astride the horizon, saying, 'O Muhammad! You are the apostle of Allah and I am Gabriel.' I stood gazing at him moving neither forward nor backward, then I began to turn my face away from him, but towards whatever region of the sky I looked, I saw him as before."

There is doubt about the period of time between Muhammad's first and second experiences of revelation - Ibn Ishaq writes that three years elapsed from the time Muhammad received the first revelation until he started to preach publicly - but the bottom line is these revelations resulted in the creation of the Quran, which in turn led to the entire religion of Islam which is today followed by a billion people.

At least once in his or her lifetime each Muslim is expected to undertake a pilgrimage called the "Hajj" to Mecca, the sacred city of Islam. While a visit to Mecca is considered beneficial any time of the year it must take place during the month of Dhu al-Hijja (the last month of the Islamic year) to fulfill the requirements of the Hajj. The Hajj is commanded in the Quran and its rites were established by Muhammad but Muslim tradition dates it back to Adam and Abraham whom they believe were instructed by angels in the performance of the rites, and it in part commemorates the stories of Abraham, Hagar and Ishmael and has been assigned various other meanings throughout the centuries - and it was one of the last public acts of worship performed by Muhammad before his death.

Upon arrival at the boundary of Mecca pilgrims enter the state of ihram (purity) in which they will remain throughout the Hajj. Males entering this pure state don the ihram garments - two white, seamless sheets wrapped around the body - and sandals. This aspect of the rite not only signifies the state of holiness the pilgrims have entered but serves to contribute to a sense of equality and unity by removing visual indicators of class, wealth and culture. Requirements for women are less stringent, but they usually dress in white with only faces and hands uncovered. While in the state of ihram pilgrims must not cut their nails or hair, engage in sexual relations, argue, fight or hunt.

When he or she enters the city of Mecca the pilgrim first walks around the Ka'ba (the cube-shaped monument in Mecca containing a sacred black stone which Muslims face while praying) seven times while reciting the talbiya (a ritual prayer), then kisses or touches the Black

Stone, prays twice towards the Station of Abraham and the Ka'ba and runs seven times between the small mountains of Safa and Marwa.

The second stage of the Hajj takes place between the eighth and twelfth days of Dhu al-Hijja, beginning with a sermon at the mosque on the seventh day. On the eighth day and night the pilgrim stays at Mina or Arafat, on the ninth day the ritual of wuquf (standing) takes place at the small hill of Jabal al-Rahma in Arafat and the pilgrim then returns to Muzdalifa (a small town within the Meccan boundaries) to stay the night. The tenth day is Eid al-Adha (The Feast of Sacrifice), which is a major holiday observed by all Muslims. For those participating in the Hajj the day is spent in Mina where the pilgrim sacrifices an animal to commemorate Abraham's sacrifice and throws seven small stones at each of three pillars on three consecutive days because the pillars represent sins and devils. The pilgrim then returns to Mecca where he or she once again performs the tawaf (circuit of the Ka'ba) and the head is then shaved or the hair is trimmed, which marks the end of the state of ihram.

About two million Muslims complete the Hajj each year and the reason it and the origins of Islam have just been described is twofold - to educate those who know nothing about the religion and to offer a simple comparison. Are Muslims insane and/or delusional because they believe the obviously made up story of Muhammed meeting the Angel Gabriel? If so, how is that any different from a Polish nun meeting Jesus or Portuguese children conversing with the Virgin Mary? Are Muslims wasting their time when they make the pilgrimage to Mecca? If so, how is that different from millions of Christians making a pilgrimage to Lourdes or Fatima? The obvious question which comes to mind is where did all of the books and Gospels come from in the first place if not from divine revelation? More to the point, what about the voices and dreams and images on which Scripture is based?

To begin with there is internal monologue, also known as inner voice, internal speech or verbal stream of consciousness, which is essentially thinking in words. It also refers to the semi-constant internal monologue one has with oneself at a conscious or semi-conscious level. Much of what people consciously report thinking about may be thought of as an internal monologue, i.e. a conversation with oneself. Some of this can be considered speech rehearsal.

In the Zen tradition of Buddhism there is the phrase "Nen nen ju shin ki," which means "thought following thought." Sometimes this concept is translated with the help of the words "first nen" and "second nen" where each "nen" is a reaction to the previous one. We can think of our thoughts, memories, visualizations or sensations as good or bad and as true or false. Particularly with the judgment of word-thought as true or false we continue this reactionary "nen" process. Another way to think of thoughts is in a context somewhat like a Jenga puzzle or concept map where each thought is part of a system and is related to other thoughts.

There is uncertainty about what the source of these internal sentences are in some conditions. Attribution for a recently produced internal sentence may lead to concerns over schizophrenia, hallucinations or hearing voices. Experiments have shown cerebral asymmetry is reduced in schizophrenia, that is while performing verb-generation and semantic decision tasks people with schizophrenia show an increased activation in the right hemisphere of the brain, while in psychosis a typical schizophrenic may speak in "word salads" and/or write profusely.

In the philosophical field of language there is much research about internal speech in correlation with the building and usage of phrases in one's own idiom and thus the importance of language in the process of thinking. The bottom line is when someone "hears voices" in their head it is not coming from an outside source, but rather from their own subconscious.

A related phenomenon, the hallucination, is a perception in the absence of a stimulus which has qualities of real perception. Hallucinations are vivid, substantial and located in external objective space. They are distinguished from the related phenomena of dreaming, which does not involve wakefulness, illusion, which involves distorted or misinterpreted real perception, imagery, which does not mimic real perception and is under voluntary control, and pseudo-hallucination, which does not mimic real perception but is not under voluntary control. Hallucinations also differ from "delusional perceptions" in which a correctly sensed and interpreted stimulus, i.e. a real perception, is given some additional and typically bizarre significance. Hallucinations can occur in any sensory modality - equilibrioceptive, visual, auditory, tactile, olfactory, gustatory, proprioceptive, nociceptive, thermoceptive and chronoceptive. Those are certainly a bunch of big words, so to put them in layman's terms there are a lot of ways in which our minds can deceive us.

A mild form of hallucination is known as a disturbance and can occur in any of the senses above. These may be things like seeing movement in peripheral vision or hearing faint noises and/or voices. Auditory hallucinations are very common in paranoid schizophrenia. They may be benevolent, i.e. telling the patient good things about themselves, or malicious, i.e. cursing the patient etc. Auditory hallucinations of the malicious type are frequently heard as if people are talking about the patient behind their back. Like auditory hallucinations, the source of their visual counterpart can also be behind the patient's back. Their visual counterpart is the feeling of being looked or stared at, usually with malicious intent. Frequently auditory hallucinations and their visual counterpart are experienced by the patient together.

Hypnagogic and hypnopompic hallucinations are considered normal phenomena. Hypnagogic hallucinations can occur as one is falling asleep and hypnopompic hallucinations occur when waking up. Hallucinations can be associated with drug use (particularly deliriants), sleep deprivation, psychosis, neurological disorders and delirium tremens. Visual hallucination is the "seeing of things that are not there" which can according to some definitions also include "seeing things that are there, but incorrectly," i.e. illusions. Command hallucinations are hallucinations in the form of commands and can be auditory or inside of the persons mind and/or consciousness. The contents of the hallucinations can range from the innocuous sort to commands to cause harm to one's self or others and are often associated with schizophrenia, although people experiencing them may or may not comply with the hallucinated commands depending on circumstances.

Compliance is more common for non-violent commands however command hallucinations are sometimes used in defense of a crime, often homicides. It is essentially a voice one hears which tells them what to do. Sometimes they are quite benign directives such as "stand up" or "shut the door," but whether it is a command for something simple or something which is a threat it is still considered a command hallucination. Some helpful questions which can assist one in figuring out if they may be suffering from this includes deciding what are the voices telling you to do, when did your voices first start telling you to do things, do you recognize the person who is telling you to harm yourself or others and do you think you can resist doing what the voices are telling you to do?

Schizophrenia is a mental disorder characterized by a breakdown of thought processes and by a deficit of typical emotional responses. Common symptoms include auditory hallucinations, paranoid or bizarre delusions or disorganized speech and thinking, and it is accompanied by significant social or occupational dysfunction. The onset of symptoms typically occurs in young adulthood with a global lifetime prevalence of about 0.3–0.7% and diagnosis is based on observed behavior and the patient's reported experiences.

Genetics, early environment, neurobiology and psychological and social processes appear to be important contributory factors, and some recreational and prescription drugs appear to cause or worsen symptoms. Current research is focused on the role of neurobiology, although no single isolated organic cause has been found. The many possible combinations of symptoms have triggered debate about whether the diagnosis represents a single disorder or a number of discrete syndromes. Despite the etymology of the term from the Greek roots "to split" and "mind," schizophrenia does not imply a split personality or multiple personality disorder (which is known these days as dissociative identity disorder), a condition with which it is often confused in public perception. Rather, the term means a "splitting of mental functions" because of the symptomatic presentation of the illness.

A person diagnosed with schizophrenia may experience hallucinations (most reported are hearing voices), delusions (often bizarre or persecutory in nature) and disorganized thinking and speech. The latter may range from a loss of train of thought to sentences only loosely connected in meaning to incoherence known as "word salad" in severe cases. In one uncommon subtype the person may be largely mute, remain motionless in bizarre postures or exhibit purposeless agitation - all signs of catatonia. In the religious these can be interpreted as "trances." About thirty to fifty percent of people with schizophrenia do not have insight, in other words they do not accept their condition or its treatment. Psychotic symptoms may also be present in several other mental disorders including bipolar disorder, borderline personality disorder, drug intoxication and drug-induced psychosis. Currently the "Hearing Voices Movement" is a philosophical trend in how people who hear voices are viewed. It was begun by Marius Romme, a professor of social psychiatry at the University of Limburg in the Netherlands and Sandra Escher, a science journalist who began this work after being challenged by a voice hearer as to why they could not accept the reality of her voice hearing experience.

Another way the mind can be deceived is via the mirage, which is a naturally occurring optical phenomenon in which light rays are bent to produce a displaced image of distant objects or the sky. The word comes to English via French and from the Latin "mirari," meaning "to look at, to wonder at." This is the same root as for "mirror" and "to admire."

In contrast to a hallucination, a mirage is a real optical phenomenon which can be captured on camera since light rays actually are refracted to form the false image at the observer's location. What the image appears to represent, however, is determined by the interpretive faculties of the human mind. For example inferior images on land are very easily mistaken for the reflections from a small body of water.

Mirages can be categorized as "inferior" (meaning lower), "superior" (higher) and "Fata Morgana" - one kind of superior mirage consisting of a series of unusually elaborate, vertically stacked images which form one rapidly changing mirage. A Fata Morgana, the name of which comes from the Italian translation of Morgan le Fay, the fairy shape-shifting half-sister of the legendary King Arthur, is a very complex superior mirage. It appears with alternations of compressed and stretched zones, erect images and inverted images. A Fata Morgana is also a fast-changing mirage. They are most common in polar regions, especially over large sheets of ice with a uniform low temperature, but they can be observed almost anywhere. While in polar regions a Fata Morgana may be observed on cold days, and in desert areas and over oceans and lakes one may be observed on hot days. For one to occur temperature inversion has to be strong enough that light rays' curvatures within the inversion are stronger than the curvature of the Earth since the rays will bend and create arcs. An observer needs to be within an atmospheric duct to be able to see a Fata Morgana, and such mirages may be observed from any altitude within the Earth's atmosphere including from mountaintops or airplanes.

A Fata Morgana can go from superior to inferior mirage and back within a few seconds depending on the constantly changing conditions of the atmosphere. For instance sixteen frames of the mirage of the Farallon Islands, which cannot be seen from sea level at all under normal conditions because they are located below the horizon, were photographed on the same day. The first fourteen frames have elements of a Fata Morgana display - alternations of compressed and stretched zones. The last two frames were photographed a few hours later around sunset. The air was cooler while the ocean was probably a little bit warmer, which made temperature inversion lower. The mirage was still present, but was not as complex as it had been a few hours before sunset and corresponded no longer to a Fata Morgana but rather to a superior mirage display.

Distortions of image and bending of light can produce spectacular effects. In his book *Pursuit: The Chase and Sinking of the Bismarck*, author Ludovic Kennedy describes an incident which took place below the Denmark Strait during 1941 following the sinking of British battleship *HMS Hood.* The *Bismarck,* while being pursued by British cruisers *Norfolk* and *Suffolk,* passed out of sight into a sea mist - and within a matter of seconds the ship re-appeared, seemingly steaming toward the British ships at high speed. In alarm the cruisers separated in anticipation of an imminent attack and observers from both ships watched in astonishment as the German battleship fluttered, grew indistinct and faded away. Radar watch during these events indicated the *Bismarck* had in fact made no changes of course.

The foregoing explain different ways ancient peoples may have been mistaken about what they thought they saw so why, if Moses or Muhammed or any of the other prophets were suffering from hallucination, schizophrenia or some other affliction, did no one realize it? The answer should be obvious - sciences such as psychoanalysis and meteorology would not be invented for millennia and in fact the very idea of psychoanalysis would not come into full prominence until Freud formulated his theory of psychoanalysis in the 1890s.

Psychoanalysis is a psychological and psychotherapeutic theory which has its roots in the ideas of Austrian neurologist Sigmund Freud and since then it has expanded and been revised, reformed and developed in different directions. This was initially done by Freud's colleagues and students such as Alfred Adler and Carl Gustav Jung, who went on to develop their own ideas independently from Freud. In line with Freudian thought, psychoanalysis was revised and developed by neo-Freudians such as Erich Fromm, Karen Horney, Harry Stack Sullivan and Jacques Lacan.

The basic tenets of psychoanalysis include the understanding that besides the inherited constitution of personality a person's development is determined by events in early childhood, human behavior is largely influenced by irrational drives such as a desire for immortality, irrational drives are unconscious and attempts to bring these drives into awareness meet with psychological resistance in the form of defense mechanisms such as apologetics and the invocation of "faith." When viewed in that light it is much easier to understand the widespread theistic acceptance of "revelation" as the basis of religion.

The next source of "revelation" is dreams, which are successions of images, ideas, emotions and sensations which occur involuntarily in the mind during certain stages of sleep. Many purported biblical and quranic revelations are said to take place in them, and while the content and purpose of dreams are not definitively understood they have been a topic of scientific speculation and a subject of philosophical and religious interest throughout recorded history.

Dreams mainly occur in the rapid-eye movement (REM) stage of sleep when brain activity is high and resembles that of being awake. REM sleep is revealed by continuous movements of the eyes during which time the release of the neurotransmitters norepinephrine, serotonin and histamine is completely suppressed. At times they may occur during other stages of sleep, however these dreams tend to be much less vivid or memorable. Dreams can last for a few seconds or as long as twenty minutes and people are more likely to remember the dream if they are awakened during the REM phase. The average person has three to five dreams per night but some may have up to seven and they tend to last longer as the night progresses - during a full eight-hour night of sleep, two hours of it is spent dreaming.

In modern times dreams have been seen as a connection to the unconscious and range from normal and ordinary to overly surreal and bizarre. They can have varying natures such as frightening, exciting, magical, melancholic, adventurous or sexual, and the events in dreams are generally outside the control of the dreamer with the exception of lucid dreaming where the dreamer is self-aware.

Opinions about the meaning of dreams have varied and shifted through time and culture, and interpretations date back to 5000-4000 BCE. The earliest recorded dreams were found in materials dating back approximately five thousand years in Mesopotamia where they were documented on clay tablets. In the classic Greek and Roman eras people believed dreams were direct messages from the gods or from the dead and that they predicted the future, and some cultures have even practiced dream incubation with the intention of cultivating dreams which were prophetic. One example is “The Dreaming,” which is a common term within the animist creation narrative of indigenous Australians commonly referred to as aboriginals, for what may be understood as the “timeless time” of formative creation and perpetual creating.

The Sumerians in Mesopotamia left evidence of dreams dating back to 3100 BCE and according to these early recorded stories gods and kings such as the 7th Century BCE scholar-king Assurbanipal paid close attention to them. The Mesopotamians believed the soul, or some part of it, moves out from the body of the sleeping person and actually visits the places and persons the dreamer sees in his or her sleep and sometimes the “god of dreams” was said to actually carry the dreamer there.

Babylonians and Assyrians divided dreams into "good," which were sent by the gods, and "bad," those sent by demons, and also believed their dreams were omens and prophecies. It's no wonder other religions including Judaism, Christianity and Islam adopted similar beliefs.

In ancient Egypt as far back as 2000 BCE the Egyptians wrote down their dreams on papyrus and people with vivid and significant dreams were thought blessed and considered special. Ancient Egyptians believed they were like oracles bringing messages from the gods, thought the best way to receive divine revelation was through dreaming and thus they would induce or "incubate" dreams by going to sanctuaries and sleeping on special "dream beds" in the hope of receiving advice, comfort or healing from the gods.

In Chinese history people wrote of two vital aspects of the soul, one of which is freed from the body during slumber to journey to a dream realm while the other remained in the body. The Indian text *Upanishads*, written between 900 and 500 BCE, emphasizes two meanings of dreams. The first says dreams are merely expressions of inner desires, while the second is a belief the soul is leaving the body and being guided until awakened. Which of those ideas make the most sense, I wonder?

The Greeks shared their beliefs with the Egyptians on how to interpret good and bad dreams and the idea of incubation. Morpheus, the Greek god of dreams, also was thought to send warnings and prophecies to those who slept at shrines and temples. The earliest Greek believed their gods physically visited dreamers by entering through a keyhole and exiting the same way after the divine message was given.

Antiphon wrote the first known Greek book on dreams in the 5th Century BCE and in that century other cultures influenced the Greeks to develop the belief souls left the sleeping body. Hippocrates (469-399 BCE) had a simple dream theory - during the day the soul receives images, and during the night it produces them. Greek philosopher Aristotle (384-322 BCE) believed dreams caused physiological activity and thought they could analyze illness and predict diseases while Marcus Tullius Cicero, for his part, believed all dreams are produced by the thoughts and conversations a dreamer had during the preceding days, something which actually makes a great deal of sense since it forms the basis for dream incubation.

In Judaism dreams are considered part of the experience of the world which can be interpreted and from which lessons can be garnered. The ancient Hebrews connected their dreams heavily with their religion, though they were monotheistic and believed dreams were the voice of one god alone. Hebrews also differentiated between good dreams from God and bad dreams from evil spirits, and like many other ancient cultures incubated dreams in order to receive "divine revelation." For example the Hebrew prophet Samuel, or more accurately whoever wrote the Scriptures attributed to him, would "lie down and sleep in the temple at Shiloh before the Ark and receive the word of the Lord," although most of the dreams in the Bible are found in the Book of Genesis.

Christians mostly shared their beliefs with the Hebrews and thought dreams were of the supernatural because the Old Testament had frequent stories of dreams with divine inspiration. The most famous of these was Jacob's dream of a ladder which stretched from Earth to Heaven, and since then many Christians have preached that God talks to his people through their dreams.

Dreams also play an important role in the history of Islam and the lives of Muslims because dream interpretation is the only way Muslims have been able to receive revelations from God after the death of the "one true prophet" Muhammed, who had himself "received" much of the Quran from Allah while dreaming.

Some indigenous American tribes and Mexican civilizations believe dreams are a way of visiting and having contact with their ancestors. In fact some Native American tribes used vision quests, often accompanied by the use of hallucinogens such as peyote, as a rite of passage, fasting and praying until an anticipated guiding dream was received to be shared with the rest of the tribe.

The Middle Ages brought a harsh interpretation of dreams. They were seen as evil and the images as temptations from the devil, since many believed during sleep the devil could fill the human mind with corrupting and harmful thoughts. For example the founder of Protestantism, Martin Luther, believed dreams were the work of the devil, however Catholics such as St. Augustine and St. Jerome claimed the direction of their lives were heavily influenced in a positive way by their dreams.

Sigmund Freud wrote extensively about dream theories and interpretations and explained them as manifestations of our deepest desires and anxieties, often relating to repressed childhood memories or obsessions. In *The Interpretation of Dreams* Freud developed a psychological technique to interpret dreams and devised a series of guidelines to understand the symbols and motifs which appear in them since dream interpretation can often be a result of subjective ideas and experiences. A recent study conducted by the *Journal of Personality and Social Psychology* concluded many people believe "their dreams reveal meaningful hidden truths." The study was conducted in the United States, South Korea and India and according to its findings we are irrational about dreams in the same way we are irrational in our everyday decisions. In their search for meaning, humans can turn to dreams in order to find answers and explanations, and the studies found that dreams reflect the human trait of optimistic thinking since the results show people tend to focus more on dreams in which good things take place.

According to surveys it is common for people to feel their dreams are predicting subsequent life events but psychologists have explained these experiences in terms of memory biases, namely a selective memory for accurate predictions and distorted memory. In other words dreams are retrospectively fitted into life experiences and their multi-faceted nature make it easy to find connections between their content and real events. In one experiment subjects were asked to write down their dreams in a diary to prevent the selective memory effect, and the dreams no longer seemed accurate about the future. Another experiment gave subjects the fake diary of a student with apparently precognitive dreams which described events from the person's life as well as some predictive dreams and some non-predictive dreams, and when subjects were asked to recall the dreams they had read they remembered more of the successful predictions than unsuccessful ones.

The recall of dreams is extremely unreliable although it is a skill which can be developed, and they can usually be recalled if a person is awakened while dreaming. Often a dream may be recalled upon viewing or hearing a random trigger or stimulus, and the salience hypothesis proposes that dream content which is salient - that is novel, intense or unusual - is more easily remembered. There is also considerable evidence vivid, intense or unusual dream content is more frequently recalled, and in line with the salience hypothesis people who have more vivid, intense or unusual dreams show better recall. There is also evidence continuity of consciousness is related to recall, in other words people who have vivid and unusual experiences during the day tend to have more memorable dream content and hence better dream recall and those who score high on measures of personality traits associated with creativity, imagination and fantasy such as openness to experience, daydreaming, fantasy proneness, absorption and hypnotic susceptibility tend to show more frequent dream recall. There is also evidence for continuity between the bizarre aspects of dreaming and waking experience, that is people who report more bizarre experiences during the day such as people high in schizotypy (psychosis proneness) have more frequent dream recall and also report more frequent nightmares. There are many theories about the mechanism of how dreams occur in the brain, but they are complicated and outside the scope of this book. The important point is they do occur and are sometimes difficult to differentiate from reality.

Another factor to consider is cryptomnesia, which is literally "hidden memory." The term was coined by psychology professor Théodore Flournoy and is used to explain the origin of experiences people believe to be original but which are actually based on memories of events they've forgotten. It seems likely most so-called past life regressions induced through hypnosis are confabulations fed by cryptomnesia. For example Virginia Tighe's hypnotic recollections of "Bridey Murphy of Cork, Ireland," if not deliberately fraudulent, are most likely recollections of events which happened in this life but had been forgotten. If you are not familiar with the case in 1952 Tighe, who lived in Pueblo, Colorado, was hypnotized by local businessman Morey Bernstein. She allegedly spoke in an Irish brogue and claimed to be Bridey Murphy, a 19th Century woman from Cork. Bernstein says he encouraged past life regression, his subject cooperated and he hypnotized Tighe many times. While under hypnosis she sang Irish songs and told Irish stories, always as Bridey Murphy. She also gave her birth date as 1798, described her childhood in a Protestant family in Cork and marriage to Sean Brian Joseph McCarthy and even detailed her own burial in Belfast in 1864. Bernstein's 1956 book *The Search for Bridey Murphy* became a best-seller and newspapers sent reporters to Ireland to investigate whether there was had been a red-headed Bridey Murphy who lived in Ireland in the 19th Century - but no records were found which matched Tighe's claims regarding Bridey's birth, upbringing, marriage or death. One newspaper, the *Chicago American*, did however find a Bridie Murphey Corkell… but in Wisconsin and in the 20th Century. In fact she lived in the house across the street from where Virginia Tighe grew up, so obviously what she reported while hypnotized were not memories of a previous life but memories from her early childhood. Many people had been easily and credulously impressed with the details of Tighe's hypnotic memories but they were not evidence of past life regression, reincarnation or channeling but were instead evidence of a vivid imagination, confused memory, fraud or some combination of the three.

Likewise the "past-life memories" of "Jane Evans" produced while under hypnosis by Arnall Bloxham were almost certainly unconsciously produced confabulations. Bloxham was a British hypnotherapist who developed a strong interest in reincarnation, and inspired by the just debunked Bridey Murphy case he dedicated more than twenty years of his life to studying past-life regression. Beginning in the 1950s Bloxham carried out past-life regression experiments on more than four hundred subjects with his star patient being a Welsh housewife who was only identified under the pseudonym of "Jane Evans." While hypnotized she recalled seven different lives including a Roman matron named Livonia who happened to be married to the tutor of the future Emperor Constantine, and most famously a 12th Century Jewish woman named Rebecca who lived in the English city of York.

During the 1970s British television producer Jeffrey Iverson took great care in verifying the extensive details "Rebecca of York" had provided of her life and the savage persecution Jews of her era often faced such as hiding with one of her children in a crypt beneath a small church "near a big copper gate" before they were found and brutally murdered. Iverson was able to establish that "Rebecca's" recall matched known historical accounts of Jewish persecution during that time period and also identified the church she described as St. Mary's Church near Coppergate in York. Even more astounding, an actual crypt was discovered beneath the church in 1975 which had been previously unknown, and Iverson published his findings in a 1976 book titled *More Lives Than One?* which was presented as absolute proof of reincarnation.

Unfortunately for Bloxham and Iverson researcher Ian Wilson pointed out in his 1982 book *Reincarnation? The Claims Investigated* all of the evidence Bloxham and Iverson had presented could be explained by the phenomenon of cryptomnesia. As for Jane Evans and "Rebecca of York," Wilson raised the rather obvious point that while the persecution of Jews in the 12th Century was quite real, Rebecca of York was a fictional character and central figure in Sir Walter Scott's classic novel *Ivanhoe* and many of the details "recalled" by Evans matched points in Scott's book as well as the 1952 movie of the same name featuring Elizabeth Taylor as Rebecca. As for the previously undiscovered crypt under St. Mary's Church, such crypts are a common feature in many medieval church buildings and the presence of a previously unknown one is not remarkable. Plus Evans' description was vague at best, so it was guesswork on Iverson's part that St. Mary's was the building she identified. In fact there is no evidence St. Mary's ever had a copper gate and the "Coppergate" in York referred not to an actual gate but instead to the name of the local road. None of the other evidence Iverson raised stood up to careful scrutiny either, but even so this case is still cited as "evidence" for past-life recall by true believers.

Cryptomnesia may also explain how apparent plagiarisms by such people as deafblind author Helen Keller and songwriter George Harrison of the Beatles might actually be cases of hidden memory. Harrison likely didn't intend to plagiarize the Chiffon's *He's So Fine* in his song *My Sweet Lord*, nor did Keller intend to plagiarize Margaret Canby's *The Frost Fairies* when she wrote *The Frost King*. Both may simply be cases of not having a conscious memory of experiencing the works in question.

The first recorded instance of cryptomnesia occurred in 1874 and involved William Stanton Moses, a medium who during a séance claimed to be in contact with the spirits of two brothers who had recently died in India. The deaths were verified but further research showed that the obituary ran in a newspaper six days before the séance and all information in the obituary was given in the séance and nothing more was added. Is it any wonder we so often have difficulty deciding whether an event was dreamt or had actually occurred?

This also goes a long way towards explaining Déjà vu, which is French for "already seen." Déjà vu is an uncanny feeling or illusion of having already seen or experienced something which is being experienced for the first time. If we assume the experience is actually of a remembered event, then déjà vu probably occurs because an original experience was neither fully attended to nor elaborately encoded in memory. If so, then it would seem most likely that the present situation triggers the recollection of a fragment from one's past and the experience may seem uncanny if the memory is so fragmented that no strong connections can be made between the fragment and other memories.

Thus the feeling one has been there before is often due to the fact one has indeed been there before but has simply forgotten most of the original experience because they were not paying close attention the first time. The original experience may even have occurred only seconds or minutes earlier. On the other hand the déjà vu experience may be due to having seen pictures or heard vivid stories many years earlier. The experience may even be part of the dim recollections of childhood, however it is possible the déjà vu feeling is triggered by a neurochemical action in the brain which is not connected to any actual experience in the past. One feels strange and identifies the feeling with a memory even though the experience is completely new, and yet it all seems so real.

An excellent example of how all of these things influence our beliefs can be found in Todd Burpo's book *Heaven Is For Real: A Little Boy's Astounding Story of His Trip to Heaven and Back* which purports to tell of four-year-old Colton's journey to Heaven during a surgical procedure for a severely ruptured appendix. Following the procedure, and over a period of months and years, Colton gradually "revealed" bits and pieces of his alleged journey to Heaven, claiming among other things that he was sitting on Jesus' lap, Jesus has a rainbow colored horse and wears a golden crown with a pink diamond, he was given "homework" to do by his deceased grandfather (whom he had never met), everyone in Heaven has wings and flies around from place to place (except for Jesus who levitates up and down like an elevator), the gates of Heaven are made of gold and pearls and so on.

There are a number of reasons one could and should be highly skeptical of this story. Firstly, Colton was just four years old when he began to talk about his experience and he was mostly prompted by his father. Four-year-old children are renowned for making up stories and not being able to distinguish fantasy from reality. After all many children have imaginary friends and use their imagination constantly in making up stories while engaging in play. I for one had an imaginary friend when I was that age and was so convinced he was real made my mother set a place for him at the dinner table. It seems to me the parents were thinking like four-year-olds if they took what their child said as being literally true. Comedian Jimmy Carr put a humorous and quite apropos spin on that when he quipped, "When I was a kid I had an imaginary friend and I used to think that he went everywhere with me, and that I could talk to him and that he could hear me, and that he could grant me wishes and stuff. And then I grew up, and stopped going to church."

Why did it take so many months and years for Colton's story to develop and why did it require the prompting of his parents? Surely if a child visited Heaven he would come back and begin talking about it excitedly all at once, at least to start with. Haven't we all heard children bubble over with enthusiasm after having an exciting experience? But not Colton. He doesn't even mention it until he happens to say something about where his parents were during his operation, but given that it took years for his whole story to "come out" one has to wonder how much of it was constructed in response to his father's questioning.

The "information" provided by Colton is so obviously consistent with an evangelical fundamentalist view it is easy to see it was informed by the culture he grew up in. Colton's father is a pastor and admits to reading Bible stories to Colton as he grew up so he would have been previously exposed to all of the of details he described, even if unconsciously, and it's not surprising his description of Heaven draws on that culture. What would have lent credibility to the story is if the Heaven he had described had been totally different from what fundamentalist Christians imagine. For instance Colton's father holds to a literalist reading of the biblical book of Revelation which most people quite rightly understand to be highly symbolic and figurative and as a result Colton describes things such as swords and horses in Heaven, rainbow colored no less similar to the children's Rainbow Brite toy, and since his father believes such things are truly in Heaven because verses in Revelation "confirm" it he believes it too.

If Colton's descriptions of God on a throne with angels using swords to keep Satan out of heaven are taken literally then God has been caught in an Old Testament era time warp. Are they really suggesting God has eternally sat on thrones, ridden horses and fought with swords against real dragons? Most biblical scholars and indeed most Christians have a much more mature view of these issues than the childish view Colton and his parents have, but according to this book we are to become "as little children in our faith" and accept all this without question.

The claim Colton told them a few things which he couldn't have known about is also highly unlikely. Church communities are renowned gossiping communities and it is much more reasonable to assume he heard or overheard some of these things than believe they were supernaturally revealed. The disturbing thing is this book became extremely popular and was believed by many, which doesn't say much for the people who swallowed it whole without a second thought.

Naturally Colton Burpo is not the only child given to telling tall tales. Nearly five years after it hit bestseller lists a book titled *The Boy Who Came Back from Heaven*, which purported to be a six-year-old boy's story of visiting angels and heaven, was pulled from shelves by publisher Tyndale House. It had been promoted as "a supernatural encounter that will give you new insights on Heaven, angels and hearing the voice of God" and in a review the *Washington Post* called it a "spiritual memoir," noting it "became part of a popular genre of 'heavenly tourism,' which has been controversial among orthodox Christians." The aptly named Alex Malarkey, now a teenager, was paralyzed at the age of six when he was in a car wreck, spent two months in a coma and later co-authored the book with his father ala Todd and Colton Burpo, but in January of 2015 admitted the story was all made up. In an open letter to book retailer LifeWay and others who sell Christian books and religious materials he wrote, "I did not die. I did not go to Heaven. I said I went to Heaven because I thought it would get me attention… people have profited from lies, and continue to." One must wonder how those who believed his story and defended it to skeptics must have felt upon reading that. A bit foolish, perhaps?

As you can see one other explanation for a purported revelation is intentional deception. Think about it. If someone wants a group of people to do or not do a certain thing or believe in a particular concept and can convince them they have received marching orders from a "higher power" they will be far more likely to follow instructions. As for the fact so many revelations come from young children such as Bernadette, Lúcia, Colton and Alex, naturally no child with an active imagination would ever be mistaken or for that matter tell a fib, would they? This explanation is often not considered because people tend to avoid calling other people liars, even though many of them most certainly are.

Another interesting theory concerning the source of some revelations was put forward by an Israeli researcher who claimed in a published study that Moses was on psychedelic drugs when he heard God deliver the Ten Commandments on Mount Sinai and further opined that such mind-altering substances formed an integral part of the religious rites of Israelites in biblical times. Professor of cognitive psychology at the Hebrew University of Jerusalem Benny Shanon wrote in the *Time and Mind* journal of philosophy, "As far as Moses on Mount Sinai is concerned it was either a supernatural cosmic event, which I don't believe, or a legend, which I don't believe either, or finally, and this is very probable, an event that joined Moses and the people of Israel under the effect of narcotics." Moses was probably also on drugs when he saw the "burning bush," suggested Shanon, who said he himself has dabbled with such substances. "The Bible says people see sounds, and that is a classic phenomenon," he said citing the example of religious ceremonies in the Amazon in which drugs are used and induce people to "see music." He mentioned his own experience and talked about how he had used ayahuasca, a powerful psychotropic plant, during a religious ceremony in Brazil's Amazon forest in 1991. "I experienced visions that had spiritual-religious connotations," Shanon said, and he added that the psychedelic effects of ayahuasca were comparable to those produced by concoctions based on the bark of the acacia tree, something which is frequently mentioned in the Bible.

The point in mentioning this is not to prove Moses was under the influence of hallucinogens, assuming he existed in the first place, because that would be impossible. It is to ask the reasonable and equally unanswerable question, how do we know he was not? Consider what your initial reaction would be to a neighbor who claimed to be acting on the direction of a flaming plant. Would you think he might be high? Of course you would. Why not Moses?

We have examined a number of ways in which the human mind can be deceived, but there is one more which needs to be discussed in more detail - intentional deception. A good example is the phenomenon of so-called "weeping statues" which have been claimed to be shedding tears or weeping by supernatural means tears of a substance which appears to be human tears, blood, oil and scented liquids, all of which have been reported. Other claimed phenomena sometimes associated with weeping statues are miraculous healing, the formation of figures in the tear lines and the scent of roses. These events are generally reported by Christians and initially attract some pilgrims but are in most cases are disallowed by the upper levels of the Church and/or proven as hoaxes outright.

Reported weeping statues are most often of the Virgin Mary and are at times accompanied by claims of Marian apparitions, however to date only one single example of a combined weeping statue and apparition, namely Our Lady of Akita, has been "approved" by the Vatican and the rest have been dismissed as hoaxes. This is because authorities of the Catholic Church have been very careful in their approach and treatment of these statues and have generally set high barriers for their acceptance. For instance when a statue of the popular Saint Padre Pio in Messina, Sicily was found to have tears of blood one day in 2002 Church officials quickly ordered tests which showed the blood actually belonged to a woman and dismissed the case as a hoax.

Making a fake weeping statue is relatively easy and believe it or not do it yourself weeping statue kits have actually been sold. Such statues have of course been dismissed by rationalists as a purely psychological and/or fraudulent phenomenon and witnesses are said to be deluded by their own state of mind or strong group suggestion - and in this altered state of mind they believe they see something which isn't really there.

Another possible explanation attributes the so-called tears to condensation and the drops statues appear to weep are said to actually be beads of water from microscopic cracks in the surface of the statues. Unpublished reports of testing have supposedly been able to verify this theory, but peer reviewed scientific research is rarely if ever carried out into this sort of phenomenon since most researchers feel such things are not worth their time.

A number of weeping statues have been declared fake by Catholic Church officials, for example in 1995 a Madonna statue appeared to weep blood in the town of Civitavecchia in Italy with about sixty witnesses testifying to the miracle and the local bishop saying he himself had seen it weep… but the blood on the statue was later found to be male and the statue's owner, Fabio Gregori, refused to take a DNA test. After the Civitavecchia case dozens of reputedly miraculous statues were reported and all were proven to be hoaxes where blood, red paint or water was splashed on the faces of the statues and in fact in 2008 church custodian Vincenzo Di Costanzo went on trial in northern Italy for faking blood on a statue of the Virgin Mary when his own DNA was matched to the blood. So why all the deceptions? The only logical explanation is some people feel it is possible and/or necessary to "prove" the "truth" of their beliefs using lies.

Of course some people do truly believe they have experienced something divine, although it is quite possible they are mistaken. In article titled *Ecstatic Epilepsy: How Seizures Can Be Bliss* in a January 2014 edition of *New Scientist* the author provided a description of a purported "religious experience" along with several descriptions of the type of the aura experienced by some epilepsy sufferers. See if you can divine which is which.

In the first a sixty-four-year-old woman said, "The immense joy that fills me is above physical sensations. It is a feeling of total presence, an absolute integration of myself, a feeling of unbelievable harmony of my whole body and myself with life, with the world, with the 'All.'" In the second a fifty-three-year-old female teacher claimed, "...it is as if I were very, very conscious, more aware, and the sensations, everything seems bigger, overwhelming me." The third involved a middle-aged woman's assertion, "...the most amazing feeling came over me... a feeling of complete and utter love - I felt as if I were radiating like the heat of the sun..." In the fourth a forty-one-year-old architect said, "You are just feeling energy and all your senses. You take in everything that is around, you get a fusion." Finally, a thirty-seven-year-old man offered, "...a sensation of velvet, as if I were sheltered from anything negative."

Before revealing which is which it should be pointed out that M.E. Nielson of the Department of Psychology at Georgia Southern University has produced a list of adjectives which sixty-six adults rated as representing how their perceived "religious experiences" felt with adjectives representing positive affect (enthusiastic and/or, at ease), low neuroticism (calm and/or, relaxed), high agreeableness (soft-hearted and/or, sympathetic), conscientiousness (conscientious and/or, reliable) and extraversion (sociable and/or talkative). Famed Russian author Fyodor Dostoyevsky, himself an epileptic, gave a vivid account of an epileptic seizure in his book *The Idiot*: "He remembered that during his epileptic fits, or rather immediately preceding them, he had always experienced a moment or two when his whole heart, and mind and body seemed to wake up with vigor and light; when he became filled with joy and hope, and all his anxieties seemed to be swept away forever; these moments were but presentiments, as it were, of the one final second… in which the fit came upon him. That second, of course, was inexpressible. Next moment something appeared to burst open before him: a wonderful inner light illuminated his soul. This lasted perhaps half a second, yet he distinctly remembered hearing the beginning of a wail, the strange, dreadful wail, which burst from his lips of its own accord, and which no effort of will on his part could suppress. Next moment he was absolutely unconscious; black darkness blotted out everything. He had fallen in an epileptic fit."

A Carmelite Nun, Saint Teresa of Ávila, described one of her many "visions" as follows: "I saw in his hand a long spear of gold, and at the point there seemed to be a little fire. He appeared to me to be thrusting it at times into my heart, and to pierce my very entrails; when he drew it out, he seemed to draw them out also, and to leave me all on fire with a great love of God. The pain was so great, that it made me moan; and yet so surpassing was the sweetness of this excessive pain, that I could not wish to be rid of it..."

Setting aside the obvious sexual fantasy which is understandable in a celibate young woman who went into a nunnery at the age of fourteen there is that sense of presence, well-being and ecstasy again, so clearly there is a close similarity, if not an identicality, between a "religious experience" and some forms of pre-epileptic aura. These have been associated with temporal lobe epilepsy in particular and sufferers often describe a feeling of great peace and well-being and the belief someone else is present. In a religious person with a pre-existing belief in a god this presence is often interpreted as a god or saint or other person of some significance in their religion. The problem was in identifying the precise area of the temporal lobe because the wave of excitation propagates so rapidly. In fact some agnostic patients have said they could understand how after such a seizure a person can develop faith and belief because it has some spiritual meaning.

A team led by Fabienne Picard, a neurologist at the University Hospital in Geneva, Switzerland, has shown this phenomenon may not originate in the temporal lobe but in a small area of the cerebral cortex called the "insula," the area thought to be responsible for integrating internal sensations such as the heartbeat with external sensations such as touch. The anterior portion of the insula deals with how we feel about ourselves, in other words our sense of self or awareness of "being." Picard's team went one step further and electrically stimulated the insula of a patient suffering from "ecstatic epilepsy" via implanted electrodes. The patient, a twenty-three-year-old woman, confirmed the feelings she experienced during artificial stimulation were identical to those she experienced immediately prior to a fit. The number of people with ecstatic epilepsy are probably underestimated because the emotions are so strong and strange, so perhaps they feel embarrassed to speak about them.

Given how much store religions tend to give to mystical religious experiences and how many people claim they are religious, not because of any physical evidence they can produce but because of a personal experience they have had, these findings make it difficult to seriously accept them as reliable testimonies. Of course many can be dismissed as fantasies at best, if not downright lies told to impress others (after all how special someone must be for the creator of the universe to have paid them a special visit), but despite that logic a substantial number of pivotal moments in the official histories of religions turn on a "revelation," often to someone who was fasting. As comedian Billy Connolly said, "He was fasting in the desert for forty days and a burning bush started talking to him! You try it!" Think about the often deranged prophecies of the Old Testament, some of which read like the psychotic ravings of paranoid schizophrenics. Now consider the tale of Paul's alleged conversion. At least part of it was a figment of the author's imagination because he didn't know the geography or politics of the place and time he set his tale in since Judea did not extend to Damascus in Phoenicia, therefore Saul could not have been going there for the reason stated, but his writings suggest he was familiar with ecstatic epilepsy since he describes it almost exactly. In fact the conversion on the road to Damascus may well be the first written description of this neurological disorder, and then there is the Book of Revelation… of which the less said, the better.

Thomas Paine correctly pointed out in his *Age of Reason* that when someone "gets a message" directly from a higher power it can be viewed as revelation, but when that person turns around and tell it to someone else it immediately becomes second hand information, i.e. hearsay. Paine used the example of the apostle Thomas, who didn't believe Jesus had risen and that other people had seen him. He instead said he had to see it for himself and wasn't going to believe it simply because someone else had told him. This shows us precisely why we should be skeptics about what others say, especially when it comes to religion and the supernatural, and the lesson here is being a "Doubting Thomas" should be considered a virtue rather than a fault because claiming divine revelation and using it as a tool to influence and control others can be a very dangerous thing indeed. This was perfectly articulated by Paine who observed, "The most detestable wickedness, the most horrid cruelties and the greatest miseries that have afflicted the human race have had their origin in this thing called revelation, or revealed religion."

So now, in the absence of physical evidence and with personal testimony looking more and more like a pathological brain malfunction as we discover more about how the brain works, what does that mean for religion? In the words of Thomas Szasz, Professor Emeritus of Psychiatry at the State University of New York, "If you talk to God, you are praying… but if God talks to you, you have schizophrenia." By the way, the third description mentioned earlier was the religious experience. The others were all Fabienne Picard's patients. Did you guess right?

Myth

Or, Once Upon a Time

"The great enemy of the truth is very often not the lie, deliberate, contrived and dishonest, but the myth, persistent persuasive and unrealistic." ~ John F. Kennedy

Do you think you are able to tell myth from truth? Most people think they can, but don't realize there is a blurry line between legend and fact. Take for instance the myth that Saint Patrick was Irish. That's right Saint Patrick, the most venerated of all Irishmen and namesake of St. Patrick's Day, was actually born in what is now western Britain to a well-to-do Christian family of Roman heritage. When he was about sixteen he was captured by a band of marauders and sold to an Irish chieftain whom he served as a shepherd for about six years and during that period spent considerable time learning the local language and customs before escaping and returning to Great Britain. Several years later he started his studies for the priesthood and around 433 went back to Ireland, built churches, converted thousands and in the 8th Century became Ireland's patron saint. As for stories of driving out the snakes and using a three-leaf clover to explain the Trinity, they are of course nothing but fanciful folklore.

Mythology is a body or collection of myths as well as the study of them and in "folkloristics" myths are sacred narratives which usually explain how the world or humankind came to be in its present form, although in a very broad sense the word can refer to any traditional story. Bruce Lincoln, Professor of the History of Religions in the Divinity School of the University of Chicago, defines myth as "ideology in narrative form." Myths tend to arise as either truthful depictions or overelaborated accounts of historical events, allegory for or personification of natural phenomena or an explanation of ritual. Once established, they are then transmitted to convey religious or idealized experience, establish behavioral models and/or teach.

Early classifications of Greek myths were developed by the "Neoplatonists" and revived by Renaissance mythographers as in the *Theologia Mythologica* of 1532. 19th Century comparative mythology reinterpreted myth as evolution toward science, a "disease of language" or the misinterpretation of magical ritual. Later interpretations rejected opposition between myth and science and modern mythopoeia such as fantasy novels, manga and urban legend - with many competing artificial myths acknowledged as fiction - supports the idea of myth as ongoing social practice.

The main characters in myths are usually gods, supernatural heroes and humans and as sacred stories they are often endorsed by rulers and priests and closely linked to religion or spirituality. In the society in which it is told a myth is usually regarded as a true account of the remote past and in fact many societies have two categories of traditional narrative, "true stories" or myths and "false stories" or fables, although creation myths generally take place in a primordial age when the world had not yet achieved its current form and attempt to explain how the world came to be and how customs, institutions and taboos were established so there is no way to prove they contain truth.

It should be pointed out that myths, legends and folktales are different types of traditional stories. Unlike myth, folktales can be set in any time and any place and are not considered true or sacred by the societies which tell them, but like myth, legends are stories which are traditionally considered true but are set in a more recent time when the world was much as it is today. Legends also generally feature humans as their main characters, whereas myths generally focus on superhuman characters. This distinction between myth, legend and folktale is a useful tool for grouping traditional stories because in many cultures it is difficult to draw a sharp line between myths and legends. Instead of dividing their traditional stories into myths, legends and folktales some cultures instead divide them into just two categories, one which roughly corresponds to folktales and one which combines myths and legends. Even myths and folktales are not completely distinct since a story may be considered true (and therefore a mythos) in one society but considered fictional (and therefore a folktale) in another. In fact when a myth loses its status as part of a religious system it often takes on traits more typical of folktales, with its formerly divine characters reinterpreted as human heroes, giants or fairies.

One theory asserts that myths are essentially distorted accounts of real historical events and suggests storytellers repeatedly elaborated upon historical accounts until the figures in those accounts gained the status of gods. For example one might argue the myth of the wind-god Aeolus evolved from a historical account of a king who taught his people to use sails and interpret the winds. Herodotus (5th Century BCE) and Prodicus made claims of this kind. A more familiar example is the story of Jesus, which may well have started out as a factual account of an actual Jewish rabbi and morphed into the supernatural story Christians are familiar with after being handed down through the years through oral tradition. This theory is named "euhemerism" after the mythologist Euhemerus (circa 320 BCE) who suggested the Greek gods developed from legends about human beings, and clearly this theory can be applied to the gods of other faiths as well.

Some theories propose myths began as allegories, which are literary devices in which characters or events in a literary, visual or musical art form represent or symbolize ideas and concepts. Allegory has been used widely throughout history in all forms of art with a major reason being its immense power to illustrate complex ideas and concepts in ways which are easily digestible and tangible to its viewers, readers or listeners. In essence they convey hidden messages through symbolic figures, actions, imagery and/or events. Allegory is generally treated as a figure of rhetoric, since a rhetorical allegory is a demonstrative form of representation conveying meaning other than the words which are spoken. According to one view myths began as allegories for natural phenomena, for example Apollo represents the sun, Poseidon the water and so on. According to another theory myths began as allegories for philosophical or spiritual concepts with Athena representing wise judgment, Aphrodite being desire, etc. The 19th Century Sanskritist Max Müller supported an allegorical theory of myth, believing they began as allegorical descriptions of nature but gradually came to be interpreted literally. For example a poetic description of the sea as "raging" was eventually taken literally and the sea was then thought of as a raging god.

Many Christians, notably commentator Bill O'Reilly among them, contend stories in the Bible which would be considered supernatural or nonsensical are actually allegorical while others steadfastly hold to the belief they literally happened as written. Good examples of those sorts of stories are God sending two bears to kill forty-two children because they had made fun of the prophet Elijah's bald head (2 Kings 2:23-4) and Balaam's donkey complaining about being whipped (Numbers 22:28-30). If you view those stories as allegorical the message from the first might be it is wrong to make fun of someone and the second could be an entreaty not to abuse animals and seen in that light a case could be made for those stories as fanciful cautionary tales much like those found in *Aesops's Fables* such as *The Wolf in Sheep's Clothing* and *The Hare and the Tortoise*, but if you take the literalist view that presents a problem. For instance you would be forced to rationalize why a benevolent God would slaughter children who are acting as children do in such a horrific manner for such a minor offense and would also have to accept the premise of a talking donkey. With regard to that last scenario an apologist will point out it would in fact be possible for God to make a donkey talk because he can do anything. Okay, fine. Now ask yourself if you have ever seen such a thing or for that matter if you know, or even know of, anyone who has? The answer is obviously no, which will force you to make an additional rationalization such as, "God doesn't do that sort of stuff anymore." How do you know? Now ask yourself what your reaction would be if someone told you he or she had just engaged in a two way conversation, in English, with an animal? Would you think to yourself they are modern day prophets who have received a vision from God or would you consider them to be crazy as a loon? Be honest. So why then believe a story written thousands of years ago by an anonymous author who doesn't even claim to be an eyewitness?

Some thinkers believe myths result from the personification of inanimate objects and forces. According to this school of thought the ancients worshipped natural phenomena such as fire and air, gradually coming to describe them as gods. For example according to the Theory of Mythopoeic Thought the ancients tended to view things as persons rather than mere objects, thus they described natural events as acts of personal gods and in doing so gave rise to myths.

According to the Myth-Ritual Theory the existence of myth is tied to ritual and in its most extreme form claims myth arose to explain rituals. This idea was first put forward by biblical scholar William Robertson Smith, according to whom people begin performing rituals for some reason not related to myth and later, after having forgotten the original reason for a ritual, tried to account for the ritual by inventing a myth and claiming the ritual commemorates the events described in it. Anthropologist James Frazer had a similar theory, believing primitive man started out with a belief in magical laws and later, when he began to lose faith in magic, invented myths about gods and claimed his formerly magical rituals were religious rituals intended to appease the gods.

Religious historian Mircea Eliade argued one of the foremost functions of myth is to establish models for behavior and said they may also provide a religious experience, with the idea being by telling or reenacting myths members of traditional societies detach themselves from the present and return to the mythical age - and in doing so bring themselves closer to what they perceive as the divine. Folklorist Lauri Honko asserted that in some cases a society will reenact a myth in an attempt to reproduce the conditions of the mythical age, for example it will reenact the healing performed by a god at the beginning of time in order to heal someone in the present. Similarly, Semioticist (semiotics is the study of signs and symbols and how they are used) Roland Barthes argued modern culture explores religious experience and because it is not the job of science to define human morality a religious experience is an attempt to connect with a perceived moral past which contrasts with the technological present.

Mythologist Joseph Campbell wrote, "In the long view of the history of mankind, four essential functions of mythology can be discerned. The first and most distinctive - vitalizing all - is that of eliciting and supporting a sense of awe before the mystery of being. The second function of mythology is to render a cosmology, an image of the universe that will support and be supported by this sense of awe before the mystery of the presence and the presence of a mystery. A third function of mythology is to support the current social order, to integrate the individual organically with his group; The fourth function of mythology is to initiate the individual into the order of realities of his own psyche, guiding him toward his own spiritual enrichment and realization."

There are comparatively recent examples of this phenomenon which demonstrate how they began and evolved over time. Legends of the American West, for instance, are almost always based upon real people and events but often facts got obfuscated and embellishments were added in the retelling. We aren't sure what is fact or fiction in many cases even though these events only took place a little over a century ago, while in comparison the stories of Jesus had many centuries to develop. Consider the story of Wyatt Earp and the infamous shootout at the O.K. Corral. We all know the story, or at least think we do. The gunfight took place on Wednesday, October 26, 1881 in Tombstone, Arizona and is generally regarded as the most famous gunfight in the history of the American Old West. That much is fact, but despite its current notoriety the event was actually not well known to the American public until 1931 when author Stuart Lake published what has since been determined to be a largely fictionalized biography titled *Wyatt Earp: Frontier Marshal* two years after Earp's death. He retold this story in a 1946 book which director John Ford developed into the movie *My Darling Clementine* but it was only after the movie *Gunfight at the O.K. Corral* was released in 1957 that the shootout came to be known by that name - but despite its name, the gunfight actually occurred in a narrow lot six doors west of the rear entrance to the O.K. Corral on Fremont Street as well as out in the street. Since then the conflict has been portrayed with varying degrees of accuracy in numerous Western films and books such as *Wyatt Earp* and *Tombstone* and no two stories are the same. Many of the facts surrounding the actual events leading up to the gunfight and details of the event itself are uncertain largely because the newspapers of the day were not above taking sides with news reporting often editorializing on issues to reflect the publisher's interests, much like the treatment of the various Gospels by different Christian denominations. Much of what is known of the event is based on a month-long preliminary hearing held afterward generally known as the "Spicer Hearings." Reporters from two newspapers covered the hearings and recorded the testimony at the coroner's inquest but the way they reported what they heard was totally different. According to one version the fight was in self-defense, and the other claimed the Cowboys were shot in cold blood by the Earps. Sorting out who was telling the truth then and now remains difficult if not impossible, but that was not unusual since other western legends such as Billy the Kid, Bat Masterson, Davy Crockett and many others morphed in a similar fashion through the years. The point is the event was comparatively recent, we know the names of the people involved, we have records and eyewitness accounts, we know who recorded it for posterity and yet what actually happened is *still* unclear. So why is it so difficult for some people to accept the fact scriptural stories changed and those changes are the result of time, error and/or intentional bias?

In short storytelling is common to every culture, most people enjoy listening to stories and storytellers have catered to the need for a "good story" since the beginning of civilization - and these stories include legends and myths. As previously discussed a legend is a semi-true story with some basis in fact which has been passed on from person-to-person, has important meaning or symbolism for the culture in which it originates and usually includes an element of truth. Either that or it is based on historical facts but with "mythical qualities" added. For example you probably were taught Thomas Edison invented the lightbulb, Samuel Morse invented the telegraph and Alexander Graham Bell invented the telephone, but those stories are not exactly true. Legends sometimes involve heroic characters or fantastic places and often encompass the spiritual beliefs of the culture in which they originate, while a myth is a story based on tradition or a legend which has a deep symbolic meaning. In contrast a myth "conveys a truth" to those who tell and hear it rather than necessarily recording a true event and although some can be accounts of actual events they have become transformed by symbolic meaning or shifted in time or place and are often used to explain universal and local beginnings and involve supernatural beings. The great power of the meaning of these stories to the culture in which they developed is a major reason why they survive as long as they do - sometimes for thousands of years.

Let's look at a religious example and see if there is reason to believe it. Mormonism originated in the 1820s in western New York during a period of religious excitement known as the Second Great Awakening. Founded by Joseph Smith, Jr., the faith drew its first converts while Smith was allegedly dictating the text of the *Book of Mormon* from Golden Plates he said he found buried on September 22, 1823 at a hill near his home in Manchester, New York after being directed to their location by an angel. Some witnesses described the plates as weighing from thirty to sixty pounds, being golden in color and composed of thin metallic pages engraved on both sides and bound with three D-shaped rings. The book described itself as a chronicle of early indigenous peoples of the Americas (i.e. Native Americans), portraying them as pious Israelites who had a belief in Christ many hundreds of years before his birth. Smith dictated the book of 584 pages over a period of about three months, saying he had translated it from an ancient but unknown language called Reformed Egyptian "by the gift and power of God." He did this by using a "seer stone" which he placed in the bottom of a hat and then placed the hat over his face to view the words written within the stone. Smith published the translation in 1830 as the *Book of Mormon.* After the translation was complete Smith said he returned the plates to the Angel Moroni, therefore if they ever actually existed they cannot now be examined. Latter Day Saints accept the account of the golden plates as a matter of faith, while critics often assert Smith either manufactured the plates himself or the *Book of Mormon* witnesses (to be discussed shortly) based their testimonies on visions rather than an actual physical experience. In any event during production of this work in mid-1829 Smith and his close associate Oliver Cowdery, along with other early followers, began baptizing new converts into a Christian primitivist church formally organized in 1830 as the Church of Christ. As a result of all this Smith was seen by his followers as a modern-day prophet.

Joseph Smith later wrote that he had seen a vision of God the Father and Jesus Christ in the spring of 1820 in answer to his question of which denomination he should join. Sometimes called the "First Vision,"

Smith's vision of God the Father and Jesus Christ as two separate beings was reportedly the basis for the difference in doctrine between Mormonism's view of the nature of God and that of orthodox Christianity. Smith further claimed in answer to his prayer the Lord had instructed him to join none of the existing churches because they were all wrong, during the 1820s reported having several angelic visitations and by 1830 claimed to have been told God would use him to re-establish the true Christian church and the *Book of Mormon* would be the means of establishing correct doctrine for the restored church.

Smith eventually obtained testimonies from eleven men now known as the *Book of Mormon* Witnesses who said they had seen the plates. The "Three Witnesses" were a group of early leaders of the Latter Day Saint movement who wrote in a statement of 1830 that an angel had shown them the golden plates from which Smith translated the *Book of Mormon* and further stated they had heard God's voice testifying that the book had been translated by the power of God. These Three Witnesses were Oliver Cowdery, Martin Harris and David Whitmer and their joint testimony, in conjunction with a separate statement by an additional Eight Witnesses, has been printed with nearly every edition of the *Book of Mormon* since its first publication in 1830.

Unlike the Three Witnesses, "The Eight" testified they saw and handled the plates but said they were shown to them by Joseph Smith rather than by an angel as had "The Three." In the words of LDS historian Richard Bushman, "For most modern readers, the [golden] plates are beyond belief, a phantasm, yet the Mormon sources accept them as fact." Non-believers and some liberal Mormons have advanced naturalistic explanations for the story of the plates, for example it has been theorized they were fashioned by Smith or one of his associates, Smith had the ability to convince others of their existence through illusions or hypnosis or the plates were mystical and should be understood in the context of Smith's historical era when magic was an accepted part of reality... and if magic was accepted during the 1800s, imagine how it must have been viewed two thousand years ago when the Gospels were written.

So why mention Mormon beliefs at all? Because they serve as an excellent point of comparison when considering the historical accuracy of the Gospels. Consider that the events surrounding Mormonism occurred less than two hundred years ago, have had relatively little opportunity to change or be modified over time, involved actual documented persons and were "verified" by signed, sworn attestations.

By way of comparison the stories in the Bible allegedly took place thousands of years in the past, featured many people otherwise unknown to history, were written by largely anonymous authors and must be believed on faith alone. While the existence and authenticity of the golden plates are certainly questionable and only can be verified through hearsay, and as a result are dismissed as legend by nonbelievers and mainstream Christians alike, let's put that into perspective. No more believable is the story of the Ten Commandments, which the Bible tells us were carved into stone tablets by the finger of God himself and presented to the prophet Moses. Like the plates they are nowhere to be found and yet the very same Christians who ridicule belief in the plates readily accept the story of the tablets without question. Why? After all Joseph Smith was a real person, there are even pictures of his likeness and he had witnesses who testified to the truth of his claims, while there is no extra-biblical basis at all for a person named Moses. It makes no sense to an objective observer.

In modern times we have a new version of myth known as urban legends, and thanks to modern technology they tend to spread like wildfire via the internet. For example the headline "Woman's Butt Implants Explode While Doing Squats for an Instagram Workout Video" recently appeared on a fake news website only to be heedlessly picked up by reputable media outlets, thereby initiating what can only be described as a cringe-inducing urban legend.

What leads a piece of modern folklore to gain such traction? Studies have shown humans tend to remember certain kinds of information better than others such as knowledge which might keep us alive or help us find a mate. In one study subjects were asked to read an urban legend, rewrite it from memory and then pass their version to the next person - a sequence resembling a game of telephone. At the end of the chain the legends whose themes could have social or survival related utility such as life after death were recalled most accurately, exactly as evolutionary theory might predict.

One theory of cultural transmission argues stories, myths and religious concepts are most likely to endure when they have enough familiar elements to feel plausible but also have two to three "counterintuitive" elements which make them memorable, a phenomenon known as minimally counterintuitive (MCI) bias. One study analyzed forty-five online versions of the ubiquitous Bloody Mary story which claims chanting "Bloody Mary!" thirteen times in front of a candlelit mirror will summon the vengeful spirit of Mary Worth, a woman who was supposedly executed for being a witch, and found the average number of counterintuitive elements was 2.36.

Suspecting or even knowing an urban legend isn't true won't necessarily inoculate you against its virality because a recent study to be published in the *Journal of Experimental Psychology: General* found that reading a false statement such as, "The Atlantic Ocean is the largest ocean on Earth" made people more likely to rate the statement as true when they encountered it a second time even if they were told on both readings it might be false and even if they later demonstrated they knew the Pacific was in fact the largest ocean. Clearly exposure breeds familiarity, which in turn fosters credulity, even when you know better.

Naturally the internet is rife with religious urban legends which purportedly present evidence for a variety of beliefs and almost without exception these stories are fabricated, and yet the faithful are eager to hit the "forward" button without bothering to fact check because such stories feed their innate desires and appear to bolster preexisting beliefs. These include inspirational tales which hype the astoundingly miraculous, allege the government is planning to curtail religious freedoms if the reader does not sign a petition and forward the message to everyone they know, as well as amazing "historical incidents" such as oil drillers dropping a microphone down a well and hearing the screams of tormented souls in Hell. That the religious are especially gullible when it comes to such things is not surprising, but they would certainly save themselves a lot of embarrassment if they would only do a bit of research on sites designed to vet hoaxes, rumors, myths, fallacies and urban legends such as *Snopes* before forwarding them to less credulous friends who will only laugh and shake their heads. There is even a book titled *Christians Believe the Darndest Things* which examines the foundation of the most pervasive internet myths and gives the true story behind them - but such resources are useless to those who are content to wallow in their own ignorance.

Prophecy

Or, Let Me Look Into My Crystal Ball

"Physics is the only profession in which prophecy is not only accurate, but routine." ~ Neil DeGrasse Tyson

It almost goes without saying the fulfillment of any sort of prophecy, from your daily horoscopes to those in the Bible, largely depends on how one interprets vague allusions and connects them to even more vague events or people. For example the line from Nostradamus, "In the city of York there will be a great collapse, two twin brothers torn apart by chaos" seems perfectly built for 9-11 until you look at the whole thing in context. Thus, although it is possible to identify parallels between Bible verses and subsequently occurring events, alleged prophecy fulfillment is not sufficient to compel belief in the inerrancy of the Bible. In order to believe it is necessary to first accept the Bible and/or Quran or other religious text as true, and since they are filled with so many absurd stories and so much incorrect science the only way to do so is by claiming "fulfilled prophecy" - something which was touched on earlier in this book. Absent that there is no reason for anyone to accept the contention the prophets who wrote them were actually inspired by an omniscient being, and as a result they are cornerstones of faith.

Most world religions, especially the Abrahamic faiths, promote the idea God has spoken to man in the past and present and if they are correct we should find strong evidence that future knowledge was handed down to man in the form of prophecy. It is also claimed God may also have spoken scientific facts to a prophet which he could not possibly have known at the time. As you might guess Christians, Jews and Muslims all believe only their holy books contain such knowledge, and in fact this is a key element to discussing the authenticity and accuracy of holy writings in general and the Bible in particular since there is no other way for apologists to validate the authorship of Scripture other than through knowledge of the future which only an omniscient being could possess. In effect, if they fail to prove the Bible could only have been written by God there is no longer any reason to believe anything contained in it as being true - however a careful examination reveals there is no strong evidence of prophecy and also shows the Bible and Quran and Torah all contain falsehoods concerning both history and science.

Before we can consider a prophecy genuine there are a few standards which must be met.

1) **The prophecy must be specific**. This criterion rules out the vast majority of prophecies. Take for example those in the biblical Book of Revelation which are so vague they have many different interpretations. For instance the number "666" is said to refer to the Roman Emperor Nero by Roman Catholics while Seventh-Day Adventists maintain this number refers to the Pope. Also, in order to be precise the prophecy should give or imply a date by which it is to be fulfilled, otherwise any group can make a prophecy such as "City X will be destroyed" and claim victory for their prophecy if City X is destroyed hundreds or even thousands of years later. Alternately, a group could always claim the prophecy will be fulfilled "sometime in the future" and as a result such a claim would risk nothing. An example of this is in the Book of Ezekiel (Chapter 26) which says the city of Tyre would be completely destroyed by Nebuchadnezzar. This is a false prophecy since Tyre was still standing centuries later when Alexander the Great came through and conquered it.

2) **The prophecy must be made before the prophesied event.** This is another criterion which rules out a very high percentage of alleged prophecies. To be certain a prophecy was made before the predicted event we must have documentation and this documentation must be datable by carbon-dating or some other trusted method to a time well before the event happened. Such prophecies appear accurate because, quite simply, they were actually written after the event they purport to have foreseen. The Book of Daniel is a good example of this. It pretends to have been written during the time of the exile (around the 6th Century BCE) but has been shown to likely have been written around the 2nd Century BCE. Another is Lúcia Santos claiming in 1941 that the Virgin Mary had predicted the 1920 deaths of her two cousins, two decades after it had actually happened.

3) **The prophecy must be verified extra-biblically as having been fulfilled and must not simply appear in the same book as a text containing false prophecies**. We must be able to verify the prophecy came true. It is not enough that it says something in one

part of the Bible and then that "prediction" is "fulfilled" in another part. Using that low standard of proof anyone could "predict" anything. In other words we would not expect a God-given prophecy to predict something other than what actually happened.

4) **The prophecy must not be something which could plausibly be attributed to a guess.** Years before the Soviet Union collapsed many people predicted the collapse itself. This makes sense and was a logical deduction since the Soviet Union had been unstable for years. While there is nothing miraculous about these predictions, any such alleged prophecy must likewise be this specific.

5) **The prophecy must not be self-fulfilling.** A self-fulfilling prophecy is an assumption or prediction which, purely as a result of having been made, causes the expected or predicted event to occur and thus confirms its own "accuracy." The most glaring and commonly cited example of this phenomenon is the formation of the nation of Israel, and today there are those who are actively *trying* to fulfill other prophecies. For example in order for several end time prophecies (Revelation 11:2, Daniel 9:26-27) to be fulfilled the temple in Jerusalem will have to be rebuilt and according to some who just can't seem to wait until the end of the world "there are many groups already working on preparations for the new temple." As if that were not enough, others have been hard at work trying to breed an unblemished red heifer because they believe it is necessary to sacrifice such an animal in order to bring about Armageddon. If those are not self-fulfilling prophecies, I don't know what are.

Christians say we can evaluate the Bible's claims of divine inspiration by whether or not it accurately records actual instances of fulfilled prophecy. CARM (Christian Apologetics and Research Ministry) continues, "If just one prophecy failed, then we would know God is not the true God, because the creator of all things, which includes time, would not be wrong about predicting the future."

So, can we find just one bogus prophecy? Well, here's where it gets tough - choosing *just* one. Let's start in Matthew, who is prolific in his quotation of Old Testament prophecies and his application of them to Jesus. Should we build our case on a passage like Matthew 2:23? It says of Jesus, "And he came and dwelt in the city called Nazareth, that it might be fulfilled which was spoken by the prophets, 'He shall be called a Nazarene.'" The problem with this passage is it makes reference to a prophecy which doesn't even exist. Try as you may you will not find a place in the Old Testament where it unambiguously declares the Messiah would be a Nazarene and even if that were not the case this would fall into the category of self-fulfilling prophecy because the author of Matthew, having read earlier Scriptures, could say Jesus lived anywhere which fell into line with that prediction whether it was true or not.

How about the (in)famous example of Isaiah 7:14? Matthew uses this prophecy as the cornerstone of his Gospel, quoting Isaiah as saying "Behold, the virgin shall be with child." However, the word Matthew translates as "virgin" would be more accurately translated as "young woman." The Jews had a very specific word for virgin (bethulah), but it was not the word Isaiah chose (ha-almah). Further examination of the chapter reveals the promised child of Isaiah 7:14 was actually to be a sign to Ahaz, a Judean king who lived centuries before Jesus was born.

How about Matthew's claim that King Herod slaughtered "all the male children who were in Bethlehem and its vicinity, from two years old and under" (Matthew 2:16). Every Sunday school student knows this story and one Bible class lesson even titles this episode "Babies Give Their Lives for Jesus." Many ministers have searched desperately to substantiate this story with the Jewish histories of Josephus or any secular historian of that era only to realize there is not a shred of historical or archaeological evidence behind it. To add insult to injury, Matthew (or whoever wrote under his name) would have us believe this fanciful tale was a fulfillment of ancient prophecy. He quotes Jeremiah 31:15: "A voice was heard in Ramah, weeping and great mourning, Rachel weeping for her children; and she refused to be comforted, because they were no more." Once again, a careful reading of the entire chapter in its context reveals Jeremiah is talking about a situation far removed from Bethlehem, Herod and the Magi. Jeremiah is instead describing the struggles of the Israelites during the Babylonian Captivity.

Ezekiel 29:8-12 states Egypt will be desolate for forty years, saying "Therefore thus saith the Lord GOD; Behold, I will bring a sword upon thee, and cut off man and beast out of thee. And the land of Egypt shall be desolate and waste; and they shall know that I am the LORD: because he hath said, The river is mine, and I have made it. Behold, therefore I am against thee, and against thy rivers, and I will make the land of Egypt utterly waste and desolate, from the tower of Syene even unto the border of Ethiopia. No foot of man shall pass through it, nor foot of beast shall pass through it, neither shall it be inhabited forty years. And I will make the land of Egypt desolate in the midst of the countries that are desolate, and her cities among the cities that are laid waste shall be desolate forty years: and I will scatter the Egyptians among the nations, and will disperse them through the countries." This passage is one of the most erroneous in the entire Bible since Egypt has never been a desolate waste, there has never been a time when people have not walked through it, there has never been a period of forty years when Egypt was uninhabited and it has never been surrounded by other desolate countries.

Isaiah 17:1-2 says, "Damascus will not be a city any longer; it will be only a pile of ruins. The cities of Syria will be deserted forever. They will be a pasture for sheep and cattle, and no one will drive them away." Because of recent developments in Syria prophecy prognosticators came gleefully out of the woodwork and claimed, "Isaiah 17 was being fulfilled right before our eyes." Things there have since calmed down, and not surprisingly those same people are now nowhere to be found. While Damascus certainly has been sacked numerous times throughout history this prophecy explicitly states it would cease to be a city forever, so the prophecy is explicitly wrong. It is now almost three millennia since that prediction was made and Damascus remains a vibrant city to this day, thus the prophecy which says it will cease to be a city forever is obviously false.

Isaiah 19:5-7 foretold the drying up of all the waters of the Nile and the destruction of all land used for planting as a result saying, "And the waters of the Nile will be dried up, and the river will be parched and dry; and its canal will become foul, and the branches of Egypt's Nile will diminish and dry up, reeds and rushes will rot away. There will be bare places by the Nile, on the brink of the Nile, and all that is sown by the Nile will dry up, be driven away, and be no more." This part of Isaiah, widely accepted by scholars to be written around the 8th Century BCE, is now about 2750 years old and in all this period of two and three quarters millennia this prophecy has yet to be fulfilled. Moreover it is clear from the context that Isaiah's prophecy was meant for the Egypt of his time, for it was that Egypt which Isaiah and his people had a grievance against and the prophecy was meant as a warning to them. This is a clear example of an unfulfilled prophecy.

The aforementioned Book of Daniel is particularly disingenuous and consists of twelve chapters of which only the first half, the narrative portion, concerns us here. Like Jonah its pretense at being a historical work is foiled by the author's poor knowledge of history. That the author, whoever he was, was profoundly ignorant of the history of the 6th

Century BCE can be seen in the following errors regarding the fall of Jerusalem, Belshazzar and the succession of Babylonian kingdoms.

Daniel 1:1-2 says, "In the third year of the reign of Jehoiakim king of Judah, Nebuchadnezzar king of Babylon came to Jerusalem and besieged it. And the Lord gave Jehoiakim king of Judah into his hand, with some of the vessels of the house of God; and he brought them to the land of Shinar, to the house of his god, and placed the vessels in the treasury of his God." That passage is filled with historical errors and anachronisms. First of all he got the name of the king of Judah during the siege wrong. II Kings 8-13 says it was during the reign of Jehoiachin (Jehoiakim's son) that Nebuchadnezzar laid siege to Jerusalem. Furthermore, the third year of Jehoiakim's reign would be 606 BCE and Nebuchadnezzar was not yet king of Babylon at that time. Nebuchadnezzar would become king in 605 BCE, the fourth year of Jehoaikim's reign.

Next, the use of the term "Shinar" is an anachronism since the name was used to refer to Sumeria during the time of Abraham and during the exilic period. Around the time the book of Daniel was supposedly written the correct term would have been Chaldea rather than Shinar. Finally, the correct spelling for the neo-Babylonian king was Nebuchadrezzar. Notice that books actually written during the exilic period such as Jeremiah (25:9) and Ezekiel (26:7) got this spelling right at least some of the time, but Daniel always incorrectly spells the name with an "n" rather than "r." This is the case even in the original Hebrew. It is also interesting to note part of Daniel was written in Hebrew and part in Aramaic, which is hard to explain if one person was the writer.

Next, Daniel 5:1-2 says, "King Belshazzar made a great feast for a thousand of his lords, and drank wine in front of the thousand. Belshazzar, when he tasted the wine, commanded that the vessels of gold and silver which Nebuchadnezzar his father had taken out of the temple in Jerusalem be brought..." This innocent looking passage is simply loaded with historical errors. Belshazzar, or more correctly Bel-shar-utsur ("Bel, Protect the King") was never a king. He was a crown prince but did not become king of Chaldea, for the kingdom collapsed during the reign of his father. Plus Nebuchadnezzar was not the father of Belshazzar and in fact there was no family relation at all between the two. Nebuchadnezzar died in 562 BCE and left the kingdom to his son Amel-Marduk, who in turn was murdered by his brother-in-law Nergal-ashur-usur two years later. Nergal-ashur-usur reigned for only four years and after his death in 560 BCE his son, Nebuchadnezzar's grandson Labashi-Marduk, became king. There was a revolt, Labashi Marduk was dethroned and the new king was Nabu-naido ("Nabu is glorious") or, in its Greek form, Nabudonius. He was not related in any way to Nebuchadnezzar, was the last king of the Chaldean Empire and Belshazzar was actually *his* son.

Now let's examine Daniel 5:30-31 which says, "That very night Belshazzar the Chaldean king was slain. And Darius the Mede received the kingdom..." Again a statement which is historically false. In the first place the Chaldean Kingdom fell not to the Medes but to the Persians in 538 BCE and the King who conquered Chaldea was Cyrus the Persian. There was no historical Darius the Mede who conquered Chaldea. There was however a Persian king name Darius who became king in 521 BCE - seventeen years after the fall of Babylon. Darius was a renowned king in antiquity and it is obvious the author of Daniel erroneously thought he was the conqueror of the Chaldean Empire.

The author of Daniel further revealed his ignorance of history when he wrote in Daniel 9:1, "In the first year of Darius the son of Ahasuerus, by birth a Mede..." If he was referring to the historical Darius the Persian this is another false statement. The father of Darius was Hystaspes, and while Ahasuerus (based on Ezra 4:5-6) can be correctly identified with Xerxes I he was the *son* of Darius, not his father. As a final indictment the author of Daniel wrote in Daniel 6:28, "So this Daniel prospered in the reign of Darius and in the reign of Cyrus the Persian" which is a fitting tribute to Daniel's monumental ignorance of history. The passage clearly shows he believed the Chaldean empire fell first to the Median Empire and in turn fell to the Persians, but history tells us the Chaldean and Median empires existed together and both fell to the Persians.

The book of Daniel is so filled with historical errors and inaccuracies most biblical scholars, excepting the fundamentalists of course, now conclude it was written very much later (between 167 and 164 BCE) than the period it pretends (6th Century BCE). How do they know this? The book could not have been written in the 6th Century BCE because as previously discussed it made errors which anyone living during that time would know. Even more telling is the revealing statement from Daniel 9:2, "I was studying the sacred books and thinking about the seventy years that Jerusalem would be in ruins, according to what the Lord had told the prophet Jeremiah." The prophet Jeremiah lived during the fall of Jerusalem to Nebuchadnezzar in 587 BCE and thus was a very near contemporary of Daniel. The time of the supposed Daniel was simply too soon for the book of Jeremiah to be considered Scripture (i.e. "sacred books") and in fact we know the book of Jeremiah was not canonized and considered Scripture until around 200 BCE. As a result Daniel could not possibly have been written any earlier than that.

Daniel was very accurate however in "predicting" events leading to and including the desecration of the Jerusalem temple by Antiochus in December of 167 BCE, but after this he starts to go wrong again. Daniel 11:45 predicted that Antiochus IV would die "between the sea and the mountain on which the temple stands," i.e. between Jerusalem and the Mediterranean Sea, yet Antiochus IV died in Persia in 164 BCE.

To summarize, Daniel made errors regarding events in the distant past, was remarkably accurate in describing details of the events leading to the desecration of the temple and then made errors about events after that, so it is obvious he must have written at a time after the temple desecration but before the death of Antiochus IV - in short, between 167 and 164 BCE. The question then is why did the author adopt this pretense of writing in the 6th Century BCE? The answer is both simple and obvious. By the time it came to be read many of his so-called "prophecies" would have already been "fulfilled" and thus lend credence to the book and add more weight to prophecies yet to be fulfilled. In a nutshell, the author of Daniel fooled his readers into believing his book was of an ancient origin in order to have them believe his future prophecies. To give a contemporary analogy, if we were to today find a detailed and accurate prophecy about 9-11 dated 1962 (before the WTC was even built) which went on to make predictions about some event in 2058, would it be more likely someone knew in advance what would happen in 2001 and 2058 or that someone had perpetrated a hoax by writing about an event which had already occurred (9-11) and backdated it to lend credence to the prediction about 2058? Think about that.

Historian Robin Fox summarized the Book of Daniel quite aptly when he remarked, "The book (of Daniel) has the familiar ingredients of a biblical success story: its hero probably never existed; he was credited with visions he never saw and actions he never did; ...while its dates and kings are incorrect and its setting is a fiction, posing as history." In short, the author of Daniel was a fraud.

Jeremiah 33:17 says, "David shall never want a man to sit upon the throne of the house of Israel" and Psalms 89:3-4 adds, "I have sworn to David my servant, I will establish your seed forever, and build up your throne for all generations." According to the speaker of this prophecy (i.e. God) a descendant of David will always be on the throne of Israel, but this is obviously not the case since David's line ended twenty-one generations later with Zedekiah, no king returned to David's throne for the next 450 years and no king of David's line has occupied any throne anywhere for the last couple of thousand years.

Isaiah 52:1 proclaims, "Put on your beautiful garments, O Jerusalem, the holy city: from now on no one shall enter you who is uncircumcised or unclean." This failure is pretty self-explanatory as Jerusalem has been filled with many uncircumcised people from the time this prophecy was uttered until this very moment.

Genesis 49:13 tells us, "Zebulon shall dwell at the shore of the sea; he shall become a haven for ships, and his borders shall be at Sidon." This prophecy is said to have been made by Joseph as he lay dying in Egypt, but in actual fact the borders of Zebulon never extended to the sea or reached to the city of Sidon. Amusingly, one Christian apologist named John F. Walvoord acknowledged this in his book *Every Prophecy in the Bible* but went on to rationalize, "Though Zebulon would not actually be bordered on the sea, it would be near enough so that they would benefit from seaborne trade." In other words Walvoord freely admits the prophecy failed but then goes ahead and chalks it up in the "win" column anyway. This is akin to predicting your child will one day live in New York City but when he never gets any closer than Philadelphia rationalize by saying, "Well, he got close enough to pick up a couple of New York radio stations, so same difference."

Isaiah 13:19-22 and Jeremiah 50:39-40 contain the prophecy, "Babylon... shall be as when God overthrew Sodom and Gomorrah. It shall never be inhabited, neither shall it be dwelt in from generation to generation: neither shall the Arabian pitch tent there; neither shall the shepherds make a fold there. But wild beasts of the desert shall lie there; ...and satyrs shall dance there... and her time is near to come, and her days shall not be prolonged." There has never been a time since then during which Babylon (modern day Iraq) was uninhabited since people lived there during New Testament times according to Matthew 1:11-12, 17, Acts 7:43 and I Peter 5:13. Obviously it is still inhabited today, Arabians still visit there, shepherds still make their folds there... and Iraq has never to my knowledge been known for its dancing satyrs.

Genesis 15:18 says, "On that day the LORD made a covenant with Abram and said, 'To your descendants I give this land, from the river of Egypt to the great river, the Euphrates.'" Though Israel's western border never got anywhere close to the Nile river that was still a lot closer than it ever got to the Euphrates to the east.

Isaiah 19:23-24 predicts, "In that day there will be a highway from Egypt to Assyria. The Assyrians will go to Egypt and the Egyptians to

Assyria. The Egyptians and Assyrians will worship together. In that day Israel will be the third, along with Egypt and Assyria, a blessing on the earth." This is yet another one which never happened and it seems rather unlikely to ever occur in the future since Assyria vanished from the earth around 600 BCE.

The New Testament fares little better. In Luke 9:27 Jesus falsely predicts some of his listeners would live to see him return and establish the kingdom of God saying, "But I tell you of a truth, there be some standing here, which shall not taste of death, till they see the kingdom of God," and he makes similar claims in Matthew 16:28 and 25:33-36. The Christian apologist will rationalize he was referring not to the end times but to his resurrection but Mark 9:1 plainly states, "And he said to them, 'I tell you the truth, some who are standing here will not taste death before they see the kingdom of God come with power.'" Since two thousand years has since passed it is clear that not only was this prophecy not fulfilled, it never can be.

Even things which have not occurred are touted by apologists as being fulfilled prophecy through a mechanism of selective observation which rationalizes current events and shoehorns them into the narrative. For example one so-called prophecy concerning the "last days" comes from Revelation 9:13-19 in which John describes an army of two hundred million soldiers crossing the Euphrates River from the east. The rationalization here is that in John's time there were not two hundred million people on the entire earth let alone in one army and although China does not now have an army that size (in actual fact China has an army of less than three million) it *could* at some point produce an army of two hundred million which would make it more than sixty-six times its current strength. This "amazing" claim goes on to tell us John predicted that giant army would be riding horses with breastplates which belch fire, smoke and sulfur from their mouths and would kill a third of all mankind while concluding, "It sounds like John is describing modern warfare with tanks." That is exactly the sort of cryptic revelation which might be attributed to Nostradamus and would be scoffed at for being loony, but since it comes from the Bible, well then, it must be accurate. An even bigger stretch is the assertion from Revelation 13 which describes a one-world government using a cashless money system which works with a mark on each person's hand or forehead. Setting aside the obvious fact we can barely manage to keep nations cooperating in the United Nations let alone form a one world government, the rationalization here is we now use debit cards and an implant would be more practical because it could not be stolen or lost, but whomever came up with this nutty idea seems to be unaware that the vast majority of people on this planet do not even have debit cards or anywhere to use them and for that matter some don't use money in any form.

There are many more examples of unfulfilled prophecy but to list them all is unnecessary and would belabor the point because as CARM correctly pointed out, "If just one prophecy failed, then we would know God is not the true God, because the creator of all things, which includes time, would not be wrong about predicting the future." And yet as we have seen that is what an honest evaluation of the Bible reveals.

The bottom line is human beings are credulous by nature and prepared to believe virtually anything which supports their beliefs. For example in Leeds, England back in 1806 a hen which became known as the "Prophet Hen of Leeds" began laying eggs on which the phrase "Christ is coming" was found to be written but not surprisingly it was eventually discovered to be a hoax. The hoaxer had written on the eggs in a corrosive ink so as to etch them, and had then cruelly reinserted them back into the hen.

According to Charles Mackay's 1841 book *Extraordinary Popular Delusions and the Madness of Crowds,* "Great numbers visited the spot and examined these wondrous eggs, convinced the Day of Judgment was near at hand. Like sailors in a storm, expecting every instant to go to the bottom, the believers suddenly became religious, prayed violently and flattered themselves that they repented them of their evil courses. But a plain tale soon put them down, and quenched their religion entirely. Some gentlemen, hearing of the matter, went one fine morning and caught the poor hen in the act of laying one of her miraculous eggs. They soon ascertained beyond doubt that the egg had been inscribed with some corrosive ink and cruelly forced up again into the bird's body. At this explanation those who had prayed now laughed and the world wagged as merrily as of yore."

Some years later on the other side of the pond Dorothy Martin, a Chicago housewife and student of Dianetics (a set of practices developed by science fiction author and Scientology founder L. Ron Hubbard) predicted the world would end on December 21, 1954. Through a process she called "automatic writing" Martin claimed to have come into contact with beings from the planet Clarion who told her the world would be destroyed by flood and the faithful would be rescued at midnight by flying saucers.

Martin's followers, many of whom had quit their jobs and given away their possessions, gathered in her home to await the aliens. In the meantime her husband, who was a nonbeliever, slept upstairs through the whole thing. To avoid being burned by the flying saucer her followers removed all metal from their persons including zippers and bra straps. As the prophesized midnight hour came and went the group became increasingly agitated and finally at 4:45 AM Martin said she had received yet another message from the Clarions informing her God was so impressed by her group's actions he had changed his mind and decided to spare the earth. As an interesting footnote, the group had been infiltrated by a psychologist named Leon Festinger who used his observations to develop the theory of cognitive dissonance, a subject which is discussed elsewhere in this book.

There are of course many other forms of prophecy such as horoscopes, which are astrological charts or diagrams representing the positions of the sun, moon, planets, astrological aspects and sensitive angles at the time of an event such as the moment of a person's birth. The word "horoscope" itself is derived from Greek words meaning "time" and "observer" and it is used as a method of divination regarding events relating to the point in time it represents and forms the basis of astrology.

In common usage horoscope often refers to an astrologer's interpretation, usually based on a system of solar sign astrology centered strictly on the position of the sun or the calendar significance of an event as is the case in Chinese astrology. Many newspapers and magazines carry predictive columns based on celestial influences in relation to the zodiacal placement of the sun, cusp (two days before or after any particular sign, an overlap) or decante (the month divided into three ten day periods) of a person's month of birth which identify the individual's "star sign."

Not surprisingly, no scientific studies have shown support for the accuracy of horoscopes and the methods used to make interpretations are generally considered pseudo-scientific. In modern scientific framework no known interaction exists which could be responsible for the alleged influence between the apparent position of stars in the sky and a person at the moment of their birth, and all tests done so far which employ a strict control group and proper blinding between experimenters and subjects have shown no effect beyond pure chance. Further, some psychological tests have shown it is possible to construct personality descriptions and foretelling which are generic enough to satisfy most members of a large audience simultaneously. This is referred to as the "Forer" or "Barnum" effect after P. T. Barnum's comment, "We've got something for everyone." These descriptions of their personalities which are supposedly tailored specifically for each of them are in fact vague and general enough to apply to a wide range of people, and even so duped individuals give them high accuracy ratings. In spite of all that, according to a 2009 Harris Poll twenty-six percent of Americans believe in astrology and according to a 2005 Gallup poll a similar percentage believe astrology and/or the position of the planets and stars can affect people's lives... and based on demographics most of those same people *also* believe in Christianity. What does that tell you?

Then there is fortune-telling, which is the practice of predicting information about a person's life. It is in principle identical with divination, with the difference being divination is the term used for predictions considered to be part of a religious ritual such as invoking deities or spirits. Historically fortune-telling has grown out of folkloristic reception of Renaissance magic, specifically that associated with the Romani people. During the 19th and 20th Century methods of divination from non-Western cultures such as the I Ching were also adopted as methods of fortune-telling in western popular culture. Common methods used in Europe and the Americas include astromancy, horary astrology, pendulum reading, spirit board reading, tasseography (reading tea leaves in a cup), cartomancy (fortune telling with cards), tarot reading, crystallomancy (reading of a crystal sphere) and chiromancy (palmistry, reading of the palms). The last three have traditional associations in the popular mind with the Roma and Sinti people who are better known as "gypsies." Another form of fortune-telling sometimes called "reading" or "spiritual consultation" does not rely on specific devices or methods, but rather the practitioner gives the client advice and predictions which are said to have come from spirits or in visions.

Speaking of visions, have you ever wondered why liquors are known as spirits? Two thousand years ago before any kind of mainstream science existed everything was believed to be of magical origin and alcohol was believed to be made of literal spirits because the very adept Greeks realized alcohol evaporated rapidly and figured it did so because it was getting up and going "somewhere else." This may have also been the origin of the concept of a genie since people realized some spirits were more potent than others and created myths that some were very powerful but could be imprisoned in a bottle since they were made of air.

Throughout history artists, poets and such have sought inspiration from "spirits" and thus we have the stereotype of the drunken poet and in modern culture the musician seeking his muse in things such as LSD or THC. In a bit of arcane trivia I came across some years back on this subject the archaic definition of "inspire" was "to breathe into, as by a spirit," so it's not surprising where some of these beliefs came from. All inspiration was once believed to be supernatural, with biblical inspiration being just one example. For example in the Bible when Christ was crucified the apostles were reasonably depressed and then all of a sudden they were running around telling everyone they had seen Christ risen from the dead, but nobody believed them. Some accused them of being drunk and they replied that they were not drunk but instead, "filled with the holy spirit." There may be some truth to that, but not in the way it was intended.

In the eyes of Christians one of the things which irrefutably "proves" Jesus is God is the claim he fulfilled many prophesies from the Old Testament. For example if you look at the website of the *Campus Crusade for Christ* you will find, "More than 300 prophecies like this were made in the Old Testament and then fulfilled through Jesus' life, death and resurrection. The chances of one person fulfilling a mere eight of these prophecies are one in 100,000,000,000,000,000. For one person to fulfill forty-eight of these prophecies, the number becomes staggering -one chance in ten to the 157th power (1 with 157 zeros after it). Add to that the 250 other prophecies and it becomes impossible for any other person except Jesus to ever fit that particular sequence of time and events."

Sounds impressive and authoritative, doesn't it? Three hundred certainly is a huge number of prophesies and Christians put a lot of stock in them, however the "prophesies" Jesus fulfilled are actually a collection of oblique references scattered throughout the Old Testament which some people have interpreted as somehow having something to do with Jesus, although it is not clear why. Let's look at several.

Isaiah 7:1-25 states, "When Ahaz son of Jotham, the son of Uzziah, was king of Judah, King Rezin of Aram and Pekah son of Remaliah king of Israel marched up to fight against Jerusalem, but they could not overpower it. Now the house of David was told, 'Aram has allied itself with Ephraim'; so the hearts of Ahaz and his people were shaken, as the trees of the forest are shaken by the wind. Then the Lord said to Isaiah, 'Go out, you and your son Shear-Jashub, to meet Ahaz at the end of the aqueduct of the Upper Pool, on the road to the Washerman's Field. Say to him, 'Be careful, keep calm and don't be afraid. Do not lose heart because of these two smoldering stubs of firewood-because of the fierce anger of Rezin and Aram and of the son of Remaliah. Aram, Ephraim and Remaliah's son have plotted your ruin, saying, 'Let us invade Judah; let us tear it apart and divide it among ourselves, and make the son of Tabeel king over it.' Yet this is what the Sovereign Lord says: 'It will not take place, it will not happen, for the head of Aram is Damascus, and the head of Damascus is only Rezin. Within sixty-five years Ephraim will be too shattered to be a people. The head of Ephraim is Samaria, and the head of Samaria is only Remaliah's son. If you do not stand firm in your faith, you will not stand at all.' Again the Lord spoke to Ahaz, 'Ask the Lord your God for a sign, whether in the deepest depths or in the highest heights.' But Ahaz said, 'I will not ask; I will not put the Lord to the test.' Then Isaiah said, 'Hear now, you house of David! Is it not enough to try the patience of men? Will you try the patience of my God also? Therefore the Lord himself will give you a sign: The virgin will be with child and will give birth to a son, and will call him Immanuel. He will eat curds and honey when he knows enough to reject the wrong and choose the right. But before the boy knows enough to reject the wrong and choose the right, the land of the two kings you dread will be laid waste. The Lord will bring on you and on your people and on the house of your father a time unlike any since Ephraim broke away from Judah-he will bring the king of Assyria.' In that day the Lord will whistle for flies from the distant streams of Egypt and for bees from the land of Assyria. They will all come and settle in the steep ravines and in the crevices in the rocks, on all the thornbushes and at all the water holes. In that day the Lord will use a razor hired from beyond the River-the king of Assyria-to shave your head and the hair of your legs, and to take off your beards also. In that day, a man will keep alive a young cow and two goats. And because of the abundance of the milk they give, he will have curds to eat. All who remain in the land will eat curds and honey. In that day, in every place where there were a thousand vines worth a thousand silver shekels, there will be only briers and thorns. Men will go there with bow and arrow, for the land will be covered with briers and thorns. As for all the hills once cultivated by the hoe, you will no longer go there for fear of the briers and thorns; they will become places where cattle are turned loose and where sheep run."

I realize that is a lot of information, but ask you to read it closely and then read it again. Much of it is nonsensical to the average person and most people probably cannot get halfway through it without their eyes glazing over, but somewhere in there is an important prophecy of Jesus' life. Can you find it? The sentence is, "Therefore the Lord himself will give you a sign: The virgin will be with child and will give birth to a son, and will call him Immanuel."

According to Christians this sentence prophesizes Jesus will be born of a virgin mother and is one of the three hundred prophecies in the Old Testament which prove Jesus is the son of God. You have just read the entire chapter. Did you see anything which indicates anyone is talking about Jesus? Then there are all the other "prophesies" in this same chapter - the flies and bees, curds and honey, the razor from across the river, the cow and the goats, briers and thorns, etc. What is the relationship between curds and honey and Jesus?

In Hosea 11:1-12 there is another important prophecy about Jesus. "When Israel was a child, I loved him, and out of Egypt I called my son. The more I called them, the more they went from me; they kept sacrificing to the Ba'als, and burning incense to idols. Yet it was I who taught E'phraim to walk, I took them up in my arms; but they did not know that I healed them. I led them with cords of compassion, with the bands of love, and I became to them as one, who eases the yoke on their jaws, and I bent down to them and fed them. They shall return to the land of Egypt, and Assyria shall be their king, because they have refused to return to me. The sword shall rage against their cities, consume the bars of their gates, and devour them in their fortresses. My people are bent on turning away from me; so they are appointed to the yoke, and none shall remove it. How can I give you up, O E'phraim! How can I hand you over, O Israel! How can I make you like Admah! How can I treat you like Zeboi'im! My heart recoils within me, my compassion grows warm and tender. I will not execute my fierce anger, I will not again destroy E'phraim; for I am God and not man, the Holy One in your midst, and I will not come to destroy. They shall go after the LORD, he will roar like a lion; yea, he will roar, and his sons shall come trembling from the west; they shall come trembling like birds from Egypt, and like doves from the land of Assyria; and I will return them to their homes, says the LORD. E'phraim has encompassed me with lies, and the house of Israel with deceit; but Judah is still known by God, and is faithful to the Holy One."

Read it, and read it again. Once again the material is nonsensical. Verse 1 is the prophecy which supposedly says Jesus will be called out of Egypt after God sends him there to avoid the murder of thousands of babies, but do you see anything which indicates we are talking about Jesus besides the random pair of words "my son"? Even verse 2 makes no sense. Then there are all the other "prophesies" in this same chapter - the Ba'als, the incense, E'phraim, the bands of love, the return to the land of Egypt, the kingdom of Assyria, the sword, the yoke, Admah, Zeboi'Im, the lion, the birds, the doves of Assyria and so on. What is the relationship between all of that and Jesus?

In Zechariah 9:1-13 there is a prophecy which supposedly says Jesus will ride into Jerusalem on a donkey. "The word of the Lord is against the land of Hadrach and will rest upon Damascus - for the eyes of men and all the tribes of Israel are on the Lord - and upon Hamath too, which borders on it, and upon Tyre and Sidon, though they are very skillful. Tyre has built herself a stronghold; she has heaped up silver like dust, and gold like the dirt of the streets. But the Lord will take away her possessions and destroy her power on the sea, and she will be consumed by fire. Ashkelon will see it and fear; Gaza will writhe in agony, and Ekron too, for her hope will wither. Gaza will lose her king and Ashkelon will be deserted. Foreigners will occupy Ashdod, and I will cut off the pride of the Philistines. I will take the blood from their mouths, the forbidden food from between their teeth. Those who are left will belong to our God and become leaders in Judah, and Ekron will be like the Jebusites. But I will defend my house against marauding forces. Never again will an oppressor overrun my people, for now I am keeping watch. *Rejoice greatly, O Daughter of Zion! Shout, Daughter of Jerusalem! See, your king comes to you, righteous and having salvation, gentle and riding on a donkey, on a colt, the foal of a donkey.* I will take away the chariots from Ephraim and the war-horses from Jerusalem, and the battle bow will be broken. He will proclaim peace to the nations. His rule will extend from sea to sea and from the River to the ends of the earth. As for you, because of the blood of my covenant with you, I will free your prisoners from the waterless pit. Return to your fortress, O prisoners of hope; even now I announce that I will restore twice as much to you. I will bend Judah as I bend my bow and fill it with Ephraim. I will rouse your sons, O Zion, against your sons, O Greece, and make you like a warrior's sword."

Once again this material is irrelevant and nonsensical. The "prophecy" is contained in verse 9 (italicized). Do you see anything there which indicates we are talking about Jesus? In Micah Chapter 5 verse 2 there is a "prophecy" Jesus will be born in Bethlehem. "Now you are walled about with a wall; siege is laid against us; with a rod they strike upon the cheek the ruler of Israel. *But you, O Bethlehem Eph'rathah, who are little to be among the clans of Judah, from you shall come forth for me one who is to be ruler in Israel, whose origin is from of old, from ancient days.* Therefore he shall give them up until the time when she who is in travail has brought forth; then the rest of his brethren shall return to the people of Israel. And he shall stand and feed his flock in the strength of the LORD, in the majesty of the name of the LORD his God. And they shall dwell secure, for now he shall be great to the ends of the earth. And this shall be peace, when the Assyrian comes into our land and treads upon our soil, that we will raise against him seven shepherds and eight princes of men; they shall rule the land of Assyria with the sword, and the land of Nimrod with the drawn sword; and they shall deliver us from the Assyrian when he comes into our land and treads within our border."

Look closely at this "prophecy." There is the wall, the siege, the rod, the cheek, the flock, the Assyrians, the Nimrods, the sword, the seven shepherds, the eight princes and so on - the only things missing are three French hens, two turtle doves and a partridge in a pear tree. Once again all of this material is irrelevant. There is something else you may notice. Look at the phrase, "With a rod they strike upon the cheek the ruler of Israel." Let's say that at some point in the Gospels Pontius Pilate had struck Jesus with a rod on the cheek. If that had happened Micah 5:1 might be a prophecy about Jesus' coming but since he is never struck on the cheek with a rod in the New Testament that "prophecy" is never mentioned. The only recourse Christian apologists have to that omission is the rationalization that not mentioning it does not mean it didn't happen. Once you understand that, you completely understand the "three hundred fulfilled prophecies of Jesus."

The Old Testament contains thousands and thousands of words, most of them nonsense, and out of those thousands of words you are going to find some which happen to match up with New Testament accounts of Jesus in some obscure way, however you are going to find far more like the rod and cheek, curds and the honey, razor from across the river, Nimrods and all the rest which do not. If you look for ones which seem to randomly match up and ignore the thousands which do not you can claim the Old Testament prophesizes the coming of Jesus, but an objective person sees it all as gibberish. These prophecies are the product of a process known as hermeneutics which determines how Scripture is to be interpreted, something discussed elsewhere.

Christians claim over and over, "Jesus' coming was prophesized hundreds of times in the Old Testament, centuries before his birth, the only way that could have happened is if God wrote the Bible and Jesus was sent by God and the chances of one man fulfilling all of these prophecies together are infinitesimally small, so Jesus *must* be God." But how many people ever actually take the time to read the Bible and check out these "prophecies" or examine their context? They are scattered far and wide throughout the Old Testament without a single thing tying them together and absolutely nothing to indicate they point to Jesus, and there are thousands of other prophesies which never came to pass and are therefore ignored. These prophecies are as random and arbitrary as a horoscope in the newspaper and so vague and filled with irrelevant material that they are completely meaningless. Therefore, as CARM correctly pointed out, "If just one prophecy failed, then we would know God is not the true God."

Explaining the Unexplainable

Or, It's a Miracle!

"A miracle signifies nothing more than an event... the cause of which cannot yet be explained by another familiar instance, or.... which the narrator is currently unable to explain." ~ Baruch Spinoza

In the 1960s the expansion New York Mets were the laughingstock of Major League Baseball and were referred to as the "Amazin' Mets," a nickname coined by manager Casey, because they were so awful. In their first seven seasons the Mets had never finished higher than ninth place in the ten team National League, had never had a single winning season and had in fact lost at least one hundred games in five of their seasons, but in 1969 they went 100–62 to win the Eastern Division of the National League, beat the Western Division champion Atlanta Braves in the National League Championship Series and went on to defeat the heavily favored American League champion Baltimore Orioles in the World Series. In the process they became known as the "Miracle Mets."

Similarly, in the medal round of men's ice hockey during the 1980 Winter Olympics at Lake Placid the United States national team, made up exclusively of amateur and collegiate players, defeated the powerful Soviet Union national team which had won the gold medal in six of the seven previous Olympics including the previous four dating back to 1964. In the last exhibition game before the Games the Americans were crushed by the Soviets at Madison Square Garden by a score of 10-3 so nobody gave them a chance in the Olympics and ever since their improbable victory has been known as the "Miracle on Ice" in American popular culture with a movie by the same name being made in 1981.

In today's world words like "star" and "hero" tend to get bandied about so much they have become virtually meaningless and the word "miracle" is little different because people are confusing the impossible with the improbable. As a result before anyone attempts to use the Argument From Miracles they must define what they think a "miracle" is and why because if they cannot explain why a natural cause for an event is impossible their argument won't work and if they cannot explain how they can distinguish between, for instance, rainfall which occurred naturally and rainfall which occurred due to supernatural intervention their argument is equally ineffective.

Saint Thomas Aquinas spoke of three types of miracles - God doing something which nature could never do (e.g. creation *ex nihilo*), God doing something which nature could do but not in order (i.e. nature can give life but not after physical death) and God doing something which nature could do in order without the usual mediating event(s) or time (i.e. a broken bone healing overnight). I suspect a hypothetical limb regeneration miracle such as those discussed in a previous chapter would be a miracle of the second type since nature can grow limbs but not after amputation, at least in the case of mammals, so we can say limbs growing back spontaneously after amputation, if it were to occur, would be a category two miracle.

Even if we grant that a "miraculous" event is indeed exceptional enough to warrant an exceptional explanation it cannot be assumed this supports theism. We could for example postulate the event was caused by the incredible power of human minds rather than the incredible power of a god's mind. This explanation is no less credible and in fact has the advantage because we know human minds actually exist whereas the existence of a god's mind is questionable. The point is if someone is going to advance a supernatural, paranormal or unusual explanation for an exceptional event they have to be willing to first consider every other supernatural, paranormal or unusual explanation.

The question which thus faces the believer is how can we possibly compare all of these different explanations? How on earth can one reasonably support the idea something occurred because of a god rather than human telepathy or ghosts or extraterrestrials? Unless the believer is able to show why their supernatural explanation is preferable to all the others their claim fall flat. This cuts to the very nature of what a valid explanation is. When you can't show why your attempted explanation does a better job than another you reveal what you are saying does not really explain anything at all and does not lead us to better understand the nature of the event and our universe in general.

Another problem with the Argument From Miracles is something which argues for the existence of "a" god does not necessarily support the likely existence of any particular one, but although this is a problem for many arguments it does not immediately appear to be the case in this instance because while any god might have created the universe, it seems likely only the Christian God would be causing miraculous healings in Lourdes. The difficulty here lies in the fact every religion seems to make claims of miraculous events. If one religion's claims are correct and that religion's god exists what is the explanation for all the miracles claimed by other religions? After all, it seems unlikely the Christian God was causing miraculous healings in the name of ancient Greek gods at one time so any attempt to rationally explain away the miracle claims of other religions opens the door for similar explanations for yours, and any attempt to explain away other miracles as the work of Satan undermines the truth claims of the religion in question.

When assessing claims about miracles it is important to consider how we judge the likelihood of any reported event. When someone tells us something happened we need to weigh three general possibilities against each other - the event happened exactly as reported, some event happened but the report is somehow inaccurate or we are simply being lied to. Without knowing anything about the reporter we have to make our judgments based upon two other things - the importance of the claim and the likelihood of the claim happening.

When claims aren't very important our standards don't need to be as high and the same is true when the reported event is mundane. This can be illustrated by three similar examples. Imagine I told you I visited Canada last month. How likely is it you would doubt my story? Probably not very since people visit Canada all the time so it's not hard to believe I did as well. And what if I didn't actually go? Does it really matter? In such a case my word is enough to believe. Imagine however I am a suspect in a murder investigation and claim I couldn't have committed a crime because I was visiting Canada when it occurred. Once again, how likely is it you would doubt my story? Doubts would come more easily this time because although it is still not difficult to imagine me in Canada the consequence of error is much more serious, thus you'll need more than just my word to believe my story, will request more proof in the form of tickets and such and the stronger the evidence is against me as a suspect the stronger the evidence you will demand for my alibi. In this instance we can see how the increasing importance of an event causes our standards for believing to grow stricter. Finally, imagine I am once again claiming to have visited Canada but instead of using normal transportation say I traveled there using a Star Trek style transporter beam. Unlike the second example the mere fact I was in Canada now isn't so important and is still very believable, but while the importance of the claim being true is low the likelihood is as well and because of this you would be justified in demanding quite a bit more than just my word before believing me.

Of course there is a tangential issue of importance too. While the immediate claim might not itself be important, the implication that travel via energy beam is possible is quite significant because it is so unlikely given the current level of scientific understanding. This dictates how strict our standards for belief of this claim must be and as a result we are justified in approaching different claims with differing standards of evidence since in the words of Carl Sagan, "Extraordinary claims require extraordinary evidence."

Where to miracles fall into this spectrum? According to famed Scottish philosopher David Hume they fall way out at the end of the unlikely and unbelievable. In fact according to Hume reports of miracles are never believable because the possibility of a miracle actually having happened is always lower than the possibility the reporter is somehow mistaken or simply lying and because of this we should always assume one of the two latter options is more likely true. Although he may be going too far in suggesting miracle claims are never believable Hume makes a good case that the likelihood of a miracle claim being true is vastly inferior to the likelihood of the other two options in accordance with Occam's Razor. In light of this anyone claiming the truth of a miracle has a significant burden of proof to overcome.

We can thus see the Argument From Miracles fails to offer a solid and rational basis for theism. First, the very definition of a miracle makes it almost impossible to demonstrate a miracle claim is credible and second miracles are so unlikely in comparison to other possible alternatives that accepting the truth of a miracle would require a miraculous amount of evidence. Indeed, the truth of a miracle is so unlikely that if one turned out to be true that in and of itself would be a miracle. As Elbert Hubbard wrote in *The Philistine,* "A miracle is an event described by those to whom it was told by people who did not see it." That is a perfect explanation for the ones found in the Gospels.

Let's look at a recent example of a claimed miracle, the 2010 Copiapó mining accident also known as the "Chilean mining accident," which occurred at the San José copper-gold mine in northern Chile. The buried men who became known as "the thirty" were trapped deep underground and survived for a record sixty-nine days before their rescue. Due to the mine's history it was originally thought the miners had probably not survived the collapse or would starve to death before they were found. Chile had just endured two major "Acts of God," the 2010 earthquake and its associated tsunami, which happened less than six months before the accident. The Chilean people's strong empathy for the workers and their grief-stricken families and the nation's outpouring of public concern led the national government to take over the faltering search and rescue operation from the mine's financially strapped owners. With those significant resources the state-owned mining company was able to hastily drill eight exploratory boreholes in an attempt to find the miners. Out of date mine shaft maps complicated rescue efforts, and several drifted off target due to the extreme drilling depth and the notoriously hard rock which exacerbated the drills' tendency to drift. Fourteen days into the rescue operation one of the probes reached a space where the miners were believed to be trapped and found no signs of life, but seventeen days after the accident a note from the trapped workers appeared taped to a drill bit when it was pulled to the surface.

Once the rescuers knew the men were alive Chile implemented a comprehensive plan to rescue the miners which included the deployment of three large international drilling teams, nearly every Chilean government ministry, the expertise of the NASA space agency and more than a dozen multi-national corporations from nearly every continent. Private donations covered one-third of the twenty million dollar cost of the rescue, with the rest coming from the mine owners and government.

The trapped miners, most of whom were Roman Catholic, asked for religious items including Bibles, crucifixes, rosaries and statues of the Virgin Mary and other saints to be sent down to them and set up a makeshift chapel in the mine. Mario Gómez, the eldest miner, spiritually counseled his companions, led daily prayers and a number of the men later attributed religious significance to what transpired. Mónica Araya, the wife of the first man rescued, noted, "We are really religious, both my husband and I, so God was always present. It is a miracle, this rescue was so difficult, it's a grand miracle." As one story in the British newspaper *Daily Mail* reported, "A deep religious faith powered this rescue; miners and families and rescuers alike believe their prayers were answered." Government representatives and the Chilean public credited Divine Providence with keeping the miners alive while the Chilean public viewed their subsequent rescue as a miracle. Chile's President Sebastián Piñera stated, "When the first miner emerges safe and sound, I hope all the bells of all the churches of Chile ring out forcefully, with joy and hope. Faith has moved mountains."

A tent city called Camp Hope sprang up in the desert as word of the mine's collapse spread and many members of the miners' families arrived there, lit candles and prayed almost constantly for the men. According to Jose Henriquez, one of the miners, their rescue was a miracle "even atheists could not deny." When it became evident only a miracle would get them out alive Henriquez, known as the pastor of the group, said the men approached him to guide them in prayer. The miners came from different denominations and some were atheists, but he said all took part in the prayer meetings. "We all were praying, 'Lord open up a door of escape. There's no other way unless you do it.' The first big test of faith came when the first drill missed the mark, but rather than giving up it only spurred us to pray harder that God would help the rescuers locate us. When the second drill came down, it glanced off a rock at just the right angle to enter the chamber we were in. Everyone, even atheists, agreed that it was a miracle." Television cameras captured the moment Henriquez and the other miners emerged one by one from the rescue capsule wearing T-shirts saying 'Thank you God,' with some getting down on their knees to pray. Sounds pretty compelling, doesn't it? Still, it is odd there was no mention of the massive rescue effort and its many human participants. Let's put this event into perspective.

Another mine disaster, the Upper Big Branch Mine disaster in Raleigh County, West Virginia, also occurred in 2010 but turned out quite differently with twenty-nine of thirty-one miners being killed. There were two rescue chambers - ventilated rooms with basic supplies for survival - in the mine but high levels of methane and carbon monoxide were detected which forced the team of rescuers to higher ground and delayed the search. By April 7th eleven bodies had been recovered while fourteen still had not been found, and although there were no indications the four missing miners were still alive operations continued in rescue mode. Governor Joe Manchin of West Virginia said at the time, "Everyone is praying and holding on to the hope that is their father, their son," but on the morning of April 8th the rescue efforts were suspended due to dangerous levels of methane in the mine. There was no miracle and references to God were nowhere to be found.

The Pike River Mine disaster was yet another mining accident in 2010, this one in New Zealand. At the time of the explosion thirty-one miners and contractors were present in the mine. Two managed to walk from the shaft, but the remaining twenty-nine died five thousand feet from the mine's entrance. Once again there was no miracle and no mention of God.

The Sago Mine disaster was a coal mine explosion in January of 2006 in Upshur County, West Virginia which trapped thirteen miners for nearly two days. Rescue operations were underway when news came to some of the relatives who were waiting and desperately praying at the

Sago Baptist Church. A man burst up to the front of the church shouting, "They're alive!" and everyone was instantly on their feet, pressing their hands to their mouths or clenching their hair or one another's shoulders. Hollering and joyful screaming begin to swirl around the room until everyone was caught up in it. The church bells start to clang. Men were dancing. Everywhere people shouted, "The Lord is merciful! Praise God! Praise Jesus!" Relatives ran out of the building screaming in delight shouting "They're alive! They're alive!" A group of several hundred then broke into a chorus of the hymn *How Great Thou Art*. Governor Manchin started crying and stooped to hug one of the wives saying, "I told you miracles happen in West Virginia!" He said it to everyone he saw and gave everyone a thumbs-up. "It is a miracle, there's no other explanation," the governor told several major news organizations by phone and half of America's daily newspapers had the miracle story on their front pages the next morning - but they were wrong.

Anger and grief replaced jubilation as the families of the trapped miners learned initial reports of the men's survival were wrong and all but one had died. John Groves, whose brother Jerry was one of the trapped miners, said the families' hopes had been dashed when Ben Hatfield, CEO of the company which owned the mine, said there had been "a lack of communication, that what we were told was wrong and that only one survived." Chaos broke out in the church and a fight started. Tamila Swiger, a Red Cross volunteer, told CNN people were breaking down and suffering panic attacks.

The sole survivor, Randal McCloy Jr., was taken to the hospital in serious condition while the rest of the miners were found together near an air hole the company had drilled in an attempt to contact them. They were behind a barrier they had built to block the gas, indicating they had survived the blast. "I think we can confirm with certainty the miners survived for a certain amount of time, but we have no way of knowing exactly how long," Hatfield said.

Of course there are other sorts of disasters besides those which take place in mines where God might intervene. On January 15, 2009, US Airways Flight 1549 piloted by Captain Chesley B. "Sully" Sullenberger made an unpowered emergency water landing in the Hudson River after multiple bird strikes caused both jet engines to fail. All 155 passengers and crew successfully evacuated from the partially submerged airframe as it sank into the river and were rescued by nearby watercraft, with several suffering injuries but only one requiring hospitalization overnight. The incident came to be known as the "Miracle on the

Hudson" and Captain Sullenberger was soon regarded as a hero by some accounts… but naturally some of the passengers were praying, so others took the miracle headline to heart and gave all of the credit to God. So let's look at a different flight from around that same time.

On February 12, 2009, just twenty-eight days after the Miracle on the Hudson, Colgan Air Flight 3407 crashed while enroute from Newark, New Jersey to Buffalo, New York after entering an aerodynamic stall from which it did not recover and crashing into a house in Clarence Center, New York, killing all forty-nine passengers and crew as well as one person inside the house. There is little doubt many if not all of the people aboard that aircraft were frantically praying as it hurtled towards the ground, so what happened? Where was the miracle this time? Where was God?

What we have here is a blatant example of selective observation. If everything works out God gets the credit, the survivors sing his praises, books are written and movies are made as was the case with the Chilean mine collapse, but if things go badly a heavy dose of apologetics telling us God "works in mysterious ways" and "has purposes we cannot understand" must be applied and the incident is wiped from the memory banks. If you think that is cynical consider this - most people have heard about the Miracle on the Hudson and the Chilean mine rescue but how many are familiar with or remember the Non-Miracles in Clarence Center and Upshur County? How about you?

Transubstantiation

Or, Swallow the Leader

☥☸☯⛩ॐ✋☸✡✝☪☬🔥✡⚕☤⚛☸♆☸

"[Religion] allows perfectly decent and sane people to believe by the billions what only lunatics could believe on their own. If you wake up tomorrow morning thinking that saying a few Latin words over your pancakes is going to turn them into the body of Elvis Presley, you have lost your mind. But if you think more or less the same thing about a cracker and the body of Jesus, well, you're just a Catholic."
~ Sam Harris

Sacrifice was a common theme in Central American cultures and although human sacrifice is the most talked about there were actually many types practiced. The people believed they owed a blood-debt to the gods and wanted to avert disaster by paying the endless debt. Blood was a common theme - it was the sacrifice the gods required - so animals were sacrificed as well as humans. In the Aztec *Legend of the Five Suns* it was believed all of the gods sacrificed themselves so that mankind could live, so for each ritual at least one of the victims took on the paraphernalia, habits and attributes of the god or goddess whom they were dying to honor or appease and in the process became the Aztec equivalent of a celebrity, being greatly revered and adored to the point of people "kissing the ground" when he passed by. And of course the Aztecs were famous for eating the still beating hearts of their "honorees." In fact in some societies, especially tribal societies, cannibalism has been a cultural norm and it was sometimes done as part of a religious ritual. Sounds pretty bizarre, doesn't it? I mean the whole idea of someone having to die to pay a blood debt to placate a god, and of someone eating human flesh and drinking their blood.

So why bring up pagan sacrifices and cannibalism, you may ask? Elsewhere we discussed the phenomenon known as Cafeteria Catholics - people who pick and choose what parts of their faith to accept while ignoring other aspects which are either inconvenient or uncomfortable - but there is another reason this happens. Many don't even know about or understand much of the dogma which they claim to believe in and the doctrine of transubstantiation is a good example of that.

For the benefit of the uninitiated, transubstantiation is the belief in some Christian denominations, primarily the Catholic Church, that the bread and wine given at Communion becomes the actual body and blood of Jesus Christ when they are blessed, although their appearance is not altered. As someone who was raised Catholic and took Communion on numerous occasions I think it would have been nice if someone had told me I was essentially engaging in cannibalism before putting the Eucharist wafer in my mouth because absent that explanation I naturally and understandably thought the whole "this is my body, this is my blood" thing was purely symbolic. For a long time I thought it had been a simple oversight until years later when I discussed the subject with a friend who is a practicing Catholic and also ignorant of the doctrine, When I explained it to her she refused to believe me so I suggested she ask her parish priest, but I doubt she ever did because sometimes people prefer comfort to truth. As it turns out she is not alone in her ignorance. A nationwide poll conducted by the Pew Research Center in 2010 found more than four-in-ten Catholics (45%) do not know their church teaches the bread and wine used in Communion do not merely symbolize, but are actually believed to become, the actual body and blood of Christ.

The Catholic Church also teaches sterilization, artificial contraception and abortion are intrinsically immoral and Catholics cannot be involved in them period, and yet people professing to be Catholics do those things all the time. Nearly fifty percent of married Christian-Catholics get divorced at some point which flies in the face of biblical teachings and many use birth control or engage in homosexual relationships, while other doctrines such as the prohibition against eating meat on Friday have since been inexplicably modified or eliminated. So the question is if you don't think the wafer turns into Jesus or choose not to follow other tenets of Church doctrine, are you really a Catholic?

An *Irish Times* poll found many Catholics in Ireland don't believe in some tenets of their own faith. In that survey a total of eighty-nine per cent of respondents were Catholic and the remainder were either not religious (six percent), Protestant (three per cent) or of other faiths. It showed that when it comes to the church's teachings many Catholics do not subscribe to key tenets such as transubstantiation with almost two-thirds (sixty-two percent) believing the blessing of bread and wine during Mass only represents the body and blood of Christ while just over a quarter (twenty-six percent) believe it is transformed. In other words only twenty-six percent of Irish Catholics believe what the Catholic Church teaches - that after being blessed, the wafer and wine become the actual body and blood of Christ.

Richard Dawkins remarked on that discrepancy with what should have been a non-controversial statement when he observed, "If they don't believe in transubstantiation then they are not Roman Catholics… if they are honest they should say they are no longer Roman Catholics." That makes sense. Maybe someone can call themselves a cultural Catholic, a non-practicing Catholic, a bad Catholic or just a run of the mill Christian, but you're not a true Catholic if you deny one of the basic Sacraments. It's the same reason I don't call myself a Jain - if I don't believe in supernatural deities or the afterlife or karma or reincarnation, i.e. what the faith tells me I'm supposed to believe, I don't belong in that faith and for that matter if you don't believe Jesus came back to life three days after Crucifixion you have no business calling yourself a Christian. Dawkins didn't say anything wrong, and yet some Catholics are taking him to task for it and in doing so make no sense at all.

Colum Kenny of the *Independent* backtracked and said of course Catholics don't believe in transubstantiation but "…generations of Irish people have found consolation and meaning in the act of Communion, while not understanding or not fully accepting convoluted medieval theories about it. Such Christians have been as much a part of the Church as is any bishop. Such an idea of "transubstantiation" seems barbaric to some people, with its echoes of human sacrifice and cannibalism, and simply unnecessary to others. Transubstantiation never made much sense to many believers. It makes even less sense today unless it can be reinterpreted and integrated into our scientific knowledge of physics and psychology."

Well, no kidding it doesn't make sense. It's a silly theory which never had any substance to it but it is still part of Catholicism and any basic understanding of the faith includes accepting that particular belief. I don't see how you can deny it and still claim you are a Catholic.

Irish Times columnist John Waters took a different angle on this story by pinning the blame for this discrepancy on bad polling saying, "… when Ipsos MRBI conducts a survey on behalf of *The Irish Times*, how many believe that the views of its sample of 1,000 people are representative of those of the entire population? Does 'rationality' involve a requirement to understand the processes you claim to believe in or trust? If so, how many people could tell you, off the top of their heads, that the margin of error in any particular aspect of an opinion poll is calculated by multiplying by two the square root of the result obtained when the quantum at issue is multiplied by 100 minus itself and the answer divided by the sample? Give me transubstantiation any day - much easier on brain, mind and reason."

Waters doesn't like the results of a poll so he blames the math for being difficult? Someone needs to teach him how statistics and surveys work. Meanwhile transubstantiation requires little thought, so he'll take it. Sounds like the typical religious mindset. And in fact the small margin of error for the poll means it is pretty reliable.

Transubstantiation, unlike math, isn't based in evidence because the makeup of the wafer and wine don't change before and after a blessing although according to the *Catholic Encyclopedia* it is based on "proof from Scripture" and "proof from tradition." It's all about belief, and if you don't believe it's actually the body and blood of Christ you're denying your own faith. Taken a bit further, if you don't agree with everything the Catholic Church dictates you might indeed still be Christian but you don't belong in the Catholic Church so you might as well just take the next step and abandon the Church altogether.

Forget transubstantiation for a moment. What about the articles which came out a while ago about how so many Catholic women are taking birth control? Are they really Catholic? You could argue that even if Church leaders were against it they were misinterpreting what the Bible says, or that not using birth control isn't one of the "official rules" of being Catholic. I'm not saying I buy those arguments, but those are some of the ways around it.

Perhaps you might argue being a Catholic is like being a Republican. There are Republicans who don't necessarily like the current ideology of the GOP (i.e. Andrew Sullivan), and even though people might accuse him of being a RINO (Republican In Name Only) I think it's fair to point out Republicans today are very different from Republicans a few decades ago since platforms change and can change back. Unlike politics however, religious beliefs aren't supposed to be flexible. Different faiths have different rules you must follow and if you break the rules for your faith you can call yourself an adherent all you want but you're lying to yourself if you do.

Dawkins is right. It's time for people who don't believe the tenets of their supposed faith to be honest and admit it. Stop saying you belong to faith X when you don't believe what faith X teaches. There may be ambiguity in some cases such as the evangelical Christian debate over whether or not women should be able to take on leadership roles, but every faith has rules which are all or nothing and you either accept them or you don't.

There is no ambiguity when it comes to transubstantiation. If you don't believe you're eating Jesus when you play "swallow the leader" stop deluding yourself and shed the Catholic label, and now that I think about it I think the Church must be keeping the rank and file in the dark intentionally because even they know the concept is ridiculous and will make their creed less believable if people knew about it… but of course it is now too late to change and they are stuck with the absurdity.

The Slave Trade

Or, Uncle Yahweh's Cabin

"The slave should be resigned to his lot, for in obeying his master he is obeying God." ~ Saint John Chrysostom, commenting on I Timothy 6:1-5 and other biblical mandates for human slavery

Sir John Hawkins had the dubious distinction of becoming the first slave-ship captain to bring Africans to the Americas. Hawkins was a religious gentleman who insisted that his crew "serve God daily" and "love another." His ship, ironically called "the good ship *Jesus*," left the shores of his native England for Africa in October 1562. He arrived at Sierra Leone and in a short time had three hundred blacks in his possession. Hawkins claimed to have acquired them "partly by sword and partly by other means."

Hawkins wrote a description of a typical slave raid at Cape Verde in 1564 saying, "I assaulted the town, both by land and sea, and very hardly with fire (their houses being covered with dry palm leaves) obtaining the town, put the inhabitants to flight, where we took two hundred and fifty persons, men, women and children." An officer on the ship added, "In the cargo there were over seven hundred men, women, boys and young girls. Not even a waist cloth can be permitted among slaves aboard ship, since clothing even so light would breed disease. To ward off death I ordered that at daylight the Negroes should be taken in squads of twenty and given a salt-bath by the hose pipe... And when they were carried below, trained slaves received them one by one, and laying each creature on his side, packed the next against him, and so on, till, like so many spoons packed away, they fitted onto one another, a living mass."

What has come to be referred to as "the good ship *Jesus*" was in fact *Jesus of Lubeck*, a 700-ton ship purchased by King Henry VIII from the Hanseatic League, a merchant alliance between the cities of Hamburg and Lubeck in Germany. Twenty years after its purchase the ship, in disrepair, was leant to Sir John Hawkins by Queen Elizabeth. Hawkins, a cousin of Sir Francis Drake, was granted permission by the Queen for his first voyage in 1562. He was allowed to carry Africans to the Americas "with their own free consent" and he agreed to this condition. Drake, who accompanied Hawkins on this voyage and subsequent others, was himself devoutly religious and services were held on board twice a day.

A bound slave adorns John Hawkins' coat of arms. Off the coast of Africa near Sierra Leone he captured 300-500 slaves, mostly by plundering Portuguese ships, but also through violence and subterfuge by promising Africans free land and riches in the new world. He sold most of the slaves in what is now known as the Dominican Republic and returned home with a profit and a ship laden with ivory, hides and sugar. Thus began the British slave trade.

On his return to England a livid Queen Elizabeth assailed Hawkins, charging that his endeavor "was detestable and would call down vengeance from Heaven upon the undertakers." When Elizabeth became fully aware, however, of the profits to be made she joined in partnership with Hawkins and provided him with *Jesus of Lubeck* for future voyages. Let's now look at how the practice of slavery was justified in the New World.

Frederick Douglass started his life as a slave, born to a slave mother in 1818 at a time when slavery was practiced almost universally throughout the United States, but at the age of twenty he was able to escape, educate himself and transcend his humble origins - and that transformation gave him a unique perspective on slavery. Douglass wrote an autobiography entitled *Narrative of the Life of Frederick Douglass* in which he described many of his experiences in graphic detail. He was a person who had experienced the atrocities firsthand, describing the violence of his master in this way: "He was a cruel man, hardened by a long life of slaveholding. He would at times seem to take great pleasure in whipping a slave. I have often been awakened at the dawn of day by the most heart-rending shrieks of an own aunt of mine, whom he used to tie up to a joist, and whip upon her naked back till she was literally covered with blood. No words, no tears, no prayers, from his gory victim, seemed to move his iron heart from its bloody purpose. The louder she screamed, the harder he whipped; and where the blood ran fastest, there he whipped longest. He would whip her to make her scream, and whip her to make her hush; and not until overcome by fatigue, would he cease to swing the blood-clotted cowskin. I remember the first time I ever witnessed this horrible exhibition. I was quite a child, but I well remember it. I never shall forget it whilst I remember anything. It was the first of a long series of such outrages, of which I was doomed to be a witness and a participant. It struck me with awful force. It was the blood-stained gate, the entrance to the hell of slavery, through which I was about to pass."

He spoke of the slave trade in this way: "We were all ranked together at the valuation. Men and women, old and young, married and single, were ranked with horses, sheep, and swine. There were horses and men, cattle and women, pigs and children, all holding the same rank in the scale of being, and were all subjected to the same narrow examination. Silvery-headed age and sprightly youth, maids and matrons, had to undergo the same indelicate inspection. At this moment, I saw more clearly than ever the brutalizing effects of slavery upon both slave and slaveholder."

Now that you have a clear image of slavery, how would you imagine God feels about the practice? As the all-loving creator of the universe and of each human soul you would expect him to be opposed to the enslavement of human beings and despise slavery in the same way any decent person does. What other position could a good and perfect God take? It is therefore surprising to discover the Bible tells a different story. If you take the time to read it you will find instead a God who embraces slavery. In fact the Bible is so supportive it was frequently used as divine justification for American slavery prior to the Civil War.

For instance Richard Furman of Baptist State Convention, in a letter to the Governor of South Carolina in 1822 wrote, "...the right of holding slaves is clearly established in the Holy Scriptures, both by precept and example... had the holding of slaves been a moral evil, it cannot be supposed that the inspired Apostles... would have tolerated it for a moment in the Christian Church. In proving this subject justifiable by Scriptural authority (Luke 12:47), its morality is also proved; for the Divine Law never sanctions immoral actions."

Thomas Smyth, minister of 2nd Presbyterian Church of Charleston, S.C. wrote in 1861, "God is introduced to give dignity and emphasis... and then He is banished. It was this very atheistic Declaration (of Independence) which had inspired the 'higher law' doctrine of the radical antislavery men. If the mischievous abolitionists had only followed the Bible instead of the godless Declaration, they would have been bound to acknowledge that human bondage was divinely ordained. The mission of southerners was therefore clear; they must defend the word of God against abolitionist infidels."

The Vatican for its part issued a statement in 1866 saying, "Slavery itself... is not at all contrary to the natural and divine law... the purchaser (of the slave) should carefully examine whether the slave who is put up for sale has been justly or unjustly deprived of his liberty, and that the vendor should do nothing which might endanger the life, virtue or Catholic faith of the slave."

On what did they base such sentiments, you may wonder? For starters let's look at Genesis 17:12. In this passage God explains he wants slaves circumcised in the same way as non-slaves, so he obviously understands that people buy other people and is fine with the concept. "And he that is eight days old shall be circumcised among you, every man child in your generations, he that is born in the house, or bought with money of any stranger, which is not of thy seed. He that is born in thy house, and he that is bought with thy money, must needs be circumcised."

Exodus 12:43 singles out slaves for special treatment. "The Lord said to Moses and Aaron, 'These are the regulations for the Passover: No foreigner is to eat of it. Any slave you have bought may eat of it after you have circumcised him, but a temporary resident and a hired worker may not eat of it.'"

In Exodus 21:1 God describes how to become a slave for life, shows it is completely acceptable to separate slaves from their families and endorses the branding of slaves through mutilation. "Now these are the ordinances which you shall set before them. When you buy a Hebrew slave, he shall serve six years, and in the seventh he shall go out free, for nothing. If he comes in single, he shall go out single; if he comes in married, then his wife shall go out with him. If his master gives him a wife and she bears him sons or daughters, the wife and her children shall be her master's and he shall go out alone. But if the slave plainly says, 'I love my master, my wife, and my children; I will not go out free,' then his master shall bring him to God, and he shall bring him to the door or the doorpost; and his master shall bore his ear through with an awl; and he shall serve him for life."

Exodus 21:20 tells us not only does God condone slavery, he is also comfortable with the practice of beating your slaves as long as you don't kill them. "If a man beats his male or female slave with a rod and the slave dies as a direct result, he must be punished, but he is not to be punished if the slave gets up after a day or two, since the slave is his property."

In Exodus 21:32 God places a value of thirty shekels of silver on slaves. "If the bull gores a male or female slave, the owner must pay thirty shekels of silver to the master of the slave, and the bull must be stoned." Note that despite being omniscient God is seemingly not sophisticated enough to understand the concept of inflation since it is now thousands of years later and a gored slave is apparently still worth thirty shekels of silver according to his word.

Leviticus 22:10 demonstrates that according to God the children of slaves are slaves themselves saying, "No one outside a priest's family may eat the sacred offering, nor may the guest of a priest or his hired worker eat it. But if a priest buys a slave with money, or if a slave is born in his household, that slave may eat his food."

Leviticus 25:44 states where you may purchase your slaves and clearly specifies they are property to be bought, sold and handed down. "Your male and female slaves are to come from the nations around you; from them you may buy slaves. You may also buy some of the temporary residents living among you and members of their clans born in your country, and they will become your property. You can will them to your children as inherited property and can make them slaves for life, but you must not rule over your fellow Israelites ruthlessly."

Are you thinking those verses no longer matter because they are from the Old Testament? The question should be why were such practices ever allowed by a loving and just God and in any case in the New Testament (Luke 7:2) Jesus shows he too is nonplussed by the concept of slavery because he heals a slave without any thought of freeing him or admonishing the slave's owner for owning another human being. "Now a centurion had a slave who was dear to him, who was sick and at the point of death. When he heard of Jesus, he sent to him elders of the Jews, asking him to come and heal his slave. And when they came to Jesus, they besought him earnestly, saying, 'He is worthy to have you do this for him, for he loves our nation, and he built us our synagogue.' And Jesus went with them. When he was not far from the house, the centurion sent friends to him, saying to him, 'Lord, do not trouble yourself, for I am not worthy to have you come under my roof; therefore I did not presume to come to you. But say the word, and let my servant be healed. For I am a man set under authority, with soldiers under me: and I say to one, 'Go,' and he goes; and to another, 'Come,' and he comes; and to my slave, 'Do this,' and he does it.' When Jesus heard this he marveled at him, and turned and said to the multitude that followed him, 'I tell you, not even in Israel have I found such faith.' And when those who had been sent returned to the house, they found the slave well."

Also in the New Testament, Colossians 3:22 encourages slaves to work hard when it says, "Slaves, obey in everything those who are your earthly masters, not with eyeservice, as men-pleasers, but in singleness of heart, fearing the Lord. Whatever your task, work heartily..." and this sentiment is repeated in Titus 2:9: "Bid slaves to be submissive to their masters and to give satisfaction in every respect; they are not to be refractory, nor to pilfer, but to show entire and true fidelity."

If the Bible was actually written or inspired by God and those are the words of the Lord then you can only reach one conclusion - slavery is acceptable to God. The fact that after many centuries the wording in some translations has been changed from slaves to servants is just semantics, and another way Christians attempt to explain away what the Bible says about slavery is by rationalizing that the practice needs to be understood "in the context of the time it was written" as if owning another human being was ever moral.

These passages demonstrate God, at least not the one worshipped by Christians, could not possibly have written the Bible because there is no way an omnibenevolent deity would endorse the subjugation of one human by another. If God had written the Bible shouldn't it say slavery is wrong? Shouldn't one of the Commandments be "Thou shalt not enslave?" And in spite of what Scripture says or rather does not say our society has determined slavery is wrong and as a result the practice is now illegal throughout the developed world. This highlights one of the major problems with Scripture - once something is in there it is in there for good and there can be no retraction. There are no revised editions of the perfect word of God, so true believers have no choice but to rationalize, obfuscate or ignore these embarrassing issues.

If you do not believe God wrote the slavery passages in the Bible how can you possibly know which parts came from him and which were inserted by men? There can be no middle ground because if part of the Bible came from God and part came from men you cannot possibly know which is which. If part of the Bible has been polluted by slave owning men you have to reject the whole thing because there is no way to know who wrote what. You must assume every sentence is the product of men. To use an analogy, imagine someone has inserted capsules containing cyanide into random bottles of Tylenol on store shelves. The poisoned capsules look identical to normal capsules and the tainted bottles are indistinguishable. Knowing that, if someone were to hand you a bottle off a store shelf would you take one of the pills? Of course not, because you must assume every pill contains poison. This actually happened in 1982 and is the reason bottles of over-the-counter medicine now have tamper-proof seals. The lesson is simple. Since every capsule could have contained poison we had to assume every capsule did and threw out millions of good ones along with the bad. The Bible suffers from the same problem.

Given the stance of both the Bible and Quran on slavery I'm amazed so many African-Americans venerate them the way they do. How did that come to be? Part of the rationalization of the slave trade was to "civilize" and "Christianize" Africans, and missionary efforts among the slaves were allowed because owners assumed Christianity would make slaves better workers. In the course of this instruction the slaves discovered the Bible taught "Slaves, obey your earthly masters with respect and fear" which one would think would give them pause, but some have claimed because it also said "...and masters, treat your slaves in the same way. Do not threaten them, since you know that he who is both your Master and theirs is in Heaven and there is no favoritism with him" that made it all okay. Some masters believed Africans were too brutish to comprehend the gospel, others doubted Africans had souls and as Anglican missionary to South Carolina Francis Le Jau reported in 1709, "Many masters can't be persuaded that Negroes and Indians are otherwise than beasts, and use them like such."

Not being African-American myself some might say I am not qualified to comment further so I will defer to Butterfly McQueen, best remembered for her role as Scarlett O'Hara's maid Prissy in the 1939 film *Gone with the Wind* who declared, "Christianity appears to me to be the most absurd imposture of all the religions, and I'm puzzled that so many people can't see through a religion that encourages irresponsibility and bigotry. As my ancestors are free from slavery, I am free from the slavery of religion." Even so as recently as 1962 Congressman George Andrews, in response to the U.S. Supreme Court's verdict in *Engle v. Vitale* which barred school-sponsored prayer said, "They put the Negroes in the schools, and now they've driven God out."

Burnt Offerings

Or, Blessed Barbeques

"Compared to the Bible, *The Wizard of Oz* is much more believable... and much more fun." ~ James Randi

The dictionary defines "sacrifice" as the act of offering something to a deity in propitiation or homage, especially the ritual slaughter of an animal or a person, and to most civilized people the idea of animal and/or human sacrifice is understandably nauseating because it is something primitive savages would do. Sacrificing and burning an animal on an altar does not have any beneficial effect for anyone, and yet the practice of sacrifice was common in many religious traditions.

For example there are many early Roman references to the practice of human sacrifice by the Celtic Druids and Caesar himself explained the slaves and dependents of high-ranking Gauls would usually be burnt alive along with the body of their deceased master. Other types of sacrifices included hangings for the god Esus and drownings for the god Teutates, but the most well-known form was the "wicker man" method in which a large effigy made of sticks in the shape of a man was erected and living people were placed within it. The creation would then be set ablaze along with all those inside.

According to various accounts the Phoenician and Carthaginian civilizations religiously sacrificed children to protect their communities. The Phoenicians' sacrificial areas were known as "topheth" (the roasting place) and the sacrifices themselves were referred to as "mulk" (or "King") offerings. According to Diodorus Siculus' account of the Carthaginians, "There was in their city a bronze image of the god Cronus extending his hands, palms up and sloping toward the ground, so that each of the children when placed thereon rolled down and fell into a sort of gaping pit filled with fire."

The Mayans strongly believed in a divine power they thought was contained deep within limestone sinkholes or "cenotes" as they called them. They thought these to be portals which led to the underworld and would cast their own people into them because according to their beliefs those thrown into the cenote would not die - but of course they were never seen again either.

The Aztecs are infamous for the sacrificial rituals performed at the height of their civilization with one of the most famous involving the removal of a living person's heart in honor of the sun god Huitzilopochtli, however there were also several other types such as offerings made to Tlaloc, Xipe Totec and the "Earth Mother" Teteoinnan. Tlaloc's offering required "weeping boys" to be ritually murdered, sacrifice offerings made to Xipe Totec were bound to a post and shot full of arrows before being skinned by a priest and the Earth mother Teteoinnan's offerings generally required skinned female victims.

The deaths of these people of course did nothing to improve crop yield or rainfall nor did it appease the gods, because as I'm sure you'll agree those gods were imaginary. Why did they engage in such bizarre practices? Was it mass delusion? Rampant superstition? Desperation? There is no way to know, but we do know it was insane. The idea of religious sacrifice is ridiculous to most of us and one would think God would feel the same way since ritual slaughter should have nothing to do with an all-powerful, all-knowing, all-loving creator of the universe. The idea of killing an animal, splattering its blood and burning its flesh is bizarre so obviously God would have nothing to do with animal sacrifice, but when we examine the Bible we find passages like Leviticus 1 which says, "The Lord called to Moses and spoke to him from the Tent of Meeting. He said, 'Speak to the Israelites and say to them: 'When any of you brings an offering to the Lord, bring as your offering an animal from either the herd or the flock. If the offering is a burnt offering from the herd, he is to offer a male without defect. He must present it at the entrance to the Tent of Meeting so that it will be acceptable to the Lord. He is to lay his hand on the head of the burnt offering, and it will be accepted on his behalf to make atonement for him. He is to slaughter the young bull before the Lord, and then Aaron's sons the priests shall bring the blood and sprinkle it against the altar on all sides at the entrance to the Tent of Meeting. He is to skin the burnt offering and cut it into pieces. The sons of Aaron the priest are to put fire on the altar and arrange wood on the fire. Then Aaron's sons the priests shall arrange the pieces, including the head and the fat, on the burning wood that is on the altar. He is to wash the inner parts and the legs with water, and the priest is to burn all of it on the altar. It is a burnt offering, an offering made by fire, an aroma pleasing to the Lord. If the offering is a burnt offering from the flock, from either the sheep or the goats, he is to offer a male without defect. He is to slaughter it at the north side of the altar before the Lord, and Aaron's sons the priests shall sprinkle its blood against the altar on all sides. He is to cut it into pieces, and the priest shall arrange them, including the head and the fat, on the burning wood that is on the altar. He is to wash the inner parts and the legs with water, and the priest is to bring all of it and burn it on the altar. It is a burnt offering, an offering made by fire, an aroma pleasing to the Lord. If the offering to the Lord is a burnt offering of birds, he is to offer a dove or a young pigeon. The priest shall bring it to the altar, wring off the head and burn it on the altar; its blood shall be drained out on the side of the altar. He is to remove the crop with its contents and throw it to the east side of the altar, where the ashes are. He shall tear it open by the wings, not severing it completely, and then the priest shall burn it on the wood that is on the fire on the altar. It is a burnt offering, an offering made by fire, an aroma pleasing to the Lord."

So burning flesh is an aroma pleasing to the Lord? Does this make any sense? That sounds like something we might expect to find in a Wes Craven movie. There is another example in Leviticus 5 which says, "If a person sins because he does not speak up when he hears a public charge to testify regarding something he has seen or learned about, he will be held responsible. Or if a person touches anything ceremonially unclean - whether the carcasses of unclean wild animals or of unclean livestock or of unclean creatures that move along the ground - even though he is unaware of it, he has become unclean and is guilty. Or if he touches human uncleanness - anything that would make him unclean - even though he is unaware of it, when he learns of it he will be guilty. Or if a person thoughtlessly takes an oath to do anything, whether good or evil - in any matter one might carelessly swear about - even though he is unaware of it, in any case when he learns of it he will be guilty. When anyone is guilty in any of these ways, he must confess in what way he has sinned and, as a penalty for the sin he has committed, he must bring to the Lord a female lamb or goat from the flock as a sin offering; and the priest shall make atonement for him for his sin. If he cannot afford a lamb, he is to bring two doves or two young pigeons to the Lord as a penalty for his sin - one for a sin offering and the other for a burnt offering. He is to bring them to the priest, who shall first offer the one for the sin offering. He is to wring its head from its neck, not severing it completely, and is to sprinkle some of the blood of the sin offering against the side of the altar; the rest of the blood must be drained out at the base of the altar. It is a sin offering. The priest shall then offer the other as a burnt offering in the prescribed way and make atonement for him for the sin he has committed, and he will be forgiven."

Think about that. What it essentially said was, "Today I accidentally touched something that was 'ceremonially unclean' and didn't know about it at the time, but fortunately a priest brought it to my attention and I am guilty. I can't afford a lamb, but can get two young pigeons and take them to the priest. He will wring the head from the neck of one of them but not sever it completely, and will sprinkle the blood and drain the rest. Then the priest will burn the other pigeon and I will be forgiven." Why in the world would a God powerful enough to create the entire universe demand such a thing in order to forgive someone for accidentally touching something?

There is another example in Leviticus 7 which is known as "the priest's share." It says, "The Lord said to Moses, 'Say to the Israelites: Anyone who brings a fellowship offering to the Lord is to bring part of it as his sacrifice to the Lord. With his own hands he is to bring the offering made to the Lord by fire; he is to bring the fat, together with the breast, and wave the breast before the Lord as a wave offering. The priest shall burn the fat on the altar, but the breast belongs to Aaron and his sons. You are to give the right thigh of your fellowship offerings to the priest as a contribution. The son of Aaron who offers the blood and the fat of the fellowship offering shall have the right thigh as his share. From the fellowship offerings of the Israelites, I have taken the breast that is waved and the thigh that is presented and have given them to Aaron the priest and his sons as their regular share from the Israelites."

Does it seem more likely God commanded this or that primitive men looking for the "priest's share" wrote it? Yet another example from Leviticus 9 says, "[Moses] then presented the other ram, the ram for the ordination, and Aaron and his sons laid their hands on its head. Moses slaughtered the ram and took some of its blood and put it on the lobe of Aaron's right ear, on the thumb of his right hand and on the big toe of his right foot. Moses also brought Aaron's sons forward and put some of the blood on the lobes of their right ears, on the thumbs of their right hands and on the big toes of their right feet. Then he sprinkled blood against the altar on all sides. He took the fat, the fat tail, all the fat around the inner parts, the covering of the liver, both kidneys and their fat and the right thigh. Then from the basket of bread made without yeast, which was before the Lord, he took a cake of bread, and one made with oil, and a wafer; he put these on the fat portions and on the right thigh. He put all these in the hands of Aaron and his sons and waved them before the Lord as a wave offering. Then Moses took them from their hands and burned them on the altar on top of the burnt offering as an ordination offering, a pleasing aroma, an offering made to the Lord by fire. He also took the breast - Moses' share of the ordination ram - and waved it before the Lord as a wave offering, as the Lord commanded Moses."

What we have here is Moses putting the blood of a freshly slaughtered animal on the ears, thumbs and toes of other people. Does that make any sense? Why would God wants people to kill animals, splatter their blood, cut them up into pieces, arrange the pieces on an altar and burn them so he can "smell the pleasing aroma." There is little difference between the Bible's book of Leviticus and the insanity of the Aztecs.

For those apologists who would point out, "All of this material about animal sacrifice is found in the Old Testament of the Bible" that's true, but this is the same place where we find the Ten Commandments and in fact only about twenty pages separate Exodus 20, the source of the Ten Commandments, from Leviticus 1. Does that mean we should cherry pick the parts we'd like to believe?

How should we view these passages? It is hard to put faith in a book filled with numerous passages in which God demands animal sacrifice. As with the slavery issue there are three possible ways to look at it. Pretend the passages are not there, change the subject when they are mentioned or develop a rationalization to explain them. Many Christians tend to take the latter approach and surprisingly some actually embrace these parts of the Bible because only in the context of this bizarre practice does the death of Jesus on the cross, as portrayed in the movie *The Passion of the Christ*, make even a modicum of sense.

Christians believe the human race had to engage in human sacrifice to appease God. A Christian minister might say, "If you read all those dry regulations for sin sacrifices in Leviticus and the requirements for the Passover lamb you will realize Jesus is the perfect sacrifice for sin. He is the first-born son not of a sheep or goat, but of God. He is innocent of all sin and volunteers of His own free will - that is, He was convicted only by His own confession. He freely submitted to His Father's will. He is, by the Levitical code, a perfect sacrifice, and therefore He perfectly removes all sin. He meets all the requirements for a fellowship offering, and thus places us in fellowship with God. Since even on the cross none of His bones were broken He also meets all the requirements for a Passover lamb whose blood protects us from the angel of death, thus He prepares us for the Resurrection."

As ridiculous as that sounds to the objective person that is the core belief of Christianity. Christ had to die as a human sacrifice for our sins to appease the God of Leviticus and the most prominent religion on this planet, practiced by two billion people, has a human sacrifice as its central tenet. In other words, Christians are not all that different from the virgin-killing Aztecs.

Have you ever thought about how bizarre the crucifixion story is? The creator of the universe looked down and said to himself, "Those evil humans down on earth. All this sin. So here's what I am going to do. I will artificially inseminate a virgin, she will give birth to an incarnated version of me, the humans will eventually crucify and kill the incarnated me and that will make me happy." It makes no sense. Why would an all-knowing being need to have humans kill himself (Jesus is God, after all) to make himself happy? Especially since it was this perfect God who set the whole thing in motion exactly the way he wanted it. The story of the crucifixion is absurd if you think about it. Have you ever done that? Have you ever thought about how nonsensical it is to worship a God who demanded animal sacrifice and then was finally appeased by a human sacrifice… of himself? Many Christians seem to actually revel in it. How else can we explain the millions who flocked to see *The Passion of the Christ?* It also makes no sense in another way. As Dr. Colleen M. Conway has said about the alleged statement of Jesus from the cross in Matthew 27:46 of "'My God, my God, why hast thou forsaken me!' that cry could never be wrung from the lips of a man who saw in his own death a prearranged plan for the world's salvation, and his own return to divine glory temporarily renounced for transient misery on earth. The fictitious theology of a thousand years shrivels beneath the awful anguish of that cry."

Godly Misogyny

Or, You Haven't Come a Long Way Baby

"It will yet be the proudest boast of women that they never contributed a single line to the Bible." ~ George W. Foote

In October of 2013 the principal of the Wisconsin Evangelical Lutheran Synod Church, John Hartwig, was fired primarily due to his belief that women should be respected more in the church, and at the meeting to decide his fate those same women were ironically told to "shut up" while the men voted to oust him by a margin of 76-74. Church leaders argued they were not at all disrespectful to women and pointed out that any woman who wanted to ask questions during the meeting had been told to write them on a piece of paper and have a man read them aloud but some, including Hartwig's daughter, said their questions were never read. Clearly women do not possess the capacity to develop their own opinions, or at the very least must speak through a male translator. In a statement Reverend Carl Schroeder said, "Our congregational president was not trying to disrespect anyone. We have a wide number of households and a representative spiritual leadership of males who were asked to speak on behalf of their families so the meeting would not be over five hours," which might have made sense except it is only logical to assume the process of having to write questions down and have someone else read them would actually take more time. Thankfully a few of the women came to their senses, because those who didn't have a voice at the meeting said they hope they are heard loud and clear when they move their children to public school. As a mother named Julie Cutrell put it, "They're willing to take our money and take our time to ask us for more, but when it comes to our opinion it's not really needed."

I am always amazed by women who profess to be devout Christians. The best explanation for most of them is they, like most believers, have never actually read the Bible. There are however some who have indeed read the "good book" and somehow accept or in some cases even embrace their role as second class citizens who are subservient to men.

Do Christian and/or Islamic women think they are worshipping a sexist or misogynist? Probably not. After all, why would they worship

God or Allah if that were the case? When people think of God they generally do not imagine him hating anyone but instead are trained to think of him as an all-knowing and all-loving father who is fair and loves each of his "children" equally regardless of any distinction such as skin color or gender, and yet for some strange reason God treats women differently from the way he treats men.

The dictionary defines a misogynist as "one who hates women" and explains the word sexism means "discrimination based on gender, especially discrimination against women; attitudes, conditions, or behaviors that promote stereotyping of social roles based on gender." That is exactly what we find when we examine the Bible and Quran. In Genesis chapter 17 God says, "This is my covenant, which you shall keep, between me and you and your descendants after you: Every male among you shall be circumcised. You shall be circumcised in the flesh of your foreskins, and it shall be a sign of the covenant between me and you" but it makes no mention of forming any sort of covenant with women.

In Genesis 3 God punished Eve and all women who have lived since, including those in the animal kingdom, with greatly increased pain during childbirth while no such pain was inflicted on Adam or men. All they were required to do was till the fields and grow crops.

In Deuteronomy 22:28-29 it says, "If a man meets a virgin who is not engaged, and seizes her and lies with her, and they are caught in the act, the man who lay with her shall give fifty shekels of silver to the young woman's father, and she shall become his wife. Because he violated her he shall not be permitted to divorce her as long as he lives." So what God is saying is if a man rapes a girl she gets to be his wife. How nice.

Numbers 31:14-18 contains the passage, "Moses was angry with the officers of the army - the commanders of thousands and commanders of hundreds - who returned from the battle. 'Have you allowed all the women to live?' he asked them. 'They were the ones who followed Balaam's advice and were the means of turning the Israelites away from the LORD in what happened at Peor, so that a plague struck the LORD's people. Now kill all the boys. And kill every woman who has slept with a man, but save for yourselves every girl who has never slept with a man.'" Making sex slaves of female virgins is apparently God's will.

You are probably thinking sure, but those verses come from the Old Testament and we are now living under a new covenant which supersedes the old Law. That is the standard apologetic used to explain away the archaic practices outlined in the OT, but in this instance there is a problem. There are many, many examples like these throughout both the Old and New Testaments and there are other, broader examples of misogyny which are readily apparent as well. For instance were any of Jesus' disciples women? No. Are any of the elders in the book of Revelation women? No. Were any of the books of the Bible written by women? No.

As for the New Testament we find in 1 Corinthians 14, "As in all the congregations of the saints, according to the Bible women should remain silent in the churches. They are not allowed to speak, but must be in submission as the Law says. If they want to inquire about something they must ask their husbands at home for it is disgraceful for a woman to speak in church." This seems like a straightforward passage. We have God in his eternal and perfect word saying it is disgraceful for a woman to speak in church. Why would God create man and woman in his own image and then silence women? What possible reason does God have to be sexist? Could it be because men rather than God were the exclusive authors of the Bible? Even more interesting is the question of why would a woman worship such a God?

There are many more places in the New Testament where God talks about women. 1 Corinthians 11 is particularly noteworthy: "But I want you to understand that the head of every man is Christ, the head of a woman is her husband, and the head of Christ is God. Any man who prays or prophesies with his head covered dishonors his head, but any woman who prays or prophesies with her head unveiled dishonors her head - it is the same as if her head were shaven. For if a woman will not veil herself, then she should cut off her hair; but if it is disgraceful for a woman to be shorn or shaven, let her wear a veil. For a man ought not to cover his head, since he is the image and glory of God; but woman is the glory of man (for man was not made from woman, but woman from man. Neither was man created for woman, but woman for man). That is why a woman ought to have a veil on her head, because of the angels."

What exactly is God saying? You may find it hard to believe something like that is in the Bible, yet if you look it up you will find it. Then in 1 Timothy 2 we find, "Also that women should adorn themselves modestly and sensibly in seemly apparel, not with braided hair or gold or pearls or costly attire but by good deeds, as befits women who profess religion. Let a woman learn in silence with all submissiveness. I permit no woman to teach or to have authority over men; she is to keep silent." It is hard to miss God's meaning when he says something as direct as, "I permit no woman to teach or to have authority over men; she is to keep silent," and yet some Christian apologists work diligently to find a way to reinterpret those words while other Christians take them quite literally.

In Matthew 25:1 Jesus says, "At that time the Kingdom of Heaven will be like ten virgins who took their lamps and went out to meet the bridegroom" and in John 20:17 he says to Mary, "Touch me not; for I am not yet ascended to my Father" as though the touch of a woman, in this case his own mother, is somehow improper but a few verses later he has no problem with a man (Thomas) touching him.

In Ephesians 5:22-24 we find, "Wives, submit to your husbands as to the Lord. For the husband is the head of the wife as Christ is the head of the church, his body, of which he is the Savior. Now as the church submits to Christ, so also wives should submit to their husbands in everything." John 2:13 says, "I write to you, fathers, because you have known him who is from the beginning. I write to you, young men, because you have overcome the evil one. I write to you, dear children, because you have known the Father." No mention is made of women.

How do women feel about all this sexism? Keep in mind God's misogyny as portrayed in the Bible has affected society for centuries. For example the Constitution was originally drafted to specifically deny rights to women and in fact they could not even vote in the United States until 1920, and only then after decades of battle in the women's suffrage movement. Fittingly, women today owe their right to cast a ballot in large part to agnostic Susan B. Anthony who once observed, "I distrust those people who know so well what God wants them to do, because I notice it always coincides with their own desires."

In spite of the Bible and its far-reaching effects and in spite of the fact it is supposed to be God's eternal Word we as a society have advanced beyond the Bible's teachings. We reject sexism and for the most part ignore these biblical teachings. Today women are the CEOs of major corporations, are elected to high government office and are appointed as presidents of universities. We fill our schools with female teachers, allow women to speak freely in most churches and they even become pastors in some denominations. We do all this in direct defiance of God's Law in the Bible because we know "his eternal word" is wrong. Could that be because the Bible's attitude toward women is irrational? After all there is no reason for women to be treated differently from men and through our actions we mere mortals have told an all-powerful God he is wrong, yet despite that billions of Christians still worship him and claim the Bible is his word. Women happily stand up in church and proclaim how much they love God… in defiance of Scripture. Is this out of ignorance of what it says, or are they just cherry picking?

Supreme Court Justice Antonin Scalia has trumpeted his support for the Ten Commandments, which come from the very same book which tells women to be subservient. According to him "ninety-nine percent of Americans believe in the Ten Commandments" and they are "a symbol of the fact that government derives its authority from God…" and yet we have female Justices sitting on the Supreme Court right alongside Justice Scalia. How ironic.

Religious people might and in fact do rationalize this by saying, "God had to 'fit in' with the customs of the time" but that is absurd. Didn't he understand how it would look in the 21st Century? The fact is we are forced to ignore it when the Bible says, "I permit no woman to teach or to have authority over men; she is to keep silent." No one believes that, especially the fifty-one percent of the population which happens to be female, or at least most of them. If the creator of the universe wanted women treated equally all he had to do was say so when he created Adam or write a Commandment which said, "Thou shalt treat men and women equally." He could have portrayed men and women as equals throughout the Bible and half of Jesus' apostles, or at least one of them, could have been female. That would have made things clear. If God wanted men and women to be equal he would have made it happen.

In a 1992 fundraising letter evangelist Pat Robertson wrote, "The feminist agenda is not about equal rights for women. It is about a socialist, anti-family political movement that encourages women to leave their husbands, kill their children, practice witchcraft, destroy capitalism and become lesbians." Not to be outdone Pat Buchanan said, "Rail as they will about 'discrimination,' women are simply not endowed by nature with the same measures of single-minded ambition and the will to succeed in the fiercely competitive world of Western capitalism," and Phyllis Schlafly added her two cents about the superiority of fear over contraception when she opined, "It's very healthy for a young girl to be deterred from promiscuity by fear of contracting a painful, incurable disease, or cervical cancer, or sterility, or the likelihood of giving birth to a dead, blind or brain-damaged baby (even ten years later when she may be happily married)." Where do they get such warped ideas? From Scripture.

There are two ways to explain sexism in the Bible. One can believe God actually did write or inspire it and truly is sexist and misogynistic, and in that case we are directly defying his word by allowing women to be equal to men, or we can assume God had nothing to do with it. In that case it is meaningless and can be discarded. One need only look at how men in Muslim countries like Afghanistan treat women today to understand those are the kind of people who wrote the Bible.

As the story of the Wisconsin Evangelical Lutheran Synod Church illustrated if you think biblical misogyny is a thing of the past which "must be viewed in the context of the times when the Bible was written" you must think again. Even worse is Christian Patriarchy, which is the modern, Bible-based belief that God has ordained a specific family order in which the husband leads, the wife submits and the children obey - period - and it derives its authority from I Corinthians 11:3 which says, "But I want you to understand that the head of every man is Christ, the head of a wife is her husband, and the head of Christ is God."

Christian Patriarchy holds that women must always be under male authority or "headship" and can never be independent of male authority. First she is under her father's authority and then her husband's and believe it or not a widow would be under her son's authority, or if she had no sons or they were young she would return to her father's authority, and if that is not possible some argue she should place herself under the authority of a church elder or pastor. Furthermore, in addition to preaching absolute female submission there is also a rejection of higher education for women and the shunning of contraception in favor of trying to have as many children as humanly possible.

A good example of this practice is Jim Bob and Michelle Duggar, who have put many years and a lot of work into putting a smiling, nearly normal-seeming face on the extreme Christian right while adhering to this strain of fundamentalist Christianity which is also sometimes known as the "Quiverfull movement." While the movement is controversial even within Christian right circles the Duggars have tried to counter that with their popular reality TV show *19 Kids & Counting* where they present themselves as a wholesome everyday family which just happens to be a little more conservative than average, but while adherents to this form of Christianity like to paint an uber-wholesome face on their families and beliefs ugly truths are finally starting to leak out regarding the problems of infidelity and alleged sexual abuse in the community.

In November 2013 Doug Phillips, who in his capacity as the president of *Vision Forum Ministries* is probably the most important leader in the world of biblical patriarchy, confessed to cheating on his wife and resigned as president of his ministry but there may be more to this entire scandal than the typical minister-caught-cheating story. The woman with whom Phillips confessed to having an "inappropriate" relationship with, Lourdes Torres-Manteufel, filed suit in Bexar County, Texas and accused the Christian leader of pushing her into a multi-year abusive relationship which allegedly featured frequent sexual assault. While the complaint never mentions sexual intercourse, it does claim he repeatedly groped and masturbated on her while she protested.

The scandal around Phillips is just the latest in a long line of ugly shocks to the far Christian right which threaten to destabilize and possibly capsize the community. As *The Wire* reported Bill Gothard, leader of the Institute in Basic Life Principles, resigned his position in the wake of a series of accusations of alleged sexual abuse from dozens of women in the organization. IBLP, like *Vision Forum Ministries*, is a major clearinghouse for adherents to biblical patriarchy, teaching members to shun contraception, embrace extreme forms of female submission and of course use homeschooling to "shelter" young people from the outside world (and deny them access to science).

Similarly, both Bob Jones University and Patrick Henry College, schools which were established in no small part to give homeschooled and sheltered kids from far Christian right backgrounds a place to go to college, have been at the center of accusations of indifference and even of allegedly covering up reported sexual abuse on campus. Bob Jones received a lot of heat when they fired an outside firm which had been brought in to investigate accusations of sexual abuse, only to rehire them when it looked like they were punishing the firm for being too thorough in exposing the problem. Patrick Henry College was the recent target of an exposé in *The New Republic* which explored how young women who brought sexual abuse complaints to the school were frequently drummed out of the college or made to feel that they had somehow brought the abuse on themselves.

Latin Philosopher and Theologian Saint Augustine of Hippo once proclaimed, "Women should not be enlightened or educated in any way. They should, in fact, be segregated as they are the cause of hideous and involuntary erections in holy men." Correct me if I am wrong, but that sure sounds like something a Muslim cleric operating under Sharia might say, doesn't it? But it isn't, because as Annie Besant observed in *The Freethinker's Textbook*, "For centuries the leaders of Christian thought spoke of women as a necessary evil, and the greatest saints of the Church are those who despise women the most."

Infanticide

Or, Save the Children

"It is time we recognized the boundless narcissism and self-deceit of the saved. It is time we acknowledged how disgraceful it is for the survivors of a catastrophe to believe themselves spared by a loving God, while this same God drowned infants in their cribs." ~ Sam Harris

Aisha was the six-year-old girl who was betrothed to the Prophet Muhammad, married him at the age of nine and became one of his eleven (or thirteen, depending on the source) wives, and while most Muslims do not object to this marriage it is a source of great scandal to many non-Islamic people because pedophilia, the sexual attraction of adults to prepubescent children, is considered taboo in most Western societies and is in fact viewed as a psychiatric disorder - however in Islamic tradition she is attributed as the source of many stories about the life of Muhammad and it is believed she was his favorite wife.

If you think that's bad, and of course it is, there is also ample historical evidence to document the propensity of parents to actually murder their own children. In 19th Century England for example, infanticide was so rampant a debate over how to correct the problem was conducted in both the lay and medical press. An editorial in the respected medical journal *Lancet* noted, "To the shame of civilization it must be avowed that not a State has yet advanced to the degree of progress under which child-murder may be said to be a very uncommon crime."

Infanticide has pervaded almost every society of mankind from the Golden Age of Greece to the splendor of the Persian Empire and the colonists brought it to America from England while at the same time finding the Indians practiced it as well. Extreme discipline characterized family life in puritanical colonial America and parents were given extensive liberty to punish their children, even to the point of death. In 1646 the General Court of Massachusetts Bay enacted a Bible-based law whereby, "A stubborn or rebellious son of sufficient years and understanding" would be brought before the Magistrates in court and "such a son shall be put to death," and similar "stubborn child laws" were enacted in Connecticut in 1650, Rhode Island in 1668 and New Hampshire in 1679.

More recently in 1966 the United States had 10,920 murders and one out of every twenty-two was a child killed by a parent, so despite our predilection for considering modern civilization "advanced" the crime of infanticide has continued to pervade most contemporary cultures. If you are anything like me, especially if you are a parent, you must find that disgusting. Who or what could possibly sanction the killing of innocent children? How can a human being justify such a heinous act? What reason can they give?

One example immediately comes to mind. In her confession letter after drowning her two children Susan Smith wrote, "My children, Michael and Alex, are with our Heavenly Father now, and I know that they will never be hurt again. As a mom, that means more than words could ever say… my children deserve to have the best, and now they will have it… I have put my total faith in God, and He will take care of me."

In Exodus 12:28 the Bible tells us of about one of God's earliest and most horrific massacres. "So the people of Israel did just as the LORD had commanded through Moses and Aaron. And at midnight the LORD killed all the firstborn sons in the land of Egypt, from the firstborn son of Pharaoh, who sat on the throne, to the firstborn son of the captive in the dungeon. Even the firstborn of their livestock were killed. Pharaoh and his officials and all the people of Egypt woke up during the night, and loud wailing was heard throughout the land of Egypt. There was not a single house where someone had not died."

Here the death of the children is directly by the hand of God and it is important to note this is not the only place in the Bible where God caused or allowed children to die. To put this into a modern context this is akin to today slaughtering the first born infants of every family in a foreign country to punish the leader of that nation for some decision he has made and then extending that punishment to the offspring of every animal whether they be in the wild or the zoo. Does that make any sense at all?

Isaiah 13 paints quite a word picture in saying, "Anyone who is captured will be run through with a sword. Their little children will be dashed to death right before their eyes. Their homes will be sacked and their wives raped by the attacking hordes. For I will stir up the Medes against Babylon, and no amount of silver or gold will buy them off. The attacking armies will shoot down the young people with arrows. They will have no mercy on helpless babies and will show no compassion for the children." What a lovely image. In Jeremiah 49:20 he paints a similar picture with, "Therefore hear the plan which the LORD has made against Edom and the purposes which he has formed against the inhabitants of Teman: Even the little ones of the flock shall be dragged away; surely their fold shall be appalled at their fate. At the sound of their fall the earth shall tremble; the sound of their cry shall be heard at the Red Sea." In Hosea 13 he does it yet again with, "Samaria shall bear her guilt, because she has rebelled against her God; they shall fall by the sword, their little ones shall be dashed in pieces, and their pregnant women ripped open."

In Numbers 31 Moses, God's prophet and leader of the Tribes of Israel, said to them, "Have you let all the women live? Behold, these caused the people of Israel, by the counsel of Balaam, to act treacherously against the LORD in the matter of Pe'or, and so the plague came among the congregation of the LORD. Now therefore, kill every male among the little ones, and kill every woman who has known man by lying with him. But all the young girls who have not known man by lying with him, keep alive for yourselves." Here Moses, acting as an agent of God, commands that thousands of male babies and children be killed as well as thousands of women. The Bible states in verse 35 that the captured women numbered "thirty-two thousand persons in all, women who had not known man by lying with him," so this was no small thing. In Deuteronomy 3 they massacred all of the men, women and children in sixty cities at God's behest and of course there is also Noah's flood in which God drowned every single infant and child on the face of the earth.

In Matthew 2, mixed into the Christmas story, the Bible describes the massacre of more babies. "Herod, angel of the Lord appeareth to Joseph in a dream, flee into Egypt, and be thou there until I bring thee word: Then Herod, when he saw that he was mocked of the wise men, was exceeding wroth, and sent forth, and slew all the children that were in Bethlehem, and in all the coasts thereof, from two years old and under..." Think about the families who were affected by this massacre. The Bible describes their suffering. They wept and could not be comforted. Of course they couldn't. If you are a parent, you know exactly how you would feel if an agent of the government came to your door one morning and slaughtered your children.

Of course God knew this would happen. In fact according to the Bible he acted on this knowledge, but why would he reach down and save his own child while allowing other innocent children to die? If God is love, where is the love in that? Think about how easy it would have been for him to prevent all of this. He could have appeared to Herod in a dream and told him not to kill these children, killed Herod, protected the babies, spoken to the murdering soldiers, sent all of the families to Egypt when he sent Jesus and his family there, made it so no male child besides Jesus was born during that time, changed history so Herod was not king or a thousand other things and yet God did nothing even though sending his son to earth was the direct cause of this massacre. God took action to save Jesus, but instead of saving the other children he stood by and watched as they were slaughtered. Why would a loving being act this way? In the case of Herod's massacre a religious person might say, "God had to do it to fulfill a prophecy in the Bible," but that makes no sense because he could have left the prophecy out or changed it. And why would an omnipotent God *have to* do *anything*?

On a more personal level Deuteronomy 21:18-21 commands. "If a man have a stubborn and rebellious son, which will not obey the voice of his father, or the voice of his mother, and that, when they have chastened him, will not hearken unto them: Then shall his father and his mother lay hold on him, and bring him out unto the elders of his city… they shall say unto the elders of his city, 'This our son is stubborn and rebellious, he will not obey our voice…' and all the men of his city shall stone him with stones, that he die…"

If you are a parent you undoubtedly know that virtually all children become rebellious at some point, especially when in their early teens. For that matter you were most likely a difficult child yourself at some point. I know I was. Ask yourself if you would follow this directive from God. It does not matter that this is in the Old Testament. The question you must ask is was this ever the right thing for anyone to do at *any* time? I am amazed how otherwise rational and decent human beings can read such passages and not feel a sense of disgust, and will instead think up ways to excuse them. Why would anyone worship such a being? A loving God would not condone these acts and therefore these parts of the Bible could not possibly have been written by one and if that is the case it is fair to ask how much else did not come from the hand of God? Most Christians have never read the Bible and know about none of this because these passages are never mentioned in church so they can be excused to some degree for their ignorance, but once they do know the questions become how and why do human beings living in the modern world continue to worship and make excuses for such a God?

A Christian Nation

Or, Is America God's Country?

"Christianity neither is, nor ever was, a part of the Common Law."
~ Thomas Jefferson, in a letter to Dr. Thomas Cooper, 1814

I have lost count of the number of times I have seen someone post a comment on social media which reads something along the lines of, "This is a Christian nation founded on Judeo-Christian principles and anyone who isn't a Christian or who objects to school prayer and having the Ten Commandments posted outside courthouses should just leave!" Naturally I take exception to that sort of rhetoric given that I served honorably for twenty-five years in the Marine Corps and when I point out the incongruity of such remarks I am generally greeted with incredulity followed by statements such as "I will pray for you" and questions like "Where did you go wrong in life?" The bottom line is I am living proof of someone who is a patriot but not a Christian or for that matter a believer in any religion at all. Even a Born Again believer like President George W. Bush understood that when he said, "You can be a patriot if you don't believe in the Almighty. You can honor your country and be as patriotic as your neighbor."

A Christian evangelist named Mark Baird recently stated in an online article, "The writers of the U.S. Constitution were not God-haters as many would represent them. The truth is that they ALL believed in God. And they ALL believed that religious instruction was essential to preserving our nation and its freedoms." That is of course not accurate, but he banks on nobody checking the facts. Certainly some of the Founding Fathers were just as he said, but far from all. Notice that he carefully avoided calling them Christians because many if not most of the Founders were Deists. For those unfamiliar with the term Deists believe the universe had a creator but that "he" does not concern himself with the daily lives of humans and does not directly communicate with us either by revelation or through sacred books. They spoke often of "God" using language such as Nature's God or the God of Nature, but this was most certainly not the God of the Bible.

The seven men considered by historians to be the Founders were John Adams, Benjamin Franklin, Alexander Hamilton, John Jay, Thomas Jefferson, James Madison and George Washington. Of these only John Jay can be considered an orthodox Christian and it is he modern Christians have in mind when they talk about the Founding Fathers being devout. James Madison wrote, "Religious bondage shackles and debilitates the mind and unfits it for every noble enterprise" and John Adams said, "The divinity of Jesus is made a convenient cover for absurdity. Nowhere in the Gospels do we find a precept for Creeds, Confessions, Oaths, Doctrines, and whole cartloads of other foolish trumpery that we find in Christianity." Adams also wrote, "God is an essence that we know nothing of. Until this awful blasphemy is got rid of, there will never be any liberal science in the world" and most famously offered, "This would be the best of all possible worlds, if there were no religion in it."

George Washington for his part was very private about his beliefs but is widely considered a Deist. Historian Barry Schwartz wrote, "George Washington's practice of Christianity was limited and superficial because he was not himself a Christian... he repeatedly declined the church's sacraments. Never did he take communion, and when his wife Martha did he waited for her outside the sanctuary... even on his deathbed Washington asked for no ritual, uttered no prayer to Christ, and expressed no wish to be attended by His representative." In addition, according to Paul F. Boller in his anthology on Washington (which was based on exhaustive research), "There is no mention of Jesus Christ anywhere in his (Washington's) extensive correspondence."

Benjamin Franklin, an avowed Deist, said "I looked around for God's judgments, but saw no signs of them," and "In the affairs of the world, men are saved not by faith, but by the lack of it." In Poor Richard's Almanac he famously wrote, "Lighthouses are more helpful than churches" and "The way to see by faith is to shut the eye of reason." Priestley's Autobiography said of Franklin, "It is much to be lamented that a man of Franklin's general good character and great influence should have been an unbeliever in Christianity, and also have done as much as he did to make others unbelievers."

Thomas Paine, known as the "Firebrand of the American Revolution" and author of the book *Age of Reason*, was far more scathing in his assessments. He wrote, "Whenever we read the obscene stories, the voluptuous debaucheries, the cruel and torturous executions, the unrelenting vindictiveness, with which more than half of the Bible is filled, it would be more consistent that we call it the word of a demon than the word of God. It is a history of wickedness that has served to corrupt and brutalize mankind." He added, "Take away from Genesis the belief that Moses was the author, on which only the strange belief that it is the word of God has stood, and there remains nothing of Genesis but an anonymous book of stories, fables and traditionary or invented absurdities, or of downright lies… the story of Jesus Christ appearing after he was dead is the story of an apparition, such as timid imaginations can always create in vision, and credulity believe. Stories of this kind had been told of the assassination of Julius Caesar." Finally he opined, "All national institutions of churches, whether Jewish, Christian or Turkish, appear to me no other than human inventions, set up to terrify and enslave mankind, and monopolize power and profit."

Thomas Jefferson is the Founding Father most often claimed by Christians as one of their own but although he absolutely did believe in a God it was not the God of orthodox Christianity. He was a Deist who believed in Nature's God rather than a Christian who followed the God of Abraham and Isaac. Jefferson is of course the author of the *Jefferson Bible*, which came into existence when he took a razor to the New Testament. He omitted the Old Testament in its entirety because he considered it absurd and removed every verse dealing with the virgin birth, miracles, resurrection, claims of Jesus' divinity and other puerile superstition because he believed none of that. His reasons for doing this became clear when he said, "We discover in the Gospels a groundwork of vulgar ignorance, of things impossible, of superstition, fanaticism and fabrication." He also wrote to John Adams of the virgin birth, "And the day will come when the mystical generation of Jesus, by the supreme being as his father in the womb of a virgin will be classed with the fable of the generation of Minerva in the brain of Jupiter." Do those sound like the writings of a devout Christian?

Jefferson wrote of the separation of church and state in his letter to the Danbury Baptist Association, but in saying all religions should be able to practice freely he in no way endorsed a national motto invoking a God - any God. Christians who consider the U.S. to be a Christian nation like to point out "In God We Trust" is the official U.S. motto but mislead others by implying it was the Founders who first invoked it. In truth the Founder's original motto of "E Pluribus Unum" (from many, one), which I find far more appropriate for our melting pot, was adopted by an Act of Congress in 1782 and wasn't changed until 1956 at the height of McCarthyism and the "Red Scare." That is also when the words "Under

God" were added to the Pledge and for the same reason. I would suspect if the Founders had intended this to be a Christian nation those things would have been in place from the very beginning.

If you need definitive proof the 1796 Treaty with Tripoli clearly states the United States was "not in any sense founded on the Christian religion." This was not an idle statement meant to satisfy Muslims - they believed it, and meant it. This treaty was written during the presidency of George Washington, signed by President John Adams and unanimously ratified by the Senate.

Christians also frequently point to the Supreme Court building as evidence the United States is a Christian nation but are either grossly misinformed or willfully ignorant of the facts. Moses is presented not as a religious figure as they claim but as an example of one of the historical lawgivers of eastern civilizations. They probably never noticed this because it doesn't fit with their argument, but he is depicted along with Confucius and Solon, the Greek credited with having laid the foundations for Athenian democracy. Does that serve as an endorsement of Confucianism or the Gods of Ancient Greece? Of course not.

Other figures depicted inside and outside the Court building include Octavian, Napoleon, Charlemagne and Muhammed (yes, Muhammed!) amongst others. You may also find it interesting to note upon closer inspection the tablets Moses is holding on the building's exterior are blank and where he is shown inside the tablets list only Commandments 6-10 because they are considered secular. The first five which refer to God were purposely omitted.

Another misconception surrounds the Roman numerals I through X which are found on the doors and behind the Justices. They do not represent the Ten Commandments as some think but rather the Bill of Rights, not according to me but according to the sculptor who designed them, Adolph Weinman. In short if this was a Christian nation the Supreme Court, which is charged with interpreting and enforcing the provisions of the Constitution and whose building Christians like to use as an example, would not have refused an appeal to reverse a lower court ruling which directed the removal of the Ten Commandments from in front of the Alabama Supreme Court building in 2003.

As for the oft-cited notion that the United States was founded on Judeo-Christian principles consider the words of then-Senator Barack Obama who said in 2006, "And even if we did have only Christians in our midst, if we expelled every non-Christian from the United States of America, whose Christianity would we teach in the schools? Would we go with James Dobson's, or Al Sharpton's? Which passages of Scripture should guide our public policy? Should we go with Leviticus, which suggests slavery is okay and eating shellfish is abomination? How about Deuteronomy, which suggests stoning your child if he strays from the faith? Or should we just stick to the Sermon on the Mount, a passage that is so radical that it's doubtful our own Defense Department would survive its application? So before we get carried away, let's read our Bibles. Folks haven't been reading their Bibles."

Evangelism

Or, Knock Knock…

☥☬☯⛩ॐ✋☸✡✝☪☬☫✡☥

"People who want to share their religious views with you almost never want you to share yours with them." ~ Dave Barry

Believers of various religions and denominations are generally commissioned to spread the "good news" but some groups are more committed to door to door proselytization and street evangelism than others. Born Again Christians, Jehovah's Witnesses, Mormons, Hare Krishnas and Muslims are among the most active, while Judaism for example does not as a rule seek converts.

According to one Christian who goes door to door, "We are following the commandment that the savior gave in Mark 16:15, 'And he said unto them, Go ye into all the world, and preach the gospel to every creature.' We believe that we have a unique understanding of God's plan for all of us and that it is important that everybody have the opportunity to accept or reject his plan, so we go to every place we are allowed and give as many people the opportunity to hear the message as we can."

Clearly that person is convinced he has been called by God but the problem here is threefold. First of all he claims to have a unique understanding of God's Plan but if challenged to explain what that is will not have a coherent answer, second he accepts Scripture without question and third what about all of the other religions which would like to give him the opportunity to accept or reject *their* tenets? Would they be receptive to that? Of course not. British columnist Katharine Whitehorn made an excellent point about this when she said, "Why do born again people so often make you wish they'd never been born the *first* time?"

One of the most aggressive sects is the Jehovah's Witnesses for whom "pioneering" is the most important aspect of their faith. Whether you agree with them theologically or not they, like the previously quoted Born Again believer, honestly think only those who believe as they do will get to enjoy eternal life after the resurrection, therefore if they made no effort to get the word out they would be letting everyone go to their permanent deaths.

Mormon men ages nineteen to twenty-five are expected to serve a two year full time mission for the church. In fact that is all they do six days a week and despite their age they call themselves Elders because that is the priesthood office they hold, presumably because it lends credibility to these young men. They are required to wear white shirts and ties, spend mornings studying, afternoons going door-to-door, evenings teaching and always work in pairs, and while young women also occasionally serve missions they have to be at least twenty-one years old. Missions are usually financed by the missionaries themselves or their families because they don't have jobs while on their missions and that is interesting because what they are essentially doing is fundraising for the church since Mormons are required to tithe ten percent of their incomes.

Many people don't answer the door, but occasionally someone will ask them to sit down and then aggressively challenge their religious beliefs for as long as they'll stay. This is significant because freethinkers and atheist/agnostics tend to be far better educated on the topic, while in contrast most door-to-door religious proselytizers are poorly equipped to defend their prepackaged propaganda when challenged and if someone else takes the lead in the conversation don't know how to handle it because they are usually incapable of thinking independently.

Proselytizing is not by any means unique to Christianity. Da'wah, meaning "the issuing of a summons, call or invitation," is the duty of every Muslim and involves inviting people to their faith or recalling lapsed or nominal Muslims to a deeper faith. A Muslim preacher who seeks to evangelize is called a sheikh or imam and a Muslim who practices da'wah, either as a preacher, religious worker or someone engaged in a faith-building community activity, is called a da'i. A more aggressive approach for spreading the faith is of course Jihad or holy war, which is essentially the Muslim equivalent of the Christian Crusades and Inquisition.

It seems to be working, since Islam is growing at an annual rate of about three percent. In 1900 Muslims comprised about 12.4 percent of the world's population but as of 2001 Muslims comprise about twenty-two percent. How is that possible if Christianity is true? A website called Christian Answers explains, "The average Muslim around the world has a tremendous misunderstanding of Christianity… the factors that hold a Muslim to his religion are usually only about ten percent theological and ninety percent cultural. Muslims have to fit into a larger group of people in order to feel secure and belong. This could be an extended family, a network of friends, etc… when Muslims are confronted with the claims of Christ they may know it to be 'truth,' but are more worried about leaving their community than they are about not having the truth."

There's that word "truth" again. Let's turn that view on its head and look at it from the Muslim perspective. They will say, "The average Christian around the world has a tremendous misunderstanding of Islam… the factors that hold a Christian to his religion are usually only about ten percent theological and ninety percent cultural. Christians have to fit into a larger group of people in order to feel secure and belong. This could be an extended family, a network of friends, etc… when Christians are confronted with the claims of Allah they may know it to be truth, but are more worried about leaving their community than they are about not having the truth."

What is the difference between the two? Virtually nothing aside from perspective. Each faith misunderstands the other. Each is a product of enculturation. Each believes it possesses the "truth." And each seeks to spread its dominance by recruiting followers and vilifying the infidels in the opposing camp. In the words of George Carlin, "Religion is sort of like having lifts in your shoes. If it makes you feel better, fine. Just don't ask me to wear *your* shoes."

There are many variations used by different cults. For example one of the common tactics for recruiting people into Scientology is use of a "Stress Test" or "Personality Analysis." Kiosks can be found around the world along public walkways and inside malls where passersby are invited to sit down and participate in a process which claims to identify the origin(s) of stress in their lives using a device called an E-meter and a series of questions. When the dial of the meter moves the interviewer claims he/she has found a source of stress, but it is a scam. The aim is actually finding a person's "ruin," i.e. weakness, and exploit it. After all, in order to sell someone a solution one first has to convince him there is a problem. Your first reaction is probably that this strategy is disingenuous and typical of cults, but if you stop to think about it mainstream religions do the same thing by creating a problem called sin and then offering their dogma as the solution.

Standard practice is for missionaries to keep track of where they "tract," or knock on doors and they keep lists of people they want to follow up with much like salesmen do. The difference is the "product" they are selling is intangible. The obvious question is why would God need a sales force? Isn't he everywhere? Then there is the street preacher who does not interact with targets one on one but instead bombards pedestrians with threats of eternal damnation if they do not repent and embrace the one "true" God.

On a global scale missionaries have long been sent overseas to spread the word, build churches and recruit indigenous populations and it is no accident they operate primarily in the third world where they can target the superstitious, destitute and poorly educated masses. The low hanging fruit is always the easiest to pick. I witnessed this firsthand during the two years I lived in the Congo. Don't get me wrong, the missionaries I met were wonderful people and I counted them as friends, but then again we never discussed theology - they probably thought I was already a Christian and did not need to be recruited - and when I saw the way they took advantage of the local villagers' ignorance it made me cringe. In a broader sense missionaries were used as a tool of conquest in the political as well as the spiritual realm. As Bishop Desmond Tutu put it, "When the missionaries came to Africa they had the Bible and we had the land. They said, 'Let us pray.' And we closed our eyes. When we opened them we had the Bible and they had the land."

With the advent of social media such as Facebook religious evangelism is no longer confined to those who choose to walk through neighborhoods, knock on doors or stand on street corners. There are of course pages created for and devoted to religion which are visited by the faithful and that is fine because it is their choice, but many individuals also post memes about Jesus on a regular basis, some *ad nauseum*, and ask people to "like" them or comment "amen" if they agree and woe be unto anyone who speaks up with a differing opinion and does not automatically agree like a sheep.

Sam Harris identified this root of evangelism when he opined, "My concern with religion is that it allows us by the millions to believe what only lunatics could believe on their own" and former Governor Jesse Ventura bluntly cut to the heart of the insecurity and herd mentality of evangelism when he said, "Organized religion is a sham and a crutch for weak-minded people who need strength in numbers."

The irony is atheists don't as a rule knock on doors or preach on street corners, but should they openly express their skepticism or casually challenge even the most bizarre of beliefs they will be shouted down by the faithful and asked why they cannot just "keep their disbelief to themselves." The Sunday television airwaves are dominated by shows and in fact entire networks devoted to evangelism and have been for years, but when a group of rationalists created a show called *The Atheist Experience* on a local public access channel in Austin, Texas a few years ago which explores different facets of religion and in fact encourages religious viewers to call in and discuss their beliefs it was condemned. This time the question being asked was more along the lines of why can't you just keep your logic to yourself." What are the faithful so afraid of, one must wonder?

The Christmas Story

Or, The Real Reason For the Season

"It's probably worth noting that Christmas is a Pagan tradition and was banned by the Pilgrims." ~ Michael Hayne

Every year some people in the public eye, most notably television personality Bill O'Reilly, complain about the "War on Christmas" they believe is being waged by "secular forces" in America, but what exactly is the holiday they are supposedly waging war against about in the first place? Let's examine the tradition and where it came from.

After Thanksgiving most people's thoughts turn to Christmas because it has become an integral part of our culture aside from the fact it is the time professing Christians are supposed to focus on Jesus Christ. After all it is the "Christ-mas" season, although non-religious aspects such as Rudolph the Red-nosed Reindeer, holly wreaths, mistletoe, decorated trees, Season's Greetings, seasonal music, chestnuts roasting on an open fire, exchanging gifts and Santa Claus are all associated with and dominate this holiday and bring warm feelings to those who celebrate it... including non-Christians.

The celebration of Christmas in a secular sense can be a lot of fun but those who see it as a celebration of Christ's birth are a good example of the credulous mentality associated with religion because many if not most of the traditions associated with the holiday are either secular in nature or are of pagan origin. Even the very date on which it is celebrated is in question, but most people simply accept the traditions passed down to them by their predecessors and never reflect on why they believe what they believe or do what they do. We live in a world filled with customs and traditions but few ever seek to understand their origins and instead tend to accept them without question. Most simply follow the crowd and do what everyone else does.

Let's examine the roots of Christmas and look at why people follow the customs associated with it. For instance why is it kept on December 25th and did the early New Testament Church keep it? Let's avoid all assumptions and only accept what can be proven. To begin with exactly when was Jesus born, assuming he existed at all? Questions abound about both the year and day and popular myth puts his birth on December 25th in the year 1 CE but the New Testament, the only "record" of the event although it was not written until several decades later, gives no date or year. The Gospel of Mark, written about 65 CE and therefore the earliest, begins with the baptism of an adult Jesus which suggests the earliest Christians lacked interest in or knowledge of Jesus' birthdate.

The year of his birth was eventually "determined" by someone named Dionysius Exiguus, a Scythian monk and abbot of a Roman monastery. His calculation went as follows: In the Roman, pre-Christian era years were counted from *Ab Urbe Condita* ("the founding of the City," i.e. Rome), thus 1 AUC signifies the year Rome was founded, 5 AUC signifies the 5th year of Rome's reign, etc. Dionysius figured since Roman Emperor Augustus reigned forty-three years and was followed by the Emperor Tiberius, Luke 3:1-23 indicates when Jesus turned thirty years old it was the fifteenth year of Tiberius reign and since he lived fifteen years under Augustus (placing Jesus birth in Augustus' 28th year of reign since he took power in 727 AUC) that put Jesus' birth in 754 AUC - however Luke 1:5 places his birth in the days of King Herod and he died in 750 AUC, four years before the year in which Dionysius places Jesus' birth. Professor Emeritus of Biblical Studies at the Catholic University of America Joseph A. Fitzmyer, a member of the Pontifical Biblical Commission and former president of the Catholic Biblical Association, wrote in the Catholic Church's official commentary on the New Testament, "Though the year (of Jesus' birth) is not reckoned with certainty, the birth did not occur in 1 CE. The Christian era, supposed to have its starting point in the year of Jesus birth, is based on a miscalculation introduced circa 533 by Dionysius Exiguus."

So exactly how did Christmas come to be celebrated on December 25? The *DePascha Computus*, an anonymous document believed to have been written in North Africa around 243 CE, placed Jesus' birth on March 28 while Clement, a Bishop of Alexandria circa 215 CE, thought he was born on November 18, but based on other historical records Fitzmyer guesses Jesus' birth occurred - ironically, as it later turned out - on September 11 in the year 3 BCE.

The Christmas holiday as it is celebrated today evolved over a long period of time and its traditions are drawn from a wide variety of sources. Roman pagans first introduced the holiday of Saturnalia, a week long period of lawlessness which was celebrated between December 17 and 25, during which Roman courts were closed and Roman law dictated no one could be punished for damaging property or injuring people during the celebration. The festival began when Roman authorities chose "an enemy of the Roman people" to represent the "Lord of Misrule." Each Roman community selected a victim whom they forced to indulge in food and other physical pleasures throughout the week and at the festival's conclusion on December 25th Roman authorities believed they were destroying the forces of darkness by brutally murdering this innocent man or woman. Ancient Greek writer, poet and historian Lucian described the festival's observance in his dialogue entitled *Saturnalia* and in addition to human sacrifice he mentioned the customs of widespread intoxication, going from house to house while singing naked, rape and other sexual license and even the consumption of human-shaped biscuits which are incidentally still produced today in some English and most German bakeries during the Christmas season.

In the 4th Century CE Christianity imported the Saturnalia festival and in doing so hoped to absorb the pagan masses along with it, and in fact Christian leaders succeeded in converting large numbers of pagans by promising them they could continue to celebrate the Saturnalia as Christians. The problem was there was nothing intrinsically Christian about Saturnalia so to remedy this Christian leaders identified Saturnalia's concluding day of December 25th as Jesus' birthday, however they had little success in refining the practices of the festival. As Professor of History at the University of Massachusetts in Amherst Stephen Nissenbaum observed, "In return for ensuring massive observance of the anniversary of the Savior's birth by assigning it to this resonant date, the Church for its part tacitly agreed to allow the holiday to be celebrated more or less the way it had always been." As a result the earliest Christmas holidays were celebrated by drinking, sexual indulgence and singing naked in the streets, a precursor of modern caroling. An article in *The Toronto Star* in December of 1984 observed, "The Reformation cast a blight on Christmas. By then, of course, clever ecclesiastical politicians had adopted the Pagan mid-winter festival as the alleged birthdate of Jesus of Nazareth and thrown in a few other Pagan goodies to make their takeover more palatable." In other words December 25th was not selected because it was the birth date of Christ or even near it but was chosen because it coincided with the Pagan festival of Saturnalia. Naturally Christian apologists have explained away this mystery by saying things such as "...we do not know the exact date of Christ's birth... (but) while God certainly could have made it known, He chose to hide it from the world's eyes." For what purpose, one must wonder?

The Reverend Increase Mather of Boston observed in 1687 that, "The early Christians who first observed the Nativity on December 25 did not do so thinking that Christ was born in that month, but because the heathens' Saturnalia was at that time kept in Rome and they were willing to have those Pagan holidays metamorphosed into Christian ones." Because of its known Pagan origin Christmas was actually banned by the Puritans and its observance was illegal in Massachusetts between 1659 and 1681 although it was and still is celebrated by most Christians in spite of that.

Some of the most depraved customs of the Saturnalia carnival were intentionally revived by the Catholic Church in 1466 when Pope Paul II, for the amusement of Roman citizens, forced Jews to race naked through the streets of the city. An eyewitness account reported, "Before they were to run, the Jews were richly fed so as to make the race more difficult for them and at the same time more amusing for spectators. They ran… amid Rome's taunting shrieks and peals of laughter, while the Holy Father stood upon a richly ornamented balcony and laughed heartily."

As part of the Saturnalia carnival throughout the 18th and 19th Centuries rabbis of the ghetto in Rome were forced to wear clownish outfits and march through the city streets to the jeers of the crowd while being pelted by a variety of missiles, and when the Jewish community of Rome sent a petition to Pope Gregory XVI in 1836 begging him to stop the annual abuse of the Jewish community he responded, "It is not opportune to make any innovation," and on December 25, 1881 Christian leaders in Poland whipped the masses into Anti-Semitic frenzies which led to riots across the country. In Warsaw twelve Jews were brutally murdered, huge numbers maimed and many Jewish women raped.

December 25 was also regarded as the birth date of the Iranian mystery god Mithra known as the Sun of Righteousness, and on the Roman New Year of January 1 houses were decorated with greenery and lights and gifts were given to children and the poor. To these observances were added the German and Celtic Yule rites when the Teutonic tribes penetrated into Gaul, Britain and central Europe with food, good fellowship, the Yule log and Yule cakes, greenery and fir trees, gifts and greetings, all commemorating different aspects of this festive season. In fact fires and lights, symbols of warmth and lasting life, have always been associated with winter festivals both Pagan and Christian.

Christ, if he was born at all, was almost certainly born in the fall if the Gospels are to be believed. Many still mistakenly think he was born around the beginning of winter and they are wrong. The *Adam Clarke*

Commentary points out, "It was custom among Jews to send out their sheep to the deserts about the Passover (early spring) and bring them home at the commencement of the first rain." The first rains began in early-to-mid fall. Continuing with this same quote, "During the time they were out, the shepherds watched them night and day. As... the first rain began early in the month of March-esvan, which answers to part of our October and November (begins sometime in October), we find that the sheep were kept out in the open country during the whole summer. And as these shepherds had not yet brought home their flocks, it is a presumptive argument that October had not yet commenced, and that, consequently, Jesus was not born on the 25th of December when no flocks were out in the fields; nor could he have been born later than September as the flocks were still in the fields by night. On this very ground, the nativity in December should be given up. The feeding of the flocks by night in the fields is a chronological fact... see the quotations from the Talmudists in Lightfoot."

Luke 2:8 says when Christ was born, "And there were in the same country shepherds abiding in the field, keeping watch over their flock by night." Note that they were "abiding" in the field. This never happened in December. Both Ezra 10:9-13 and the Song of Solomon 2:11 show that winter was the rainy season and shepherds could not stay in cold, open fields at night. Numerous encyclopedias plainly state Christ was not born on December 25th and in fact the *Catholic Encyclopedia* directly confirms this, yet every year millions of people celebrate on that day simply because it is what they have always done.

Nearly all aspects of Christmas observance have their roots in Roman custom and religion. In 1984 *The Buffalo News* opined, "The earliest reference to Christmas being marked on December 25 comes from the second century after Jesus' birth. It is considered likely the first Christmas celebrations were in reaction to the Roman Saturnalia, a harvest festival that marked the winter solstice - the return of the sun - and honored Saturn, the god of sowing. Saturnalia was a rowdy time, much opposed by the more austere leaders among the still-minority Christian sect. Christmas developed, one scholar says, "As a means of replacing worship of the 'sun' with worship of the 'Son.' By 529 A.D., after Christianity had become the official state religion of the Roman Empire, Emperor Justinian made Christmas a civic holiday and the celebration of Christmas reached its peak - some would say its worst moments - in the medieval period when it became a time for conspicuous consumption and unequaled revelry."

Consider these quotes from the *Catholic Encyclopedia*, 1911 edition: "Christmas was not among the earliest festivals of the Church... the first evidence of the feast is from Egypt." Further, "Pagan customs centering round the January calendar gravitated to Christmas." Under "Natal Day" Origen, an early Catholic writer, admitted, "...in the Scriptures, no one is recorded to have kept a feast or held a great banquet on his birthday. It is only sinners (like Pharaoh and Herod) who make great rejoicings over the day on which they were born into this world." The *Encyclopedia Americana* 1956 edition adds, "Christmas... was not observed in the first centuries of the Christian church, since the Christian usage in general was to celebrate the death of remarkable persons rather than their birth... a feast was established in memory of this event (Christ's birth) in the 4th Century. In the 5th Century the Western church ordered the feast to be celebrated on the day of the Mithraic rites of the birth of the sun and at the close of the Saturnalia, as no certain knowledge of the day of Christ's birth existed."

There is no mistaking the origin of the modern Christmas celebration and although many additional sources could be cited we will return to this later, so let's begin to tie some other facts together because it was three hundred years after Christ before the Roman church kept Christmas and not until the 5th Century that it was mandated to be kept throughout the empire as an official festival honoring "Christ" - and the trappings we know today would be gradually added through the centuries.

For example no discussion of Christmas traditions would be complete without some explanation of the "Christmas tree." Just as early Christians recruited Roman pagans by associating Christmas with the Saturnalia, so too worshippers of the Asheira cult and its offshoots were recruited by the Church sanctioning "Christmas trees." Pagans had long worshipped trees in the forest and even brought them into their homes and decorated them so this observance was adopted and painted with a Christian veneer by the Church. The modern Christmas tree originated in Germany but the Germans got it from the Romans, who in turn got it from the Babylonians and the Egyptians. The following excerpt from Walsh's *Curiosities of Popular Customs* demonstrates what the Babylonians believed about the origin of the Christmas tree: "An old Babylonish fable told of an evergreen tree which sprang out of a dead tree stump. The old stump symbolized the dead Nimrod, the new evergreen tree symbolized that Nimrod had come to life again in Tammuz! Among the Druids the oak was sacred, among the Egyptians it was the palm and in Rome it was the fir, which was decorated with red berries during the Saturnalia!" Frederick J. Haskin's *Answers to Questions* states, "The Christmas tree is from Egypt, and its origin dates from a period long anterior to the Christian Era." Did you know the Christmas tree long preceded Christianity? I certainly didn't.

Most aspects of Christmas are not referred to in the Bible because the traditions have been adapted from paganism or simply invented later on but "Christmas trees" are indeed directly mentioned, although not in the way a Christian might think. Jeremiah 10:2-5 says, "Thus says the Lord, Learn not the way of the heathen... for the customs of the people are vain: for one cuts a tree out of the forest, the work of the hands of the workman, with the axe. They deck it with silver and with gold; they fasten it with nails and with hammers, that it move not. They are upright as the palm tree, but speak not: they must needs be borne, because they cannot go. Be not afraid of them; for they cannot do evil, neither also is it in them to do good." This plain description of the modern Christmas tree is clear and even the Bible directly refers to them as "the way of the heathen" and yet Christians ignorant of that Scripture erect and decorate them every year simply because that's what everyone else does.

Another common Christmas tradition is mistletoe. Norse mythology recounts how the god Balder was killed using a mistletoe arrow by his rival god Hoder while fighting for the female Nanna, Druid rituals use mistletoe to poison their human sacrificial victim and the Christian custom of kissing under the mistletoe is a later synthesis of the sexual license of Saturnalia with the Druidic sacrificial cult. The Pagan custom of kissing under the mistletoe was natural on a night which involved much revelry done in the spirit of drunken orgies and just like today this kissing usually occurred at the beginning of the Saturnalia/Christmas celebration. Mistletoe was even considered to have special powers of healing for those who reveled under it. The *Encyclopedia Britannica*, under "Santalales" states, "The European mistletoe is thought to have had special ritual significance in Druidical ceremonies and lives in folklore today, its special status as the Christmas mistletoe having come from Anglo-Saxon times." In fact mistletoe is a parasite which lives on oak trees, and not coincidentally the Druids worshipped in oak tree groves.

The same is true of holly wreaths and Yule logs. The *Encyclopedia Americana* states, "The holly, the mistletoe, the Yule log... are relics of pre-Christian times." In other words they stem from Paganism. For example the Yule log was commonly used in a rite of Teutonic nature worship and the Christmas wreath is traceable to the pagan custom of decorating buildings and places of worship at the feast which took place during the winter solstice. The *Encyclopedia Britannica* under "Celastrales" tells us, "European pagans brought holly sprays into their homes, offering them to the fairy people of the forests as refuges from the harsh winter weather, and during the Roman winter festival of Saturnalia branches of holly were exchanged as tokens of friendship. The earliest Roman Christians adopted that practice, and apparently used holly as a decoration at the Christmas season." Like mistletoe, holly berries were also thought to be sacred to the sun god. The original "sun log" came to be called the Yule log. "Yule" simply means "wheel," which has long been a Pagan representation of the sun. People today commonly speak of the "sacred yule-tide season," and yet none of it has anything to do with the birth of Jesus.

So what about Christmas presents? Is it scriptural to exchange gifts? Merchants regularly report that over sixty percent of their annual retail sales occur during the Christmas shopping season, which represents a tremendous amount of gift buying. Most today believe gift-giving comes from the biblical example of the "three wise men" - the Bible gives no number - presenting gifts to Christ. Is this true, and if not where did the practice of exchanging gifts come from?

The *Bibliotheca Sacra* states, "The interchange of presents between friends is a like characteristic of Christmas and the Saturnalia and must have been adopted by Christians from the pagans, as the admonition of Tertullian plainly shows." How so? In pre-Christian Rome the emperors compelled their most despised citizens to bring offerings and gifts in December during the Saturnalia and during Kalends in January. Later this ritual expanded to include gift-giving among the general populace and the Catholic Church gave this custom a Christian flavor by re-rooting it in the supposed gift-giving of Saint Nicholas, aka "Santa Claus."

Nicholas was born in Parara, Turkey in 270 CE, later became Bishop of Myra, died on December 6th in 345 CE and was not named a saint until the 19th Century. He was also among the most senior bishops who convened the Council of Nicaea in 325 CE and created the New Testament. In 1087 a group of sailors who idolized Nicholas moved his bones from Turkey to a sanctuary in Bari, Italy and there he supplanted a female boon-giving deity called "The Grandmother" or "Pasqua Epiphania" who used to fill the children's stockings with gifts. The Grandmother was ousted from her shrine at Bari, which became the center of the Nicholas cult, and members of this group gave each other gifts during a pageant they conducted annually on the anniversary of Nicholas' death. The Nicholas cult spread north until it was adopted by

German and Celtic pagans. These groups worshipped a pantheon led by Woden, aka Odin, their chief god and the father of Thor, Balder and Tiw. Woden had a long white beard and rode a horse through the heavens one evening each autumn, so when Nicholas merged with Woden he shed his Mediterranean appearance, grew a beard, mounted a flying horse (later exchanged for eight flying reindeer), rescheduled his flight for December and donned heavy winter clothing. It wasn't long before, in a bid for pagan adherents in Northern Europe, the Catholic Church adopted the Nicholas cult and taught that he did - and they should - distribute gifts on December 25th instead of December 6th.

In 1809 novelist Washington Irving, who is most famous for *The Legend of Sleepy Hollow* and *Rip Van Winkle*, wrote a satire of Dutch culture entitled *Knickerbocker History*. The satire refers several times to the white bearded, flying-horse riding Saint Nicholas using his Dutch name "Santa Claus." Dr. Clement Moore, a professor at Union Seminary, read *Knickerbocker History* and in 1822 published a poem based on the character Santa Claus you are probably familiar with: "T'was the night before Christmas, when all through the house, not a creature was stirring, not even a mouse. The stockings were hung by the chimney with care, in the hope that Saint Nicholas soon would be there…" Moore innovated by portraying a Santa with eight reindeer who descended through chimneys.

Bavarian illustrator Thomas Nast then almost completed the modern picture of Santa Claus. From 1862 through 1886, based on Moore's poem, Nast drew more than 2,200 cartoon images of Santa for *Harper's Weekly*. Before Nast, Saint Nicholas had been pictured as everything from a stern looking bishop to a gnome-like figure in a frock. Nast also gave Santa a home at the North Pole, a workshop filled with elves and his list of the good and bad children of the world. All he was missing was his red outfit, but it wouldn't be long before that appeared also. In 1931 the Coca Cola Corporation contracted Swedish commercial artist Haddon Sundblom to create a coke-drinking Santa and Sundblom modeled him on his friend Lou Prentice who was chosen for his cheerful, chubby face. The corporation insisted that Santa's fur-trimmed suit be bright "Coca Cola red" and the Santa we know today was born - a blend of Christian crusader, pagan god and commercial idol.

Parents reason they owe the whole Christmas myth to their children because such traditions are focused primarily on kids. In fact some years ago when a priest in New Jersey told his Sunday school class Santa was a myth the outrage from parents and his supervisors was swift. He had "killed Santa, destroyed family tradition, usurped family authority," and was officially censored by his superiors for being "overzealous and insensitive." His crime? He told the truth.

If you once accepted Santa as being real that is a perfect example of following the crowd without question or thought. According to Langer's *Encyclopedia of World History* "Santa" was a common name for Nimrod throughout Asia Minor - the very same resurrected fire god who came down the chimneys of the ancient Pagans and to whom infants were burned and eaten in human sacrifice among those who were once "God's people." Like virtually every other aspect of Christmas the shocking truth is even this supposedly Christian custom does not come from the Bible and it is ironic people believe they are following the custom of "the wise men giving to Christ" when actually they are giving almost exclusively to each other.

Speaking of the "wise men," the Scripture describing them is Matthew 2:1-11. "Now when Jesus was born in Bethlehem of Judaea in the days of Herod the King, behold, there came wise men (no number given) from the east to Jerusalem, saying 'Where is he that is born King of the Jews?... and when they were come into the house (rather than manger), they saw the young child with Mary his mother, and fell down, and worshipped him... and when they had opened their treasures, they presented unto him gifts; gold, and frankincense and myrrh."

It is commonly supposed these were birthday presents for Baby Jesus but is this what the Bible says? Absolutely not. It is important to note they gave gifts to Jesus and did not stand in his presence and exchange gifts amongst themselves or give them to others as people celebrating Christmas do today. They also arrived well after his "birthday" and that is another reason these could not have been birthday presents.

Some accounts of the "three wise men" are accompanied with their names: Caspar, Melchior, and Balthasar. The earliest reference to these names is from *Excerpta Latina Barbari*, which is a Latin translation of an early 6th Century Greek manuscript. The names are purely tradition as they do not appear in Scripture or have any early witness. In other words they were made up much, much later.

In 1990 in the Cleveland suburb of Solon, Ohio the local school board banned all nativity and other Christmas scenes on school property because they felt it violated the separation of church and state and were challenged in court by outraged parents who felt Christmas was being stolen from their children. The board lost the case because the citizenry ironically contended Christmas was a worldwide tradition which was *not* part of, and transcended, any religion. In the end it was deemed to be secular and a part of virtually all cultures worldwide. The court decision affirmed from a legal perspective that Christmas has no Christian roots, although the opinion also noted that Bible reading and prayer obviously are associated with Christianity. The court concluded Christmas-keeping and manger scenes could remain because they are not really part of either Christianity or religion but prayer and Bible reading, which are, must remain excluded from schools.

Previous discussion introduced the subject of the Saturnalia so let's examine just exactly who Saturn was. Consider the following quote from another large American newspaper, the *Democrat and Chronicle* of Rochester, New York in December of 1984. "The Roman festival of Saturnalia, Dec. 17-24, moved citizens to decorate their homes with greens and lights and give gifts to children and the poor. The Dec. 25 festival of natalis solis invicti, the birth of the unconquered sun, was decreed by the emperor Aurelian in A.D. 274 as a Winter Solstice celebration, and sometime (later)... was Christianized as a date to celebrate the birth of the Son of Light."

Dr. William Gutsch, chairman of the American Museum of Natural History and the Hayden Planetarium, further confirmed the original name of Christmas with this quote on December 18, 1989 in a Westchester, New York newspaper, *The Reporter Dispatch*. "The early Romans were not celebrating Christmas but rather a pagan feast called the Saturnalia. It occurred each year around the beginning of winter, or the winter solstice. This was the time when the sun had taken its lowest path across the sky and the days were beginning to lengthen, thus assuring another season of growth. The Saturnalia, of course, celebrated Saturn the fire god. Saturn was the god of sowing (planting) because heat from the sun was required to allow for planting and growth of crops. He was also worshipped in this dead-of-winter festival so that he would come back (since he was the "sun") and warm the earth again so that spring planting could occur. The planet Saturn was later named after him because, among all of the planets, with its rings and bright red color, it best represented the god of fire. Virtually every civilization has a fire/sun god. The Egyptians and sometimes the Romans called him Vulcan. The Greeks named him Kronos, as did the Phoenicians - but they also called him Saturn. The Babylonians called him Tammuz (as Nimrod, resurrected in the person of his son), Molech or Baal, as did the Druids. These were all simply the various names for Nimrod. Nimrod was considered the father of all the Babylonian gods."

Let's more closely examine the actual history and origins of some of the Saturnalia customs still practiced today. Notice the following quote from the *Dictionary of Greek and Roman Antiquities*, "Oscilla" 3rd Edition, Volume II: "...all ranks devoted themselves to feasting and mirth, presents were exchanged among friends, and crowds thronged the streets, shouting 'Lo Saturnalia.' An offering was made beneath a decorated evergreen tree according to the pagan poet Virgil. Figurines and masks called 'oscilla' were hung on the tree, as are Christmas decorations today. History admits... there can be no doubt that we have in these 'oscilla' a relic of human sacrifice..." Modern oscilla look like chubby little "angels" when hanging on a tree. In fact you may have placed these little "angel babies" on your tree. Did you ever stop to wonder what they really represent? Of course not. Doesn't all of this sound familiar? Presents, singing in the streets, evergreen trees, decorations, offerings under the tree, merrymaking, feasting? They may sound wonderful, but they represent things that are pagan in origin."

One additional source demonstrates how this all came to be a heritage practiced so innocently by millions. The following quote is from the *Encyclopedia Britannica*, 15th Edition, Volume 10. "Christianity... by a complex and gradual process... became the official religion of the [Roman] empire. For a time, coins and other monuments continued to link Christian doctrines with worship of the sun, to which Constantine had been addicted previously. But even when this phase came to an end, Roman paganism continued to exert other, permanent influences, great and small... The ecclesiastical calendar retains numerous remnants of pre-Christian festivals, notably Christmas, which blends elements including both the feast of the Saturnalia and the birthday of Mithra. But, most of all, the mainstream of Western Christianity owed ancient Rome the firm discipline that gave it stability and shape." An authority as reputable as the *Encyclopedia Britannica* actually acknowledges, for anyone willing to look, that the Saturnalia and ancient Rome are what defined the "discipline... stability and shape" of Western Christianity.

The next quote reveals how this idolatrous, pagan festival slipped into the Christian world. It is from the *New Schaff-Herzog Encyclopedia of Religious Knowledge* under the heading "Christmas." "How much the date of the festival depended upon the pagan Brumalia (December 25) following the Saturnalia (Dec. 17-24), and celebrating the shortest day of the year and the 'new sun'... cannot be accurately determined. The pagan Saturnalia and Brumalia were too deeply entrenched in popular custom to be set aside by Christian influence... The pagan festival with its riot and merry-making was so popular that Christians were glad of an excuse to continue its celebration with little change in spirit and in manner. Christian preachers of the West and the Near East protested against the unseemly frivolity with which Christ's birthday was celebrated, while Christians of Mesopotamia accused their Western brethren of idolatry and sun worship for adopting as Christian this pagan festival."

One additional source reveals how the Roman church absorbed Christmas into an official celebration. The *Encyclopedia Britannica* 1946 edition states, "Christmas was not among the earliest festivals of the church... certain Latins, as early as 354, may have transferred the birthday from January 6th to December 25, which was then a Mithraic feast... or birthday of the unconquered SUN... the Syrians and Armenians, who clung to January 6th, accused the Romans of sun worship and idolatry, contending... that the feast of December 25th had been invented by disciples of Cerinthus..." Thus a pagan festival celebrated long before Christ's birth found its way into recognized Christianity.

The following quote reveals how this has happened. It also comes from the *Encyclopedia Britannica* under the heading "Christianity." "Thus, the Easter liturgy has been developed more highly in the Eastern Orthodox Church, and the Christmas liturgy more highly in the Roman Catholic Church... The Christian calendar is the most widely disseminated Christian institution. The seven-day week and the rhythm of the Christian festivals have been accepted even by most of the non-Christian countries. Despite energetic attempts at the introduction of a sliding work week, the seven-day week with work-free Sunday could not be eliminated even in Communist states with a secular worldview. Even in atheist circles and organizations throughout the world Christian holidays enjoy an undisputed popularity as work-free days, especially Christmas." Truly, it has been the "ecclesiastical politicians" referred to earlier who have sought to impose the modern "Christian" calendar on an unknowing world. It is these leaders who have "thought to change times and laws."

In contrast the Pilgrims who came to America in 1620 were strict Puritans with firm views on religious holidays such as Christmas and Easter. Scripture did not name any holiday except the Sabbath, they argued, and the very concept of holy days implied that some days were not holy. "They for whom all days are holy can have no holiday," was a common Puritan maxim. Puritans were particularly contemptuous of

Christmas, nicknaming it "Foolstide" and banning their flock from any celebration of it throughout the 17th and 18th Centuries.

The main reason Puritans didn't like Christmas was it was a raucously popular holiday in late medieval England. Each year rich landowners would throw open their doors to the poor and give them food and drink as an act of charity, the poorest man in the parish was named the "Ord of Misrule" and the rich would wait upon him at feasts which often descended into bawdy drunkenness. Such decadence never impressed religious purists. "Men dishonor Christ more in the twelve days of Christmas," wrote 16th Century clergyman Hugh Latimer, "than in all the twelve months besides."

Puritans in the English Parliament eliminated Christmas as a national holiday in 1645 amid widespread anti-Christmas sentiment and settlers in New England went even further, outlawing Christmas celebrations entirely in 1659. Anyone caught shirking their work duties or feasting was forced to pay a significant penalty of five shillings. Christmas returned to England in 1660, but in Massachusetts remained banned until the 1680s. In 1686 the royal governor of the colony, Sir Edmund Andros, sponsored a Christmas Day service at the Boston Town House and fearing a violent backlash from Puritan settlers was flanked by redcoats as he prayed and sang Christmas hymns.

The Puritans kept up their boycott of Christmas in Massachusetts for decades with Cotton Mather, New England's most influential religious leader, telling his flock in 1712, "The feast of Christ's nativity is spent in reveling, dicing, carding, masking, and in all licentious liberty... by mad mirth, by long eating, by hard drinking, by lewd gaming, by rude reveling!" European settlers in other American colonies continued to celebrate it however, both as a pious holiday and a time for revelry.

Anti-Christmas sentiment flared up again around the time of the American Revolution when Colonial New Englanders began to associate Christmas with royal officialdom and refused to mark it as a holiday. Even after the U.S. Constitution came into effect the Senate assembled on Christmas Day in 1797 as did the House in 1802, and it was only in the following decades that disdain for the holiday slowly ebbed away. In 1836 Alabama became the first state to declare Christmas a public holiday and other states soon followed suit, but New England remained defiantly Scrooge-like and as late as 1850 schools and markets remained open on Christmas Day. It was not until 1870 that Christmas Day was formally declared a federal holiday by President Ulysses S. Grant.

As was mentioned previously some now claim a "war on Christmas" is being waged but naturally those making that charge are ignorant of the true origins of the holiday. This was highlighted by the following response retailer WalMart gave to a customer who complained that a cashier had said Happy Holidays rather than Merry Christmas. "Christmas traditions are rooted in Siberian shamanism and Santa is also borrowed from the Caucuses, mistletoe from the Celts, yule log from the Goths, the time from the Visigoth and the tree from the worship of Baal. It is a wide world." In other words not pandering to one group does not amount to discrimination and the bottom line is take away all of the secular, pagan and invented elements which have been added to the celebration of Christmas over the years from Santa Claus and his elves to Rudolph the red-nosed flying reindeer, Frosty the Snowman, Christmas trees, the Yule log, gift giving and even the Nativity scene and there is little doubt the day would lose its luster and pass without much fanfare for most people.

The Easter Story

Or, Chocolate, Bunnies, Eggs and... Ishtar

"Before representatives of Christianity begin to answer modern questions about the resurrection with biblical assertions as the source of their authority, they should face the possibility that the Bible might be wrong about the literal details of Easter." ~ Bishop John Shelby Spong

It's springtime. Flowers and bunnies decorate the home. Fathers help children paint beautiful designs on eggs dyed in various colors. These eggs, which will later be hidden and searched for, are placed into lovely seasonal baskets. The aroma of fresh baked hot cross buns wafts through the house. Forty days of abstaining from special foods will finally end the next day. The whole family picks out their Sunday best to wear to the next morning's sunrise worship service to celebrate the savior's resurrection and the renewal of life. Everyone looks forward to a succulent ham with all the trimmings. It will be a thrilling day because after all it is one of the most important religious holidays of the year. Sound familiar?

If you are a Christian you no doubt think that was a description of Easter, but you would be wrong. It was actually a description of an ancient Babylonian family two thousand years before Christ honoring the resurrection of their god Tammuz who was brought back from the underworld by his mother/wife Ishtar, after whom the festival was named. As Ishtar was actually pronounced "Easter" in most Semitic dialects it could be said the event portrayed is in a sense Easter. Of course the occasion also could have easily been a Phrygian family honoring Attis and Cybele or perhaps a Phoenician family worshipping Adonis and Astarte. Also fitting the description would be a heretic Israelite family honoring the Canaanite Baal and Ashtoreth or this depiction could just as easily represent any number of other pagan fertility celebrations of death and resurrection including the modern Easter celebration as it has come to us through the Anglo-Saxon fertility rites of the goddess Eostre or Ostara. These are all the same festivals, separated only by time and culture.

What is the origin of Lent and sunrise services? How did rabbits, eggs and hot cross buns become associated with Christ's resurrection? Is Easter mentioned in the Bible? Did the apostles and early Church keep it? Most people follow along as they have been taught, assuming what they believe and do is right. They take their beliefs for granted and most do not take time to understand why they do the things they do. Why do you believe what you believe? Where did you get your beliefs? Is the source of your religious beliefs the Bible, or some other authority? Are you sure? Take Easter for example. Since hundreds of millions keep it, supposedly in honor of Jesus' resurrection, then certainly the Bible must have much to say about it. Surely there are numerous verses mentioning rabbits, egg hunts, baskets of candy, hot cross buns, Lent, Good Friday and sunrise services, not to mention Easter itself.

If Easter is not found in the Bible, and it is not, where did it come from? The vast majority of ecclesiastical and secular historians agree the name Easter and the traditions surrounding it are deeply rooted in pagan religion. The following quotes demonstrate more about the true origin of how the modern Easter celebration got its name.

The *New Catholic Encyclopedia* tells us, "Since Bede the Venerable, the origin of the term for the feast of Christ's Resurrection has been popularly considered to be from the Anglo-Saxon Eastre, a goddess of spring... the Old High German plural for dawn, eostarun; whence has come the German Ostern, and our English Easter."

Albert Henry Newman's *A Manual of Church History* explains, "The fact that vernal festivals were general among pagan peoples no doubt had much to do with the form assumed by the Eastern festival in the Christian churches. The English term Easter is of pagan origin."

In *Festival, Holy Days, and Saints Days* Ethel L. Urlin says, "On this greatest of Christian festivals, several survivals occur of ancient heathen ceremonies. To begin with, the name itself is not Christian but pagan. Ostara was the Anglo-Saxon Goddess of Spring."

According to Alice Hazeltine in the *Easter Book of Legends and Stories,* "The name Easter comes to us from Ostera or Eostre, the Anglo-Saxon goddess of spring for whom a spring festival was held annually, as it is from this pagan festival that some of our Easter customs have come."

Steve Englehart's *Easter Parade* points out, "In Babylonia... the goddess of spring was called Ishtar. She was identified with the planet Venus, which, because... (it) rises before the sun or sets after it and appears to love the light (which means Venus loves the sun-god)... in Phoenicia she became Astarte, in Greece, Eostre (related to the Greek word Eos or 'dawn') and in Germany 'Ostara' from the German word "Ost" (east) which is the direction of dawn."

Many names are interchangeable for the more well-known Easter and pagans typically used many different names for the same god or goddess. Nimrod, the Bible figure who built the city of Babylon according to Genesis 10:8-10, is an example. He was worshipped as Saturn, Vulcan, Kronos, Baal, Tammuz, Molech and others but was always the same fire or sun god universally worshipped in nearly every ancient culture. The goddess Easter was no different. She was the goddess of fertility with many names who was worshipped in spring when all life was being renewed.

Well known historian Will Durant wrote in his famous and respected work *Story of Civilization*, "Ishtar (Astarte to the Greeks, Ashtoreth to the Jews) interests us not only as analogue of the Egyptian Isis and prototype of the Grecian Aphrodite and the Roman Venus, but as the formal beneficiary of one of the strangest of Babylonian customs... known to us chiefly from a famous page in Herodotus: Every native woman is obliged, once in her life, to sit in the temple of Venus (Easter) and have intercourse with some stranger." Is it any wonder the Bible speaks of the religious system which has descended from that ancient city as "Mystery, Babylon the great, the mother of harlots and abominations of the earth" (Rev. 17:5)?

Let's look more closely at the origin of other customs associated with the modern Easter celebration. As previously noted "Ishtar" was a day which commemorated the resurrection of the Babylonian god "Tammuz" who was believed to be the only begotten son of the moon-goddess and the sun-god. In those ancient times there was a man named Nimrod who was the grandson of Noah's son Ham. Ham had a son named Cush who married a woman named Semiramis and they then had a son and named him Nimrod. After the death of his father Nimrod married his own mother and became a powerful King.

Nimrod became a god-man to the people and his wife/mother Semiramis became the powerful Queen of ancient Babylon. Nimrod was eventually killed by an enemy and his body was cut in pieces and sent to various parts of his kingdom, so Semiramis had all of the parts gathered except for one part which could not be found - his penis. She claimed Nimrod could not come back to life without it and told the people of Babylon he had ascended to the sun and was now to be called "Baal" the sun god, and also proclaimed Baal would be present on earth in the form of a flame, whether candle or lamp, when used in worship.

Semiramis claimed to have been immaculately conceived, taught the moon was a goddess which went through a twenty-eight day cycle and ovulated when full and further said she had come down from the moon in a giant moon egg which fell into the Euphrates River at the time of the first full moon after the spring equinox. She became known as "Ishtar," and her moon egg became known as "Ishtar's egg."

Ishtar soon became pregnant, claimed it was the rays of the sun-god Baal which had caused her to conceive and the son she brought forth was named Tammuz. He was noted to be especially fond of rabbits and they became sacred in that ancient religion because Tammuz was believed to be the immaculately conceived son of the sun-god Baal and like his supposed father became a hunter. One day Tammuz was killed by a wild pig and Queen Ishtar told the people he was now ascended to his father Baal and the two of them would be with worshippers in the sacred candle or lamp flame as Father, Son and Spirit.

Ishtar, who was now worshipped as the "Mother of God and Queen of Heaven," continued to build her mystery religion. She told worshippers when Tammuz was killed by the pig some of his blood fell on the stump of an evergreen tree and the stump grew into a full new tree overnight, which made the evergreen sacred by his blood. She also proclaimed a forty day period of sorrow each year prior to the anniversary of the death of Tammuz during which no meat was to be eaten. Worshippers were to meditate upon the sacred mysteries of Baal and Tammuz, make the sign of the "T" in front of their hearts as they worshipped and eat sacred cakes with the marking of a "T" or cross on the top. Every year on the first Sunday after the first full moon following the spring equinox a celebration was made. This was Ishtar's Sunday, and it was celebrated with rabbits and eggs.

By now it should be obvious paganism is the basis for many Christian rituals, further study indicates they happened by way of the Roman Catholic System and therefore Easter has nothing whatsoever to do with the resurrection of Jesus Christ. We also know Easter can be as much as three weeks away from the Passover because the pagan holiday is always set as the first Sunday after the first full moon after the spring equinox. While it is true the word "Easter" appears in Acts 12 of the King James Bible (called the "Festival of Unleavened Bread" in other translations) it says it was the evil King Herod who was planning to celebrate Easter rather than the Christians and the truth is the forty days of Lent, eggs, rabbits, hot cross buns and the Easter ham have everything to do with the ancient pagan religion of Mystery Babylon.

In Acts 12:1 King Herod began to persecute the Church, culminating in the brutal death of the apostle James by sword. This pleased the Jews so much the apostle Peter was also taken prisoner by Herod and the plan was to later deliver him to the Jews. Verse 3 says, "Then were the days of unleavened bread," which was incorrectly translated in the King James Bible as "Easter." The New Testament Church was actually observing these feast days described in Leviticus 23 rather than talking about Easter. How do we know? The word translated to Easter is the Greek word "pascha" (derived from the Hebrew word pesach; there is no original Greek word for Passover) and it has only one meaning. It always means Passover and can never mean Easter. For this reason we find a Hebrew word used in the Greek New Testament and once again this Hebrew word can only refer to Passover and translations including the *Revised Standard Version* correctly render this word as Passover. Instead of endorsing Easter this verse proves the Church was still observing the supposedly Jewish Passover ten years after the alleged death of Christ.

At this point we should look at other Scriptures authorizing Easter but the problem is there are none. That's right there are absolutely no verses anywhere in the Bible which direct or endorse the keeping of an Easter celebration. It also says nothing about Lent, eggs and egg hunts, baskets of candy, etc. although according to fundamentalist "Bible Christians" it does mention hot cross buns and sunrise services as abominations which God condemns. They point out buns had been made in the spring for hundreds of years before Jesus Christ by most cultures and nations in the world and that Jeremiah 7:18 and 44:19 talk about pagans making cakes to the "queen of heaven." As for sunrise services Ezekiel 8:15-18 prohibits any connection to the sun while worshipping and in any case Jesus supposedly rose the night before at the end of three days and three nights and when the women arrived at his tomb the following morning he was already long gone. More paganism.

Once again the name itself originated with the names of ancient gods. The Venerable Bede (672-735 CE), a Christian scholar, first asserted in his book *De Ratione Temporum* that Easter was named after Eostre, a.k.a. Eastre, the Great Mother Goddess of the Saxon people in Northern Europe. Similarly the Teutonic dawn goddess of fertility was known variously as Ostare, Ostara, Ostern, Eostra, Eostre, Eostur, Eastra, Eastur, Austron and Ausos. Her name was derived from the ancient word for spring which was "eastre." Similar goddesses were known by other names in ancient cultures around the Mediterranean and were celebrated in the springtime. Some were Aphrodite of Greece and Cyprus, Ashtoreth from ancient Israel, Astarte from ancient Greece, Demeter from Mycenae, Hathor from ancient Egypt, Ishtar from Assyria, Kali from India and the Norse goddess of fertility, Ostara.

An alternative explanation has been suggested in which the name given by the Frankish church to Jesus' resurrection festival included the Latin word "alba" which means "white," a reference to white robes worn during the festival. "Alba" also means "sunrise" and when the name of the festival was translated into German the sunrise meaning, which became "ostern" in German, was selected in error.

There are also two popular beliefs about the origin of the English word "Sunday." The first says it is derived from the name of the Scandinavian sun goddess Sunna (a.k.a. Sunne or Frau Sonne) and the second suggests it is derived from "Sol," the Roman God of the Sun, since their phrase "Dies Solis" means "day of the sun." The Christian saint Jerome commented, "If it is called the day of the sun by the pagans, we willingly accept this name, for on this day the Light of the world arose, on this day the Sun of Justice shone forth."

Many if not most Pagan religions in the Mediterranean area had a major seasonal day of religious celebration at or following the Spring Equinox. For example the Phrygian fertility goddess Cybele had a consort named Attis who was said to have been born via a virgin birth and was believed to have died and been resurrected each year during the period of March 22 to March 25. Gerald L. Berry, author of *Religions of the World*, wrote, "About 200 B.C. mystery cults began to appear in Rome just as they had earlier in Greece. Most notable was the Cybele cult centered on Vatican hill. Associated with the Cybele cult was that of her lover, Attis (the older Tammuz, Osiris, Dionysus or Orpheus under a new name). He was a god of ever-reviving vegetation. Born of a virgin, he died and was reborn annually. The festival began as a day of blood on Black Friday and culminated after three days in a day of rejoicing over the resurrection." It seems wherever Christian worship of Jesus and Pagan worship of Attis were active in the same geographical area in ancient times Christians "...used to celebrate the death and resurrection of Jesus on the same date; and pagans and Christians used to quarrel bitterly about which of their gods was the true prototype and which the imitation."

Many religious historians and liberal theologians believe the death and resurrection legends were first associated with Attis many centuries before the birth of Jesus and were simply grafted onto stories of Jesus' life in order to make Christian theology more acceptable to Pagans while others suggest many of the events in Jesus' life which were recorded in the Gospels were lifted from the life of Krishna, the second part of the Hindu Trinity. Of course ancient Christians had an alternative explanation, claiming Satan had created counterfeit deities in advance of the coming of Christ in order to confuse humanity, but that is obviously a completely fabricated rationalization because it isn't contained anywhere in Scripture and presumably God would have known this and warned us. It also raises the question of how Satan could have known ahead of time this would be necessary. Did God give him a heads up? Or is the Devil omniscient too? Of course modern Christians generally regard the Attis legend as a pagan myth of little value with no connection to Jesus and Jesus' death and resurrection account as being true and unrelated to earlier traditions.

That aside, Wiccans and other modern-day Neopagans continue to celebrate the Spring Equinox as one of their eight yearly Sabbats or holy days of celebration. In the Mediterranean this is a time of sprouting the summer's crop and farther north it is the time for seeding. Their rituals at the Spring Equinox are related primarily to the fertility of the crops and balance of the day and night times. In those places where Wiccans can safely celebrate the Sabbat outdoors without threat of religious persecution they often incorporate a bonfire into their rituals and jumping over the dying embers is believed to assure fertility of people and crops.

Early Christians kept the Passover, not Easter. From the *Encyclopedia Britannica*, 11th edit., Vol. 8: "There is no indication of the observance of the Easter festival in the New Testament, or in the writings of the Apostolic Fathers... the first Christians continued to observe the Jewish festivals (of Leviticus 23) though in a new spirit, as commemorations of events which those festivals had foreshadowed. Thus the Passover, with a new conception added to it, of Christ as the true Paschal Lamb... continued to be observed."

Despite the clear intention that the "holy days" as listed in Leviticus 23 be kept by Christians today (Acts 2:1; 12:3; 18:21; 20:6, 16; I Cor. 5:7-8; 16:8) almost no one who claims to believe in the God of the Bible keeps them and almost no one who professes to worship Jesus Christ observes the Passover eternally as the Bible commands. Why?

Easter has long been known to be a pagan festival and moreover America's founders knew this. A children's book about the holiday, *Easter Parade: Welcome Sweet Spring Time!* by Steve Englehart states, "When the Puritans came to North America, they regarded the celebration of Easter - and the celebration of Christmas - with suspicion.

They knew pagans had celebrated the return of spring long before Christians celebrated Easter... for the first two hundred years of European life in North America only a few states, mostly in the South, paid much attention to Easter." It was not until after the Civil War that Americans begin celebrating it and Easter first became an American tradition in the 1870s. That means the original thirteen colonies of a supposedly Christian nation did not observe Easter for the first century of its existence. What happened to change this?

According to theologian Johannes Cassianus, who wrote in the 5th Century, "Howbeit you should know, that as long as the primitive church retained its perfection unbroken, this observance of Lent did not exist," and since there is no instruction to observe Lent in the Bible where did it come from? According to John Landseer and *Sabaean Researches* a forty-day abstinence period was anciently observed in honor of the pagan gods Osiris, Adonis and Tammuz. In *The Two Babylons* Alexander Hislops says of the origin of Lent, "The forty days abstinence of Lent was directly borrowed from the worshippers of the Babylonian goddess. Such a Lent of forty days in the spring of the year is still observed by the Yezidis or Pagan Devil-worshippers of Koordistan who have inherited it from their early masters, the Babylonians. Such a Lent of forty days was held in spring by the Pagan Mexicans... (and it) was observed in Egypt..." Clearly Lent came from paganism rather than the Bible.

Eggs have always been associated with the Easter celebration and nearly every culture in the modern world has a long tradition of coloring eggs in beautiful and different ways. Francis X. Weiser's *Handbook of Christian Feasts and Customs* explains, "The origin of the Easter egg is based on the fertility lore of the Indo-European races... the egg to them was a symbol of spring... in Christian times the egg had bestowed upon it a religious interpretation, becoming a symbol of the rock tomb out of which Christ emerged to the new life of His resurrection." This is a direct example of exactly how pagan symbols and customs are "Christianized," i.e., Christian-sounding names are superimposed over pagan customs.

In the *Encyclopedia Britannica* we find, "Around the Christian observance of Easter... folk customs have collected, many of which have been handed down from the ancient ceremonial... symbolism of European and Middle Eastern pagan spring festivals... for example, eggs... have been very prominent as symbols of new life and resurrection."

Finally, the following comes from *Egyptian Belief and Modern Thought* by James Bonwick: "Eggs were hung up in the Egyptian temples. Bunsen calls attention to the mundane egg, the emblem of generative life, proceeding from the mouth of the great god of Egypt. The mystic egg of Babylon, hatching the Venus Ishtar, fell from Heaven to the Euphrates. Dyed eggs were sacred Easter offerings in Egypt, as they are still in China and Europe. Easter, or spring, was the season of birth, terrestrial and celestial." What could more plainly demonstrate the true origin of the Easter egg? It naturally progressed that the egg, representing spring and fertility, would be merged into an already pagan springtime festival but connecting this symbol to Christ's resurrection in the spring required much creativity and rationalizing.

As for the origin of the "Easter Bunny" the Reverend Francis Weiser wrote, "In Germany and Austria little nests containing eggs, pastry and candy are placed in hidden spots and the children believe that the Easter Bunny, so popular in this country too, had laid the eggs and brought the candy" and "The Easter Bunny had its origin in pre-Christian fertility lore… has never had religious symbolism bestowed on its festive usage… however, the bunny has acquired a cherished role in the celebration of Easter as the legendary producer of Easter eggs for children in many countries." John Bradner wrote in *Symbols of Church Seasons and Days*, "The Easter Bunny is not a true Christian symbol" and according to *The Encyclopedia of Religion,* "Although adopted in a number of Christian cultures, the Easter Bunny has never received any specific Christian interpretation." This demonstrates how no one has ever been able to connect the Easter Bunny to anything Christian, let alone to the Bible, but none of this will stop millions of professing Christians from decorating their lawns and houses with Easter bunnies each spring. Consider this last quote from the *Encyclopedia Britannica*: "The hare, the symbol of fertility in ancient Egypt, a symbol that was kept later in Europe… its place has been taken by the Easter rabbit." Even in modern times rabbits have remained common symbols of fertility but while their rapid rate of reproduction is well known another problem arises - they do not lay eggs. While both are clearly fertility symbols there is no logical way to connect them, however in a world filled with pagan tradition truth and logic can be lost and merging these symbols with Christianity makes an already idolatrous practice even worse.

There is nothing Christian about any of these symbols yet they are blindly embraced by the faithful and the true history of these fertility symbols is unknown to children who have been led by adults to think them so special. The belief these are Christian is a lie foisted on innocent children who will believe "the moon is made of cheese" just because someone tells them so. So why are these thing perpetrated? Simply because they help maintain interest among the masses.

One of the central themes of the New Testament is Jesus Christ came to die for mankind's sins but is he the real savior central to the Easter Sunday tradition? Is it the Jesus Christ of the Bible? If you say "yes," are you sure? History answers this question plainly. John M. Robertson writes in *Christianity and Mythology,* "The conception of a Savior-God was quite normal in the ancient pagan world... a conception of salvation underlies the notion of such Gods as Osiris, Attis, and Adonis..." and Arthur Nock says in *Early Gentile Christianity and its Hellenistic Background,* "It has often been urged that this belief in the Resurrection of Jesus is due to ideas of divine resurrection current in the contemporary world... stories of Attis, Adonis, and Osiris... In the pagan stories the rising again is a joyous reversal of defeat; in the Christian story it is the complement of victorious death. It may be said that Attis and Osiris saved by rising again, Jesus by dying... the Easter observance did not arise at once out of belief in the resurrection, but developed later by gradual stages out of the Jewish Pasch. The notion implied in the Easter greeting Christ is risen is a secondary development; the idea comes from this festival and from its occurrence in spring; the festival does not come from the idea. The idea of Christ's resurrection was injected into the old practice of Easter observance and not the other way around."

Famous historian James George Frazer put his into context in *The Golden Bough* when he observed, "Now the death and resurrection of Attis were officially celebrated at Rome on the 24th and 25th of March, the latter being regarded as the spring equinox, and... according to an ancient and widespread tradition Christ suffered on the 25th of March... the tradition which placed the death of Christ on the 25th of March... is all the more remarkable because astronomical considerations prove that it can have had no historical foundation... when we remember that the festival of St. George in April has replaced the ancient pagan festival of the Parilia; that the festival of St. John the Baptist in June has succeeded to a heathen Midsummer festival of water; that the festival of the Assumption of the Virgin in August has ousted the festival of Diana; that the feast of All Souls (following Halloween) in November is a continuation of an old heathen feast of the dead; and that the Nativity of Christ himself was assigned to the winter solstice in December because that day was deemed the Nativity of the Sun; we can hardly be thought to be rash or unreasonable in conjecturing that the other cardinal festival of the Christian church - the solemnization of Easter - may have been in like manner, and from like motives of edification, adapted to a similar celebration of the Phrygian god Attis at the vernal equinox... it is a remarkable coincidence... that the Christian and the heathen festivals of the divine death and resurrection should have been solemnized at the same season... (and) it is difficult to regard the coincidence as purely accidental." To summarize, the Roman Catholic Church had a practice of incorporating pagan festivals, i.e. of pasting Christian names over them and calling them Christian in order to make Christianity more palatable and familiar to heathen worshippers whom the Church was trying to attract. The entirety of traditional Christianity is actually worshipping Baal and people can worship in ways representing things which are far different from what they sincerely believe or intend. The bottom line is ancient sun worship, dressed up in Easter finery and bonnets, is just modern packaging of a very old pagan custom. It has been said, "The only thing man has learned from history is that no one learns from history." George Santayana took it further saying, "Those who do not learn the lesson of history are doomed to repeat it."

According to Scripture it was ordained that the Passover should be kept once a year, forever. The New Testament Passover also includes an ordinance of humility called the footwashing. This instruction is found in John 13:2-15 and was commanded by Christ to be taught to all who would learn God's doctrines. In Matthew 28:19-20 Christ commanded his disciples, "Go you therefore, and teach all nations, baptizing them... Teaching them to observe all things whatsoever I have commanded you." This instruction includes the Passover complete with the footwashing and symbols of the bread and wine as well as keeping the Days of Unleavened Bread and the rest of God's annual feast days.

A modern Christian reading this might say, "I know Easter comes from paganism, but I'm not pagan. I celebrate it in honor of Christ. I focus on Him." Be that as it may, the Sunday Resurrection idea came into use as a means of endorsing Sunday-keeping, in other words worshipping on the day of the sun, in place of keeping the "true" Sabbath day of Saturday. Modern scholarship is reflected in the words of Bishop John Shelby Spong who wrote, "We need to remember first that the Easter experience occurred around 30 CE, while the Gospel stories about that experience were not written until sometime between the years 70 and 100 CE. This means the Gospels were not eyewitness accounts. When the New Testament is read in the order it was written it is also easy to see how those stories grew and exactly when miraculous new details were added to the narratives and as the literal accuracy of the resurrection narratives becomes suspect the foundations of Christianity itself began to tremble. Before we can begin positive speculation about the meaning of Easter, we must clear the debris of literalism and the fanciful claims of pre-modern people. Let me be specific about the following parts of the resurrection story: An angel did not descend from the sky on the wings of an earthquake to roll away the stone from the door of the tomb in order to make the resurrection announcement. A deceased man did not walk out of his grave physically alive three days after his execution by crucifixion. The risen Jesus did not walk, talk, eat, teach or invite the disciples to handle his physical flesh. Jesus did not literally defy gravity and ascend to the top of a three-tiered universe. These legendary aspects of the Easter story are no longer viewed as literally true in the academic world of biblical scholarship."

It is important to note those words did not come from the pen of an atheist, but instead from a respected theologian.

Jesus Christ

Or, Lord, Liar, Lunatic… or Legend

"It was only much later that he was made flesh and blood [in the Gospels] on paper. Thus Christ was created as a literary creation."
~ Paul Louis Couchoud

A point first raised by apologist C.S. Lewis and often made today by Christians when someone questions the divinity of Jesus Christ is if he was not the Lord incarnate as claimed then he must have been either a Liar or a Lunatic… but there is one other possibility, another "L," and as it happens it is the most likely. That word is Legend. The central tenet of Christianity is of course the belief Jesus Christ is the Son of God and died for our sins, and as a boy I never had reason to doubt that. After all, it was right there in the Bible and the Bible is, well… the Bible! Plus my parents told me it was true, pretty much everyone we knew believed the same thing and the message was reinforced in church every Sunday. As if that were not enough, to seal the deal I was terrified by the prospect of eternal damnation in Hell and enamored by the promise of eternal life in a perfect place like Heaven. Hmmm… choose Heaven or Hell? It was a no-brainer. After all as a Catholic I simply had to be good to get there, and if I did mess up all I had to do was go to confession and get absolved. What could be easier? An added benefit to my good behavior was I still believed Santa was watching to see whether or not I was naughty or nice and I liked getting presents.

Like most Christian children I said my prayers every night at bedtime but even then questioned the necessity of the line, "if I die before I wake, I pray the Lord my soul to take." Why, I wondered, do I need to ask? From a psychological standpoint that planted a seed in my mind and caused me to think about the possibility of dying in my sleep, something which should be the farthest thing from a child's mind, but it had never occurred to me to question my parents because I knew they would never lie to me… at least until the day I figured out the truth about Santa and soon thereafter the Easter Bunny and for the first time had a difficult time separating fantasy from reality.

The basis for my beliefs was of course the Bible but since I was young I had to rely upon what I'd heard at Mass and was taught during Catechism. My parents' solution was to buy me a beautifully illustrated book called *The Bible Story* which explained the narrative in a way even a child could understand. I loved reading the stories of Noah's Ark, David and Goliath, the walls of Jericho coming down and of course Jesus' life as only a child can and it never once occurred to me they had been sanitized... although I still had some questions for my parents. Why, I asked, could a God powerful enough to create the whole universe only have one son? Why was it necessary for that son to be sacrificed in order for God to forgive? Couldn't he just forgive as I had been taught to do? And if God had given his only son, but now he was up in Heaven with his father, what did he actually sacrifice? It was then I learned neither of my parents and for that matter no one in my entire family had ever actually read the Bible. Like many Christians they were good, simple hardworking people who earnestly believed based upon what they had been told by others and had heard in church, but like ninety percent or more of the people in my congregation they had decided the Bible was either too long, too difficult to understand or there simply wasn't enough time to read it.

It was around this time we switched churches and went from being Catholics to Lutherans and everything changed for me. One minute my eternal soul was dependent upon my conduct and the next it was simply a matter of believing in and accepting Jesus. Both could not possibly be true at the same time, I reasoned. The explanation my parents gave for the change was much of the Catholic Mass was conducted in Latin while Lutheran services were exclusively in English and they also felt the Pastor at *Our Redeemer* church was more down to earth and approachable than Priests at the *St. William the Abbott* parish. One of the side effects of the transition was having the Catholic doctrine of transubstantiation explained to me for the first time. I had naturally assumed the wafer and wine were purely symbolic but when I found out it was believed to be the actual body and blood of Jesus I was shocked - I had for all intents and purposes been practicing cannibalism. Another thing which I had always taken for granted and done by rote, but was now viewing from a new perspective, was the Lord's Prayer and Hail Mary. When I now heard them recited over and over again it reminded me of a mind control technique which might be used by some sort of cult. It was all quite confusing and I decided there was only one way I could make sense of it all, so I sat down and read the Bible from cover to cover. I had always been told it was the "perfect, inerrant and living Word of God," but as I made my way through it became quite disillusioned. My mouth was agape as I read of the genocide, infanticide, racism, misogyny and fratricide which fills the pages of the "good book," so I sought out my Pastor for guidance. He assured me that while the God of the Old Testament was indeed angry and vengeful I would find a loving Jesus once I reached the New Testament, so I kept on reading. He was of course right but then a new question arose in my mind. Was there any reason to believe the fantastic claims being made about Jesus? I wasn't sure, so I did the only thing an honest young man could do in such a situation - I investigated for myself, weighed the facts and arrived at a conclusion based upon those facts. I made it a point to take into account my natural biases and did my best to remain objective, but that wasn't always easy. Naturally, I wanted the story which would potentially lead to salvation and immortality for both myself and my loved ones to be true, so I gave it the benefit of the doubt before getting started.

Now that I had read the Bible for myself I made a concerted effort to understand it. It seemed to me everyone I spoke with had a different interpretation of what it said and they all couldn't possibly be right so I began to read books by leading Christian apologists which might clear things up. What I discovered was they too disagreed about many things and much of what they said was not only contradictory but illogical so I turned to the other side of the question to see what they had to say. Keep in mind back in those days there wasn't a lot out there to go by because atheism was still viewed as a cult of devil worshippers by many and most such people were in the closet for fear of ostricization and even persecution, and of course proponents of the so-called "new atheism" such as Dawkins, Hitchens and Harris were yet to be heard from. As a result my reading was limited to such things as Thomas Paine's *Age of Reason*, science textbooks and the observations of philosophers and scientists like Voltaire, Albert Einstein, Bertrand Russell, Ayn Rand and others. What I discovered was there was very little disagreement amongst them but instead unanimity of thought and very little of what they said required interpretation or rationalization. I felt that sort of conformity was the bedrock upon which truths are built but there was still one hurdle to get over - I was clinging to that little, irrational voice in the back of my mind known as "faith." At this point what it all came down to was an objective examination of the Gospels. I decided to accept them if there was a reasonable chance they were true and factual but in the back of my mind dreaded going down that road because I knew where it might lead. Here is what I discovered.

Although the majority of scholars today believe a man named Jesus lived on earth the reasons for this appear suspicious once you consider the history and evolution of Jesus scholarship. Although some secular freethinkers accept a historical Jesus minus the miracles they, like most Christians, simply accept the traditional view without question but as time goes on more and more scholars have begun to open the way to a more honest look at the evidence, or should I say lack of evidence. No physical evidence exists of a historical Jesus - no artifacts, dwellings, works of carpentry or self-written manuscripts - and as a result all claims about his existence must be derived from the writings of other people. There is no contemporary Roman record which mentions Pontius Pilate executing a man named Jesus and more to the point there is not a single contemporary writing which mentions him. All documents about Jesus came well after his life from either unknown authors, people who had never met an earthly Jesus or in demonstrably fraudulent, mythical or allegorical writings. In other words all of the sources derive from hearsay accounts.

Hearsay means information derived from other people rather than based upon a witnesses' own knowledge. Courts of law do not generally allow hearsay as testimony nor does honest modern scholarship because it does not provide reliable evidence. If you do not understand this, imagine yourself being charged with a crime you know you did not commit. You feel confident no one can prove guilt because you know there can exist no evidence for the charge against you. Now imagine standing in a court of law which allows hearsay as evidence and when the prosecution presents its case everyone who takes the stand claims you committed the crime. They are not as eyewitness themselves mind you, but instead claim other people told them so and none of those other people ever show up in court. Clearly hearsay does not work as evidence because there is no way of knowing whether or not the person based his or her information on errors, faulty memory, wrongful belief or biases or simply lied.

Contemporary authors of ancient history can of course only write from indirect observation about times which are long past so a valid historian's writings must be cited with sources which trace to the subject themselves or to eyewitnesses and artifacts. For example a modern historian who writes about the life of George Washington cannot serve as an eyewitness but can provide citations to documents which give personal or eyewitness accounts not to mention having access to Washington's home at Mount Vernon, personal artifacts used or worn by the subject and the writings of Washington himself - and despite all this information unfounded myths such as the famous "cherry tree" incident manage to find their way into the narrative. In contrast none of the historians who wrote about Jesus were eyewitnesses or cite reliable sources so all of their writings remain pure hearsay.

The most "authoritative" accounts of Jesus naturally come from the four canonical Gospels of the Bible. Note that these Gospels were not added to the Bible as original and authoritative by the authors themselves but rather through the influence of early church fathers. The most influential of them all was Irenaeus of Lyon, who lived in the middle of the 2nd Century. Many heretical gospels existed by that time but Irenaeus considered only some of them for mystical reasons and claimed only four in number which were according to British Egyptologist, historian and archaeologist John Romer, "like the four zones of the world, the four winds, the four divisions of man's estate, and the four forms of the first living creatures - the lion of Mark, the calf of Luke, the man of Matthew, the eagle of John (see Iranaeus' *Against the Heresies*). The four Gospels then became Church canon for the orthodox faith and most of the other claimed gospel writings were burned, destroyed or lost."

Professor of Religion at Princeton University Elaine Pagels wrote, "Although the Gospels of the New Testament - like those discovered at Nag Hammadi (a collection of Gnostic writings discovered in Egypt in 1945 which will be discussed later) - are attributed to Jesus' followers, no one knows who actually wrote any of them." Not only do we not know who wrote them, consider that none of the Gospels existed during the alleged life of Jesus nor do any of the unknown authors ever claim to have actually met an earthly Jesus plus none of the original Gospel manuscripts or "signatures" exist and we only have copies of copies.

The consensus of most biblical historians put the dating of the earliest Gospel, that of Mark, sometime after 70 CE and the last Gospel, John, after 90 CE. This would make it some forty years after the alleged crucifixion of Jesus before there were any Gospel writings which mention him. Elaine Pagels writes, "The first Christian Gospel was probably written during the last year of the war, or the year it ended. Where it was written and by whom we do not know; the work is anonymous, although tradition attributes it to Mark..."

The traditional Church has of course portrayed the authors as the apostles Mark, Luke, Matthew and John but scholars know from critical textural research there is simply no evidence the Gospel authors could have served as the apostles described in the Gospel stories, and yet even today priests and ministers describe these authors as the actual disciples of Christ. Many Bibles still continue to label the stories as "The Gospel according to St. Matthew, St. Mark, St. Luke and St. John" although no apostle could or would have announced his own sainthood before the Church established the doctrine of canonization. As an experiment to determine authorship for yourself imagine the Gospels without their titles and see if you can figure out from the texts who wrote them. Those names appear nowhere. The "clues" about authorship require huge doses of interpolation and rationalization and the bottom line is those names were added sometime in the 2nd Century simply to lend authenticity to the accounts.

The Gospel of Mark describes the first written Bible Gospel and although it appears deceptively after the Matthew Gospel in the Bible it was written at least a generation before Matthew. From its own words one can deduce the author of Mark had neither heard Jesus speak nor served as his personal follower and whoever wrote it simply accepted the legend of Jesus without question and wrote a crude and ungrammatical account of a story which was popular at the time. Historians tell us of the three Synoptic Gospels (Matthew, Mark, Luke) Mark clearly served as the common element between Matthew and Luke and provided the main source for both because of Mark's 666 verses some 600 appear in Matthew and 300 in Luke. It is revealing to note most Bibles actually show 678 verses for Mark rather than 666, but many biblical scholars think the last twelve verses came from later interpolation because the earliest manuscripts and other ancient sources do not include Mark 16:9-20. Moreover the text style does not match and the transition between verse eight and nine appears awkward. That serves as an example of how biblical texts could have been and in fact were altered and the fact that some of today's Bibles such as the New International Version exclude the last twelve verses can be viewed as a tacit admission of that.

The author of Matthew obviously got much of his information from Mark's Gospel, used them for his own purposes and fashioned his narrative to appeal to Jewish tradition and Scripture although he did improve on the grammar of Mark's Gospel, corrected what he felt was theologically important and heightened the miracles and magic.

The author of Luke, for his part, actually admitted he was acting as an interpreter of earlier material and was not an eyewitness (Luke 1:1-4). Many scholars think he lived as a gentile or at the very least a Hellenized

Jew. Many modern scholars also believe the Gospels of Matthew and Luke came from both the Mark Gospel and a hypothetical document called "Q" (German *Quelle* which means "source") but since we have no manuscript from Q no one could possibly determine its author, where or how he got his information or the date of its authorship. Moreover some scholars challenge its existence and those who do think Q existed have problems explaining it. Again we are faced with unreliable methodology and obscure sources.

John, the last Gospel, presents us with long theological discourses which could not possibly have come as literal words from a historical Jesus. It also disagrees with events described in Mark, Matthew and Luke and moreover the unknown author(s) of this Gospel wrote it in Greek near the end of the 1st Century. Even more problematic, according to Bishop John Shelby Spong, the book "carried within it a very obvious reference to the death of John Zebedee (John 21:23)," its supposed author.

Naturally there are those who will vehemently deny the Gospels are in conflict with one another because they are the "perfect and inerrant word" so let's take a look at one event and place the four stories side by side for comparison. Not just any story mind you, but the very lynchpin of Christianity - the story of the resurrection. Before getting started keep in mind the "evidence" for this event is to be found in the Bible and nowhere else and of course it is not a neutral or objective source because it was written by individuals who wanted people to believe Jesus was the Jewish Messiah and was still alive. I'll say it again - no evidence of this purported event exists outside the Bible and no contemporaneous written accounts of it appear anywhere in any records or non-biblical sources whatsoever. The accounts in the first four books of the New Testament in the Christian Bible is all there is. Of course Christians would have you believe all of the Gospels were written by eyewitnesses to the events who were close associates of Jesus but can offer no evidence to support this and in any case that is covered elsewhere in this chapter. In the end we are expected to take it on faith or at best some very shaky rationalizing. The entire thing hangs on two alleged events: Jesus' tomb being found empty and Jesus appearing to some of his followers soon afterwards before then going bodily up to Heaven. Let's now look at the four accounts one at a time.

Matthew 28:1-20 tells us Mary Magdalene and "the other" Mary arrive at the tomb and an earthquake occurs. Then an angel appears and rolls back the stone from the mouth of the tomb and sits upon it. The keepers (i.e. the guards who had been placed there to make sure the body wasn't stolen) "became like dead men." The angel says Jesus has risen and takes them to see where he had been. He then tells them to go and tell the disciples. On the way Jesus appears and tells them to tell the disciples to go to Galilee where they will meet him. The keepers are then bribed by their officers to say they fell asleep but nonetheless somehow saw Jesus' followers come and steal the body and we are not told if anyone believed this story. All eleven of Jesus' disciples then go to Galilee and meet Jesus on a mountain and Matthew says nothing about Jesus ascending to Heaven.

Mark 16:1-20 says Salome, Mary Magdalene and Mary the Mother of James go to the tomb but this time the stone has already been rolled back. There is no earthquake and no angel sitting upon the rolled-back stone. Instead they find a young man sitting inside the tomb. He tells them Jesus is not there but has risen. He then tells them to go and tell the disciples and Peter what has happened and to make their way to Galilee where they would meet Jesus however the women were afraid, fled and said nothing to anyone. Jesus then appeared to Mary Magdalene but when she told the disciples they didn't believe her. He then appeared to two of the disciples as they walked in the country and they told the others but still no one believed them. Afterwards Jesus appeared to all eleven in a room and told them they were to go and preach and all those who believed them could cast out devils, speak new languages, handle serpents, drink poison with impunity and heal the sick just by touching them. Jesus then goes to Heaven but we are not told how or when.

Luke 24:1-53 claims Mary Magdalene, Joanna and Mary the Mother of James (and maybe other women; it's not clear) go to the tomb and find it open and empty. Two men appear standing near them who tell the women Jesus has risen. The women then go and tell the eleven disciples but they don't believe them so Peter goes to check and wonders what has happened. Two men then go to Emmaus, about 7.5 miles from Jerusalem, we aren't told why, and there Jesus appears but they don't recognize him. He then spends all day with them and has a meal, suddenly they recognize him and then he vanishes. They then go back to Jerusalem and tell the eleven disciples Jesus had appeared... to Simon. Jesus then appears and they give him some fish and honeycomb. He then takes them to Bethany and ascends to Heaven.

Finally, John 20:1-21:25 relates that Mary Magdalene went alone to the tomb. It was open so she ran to get Simon Peter and "the other disciple who Jesus loved" and they ran back to the tomb with Peter arriving last. Then the disciples went home and left Mary Magdalene alone at the tomb. When she looked in she saw two angels sitting down. Then she turned around and saw Jesus standing there but didn't recognize him. Later she recognized him but wasn't allowed to touch him. Jesus tells Mary to go and tell the disciples he is going to ascend to Heaven. That evening Jesus appears to all the disciples in a closed room except Thomas Didymus. Thomas doesn't believe them so after eight days Jesus appears again and convinces (Doubting) Thomas. Jesus then appears a couple of more times during which he helps them catch some fish. After that John seems to get bored with the tale and finishes it like a schoolboy ending a bad essay with "And there are also many other things which Jesus did, which if they be written every one, I suppose that even the world itself could not contain the books that should be written." He also makes no mention of Jesus ascending to Heaven.

Can you imagine presenting four "eyewitness statements" as confused as these before a court and expecting to get a conviction? They can't agree whether the tomb was open or closed when the women arrived, how many women there were, how many angels there were, whether the angels were inside or outside the tomb, whether they were standing up or sitting down, who said what to whom and whether Jesus appeared to them and told them to go tell the others or whether an angel did. They can't agree on who told whom what happened or for that matter whether the women actually told anyone or not. We're even expected to believe, according to one account, the women told no one at all because they were too afraid and yet somehow someone was able to relate in writing what they had witnessed decades later.

The "eyewitnesses" who were supposedly amongst the eleven disciples, for their part, can't agree on whether they went to Galilee to meet Jesus or whether he appeared amongst them in a room in Jerusalem. Two of the eleven appear to have been in Emmaus with Jesus all day but didn't recognize him yet others say all eleven went to Galilee. Another account has all eleven together in the room in Jerusalem but one says Thomas was missing. Two accounts say nothing about Jesus ascending to Heaven, another places it in Bethany a few days after the alleged resurrection and the third mentions it in passing but doesn't say where it happened nor can they agree on how long it was before Jesus ascended. John has him hanging around long enough to work all manner of miracles, "enough to fill more books than the world could contain" apparently, and he never does get to the actual ascension. Plus none of the others, just like contemporary historians, seemed to have noticed all of these additional but unstated miracles.

It's hard to believe these confused, contradictory, highly embroidered and quite obviously *not* eyewitness accounts are the foundation of the entire Christian faith. Clearly these statements are hearsay at best and cannot possibly be the statements of eyewitnesses to the same events. They cannot even agree amongst themselves which town they were in at the time and since these statements are the only "evidence" offered there is no case to answer. No wonder such a huge premium is placed on believing by "faith" and not looking too closely, if at all, at the "evidence" and no wonder the church portrays questioning this "evidence" and not being gullible enough to accept it without question as some sort of character defect.

Naturally I am aware that apologetics have been constructed to try to explain away these discrepancies so now would be a good time to look at some. The first states, "When Jesus was crucified, a superscription was placed above his head proclaiming, 'This is Jesus of Nazareth, King of the Jews.' It was written in three tongues - Hebrew, Latin, and Greek. These languages represented the three dominate cultures of the Mediterranean world when the New Testament was produced. Why would the Romans do this? It is not without significance that there is a Gospel record designed for each of these societal elements. Matthew was directed to the Hebrews, Mark was written for the Romans and Luke was designed to address the Greeks."

That apologetic tries to explains the need for multiple accounts of the same events, but what about the rest of the world? It's as if Asia, Africa and the other continents and nations didn't exist, and from the narrow perspective of the Gospel writers they didn't. Plus that in no way addresses the factual discrepancies previously noted.

Next we are offered, "Though the book does not bear his name, early Christian tradition is unanimous in affirming that Matthew was the inspired author of the first Gospel account. Matthew Levi was a Jew who had been called from his position as a tax collector to become an apostle of Jesus Christ (Matthew 9:9). There are indications within the book that the author was very familiar with finances, and there are more references to money in this account than in the other three Gospel records."

When you hear the words "Christian tradition," that is code for "there is no basis for an assertion in fact and myth is being accepted in its place." It is an incredible leap from a Gospel simply mentioning money to identifying an anonymous author based upon that thin premise.

Matthew 9:9 says, "As Jesus went on from there, He saw a man called Matthew, sitting in the tax collector's booth," Mark 2:14 says, "As he walked along, he saw Levi son of Alphaeus sitting at the tax collector's booth" and Luke 5:27 says, "After this, Jesus went out and saw a tax collector by the name of Levi sitting at his tax booth." So, was his name Matthew or Levi? The apologetic here is, "Both are true because Matthew and Levi are the same person. Matthew is the Greek name and Levi was the Hebrew name. Both names are used because as a tax collector Matthew worked for the Greek speaking Romans and gathered taxes from Hebrew speaking Jews." Then why did he write about himself in the third person, and if he truly was an eyewitness why did he need to copy so much of his narrative virtually word for word from Mark?

The next apologetic tells us, "Mark was the son of a woman named Mary (Acts 12:12) and the cousin of the evangelist Barnabas (Colossians 4:10). Apparently, Mark had a close relationship with Peter (1 Peter 5:13) and there is considerable evidence he wrote his Gospel account under the influence of that apostle."

That is another giant interpolation since the Gospel of Mark does not name its author. A tradition evident in the 2nd Century ascribes it to Mark the Evangelist (also known as John Mark) the companion of Peter on whose memories it is supposedly based, plus according to William Lane an "unbroken tradition" identifies him with Mark the Evangelist and John Mark is mentioned several times in the Acts of the Apostles, however according to the majority view the author is an otherwise unknown figure and his use of varied sources go against the traditional account. According to Papias of Hierapolis, writing in the early 2nd Century, this Gospel was by "Mark, (who) having become the interpreter of Peter, wrote down accurately, though not in order, whatsoever he remembered of the things said or done by Christ." Once again we are faced with the same problem for "eyewitnesses" to Jesus. This is pure hearsay because Papias lived between 70 CE and 155 CE and had no way of knowing that firsthand, plus as previously noted most scholars believe the original text of the Gospel ends at Mark 16:8 with the discovery of Jesus' empty tomb and the following account of the resurrection was a later addition.

Next we are told Luke is the solitary Gentile writer of the Bible, his dual books of the Gospel of Luke and the book of Acts constitute about one-fourth of the New Testament and by training he was a physician (Colossians 4:14). It is also claimed he joined Paul on the apostle's second missionary campaign (Acts 16:10) and was with him periodically during the tireless preacher's ministry (note the "we" sections in Acts).

The author is traditionally identified as "Luke the Evangelist" but modern scholarship generally rejects the view Luke was the original author with the most that could be said being Lukan authorship is "not impossible." While the traditional view that Luke authored the Gospel is still often put forward a number of possible contradictions between Acts and Paul's letters lead many scholars to dispute this. Biblical scholars are in wide agreement that the author of the Gospel of Luke, whoever he was, also wrote Acts but the traditional view based upon his own admission is Luke was not an eyewitness of Jesus' ministry and wrote his Gospel after gathering the best sources of information within his reach. In Luke 1:1-4 he writes, "Many have undertaken to draw up an account of the things that have been fulfilled among us, just as they were handed down to us by those who from the first were eyewitnesses and servants of the word. With this in mind, since I myself have carefully investigated everything from the beginning, I too decided to write an orderly account for you, most excellent Theophilus, so that you may know the certainty of the things you have been taught." Some critical scholarship suggests the two-source hypothesis as probable, which argues that the author used the Gospel of Mark and the hypothetical Q document in addition to unique material as sources for this Gospel. The Church Fathers, witnessed by the Muratorian Canon, Irenaeus (c. 170), Clement of Alexandria, Origen and Tertullian, held that the Gospel of Luke was written by Luke purely on the basis of tradition. The problem there is the oldest surviving copy of Luke (circa 200 CE) carries the attribution "the Gospel according to Luke" however another manuscript (P4) from about the same time period has no such attribution and like Matthew, why the need to copy so much from Mark if he was truly an eyewitness?

According to the majority view the evidence against Luke's being the author is strong enough that the author is unknown and the Book of Acts in fact contradicts the letters of Paul on many points such as Paul's second trip to Jerusalem for an apostolic council. Paul placed an emphasis on Jesus' death while the author of Luke instead emphasizes Jesus' suffering and there are other differences regarding eschatology and the Law. Paul described Luke as "the beloved physician" leading Hobart to claim in 1882 that the vocabulary used in Luke-Acts suggests its author may have had medical training, however this assertion was contradicted by an influential study by Cadbury in 1926 and has since been abandoned. Instead it is now believed this language merely reflects a common Greek education.

Finally we are told John, the son of Zebedee and brother of James (Mark 1:19) was the author of the fourth Gospel, part of the inner circle of disciples (Mark 5:37; 9:2; 14:33) and of all the apostles was closest to the Lord (John 13:23; 19:26, 27). The claim is made that, "This inspired record is in a class by itself. It is designed to appeal to all ethnic groups. Its basic purpose is to offer the evidence (although it merely tells the story) of certain signs which prove that Jesus is the Christ, the Son of God, which facts lead to eternal life (20:30, 31)."

John is actually an anonymous account of the public ministry of Jesus since the Gospel derives from the testimony of the "disciple whom Jesus loved." Along with Peter, the unnamed disciple is especially close to Jesus and early church tradition identified him as John the Apostle, one of Jesus' Twelve Apostles. The Gospel is closely related in style and content to the three surviving Epistles of John such that commentators treat the four books, along with the Book of Revelation, as a single body of Johannine literature but according to most modern scholars John was not the author of any of these books.

Despite the foregoing apologists somehow manage to spin things and conclude, "Yes, the four Gospel writers are inspired of God and provide different but not contradictory details of the life of Jesus. Inspiration does not mean they must have identical accounts. Inspiration means they have different but not contradictory accounts. When put together they complement nicely and fill in details the others leave out. That is what we have in the Gospels. The writers include different but not contradictory details. Inspiration does not mean the four Gospels must be identical in every way. It would be quite boring to read four accounts that are exactly the same. Each writer includes details he feels are necessary for the audience he is addressing. Matthew, writing to the Jews, must include all the Old Testament prophecies while Mark, writing to the Greeks, does not include many prophecies but writes on the action of Jesus' life. Is that a contradiction? No, it's just that each writer included details he felt were necessary and left out others he felt would not be necessary for his audience. Alleged contradictions are explained when one studies the accounts and puts each event of Christ in its chronological order. Matthew records one angel, Luke and John record two. The answer is this. Where there are two there must be one. There were two angels at the tomb but Matthew only writes about one in his account. Is this a contradiction? No, because where there are two, there must be at least one. Luke includes two, but Matthew only includes the one that spoke with Mary. He keyed in on that one and left the other angel out. Luke and John include the other one."

To an objective person that is clearly nothing but a huge rationalization. More importantly, we need to remember regardless of who the writers were the stories themselves cannot serve as eyewitness accounts since they came about as products of the minds of the authors rather than from the characters themselves. The Gospels are narrative stories written almost virtually in the third person and people who wish to portray themselves as eyewitnesses write in the first person rather than the third, plus many of the passages attributed to Jesus could only have come from the invention of its authors. For example many of the statements of Jesus were allegedly uttered while he was alone. If so, who was around to hear him? It becomes even more unbelievable when the authors report what Jesus thought. To whom did Jesus confide his thoughts? Clearly the Gospels employ techniques which fiction writers use so they can only serve at best as hearsay and at worst as fictional or mythological stories.

So if none of the Gospel writers were eyewitnesses and if oral tradition is not responsible for what they wrote as some claim where did the information contained in the Gospels come from? Christian apologists, with nowhere else to turn, cite "divine inspiration," in other words the belief God used human writers as instruments to record history. As for how it was decided what to include in the canon and what not to include (despite the fact that all books and Gospels, both canonical and non-canonical, claim divine inspiration) apparently that was divinely inspired as well. Talk about conjecture and blind faith.

The fact of the matter is all of the Gospels and most of the canon for that matter contain nothing but hearsay which had been passed down from generation to generation via oral tradition and as anyone who has ever played a game of "Chinese Whispers" knows stories tend to change with each retelling until reaching the point where they become almost unrecognizable. For example person one tells a story which contains many details and direct quotes to someone else and just a week later that person repeats what he heard to a third party without the benefit of written notes. Invariably some of the details will differ, some will be omitted and in many cases some will be added since one of the hallmarks of oral tradition, which is essentially storytelling, is embellishment and that is magnified when the people relating those stories are superstitious as was the case two thousand years ago. Try it for yourself. Now take that same scenario and imagine it occurring over several decades. Despite this pervasive and demonstrably true phenomenon many apologists make a "special pleading" for the stories associated with the Gospels by claiming no such errors, changes or embellishments occurred. In fact one theologian of my acquaintance claimed the unknown persons who passed down Bible stories were "extremely careful and diligent" and as a result the stories were never altered in any way. Obviously he has no basis for such a statement because there is no way of knowing what any one person did or did not do a couple of millennia ago and that is doubly true if you cannot even identify who they were. Naturally the fallback position to that logic is mystical, i.e. "God inspired each and every one of them to carry his word without error." It goes without saying such a claim is a huge assumption but it also raises the question of why an all-powerful deity would have such important information passed down orally from generation to generation rather than simply having some literate person write it all down at the time the events occurred so as to avoid all of these problems and questions? For that matter why use people at all? Presumably to a being capable of creating universes writing a book would be child's play.

Even if the Gospel writers and for that matter the authors of virtually all of the Bible had actually been eyewitnesses to the events they wrote about, and clearly they were not, eyewitness testimony has been proven to be anything but accurate. This is especially true in the case of Scripture because none of the "witnesses" are around to be cross examined. Memory recall has been considered a credible source in the past but has recently come under attack as forensics now support psychologists in their claim memories and individual perceptions are unreliable, easily manipulated, can be altered and are often biased. For example in the case of criminal convictions in the United States it was not until forensic DNA testing began exonerating innocent people in the 1990s that the relationship between wrongful convictions and eyewitness testimony was confirmed. Why would such testimony have been any more accurate two thousand years ago?

Even in antiquity Christian leaders like Origen and Eusebius raised doubts about the authenticity of books in the New Testament such as Hebrews, James, 2 & 3 John, 2 Peter, Jude and Revelation. Martin Luther rejected the Epistle of James, calling it worthless and an "epistle of straw," and questioned Jude, Hebrews and the Apocalypse in Revelation. Nevertheless all New Testament writings came well after the alleged death of Jesus from anonymous authors with the possible exception of Paul. Paul's biblical letters or "epistles" serve as the oldest surviving

Christian texts and were probably written around 60 CE. Most scholars have little reason to doubt that Paul wrote some of them himself but of the thirteen epistles Bible scholars think he only wrote eight, and even here there occur interpolations. In not a single instance in any of Paul's writings does he ever claim to have met or even seen an earthly Jesus nor does he give any reference to Jesus' life on earth other than a few well known interpolations, therefore his accounts of Jesus could only have come from other believers or his own imagination. More hearsay.

Of the remaining books and letters in the Bible there occur no claims of eyewitness accounts of a historical Jesus and therefore they are not germane to this discussion. As for the existence of original New Testament documents, none exist. No book of the New Testament survives in the original autograph copy so what we have come from copies and copies of copies of questionable originals and if the stories came piecemeal over time as it appears they have then one may never have existed. The earliest copies in existence came more than a century later than the autographs and these exist only on fragments of papyrus. According to Hugh Schonfield, a British Bible scholar specializing in the New Testament and the early development of the Christian religion, "It would be impossible to find any manuscript of the New Testament older than the late 3rd Century, and we actually have copies from the fourth and fifth."

Many people claim the Bible is proven true in part due to its consistency saying, "It is a collection of sixty-six books written by about forty authors, in three different languages, on three different continents, over approximately 1600 years." Apologists use that rationale frequently and often word for word as if it had been rehearsed but fail to mention how the work of all those authors was assembled. It is a case of not wanting to reveal "how the sausage was made." In spite of that apologetic a surprising number of people seem to think the Bible was written all at once and even more, usually Americans, assume it was written in English. In reality the editing and formation of the Bible came from members of the early Christian Church and since the fathers of the Church possessed the scriptoria and determined what would appear in the Bible there occurred plenty of opportunity and motive to change, modify or even create texts which might bolster the position of the Church or the members of the Church themselves.

The Orthodox Church also fought against competing Christian cults. Irenaeus, who determined the inclusion of the four now canonical Gospels, wrote his infamous book *Against the Heresies* and according to historian and archaeologist John Romer, "Irenaeus' great book not only became the yardstick of major heresies and their refutations, the starting-point of later inquisitions, but simply by saying what Christianity was not it also, in a curious inverted way, became a definition of the orthodox faith." If a Jesus did exist perhaps eyewitness writings got burnt along with them because of their "heretical nature," but we will never know.

In attempting to salvage the Bible respected revisionist and scholar Dr. Bruce Metzger of Princeton Theological Seminary has written extensively on the problems of the New Testament. In his book *The Text of the New Testament - Its Transmission, Corruption and Restoration* Metzger addresses errors arising from faulty eyesight, faulty hearing and errors of the mind or judgment in an effort to clear up historical and geographical difficulties and alterations made due to doctrinal considerations. For those who may feel uncomfortable with this sort of criticism I should point out Metzger is not seeking to undermine belief in the Scriptures, in fact he is the editor of the New Revised Standard Version of the Bible, however he does not allow his beliefs to interfere with his objective examination of the evidence.

Christians are fond of pointing to the *Dead Sea Scrolls* as evidence for the "truth" of Scripture and many consider them to be prophetic in nature but what are they really and how do they fit into this discussion? The *Scrolls* themselves are a collection of 972 texts discovered between 1946 and 1956 in the West Bank, found in caves about a mile inland from the northwest shore of the Dead Sea from which they derive their name. They are of great historical, religious and linguistic significance because they include the earliest known surviving manuscripts of works later included in the Hebrew Bible canon along with extra-biblical manuscripts which preserve evidence of the diversity of religious thought in late Second Temple Judaism. The manuscripts have been dated to various ranges between 408 BCE and 318 CE and bronze coins found on the site form a series beginning with John Hyrcanus (135-104 BCE) and continuing until the First Jewish-Roman War (66–73 CE).

The scrolls which have been identified can be divided into three general groups: some forty percent of them are copies of texts from the Hebrew Bible, approximately thirty percent are texts from the Second Temple Period and ultimately were not canonized in the Hebrew Bible and the remaining thirty percent are sectarian manuscripts of previously unknown documents which shed light on the rules and beliefs of a particular group or groups within greater Judaism. So the majority of the texts found among the *Dead Sea Scrolls* are non-biblical in nature and were thought to be insignificant for understanding the composition or canonization of the biblical books, but a different consensus has emerged which sees many of these works as being collected by the Essene community instead of being composed by them because scholars now recognize some of these works were composed earlier than the Essene period when some of the biblical books were still being written or redacted into their final form. What is most germane to this discussion is the fact the *Scrolls* do not include any of the Gospels, make no mention of Jesus and in any case the fact something is ancient proves nothing. The Hindu *Vedas* and Homer's *Iliad* are also quite old, but what does that prove? As Piyush Loda once put it, "'Ancient' or 'Age-old' are not synonyms for 'Facts' or 'Evidence.'"

There was actually another major find around the same time which does mention Jesus but not surprisingly very few Christians mention or for that matter even know about it. In 1945 an Arab in Upper Egypt made an archeological discovery of several ancient papyrus books which have since been referred to as the *Nag Hammadi* texts. They contain fifty-two heretical books written in Coptic script which include the Gospels of Thomas, Philip, James, John and many others. Other Gnostic Gospels such as the Gospel of Judas, found near the Egyptian site of the *Nag Hammadi* texts, show a diverse pattern of storytelling - the mark of myth. The Judas Gospel tells of Judas Iscariot as Jesus' most loyal disciple, exactly the opposite of what the canonical Gospel stories say, which actually makes some sense because without his "betrayal" (perhaps Jesus instructed him to do it?) there would have been no crucifixion, no resurrection and no Christianity. In any case since these Gnostic texts could only have been written by unknown authors well after the alleged life of Jesus they cannot serve as historical evidence of Jesus any more than the canonical versions. Here we have what can be termed "heretical hearsay."

Virtually all other mentions of Jesus come from sources outside of Christian writings but what is devastating to the claims of Christians is all of these accounts come from authors who lived after the alleged life of Jesus and as a result none of their accounts serve as eyewitness evidence as is the case with the Gospel stories. More importantly, none mention anything which would substantiate or even hint at his supposed divinity. Jewish historian Josephus Flavius, the most often cited "non-Christian witness," mentions Jesus, although many scholars think Josephus' short accounts of Jesus in his *Antiquities of the Jews* came from interpolations perpetrated by a later Church father, most likely Eusebius. I will explain why that is the case in some detail, both to show why Josephus should never be used as evidence for Jesus and to demonstrate how and why documents can and were altered to unscrupulously create "evidence" where there was none.

The notorious passage in question is called the *Testimonium Flavanium* and reads, "Now, there was about this time, Jesus, a wise man, if it be lawful to call him a man, for he was a doer of wonderful works, - a teacher of such men as receive the truth with pleasure. He drew over to him both many of the Jews, and many of the Gentiles. He was (the) Christ; and when Pilate, at the suggestion of the principal men amongst us, had condemned him to the cross, those that loved him at the first did not forsake him, for he appeared to them alive again the third day, as the divine prophets had foretold these and ten thousand other wonderful things concerning him; and the tribe of Christians, so named from him, are not extinct at this day."

This surprisingly brief and simplistic passage constitutes the "best extra-biblical proof" of Jesus' existence in the entire ancient non-Christian library comprising the works of dozens of historians, writers, philosophers, politicians and others who never mentioned the great sage and wonderworker Jesus Christ even though they lived contemporaneously with or shortly after his purported advent. I will now address this claim at length because it has recently reemerged as a commonly asserted "proof" - so please bear with me.

Despite the best wishes of sincere believers and the erroneous claims of truculent apologists, the *Testimonium* has been demonstrated continually over the centuries to be a forgery. In fact so thorough and universal has been this debunking very few scholars of repute continued to cite the passage after the turn of the 19th Century. Indeed it was rarely mentioned except to note that it was a forgery and numerous books by a variety of authorities over a period of two hundred or so years basically took it for granted that the *Testimonium* in its entirety was spurious, an interpolation and a forgery. As Dr. Gordon Stein relates: "...the vast majority of scholars since the early 1800s have said that this quotation is not by Josephus, but rather is a later Christian insertion in his works. In other words, it is a forgery, rejected by scholars." So well understood was this fact of forgery these numerous authorities did not spend their precious time and space rehashing the arguments against the *Testimonium's* authenticity. Nevertheless in the past few decades apologists of questionable integrity and credibility have glommed onto it once again because this short and dubious passage represents the most "concrete" secular, non-biblical reference to a man who purportedly shook up the world. In spite of the past debunking the debate is currently confined to those who think the *Testimonium* was original to Josephus but was Christianized as well as those who credulously and self-servingly accept it as genuine in its entirety.

To repeat, this passage was so completely dissected by scholars of high repute and standing, the majority of them pious Christians mind you, that it was for decades understood by subsequent scholars as having been proved *in toto* a forgery such that these succeeding scholars did not even mention it unless to acknowledge it as false. The scholars who so conclusively proved the *Testimonium* a forgery made their mark at the end of the 18th Century and into the 20th when a sudden reversal was implemented with popular opinion hemming and hawing its way back first to the "partial interpolation theory" and in recent times among third-rate apologists to the notion the entire *Testimonium* is genuine. As Earl Doherty says in *Josephus Unbound*: "Now, it is a curious fact that older generations of scholars had no trouble dismissing this entire passage as a Christian construction. Charles Guignebert, for example, in his *Jesus*, calls it 'a pure Christian forgery.' Before him Lardner, Harnack and Schurer, along with others, declared it entirely spurious. Today, most serious scholars have decided the passage is a mix: original parts rubbing shoulders with later Christian additions."

The earlier scholarship which proved the *Testimonium* to be fraudulent was determined by intense scrutiny by some of the most erudite, and mainly Christian, writers of the time. Their general conclusions, as elucidated by Christian authority Dr. Nathaniel Lardner in his work *Jewish Testimonies* and related here by the author of *Christian Mythology Unveiled,* include the following reasons for doubting the authenticity of the *Testimonium* as a whole: "Mathias, the father of Josephus, must have been a witness to the miracles which are said to have been performed by Jesus, and Josephus was born within two years after the crucifixion, yet in all the works he says nothing whatever about the life or death of Jesus Christ; as for the interpolated passage it is now universally acknowledged to be a forgery. The arguments of the 'Christian Ajax,' even Lardner himself, against it are these: It was never quoted by any of our Christian ancestors before Eusebius. It disturbs the narrative. The language is quite Christian. It is not quoted by Chrysostom, though he often refers to Josephus, and could not have omitted quoting it had it been then in the text. It is not quoted by Photius in the 9th Century, though he has three articles concerning Josephus; and this author expressly states that this historian has not taken the least notice of Christ. Neither Justin Martyr, in his dialogue with Trypho the Jew; nor Clemens Alexandrinus, who made so many extracts from ancient authors; nor Origen against Celsus, have ever mentioned this testimony. But, on the contrary, in chapter 25th of the first book of that work, Origen openly affirms that Josephus, who had mentioned John the Baptist, did not acknowledge Christ. That this passage is a false fabrication is admitted by Ittigius, Blondel, Le Clerc, Vandale, Bishop Warburton and Tanaquil Faber." Hence by the 1840's when the author of *Christian Mythology Unveiled* wrote the *Testimonium Flavanium* was already universally acknowledged to be a forgery.

In any event as G.A. Wells points out in *The Jesus Myth*, not only do several Church fathers from the 2nd, 3rd and early 4th Centuries have no apparent knowledge of the *Testimonium* but even after Eusebius suddenly "found" it in the first half of the 4th Century several other fathers into the 5th "often cite Josephus, but *not* this passage." In the 5th Century church father Jerome (c. 347-c.419) cited the *Testimonium* once with obvious disinterest as if he knew it was fraudulent. In addition to his reference to the *Testimonium*, in his Letter XXII to Eustochium Jerome made the following audacious claim: "Josephus, himself a Jewish writer, asserts that at the Lord's crucifixion there broke from the temple voices of heavenly powers, saying: 'Let us depart hence.'" Either Jerome fabricated this alleged Josephus quote or he possessed a unique copy of the Jewish historian's works in which this assertion had earlier been interpolated. In any case Jerome's claim constitutes "pious fraud," one of many committed by Christian proponents over the centuries, a rampant practice in fact which must be kept in mind when considering the authenticity of the *Testimonium*.

Josephus goes into long detail about the lives of numerous personages of relatively little import including several Jesuses, so it is inconceivable he would devote only a few sentences to someone even remotely resembling the character found in the New Testament. If the Gospel tales constituted "history" Josephus' elders would certainly be aware of Jesus' purported assault on the temple for example and the historian, who was obviously interested in instances of messianic agitation, would surely have reported it in detail. If Josephus had thought so highly of an historical Jesus he surely would have written more extensively about him, yet he does not. Lest it be suggested Josephus somehow could have been ignorant of the events in question the *Catholic Encyclopedia* says, "Josephus... was chosen by the Sanhedrin at Jerusalem to be commander-in-chief in Galilee. As such he established in every city throughout the country a council of judges, the members of which were recruited from those who shared his political views." Indeed, Josephus was a well-educated Jew who lived in the precise area where the Gospel tale was said to have taken place as did his parents, the latter at the very time of Christ's alleged advent. It was Josephus' passion to study the Jewish people and their history, yet other than the obviously bogus *Testimonium* and the brief "James passage" mentioned by Taylor it turns out that in his voluminous works Josephus discussed neither Christ nor Christianity. Nor does it make sense the prolific Jewish writer would not detail the Christian movement itself were Christians extant at the time in any significant numbers.

Regarding the *Testimonium* as well as the James passage which possesses the phrase, "James, the brother of Jesus, who was called Christ," Jewish writer Ben Yehoshua makes some interesting assertions: "Neither of these passages is found in the original version of the *Jewish Antiquities* which was preserved by the Jews. The first passage (XVII, 3, 3) was quoted by Eusebius writing in c. 320 CE, so we can conclude it was added in sometime between the time Christians got hold of the *Jewish Antiquities* and c. 320 CE. It is not known when the other passage (XX, 9, 1) was added... Neither passage is based on any reliable sources. It is fraudulent to claim that these passages were written by Josephus and that they provide evidence for Jesus. They were written by Christian redactors and were based purely on Christian belief."

The many reasons for concluding the Josephus passage to be a forgery have been expounded upon by numerous well-respected authorities so much so that such individuals have been compelled by honesty and integrity to dismiss the *Testimonium* as a forgery. For a more modern criticism, in *The Jesus Puzzle* and his online article *Josephus Unbound* secularist and classicist Earl Doherty leaves no stone unturned in demolishing the *Testimonium*, permitting no squirming room for future apologists whose resort to the *Testimonium* will show, as it has done in the past, how hopeless is their plight in establishing a "historical Jesus." Concerning the use of Josephus as "evidence" of Jesus' existence Doherty remarks, "In the absence of any other supporting evidence from the 1st Century that in fact the Jesus of Nazareth portrayed in the Gospels clearly existed, Josephus becomes the slender thread by which such an assumption hangs. And the sound and fury and desperate maneuverings which surround the dissection of those two little passages becomes a din of astonishing proportions. The obsessive focus on this one uncertain record is necessitated by the fact that the rest of the evidence is so dismal, so contrary to the orthodox picture. If almost everything outside Josephus points in a different direction, to the essential fiction of the Gospel picture and its central figure, how can Josephus be made to bear on his shoulders, through two passages whose reliability has thus far remained unsettled, the counterweight to all this other negative evidence?"

Other modern authors who criticize the *Testimonium* include *The Jesus Mysteries* authors Freke and Gandy who conclude, "Unable to provide any historical evidence for Jesus, later Christians forged the proof that they so badly needed to shore up their Literalist interpretation of the Gospels. This, as we would see repeatedly, was a common practice." Despite the desperate din a number of other modern writers remain in concurrence with the earlier scholarship and likewise consider the *Testimonium* a fraud. In addition to acknowledging the spuriousness of the Josephus passage many authorities agree Church historian Eusebius was the forger of the entire *Testimonium* and various reasons have been given for making such a conclusion. In *Did Jesus Really Live?* Marshall Gauvin remarks, "Everything demonstrates the spurious character of the passage. It is written in the style of Eusebius, and not in the style of Josephus. Josephus was a voluminous writer. He wrote extensively about men of minor importance. The brevity of this reference to Christ is, therefore, a strong argument for its falsity. This passage interrupts the narrative. It has nothing to do with what precedes or what follows it; and its position clearly shows that the text of the historian has been separated by a later hand to give it room."

In *Antiqua Mater: A Study of Christian Origins* Edwin Johnson remarked that the 4th Century was "the great age of literary forgery, the extent of which has yet to be exposed." He further commented that "not until the mass of inventions labeled 'Eusebius' shall be exposed, can the pretended references to Christians in Pagan writers of the first three centuries be recognized for the forgeries they are." Indeed Eusebius' character has been assailed repeatedly over the centuries with him being called a "luminous liar" and "unreliable." Like so many others Drews criticizes Eusebius stating that various of the Church historian's references "must be regarded with the greatest suspicion." As Drews relates, Swiss historian Jakob Burckhardt (1818-1897) declared Eusebius to be "the first thoroughly dishonest historian of antiquity." Eusebius' motives were to empower the Catholic Church and he did not fail to use "falsifications, suppressions and fictions" to this end.

Even if the Josephus passage were authentic, which it has essentially been shown not to be, it nevertheless would represent not an eyewitness account but rather a tradition passed along for at least six decades and long after the purported events since Josephus' birth in 37 CE was after the alleged crucifixion of Jesus and makes it impossible for him to have given an eyewitness account. As is the case with all hearsay he would have been simply repeating a story he had been told by person or persons unknown, hence the *Testimonium* would possess little if any value in establishing an "historical" Jesus. Remsburg summarizes, "For nearly sixteen hundred years Christians have been citing this passage as a testimonial, not merely to the historical existence, but to the divine character of Jesus Christ. And yet a ranker forgery was never penned... Its brevity disproves its authenticity. Josephus' work is voluminous and exhaustive. It comprises twenty books. Whole pages are devoted to petty robbers and obscure seditious leaders. Nearly forty chapters are devoted to the life of a single king. Yet this remarkable being, the greatest product of his race, a being of whom the prophets foretold ten thousand wonderful things, a being greater than any earthly king, is dismissed with a dozen lines...."

The dismissal of the passage in Josephus regarding Jesus is not based on "faith" or "belief" but on intense scientific scrutiny and reasoning. Such investigation has been confirmed repeatedly by numerous scholars who were mostly Christian. The *Testimonium*, Dr. Lardner concluded in none too forceful words, "ought, therefore... to be discarded from any place among the evidences of Christianity." With such outstanding authority and so many scientific reasons, we can at last dispense with the pretentious charade of wondering if the infamous passage in the writings of Josephus called the *Testimonium Flavianum* is forged and who fabricated it. The bottom line is no reputable apologist should ever cite Josephus as "proof" of anything related to Christ ever again.

Another so-called witness to Christ was Pliny the Younger, who was not born until 62 CE. His letter to Emperor Trajan about the Christians only proves that Christian believers existed, and they surely did, but he makes no mention of Jesus himself. Regardless, his birth date eliminates him as a possible eyewitness even if he had.

Roman historian Tacitus' birth year of 64 CE puts him well after the alleged life of Jesus. He gives a brief mention of a "Christus" in his *Annals* (Book XV, Sec. 44) which he wrote around 109 CE, although he gives no source for his material. Although many have disputed the authenticity of Tacitus' mention of Jesus it doesn't matter because the fact his birth occurred well after the alleged Jesus existed and he wrote the *Annals* during the later formation of Christianity demonstrates his writings can only be hearsay.

Suetonius, a Roman historian born in 69 CE, mentions a "Chrestus," which was a common name. Naturally apologists assume "Chrestus" means "Christ," which is certainly a disputable claim, but even if Seutonius had indeed meant "Christ" it still says nothing about an earthly Jesus and just like the others Suetonius' birth occurred well after the purported Jesus. Again, only hearsay.

Amazingly some Christians attempt to use brief portions of the Talmud, which is a collection of Jewish civil and religious law including commentaries on the Torah, as evidence for Jesus. They claim "Yeshu" in the Talmud refers to Jesus however according to Jewish scholars this Yeshu either depicts a disciple of Jehoshua Ben-Perachia at least a century before the alleged Christian Jesus or it refers to Yeshu ben Pandera, a teacher in the 2nd Century CE. Regardless of how one interprets this the Palestinian Talmud didn't come into existence until the 3rd and 5th Century CE and the Babylonian Talmud between the 3rd and 6th Century CE - at least two centuries after the alleged crucifixion. At best it can only serve as a controversial Christian or Jewish legend and cannot possibly serve as evidence for a historical Jesus.

Because the religious mind relies on belief and faith the religious person can inherit a dependence on any information which supports a belief and that includes fraudulent stories, rumors, unreliable data and outright fictions without bothering to check sources or investigate the reliability of information. If you doubt the veracity of that assertion take a moment to consider all of the "urban legends" which abound on the internet today. Even though they are not based in fact people believe them because they want to believe them and the hundreds of fraudulent claims which exist for the artifacts of Jesus are no different. Consider this - if the website *Snopes* had existed two thousand years ago Christianity as well as other religions most likely would not. Three examples follow.

Many faithful people believe the Shroud of Turin is the actual burial cloth of Jesus and claim the image on the cloth represents an actual "photographic" image left behind by his crucified body. The first mention of the Shroud comes from a treatise by Geoffroi de Charny in 1356 called *The Book of Chivalry* in which he claims to have owned the cloth and later, in the 16th Century, *poof!* it suddenly appeared in a cathedral in Turin, Italy. It should be noted during this period thousands of claimed "Jesus relics" appeared in cathedrals throughout Europe including wood from the "true cross," chalices, the blood of Jesus, etc., and these so-called "artifacts" proved popular and served as a prosperous commercial device which filled the coffers of the churches. In fact according to apocryphal gospels after baby Jesus was circumcised a Jewish woman saved his foreskin and by the Middle Ages several different foreskins were being touted as the original and were worshipped as holy relics by various churches.

Many people of faith believe there actually exists scientific evidence to support their belief in the Shroud's authenticity but considering how the Shroud's apologists use the words "science, fact, and authentic" without actual scientific justification and then go so far as to include pseudo-scientists to testify to their conclusions it should be no surprise that a faithful person would not question their information or motives. Television specials have also appeared which claim the authenticity of the Shroud but science does not operate through television specials which have a commercial interest and no qualms about deceiving the public.

Experts around the world consider the fourteen-foot-long linen sheet, which has remained in a cathedral in Turin since 1578, a forgery in part because of carbon-dating tests performed in 1988. Three different independent radiocarbon dating laboratories in Zurich, Oxford and the University of Arizona yielded a date range of 1260-1390 CE which is consistent with the time period of Charny's claimed ownership. Naturally apologists had a ready explanation. They claimed the sample tested came from a section of the Shroud which had been damaged in a fire and patched with new material and that had caused a false result. The obvious question is why did the Church provide a sample from that particular area? Perhaps, as some have postulated, they did it in order to have a ready-made excuse. Obviously the only solution would be to do a second test from a different section of the Shroud but not surprisingly the Church has declined to provide additional fibers. Joe Zias of Hebrew University of Jerusalem calls the Shroud indisputably a fake saying, "Not only is it a forgery, but it's a bad forgery." To that point how many people reading this who consider the Shroud to be authentic have actually viewed it? Because if they had they would notice it actually depicts a man whose front measures two inches taller than his back and whose elongated hands and arms would indicate he had the affliction of gigantism if he actually lived. As for the face of Jesus it has a striking resemblance to artwork created during the Middle Ages since of course no one knows what he actually looked like. Finally Walter C. McCrone discovered red ochre, a pigment found in earth and widely used in Italy during the Middle Ages, on the cloth which formed the body image and vermilion paint made from mercuric sulphide was used to represent blood. The actual scientific findings reveal the shroud as a 14th Century painting, not a two-thousand year-old cloth with Christ's image. Revealingly, no biblical scholar or scientist with any credibility cites the Shroud of Turin as evidence for a historical Jesus and yet credulous Christians continue to flock to Turin and cite it as "evidence."

To put these claims into perspective let's look at a couple made by other religions. After the Buddha died in approximately 500 BCE it's said his body was cremated and the story goes that afterwards a follower retrieved his left canine tooth from the ashes. The tooth was given to the king, became legendary and it was believed whoever possessed it would rule the land so wars were fought over custody of the tooth for centuries and now 2500 years later what's left of it is housed in a temple in Sri Lanka. Not to be outdone, from the 16th to 19th Century sultans of the Ottoman Empire collected religious items of the Islamic faith mostly said to be relics of various prophets. Included in the collection, which is now held in Istanbul, are Moses staff, a pot belonging to Abraham, a piece of the prophet Muhammed's tooth and something known as the "Blessed Mantle" which is a black wool shawl said to have been placed on a poet's shoulders by Muhammed himself. Obviously there no basis for the claims about the possessions of Moses and Abraham because their very existence is unproven and while the Buddha and Muhammed were quite real one must wonder why their teeth are so special. I think we can probably agree these claims are the products of superstition.

Getting back to Christianity, many credible theologians hungry for "evidence" of Jesus even bought into the fraudulent "burial box of James" hoax hook-line-and-sinker. The Nov/Dec 2002 issue of *Biblical Archaeology Review* magazine announced a "world exclusive" article about evidence of Jesus written in stone, claiming they had found the actual ossuary of "James, Brother of Jesus" in Jerusalem. This story exploded on the news and appeared widely on television and in newspapers around the world. Interestingly, they announced the find as the "earliest historical reference of Jesus yet found" but since they claimed the inscription on the box occurred around 70 CE that means even if the box script had proven to be authentic it would not provide evidence for Jesus because no one knew who wrote the script or why. Instead it would merely be the first indirect mention of a Jesus and could not serve as contemporary evidence because it didn't come into existence until long after his alleged death. In the end the claim for the authenticity of the burial box of James proved particularly embarrassing for *Biblical Archaeology Review* and for those who believed them without question because just a few months later archaeologists determined the inscription was an obvious forgery, found the perpetrator and had him arrested. Regrettably the news about the fraud never matched the euphoria of the original story and as a result many people still believe the story today.

Next we will look at the Letters of Pontius Pilate. Many of the faithful, especially those on the internet, have a strong belief Pontius Pilate wrote letters to Seneca in Rome in which he mentions Jesus and his reported healing miracles. Considering the lack of investigative curiosity in the average religious mind it is interesting to note the main source for the "letters of Pilate" belief is W. P. Crozier's 1928 book titled *Letters of Pontius Pilate: Written During His Governorship of Judea to His Friend Seneca in Rome*. The book cites Crozier as the editor as if he represented a scholar who edited Pilate's letters and from the title it certainly would seem to indicate Pilate wrote some letters, however unbeknownst to or ignored by the faithful this book was actually Crozier's first novel, i.e. a fictionalized account of what he thought Pilate *would* have written. The belief in Pilate's letters represents one of the more amusing mythical beliefs in evidential Jesus, however it also reveals just how easily myths, fakes and fictions can leak into religious thought and "history."

What appears most revealing of all comes not from what people later wrote about Jesus but what people did not write about him. Consider that not a single historian, philosopher, scribe or follower who lived during the alleged time of Jesus ever mentions him. Not one. If the Gospels portray a historical look at the life of Jesus then the one feature which stands out prominently is people apparently knew Jesus far and wide - not only a great multitude of followers but great priests, the Roman governor Pilate and even King Herod who according to Matthew 14:1 claims he had heard "of the fame of Jesus." One need only read Matthew 4:25 where it claims "there followed him (Jesus) great multitudes of people from Galilee, and from Decapolis, and from Jerusalem, and from Judea, and from beyond Jordan." The Gospels mention countless times the great multitude which followed Jesus and the crowds of people who congregated to hear him. In fact so crowded had some of these gatherings grown that Luke 12:1 alleges that an "innumerable multitude of people... trode one upon another" and Luke 5:15 says there grew "a fame abroad of him: and great multitudes came together to hear..." In fact the persecution of Jesus in Jerusalem drew so much attention that all the chief priests and scribes, including the high priest Caiaphas, not only knew about him but helped in his alleged crucifixion. (see Matthew 21:15-23, 26:3 and Luke 19:47, 23:13). The multitude of people thought of Jesus not only as a teacher and miracle healer but also as prophet (see Matthew14:5). So here we have the Gospels portraying Jesus as famous far and wide, a great prophet and healer with great multitudes of people who knew about him including the greatest Jewish high priests and the Roman authorities of the area, and not one person recorded his existence during his lifetime. If the poor, the rich, the rulers, the highest priests and the scribes knew about Jesus, who would not have heard of him?

Then we have a particular astronomical event which would presumably have attracted the attention of anyone interested in the heavens. According to Luke 23:44-45 there occurred "about the sixth hour, and there was darkness over all the earth until the ninth hour, and the sun was darkened, and the veil of the temple was rent in the midst." Yet not a single mention of such a three hour ecliptic event got recorded by anyone including astronomers and astrologers anywhere in the world, especially Pliny the Elder and Seneca who both recorded simple eclipses from other dates. Note also that, for obvious reasons solar eclipses can't occur during a full moon - Passovers always occur during full moons - nor does a single contemporary person write about the earthquake described in Matthew 27:51-54 where the earth shook, rocks ripped apart (rent), graves opened and "many corpses" walked the streets of Jerusalem and "appeared to many." It is strange there is no record of any of these extraordinary events - the darkness, the earthquake, the zombies - anywhere outside of the Gospels. None. In fact they were not even mentioned in all of the Gospels.

Matthew 2 describes Herod and all of Jerusalem as troubled by the worship of the infant Jesus and tells us Herod then had all of the infant children of Bethlehem slain. The obvious question is if extraordinary infanticides of this magnitude had actually occurred why didn't anyone write about something like that? In fact even the other Gospels do not mention it. Another huge inconsistency is Matthew tells us Jesus and his family fled to Egypt to escape the slaughter while the others say they simply returned to Nazareth. Some apologists attempt to work around the problem of why no one recorded anything about their savior by claiming there lived no capable historians during that period, or this was due to the lack of education of people with a writing capacity, or even sillier there was a scarcity of paper, but in actuality the area in and surrounding Jerusalem served as the center of education and record keeping for the

Jewish people. The Romans also kept many records of course and moreover the Gospels themselves mention scribes many times both as followers of Jesus and those connected with the high priests. As for historians, there lived plenty at the time who had the capacity and capability to record not only insignificant gossip but significant events, especially from a religious sect which drew so much popular attention through an allegedly famous and infamous Jesus.

Take for example the works of Philo Judaeus, who lived from 20 BCE to 50 CE. He was the greatest Jewish-Hellenistic philosopher and historian of the era and lived in the area of Jerusalem during the time of Jesus and wrote detailed accounts of the Jewish events which occurred in the surrounding area, and yet not once in all of his volumes of writings do we read a single account of a Jesus or "the Christ." Nor do we find any mention of Jesus in the writings of contemporary historians such as Seneca or Pliny the Elder. If someone as well-known as Jesus existed as the Gospels allege it is reasonable to conclude his fame would have reached the ears of one of these men, not to mention news of his alleged miracles. Amazingly there is not one Jewish, Greek or Roman writer, including those who lived in the Middle East much less anywhere else on the earth, who mention Jesus during his supposed lifetime.

To illustrate this extraordinary absence of Jesus Christ in historical records just imagine going through 19th Century literature looking for an Abraham Lincoln but unable to find a single mention of him in any writings made anywhere on earth until the 20th Century, yet straight-faced Christian apologists and historians want you to buy a factual Jesus despite a dearth of evidence and rely on nothing but hearsay written well after his purported life.

Many problems surface when it comes to the reliability of the accounts of ancient historians. Most did not provide sources for their claims, as they rarely included bibliographic listings or supporting documentation. They did not have access to modern scholarly techniques and often would include hearsay as evidence. No one today would take a modern scholar seriously who used the standards of ancient historians, yet this is the only kind of source from which Christology is derived. Couple this with the fact many historians believed as Christians themselves and were sometimes members of the Church and you have a built-in prejudice towards supporting a "real" Jesus.

In modern scholarship even the best historians and Christian apologists play the historian game but they can only use what documents they have available to them. If they only have hearsay accounts then they have to play the cards history deals them. Many historians feel compelled to use interpolation or guesses from hearsay and yet this very dubious information sometimes ends up in encyclopedias and history books as "fact." In other words biblical scholarship gets forced into a lower standard by the very sources they examine. A renowned Bible scholar illustrated this clearly in an interview in *Bible Review* magazine when he was asked about biblical interpretation. David Noel Freeman, General Editor of the *Anchor Bible Series* and many other works, responded with, "We have to accept somewhat looser standards. In the legal profession, to convict the defendant of a crime, you need proof beyond a reasonable doubt. In civil cases, a preponderance of the evidence is sufficient. When dealing with the Bible or any ancient source, we have to loosen up a little; otherwise, we can't really say anything." The implications appear obvious. If one wishes to believe in a historical Jesus he or she must accept this based on loose standards. Very loose. Couple this with the fact all of the claims come from hearsay and we have a foundation made of sand and a castle of information built out of cards.

Apologists also like to cite geography and known historical figures as "evidence." Although the New Testament certainly mentions various cities, geological sites, kings and people who existed or lived during the alleged life of Jesus these descriptions cannot serve as evidence for the existence of Jesus any more than do works of fiction which include recognizable locations and make mention of actual people. Homer's *Odyssey*, for example, describes the travels of Odysseus throughout the Greek islands. The epic describes in detail many locations which actually existed in history, but should we take Odysseus, the Greek gods and goddesses, one-eyed giants and monsters as literal fact simply because the story depicts geographic locations accurately? Of course not. The authors of mythical stories, fictions and novels almost always use familiar landmarks as placements for their stories. The authors of the Greek tragedies not only put their stories in plausible settings as if they happened in the real world but their supernatural characters took on the desires, flaws and failures of mortal human beings. Consider that fictions such as *King Kong, Superman* and *Star Trek* include recognizable cities, planets, landmarks and people with their protagonists and antagonists miming human emotions.

Likewise, just because the Gospels mention cities and locations in Judea and known historical people, with Jesus behaving like an actual human being with the added dimension of supernatural curses, miracles, etc., this says nothing about the actuality of the characters portrayed in the stories. In addition when a story uses impossible historical locations or makes geographical errors we may question the authority of the claims. For example in Matthew 4:8 the author describes Satan taking Jesus onto an exceedingly high mountain to show him all the kingdoms of the world and since there exists no spot on the spheroid earth to view "all the kingdoms" we know the Bible errs here since such a thing would only be possible on a small, flat planet. Similarly John 3:23 says, "John also was baptizing in Aenon near Salim..." although no such place as Aenon exists near Salim.

Next, no one has evidence for a city named Nazareth at the time of the alleged Jesus. Such a place does not appear in the Old Testament nor does it appear in the volumes of Josephus' writings, even though he provides a list of cities in Galilee. Oddly, none of the New Testament epistle writers ever mention Nazareth or a Jesus of Nazareth even though most of the epistles appeared before the Gospels. In fact no one mentions Nazareth until the Gospels and the first of those didn't come into existence until about forty years after the alleged death of Jesus. If a city named Nazareth existed during the 1st Century then we need at least one contemporary piece of evidence for the name, otherwise we cannot refer to it as established history. Many historians do not agree with this of course. Some think Nazareth existed, some don't think it did and still others remain skeptical but the fact historians still debate it tells us we should not use this uncertainly as a certainty. Moreover, some scholars think it a moot point because they believe "Nazareth" actually refers to a Christian movement rather than a city. For example Acts 24:5 refers to a sect of the Nazarenes. The Gospel writers then might have confused the term to mean the city, and by the time they wrote the Gospels a city did exist with that name. We have a lot of educated guesses by scholars, but no certainty. Many more kinds of errors and uncertainties like this appear in the New Testament and although one cannot use these as evidence against a historical Jesus we can certainly question the reliability of the texts because if the Scriptures make so many factual errors about geography and science and contain so many contradictions falsehoods could occur in any area.

If we couple historical people and locations then we should also have some historical reference of a Jesus in relation to these locations and people, but just the opposite proves to be the case. One of the Gospels depicts Herod, the Ruler of Jewish Palestine under Rome, as sending out men to search for and kill the infant Jesus yet nothing in history supports such a story. Pontius Pilate supposedly performed as judge in the trial and execution of Jesus yet no Roman record mentions such a trial. The Gospels portray a multitude of believers throughout the land spreading tales of a teacher, prophet and healer yet nobody who lived during Jesus' lifetime or even years afterward ever records a word about such a figure.

Many Christian apologists attempt to extricate themselves from this lack of evidence by claiming that if we cannot rely on the post chronicle exegesis of Jesus then we also cannot establish a historical foundation for other figures such as Alexander the Great, Augustus Caesar, Napoleon, etc., however there is a vast difference between such historical figures and Jesus. There are either artifacts, writings or eyewitness accounts for those historical people whereas for Jesus we have nothing. Even more to the point nobody is claiming any of those people were gods who will hold sway over all mankind for eternity, so even if the historical records are erroneous in those cases they are simply mistakes which have no effect on people living today.

Alexander, for example, left a wake of destroyed and created cities behind. We have buildings, libraries and cities such as Alexandria left in his name. We also have treaties and even a letter from Alexander to the people of Chios engraved in stone and dated from 332 BCE. For Augustus Caesar we have the *Res gestae divi augusti*, the emperor's own account of his works and deeds, a letter to his son (*Epistula ad Gaium filium*), Virgil's eyewitness accounts and much more. Napoleon left behind artifacts, firsthand reports and letters. We can establish some historicity for these people because we have evidence which occurred during their lifetimes, yet even with contemporary evidence historians have become wary of some after-the-fact stories about many of these historical people. For example some of the stories of Alexander's conquests or Nero starting the fire in Rome always get questioned or doubted because they contain inconsistencies or come from authors who wrote years after the alleged facts. In qualifying the history of Alexander historian Pierre Briant writes, "Although more than twenty of his contemporaries chronicled Alexander's life and campaigns, none of these texts survive in original form. Many letters and speeches attributed to Alexander are ancient forgeries or reconstructions inspired by imagination or political motives. The little solid documentation we possess from Alexander's own time is mainly to be found in stone inscriptions from the Greek cities of Europe and Asia." The salient point once again is even if the accounts of these historical figures were flawed or even fictitious, nobody ever claimed any of them were gods.

Inventing histories out of whole cloth or embellished from a seed of an actual historical event appears common throughout the chronicle of human thought. Theologian Robert Price, teacher of philosophy and religion at the Johnnie Colemon Theological Seminary observes, "Alexander the Great, Caesar Augustus, Cyrus, King Arthur and others have nearly suffered this fate. What keeps historians from dismissing them as mere myths, like Paul Bunyan, is that there is some residue. We know at least a bit of mundane information about them, perhaps quite a bit, so that does not form part of any legend cycle."

Consider that in 520 CE an anonymous monk recorded the life of Saint Genevieve, who had died only ten years before. In his account of her life he describes how when she ordered a cursed tree cut down monsters sprang from it and breathed a fatal stench on many men for two hours. He added tales of how while she was sailing eleven ships capsized but due to her prayers they were righted again spontaneously as well as how she cast out demons, calmed storms, miraculously created water and oil from nothing before astonished crowds and healed the blind and lame, with several people who stole things from her actually going blind instead. No one ever wrote anything to contradict or challenge these claims mind you and they were written very near the time the events supposedly happened by a religious man who probably regarded lying to be a sin, and yet do you believe any of it? Probably not, and you shouldn't. As David Hume once said, "Why do such things not happen *now*?" Is it a coincidence the very time when these things no longer occur happens to be the era when we have the means and methods to check them in the light of science and careful investigation? I've never seen monsters spring from a tree and don't know anyone who has and as far as I know there are no women today touring the country transmuting matter or levitating ships. These events look like tall tales, sound like tall tales, smell like tall tales and odds are they are tall tales. Agreed?

We should try to be more specific in our reasons and not rely solely on common sense impressions. There are specific reasons to disbelieve the story of Genevieve and they are the same reasons we have to doubt the Gospel accounts of the Resurrection of Jesus. The parallel is clear - the Gospels were written no sooner after the death of their main character, and more likely many decades later, than was the account of Genevieve and like that account the Gospels were also originally anonymous with the names now attached to them being added by speculation and oral tradition half a century after they were actually written. Both contain fabulous miracles supposedly witnessed by numerous people and both belong to the same genre of literature - what is called a "hagiography" or sacred account of a holy person regarded as representing a moral and divine ideal - and such a genre had as its principal aim not the dissemination of literal truth but instead the glorification of the religion itself and the example set by the perfect holy person represented as its central focus. Such literature was also a tool of propaganda used to promote certain moral or religious views and to oppose different points of view. For example the life of Genevieve was written to combat Arianism while the canonical Gospels on the other hand appear to combat various forms of proto-Gnosticism, so being skeptical of what they say is sensible from the start.

It is certainly reasonable to doubt the resurrection of Jesus in the flesh, an event placed sometime between 26 and 36 CE, because for this we have only a few written sources near the event with all of it being sacred writing and entirely pro-Christian. Pliny the Younger was the first non-Christian to even mention the religion in 110 CE but as pointed out elsewhere doesn't mention the resurrection. In fact no non-Christian mentions the resurrection until many decades later when Lucian, a critic of superstition, wrote during the mid-2nd Century and likely got his information from Christian sources.

Nevertheless Christian apologist Douglas Geivett declared the evidence for the physical resurrection of Jesus meets "the highest standards of historical inquiry" and claimed "if one takes the historian's own criteria for assessing the historicity of ancient events, the resurrection passes muster as a historically well-attested event of the ancient world" - as well-attested, he claims, as Julius Caesar's crossing of the Rubicon in 49 BCE.

It is common in Christian apologetics throughout history to make absurdly exaggerated claims and this is no exception. Let's look at the evidence for Caesar's crossing of the Rubicon in detail. First of all we have Caesar's own word on the subject since *The Civil War,* written by Caesar himself along with one of his generals, has been a Latin classic for two thousand years. In contrast we do not have anything written by Jesus and do not know for certain the name of any author of any of the accounts of his earthly resurrection.

Second we have many of Caesars enemies, including Cicero (a contemporary of the event), reporting the crossing of the Rubicon whereas we have no hostile or even neutral records of the resurrection until over a hundred years after the supposed event, fifty years after the Christians' own claims had been widely spread around.

Third we have a number of inscriptions and coins produced soon after the Republican Civil War related to the Rubicon crossing including mentions of battles and conscriptions and judgments which provide evidence for Caesar's march while on the other hand we have absolutely no physical evidence of any kind for the resurrection.

Fourth we have the story of the Rubicon Crossing from almost every historian of the period including the most prominent scholars of the age - Suetonius, Appian, Cassius Dio and Plutarch. Moreover, these scholars have a measure of proven reliability since a great many of their reports on other matters have been confirmed in material evidence and other sources. In addition they show a desire to critically examine claims for which there is any dispute and if that wasn't enough all cite or quote sources written by witnesses, both hostile and friendly, of the Rubicon crossing and its repercussions.

Compare this with the resurrection. Not a single established historian mentioned the event until the 3rd and 4th Centuries and then only Christian historians and of those few none show any wide reading, cite any other sources, show any sign of a skilled or critical examination of conflicting claims, have no other literature or scholarship to their credit which we can use as a benchmark for their skill and accuracy, are completely unknown and have an overtly declared bias towards persuasion and conversion.

Fifth, the history of Rome could not have proceeded as it did had Caesar not physically moved an army into Italy and even if he could have somehow cultivated the mere belief he had done this he could not have captured Rome or conscripted Italian men against Pompey's forces in Greece. On the other hand all that is needed to explain the rise of Christianity is a belief the resurrection happened because there is nothing an actual resurrection would have caused which could not have been caused by a mere belief, thus an actual resurrection is not necessary to explain all subsequent history unlike Caesar's crossing of the Rubicon. And of course there is a huge difference between claiming a human being simply crossed a river and asserting another rose from the dead.

The reasons to be skeptical do not stop there. We must consider the setting, i.e. the place and time in which these stories spread. This was an age of fables and wonder with magic and miracles and ghosts everywhere which were almost never doubted. One example which illustrates this is we have several accounts of what the common people thought about lunar eclipses. They apparently had no doubt this horrible event was the result of witches calling the moon down with diabolical spells so when an eclipse occurred everyone would frantically start banging pots and furiously blowing brass horns to confuse the witches' spells. These were superstitious people.

Only a small class of elite well-educated men adopted more skeptical points of view during that era and because they belonged to the upper class both they and their arrogant skepticism were scorned by the common people rather than respected. Plutarch laments how doctors were willing to attend to the sick among the poor for little or no fee but were usually sent away in preference for the local wizard. By modern standards almost no one had any sort of education at all and there was of course no mass media disseminating scientific facts in any form. By the estimates of William Harris, author of *Ancient Literacy*, only twenty percent of the population could read anything at all, fewer than ten percent could read well and far fewer still had access to books. The result was the masses had no understanding of science or critical thought and were neither equipped, skilled or even interested in challenging an inspiring story, especially stories like those in the Gospels which were utopian, wonderful and most importantly if believed appeared to secure eternal life. Who wouldn't have bought a ticket to that lottery? Opposition arose mainly from prior commitments to other dogmas rather than reason or evidence.

The differences between society then and now cannot be stressed enough. There didn't then exist such things as coroners, reporters, cameras, newspapers, forensic science or even police detectives and all of the technology and people we now have pursuing the truth of various claims. In those days few would even be able to check the details of a story if they wanted to, and few wanted to, while today we have a television show called *Myth Busters*. Instead people based their judgment on the display of sincerity by the storyteller and the potential rewards his story had to offer. At the same time doubters didn't care to waste time or money debunking yet another crazy cult of which there were then hundreds and so it should not surprise us we have no writings by anyone hostile to Christianity until a century after it began. Clearly no doubter cared to check or even challenge the story in print until it was too late to investigate the facts.

These are just some of the reasons why we cannot trust extraordinary reports from that time without excellent evidence, something we do not have in the case of the physical resurrection of Jesus, for on the same quality of evidence we have reports of talking dogs, flying wizards, magical statues and monsters springing from trees. Can you imagine a movement today claiming a soldier in World War II rose physically from the dead, but when you asked for proof all they offered you were a handful of anonymous religious tracts written in the 1980s? Would it be even remotely reasonable to believe such a thing on so feeble a proof? Of course not. What about alien bodies which were supposedly recovered from a crashed flying saucer in Roswell, New Mexico? Many people sincerely believe that legend in this modern age despite ample evidence against it in print which is easily accessible to anyone, and keep in mind this legend began only thirty years after the purported event.

In spite of the foregoing it is often said in objection that we can trust the Gospels more than we normally would because they were based on the reports of eyewitnesses of the event who were willing to die for their belief in the physical resurrection, for surely no one would die for a lie. To quote the Christian website *gospelcom.net* "The first disciples were willing to suffer and die for their faith... for their claims to have seen Jesus... risen bodily from the dead." Of course Matthew 28:17 actually claims some eyewitnesses didn't believe what they saw and might not have become Christians which suggests the experience was not so convincing after all, and as noted elsewhere in this book believers have been martyred for many faiths but that is not in and of itself an indication of truth but rather only speaks to what an individual believed.

Interestingly, almost all important historical people have some descriptions of what they looked like. We have the image of Augustus Caesar cast on denarius coins, busts of Greek and Roman aristocrats, artwork of Napoleon, etc. We have descriptions of facial qualities, height, weight, hair length and color, age and even portraits of most important historical figures, but for Jesus we have nothing. Nowhere in the Bible do we have a description of the human shape of Jesus. How can we rely on the Gospels as the word of Jesus when no one even describes what he looked like? How odd none of the disciple characters recorded what he looked like, and yet believers accept them as knowing exactly what he said. Indeed, this gives us a clue that Jesus came to the Gospel writers indirectly and/or through myth. Not until hundreds of years after the alleged Jesus lived did pictures emerge as to what he looked like and those likenesses came from cult Christians who certainly had no more to go on than we do today. They differed widely from a blond, clean shaven, curly haired Apollonian youth found in the Roman catacombs to the long-bearded blue-eyed Italian depicted to this day. Even so modern believers often "see his image" in grilled cheese sandwiches and cloud formations. This mimics the pattern of Greek mythological figures as their believers constructed various images of what their gods looked like according to their own cultural image.

Naturally most Christians will not even concede such a simple and obvious point. They feel the need to rationalize they somehow do know what Jesus looked like and in doing so accomplish two things. Number one they undermine their own credibility and number two they provide a glaring example of apologetic rationalization and how Scripture can be made to say anything you want it to. For example some claim 2nd Century church father Justin Martyr pointed to Isaiah 53 as evidence Jesus was unattractive, "He has no form nor glory, nor beauty when we beheld him, but his appearance was without honor and inferior to that of the sons of men," yet at the same time Origen and others cite the portrayal of God in Psalm 45 as testimony Jesus was the "most handsome of men" (Psalm 45:2). Does that mean he had a makeover at some point? St. Augustine for his part suggested everyone has a different mental image of Jesus writing, "The physical face of the Lord is pictured with infinite variety by countless imaginations, though whatever it was like He certainly had only one. Nor as regards the faith we have in the Lord Jesus Christ it is in the least relevant to salvation what our imaginations picture Him like... What does matter is that we think of Him as man." He unintentionally hit two nails right on the head, first by admitting it must be left up to one's imagination and second by pointing out it doesn't matter, and yet some Christians continue to claim they "know."

The only physical description of Jesus which does exist is supposedly contained in a copy of a letter from the Roman consul Lentulus, who was purportedly Governor of Judea before Pontius Pilate, to the Roman Emperor Tiberius which was discovered in a monastery. According to the *copy* of the letter the original (which has never been found, if indeed it existed) was dated to the twelfth year of the reign of the Emperor Tiberius. Apologists claim scholars have historical verification a Roman consul named Lentulus was in Judea at the time of Jesus' trial and crucifixion and that his family is mentioned by Jewish historian Josephus in his *Antiquities of the Jews* but as you will see in a bit that is not exactly true. Scholars are divided, however, as to the authenticity of the letter. Lentulus' letter is presented as an official report to the Emperor Tiberius and in it he describes the condemned man named Jesus of Nazareth as having "a noble and lively face, with fair and slightly wavy hair; black and strongly curving eyebrows, intense penetrating blue eyes and an expression of wondrous grace. His nose is rather long. His beard is almost blonde, although not very long. His hair is quite long, and has never seen a pair of scissors... His neck is slightly inclined, so that he never appears to be bitter or arrogant. His tanned face is the color of ripe corn and well proportioned. It gives the impression of gravity and wisdom, sweetness and good, and is completely lacking in any sign of anger." An alternate version is as follows: "Lentulus, the Governor of the Jerusalemites to the Roman Senate and People, greetings. There has appeared in our times, and there still lives, a man of great power (virtue), called Jesus Christ. The people call him prophet of truth; his disciples, son of God. He raises the dead, and heals infirmities. He is a man of medium size (keep in mind Professor Judica-Cordiglia described him as being tall at about six feet in height based upon the Shroud); he has a venerable aspect, and his beholders can both fear and love him. His hair is of the colour of the ripe hazel-nut, straight down to the ears, but below the ears wavy and curled, with a bluish and bright reflection, flowing over his shoulders. It is parted in two on the top of the head, after the pattern of the Nazarenes. His brow is smooth and very cheerful with a face without wrinkle or spot, embellished by a slightly reddish complexion. His nose and mouth are faultless. His beard is abundant, of the colour of his hair, not long, but divided at the chin. His aspect is simple and mature, his eyes are changeable and bright. He is terrible in his reprimands, sweet and amiable in his admonitions, cheerful without loss of gravity. He was never known to laugh, but often to weep. His stature is straight, his hands and arms beautiful to behold. His conversation is grave, infrequent, and modest. He is the most beautiful among the children of men."

The apologists then go one step further and try to tie that questionable description to "physical evidence" in the form of the Shroud of Turin, claiming that a "Shroud of Turin scholar" named Professor Giovanni Judica-Cordiglia was able to "complete the physical description of Christ" based upon information collected from the Shroud, but as I have already demonstrated that relic is clearly a forgery. As bad as those claims are some actually go even further by quoting a portion of the Book of Revelation (1:13-16) which described Jesus as follows: "...and among the lampstands was someone 'like a son of man,' dressed in a robe reaching down to his feet and with a golden sash around his chest. His head and hair were white like wool, as white as snow, and his eyes were like blazing fire. His feet were like bronze glowing in a furnace, and his voice was like the sound of rushing waters. In his right hand he held seven stars, and out of his mouth came a sharp double-edged sword. His face was like the sun shining in all its brilliance." All I can say to that is, in the words of biblical historian Ken Smith, "If his Epistles can be seen as John as on pot, Revelation is John on acid."

Getting back to the letter of Lentulus, it is regarded as apocryphal for a number of reasons. No Governor of Jerusalem is known to have been called Lentulus, a Roman governor would not have addressed the Senate in the way represented and a Roman writer would not have employed the expressions "prophet of truth," "sons of men" or "Jesus Christ" because the former two are Hebrew idioms and the third is taken from the New Testament therefore the letter gives a description of Jesus such as Christian piety conceived him.

The letter was first printed in the *Life of Christ* by Ludolph the Carthusian in 1474 and in the *Introduction to the Works of St. Anselm* in 1491 but it is neither the work of St. Anselm nor Ludolph. According to the manuscript of Jena a Cardinal named Giacomo Colonna found the letter in 1421 in an ancient Roman document sent to Rome from Constantinople. It was said to be of Greek origin and translated into Latin during the 13th or 14th Century. Christopher Mylius, the 18th Century librarian of Jena, stated the letter was written in golden letters on red paper and richly bound and of course, like most religious relics, it was lost. Even so copies of the letter saw widespread publication, it was accepted as an eyewitness account for a long time and gave various artists a model on which to base the face and appearance of Jesus.

Yet another legend needs to be mentioned and not only because it is germane to a discussion about an image of Jesus but because it is also an excellent example of a phenomenon covered in another part of this book, namely how a story can morph and grow over time. It tells of Abgar, King of Edessa, who was afflicted with an incurable sickness but having learned of the fame, power and miracles of Jesus wrote to him, acknowledged his divinity and asked for help while offering asylum in his own residence. The tradition states Jesus wrote a letter declining to go (one must wonder whatever happened to *that* relic) but promised that after his ascension he would send one of his disciples who was endowed with his power.

The 4th Century church historian Eusebius, Bishop of Caesarea, records a tradition concerning a correspondence on this occasion exchanged between Abgar of Edessa and Jesus. Eusebius was convinced the original letters, written in Aramaic, were kept in the archives of Edessa and also states that in due course after Christ's ascension Thaddeus, one of the seventy-two Disciples, was sent by Thomas the Apostle in 29 CE. The correspondence consisted of Abgar's letter and the answer dictated by Jesus. As the legend later expanded a portrait of Jesus painted from life suddenly began to be mentioned and this portrait, purportedly painted by a court archivist named Hannan during his visit to Jesus, is first mentioned in an Aramaic text called the *Doctrine of Addai* from the second half of the 4th Century. Here it is said the reply of Jesus was given not in writing but orally, and the event took place in 32 CE. This *Teaching of Addai* is also the earliest account of an image of Jesus painted from life and was supposedly enshrined by the ailing King Abgar in one of his palaces.

The story of the letter to Abgar, including the portrait made by the court painter Hannan, is later repeated with some additions in the mid-5th Century *History of the Armenians* compiled by Moses of Chorene who remarked that the portrait was preserved in Edessa. The myth was later elaborated even further by the church historian Evagrius, Bishop of Edessa (c. 536-600), who declared the image of Jesus was divinely wrought and not made by human hands. In sum, the documented legend developed from no image in Eusebius, to an image painted by a man named Hannan according to Moses of Chorene, to a miraculously-appearing image not made by human hands in the writings of Evagrius. A perfect example of an evolving myth.

Historical people leave us with contemporary evidence but for Jesus we have nothing. If we wanted to present a fair comparison of the type of information about Jesus to another example of equal historical value we could do no better than to compare Jesus with the mythical figure of Hercules. Why bother? Because if a person accepts hearsay and accounts from believers as historical evidence for Jesus then shouldn't they act consistently with regard to other accounts which are also based solely upon hearsay and belief?

Examine the evidence for Hercules of Greek mythology and you will find it parallels the historicity of Jesus to such an amazing degree that for Christian apologists to deny Hercules as a historical person belies and contradicts the very same methodology used for a historical Jesus. Also note that Herculean myth resembles Jesus in many areas. Just as the Virgin Mary was impregnated by the Holy Ghost acting as a surrogate for God the mortal and chaste Alcmene, mother of Hercules, gave birth to him from a union with a god (Zeus). Similar to Herod who wanted to kill Jesus, Hera wanted to kill Hercules. Like Jesus, Hercules traveled the earth as a mortal helping mankind and performing miraculous deeds. Similar to Jesus who died and rose to Heaven Hercules died, rose to Mount Olympus and became a god. Hercules is an example of perhaps the most popular hero in Ancient Greece and Rome with the point being they believed he actually lived, told stories about him, worshiped him and dedicated temples to him.

Likewise the evidence for Hercules closely parallels that of Jesus. We have historical people like Hesiod and Plato who mention Hercules in their writings. Similar to the way the Gospels tell a narrative story of Jesus, so do we have the epic stories of Homer which chronicle the life of Hercules. Aesop tells stories and quotes the words of Hercules. Just as we have a brief mention of Jesus by Josephus in his *Antiquities*, he also mentions Hercules (more times than Jesus) in the very same work (see: 1.15; 8.5.3; 10.11.1). Just as Tacitus mentions a Christus so does he also mention Hercules many times in his *Annals*. And most importantly, just as we have no artifacts, writings or eyewitnesses for Hercules we also have nothing for Jesus. All information about Hercules and Jesus come from stories, beliefs and hearsay. Should we then believe in a historical Hercules simply because ancient historians mention him and we have stories and beliefs about him? Of course not, and the same must apply to Jesus if we wish to have any consistency with regard to historicity.

Some critics doubt a historicized Jesus could develop from myth because they think there was never any precedence for it. We have many examples of myth from history, but what about the other way around? This doubt fails in the light of the most obvious example - the Greek mythologies where Greek and Roman writers including Diodorus, Cicero, Livy, etc., assumed there must have existed a historical root for figures such as Hercules, Theseus, Odysseus, Minos, Dionysus, etc. These writers even put their mythological heroes into an invented historical time chart. Herodotus, for example, actually tried to determine when rather than if Hercules lived. As Robert M. Price revealed, "The whole approach earned the name of Euhemerism, from Euhemerus who originated it." Even today we see many examples of seedling historicized mythologies: UFO adherents whose beliefs began as a dream of alien bodily invasion and then were expressed as actually having occurred, some of which have formed religious cults, beliefs of urban legends which started as pure fiction, hoaxes like Bigfoot and the Loch Ness Monster and false propaganda spread by politicians which are believed by their constituents.

People today consider Hercules and other Greek gods as myth simply because they no longer believe in the Greek and Roman stories. When a civilization dies, so do their gods. Christianity and its church authorities, on the other hand, still hold a powerful influence on governments, institutions and colleges. Anyone doing research on Jesus, even skeptics, had better allude to his existence or else risk damage to their reputations or embarrassment amongst their Christian friends. Christianity depends on establishing a historical Jesus and it will defend, at all costs, even the most unreliable sources. The faithful desperately want to believe in Jesus and belief alone can create intellectual barriers which leak even into secular thought. We have so many Christian professors, theologians and historical "experts" around the world who tell us we should accept a historical Jesus that if repeated often enough it tends to convince even the most ardent skeptic. The establishment of history should never reside with the "experts" words alone or simply because a scholar has a reputation as a historian. Truth is not a matter of what is popular and it is important to remember that historical review has yet to achieve the reliability of scientific investigation, and in fact many times ignores it. If a scholar makes a historical claim his assertion should depend primarily upon the evidence itself and not just because he or she says so. Facts do not require belief and whereas beliefs can live comfortably without any evidence at all facts depend upon evidence.

Some people actually believe just because so much voice and ink has spread the word of a character named Jesus throughout history this must mean he actually lived. This "where there's smoke there must be fire" argument simply does not hold up to scrutiny. The number of people who believe or write about something or the professional degrees they hold say nothing at all about fact. I'll say it again - facts are derived from evidence, not from hearsay or from hubris scholars and certainly not from faithful believers. Regardless of the position or admiration held by a scholar, believer or priest if he or she cannot support a hypothesis with good evidence then it can only remain a hypothesis.

While a reasonable possibility exists an actual person named Jesus lived another likely possibility reveals that a mythology could have derived out of earlier mythologies or possibly independent archetypal hero worship. Although we have no evidence for a historical Jesus we certainly have many accounts of mythologies from the Middle East during the 1st Century and before and many of these stories appear similar to the Christ savior story.

Just before and during the 1st Century the Jews had prophesied about an upcoming Messiah based on Jewish Scripture and their beliefs influenced many of their followers. We know powerful beliefs can create self-fulfilling prophesies and surely this proved just as true in ancient times. It served as a popular dream expressed in Hebrew Scripture for the promise of an "end-time" with a savior to lead them to the promised land. Indeed Roman records document the executions of several would be Messiahs but not a single record mentions a Jesus and many ancients believed there would come a final war against the "Sons of Darkness," i.e. the Romans. This could very well have served as the ignition and flame for the future growth of Christianity. Consider that biblical scholars tell us early Christians lived within pagan communities and Jewish scriptural beliefs, coupled with the pagan myths of the time, give sufficient information about how such a religion could have formed. Many of the Hellenistic and pagan myths parallel so closely the alleged Jesus that to ignore their similarities means to ignore the mythological beliefs of history. Dozens of similar savior stories had spread long before the alleged life of Jesus and as a result virtually nothing about Jesus "the Christ" came to the Christians as original or new.

For example the religion of Zoroaster, founded circa 628-551 BCE in ancient Persia, roused mankind to the need for hating a devil as well as a belief in paradise, last judgment and the resurrection of the dead. Mithraism, an offshoot of Zoroastrianism, probably influenced early Christianity since the Magi described in the New Testament appear as Zoroastrian priests, and note the word "paradise" came from the Persian word *pairidaeza.* Osiris, Hercules, Hermes, Prometheus, Perseus, Romulus and others also compare to the Christian myth. According to Patrick Campbell of *The Mythical Jesus* all served as pre-Christian sun gods, yet all had gods for fathers and virgins for mothers, had their births announced by stars, were born on the solstice around December 25th, had tyrants who tried to kill them in their infancy, met violent deaths, rose from the dead, nearly all were worshiped by "wise men" and some allegedly fasted for forty days.

Even early Christian apologist Justin Martyr recognized the analogies between Christianity and Paganism. To the Pagans he wrote, "When we say that the Word, who is first born of God, was produced without sexual union, and that he, Jesus Christ, our teacher, was crucified and died, and rose again, and ascended into Heaven; we propound nothing different from what you believe regarding those whom you esteem sons of Jupiter (Zeus)." Virtually all of the mythical accounts of a savior Jesus have parallels to past pagan mythologies which existed long before Christianity and from the Jewish Scriptures we now call the Old Testament. The accounts of these myths say nothing about historical reality but they certainly do say a lot about believers, how they believed and how their beliefs spread.

In the book *The Jesus Puzzle* biblical scholar Earl Doherty presents not only a challenge to the existence of a historical Jesus but reveals early pre-Gospel Christian documents demonstrate the concept of Jesus sprang from non-historical spiritual beliefs of a Christ derived from Jewish Scripture and Hellenized myths of savior gods. Nowhere do any of the New Testament epistle writers describe a human Jesus, including Paul. None of the epistles mention a Jesus from Nazareth, either as an earthly teacher or a human miracle worker. Nowhere do we find these writers quoting Jesus. Nowhere do we find them describing any details of Jesus' life on earth or of his followers. Nowhere do we find the epistle writers even using the word "disciple" (they of course use the term "apostle" but the word simply means messenger, as Paul saw himself). Except for a few well known interpolations Jesus always gets presented as a spiritual being who existed before all time with God and it was clear knowledge of Christ either came directly from God or as a revelation from the word of Scripture. Doherty writes, "Christian documents outside the Gospels, even at the end of the 1st Century and beyond, show no evidence that any tradition about an earthly life and ministry of Jesus were in circulation." Furthermore the epistle to the Hebrews (8:4) makes it explicitly clear the epistle writer did not believe in a historical Jesus saying, "If He (Jesus) had been on earth, He would not be a priest."

So did Christians copy pagan ideas directly into their own faith? Not necessarily. They may have gotten many of their beliefs through syncretism, the combining of different often seemingly contradictory beliefs melding practices of various schools of thought, or through independent hero archetype worship which is innate to human storytelling. If gotten through syncretism Jews and pagans could very well have influenced the first Christians, especially with regard to the ideas of salvation and beliefs about good and evil. Later, at the time of the Gospels, other myths may have entered Christian beliefs such as the virgin birth and miracles. In the 4th Century we know Christians derived the birthday of Jesus from the pagans. That is an undisputed fact. But even if it had been gotten through independent means it still says nothing about Christian originality because we know pagans had beliefs about incarnated gods long before Christianity existed. Those hero archetypes still exist in our storytelling today.

It is often claimed the A.D. (*Anno Domini*, or "year of our Lord") dating method is evidence of Christ's birth and some people actually believe it has been in use from that time on, but in reality it was derived from a monk named Dionysius Exiguus (Dennis the Little) in the 6th

Century who used it in his Easter tables. Oddly, some people seem to think this has relevance to a historical Jesus but of course it has nothing at all to do with it since in the time before and during the 6th Century people used various other dating methods. The first calendar was invented by the Egyptians three thousand years before Christ, the Romans used A.U.C. (*anno urbis conditae*, "year of the founded city," with that city being Rome), the Jews had their own dating system and in fact not until the 10th Century did most churches accept the new dating method. The A.D. system simply reset the time of January 1, 754 A.U.C. to January 1 in year 1 A.D. which Dionysius obliquely derived from the belief of the date of the "incarnation" of Jesus but that date, if one uses the Bible as history, can't possibly hold true because Dionysius believed the conception (incarnation) of Jesus occurred on March 25. This meant the conception must have occurred nine months later on December 25, probably not coincidentally the very same date in 274 CE Emperor Aurelian declared a holiday in celebration of the birth of the sun god Mithras, and by 336 CE Christians had replaced Mithras with Jesus' birth on the same date. Dionysius then declared the new year several days later on January 1, probably to coincide with the traditional Roman year. Dionysius had probably never read the Gospel account of the birth of Jesus because the Matthew Gospel says his birth occurred while Herod served as King and that meant if he did exist his birth would have had to occur in 4 BCE or earlier. He made another mistake by assigning the first year as 1 instead of 0 (everyone's birthday starts at year 0, not 1) since the concept of zero, which was invented in Arabia and India, didn't make it to Europe until about two hundred years later.

In sum the early historical documents can prove nothing about an actual Jesus but they do show an evolution of belief derived from varied and diverse concepts of Christianity starting from a purely spiritual form of Christ to a human figure who embodied that spirit as portrayed in the Gospels. The New Testament stories appear as an eclectic hodgepodge of Jewish, Hellenized and pagan stories compiled by pietistic believers to appeal to an audience for their particular religious times.

The Gospels which made it into the Bible pretty much skip from the birth of Jesus to his adulthood but unbeknownst to most Christians there are other documents which chronicle the adventures of Christ. They're part of something called the New Testament Apocrypha, a series of books and gospels deemed unfit for inclusion in the canon due to concerns over the message they would send. Most of the stories are pretty mundane - the usual healing of lepers and raising of the dead - but some are for lack of a better term insane.

As has been pointed out elsewhere the New Testament didn't simply descend from the skies onto newsstands the morning after Jesus ascended to Heaven and the twenty-seven New Testament books found in most modern Christian Bibles weren't declared official until over three hundred years after Jesus allegedly walked the earth. By that time thousands of sayings and stories about his life had to be left on the cutting-room floor. Such was the case of the Gospel of Pseudo-Matthew. The name comes from the fact it's basically an extended director's cut of the Gospel of Matthew which made it into the Bible and covers most of the same territory except for one deleted scene.

As previously mentioned two years after Jesus was born King Herod got word of a child being called the King of the Jews and ordered all two-year-old male children in Bethlehem to be killed to protect his throne, but God managed to warn Joseph in time and the family fled before Herod's men arrived. That much we already know. What you may not have known is on their way to Egypt Jesus and his family stopped to rest in a cave which to their surprise was populated by a group of dragons, which is really not so unusual considering dragons are mentioned elsewhere in the Bible. According to Chapter 18 of the Gospel of Pseudo-Matthew, "And, lo, suddenly there came forth from the cave many dragons; and when the children saw them, they cried out in great terror. Then Jesus went down from the bosom of His mother, and stood on His feet before the dragons; and they adored Jesus, and thereafter retired."

Written in the early 2nd Century, which is around the same time most scholars date the four Gospels in the Bible, the Infancy Gospel of Thomas picks up the story a few years later. Back in Nazareth now, five-year-old Jesus was playing beside a small brook with some other children who were forming pools of water to make clay. Jesus formed some sparrows out of the clay, decided to give the sculptures life and off they flew on his command. One of the other children saw this, walked up behind him and started splashing his pools with a stick. According to the Infancy Gospel of Thomas 3:2-3, "'O evil, ungodly, and foolish one, what hurt did the pools and the waters do thee? Behold, now also thou shalt be withered like a tree, and shalt not bear leaves, neither root, nor fruit.' And straightway that lad withered up wholly." With that the boy started aging rapidly and withered away much like the barren fig tree Jesus would later curse as described in Matthew 21:18-22 and Mark 11:12-14. Then later that same day as Jesus was casually strolling around town another boy accidentally bumped into him on the street and according to the Infancy Gospel of Thomas 4:1, "Jesus was provoked and said unto him, 'Thou shalt not finish thy course.' And immediately he fell down and died."

The local children now feared him so intensely they adopted him as their king, acted as his bodyguards and forced everyone who passed through town to come and worship him. One day a group of men came by carrying a small child and refused to follow the group of terrified children, explaining the boy they were carrying had been bitten by a snake and was near death. Jesus says simply, "Let us go and kill that serpent." Then, according to the First Gospel of Infancy 18:13-16, "Then the Lord Jesus calling the serpent, it presently came forth and submitted to him; to whom he said, 'Go and suck out all the poison which thou hast infused into that boy'; so the serpent crept to the boy, and took away all its poison again. Then the Lord Jesus cursed the serpent so that it immediately burst asunder, and died."

By now the parents of Nazareth were understandably upset so they gave Joseph an ultimatum: Either Jesus learns to use his powers for good or the family must leave town. Considering by this point Jesus has killed more children than a Willy Wonka tour group that was reasonable but what happened was, "Jesus said, 'I know that these thy words are not thine: nevertheless for thy sake I will hold my peace: but they shall bear their punishment.' And straightway they that accused him were smitten with blindness." Then according to the Infancy Gospel of Thomas 5:1, Joseph "grabbed (Jesus') ear" and "wrung it til it was sore." As a result Jesus ended up uncursing everybody but not out of some well-deserved sense of remorse or the slightest hint of empathy and eventually a local teacher began to frantically scream to everyone that Jesus was probably God… or so the story goes.

In the end the development of these myths is really a fascinating study in the human condition. As the Reverend Heinrich Rower pointed out, "We are all acquainted with the fact that in their mythological legends the Greeks and the Romans and other nations of antiquity speak of certain persons as the sons of the gods. An example of this is Hercules, the Greek hero who is the son of Jupiter and an earthly mother... All those men who performed greater deeds than those which human beings usually do are regarded by antiquity as of divine origin. This Greek and heathen notion has been applied to the New Testament and churchly conception of the person of Jesus. We must remember that at the time when Christianity sprang into evidence, Greek culture and Greek religion spread over the whole world. It is accordingly nothing remarkable that the Christians took from the heathens the highest religious conceptions that they possessed, and transferred them to Jesus. They accordingly called him the son of God, and declared that he had been supernaturally born of a virgin. This is the Greek and heathen influence which has determined the character of the account given by Matthew and Luke concerning the birth of Jesus."

All of the foregoing address the question of whether or not a historical figure named Jesus ever existed but even if he did there is no reason to believe he was anything more than a charismatic rabbi to whom some well-known quotes and parables have been attributed. That is because there is even less evidence for the supposed miracles which "prove" him to be the "son of God" in the minds of true believers. As has been previously noted not a single extra-biblical mention of a single "miracle" attributed to Jesus has ever been made by anyone at any time so we are left with nothing but the Gospels to substantiate those claims, and as we have already discussed those are pure hearsay and do not even corroborate one another. The three hours of darkness, earthquake and zombie infestation of Jerusalem which purportedly occurred when Jesus was crucified have already been mentioned but there are many more examples of amazing miracles which somehow escaped even a cursory mention by anyone who "saw" them. Apologists are quick to point out there were five thousand witnesses to Jesus feeding the masses with one loaf of bread and one fish and another four thousand on a separate occasion and "many witnesses" to the resurrection, but of course most are never named and in any case there are no testimonials to be found anywhere from any of those supposed witnesses. One could just as easily state there were "many witnesses" to a UFO visitation or a leprechaun and his pot of gold but without first hand attestations from at least some of those witnesses such a claim is worthless. The bottom line is not a single word was written by a single one of those thousands upon thousands of supposed witnesses to biblical events, let alone the miracles. As legends grow the stories tend to become more and more fantastic and when you consider that superstitious people lived at the time the Gospels were written it is easy to understand how such tales could take hold of the imagination. The legend of Jesus is just that, a legend. Viewed objectively, does it really make sense that the creator of the entire universe can only have one son as the famous and oft-quoted John 3:16 says? Is it reasonable to believe donkeys can talk and people can rise from the dead and a man can live inside a whale for three days? Of course not, but those are the sort of things legends are made of.

In conclusion belief cannot produce historical fact and claims which come from nothing but hearsay and faith do not amount to an honest attempt to get at the facts. Even with eyewitness accounts we must tread carefully. Simply because someone makes a claim does not mean it represents reality. For example consider some of the bogus claims which supposedly come from many eyewitness accounts of alien extraterrestrials and their spacecraft. They not only assert they are eyewitnesses but present blurry photos to boot and if we can question those firsthand accounts and physical "evidence" why should we not question claims which come from hearsay, especially when that hearsay comes from ancient and unknown people who are long dead.

Unfortunately belief and faith substitute as knowledge in many people's thinking and nothing, even direct evidence thrust at the feet of their claims, could possibly change their minds. We have many stories, myths and beliefs of a Jesus but if we wish to establish the facts of history we cannot even begin to put together an accurate narrative without at least a few reliable eyewitness accounts. Of course a historical Jesus may have existed, perhaps based loosely on a living human even though his actual history got lost, but this amounts to nothing but speculation - however we do have an abundance of evidence supporting the mythical evolution of Jesus. Virtually every detail in the Gospel stories occurred in pagan and/or Hebrew stories long before the advent of Christianity while we simply do not have a shred of evidence to determine the historicity of a Jesus "the Christ." We only have evidence for the *belief* of Jesus. So if you hear anyone claim to have evidence for a witness to a historical Jesus simply ask for the author's birth date. Anyone whose birth occurred after an event logically cannot serve as an eyewitness nor can their words alone serve as evidence for that event.

In the end, after objectively examining all the evidence for both supernatural claims and a historical figure named Jesus, the answer is clear - there is little reason to believe the Gospels and the entire Bible for that matter are anything other than fanciful tales which have been passed down from generation to generation and become so deeply rooted in our culture it is impossible to separate fact from fiction or reality from fantasy. Many people do of course ignore that and choose to believe what is familiar and comfortable and reassuring, but that is a subject covered in another chapter.

The End Times

Or, Apocalypse… When?

☥☸☯⛩🕉✋☸✡✝☪☬⚱✡⚓☸☸⚛☬☸

"Nearly half of the American population is eagerly anticipating the end of the world. This dewy-eyed nihilism provides absolutely no incentive to build a sustainable civilization." ~ Sam Harris

The year 1914 was going to be Armageddon according to Jehovah's Witnesses who had computed the date from prophecy in the book of Daniel 4 which refers to "seven times" and interpreted each "time" as being equal to 360 days for a total of 2520 days. This was further interpreted as representing 2520 years measured from the starting date of 607 BCE and gave 1914 as the target date, but when 1914 passed they changed their prediction and 1914 instead became the year Jesus had "invisibly" begun his rule.

Since late in the 19th Century they had taught what they call the "Battle of the Great Day of God Almighty" or Armageddon would happen in 1914 CE and when it didn't the next major estimate was 1925. *Watchtower* magazine predicted, "The year 1925 is a date definitely and clearly marked in the Scriptures, even more clearly than that of 1914; but it would be presumptuous on the part of any faithful follower of the Lord to assume just what the Lord is going to do during that year." The Watchtower Society then selected 1975 as its next main prediction because, "According to reliable Bible chronology Adam was created in the year 4026 BCE, likely in the autumn of the year, at the end of the sixth day of creation." They believed the year 1975 was a promising date for the end of the world as it was supposedly the six thousandth anniversary of Adam's creation and exactly one thousand years had passed for each day of the creation week. Needless to say this prophecy also failed. Realizing how stupid they were looking every time a new prediction failed they then announced the end of the world would occur six thousand years after the creation of Eve, a date which cannot be calculated even by them.

During one of his standup routines comedian Bill Maher said, "Here is a frightening statistic. One out of four Americans believes that Jesus will return to Earth in their lifetime. See, that's religion for you. Ego, masquerading as humility. Jesus is coming back, and of course he's going to want to meet *me*." He makes an excellent point because claims the Rapture is imminent fly in the face of Scripture which clearly, or at least as clearly as anything in the Bible gets, said it would happen to those alive in the time of Jesus. Even so every generation since has believed the "end times" would come in their lifetime and they would be the ones to meet Jesus… and yet here we remain. No doubt generations to come will believe the very same thing until finally one day in the future a collective light bulb goes on and the human race realizes it is never going to happen and the "no man can know the time" excuse is nothing more than a clever dodge. As one person put it, "He's dead… it's been two thousand years… he's not coming back… get over it!

The idea the end is near is certainly not new nor is it exclusive to the Abrahamic religions. An Assyrian stone tablet from circa 2800 BCE confidently asserts, "The Earth is degenerating these days. Bribery and corruption abound. Children no longer mind their parents, every man wants to write a book, and it is evident that the end of the world is fast approaching." Contrast that with the much more recent predictions made in the *Seven Signs of the Apocalypse* discussed later in this chapter. As they say, the more things change the more they stay the same. While many religions have end of the world beliefs the Christian version stems from the Book of Revelation which was purportedly written by the Apostle John. Believe me it is quite the interesting read for an objective person since it has been said, "If the Gospel of John is John on pot, Revelation is John on acid." A similar sentiment was expressed by Thomas Jefferson in an 1825 letter to Alexander Smyth when he wrote, "It is between fifty and sixty years since I read the Apocalypse, and I then considered it merely the ravings of a maniac, no more worthy, nor capable of explanation than the incoherences of our own nightly dreams... (because) what has no meaning admits no explanation."

Some people seem to be fascinated with the prospect of the end of the world and in fact many are actually hoping it will happen in their lifetime. One recent example of this obsession came via a group which claimed to know when the "end times" would occur. Their website made the claim, "Some realize that God knows how and when the end of the world will come, so they wonder if He tells us. Rather than turning to the Bible as the source of all truth for these answers, they turn to the churches and religious leaders. They may be told that the end will not come until the Antichrist rises as a political leader who will make them take the "mark of the beast." Many are told that God will rapture His people before a seven year Great Tribulation after which Christ will set up a thousand year reign from an earthly throne in Jerusalem. Others are told that Christ will come to rapture believers the same day he destroys the world. While just about every church has a different idea as to what the Bible teaches concerning the end, they all seem to agree on one thing; no man can know the day or the hour of Christ's return because the Scriptures say that He is coming as a thief in the night. But are they correct? Can We Know? This website serves as an introduction and portal to four faithful ministries which are teaching that we can know from the Bible alone that the date of the rapture of believers will take place on May 21, 2011 and that God will destroy this world on October 21, 2011."

Needless to say, they were wrong. In January of 2010 Justin Berton of the *San Francisco Chronicle* wrote an article about predictions of the impending rapture by a man named Harold Camping, the then eighty-eight year old owner of Oakland based evangelical station Family Radio, who ironically dismissed the popular belief the world would end in December of 2012 when the Mayan calendar ran out as being ridiculous saying, "That date has not one stitch of biblical authority. It's like a fairy tale." The real date for the end of times, he said, was in 2011.

The Mayans and the Hollywood movie *2012* had put the apocalypse in the popular mind that year but Camping had been at the business of prophecy for a long time, and while Armageddon is pop science or big-screen entertainment to many Camping had followers from the Bay Area to China. He had scrutinized the Bible for almost seventy years and said he had developed a mathematical system to interpret prophecies hidden within the "good book" and one night a few years ago Camping - a civil engineer by trade - crunched the numbers and was stunned at what he'd found: The world would end on May 21, 2011.

This was not the first time Camping had made a bold prediction about Judgment Day. On September 6, 1994 dozens of his followers gathered inside Alameda's Veterans Memorial Building to await the return of Christ, an event Camping had promised for two years. Followers dressed children in their Sunday best and held Bibles open-faced toward Heaven, but the world did not end. Camping allowed that he may have made a mathematical error and spent the next decade running new calculations as follows:

11,013 BCE: Creation. God created the world and man (Adam and Eve).

4990 BCE: The flood of Noah's day. All perished in a worldwide flood. Only Noah, his wife, and his three sons and their wives survived in the ark (6023 years from creation).

7 BCE: Jesus Christ was born (11,006 years from creation).

33 CE: Jesus Christ was crucified and the church age began (11,045 years from creation; 5023 calendar years from the flood).

1988 CE: The church age ended and the great tribulation period of 23 years began (13,000 years from creation).

1994 CE: On September 7th the first 2300-day period of the great tribulation came to an end and the latter reign began, commencing God's plan to save a great multitude of people outside of the churches (13,006 years from creation).

2011 CE: On May 21st Judgment Day will begin and the rapture (the taking up into Heaven of God's elect people) will occur at the end of the 23-year great tribulation. On October 21st, the world will be destroyed by fire (7000 years from the flood; 13,023 years from creation).

Camping claimed certain numbers repeat in the Bible along with particular themes, for instance the number five means "atonement," ten equals "completeness" and seventeen is "heaven." Multiply those numbers by each other and multiply the result by itself and it equals 722,500. According to Camping, "Christ hung on the cross April 1, 33 A.D. Now go to April 1 of 2011 A.D. and that's 1,978 years. If you multiply that number by 365.2422 - the number of days in the solar calendar - it equals 722,449... and if you add fifty-one - the number of days between April 1 and May 21 - to that number it equals 722,500.

From there it gets even more confusing. Camping also believed May 21 marked the seven thousand year anniversary of Noah's flood and the end of a thirty-three-year period of Tribulation during which he claimed Satan ruled the churches. He pointed to the increasing acceptance of gay clergy or the rise in charismatic and Pentecostal movements as signs that churches have gone astray. To him rituals such as baptism and confession were worthless.

When the day came and went the preacher initially didn't admit his error. Instead he offered a yet another new date, saying he hadn't looked closely enough at the Book of Jeremiah, but once again nothing happened. After a *San Francisco Chronicle* reporter asked him to explain he said, "Nothing has been negated... the Bible is based on the biblical calendar, which began in March. So 1994 runs until March 31, 1995." Well, in case you haven't noticed March 1995 has come and gone and so has 2011. For that matter so has Camping. He died in December of 2013 still awaiting the rapture and sure that it was at hand, just as many before him had done and many more will in the future.

This sort of thing is far from a unique occurrence since throughout history dozens of end-times predictions have gone unfulfilled, but some have had a lasting outcome. Keep in mind Christianity isn't the only religion which believes the world will end although its prescriptions about end times certainly tend to be more frequent and pronounced than other faiths while in non-Abrahamic religions such as Buddhism and Hinduism the idea of death and destruction is more cyclical than finite.

Christian denominations differ on the exact chronology and length of Christ's second coming but almost all say the date is unknown and point at two key passages. One is 2 Peter 3:10: "The day of the Lord will come as a thief in the night." Another is Matthew 24:36: "Of that day and hour knoweth no [man], no, not the angels of Heaven, but my Father only." Yet many Judgment Day preachers like Camping say reading these passages alone leads to misinterpretation while claiming God has only recently given humans the ability to understand the hidden code in his book.

Several years before Camping's so-called "end of days" another "prophet" named Shelby Corbitt predicted the Second Coming and wrote a book entitled *2007*. She claimed, "This book is a prophetic message from God for the world. Everyone must know and will know this warning from Him. This book tells of events to prepare for and a date that the rapture of the church will happen. Catastrophic events are about to happen, just like in the days of Noah. God is saying, 'Are you rapture ready?' This message is for every single person living in this present day and hour. I am an average American housewife and mother who loves God and has devoted my life to being a voice and vessel for God to use to speak to this world." She also maintained a website called *2007rapture.com* which naturally disappeared after the date had come and gone, but devotees of superstition have an incredible ability to take failure in stride and Shelby Corbitt is no exception. She's since launched a new site that's basically identical to the last except she no longer tries to predict a date. Of course she still insists, "I know the rapture will happen in my lifetime." As James Randi has said, people like this are "unsinkable rubber ducks" because her belief isn't driven by facts but by a desire to believe, which makes the unbroken string of prophetic failures irrelevant. The obvious question for any rational person to ask would be why would the omnipotent creator of the universe need Shelby Corbitt to act as his "voice and vessel to speak to this world"?

Long before all that in 1844 Baptist preacher William Miller gained thousands of followers by predicting Christ's return. "The Great Disappointment" as it became known was a major event in the history of the Millerite movement, a 19th Century American Christian sect which had formed out of the Second Great Awakening. Based on his interpretations of the prophecies in the book of Daniel (Chapters 8 and 9, especially Daniel 8:14, "Unto two thousand and three hundred days; then shall the sanctuary be cleansed") Miller proposed that Jesus Christ would return to earth during the year 1844. The more specific date of October 22, 1844 was then preached by Samuel S. Snow and thousands of followers, some of whom had given away all of their possessions, waited expectantly. When Jesus didn't come Miller's movement nonetheless grew into today's Seventh-Day Adventist Church while Miller himself, much like Camping, continued to wait in vain for the second coming of Jesus Christ until his death in 1849.

In the 1970s and 1980s Hal Lindsey famously promoted in *The Late Great Planet Earth* the idea end times would soon approach after being set off by a Soviet invasion of the Middle East. Lindsey, who has been continually predicting the end of the world since *The Late, Great Planet Earth* came out in 1970, wrote that Christians should not make any plans after the year 2000 in his 1996 book *Planet Earth 2000 A.D.: Will Mankind Survive?* He probably came by this date using the same method he used to calculate the date of the end of the world in his book *The 1980s: Countdown to Armageddon* which is of course now out of print. Despite his less-than-stellar track record Lindsey is amazingly still at it and in 2008 wrote a column for the conservative news site *WorldNetDaily* in which he suggested Barack Obama is setting the stage for the arrival of the Antichrist.

Even more mainstream Christians sometimes like to don the mantle of "prophet" and attempt to predict the future, with God's help of course. In a 1980 broadcast of *The 700 Club* well known televangelist Pat Robertson said, "I guarantee you by the end of 1982 there is going to be a judgment on the world." Robertson said God had told him about impending disasters on numerous occasions including a West Coast tsunami in 2006 and a terrorist attack in 2007, neither of which occurred. "I have a relatively good track record," he later said, "but sometimes I miss." While the world didn't end in 1982 as prophesized, the television show *WKRP in Cincinnati* in fact did.

Then of course there was Y2K and naturally some believers viewed that as a sign of the end but the year 2000 passed without widespread digital breakdowns. A few years later the year 2012 gained popularity among those interested in the ancient Mayan calendar and Armageddon and oodles of "proof" was put forward to validate that prediction. Even the Prophet Nostradamus seemed to know how the end of the world was coming to pass and although he published many predictive Almanacs filled with prophesies about foreseen events he actually wrote about the end of times in a letter to his newborn son Cesar in which he described how a storm of comets will destroy the earth about 5500 years after he wrote his predictions in 1553.

Famed American mysticist and devout Christian Edgar Cayce had much to say about the life of Jesus covering the "lost" years that were never addressed in the Bible but also spoke of Jesus' return and in July of 1933 said, "What is meant by 'the day of the Lord is near at hand'? That as has been promised through the prophets and the sages of old, the time - and half time - has been and is being fulfilled in this day and generation, and that soon there will again appear in the earth that one through whom many will be called to meet those that are preparing the way for His day in the earth. The Lord, then, will come, 'even as ye have seen him go.'" As usual, while invoking phrases such as "is being fulfilled in this day and generation" (keep in mind this was uttered over eighty years ago) and "soon there will again appear," there is always the ready excuse of Matthew 24:36 and Mark 13:32, "But about that day or hour no one knows, not even the angels in Heaven, nor the Son, but only the Father" to fall back on... in other words an open ended excuse which can and no doubt will be invoked indefinitely.

A good example of this doomsday cult mentality is contained in publications such as *Prophecy in Revelations - Seven Signs of the Apocalypse* which is billed as a Christian apologist's "important signs that point to the End Time." Let's look at those "signs" one by one with each shown in quotations followed by logical analysis:

"Sign #7: Increase in Knowledge, Travel, Planes, & Cars. New technology is rapidly being developed and regularly leaves us standing in awe. The benefits are numerous, the possibilities exciting, and the hope for the future of technology is high. The Bible says that there will be a great increase in knowledge during the last days. Daniel 12:4 says: 'But thou, O Daniel, shut up the words, and seal the book, even to the time of the end: many shall run to and fro, and knowledge shall be increased.' This is certainly true for the day and age we are living. It's incredible when you consider the total accumulation of all the earths' knowledge now doubles every 18-22 months. The knowledge of the world is increasing dramatically and this is exactly what the Bible says will happen in the last days. The Bible even mentions travel, planes and cars as end time signs. Wow!" Analysis: Did I miss something? Where exactly are planes and cars mentioned in that passage or anywhere in the Bible for that matter? Doesn't it stand to reason the knowledge of mankind will increase with the passage of time? That is common sense.

"Sign #6: Terrorism, Violence, Evil, Falling Away From the Faith. What will it be like during the end of the age just before the return of Christ? Jesus told us what this time will be like: 'But as the days of Noah were, so also will the coming of the Son of Man be.' (Matthew 24:37 NKJV) So the last days will be similar to Noah's day just before the worldwide flood. So to understand better the last days we need to look at how people were living during that generation. The Bible says in Genesis 6:11-13 that: 'The earth also was corrupt before God, and the earth was filled with violence. And God looked upon the earth, and, behold, it was corrupt; for all flesh had corrupted his way upon the earth. And God said unto Noah, The end of all flesh is come before me; for the earth is filled with violence through them; and, behold, I will destroy them with the earth.' The whole world during this time was filled with violence. Today we live in a world with the constant threat of terrorism. No longer is terrorism limited to one region of the world, such as the Middle East, but now it reaches around the world, even here in the United States with the horrible tragedy of September 11th. Our world is filled with violence, just like in Noah's day. The world in Noah's day was also full of corruption and evil. Today we live in a world that parallels these same conditions. Mankind's hearts are not full of love, but of greed, hate and corruption of every kind. When we really look at our world and our society we cannot help but see this is a result of people turning away from God. But it is also a Final Generation Sign." Analysis: So they are in effect saying the Hundred Years War, Dark Ages, Crusades, TWO WORLD WARS and many other periods in history were *less* violent than what we have in today's world? There has always been violence, greed and corruption in the world so claiming this as a sign is simply ridiculous and a classic example of selective observation. Someone needs to read a history book.

"Sign #5: Middle East Tension. The situation that exists today in the Middle East is another Final Generation Sign that indicates we are living in the last days before the return of Jesus Christ. Tensions today in the Middle East hinge on various religious beliefs. The current crisis in Israel is boiling over because of the hatred of the Jews by the surrounding countries. Countries around this tiny nation want Israel and the Jews wiped off the face of the earth. The truth is the Middle East and Israel will never have true peace until return of our Lord and Savior Jesus Christ." Analysis: Israel has been there since 1948 and there has always been tension in the region going back to biblical times. I must wonder how the apocalyptic crowd might spin things if a peace accord is ever reached which defuses those tensions?

"Sign #4: The Spread of Nuclear Weapons. Nuclear weapons have become a major issue in the world we live in today. Amazingly the Bible already predicted this reality ahead of time. The Bible seems to indicate that nuclear warfare will be seen during the Tribulation hour, so the fact that this is a major problem in our world shows that we're drawing near to Christ's return." Analysis: The claim is "the Bible seems to indicate that nuclear warfare will be seen during the Tribulation hour" and granted, a truly prescient God could have predicted such a thing, but nowhere does the Bible say that. The word "nuclear" appears nowhere in Scripture.

"Sign #3: The Revived Roman Empire. The Bible says in the end times there will be a Revived Roman Empire. It will be made up of a ten-nation confederacy and will seek to dominate and control the Middle East and the whole world. This will be the one-world government predicted by the prophet Daniel. 'God has provided us with signs that point to His imminent return.' With the Revived Roman Empire comes a new economic world order. The Revived Roman Empire will seek to control the economy of the world, securing its power globally. Today we are in the generation that has lived to see the beginnings of the Revived Roman Empire. A sign so amazing, it is very hard for anyone to deny that these truly are the last days." Analysis: Hard to deny the beginnings of a revived Roman Empire? Hard to understand where they came up with this fabrication is more like it. If the author is referring to the European

Union it consists of twenty-eight member states, not ten, and there is no indication it is seeking to or is capable of dominating the world.

"Sign #2: Return of the Jews to Their Land. The Bible says that Jews would be dispersed throughout the entire world until this time when they will return to their own land. We read about the return of the Jews to their homeland in many different places in the Bible including Ezekiel 36:24 which says: 'For I will take you from among the heathen, and gather you out of all countries, and will bring you into your own land.' This is stated again in Amos 9:15: 'And I will plant them upon their land, and they shall no more be pulled up out of their land which I have given them, saith the LORD thy God.' Since the re-establishment of Israel as a nation, Jews from all over the world have returned to their land. Every day more and more Jews are returning to their rightful home which is another amazing Final Sign predicted ahead of time by the Word of God." Analysis: Which came first, the chicken or the egg? Did the Bible contain a prophecy or did the Jews return to Israel because the Bible told them they were supposed to? And while some Jews have emigrated to Israel most have not and will not.

"Final Generation Sign #1: Israel as a Nation with Jerusalem as the Capital. So what does this generation have that no generation before could claim? If they knew their Bible prophecy they would know that Israel had to exist as a nation in the end times. Israel is a requirement for so many other prophecies of the Bible. So if Israel didn't exist today with Jerusalem as the capital, we could reasonably assert that we're not living in the last days." Analysis: I guess we can "reasonably assert" we're not "living in the last days" because the last time I checked Tel Aviv is the capital of Israel. So much for the so-called "Seven Signs of the Apocalypse."

Meanwhile some other proponents of "Christian prophesy" are talking about the ongoing "lunar tetrad" which began with the last lunar eclipse on the night of April 14-15, 2014. They refer to this as a "Blood Moon" and claim is a sign of the apocalypse. Pastors Mark Blitz and John Hagee, who popularized the term in his 2013 book *Four Blood Moons: Something is About to Change*, use the term to apply to the full moons of the ongoing "tetrad" - four successive total lunar eclipses with no partial lunar eclipses in between, each of which is separated from the other by six lunar months (i.e. six full moons) in 2014 and 2015.

Blitz and Hagee speak of the tetrad as representing a fulfillment of biblical prophecy because after all, the moon is supposed to turn blood red before the end times isn't it? As described in Joel 2:31, "The sun will be turned to darkness, and the moon to blood before the great and dreadful day of the LORD comes." That description, by the way, describes both a total solar eclipse and a total lunar eclipse because "the sun turned to darkness" requires the moon to be directly between the Earth and sun in a total solar eclipse and "the moon turned to blood" means the Earth is directly between the sun and moon with the Earth's shadow falling on the moon in a total lunar eclipse.

For context it is important to realize there will actually be a total of eight tetrads in the 21st Century but proponents of this biblical prophecy regard the ongoing tetrad as especially significant because it coincides with two important Jewish holidays - Passover and Tabernacles - with the April 2014 and April 2015 total lunar eclipses aligning with the feast of Passover and the October 2014 and September 2015 total lunar eclipses coinciding with the feast of Tabernacles. One problem with that is it is now 2016 as I write this.

Keep in mind the Jewish calendar is a lunar calendar so in any given year it's inevitable a full moon should fall on or near the feasts of Passover (15 Nissan) and Tabernacles (15 Tishri), with Nissan and Tishri being the first and seventh months of the Jewish calendar respectively, so depending upon the century in which you live a lunar tetrad may happen fairly frequently or not at all. For instance in the 21st Century there are a total of eight but in the 17th, 18th and 19th Centuries there were none at all and if we include all centuries from the 1st through the 21st there are a total of sixty-two with the last one occurring in 2003-2004 and the next one after the 2014-2015 event happening in 2032-2033 - however if we want to know which tetrads specifically fell on the Jewish feasts of Passover and Tabernacles and thereby "fulfill the prophecy" there are actually a total of eight in these twenty-one centuries and during all seven absolutely nothing happened:

1. 162-163 CE
2. 795-796 CE
3. 842-843 CE
4. 860-861 CE
5. 1493-1494 CE
6. 1949-1950 CE
7. 1967-1968 CE
8. 2014-2015 CE

Hagee's sensationalism and interpolation aside the full moon nearly always appears coppery red during a total lunar eclipse because the dispersed light from the Earth's sunrises and sunsets fall on the face of the moon at mid-eclipse so the term "blood moon" can be and probably is applied to any and all total lunar eclipses. It's only in years where volcanic activity is pronounced that the moon's face during a total lunar eclipse might appear more brownish or gray in color, but the moon usually looks red and in fact astronomy writers often say it looks blood red simply because it sounds dramatic and a lunar eclipse is indeed a dramatic natural event. What's more in folklore all full moons have names which typically coincide with months of the year or seasons. One of the most famous is the Hunter's Moon, the full moon immediately following the Harvest Moon (the full moon occurring most closely to the autumnal equinox) and in "skylore" it is also sometimes called the Blood Moon. Why? Probably because it's a characteristic of these autumn full moons that they appear nearly full and rise soon after sunset for several evenings in a row. As a result many people see them when they are low in the sky shortly after they've risen at which time there's more atmosphere between them and the moon than is the case when the moon is overhead and that extra air makes the moon look reddish. Voila! Blood Moon. Add Scripture to the mix and this simple and easily explained celestial event becomes cause for panic.

Such unfounded hysterics are by no means a new or unknown phenomenon. Take for example the story of Henny Penny, more commonly known as "Chicken Little," which is a folk tale with a moral in the form of a cumulative story about a chicken who becomes convinced the world is coming to an end and the sky is falling when an acorn falls on its head. The phrase "The sky is falling!" features prominently in the story and has since become a common idiom indicating a hysterical or mistaken belief disaster is imminent. It has now been applied to people accused of being unreasonably afraid or those trying to incite an unreasonable fear in those around them. The *Merriam-Webster Dictionary* records the first application of the name Chicken Little as "one who warns of or predicts calamity, especially without justification" and dates it from 1895 although idiomatic use of the name significantly predates that attestation. Versions of the story go back more than twenty-five centuries with a very early example containing the basic motif and many of the elements appearing in the Buddhist Scriptures as the *Daddabha Jataka* in which the Buddha, upon hearing about some particular religious practices, comments there is no special merit in them but rather they are "like the noise the hare heard." He then tells the story of a hare disturbed by a falling fruit who believes the earth is coming to an end.

The moral to be drawn changes depending on the version. Where there is a happy ending the moral is not to be a "Chicken" but have courage, and in other versions where the birds are eaten by the fox the fable is interpreted as a warning not to believe everything you are told. Fear mongering, whether justified or not, can sometimes elicit a societal response called "Chicken Little syndrome" which is described as "inferring catastrophic conclusions possibly resulting in paralysis" - but it sure does sell a lot of books as Pastor Hagee can attest.

All of this talk of the Apocalypse is of real concern for two reasons. First of all those who buy into it have no reason to make the world we live in a better place. After all what's the point if it is all going to come to a screeching halt "any day now"? As former Secretary of the Interior James Watt put it, "We don't have to protect the environment (because) the Second Coming is at hand," and that sort of attitude is not conducive to things such as recycling, college degrees and lawn care. Far more chilling is the possibility of a born again "true believer" who thinks he is simply fulfilling a prophecy about the end of the world having access to weapons of mass destruction and turning it into a self-fulfilling prophecy. As someone once put it, "Most religions prophecy the end of the world and then consistently work together to ensure these prophecies come true."

Fortunately there is a much more rational explanation for the book of Revelation. United Methodist minister Rich Lang has explained these writings are not prophetic in nature but were instead based on a political movement of rebellion within Judaism against the Roman Empire which culminated in Roman legions marching into Judea, destroying Jerusalem and burning down the temple. The author employed metaphorical images such as dragons to represent Rome, much like our political cartoons have used an eagle and a bear to symbolize the United States and Soviet Union, and he used images largely out of Hebrew Scripture to convey what the Roman Empire was and what he believed would happen to the early Christian movement. The notion of people being raptured out of their clothes and cars began in the 19th Century when an Anglo-Irish theologian named John Darby created a new interpretive lens for the Bible called Dispensationalism. In his system history is divided into seven "dispensations" or ages within an age and the Rapture leads to the Millennium when Jesus reigns on Earth for one thousand years but first comes the reign of the antichrist which can be interpreted to be different people or entities at different historical junctures as time goes on. In the 1970's it was Russia thanks to Hal Lindsey's aforementioned book *The Late Great Planet Earth*, and more recently Barack Obama and the ten nations of the European Union are seen as the Beast. This is classic Chicken Little. The sky is falling!

So after all that what is the bottom line? According to Ecclesiastes 1:4 "One generation passeth away, and another generation cometh: but the earth abideth for ever," but the sad fact is the world and for that matter our entire solar system will indeed end... about seven billion years from now. All stars die and our sun is just another star. Once it has consumed all of the hydrogen fuel in its core it will reach the end of its life and for a few million years will expand from a yellow dwarf into a red giant (it doesn't have enough mass to supernova) and in the process engulf the Earth before collapsing down into a white dwarf and slowly cooling to the background temperature of the Universe.

The Road to Damascus

Or, Why Doesn't Jesus Appear To Us All?

"Now faith is the substance of things hoped for, the evidence of things not seen." ~ Hebrews 11:1

"Who are you going to believe, me or your own lying eyes?" is a quip attributed to Groucho Marx although it was actually his brother Chico who was dressed like Groucho and said those words in the movie *Duck Soup*. Regardless of who said it, it's funny and makes an excellent point. John 6:1-15 tells us Jesus had just fed the five thousand with bread and fish but despite having seen it with their own eyes the people still didn't believe and having just seen an amazing miraculous sign they asked for another since they obviously thought their eyes were lying to them, so Jesus then confronts the crowd and said, "…you have seen me but yet do not believe."

Let's set aside the fact there is no proof or even an attestation outside of the Bible which confirms this event ever took place. For the sake of argument let's say it did. Why is it all of those people who met Jesus personally and got an actual demonstration of his divinity still did not believe and yet we are expected to believe those same claims two thousand years later without benefit of such a demonstration? Moreover, this Scripture also debunks the notion God must remain hidden because it would "take away our faith" and "make us into robots" with no free will to believe. Clearly this dog and pony show did not take away the free will of the five thousand, so why would it take away ours?

Going back to the Old Testament the Israelites saw demonstration after demonstration of God's existence such as the parting of the Red Sea and manna raining from the sky and yet still chose to worship a golden calf after being left to their own devices for a few days, so their free will was clearly unaffected as well. And no figure in the Bible is more aware of the existence and omnipotence of God than Satan, yet he managed to retain his free will, chose not to worship his creator and even challenged his authority in spite of knowing he was destined to lose.

Paul, for his part, never met an earthly Jesus and certainly possessed no faith concerning his existence. The only reason he adopted his belief is because according to Scripture he was the beneficiary of a personal appearance by the disembodied Jesus as he traveled the road to Damascus. That contradicts the argument faith is the substance of things hoped for, the evidence of things not seen because Paul allegedly saw it.

Then there is the case of Doubting Thomas. "Seeing is believing" is an idiom first recorded in this form in 1639 which means only physical or concrete evidence is convincing. That is the essence of Thomas' claim to believing in Jesus Christ, to which the latter responded there were those who had not seen but believed anyway and that leads to a sophistry that seen evidence can be easily and correctly interpreted when in fact interpretation may be difficult. It should not be lost on us that Thomas was depicted as no less righteous (after all, they made him a saint) for refusing to believe so wild a claim without physical proof and we have as much right and ought to follow his example. He got to see and feel the wounds before believing and so should we, and since I haven't - in fact none of us have - we should not be expected to believe on faith alone.

In previous chapters we discussed Jesus' miracles but there is one which deserves special discussion - the resurrection after his death, which is viewed by Christians as the ultimate and defining proof of his divinity. Just about everyone knows the story summarized in the Apostles' Creed of Jesus' death and resurrection. He was crucified, died, was buried, descended into Hell, on the third day arose from the dead, ascended into Heaven and now sits at the right hand of God the Father Almighty. There was only one way for Jesus to prove he rose from the dead - he had to appear to people - and therefore several parts of the Bible describe him as appearing after his death, specifically Matthew 28, Mark 16, Luke 24 and John 20-21.

1 Corinthians 15:3-6, written by Paul, provides a summary of those passages. "For I delivered to you as of first importance what I also received, that Christ died for our sins in accordance with the Scriptures, that he was buried, that he was raised on the third day in accordance with the Scriptures, and that he appeared to Cephas, then to the twelve. Then he appeared to more than five hundred brethren at one time, most of whom are still alive, though some have fallen asleep. Then he appeared to James, then to all the apostles. Last of all, as to one untimely born, he appeared also to me." As you can see according to this passage Jesus appeared to hundreds of people a number of different times but it raises the question of why has he stopped making these appearances? Specifically, why isn't he appearing to us today?

Obviously Paul, who was "untimely born," benefitted from a personal meeting with the resurrected Christ and because of that personal visit could see for himself the "truth" of the resurrection and could even ask Jesus questions. So why doesn't Jesus appear to everyone to prove he is resurrected as he did for Paul? There is nothing to stop him from materializing right now to have a personal chat with you, and if you think about it Jesus really does need to appear to each of us because if Paul needed a personal visit to know he was resurrected why wouldn't you or I? Such a thing is clearly not unprecedented and would not take away our free will as some apologetics claim because it was okay for Jesus to appear to hundreds of other people and it did not affect theirs.

There is a legend in the technology community about the man who invented elevator safety brakes which serves as an excellent analogy. He claimed any elevator fitted with his brakes, even if all the cables broke, would be safely and swiftly stopped by his new invention but still no one trusted it. Did he get angry or indignant? No. He simply put himself in an elevator, ordered the cables cut and proved to the world his brakes worked by risking his own life. This is the principle which has delivered us from superstition to science. Any claim can be made about a drug, but people are rightly wary of swallowing something which hasn't been thoroughly tested and re-tested and then tested again and since I have no such proofs regarding the resurrection story I'm not going to swallow it - and it would be cruel for a benevolent God to expect otherwise. I can reason rightly that a God of all humankind would not appear in one tiny backwater of the Earth in a comparatively primitive time, reveal himself to a hitherto unknown few and then expect billions of us to take their word for it - and not even their word, but the word of some unknown person many times removed who wrote about it in an ambiguous book.

This is the difference between faith and proof. Some argue conversion is entirely about faith rather than evidence, but this is a moot point since it is addressed to those who believe the claim is sufficient to convince rather than those who think belief cannot be warranted without sufficient evidence. This is a thoroughly unacceptable way to approach questions of truth in any case. For example apologist Ryan Renn once asserted he does not desire to be 'just as right' as Thomas was in the Gospel of John, meaning he does not want to ask for sufficient evidence as Thomas did. This is an issue of the ethics of belief, i.e. it's what Renn thinks a person ought to believe given certain reasons and is based upon his own subjective values, however in my opinion Thomas behaved far more ethically than any other character in the stories we have. Others have said reason and facts don't belong in questions of faith because they are barriers to a personal relationship with Jesus but this is also a claim about the ethics of belief and is quite immoral. In other words it would make far more sense to establish the existence of Jesus before pursuing a relationship with him and doing it the other way around amounts to blatant self-deception.

It would have been easy for Jesus to appear to everyone throughout history and if he did we could all know he is resurrected and in fact God. After all if Paul, Thomas and "many other people" in the Bible needed a personal visit to know Jesus was resurrected why not you and me? And yet he has not unambiguously appeared to anyone in over two thousand years. What if we were to pray to Jesus and say, "Please appear to us as you did to Paul and the five hundred brethren so we can see evidence of your resurrection." After all as we have already discussed in a previous chapter Jesus said our prayers would be answered so we should only need to ask. It is claimed Jesus is already in our midst yet when we pray and ask him to materialize as he supposedly did to hundreds of others, nothing happens.

Paul's story in the Bible must be deemed false if we look at it like a judge in a courtroom would. What his story is suggesting is unprecedented - that a man he never met was dead three days and came back to life. There is no evidence it is true, he was not there to witness the event in question and there are many alternative explanations for what Paul wrote. He could have been fabricating the story, hallucinated or dreamt the meeting, seen an imposter, seen a mirage, been the victim of a hoax, been insane and so on. Given this evidence a jury would have no choice but to conclude what Paul is saying is untrue because there is zero evidence to support the story, no reason to believe it, there is a motive to lie and plenty of alternate explanations. Every bit of evidence points to the resurrection story being a myth.

So what about Jesus' famous statement in the Bible, "Happy are those who have not seen yet still believe"? That is the perfect cover for a con because it in effect says, "I exist, and the way I am going to show you I exist is by not showing you I exist." Bernie Madoff could not have said it better. Every other thing in the universe provides evidence of its existence and if there is none we call it theoretical at best or imaginary at worst, but with Jesus the lack of evidence is turned *into* evidence. Quite clever, but still obviously a scam.

The Rule of Gold

Or, God Needs Your Money

"Religion convinced the world that there's an invisible man in the sky who watches everything you do... and he needs money! He's all powerful, but he can't handle money! Religion takes in billions of dollars, they pay no taxes, and they always need a little more."
~ George Carlin

In 1913 Charles Russell, a restorationist minister from Pittsburgh, was accused of bilking his followers on grain sales. It turned out Russell had been charging his flock exorbitant rates for a "Miracle Wheat" which upon further inspection was no different from regular wheat and the scandal, according to a newspaper editorial at the time, proved "Pastor Russell's religious cult is nothing more than a money-making scheme." Although Russell's followers, now known as Jehovah's Witnesses, still maintain his innocence the scheme has become familiar and has been repeated countless times over the past century by a steady parade of religious hucksters, snake-oil salesmen and bronzed televangelists looking to make a quick buck off of the faithful. The underlying idea is people who ignore the common sense advice "if it seems too good to be true, it probably is" when it comes to religion would likely do the same when targeted by a financial scam due to their proven credulity. After all greed is greed and unrealistic expectations are just that whether they involve money or eternal life. The scams have of course grown more sophisticated over the years from the fake revelations of revivalist preacher Peter Popoff to the false lashes of Jim and Tammy Faye Bakker but the basic idea remains the same - praise God, promise miracles and when all eyes are turned up to Him rob the flock blind.

That was the modus operandi of Ephren Taylor II, a twenty-something minister's son and self-proclaimed "social capitalist" who spent three years visiting churches with his Wealth Tour Live seminars and hawking "socially conscious" investment opportunities which he said would make believers both godly and rich. Promising low-risk, high-reward investment opportunities that would "show you how to get wealth and use it for the building of His Kingdom" in sermons and later infomercials, books and webinars, Taylor revved up the flock while quoting Scripture, exalting Jesus and making vague promises. Congregations which included powerful megachurches like New Birth Missionary Baptist Church in Atlanta and Joel Osteen's Lakewood Church in Houston ate it up while opening their doors and wallets to the black Elmer Gantry of the new millennium.

What actually happened was in classic Ponzi fashion most of the money collected was used to cover up losses and pay for other investments or was spent by Taylor himself to pay for improved branding and PR campaigns, personal credit cards and apartments and to bankroll his wife's career as an aspiring pop star. A lawsuit filed by Department of Justice prosecutors claimed Taylor defrauded investors of more than five million dollars and a 2012 complaint by the Securities and Exchange Commission accused him of running an eleven million dollar Ponzi scheme which had targeted predominately black churchgoers.

Religious groups tend to be a popular target for scammers and religious-affinity fraud is quite common but it's not discussed inside the church and that's one of the problems. No one wants to admit it occurs, and that's how these charlatans manage to do such things for so long and get away with it. A lot of people are ashamed or feel from a religious standpoint "what happens in the church stays in the church" and you shouldn't tell anyone. Researchers at the Center for Study in Global Christianity, which examines church fraud and embezzlement, found that ecclesiastical crime accounted for thirty-seven billion in losses for churches worldwide in 2013 and Alabama Securities Commissioner Joseph Borg estimated faith-based fraud accounted for about half of all affinity schemes in the South and make up a substantial portion of affinity frauds nationwide. While the form of the schemes may vary it basically boils down to this - if faith is paramount it's difficult for the faithful to know when not to believe and this demographic is more apt to suspend their critical thinking than most.

What if things were different and middlemen like Taylor were eliminated? Imagine for a moment hearing this advertisement on the radio one day: "Hello, my name is Jesus and I am God, the all-powerful creator of the universe. I created everything you see before you - the galaxies and stars in the heavens; the oceans, the mountains and the plains of earth; the sun and the moon and the skies; along with every living thing on the planet. I created you personally, and I gave you your unique soul. I created everything. And I will answer your prayers. Pray to me for anything and I will hear and answer your prayers. Anything you need, love, happiness, you name it - I am here to provide it for you. There is just one thing I need in return. I need your money. I need lots of your money. The Bible says you must send me ten percent of your gross income, but think of that as a starting point. Feel free to give more. When they pass the offering plate at church be sure to give generously because even though I created the universe and everything in it and will give you everything you ask for in prayer I can't give a cent to any church, ever. So please give generously at your place of worship today. I thank you for your support!" This is essentially what every church tells you on Sunday mornings when they pass the collection plate. It's big business. He is the all-powerful creator of the universe and everything in it, but he has no money. Why don't the ministers and deacons of the church gather every Sunday morning and pray for Jesus to deposit money into their offering plate or bank account? Why do they have to beg for money from mere mortals when it is God who should provide anything they ask for? The reason why Jesus needs lots of your money every Sunday morning should be obvious and it's not that "God uses us to do his good works."

A tithe, from an Old English word meaning "tenth," is a one-tenth part of something paid as a contribution to a religious organization or compulsory tax to government. Today tithes are normally voluntary and paid in cash, checks or stocks whereas historically they were required and paid in kind such as with agricultural products, although several European countries operate a formal process linked to the tax system allowing some churches to assess tithes.

Traditional Jewish law and practice has included various forms of tithing since ancient times and in modern Israel Jews continue to follow the laws of agricultural tithing but in Christianity some interpretations of biblical teachings conclude that although tithing was practiced extensively in the Old Testament it was never practiced or taught within the 1st Century church so instead the New Testament Scriptures 1 Corinthians 16:2 and 2 Corinthians 9:7 are seen as teaching the concept of "freewill offerings" as a means of supporting the church. Also some of the earliest groups sold everything they had and held the proceeds in common to be used for the furtherance of the Gospel in accordance with their interpretation of Acts 2:44-47 and 4:34-35, plus Acts 5:1-20 contains the account of a man and wife named Ananias and Sapphira who were living in one of these groups. They sold a piece of property and donated only part of the selling price to the church but claimed to have given the whole amount and immediately fell down and died when confronted by the apostle Peter over their dishonesty.

In Genesis 14:18-20 Abraham, after rescuing Lot, met with Melchizedek and after Melchizedek's blessing gave him a tenth of everything he has obtained from battle and in Genesis 28:12-22 Jacob, after his visionary dream of Jacob's Ladder and receiving a blessing from God, promises God a tenth.

The tithe is specifically mentioned in the Books of Leviticus, Numbers and Deuteronomy. The tithing system was organized in a three year cycle corresponding to the Shemittah-cycle (Sabbath year) which is the seventh year of the seven-year agricultural cycle mandated by the Torah for the Land of Israel. Every year Bikkurim or "First Fruits," a religious offering of the first agricultural produce of the harvest given to priests to offer to gods or God in classical Greek, Roman, Hebrew and Christian religions, were separated from the grain, wine and oil but as regards other fruit and produce the biblical requirement to tithe is a source of debate. Unlike other offerings which were restricted to consumption within the tabernacle the yearly tithe to the Levites could be consumed anywhere (Numbers 18:31). On years one, two, four and five of the Shemittah cycle God commanded the children of Israel to take a second tithe that was to be brought to the city of Jerusalem (Deuteronomy 14:23). The owner of the produce was to separate and bring one tenth of his finished produce to Jerusalem after separating Terumah and the first tithe but if the family lived too far from Jerusalem the tithe could be redeemed upon coins (Deuteronomy 14:23). Then the Bible required the owner of the redeemed coins to spend the tithe "to buy whatever you like: cattle, sheep, wine or other fermented drink or anything you wish" (Deuteronomy 14:22-27). Implicit in the commandment was an obligation to spend the coins on items meant for human consumption. According to the Hebrew Scriptures the second tithe could be brought to Jerusalem any time of the year and there was no specific obligation to bring the second tithe to Jerusalem for the Festival of Sukkot. The only time restriction was a commandment to remove all the tithes from one's house in the end of the third year (Deuteronomy 14:28). The third year was called "the year of tithing" (Deuteronomy 26:12-14) in which the Israelites set aside one tenth of the increase of the land and were to give this tithe to the Levites, strangers, orphans and widows. These tithes were in reality more like taxes for the people of Israel and were mandatory rather than optional giving. This tithe was distributed locally "within thy gates" (Deuteronomy 14:28) to support the Levites and assist the poor.

The Levites, also known as the Tribe of Levi, were descendants of Levi. They were assistants to the Israelite priests, who were the children of Aaron and therefore a subset of the Tribe of Levi, and did not own or inherit a territorial patrimony (Numbers 18:21-28). Their purpose in society was that of temple functionaries, teachers and trusted civil servants who supervised the weights and scales and witnessed agreements. The goods donated from the other Israeli tribes were their source of sustenance. They received from "all Israel" a tithe of food or livestock for support and in turn would set aside a tenth portion of that tithe for the Aaronic priests in Jerusalem.

The Book of Malachi, which will be discussed shortly, has one of the most quoted biblical verses assumed to be about tithing when isolated from the context of the chapter however when taken in context it is clear the verse is not talking about those failing to tithe but is instead actually talking about the priests who oversee the distribution of the tithe from the storehouse, took more than their equal share or who took the best portions of what was to be shared equally.

Orthodox Jews continue to follow the laws of Terumah and Ma'aser as well as the custom of tithing ten percent of one's earnings to charity. Due to doubts concerning the status of persons claiming to be Kohanim or Levi'im arising after severe Roman/Christian persecutions and exile, the Hebrew Bible tithe of ten percent for the Levites and "tithe of the tithe" (Nehemiah 10:38) of ten percent of ten percent (one percent) for the priests are dealt with in accordance with Jewish Law however the Mishnah and Talmud contain analysis of the first tithe, second tithe and poor tithe.

Many Christians support their churches and pastors with monetary contributions of one sort or another and frequently these monetary contributions are called tithes whether or not they actually represent ten percent of anything. Some claim that since tithing was an ingrained Jewish custom by the time of Jesus no specific command to tithe per se is found in the New Testament, but there are actually four references to it.

For Catholics the payment of tithes was adopted from the Old Law and early writers speak of it as a divine ordinance and an obligation of conscience rather than any direct command by Jesus Christ. Some Protestants cite Jesus' words in Matthew 23:23 and its parallel Luke 11:42 in support of tithing while others see it as a denunciation of false piety - yet another example of how Scripture can be interpreted to mean different things by different people. The final mention of tithing in the New Testament is Hebrews 7:1-10 which refers back to the tithe Abram paid to Melchizedek and although not a direct command it certainly does hint at a continuance of at least the principle of tithing for the Church. Whether that is generosity or a letter-of-the-law tenth is not mentioned.

Most New Testament discussion promotes giving but does not mention tithing. 2 Corinthians 9:7 talks about giving cheerfully, 2 Corinthians 8:12 encourages giving what you can afford, 1 Corinthians 16:1-2 discusses giving weekly (although this is a saved amount for Jerusalem), 1 Timothy 5:17-18 exhorts supporting the financial needs of Christian workers, Acts 11:29 promotes feeding the hungry wherever they may be and James 1:27 states pure religion is to help widows and orphans. That is not a bad thing by any means, but don't get the idea Christians and Jews are the only ones who give because they are not.

In Islam "Zakāt" or "alms giving," which is one of the Five Pillars of Islam, is the giving of a small percentage of one's income to charity and serves principally as the welfare contribution to poor and deprived Muslims although others may have a rightful share. It is the duty of an Islamic state not just to collect zakāt but to distribute it fairly as well. Another mechanism for voluntary charity and support for religious organizations in the Islamic States in the old days was to take one-tenth of the income or product which is called "ushar" and give it to a Mosque. To date this ushar strictly goes to the local mosques in Islamic countries such as Afghanistan and the most qualified person for the ushar is considered to be the Imam and his students. In most villages the Imam gets the ushar from the landowners and sometimes it amounts to a large sum of money. In other words the idea of ushar in Islam is a direct continuation of the Judeo-Christian idea of "tethi" or one tenth. In fact during the Taliban rule in Afghanistan the government, which considered itself protector of the state as well as religious students, collected the ushar from people in villages and towns, thus reviving an old tradition of alms giving in the Islamic states of the past.

Zakāt is payable on three kinds of assets - wealth, production and animals. The more well-known zakat on wealth is 2.5% of accumulated wealth beyond one's personal needs, whatever that means. Production (agricultural, industrial, renting, etc.), is subject to a ten or five percent zakāt (also known as Usher or "one-tenth") using the rule that if both labor and capital are involved a five percent rate is applied but if only one of the two are used for production then the rate is ten percent. For any earnings which require neither labor nor capital like finding underground treasure the rate is twenty percent. The rules for zakāt on animal holdings are specified by the type of animal group and tend to be fairly detailed.

Muslims fulfill this religious obligation by giving a fixed percentage of their surplus wealth and Zakāt has been paired with such a high sense of righteousness it is often placed on the same level of importance as performing the daily repetitive ritualized prayer or "salat." Muslims see this process also as a way of purifying themselves from their greed and selfishness and also safeguarding future business. In addition Zakāt purifies the person who receives it because it saves him from the humiliation of begging and prevents him from envying the rich. Because it holds such a high level of importance the "punishment" for not paying when able is very severe. In the second edition of the *Encyclopedia of Islam* it states, "...the prayers of those who do not pay zakāt will not be accepted." This is because without Zakāt a tremendous hardship is placed on the poor which otherwise would not be there. Besides the fear of their prayers not getting heard those who are able practice this third pillar of Islam simply because the Quran states this is what believers should do.

While the federal government of the United States has never collected a church tax or mandatory tithe on its citizens believe it or not states did collect tithes into the early 19th Century but today such a tax is prohibited by the Establishment Clause of the U.S. Constitution. The United States and its governmental subdivisions also exempt most churches from payment of income tax under Section 501(c)(3) of the Internal Revenue Code which additionally allows donors to claim donations as an income tax itemized deduction. Churches also may be permitted exemption from other state and local taxes such as sales and property taxes, either in whole or in part.

Within religious organizations actual collection procedures vary from church to church, from the common and strictly voluntary practice of "passing the plate" in Catholic and mainline Protestant churches to formal church-mediated tithing in some conservative Protestant churches and the Church of Jesus Christ of Latter-day Saints to membership fees as practiced in many Jewish congregations. There is no government involvement in church collections, but because of less-strict income and tax reporting requirements for religious groups some churches have been placed under legal and media scrutiny for their spending habits.

In Spain and Latin America both the tithe, a levy of ten percent on all agricultural production, and "first fruits" (an additional harvest levy) were collected by Spain throughout the medieval and early modern periods for the support of local Catholic parishes. The tithe crossed the

Atlantic with the Spanish Empire, however the Indians who made up the vast majority of the population in colonial Spanish America were initially exempted from paying them on native crops such as corn and potatoes which they raised for their own subsistence but after some debate they were forced to pay tithes on production of European agricultural products including wheat, silk, cows, pigs and sheep. The tithe was abolished in several Latin American countries including Mexico soon after independence from Spain in 1810, but others including Argentina and Peru still collect tithes today for the support of the Catholic Church.

In Austria a church tax has to be paid by members of the Catholic and Protestant Church which is levied by the churches themselves rather than the government, although the obligation to pay can be evaded by an official declaration to cease church membership. The tax is calculated on the basis of personal income and amounts to about 1.1% (Catholic Church) and 1.5% (Protestant Church). In Denmark all members of the Church of Denmark pay a church tax which varies between municipalities, generally around one percent of the taxable income, and in Finland members of state churches pay a church tax of between one and two percent of income depending on the municipality. In addition 2.55% of corporate taxes are distributed to state churches with church taxes being integrated into the common national taxation system.

Germany levies a church tax on all persons declaring themselves to be Christians of roughly eight to nine percent of their income tax which typically between 0.2% and 1.5% of total income with the proceeds being shared amongst Catholic, Lutheran and other Protestant Churches. This church tax actually traces its roots back as far as 1803 and was reaffirmed in the Concordat of 1933 between Nazi Germany and the Catholic Church. Today its legal basis is article 140 of the German "Constitution" in connection with article 137 of the Weimar Constitution. Originally these laws merely allowed the churches themselves to tax their members but in Nazi Germany collection of church taxes was transferred to the German government and as a result both government and employer were notified of the religious affiliation of every taxpayer. This system is still in effect today and even though mandatory disclosure of religious affiliation to government agencies or employers constituted a violation of the original European data protection directives it is now permitted after the German government obtained an exemption. Church tax is compulsory in Germany for those confessing members of a particular religious group and the duty to pay this tax theoretically starts on the day one is christened - and anyone who wants to stop paying must declare in writing at their local court of law or registry office they are leaving the Church. They are then crossed off the Church registers and can no longer receive the sacraments, confession and certain services and the Roman Catholic Church may deny such a person a burial plot. In addition to the government the taxpayer also must notify his employer of his religious affiliation or lack thereof in order to ensure proper tax withholding.

There has never been a direct church tax or mandatory tithe on Greek citizens however the state pays the salaries of the clergy of the established Church of Greece in return for use of real estate (mainly forestry) owned by the church. The remainder of church income comes from voluntary, tax-deductible donations from the faithful which are handled by each diocese independently.

Originally the Italian government of Benito Mussolini, under the Lateran treaties of 1929 with the Holy See, paid a monthly salary to Catholic clergymen called the "congrua." The "eight per thousand" law has since been created as a result of a 1984 agreement between the Italian Republic and the Holy See and under this law Italian taxpayers are able to vote how to partition the 0.8% (eight per thousand) of the total income tax levied by Italy among some specific religious confessions, or alternatively to a social assistance program run by the Italian State. The last official statement the Italian Ministry of Finance made in respect of the year 2000 singled out seven beneficiaries: the Italian State, the Catholic Church, the Waldenses, the Jewish Communities, the Lutherans, the Seventh-day Adventist Church and the Assemblies of God in Italy. In this manner the Catholic Church alone raised almost a billion euros in 2000.

Until the year 2000 Sweden had a mandatory church tax to be paid if one did belong to the Church of Sweden which had been funneling about $500 million annually to the church but because of a change in legislation the tax was withdrawn in year 2000, however the Swedish government has agreed to continue collecting from individual taxpayers the annual payment which has always gone to the church but now the tax will be an optional checkoff box on the tax return with the government allocating the money collected to Catholic, Muslim, Jewish and other faiths with each taxpayer directing where his or her taxes should go.

There is no official state church in Switzerland however all the twenty-six cantons (states) financially support at least one of the three traditional denominations - Roman Catholic, Old Catholic or Protestant - with funds collected through taxation and each canton having its own regulations regarding the relationship between church and state. In some the church tax (up to 2.3%) is voluntary but in others an individual who chooses not to contribute may have to formally leave the church.

Which brings us to Prosperity Theology, sometimes referred to as the Prosperity Gospel, Health and Wealth Gospel or the Gospel of Success. This is a Christian religious doctrine which teaches financial blessing is the will of God for Christians and that faith, positive speech and most importantly generous donations to Christian ministries will always increase one's material wealth. This doctrine is based on non-traditional interpretations of the Bible, often with emphasis on the Book of Malachi, and views the Bible as a contract between God and humans - i.e. if humans have faith in God he will deliver his promises of security and prosperity. While Malachi has generally been celebrated by Christians for its passages about the Messiah, teachers of prosperity theology instead draw attention to its descriptions of physical wealth. For example Malachi 3:10 says, "Bring to the storehouse a full tenth of what you earn so there will be food in my house. 'Test me in this,' says the Lord All-Powerful. 'I will open the windows of Heaven for you and pour out all the blessings you need,'" and other oft-quoted verses include Matthew 25:14-30 (the "parable of the talents"), John 10:10, Philippians 4:19 and 3 John 2.

It was during the Healing Revivals of the 1950s that prosperity theology first came to prominence in the United States, although some have linked the origins of its theology to the New Thought movement which began in the 1800s and prosperity teaching later figured prominently in the Word of Faith movement and 1980s televangelism.

Prosperity churches place a strong emphasis on the importance of giving - primarily to *them* - and services commonly include two sermons with one focusing on giving and prosperity to include biblical references to tithing followed by a second on another topic and church leaders often bestow a specific blessing on the money being donated with some instructing worshipers to hold their donations above their heads during prayer.

Oral Roberts began teaching prosperity theology in 1947 and explained the laws of faith as a "blessing pact" in which God would return donations "seven fold," promising donors they would receive back from unexpected sources the money they donated to him. In the 1970s Roberts characterized this blessing pact teaching as the "seed faith" doctrine, i.e. donations were a form of "seed" which would grow in value and be returned to the donor, and that term has been enthusiastically employed by those who have followed ever since. To put that claim into perspective he also once said, "I can't tell you about (all) the dead people I've raised. I've had to stop a sermon, go back and raise a dead person." Of course he did.

In 1953 faith healer A. A. Allen published *The Secret to Scriptural Financial Success* and promoted merchandise such as "miracle tent shavings" and prayer cloths anointed with "miracle oil" and by the late 1950s he increasingly focused on prosperity, teaching that faith could miraculously solve financial problems and claiming to have had a miraculous experience in which God supernaturally changed one dollar bills into twenty dollar bills to allow him to pay his debts. Allen called this the "word of faith," i.e. the power to speak something into being, saying, "I decreed a thing. God said, 'Thou shall decree a thing, and it shall be established unto thee.' I believe I can command God to perform a miracle for you financially. When you do, God can turn dollar bills into twenties." People bought it hook, line and sinker.

By the 2000s proponents of prosperity theology claimed tens of millions of Christians had accepted their doctrine and a 2006 poll by *Time* magazine reported seventeen percent of Christians in America said they identified with the movement. Mainstream evangelicalism, probably feeling the pinch at the collection plate as dollars were diverted elsewhere, have consistently opposed prosperity theology as heresy and prosperity ministries have frequently come into conflict with other Christian groups including those within the Pentecostal and Charismatic movements. Critics such as Evangelical pastor Michael Catt have argued that prosperity theology has little in common with traditional Christian theology and other prominent evangelical leaders have harshly criticized the movement. In his book *Mark: Jesus, Servant and Savior* R. Kent Hughes cites Jesus' statement in Matthew 19:24 that, "It is easier for a camel to go through the eye of a needle, than for a rich man to enter into the kingdom of God" as evidence to oppose such thinking but of course like most Bible verses there is room for alternate interpretations via the magic of hermeneutics. In fact my own brother-in-law, a pastor who aspires to be the next Joel Osteen or Joyce Meyer, has "explained" to me the "eye of the needle" actually refers to the Needle Gate which was supposedly a low and narrow after-hours entrance found in the wall surrounding Jerusalem through which a camel could go only by stripping off any saddles or packs and crawling through on its knees. The problem with this theory is there is no evidence such a gate ever existed, there is no basis in Scripture and beyond that what sane camel driver would go through such contortions when larger gates were accessible? In other words it is a classic rationalization which allows Prosperity Gospel adherents to arrive at the conclusion they desire. Plus it should be viewed in the context of the previous and far less ambiguous verse (19:23) in which Jesus tells his disciples, "Verily I say unto you, that a rich man shall hardly enter into the Kingdom of Heaven" which is unsurprisingly and dishonestly omitted.

So where did this all start and why is it so popular? It's quite simple. The Prosperity Gospel promises the two things people want most and are least likely to attain - wealth and immortality. What won't people do, or believe, to get them? As for the origins, some say it began with a religious sect known as The House of David which was founded in the early 1900s by Benjamin Franklin Purnell and his wife Mary who based their teachings on an 18th Century English group called the Philadelphians who believed they were God's appointed messengers for the second coming of Christ, men and women should imitate Jesus by never cutting their hair and the human body could have eternal life on earth. These beliefs were developed from the prophecies of a woman named Joanna Southcott who claimed she was the first of seven messengers to proclaim the Second Coming. Naturally Purnell deduced he was also one of the seven.

The Purnells traveled around the country for several years while polishing their doctrine and after being booted out of a small town in Ohio they settled in Benton Harbor, Michigan in 1903 and soon attracted a crowd of about seven hundred believers. The group was soon christened the Israelite House of David and a number of cottage industries were begun. After adopting the title "Prince of Peace" Purnell often held teaching sessions including one in which he was photographed allegedly turning water into wine. Rumors grew concerning improper relationships between Purnell and young females in the group and newspaper reports alleged rebellious group members were killed and buried on an island where the colony ran a prosperous lumber business and Purnell also kept a group of young girls there as sex slaves. In 1926 Purnell was finally arrested on charges of religious fraud and statutory rape but he was ill for most of his lengthy trial and his testimony was deemed incoherent. He died the following year at the age of sixty-six and shortly before passing told followers that he, like Jesus, would be back in three days… but as far as anyone knows he didn't show. His preserved remains were instead kept in a glass coffin on the colony grounds for decades. Some of his believers declared allegiance to his widow, she started a new colony called Mary's City of David and today many credit

Purnell with being the forerunner of later evangelical leaders such as Oral Roberts and Jim Bakker.

Bakker is one of the most notorious examples of theistic subterfuge. Not one to be discouraged by being labeled a fraud and thief, the disgraced televangelist is now peddling survivalist gear and books about the apocalypse on his website almost twenty years after he was released from prison on a conviction of bilking followers out of millions of dollars through his PTL Club ministry. That stands for Praise The Lord, but has since been rebranded by many as Pass The Loot or Pay The Lady.

Back from the evangelical wilderness, Bakker now tapes a daily TV show from the rolling Ozarks of Missouri and uses his website to pitch what he calls "love gifts," essentially a variety of odd products including "Tiffany style" jewelry, fuel-less generators and buckets of dried food. For just five hundred dollars you can get "Jim's All American Four-Star Vegetable" buckets and two grand will get you the "Jerry Jones Special" which promises "over 3,300 servings of food and enough fuel to cook 480 meals."

Preparing for the end of the world is nothing new for Bakker who served almost five years in prison following his conviction for the $158 million rip off of his followers. "Pastor Jim" as he calls himself now published a book in 1998 called *Prosperity and the Coming Apocalypse* which he sells on his site for twenty dollars and proclaims, "This is not just a book of prophecy, it is a book of survival."

His longtime wife Tammy Faye having divorced him while he was in prison, Bakker married his new wife Lori the same year he published the book. She now works beside him as a pastor at the *Jim Bakker Show* and offers her own line of products like the "Lori's Little Lambs Chrystal Necklace" for thirty-five dollars. Most of the goods, the Bakkers assure their followers, are at least partially tax deductible and amazingly credulous people actually spend their hard earned cash on this stuff. As David Hannum once said, "There's a sucker born every minute."

Peter Popoff is a German American televangelist, self-proclaimed prophet and faith healer who initially rose to prominence in the 1980s. In 1985 Popoff came to national attention when he began campaigning for money to help smuggle Bibles into the Soviet Union, claiming the Bibles would be tied to helium-filled balloons and sent floating above the Iron Curtain. When he had to account for the money being spent Popoff staged a burglary at his own headquarters and on subsequent broadcasts of his show would tearfully beg for more money to help repair the damage. During his appearances at church conventions in the 1980s

Popoff was best known for routinely and accurately stating the home addresses and specific illnesses of his audience members, a feat many believed was due to divine revelation and "God-given ability." In 1986 the Committee for Skeptical Inquiry reported Popoff was using a radio to receive messages, but of course Popoff denied it and claimed the messages came directly from God. In response skeptic groups across the United States handed out pamphlets explaining how Popoff's feats were done and naturally he responded by telling his audiences the pamphlets were "tools of the devil" because invoking Satan always comes in handy in a pinch.

Popoff's claims were debunked in 1986 when noted skeptic James Randi and his assistant Steve Shaw researched Popoff by attending revival meetings across the country for months. Randi asked crime scene analyst and electronics expert Alexander Jason for technical assistance and he was able to use a computerized scanner during a Popoff appearance in San Francisco to intercept and identify radio transmissions being sent by Popoff's wife Elizabeth from backstage where she was reading information she and her aides had gathered from earlier conversations with members of the audience. Popoff would listen to these promptings with a hidden in-ear receiver and repeat what he heard to the crowd. Randi also planted accomplices in the audience, including a man dressed as a woman pretending to have uterine cancer of which "she" was "cured" by Popoff.

Popoff at first denied he used the tactics Randi claimed and even asserted, "NBC hired an actress to impersonate Mrs. Popoff on a 'doctored' videotape," however as the media pressed with more questions, "On day three Reverend Popoff admitted the existence of the radio device, claiming that 'almost everybody' knew about the 'communicator' and adding, "my wife occasionally gives me the name of a person who needs special prayers."

On several occasions Popoff would tell his revival attendees to "break free of the Devil" by throwing their medications onto the stage and dozens of his followers obeyed, throwing away prescriptions for digitalis, nitroglycerine tablets, oral diabetes medication and other pills which might have been vital for their survival. Popoff's shows also featured audience members who were brought on stage in wheelchairs and then rose dramatically to walk without support. These were some of his most incredible "healings," but what believing audience members and television viewers did not know was wheelchairs were used by Popoff to seat people who were already able to walk.

In February of 2007 *Inside Edition* broadcast a feature on Popoff's continued faith healing and "Miracle Spring Water" which claimed Popoff's new television programs feature him "healing the sick" in a manner identical to his method prior to James Randi's exposé. These programs also included offers of free "Miracle Manna" that allegedly provide health and financial miracles but if viewers called to ask for the so-called manna they were subsequently sent letters asking for money. Then in 2009 advertisements appeared in the UK press offering a free cross which contained "blessed water" and "holy sand." The blessed water was supposedly from a source near the nuclear accident site at Chernobyl and it was claimed animals drinking from this source were purportedly free from any radiation sickness, the cross bore the inscription "Jerusalem" and requests for donations accompanied each. Up until 1987 Popoff took in almost four million dollars per year in this manner but after his exposure by Randi on *The Tonight Show* he declared bankruptcy later that year. In spite of that in 2003 Popoff's ministry received over $9.6 million and by 2005 the amount had risen to over $23 million but financial data is not available after 2005 because Peter Popoff Ministries changed from a for-profit business to a religious organization in 2006, making it tax-exempt.

Robert Gibson Tilton is another televangelist who achieved notoriety in the 1980s and early 1990s through his infomercial-style religious television program *Success-N-Life* which at its peak in 1991 aired daily in all 235 American TV markets, brought in nearly eighty million per year and was described as "the fastest growing television ministry in America." However ABC's *Primetime Live* aired an expose on Tilton's fundraising practices which triggered a series of investigations into the ministry and within two years Tilton's program was no longer being broadcast, but like Popoff and Bakker he eventually returned to television with a new version of his program.

In *Success-N-Life* Tilton regularly taught all of life's trials, especially poverty, were a result of sin and his ministry consisted mainly of impressing upon his viewers the importance of making "vows" - i.e. financial commitments to Tilton's ministry. His preferred vow, stressed frequently on his broadcasts, was one thousand dollars but occasionally Tilton would claim to have received a "word of knowledge" (among Pentecostal and charismatic Christians this is often defined as the ability of one person to know what God is currently doing or intends to do in the life of another person) for someone to give a vow of five or even ten thousand dollars. When a person made such a vow to Tilton he preached that God would recognize it and reward the donor with vast material riches. The show also ran testimonials from viewers who had given to Tilton's ministry and reportedly received miracles in return, a practice which would be used as the basis for a later lawsuit from donors charging the ministry with fraud. In 1991 Diane Sawyer and ABC News conducted an investigation of Tilton which was broadcast on ABC's *Primetime Live* and alleged Tilton's ministry threw away prayer requests without reading them while keeping only the accompanying money or valuables sent by viewers.

Tilton vehemently denied the allegations and took to the airwaves on a special episode of *Success-N-Life* entitled *Primetime Lies* to air his side of the story. Tilton asserted the prayer requests found in garbage bags shown on the *Primetime Live* investigation were stolen from the ministry and placed in the dumpster for a sensational camera shot and that he prayed over every prayer request received to the point that he "laid on top of those prayer requests so much that the chemicals actually got into my bloodstream and... I had two small strokes in my brain." Tilton remained defiant on claims regarding his use of donations to his ministry to fund various purchases asking, "Ain't I allowed to have nothing?" with regards to his ownership of multiple multimillion-dollar estates. Tilton also claimed he needed plastic surgery to repair capillary damage to his lower eyelids from ink which had seeped into his skin from the prayer requests, and yet people continued to send him money. Not to be outdone bogus faith healer Ernest Angley sends worthless prayer cloths which he claims will cure cancer to the desperate poor in exchange for donations and Benny Hinn has claimed, "I see rows of caskets lining up in front of this TV set... and I see actual loved ones picking up the hands of the dead and letting them touch the screen and people are getting raised."

Creflo Dollar, whose very name is a dead giveaway of his real agenda, uttered one of the most blatantly despicable descriptions of how tithing should work when he proclaimed, "If they were tithing, beautiful music would go off... but if they were non-tithers, the bar would lock up... the siren would go off... security would go and apprehend them, and once we got them all together we'd line them up in the front and pass out Uzis by the ushers and point our Uzis right at all those non-tithing members 'cause we want God to come to church, and at the count of three 'JESUS-es' we'd shoot them all dead. And then we'd take them out the side door there, have a big hole, bury them, and then go ahead and have church and have the anointing." And still they give.

Such subterfuge is by no means confined to the United States and Europe, for example Korean Sun Myung Moon was a self-proclaimed messiah and founder of the Unification Church. His followers, who were sometimes called "Moonies," considered him their True Father. Moon's family had rejected the Shinto faith pushed by the country's Japanese rulers and followed Confucianist beliefs until he was around ten years old when they converted to Christianity and joined the Presbyterian Church. When he was fifteen Moon said Jesus Christ appeared to him on Easter morning of 1935 and anointed him to carry out his unfinished work by becoming parent to all of humanity. After a period of prayer and consideration, Moon accepted the mission.

The Divine Principle, the main text explaining Moon's theology, blends Bible-based Christianity with Eastern philosophies like Confucianism and Korean shamanism and makes the core statement that Moon was sent from the East to be the messiah and finish Jesus' mission. It also stated Jesus was divine but not God and Moon was supposed to be the second Adam who would join with the ideal wife and create a pure family which would have begun humanity's liberation from the sinful condition caused by Eve's illicit sex with Satan. Because Jesus was crucified before marrying he had redeemed mankind spiritually but not physically, so that task was left to the "True Parents" - Moon and his future wife - who would link married couples and their families to God.

Moon was renowned for presiding over mass "blessing ceremonies," the most famous ritual of the Unification Church. The ceremonies gained international attention for joining thousands of identically dressed brides and grooms, many who had never met before, in matrimony. In church doctrine the wedding or marriage re-dedication ceremony removes couples from the lineage of sinful humanity and grafts them into God's sinless lineage, and after the third generation of intra-Unification Church blessed marriages any children born will be free from the consequences of original sin.

From its beginning the Unification Church claimed to be Christian and promoted its teachings to mainstream churches and organizations but it was labeled as heretical by Protestant churches in South Korea including Moon's own Presbyterian Church. In the United States the church was rejected by ecumenical organizations as being non-Christian with the primary objections being theological, mainly because it added material to the Bible. Protestant Christian commentators have also criticized its teachings as contrary to the Protestant doctrine of salvation by faith alone.

In 2001 the Unification Church came into conflict with the Roman Catholic Church when Catholic Archbishop Emmanuel Milingo and Maria Sung, a Korean acupuncturist, married in a Unification Church Blessing ceremony presided over by Reverend and Mrs. Moon. Following the marriage the Archbishop was called to the Vatican by Pope John Paul II, where he was asked not to see his wife anymore and to move to a Capuchin monastery.

One of the central doctrines of the Unification Church is what they call "heavenly deception." It basically says that in order to take from Satan what rightfully belongs to God you may do most anything, which is another way of saying it is permissible to tell lies in order to advance the cult. There are mainstream Christians today who use similar practices and intentionally promote inaccurate accounts of American History because it gives them political traction and advantage, with David Barton and Wallbuilders and D. James Kennedy being prominent among them.

In popular culture *Elmer Gantry* is a 1960 film about a con man and a female evangelist selling religion to small town America which was adapted from the 1927 Sinclair Lewis novel of the same name. In it Gantry, played by Burt Lancaster, is a hard-drinking, fast-talking traveling salesman with a charismatic personality who infuses biblical passages and fervor into his pitches as a way to collect money. He is drawn to the evangelical road show of Sister Sharon Falconer and is immediately attracted to the saintly revivalist, cons his way into her good graces and joins the troupe preaching something called "Christ in commerce." Gantry and Falconer develop a "good cop/bad cop" routine, with Gantry telling audience members they will burn in Hell for their sins and Sharon promising salvation if they repent - a perfect example of art imitating life.

Of course many Christians do not subscribe to the Prosperity Gospel model because they interpret Scripture differently and as a result they rightfully, but ironically, vilify adherents for their "false teachings." For example a Pastor named Rick Henderson blogged about Joyce Meyer and Joel Osteen saying, "If you listen to Joel Osteen and Joyce Meyer, if you take what they teach seriously, it will not be good for you. It will be detrimental to your long-term growth as a follower of Jesus… they both teach a twisted form of Christianity that teaches obedience, giving and faith as a way to get things from God… they are both products of what is known as the Prosperity Gospel and the Word of Faith Movement or the Seed Faith Movement…" and then, after citing some examples of what he considers to be Joyce Meyer's false doctrine he adds, "I could continue with examples of her utter misuse of Scripture, false teaching and blatant heresy… the lies that she teaches are easily lost in the hum of all the great teachers we hear… uneducated pastors, who are doing their very best and uninformed Christians have this garbage pumped into their countries through radio waves and TV broadcasts… and she can afford to spread her message with the money she makes from American Christians who buy her books, CDs and who attend her conferences." To put that into proper perspective, keep in mind Meyer and Osteen could have written many of the same words about Henderson's theology. Clearly the other guy's theology, whatever it may be, is always the wrong kind.

The good pastor then goes on to discuss the financial windfalls reaped by Prosperity Gospel preachers and on this point I could not agree more. "There is nothing wrong with being wealthy… but there is a line to how much money we as leaders should spend on ourselves. I don't know where the line is, but it is somewhere before the ministry purchasing million dollar homes… purchasing us a ten million private jet… (or) having the ministry spending $261,498 for sixty-eight pieces of furniture (which equates to $3,845.56 per item). That line is somewhere before spending so egregiously that the U.S. Senate investigates us. Joyce Meyer lands on the other side of that line… her ministry lacks real accountability. Her family and her close friends are the governing board. This is an organization that receives almost a hundred million dollars annually with no substantive accountability."

He then makes a detour from financial dealings, circles back to theological interpretations and once again loses his objectivity by saying, "Her doctrine is horrific. Her hermeneutics are horrible… (and) like Joyce Meyer, Joel Osteen is confused on theology. He has much of the same doctrinal misunderstandings as does Joyce Meyer… he frequently misunderstands important matters of faith and doctrine when being interviewed. He repeatedly gets the Gospel wrong… if we take Joel at his word, our only conclusion is that he is either incapable or unwilling to understand and explain how the Gospel intersects with all of life."

Pastor Henderson then quite unintentionally exposes the foundation of his own beliefs in the following vignette when he says, "When I was in seminary Heather and I were poor. This was an extended period of exhausting financial stress… during this time I remember reading something from Joel Osteen. He and his wife claimed by faith a new house that they wanted… sometime later, they purchased that house. Still in seminary, my wife and I were walking through our dream neighborhood and that was playing through my mind. As I walked through the neighborhood, looking at all the homes, I wanted so badly for what Joel is teaching to be true. I don't know if you can understand how desperately I wanted it to be true… I knew that my exhaustion and desperation made me emotionally vulnerable to this false gospel...but for a moment I was emotionally vulnerable to this false doctrine." Then at the end came an incredibly ironic question: "What about the millions of others who are desperate, searching, hoping and vulnerable without the discernment?" Isn't that exactly the sort of person upon which all belief systems prey?

Indeed. According to Roman Catholics when God forgives there are some sins for which he remits only eternal punishment but there are still "temporal punishments" which must be endured and if they are not suffered in this lifetime they must be endured in purgatory, but through the giving of "indulgences" the Roman Catholic Church insists it can shorten that punishment whether here on earth or in purgatory. So, you might ask, how exactly does that work?

The citizens of Europe under the rule of the Roman Catholic Church were kept in great ignorance, superstition was rampant, doctrines like purgatory were superb for keeping citizens mired in fear and ignorance lent strength to wild ideas about demons and witches. Renowned Dominican preacher of indulgences Johann Tetzel fed on those superstitious fears, and it was very easy for him to convince people who believed their dear mother, departed wife or beloved child were at that very moment burning in flames in purgatory to pay money to release them from their torment.

During the last four centuries clergymen have raised fortunes by selling indulgences. Around 1515 when Pope Leo X needed money to rebuild Saint Peter's Basilica he embraced the practice of many bishops and popes and asked Tetzel to offer a plenary indulgence to whomever donated funds for the construction. In eloquent sermons Tetzel first explained the need and efficacy of indulgences, saying even after a sin had been forgiven an obligation remained to repair or compensate for the wrong done and this debt was called the temporal punishment due for sin - and if it were not fully satisfied before death a person's soul would suffer in purgatory for an unknown time before entering Heaven. Then Tetzel informed the people they could make satisfaction for all their own past sins and also for the sins of their beloved lingering in purgatory by performing good deeds, saying prayers, fasting and of course alms giving. So in a sense the sale of indulgences was a way to get the poor to willingly pay taxes.

The Pope then offered a faster and surer way to erase the temporal punishment due for sins. He controlled the "treasury of infinite merits" accumulated by Jesus, Mary and the saints and was now granting a plenary indulgence to anyone who contributed towards the construction of Saint Peter's. Since the indulgence was plenary each donation guaranteed the immediate release of a soul from purgatory and its entrance into Heaven, so in theory these donations would build Saint Peter's basilica and at the same time empty purgatory.

It did not bother Tetzel and the Pope that Jesus and Peter had never preached indulgences, that the first claim indulgences benefited souls in purgatory appeared only in 1476 or that the theories of indulgences, temporal punishment for sin and the Church's treasury of merits had no basis in Scripture but it did bother renowned Scripture scholar Martin Luther. What disturbed him even more was those theories were being preached not for the spiritual benefit of Christians, but instead for the grandiose building plans of Pope Leo X.

To this day the Roman Catholic Church claims Jesus, Mary and the saints did many good works which left behind "merit" they didn't need and that "treasury" of merit is in the possession of the Church and can be bestowed on others as the Church wills... for a price. As Napoléon Bonaparte once observed, "I am surrounded by priests who repeat incessantly that their kingdom is not of this world, and yet they lay their hands on everything they can get."

This chapter can be best summed up with the following actual infomercial: "What does Believer's Church teach about giving? Believers love to give. We give out of a cheerful heart, confident of blessing, and without fear of condemnation. (See Genesis 14:18-20, Luke 6:38, II Corinthians 9:6-15, Galatians 2:10, Philippians 4:14-20, I John 3:16-17) Many begin with the tithes (when we speak of tithing or giving a tenth we base it on the offering of Abraham to Melchizedek and not on the requirements or curses of the Law) but all giving is strictly as the Lord leads on a voluntary basis and is only between each one and the Lord. (Please make all checks out to Danny Thompson with "Believer's Church" or "B. C." in the memo area.)

Godly Hypocrisy

Or, Do As I Say, Not As I Do

"Religious dogma creates a perfect fertilizer for the weeds of hypocrisy." ~ Steve Maraboli, *Unapologetically You: Reflections on Life and the Human Experience*

Do you know the Bible? More importantly do you believe it is the inerrant and immutable word of God which guides you in your morality as so many do? If so, consider the following. Toward the end of Genesis 18 Abraham was arguing with God over a city called Sodom which was apparently a very, very naughty place - what with "sodomy" being named after it and all. As the Old Testament God was frequently given to temper tantrums and fits of violent, destructive rage he wanted to fire-bomb Sodom but Abraham, voicing the sentiment felt by any sane reader of the Bible, asked God why he would destroy the good along with the wicked. Setting aside the obviously bizarre notion that a mere mortal could possibly argue with an omniscient, omnipotent being and win, God and Abraham then entered into a negotiation over just how many righteous people would have to be in the city before God decided not to destroy it and they finally agreed should there be at least ten good people in Sodom God would leave things be. In the following chapter God inexplicably sent down two angels to investigate the level of naughtiness in the town and directed them to stay with the righteous Lot, who was Abraham's nephew... and if you are now wondering why an allegedly omniscient God who is aware of everyone's very thoughts would need to send angels down to investigate something you are not alone. In any case after the angels arrived the men of the city surrounded the house and demanded that Lot send them out so they could rape them. Granted that is pretty awful and I'm sure most people can agree the rapists deserved to be fire-bombed, but wouldn't it also be considered pretty awful for a father to throw his young virgin daughters to a mob of rapists? And that is exactly what Lot, the only "righteous man" in Sodom according to God's idea of goodness, offered to do.

I hope you would agree that while mobs of rapists are one level of evil, a father who would throw his own daughters to those rapists represents a whole different, deeper level. In any case the angels then struck the mob of rapists blind just in the nick of time, but one must wonder why they didn't do this before Lot tried to placate them with his young daughters or for that matter if it is even possible to rape an angel in the first place. Are they anatomically correct, and if so do they actually employ those organs as humans do? If not, why do they have them at all? But I digress. The angels then warned Lot that he and his family needed to flee the city and not look back and the "not looking back" part is important later on - and this is in fact the only part of this story which most Christians know about.

Lot, his wife and two daughters left the city, the fire-bombing began and while the mob of now-blind rapists certainly got their just desserts it is not clear what the women and children of the city, especially the infants in their cribs, did to deserve being burned alive. Surely there were at least ten of them who were righteous? In any case as they were fleeing Lot's wife committed the heinous "crime" of pivoting her head and was instantly turned into a pillar of salt. So to summarize God destroyed two cities and decided the only man he considered righteous enough to escape was the one willing to throw his own daughters to rapists, and yet the man's wife was turned into a condiment simply for looking back on what was surely a great display of fireworks.

Lot and his two daughters later settled in the mountains "for he was afraid to stay in Zoar" for some reason and lived in a cave. One day the older daughter suggested to her sister getting their father drunk and sleeping with him to preserve the family line and that night she did indeed have sex with him and he was not even aware of it. The very next day the younger daughter did the same and once again he was not aware of it. Talk about a wild party. Both of Lot's daughters became pregnant by their father and the older daughter's son Moab became the father of the Moabites and the younger daughter's son Ben-Ammi the father of the Ammonites. Who the mothers of those tribes were is not exactly clear. In any event apologists try to sanitize this tale by pointing out Deuteronomy 23:3 says, "No Ammonite or Moabite or any of their descendants may enter the assembly of the LORD, not even in the tenth generation," but neglect to mention the descent of King David from Ruth, who was mentioned in Matthew's genealogy of Jesus and had Moabite blood in her veins.

If you doubt the accuracy or context of any of the foregoing I invite you to pick up a Bible and read it for yourself. My hope is someday religious fundamentalists will actually read the passages they parrot so often because if they "clearly" show homosexuality is immoral they also clearly show a father using his own daughters as bait for a mob of rapists and then later getting them pregnant after being raped himself is just fine. Is that really the message to be learned here? Incest is okay? Rape is okay? These are the sorts of stories one finds in the Bible if one bothers to read it, so is it any wonder there are so many messed up members of the clergy out there hiding behind a veil of self-righteousness?

Religious leaders should have an obligation to teach and serve as moral examples to their congregations and communities but too often they preach one thing and do another and by participating in amoral acts their secrets both destroy the lives of their victims and cause their followers to experience uncertainty and confusion - and in the process demonstrate those who have "found" and essentially "speak for" God are really no different from anyone else. The examples are legion. For example after televangelist Jimmy Swaggart attacked fellow Assemblies of God minister Marvin Gorman with charges of moral turpitude Gorman retaliated by hiring a private investigator to find dirt on Swaggart and caught him having an affair with a prostitute after which he was defrocked and forced to step down from the pulpit. Three years later Swaggart was caught with yet another prostitute and despite that his show continues to be broadcast to devoted followers both throughout the U.S. and internationally.

Bishop Eddie Long, founder of New Birth Missionary Baptist Church, settled out of court in 2011 with several young men who claimed he sexually abused them as teens in exchange for money and gifts and yet Long today remains the leader of New Birth. Bob Moorehead, a leading pastor of Overlake Christian Church for nearly thirty years, was arrested in 1996 after being charged with indecent exposure in a public restroom and stepped down after several adult members accused him of molestation during baptism and wedding ceremonies. Douglas Goodman, pastor of Victory Christian Centre, one of the largest churches in the U.K., served time in prison for sexually assaulting four members of his congregation in 2004 and returned to his church after his prison sentence. Earl Paulk, founder of Chapel Hill Harvester in Decatur, Georgia had sex with a number of female members of his congregation, was accused of child molestation, had a sexual relationship with his sister-in-law and they had a child together. Tony Alamo, leader of Tony Alamo Christian Ministries in Arkansas, is serving 175 years in prison after being convicted of rape and illegally transporting minor girls in 2010. Frank Houston, founder of Assemblies of God in Lower Hutt, New Zealand, confessed to sexually abusing male children in 2000 and also sexually abused a pastor-in-training back in the '80s but was never charged with the crimes and eventually stepped down. Those are just isolated incidents from the fringe, right? Wrong.

Ted Haggard, founder of the New Life Church in Colorado Springs and president of the National Association of Evangelicals, was much more than just another preacher - he was one of the most influential Christian leaders in America. He was also a hypocrite of the greatest magnitude. In November of 2006 a male prostitute alleged that Haggard, who strenuously campaigned for banning same-sex marriage in Colorado, had paid him for sex for three years and had also used crystal methamphetamine. Haggard of course tried to sidestep the charges but eventually confessed to "sexual immorality" and resigned from his NAE post and stepped down as senior pastor position at New Life Church, which by then had grown to 14,000 congregants. Although he owned a home reportedly valued at $700,000 and received some $200,000 in salary and bonuses in 2006 and a $138,000 severance package, in 2007 he amazingly released a letter soliciting donations to support his family before in 2009 confirming he'd had yet another inappropriate relationship with a male volunteer at his church. Haggard has since started holding prayer meetings in his Colorado Springs home and has ambitions of starting a new church.

Dr. Albert Odulele, founder of Glory House London, was sentenced to six months in prison for sexually assaulting a fourteen-year-old boy and twenty-one-year-old man, and then there are the cases of Robert Liardon, Paul Barnes, Michael Reid, Joe Barron, Pat Mesiti, John Paulo and many others - and these are just some of the ones who have been caught.

Even when there are no immediate "victims" per se the pretense of church leaders as being somehow "holier than thou" illustrates the folly and hypocrisy of the religious as was the case with Reverend Gary Aldridge, who served as Montgomery Alabama's Thorington Road Baptist Church's pastor for sixteen years and died on June 24, 2007 from "accidental mechanical asphyxia" when he was found hogtied and wearing two complete wet suits including a face mask, diving gloves and slippers, rubberized underwear and a head mask. The *Montgomery Advertiser*, which first obtained the autopsy records, reported on Aldridge's two wet suits but chose not to mention what police discovered inside the minister's rubber briefs which, according to the coroner's report, turned out to be "a dildo in the anus covered with a condom." It makes one wonder if the good pastor really believed Jesus was watching.

You have probably noticed the absence of one scandal in particular but that is because I have saved the worst, or at least the most pervasive, for last. Though its epicenter was in Boston, the Catholic Church's clergy sexual abuse scandal in 2002 reverberated across America and all the way to the Vatican. While it was horrifying enough that scores of priests had sexually molested minors, revelations that many bishops had moved guilty priests from parish to parish to conceal those crimes brought the Church to a new low and in some cases bishops allegedly entered into secret settlements to keep the allegations from becoming public.

Protests and mounting lawsuits forced Cardinal Bernard Law of Boston to resign in 2002 but inexplicably in 2004 Pope John Paul II chose him to serve as Archpriest of St. Mary Major Basilica in Rome, a move which obviously angered and dismayed Law's critics. Meanwhile Boston and other dioceses offered millions of dollars in cash settlements to victims and their families who sued, thereby hastening a financial catastrophe which forced some dioceses into bankruptcy.

The *Boston Globe* earned a 2003 Pulitzer Prize for its coverage of the scandal but as the decade wound down the story continued and in May of 2009 Ireland's Commission to Inquire into Child Abuse issued a report finding that rape and sexual abuse had been endemic in Catholic run schools in that country. All of that leaves the outsider to wonder how anyone could in good conscience continue sending their children to Catholic Churches and schools while making excuses for the institution and abusers. One can only marvel at the power of enculturation and indoctrination. Plus we are only examining well known cases involving high profile members of the clergy and the religious institutions as well, and this is but the tip of the iceberg since untold numbers of rank and file believers engage in similar hypocritical activities.

It is often claimed religion does no harm and believers will want to sweep aside the foregoing as examples of individuals who are "demon possessed" or "not true Christians" and nothing more, but the reality is religion sets the stage for such abuses by putting defenseless children and easily manipulated adults into situations where they can be exploited by those in positions of ultimate authority, i.e. people whom they believe represent God.

As Kyle Idleman, teaching pastor at Southeast Christian Church, put it in his book *Not A Fan*, "These religious types were the fans that Jesus seems to have the most trouble with. Fans who will walk into a restaurant and bow their heads to pray before a meal just in case someone is watching. Fans who won't go to R-rated movies at the theater but have a number of them saved on their DVR at home. Fans who may feed the hungry and help the needy and then make sure they work it into every conversation for the next two weeks. Fans who make sure people see them put in their offering at church but haven't considered reaching out to their neighbor who lost a job and can't pay the bills. Fans who like seeing other people fail because in their minds it makes them look better. Fans whose primary concern while raising their children is what other people think. Fans who are reading this and assuming I'm describing someone else. Fans who have worn the mask for so long they have fooled even themselves."

Clearly a great many Christians at every level of church hierarchy and in every denomination are hypocrites who either believe "just in case" as Pascal's Wager dictates or pick and choose which bits of Scripture they will adhere to and then interpret that Scripture to coincide with their own desires. How are such people better than those who believe in a different religious creed or in fact those who do not believe at all? The simple answer is they aren't. As famed Harvard lawyer and jurist Professor Alan Dershowitz, who is no stranger the concept of plea bargaining put it, "I have always considered Pascal's Wager a questionable bet to place. Any God worth believing in would surely prefer an honest agnostic to a calculating hypocrite."

Early in the movie *Tombstone* character Doc Holliday says, "My hypocrisy only goes so far" when he turns down wearing a badge as part of a posse because he knows he is more outlaw than lawman and pretending to represent the law by wearing a badge seems hypocritical to him, but then at the end after he has shot Johnny Ringo while wearing one he declares, "It appears my hypocrisy knows no bounds" as he tosses the badge onto Ringo's dead body." The point being made here is the hypocrisy of many religious people truly know no bounds.

Inescapable Realities

Or, Death and Taxes

"The 'Salvation' that religion preaches as a way to lessen the fear of death also serves as a bullying tactic against those who do not adhere to that religion's dogma." ~ Dr. Darryl Ray

Throughout history warrior societies have celebrated and exalted death in diverse ways, often adopting practices which would be considered extreme or even savage by modern western standards. For example in Micronesia during the early 19th Century Kiribati warriors who were skilled in hand-to-hand combat and close-quarters fighting conducted celebratory practices after warrior deaths, the residuals of which still exist today. When a warrior fell his body was interred after a small ceremony much like any common funeral, however several weeks later the body was exhumed, the head removed and the skull stripped, oiled, polished and offered tobacco and food. Then after the remainder of the body was re-interred fellow tribesmen would keep the warrior's skull on a shelf in their home because they believed it was pleasing to their native gods.

The Haida, an indigenous people who inhabited the American northwest long before white settlers arrived, had vastly different practices for warrior versus civilian burial. Ordinary citizens were simply left in the open behind the village for predators to consume as a sign of respect to the balance of nature, but when a warrior was killed the ceremony was quite different with the fallen warrior's body being crushed with clubs until it fit into a small wooden box about the size of a suitcase and then fitted atop a totem pole in front of the longhouse of the warrior's tribe as reverence to his sacrifice - and the various icons of the totem served as guardians for the spirit's journey to the next world.

The Maori in Polynesia regarded combat as a sacred practice conducted to honor ancestors and believed an all-encompassing life force called "mana" was passed to the living through death. So fervent was this belief that the Maori often feasted on their enemies, a practice fueled by the desire to gain the mana of an adversary defeated in battle, and unlike most native cultures the Maori were never conquered so maybe they were onto something.

In feudal Japan the warriors of Samurai culture were so ready to die they created and embraced the code of "Bushido" as their sole philosophy in life. The literal meaning of Bushido is to achieve something in the world and then be able to throw away the physical body and accept death, and perishing in battle was considered to be the most honorable way to die. Being taken prisoner imposed a shame which could never be washed away so if capture was imminent the Samurai would commit ritual suicide or "hara-kiri" rather than surrender. This kept the Samurai's legacy pure and preserved the culture as a whole because to the Samurai committing hara-kiri was just as honorable as death in combat and was exalted by fellow warriors.

Of course no discussion of death in warrior culture would be complete without including the Vikings. The funeral ceremony for a fallen Viking warrior, especially a chieftain or warrior of considerable status, was among the most elaborate in history. The warrior's body was placed in a temporary grave for several days while new clothes were fabricated for him and endowments given. Generally several of his conquered thrall women would volunteer to join him in the afterlife and were given intoxicating drinks while being bathed and pampered by fellow thralls. The chieftain's longship was docked and prepared for cremation, a practice believed to help usher the fallen warrior to Valhalla. Several horses were usually run sweaty and then slaughtered and cut to pieces and the meat thrown onto the ship. Other animals were often sacrificed as well. Meanwhile the thrall girls were passed among the tents of the warriors in the chieftain's tribe, had intercourse with them and every man would ritualistically affirm to the thralls before bedding them, "Tell your master I did this because of my love for him." Afterward the girls were brought to an altar where they were lifted from their backs into the air by tribesmen and held suspended for several minutes to allow them to receive a vision which they reported to the tribe. When the time came for cremation the chieftain's body was placed in the ship and the thralls were brought into the master's quarters where they were strangled to death by an elder female mystic of sorts who was known in Norse lore as the "angel of death." Afterward their bodies were placed next to the chieftain's, the ship was cast off and the chieftain's relatives set fire to the vessel via flaming arrows or torches. Quite a send-off.

Our perception of death may have evolved away from that over the years with the tide of Judeo-Christian dominance and political correctness in modern western society but our warrior instincts are rooted in our collective subconscious whether we acknowledge them or not. It's not that warriors have a death wish, but it is important for them to perceive the death of comrades as a righteous passage which they may be lucky enough to one day make themselves… whether it is true or not.

Of course warriors are not the only ones who face death and most do not meet their end in battle. On February 25, 1990 a twenty-six-year-old woman named Terri Schiavo collapsed in her St. Petersburg, Florida home in full cardiac arrest, suffered massive brain damage due to lack of oxygen and after two and a half months in a coma her diagnosis was changed to "vegetative state." For the next few years doctors attempted speech, physical and other experimental therapies hoping to return her to a state of awareness but when that was unsuccessful Schiavo's husband Michael petitioned the Sixth Circuit Court of Florida to remove her feeding tube. He was opposed by Terri's parents, Robert and Mary Schindler, who argued that she was conscious and claimed their daughter was a devout Roman Catholic who would not wish to violate the Church's teachings on euthanasia. This raises a few interesting points. If Heaven actually exists and is as wonderful as some people imagine why would the church and family be against her going there sooner rather than later? Plus removing a feeding tube is not the same as euthanizing someone because if God wanted her to remain in this world a bit longer surely he could cause her to wake up. On top of that what about all of those unanswered prayers over the years? What does that demonstrate? And finally the Bible is quite clear about the husband having dominion over his wife with his decisions trumping the desires of the parents, and yet the pious Schindlers took him to court in an attempt to usurp the authority of their holy book. It is clear beliefs only go so far when they do not jive with the reality of a situation.

Benjamin Franklin once quipped the only certainties in life are death and taxes but you can get out of paying taxes if you have a creative accountant or are willing to cheat. Conversely there is no cheating the Grim Reaper, although throughout history people have deluded themselves into believing a wide variety of myths which have made them think they could. After all the most powerful human instinct is self-preservation and once primitive peoples began to realize death was a fact of life they would have to face one day, in the ultimate act of desperation and self-preservation, they began searching for a "way out," real or imagined, to assuage their fear of the great unknown.

Immortality has always been a dream for humans and the desire to avoid death is universal whether due to fear, a thirst for knowledge or simply a love of living - although some see it as a curse, with journalist Herb Caen having said, "The only thing wrong with immortality is that it tends to go on forever." The subject has long fascinated humans and because of that it has become inexorably intertwined with most religions and mythologies.

For example Ambrosia was the drink of the Greek gods. Said to taste like honey, it was delivered to the Olympians by doves and was the source of their immortality. Various mortals and demigods such as Heracles were given the privilege of drinking of it while others such as Tantalus stole it and were punished. He was trapped in a pool of water with food always just out of reach and his name and story are the origin of the English word "tantalize." Others such as the hero Tydeus almost tasted it but were turned away at the last moment. As the story goes he was going to be made immortal by the goddess Athena... until she caught him eating human brains.

In Hinduism the Devas, or gods, were originally mortal or had lost their immortality because of a curse and sought a way to obtain eternal life. They teamed up with their enemies the Asuras, or anti-gods, to churn the Milk Ocean and create a nectar called "Amrita," which is a Sanskrit word which almost literally translates to "immortality" in English. The Devas ended up tricking the Asuras into not drinking any by having Vishnu disguise himself as a female goddess who could instill an uncontrollable lust in anyone's heart, but Yoga masters are said to be able to drink the potion because the Devas spilled some of it in their rush to keep it from the Asuras.

In Taoism the common ore of mercury known as Cinnabar is a central ingredient in an elixir of immortality called "huandan," which means "Reverted Elixir." They believed ingesting certain materials such as cinnabar or gold would instill some of their qualities and rid the body of the imperfections which kept it from obtaining immortality but unfortunately most of those things were poisonous and many people died, including many of the Tang Dynasty emperors. Eventually the idea of "External Alchemy" was changed to "Internal Alchemy," a way of harnessing one's natural energy through yoga and other practices in the hope of gaining immortality.

In the Sumerian *Epic of Gilgamesh* the hero is searching for the source of immortality after his friend Enkidu dies and causes him to fear dying himself. His quest leads him to Utnapishtim, a Noah-like figure who was granted immortality when he built a large boat at the gods' instructions in order to survive a great flood, which is discussed elsewhere. Utnapishtim tells Gilgamesh his immortality was a special gift but adds there is a plant of unknown origin and species which could be eaten to achieve eternal life. His description is similar to a buckthorn or a boxthorn, depending on the source, however after finding it Gilgamesh loses the plant to a snake. There always seems to be a serpent around to muck things up, so we will never know if it would have worked.

In Chinese Mythology something called the Peaches of Immortality play a very large role in the epic *Journey to the West*. The Jade Emperor and his wife Xi Wangmu were said to be the planters of a peach tree which only gave ripened fruit every three thousand years, and they gladly gave it to the other gods to keep them living forever. Sun Wukong, the Monkey King, was chosen as Protector of the Peaches and ended up consuming one of them which bestowed upon him one thousand years of life. He was later captured, but since he had also eaten the Pills of Immortality was unable to be executed. Sun Wukong eventually went to war against Heaven and the gods had to turn to the Buddha, who managed to trick and trap him for five centuries after which he went on the quest outlined in rest of the myth.

A different sort of fruit, the Golden Apples, were extremely important to the Norse deities because they needed the apples to maintain their immortality and eternal youth. Idun, the goddess of spring, was the keeper of their orchard and when she was tricked by Loki and handed over to the giant Thiassi along with the apples the other gods began to grow old and their power waned. With their last bit of strength they forced Loki to retrieve Idun and the apples so he transformed himself into a falcon, saved Idun and the apples and the gods regained their youth.

In Christian mythology there was said to be a Jewish man who taunted Jesus during his walk to be crucified by hitting him with his shoe and telling him to hurry up. Jesus responded by telling the man he would have to stay around until he returned and when he realized what had transpired the man took the name Joseph, converted to Christianity and was baptized - although the curse did come with some harmful side effects. He wasn't allowed to sit or rest at any time except for a brief respite on Christmas and every one hundred years he would get incurably sick, go into a fit for an indeterminate amount of time then return to the age of thirty. Another well-known piece of Christian mythology is the Holy Grail, the cup (or bowl) which Jesus drank from during the Last

Supper and was also believed to be the container in which Joseph of Arimathea caught Christ's blood while he was on the cross. It was a widely sought-after relic and King Arthur and his knights are said to have journeyed far and wide searching for it. Only the purest of souls were able to grasp the Grail, and Sir Galahad is said to have gained immortality by virtue of being the only man able to touch it.

Such tales, which are obviously ridiculous, have given way to various versions of the place we call Heaven. Of course no mortal has ever been there not counting Muhammed and his winged horse, something which Christians do not believe but a billion Muslims do, and yet many people are sure it is waiting for them. Even so they don't give much thought to the nuts and bolts of such a place. Let's say for a moment they are right. What are we all going to do there… for eternity? Think about that. As Susan Ertz put it, "Millions long for immortality who don't know what to do with themselves on a rainy Sunday afternoon." Think about the things in your life which make it worth living whether it be golf, sex, going to the movies, reading a new novel by your favorite author and so on. The list is virtually endless. Will you find any of those things in the great beyond? Are there golf courses, and if so will it be possible to miss a putt? Who will make the movies and write the novels? Is sex even allowed? If so, with whom? After all many people have more than one true love over the course of their lives. Another perk of Heaven is the prospect of once again seeing family and friends who have preceded us in death, but that presents a different sort of problem. I'm sure it would be wonderful to reminisce and talk about the old days, at least initially, but after the thousandth retelling those stories will become tedious and presumably there will be no new ones. To put that into perspective many of us have an older, absent minded relative who keeps telling us the same old stories over and over and we immediately look for a way to escape because it feels like Groundhog Day… but in Heaven they would be retold for eternity. As they say be careful what you ask for, because you just might get it.

The other great motivator along with fear is greed. Those who feel this life is not enough refuse to accept their impending demise and demand eternity, but by the same token many refuse to accept the tax bill the government sends them each year but still end up paying it. Similarly, we will all have to pay the piper when our time comes and I don't mean the ferryman at the River Styx on our way to the underworld.

Like it or not death is a central feature of every human life. Turn on the television any given day and most likely there will be news about the demise of some celebrity or statesman. As we live we know we will eventually die, and as a result many people find death both terrifying and mystifying. Throughout the ages this terror has been a constant. You can go all the way back to the Neanderthals and discover they buried their dead and even placed flowers and other artifacts on their graves. This was happening tens of thousands of years ago, so obviously the prospect of death has been a big deal for a very long time.

As a result the central feature of most religions, including the Christian faith, is eternal life. In John 3:16 we find the signature verse of Christianity, "For God so loved the world that he gave his only begotten son, that whosoever believes in him shall not perish but have eternal life." In other words by simply believing in Jesus you can avoid death. This is the promise of Christianity and if you are terrified by the prospect of dying it's easy to understand why the promise of eternal life is compelling. This is a fundamental reason so many people turn to religion. In the words of Gore Vidal, "The idea of a good society is something you do not need a religion and eternal punishment to buttress. You need a religion if you are terrified of death." The problem is, eternal life is a fabrication no matter which religion you follow. As Sam Harris observed, take away the prospect of death and religion all but disappears. Put another way, if you seriously believe in life after death why does everyone not react like the Abbot of Ampleforth? When Cardinal Basil Hume told the Abbot he was dying the Abbot replied delightedly "Congratulations! That's brilliant news. I wish I was coming with you." Clearly many people who profess to believe still retain a degree of uncertainty about the promise of eternal life. As Dr. Jack Kevorkian put it, "Despite the solace of hypocritical religiosity and its seductive promise of an after-life of heavenly bliss, most of us will do anything to thwart the inevitable victory of biological death."

Consider the Fountain of Youth, which is of course a spring which supposedly restores the youth of anyone who drinks of it or bathes in its waters. Tales of such a fountain have been recounted for thousands of years and appeared in writings by Herodotus (5th Century BCE), the Alexander Romance (3rd Century CE) and the stories of Prester John (early Crusades, 11th/12th Centuries CE). Stories of similar waters were also prominent among the indigenous peoples of the Caribbean during the Age of Exploration in the early 16th Century who spoke of the restorative powers of the water in the mythical land of Bimini.

The legend became particularly prominent when it became attached to Spanish explorer Juan Ponce de León, the first Governor of Puerto

Rico. According to an apocryphal combination of New World and Eurasian elements de León was searching for the Fountain of Youth when he traveled to what is now Florida in 1513. The myth is too perfect to abandon completely because we are all going to die just as Ponce did, but we will probably do so while on some kind of quest, conscious or unconscious, literal or metaphorical, for a Fountain of Youth. Aging is the only eternal thing in human life. We have raged against it from the beginning and will rage against it to the end as we should, but it makes no logical sense since it is not in any meaningful way a part of our experience. As any Buddhist will tell you we live life only in the now - a now which feels present, urgent, immediate and singular - but in fact those nows are plural and each one costs us because they accumulate. The way we know this is through age. It's not something we've done or deserve and we can't even feel it happening except abstractly over time. Our brains are justifiably confused. There must, we think, have been some mistake. We are angry. We are Ponce de León.

The Fountain of Youth, whatever it is, would feel like justice. Time is liquid which flows unfairly through and past us. We ingest it without effort, so it makes sense that we would look for a liquid to save us. A liquid cure to a liquid curse. Generation after generation, like the mythical Ponce, has chased eternity in some liquid form - fish oil, coconut water, a juice fast and lotions - as 21st Century science promises to fulfill this myth using Nanocures which will flow in our blood and restore the fluid inside our cells. Ponce's quest rages on and perhaps this is the fountain he was pointing to, the perpetually flowing quest to the horizon and then the next and the next. We turn to look where he was pointing, and then suddenly we are gone.

One thing to consider is as time marches on our understanding of the universe grows, science keeps pushing the boundaries of knowledge further and further and that raises an important question. If tomorrow it were announced that a "cure for death" were found which would essentially allow us to become immortal or at least allow us to live much longer, would you avail yourself of it? Or would you prefer to grow old, die and "go to Heaven?" When asked that question many people will hedge their bets and lie to themselves because they know no such cure currently exists, so they refuse to indulge in the hypothetical and instead cling to the "cure" provided by religious belief.

As it turns out the foregoing is not as farfetched as it may sound and believe it or not man actually discovered eternal life on the ocean floor in 1988. The discovery was made unwittingly by Christian Sommer, a

German marine-biology student in his early twenties who was spending the summer in Rapallo, a small city on the Italian Riviera where exactly one century earlier Friedrich Nietzsche prophetically conceived his philosophical novel *Thus Spoke Zarathustra* which contains the words, "Everything goes, everything comes back; eternally rolls the wheel of being. Everything dies, everything blossoms again…"

Sommer was conducting research on hydrozoans, small invertebrates which depending on their stage in the life cycle resemble either a jellyfish or soft coral, and among the hundreds of organisms he collected was a tiny, relatively obscure species known to biologists as Turritopsis dohrnii which today is more commonly known as the "immortal jellyfish." He kept his hydrozoans in petri dishes, observed their reproduction habits and after several days noticed his Turritopsis dohrnii was behaving in a very peculiar manner for which he could hypothesize no earthly explanation. It refused to die and in fact appeared to age in reverse, growing younger and younger until it reached its earliest stage of development at which point it began its life cycle anew.

Several biologists in Genoa, fascinated by Sommer's finding, continued to study the species and in 1996 published a paper called *Reversing the Life Cycle* in which they described how the species at any stage of its development could transform itself back to a polyp, the organism's earliest stage of life, "thus escaping death and achieving potential immortality." This finding appeared to debunk the most fundamental law of the natural world which says you are born and then you die. One of the paper's authors, Ferdinando Boero, likened the Turritopsis to a butterfly which instead of dying turns back into a caterpillar. The anthropomorphic analogy is that of an old man who grows younger and younger until he is again a fetus and for this reason Turritopsis dohrnii is sometimes referred to as the Benjamin Button jellyfish.

We now know the rejuvenation of Turritopsis dohrnii and some other members of the genus is connected to the fact it undergoes cellular trans-differentiation, an unusual process by which one type of cell is converted into another, for instance a skin cell into a nerve cell. This same process occurs in human stem cells. A Japanese scientist named Shin Kubota who has been culturing Turritopsis polyps in his lab has said, "Turritopsis application for human beings is the most wonderful dream of mankind. Once we determine how the jellyfish rejuvenates itself we should achieve very great things. My opinion is that we will evolve and become immortal ourselves."

In the opinion of Dartmouth molecular paleobiologist Kevin J. Peterson, "Immortality might be much more common than we think. There are sponges out there that we know have been there for decades. Sea-urchin larvae are able to regenerate and continuously give rise to new adults. This might be a general feature of these animals. They never really die." Peterson is closely following the work of Daniel Martínez, a biologist at Pomona College and one of the world's leading hydroid scholars. The National Institutes of Health awarded Martínez a five-year, $1.26 million research grant to study the hydra, a species which resembles a polyp but never yields medusas and has a body almost entirely composed of stem cells which allows it to regenerate itself continuously. As a Ph.D. candidate Martínez had set out to prove hydra were mortal but his research over the past fifteen years has convinced him they can in fact survive forever and are "truly immortal."

Those studies of immortal sea life are only some examples of what is being done. Russian scientist Anatoli Brouchkov from Moscow State University recently injected himself with a 3.5 million-year-old bacteria called Bacillus F which could hold the key to immortality. The bacteria was found in Siberian permafrost on Mamontova Gora in 2009 and since then scientists have used it to experiment on plants, mice and human blood cells with tests showing it improved longevity, fertility and appeared to heal plants and restore the ability to reproduce in older mice. The key is establishing what mechanisms kept the bacteria alive in such harsh conditions for millions of years in the hope of developing it to extend human life. Brouchkov explained, "Our cells are unable to protect themselves from damage, but these bacteria cells are able to protect themselves."

Approaching the subject from an entirely different angle, Professor Yuval Noah Harari from the Hebrew University of Jerusalem said human dissatisfaction will drive mankind to "upgrade themselves" and cyborg technology will allow them to do this stating, "I think it is likely Homo sapiens will upgrade themselves into some idea of a divine being either through biological manipulation or genetic engineering by the creation of cyborgs which are part organic and part non-organic. It will be the greatest evolution in biology since the appearance of life." Harari argued humans have become the dominant species because of our ability to invent fictions such as religion and money which help bind society together, however the departure from belief in religion will spur on a change to the human race. "God is extremely important because without religious myth you can't create society. Religion is the most important invention of humans. As long as humans believe in and rely on gods they are controllable, but you can't convince chimpanzees to give you a banana with the promise it will get twenty more bananas in chimpanzee heaven. They won't do it, but humans will. However what we have seen in the last few centuries is humans becoming more powerful and they no longer need the crutches of the gods. Now we are saying we do not need God, just technology." He added that Silicon Valley is now the most interesting place in the world from a religious perspective because they believe all problems can be solved with technology. No matter which of the forgoing bear fruit, and keeping in mind there are many other avenues being pursued, it seems inevitable that one day in the future immortality will become a reality so the question remains - if you had the chance to take advantage of such a development would you make the pragmatic choice and choose the known, or would you instead allow yourself to die and opt for the unknown. Be honest.

The reality of the human condition is simple and for now the time we have on earth is all we have. For many people this is terrifying, but like many unpleasant realities it is a fact of life. There is neither Heaven nor Hell. These two places have sprung from the human imagination and are the ultimate "carrot and stick" control mechanism - do this and go to Heaven, do that and go to Hell. Moreover, as much as we might want to we will not meet up with dead friends and family members in an afterlife.

If you are honest with yourself the truth becomes obvious. When you die, you die. Many people have trouble getting their heads around this fact of life and chances are you have heard about eternal life and your everlasting soul since you were a toddler. The concept of Heaven is as deeply ingrained in you as your native language but nonetheless everlasting life is nothing more than a pipe dream and by understanding the biochemistry you can see why. Let's start with a bacterium cell. It is a tiny membrane filled with a variety of molecules which react together to create what we call "life." Some build and repair the cell wall, some allow the cell to move, some provide energy and so on. It is a little chemical machine. One of the molecules is a long DNA strand and there are molecules floating around it which are able to copy parts of the DNA to manufacture new molecules. In other words the "miracle of life" is a chemical reaction.

What if a foreign molecule gets into the bacterium cell and interferes with the DNA chemistry or something damages the strand so the cell can no longer manufacture what it needs to survive? Eventually the chemical reactions inside the bacterium will stop. In other words it "dies." The cell walls break down and burst, the chemicals inside it float away and the bacterium ceases to exist. When that bacterium dies do you believe it goes to Heaven? Of course not.

Next let's look at a mosquito, which is much more complex than bacteria. It is a multi-cellular insect but if you look at each cell it is much like a bacterium in its basic functioning. A cell in a mosquito is also a series of DNA-based chemical reactions and when they cease the mosquito dies. I think we can agree mosquitoes don't go to Heaven either. Think of how many mosquitoes have lived and died over the years. No one imagines Heaven being full of septillions of everlasting mosquitoes, do they?

What about a mouse? It is even more complex, but the same thing applies. How about dogs and cats? Lots of vets and pet owners would argue with you here because of the emotion involved but dogs and cats do not go to Heaven either. When they die, they die, but because there are those who would argue the point this is covered in greater detail elsewhere.

What about chimps, the closest living relatives to humans? Same answer, which brings us to humans. The human body is nothing but a set of chemical reactions just like all of the life forms just discussed and when we dies those chemical reactions stop. There is no "soul" mixed in with the chemicals, just like there is no soul in a bacterium, mosquito, mouse, dog or chimp. There is no afterlife, Heaven or Hell for the chemicals which make up a human body. Furthermore the thoughts and traits which make you "you" are contained in your brain which is a physical vessel so when you die it dies and those things die with you. They do not somehow "float away" to some other plane of existence as much as you might want them to. The inescapable fact we cease to exist upon death is intolerable for some people. They cannot or will not accept or even imagine it. They think, "Me… die? I am going to cease to exist? All of my thoughts, experiences, relationships, ideas and memories simply vanish? The thing is we know this subconsciously and/or intellectually but at this point our self-preservation instinct kicks in and religious beliefs which seem to offer a way out take over. Not to beat a dead horse, but if it seems too good to be true… it probably is.

Consider that animals are not aware of their mortality and therefore do not know, as we do, that they will die one day. They do not hold elaborate funeral services, do not eulogize each other and instead of being buried in coffins or getting cremated simply lay down, die and decompose… and in the process complete the natural cycle of life. They face their demise honestly because they lack the ability to create fictions. Humans, on the other hand, are aware of what is going to happen and invent all sorts of beliefs and rituals to mitigate their fear.

That is the reality. "You" cease to exist and imagining eternal life and inventing a fantasy called Heaven does not change it, but even so people convince themselves they have souls, fabricate the concept of immortality and then picture a place called Heaven complete with mansions, streets of gold, frolicking virgins and whatever else fits their desires. They imagine it so vividly and repeat the fantasy so often they actually believe it to be reality.

How can it be a person like your Grandpa with decades of memories, hundreds of close friends, a large, happy family and seven grandkids who love him dearly can cease to exist? How can it be that in a moment *poof* all of that is gone? One minute Grandpa is alive and the next he is gone along with everything stored in his brain. We are never going to see him again. That is troubling enough, but when a person turns that logic on himself and faces his own mortality it becomes truly painful. What goes through our minds is simple. How can it be I will die? How can it be my body will turn to dust? For many people the thought is impossible to imagine or accept.

Talk to a few believers about Heaven and ask them to describe what it is like and how they will get there. This will highlight the absurdity of the concept in two different ways. First of all the creation of entirely new and obviously made up "dimensions" and "materialization processes" should tell you everything you need to know about how delusional people can be, and second there is the disconnect which comes when you compare any two people's idea of Heaven. Since no one has been there to see it naturally everyone's concept is different. For some it involves harps and clouds and halos, for others it is filled with hot and cold running virgins, for some people the actual body is transported magically to Heaven as described in the *Left Behind* books, for others your soul floats out of the body and makes its way to St. Peter and so on. People can and do make up anything they like because Heaven is an imaginary place and after listening to three or four versions the message should come through loud and clear. Heaven is an invention of the human imagination and each person's version is different.

Fly to Cairo and take a look at the Great Pyramid. It is one of the largest manmade objects on earth and was built for the express purpose of helping the Pharaoh reach the afterlife. In addition there is the mummification process, disassembled boats, sacred artwork, *Book of the*

Dead incantations and so on. We look at all that now and know with absolute certainty it was a waste of time. The Egyptian notion of the afterlife was a fantasy - and ours are no different.

It was previously stated that neither humans nor mosquitoes go to Heaven and the big difference between them is the fact humans have the brainpower to imagine such a place, but just because we can imagine something does not mean it exists. After all we can imagine a lot of things which we know without question are not real and if you stop to think about what your fantasy of Heaven is like you will realize it is just as preposterous as the Egyptian version. Neither of these places exist, and no amount of wishing can change that.

Beliefs such as the foregoing can certainly be comforting, there is no denying that, so it is time to once again ask a question posed in the very beginning of this book. Do you care if your beliefs are true? As Professor Richard Dawkins put it, "There are all sorts of things that would be comforting. I expect an injection of morphine would be comforting... but to say that something is comforting is not to say that it's true."

Many adults never outgrow their childhood fear of death and because it is so distressing they invented a "way out" by imagining eternal life in a place they call Heaven. This is where God comes in. In no one's conception of Heaven is there murder, incest, burglary, muggings, political backstabbing, office politics, gossip, rumor, PMS, arguments, anger, discontent or disease. Heaven is free of tooth decay, mosquitoes and rapists. In Heaven everyone is beautiful and eternally young and always happy. Emotion is a powerful thing so even grown, intelligent adults who should know better believe in these fantasies and go to incredible lengths to rationalize them. In his book *The Case for Faith* apologist Lee Strobel interviewed fellow apologist Norman Geisler who stated, "In sum, everything that God created was good. What changed things was the Fall [Adam and Eve eating the fruit]. When God was told, in effect, to shove off, he partially did. Romans 8 says all creation was affected - that includes plant life, human beings, animals, everything. There were fundamental genetic changes; we see, for instance, how life spans rapidly decreased after the Fall. God's plan was not designed to be this way; it's only this way because of sin."

This is the concept of original sin. The idea is by simply eating some fruit Adam and Eve infuriated God so much that as punishment he changed all living things and made them mortal and for some Christians this is the explanation for why we die rather than live forever. Why would an adult believe such a silly story and why do Christians and Jews cling to the concept of original sin? Why don't people reading the story of the talking serpent just chuckle like we do when we read about Santa and the Easter Bunny? It's because original sin tries to explain death and people are afraid of dying. The truth is we do not die because someone ate a piece of fruit. That is absurd if you really stop to think about it. We die because we are degenerating on a cellular level. When we die, we die. This secular scientific view of death was expressed by Stephen Hawking when he said, "I regard the brain as a computer which will stop working when its components fail. There is no Heaven or afterlife for broken down computers… that is a fairy story for people afraid of the dark."

But wait, what about the "proof" of an afterlife shown by so-called "Near Death Experiences" or NDEs in which people float around the operating room and look down at their own body lying on the table? When a small percentage of people are near death or "temporarily dead" either from an accident or during emergency lifesaving treatment they report eerie experiences which they interpret as meaning they have crossed the threshold into an afterlife. Some have catalogued these reports and concluded the experiences must have been real, while researchers have found they are simply the natural and expected result of a lack of oxygen to the brain. As usual our starting point when examining such tales should be the application of Occam's Razor. The supernatural explanation for near death experiences requires an assumption there is such a thing as an afterlife, but of course to many people with religious beliefs such a place is a given and the afterlife is real and thus not an assumption.

Everyone will probably agree at least to some extent the brain is capable of generating surprising experiences such as highly realistic dreams. We've all had fainting or dizzy spells and these can be pretty dramatic episodes even though to an outsider nothing notable happened physically, and shortly we will discuss how all of the major events of an NDE can be created in the brain by performing controlled experiments. Even those who believe NDEs truly represent a brush with the afterlife probably agree every experience which characterizes one could also be attributed to a natural cause. Why then is there a tendency to insist they have had an actual life after death experience?

In 1975 Dr. Raymond Moody published *Life After Life* which became the seminal work promoting NDEs as evidence of an afterlife. A strong believer in both the afterlife and reincarnation, Moody claimed he has personally lived not one but nine previous lives (one more than a cat!)

and in his book cited one hundred fifty cases of people who reported extraordinary experiences after resuscitation.

Let's take a look at some of the reports because although it's rare for any two stories to be substantially similar there are common themes. One of the most familiar is the "life flashing before the eyes," i.e. a fast-forward replay of either someone's entire life or important events, even long-forgotten events, commonly called a "life review." Perhaps the most popular report is a warm and inviting bright light and sometimes this is combined with a feeling of floating through a tunnel. Some NDEs include an out-of-body experience, usually floating in the air and seeing one's own body below being tended to by medics and sometimes reporting seeing things happen which could not have been observed from the body's position. People with physical limitations who are blind, deaf or paralyzed usually find that their bodies are whole during these experiences.

Some people report positive meetings with deceased loved ones or religious figures such as Jesus or Muhammad. Just as often however, they report terrifying encounters with monsters, evil people or the devil. So while many experiences are euphoric many are very much the opposite and the question is can we group all of these things together to find an undeniable pattern? Is there enough consistency to conclude with certainty such a thing as an afterlife must exist? It's unlikely, because NDEs are similarly complicated by many unrelated causes of characteristic experiences such as drug effects, hypoxia, trauma, brain abnormalities and simple dreaming just to name a few.

Let's take a look at out-of-body experiences. If you search the internet you'll find dozens of stories involving someone floating off the operating table and making observations about the room, actions performed by the surgical staff and even things happening outside the room. Many sound undeniable and it seems the only possible explanation is the person's consciousness was indeed outside the body but we must necessarily consider other possible explanations.

Anesthesiologists are not impressed by these stories since they know it is common for patients to be aware during general anesthesia and remember many details of the people, objects and events in the room. In fact *The Lancet* published research in 2001 which showed nearly twenty percent of patients retained memories of things which occurred when they were clinically dead and what's rarely mentioned is the fact most such "recollections" get the details wrong and were probably just imagined by the patient. When authors compile stories to promote the idea of NDEs they tend to universally exclude those and in fact the majority were never recorded to begin with.

Some stories can't be explained and include specific details the patient could not have known but unfortunately all of these are anecdotal. As an example of the value of anecdotes Dr. Penny Sartori placed playing cards in obvious places on top of operating room cabinets at a hospital in Wales in 2001 while she was working as part of a supervised experiment. Although she's a believer in the afterlife and documented fifteen cases of reported out-of-body experiences by patients during her research not one person ever reported seeing the playing cards or knowing they were there.

Life reviews, euphoria, bright lights and meetings with sacred personages have also all been correlated with high levels of carbon dioxide in the brain. Research published in the journal *Critical Care* in 2010 found that over one-fifth of heart attack patients who went into cardiac arrest and were resuscitated, all of whom would have had high CO2, reported these phenomena. These patients were all nearly dead so the NDE correlates equally well as the physiological condition so to find out which is the best correlation we need to see whether an NDE can happen when one condition is present and the other is not.

Extensive research has been done to characterize a person's experience with loss of blood to the brain when there is no risk of death, for example for fifteen years Dr. James Whinnery put hundreds of healthy young fighter pilots into centrifuges to understand what a pilot might experience under extreme gravitational loads. Once they reached the point where there was inadequate bloodflow to the brain they lost consciousness and among the frequently reported experiences were bright lights, floating through a tunnel, out of body experiences, vivid dreams of beautiful places, euphoria, rapid memories of past events, meeting with friends and family and more - an exact match with the events attributed by believers to a brush with the afterlife.

What about the reverse? Are there reliably documented reports of NDEs from people who were near death but whose brains had normal oxygen supplies? If there are I was not able to locate any. This leaves only one group of conditions which can be consistently correlated with what we call an NDE and it's not nearness to death but rather a set of brain conditions which includes hypoxia, hypercarbia and anoxia.

Other researchers have also found ways to produce the symptoms of an NDE without nearness to death being a factor. In 1996 Dr. Karl Jansen published the results of his successful attempt to induce an NDE using the drug ketamine and in 2002 *Nature* published research in which experimenters gave direct electrical stimulation to the part of the brain called the angular gyrus in the parietal lobe. In each case subjects reported being able to see themselves lying there from a vantage point near the ceiling and were able to communicate what they observed as it was happening. Some brain surgeries, most notably those for epilepsy, also produce very high rates of NDE reports from patients whose lives were not in danger.

Believers in the afterlife are quick to point out just because the reported experiences have natural explanations that doesn't prove the supernatural explanation is not also true in at least some cases, and of course that's correct. While most of the symptoms of NDEs such as seeing a bright light and feeling euphoric are too vague to serve as proof of the afterlife one isn't and that's the out-of-body experience. What science would love to find is a positive outcome in a controlled test, however no disembodied consciousness has ever successfully completed a task under controlled conditions, i.e. nobody has yet seen Dr. Sartori's hidden cards or beaten any similar tests.

NDEs can actually be explained biologically. Recessed in the center of your brain, encased snugly within the corpus colossum, wrapped tightly between the dual-hemispheres of spongy nerve bundles, encased in the quarter-inch-thick armor-plating of skull and surrounded by your main and expressive organs with which you face the world exists a tiny gland, long considered vestigial (i.e. serving little to no function) which holds the key to our interpretation of existence as we know it. This is the pineal gland. This minute spec, roughly the size of a grain of rice, is more heavily protected than even the heart with its literal cage of protection because if something happens to your heart you will die, but if something happens to your pineal gland you can't "go to Heaven."

This gland has influences on both melatonin and pinoline but our interest here is its role in the creation of the chemical dimethyltriptamine or DMT, because it may well be the reason we as a species are capable of sentience itself. DMT is a Schedule 1 narcotic largely because it is one of the most potent psychedelics known to man and yet every day your pineal produces more. It is also the chemical which elicits dreams, and what's more this gateway to dreamland is released in massive amounts at the moment of death.

The pineal's significance is neither a new idea nor an unfounded one. Spanning the expanse of human civilization there runs an undercurrent of worshipful adoration to it more widely known as the inner eye, all-seeing eye and/or the like which is considered the body's gateway to the soul. Egypt had its Eye of Horus (now emblazoned on the dollar bill), Hindu culture has its bottu (the familiar forehead dot) and even the ancient art of yoga recognizes the brow chakra or ajna as blossoming at the pineal or third eye. That's only to name a few, but the truth behind the cult of the pineal has gone largely unnoticed collectively though the symbols themselves have been downright ubiquitous. In fact Tibetan Buddhists have long carried a belief the soul enters the fetus precisely forty-nine days after conception but because you are not likely a Tibetan Buddhist - since they number less than twenty million - whether you subscribe to an eternal soul or not isn't the point because day forty-nine happens to be the moment the pineal is formed in a fledgling brain.

So what does this have to do with death? On an experiential level psychological mushrooms distort perception, cocaine produces raw energy and most notably marijuana slows time - you see time distortion seems to go hand in hand with most psychedelics as well - so time passage then is totally subjective. Meanwhile among DMT smokers two major themes emerge nearly universally. First there is a stretching of time in which they experience a hectic six or seven minutes as a near eternity or lifetime, and second they experience religious incarnations with an inclination toward whatever sect the subject is affiliated with.

After death, while this massive psychedelic dose courses through the brain, there is a mysterious several minutes where the brain still functions but with our new perspective we at last understand what these minutes are. These few minutes after death, subjectively, are experienced as an eternity engrossed in the DMT universe and the trip itself is a highly personal experience dictated by the deepest realms of the subconscious. Therefore whatever at your deepest core you *expect* to happen when you die, that's what will *appear* to happen. Is it any wonder when someone is brought back from the brink of clinical death they believe they have visited Heaven?

The bottom line is like it or not your total experience is here and now on earth and that realization should make you view a day in line at the Department of Motor Vehicles, a week preparing your taxes or a Sunday morning wasted at church a little differently. On average all we have is about thirty thousand days. When you die, what is your legacy? What do you leave behind? What contributions have you made to society? If you have done research into the cure for cancer you leave that. If you have written books or made movies you leave them. If you funded a building at your university you leave that. Images of you in photographs and on video as well as any letters, writings or recordings testify to your existence. Your children have their memories of you, as well as those you leave with friends and family. That's it. Now that you understand that death is final you may look at those things in a different light because as Ecclesiastes 1:4 tells us, "One generation passeth away, and another generation cometh: but the earth abideth for ever."

Mark Twain explained this when he observed, "The finality of death is the coldest and most difficult truth one must face. Religion makes the perfect distraction." He added, "I do not fear death. I had been dead for billions and billions of years before I was born, and had not suffered the slightest inconvenience from it," and that makes a great deal of sense. German philosopher Arthur Schopenhauer and author H. P. Lovecraft mirrored that view when they respectively wrote, "After your death you will be what you were before your birth" and "We had it (oblivion) before we were born, yet did not complain. Shall we then whine because we know it will return?"

Heaven Can Wait

Or, All Dogs Don't Go to Heaven

"We shall tell ourselves that it would be very nice if there were a God who created the world and was a benevolent Providence, and if there were a moral order in the universe and an afterlife; but it is a very striking fact that all this is exactly as we are bound to wish it to be."
~ Sigmund Freud

Early in the blockbuster film *Gladiator* General Maximus Decimus Meridius, portrayed by Russell Crowe, addressed his troops as they were about to go into battle by saying, "If you find yourself alone, riding in the green fields with the sun on your face, do not be troubled. For you are in Elysium and you're already dead!" What was he referring to?

Elysium or the Elysian Fields is a conception of the afterlife that developed over time and was maintained by certain Greek and Roman religious and philosophical sects and cults. Initially separate from the realm of Hades, admission was reserved for mortals related to the gods and other heroes but later it expanded to include those chosen by the gods as well as the righteous and heroic and it was where they would remain after death to live a blessed and happy life while indulging in whatever employment they had enjoyed in life.

According to Homer the Elysian Fields were located on the western edge of the Earth by the stream of Okeanos. In the time of the Greek oral poet Hesiod, Elysium would also be known as the Fortunate Isles or the Isles (or Islands) of the Blessed, located in the western ocean at the end of the earth. The Isles of the Blessed would be reduced to a single island by the Thebean poet Pindar who described it as having shady parks with residents indulging their athletic and musical pastimes.

In a similar fashion in Norse mythology "Valhalla," from the Old Norse Valhöll or "hall of the slain," is a majestic, enormous hall located in Asgard which is one of the "Nine Worlds" and home to the Æsir tribe of gods ruled over by the god Odin. Before the hall stands the golden tree Glasir and the hall's ceiling is thatched with golden shields.

Chosen by Odin himself, half of those who die in combat travel to Valhalla upon death led by the Valkyries while the other half go to the goddess Freyja's field Fólkvangr. In Valhalla the dead join the masses of those who have died in combat known as "Einherjar" as well as various legendary Germanic heroes and kings as they prepare to aid Odin during the events of "Ragnarök" - a series of future events which include a great final battle (like Armageddon) foretold (i.e. prophesized) to ultimately result in the death of a number of major figures including the gods Odin, Thor, Týr, Freyr, Heimdallr and Loki along with the occurrence of various natural disasters and the subsequent submersion of the world in water (much like the biblical flood). Afterward the world will resurface anew and fertile, the surviving gods will meet and the world will be repopulated by two human survivors (similar to Noah's family). Of course not all were warriors so as a result there was also "Helgafjell" or the "holy mountain" which represents another version of the afterlife. It was often manifest in a mountain formation in the vicinity and was so sacred people could not look in its direction without washing their face first. In the holy mountain it was believed members of the Norse clans would lead lives similar to the ones they had lived in the world of the living and it is said some psychics could look into the mountain and what they saw was not intimidating but instead a scene with a warm hearth, drinking and talking.

Let's compare that Norse idea of a warm hearth, drinking and talking in the afterlife with the Greco-Roman view that Elysium had shady parks filled with residents indulging their athletic and musical pastimes, the Muslim version with its rivers of wine and honey and of course the Christian notion of a perfect Heaven with mansions and streets of gold. The one thing all have in common is they give the illusion death is actually something to look forward to rather than dreaded and as Freud said, "It is a very striking fact that all this is exactly as we are bound to wish it to be." Even the ancients Greeks understood that with regard to their own beliefs, with Demosthenes writing in his *Third Olynthiac,* "A man is his own easiest dupe, for what he wishes to be true he generally believes to be true."

Have you ever noticed how people always look up when speaking about departed friends and relatives? Why is that? As George Carlin has observed, "After someone dies sooner or later somebody will say, 'I think he's up there, smiling down on us.' First of all there's no *up there*, but even if there was why is it no one ever says, 'I think he's down there, screaming up at us.' It never occurs to people their loved ones might be in Hell." Some make the excuse it would be cruel or impolite to suggest the deceased had gone to the "other place" but there is more to it than that. People look up because subconsciously that is where they hope to be themselves someday.

So how and why do we allow ourselves to be fooled into believing we are immortal? An excellent illustration can be found in the film *The Invention of Lying*. It takes place in a world much like our own except for one key difference - no one lies. It's not that humanity has dedicated itself to honesty, but simply that lying was never invented. They don't even have a word for it so whatever someone says simply *is* and the idea of saying something which isn't true is beyond the grasp of everyone on planet Earth. There's no such thing as flattery or for that matter tact. If someone is ugly you tell them so because of course it's true, but it runs much deeper than that. Without lies there is no fiction, and movies have been reduced to men on camera narrating actual historical events. In a world without lies there is also no religion because according to the premise it is really just a big lie told over and over again. This results in a heartbreaking scene in which the main character's dying mother professes an abject fear of nothingness saying, "I'm so scared, Mark. I don't want to die. You know, people don't talk about it much, but death is a horrible thing. One minute you're alive… and then just like that, it's all gone." The newly fib-empowered son (who had figured out how to lie) in a moment of weakness comforts her with a lie about death replying, "When you die you're going to go to your favorite place in the whole world. And you're going to be with all of the people you've ever loved and who have ever loved you. And you're going to be young again, and you'll be able to run through the fields and dance and jump, and there will be no sadness, no pain, just love and laughing and happiness. There will be ponies made of gold and everyone will live in giant mansions and everything will smell like cookies. And it will last for an eternity." That lie is overheard by hospital staff who of course believe it because lying is unheard of and soon the world wants to know more about this mansion filled Heaven and the "man in the sky" who takes care of you after death.

Even when I still believed in Heaven one thing which always puzzled me is why is it so important for someone to believe in order to go there? I guess the only thing which makes sense is religion is like a Ponzi scheme where you have to blindly trust the guy taking your money, with the difference being you must die in order find out you've been had. Religions are like "after-life insurance" policies you pay for now but will never be able to collect on… and by then it's too late to complain. On the other hand as Philip K. Dick once explained, "Reality is that which, when you stop believing in it, doesn't go away." On a few occasions I have been challenged on that point by believers who used what might be called the "Australia analogy" in which they claim the existence of Heaven is just as believable as that of Australia based upon the premise people believe in Australia simply because they have been told it exists. The problem with that rationale should be obvious - we have pictures and maps, can speak to people who have been there and can even buy a plane ticket to find out for ourselves, while Heaven is nothing more than an abstract concept - but what I found particularly funny was the look on their faces when I explained that I lived there for two years in the 1990s and therefore possess firsthand knowledge.

An excellent example of how people tend to choose a comforting fantasy over a painful reality is a belief called *The Rainbow Bridge* which is based on a work of poetic prose written sometime between 1980 and 1992. The poem describes an otherworldly place to which a pet goes upon its death, eventually to be reunited with its owner. The story tells of a green meadow located "this side of Heaven" (i.e., before one enters into it) and Rainbow Bridge is the name of both the meadow and an adjoining bridge connecting it to Heaven.

According to the story when a pet dies it goes to the meadow after having been restored to perfect health. The pet runs and plays all day with the others, there is always fresh food and water and the sun is always shining - however it is said that although the pet is at peace and happy they miss their owner who had to be left behind on Earth, so when their owner dies they come across the Rainbow Bridge and it is at that moment the pet stops what they are doing and sniffs at the air and looks into the distance where they see their beloved owner. Excited, they run as fast as they can until they are in their owner's arms, licking their face in joy while their owner looks into the eyes of their pet who was absent on Earth but never absent in their heart. Then side by side they cross the Rainbow Bridge together into Heaven, never again to be separated.

This tale has of course gained popularity amongst animal lovers who have lost a pet and understandably so - I for one love my cat dearly and dread the day when she leaves us - but it was probably never meant to be taken literally. Even so some broken hearted pet owners have come to believe the story is literally true, but aside from the obvious problems such as animals cannot go to Heaven because according to many belief systems they have no souls, stray animals would have no human masters to greet them, abusive people own pets too and the like - let's not forget it's just a poem and a recent one at that. We know exactly where this originated, there is zero basis in fact and still people will argue with you about how it must be true because their heart tells them so. Is it any wonder humans have invented similar destinations for their own souls?

During a weekly general audience at the Vatican in November of 2014 Pope Francis, speaking of the afterlife, appeared to suggest animals could go to Heaven by asserting, "Holy Scripture teaches us that the fulfillment of this wonderful design also affects everything around us." Italy's *Corriere della Sera* newspaper, analyzing the Pope's remarks, concluded he believed animals have a place in the afterlife and drew an analogy to the comforting words Pope Paul VI was said to have once told a distraught boy whose dog had died. "One day, we will see our animals again in the eternity of Christ. Paradise is open to all of God's creatures." Charles Camosy, a professor of Christian ethics at Fordham University, said it was difficult to know precisely what Francis meant since he spoke "in pastoral language that is not really meant to be dissected by academics" but when asked whether the remarks had caused a new debate on whether animals have souls he answered, "In a word, absolutely."

The Reverend James Martin, a Jesuit priest and editor at large of the Catholic magazine *America*, said he believed Francis was at least asserting that "God loves and Christ redeems all of creation" even though conservative theologians have said paradise is not for animals. Laura Hobgood-Oster, Professor of Religion and Environmental Studies at Southwestern University in Georgetown, Texas and an expert on the history of dog-human interaction, said she believed there would be a backlash from religious conservatives but that it would take time. "The Catholic Church has never been clear on this question. It's all over the place, because it begs so many other questions," she said. "Where do mosquitoes go, for God's sake?"

In early history there was no question dogs had souls and would be allowed into Heaven. Rameses III, who became Pharaoh of Egypt in 1198 BCE, buried his favorite dog Kami with all the ritual ceremony due to a great man including a coffin, linen, incense, jars of ointment and the ritual scroll he would need for his entrance into paradise, but the rise of Christianity seems to have ushered in the belief dogs would not make it to paradise. Despite the fact the word animal is derived from the Latin word "anima" which means "soul," Christianity (particularly the Catholic Church) has traditionally taught that dogs and other animals have no more consciousness or intelligence than rocks or trees. According to religious doctrines of the time anything which had consciousness also had a soul, anything possessing a soul could earn admission to Heaven and to grant that animals had souls was simply unacceptable to the Church. In later years they would claim support from some scientists and philosophers such as Rene Descartes, who would have described your dog as just some kind of machine filled with the biological equivalent of gears and pulleys which doesn't think but can be programmed to do certain things. Machines have no souls, and therefore one need not allow a Beagle-shaped automaton or a mechanized Maltese to pass through the pearly gates of Heaven.

These views were strongly held and Pope Pius IX, who headed the church longer than any other pope (1846–1878), led a heated campaign to try to prevent the founding of the Italian Society for the Prevention of Cruelty to Animals on the grounds animals have no souls. Pius quoted Thomas Aquinas to prove his case since Aquinas often noted animals are not beings but just "things," however Aquinas seems to have had some doubts since he warned, "We must use animals in accordance with the Divine Purpose lest at the Day of Judgment they give evidence against us before the throne," which would certainly suggest animals would be around in the afterlife.

It is ironic to note that Pope Pius, who created the doctrine of Papal Infallibility, was himself contradicted in 1990 by Pope John Paul II who said "also the animals possess a soul and men must love and feel solidarity with smaller brethren" and went on to say animals are "as near to God as men are." Although the Pope's statement was reported in the Italian press it was not widely discussed, perhaps to prevent the embarrassment of having two supposedly "infallible" popes contradicting one another.

Only three years after the death of John Paul II his successor, Pope Benedict XVI, seemed to once again close the doors of Heaven firmly to pets and other animals. Although he was personally a cat-lover, Benedict asserted the traditional doctrine that only humans have immortal souls and in a sermon he gave in 2008 stated, "For other creatures, who are not called to eternity, death just means the end of existence on Earth." He would later point out the Bible makes it clear in Mark 16:16 that only "he that believes and is baptized shall be saved." The implication was clear, since it is pretty certain the apostles never baptized or preached the gospel to dogs or cats.

Following Benedict's short tenure his successor was Pope Francis and since he adopted his papal name in honor of the patron saint of animals, Saint Francis of Assisi, it is not surprising he chose to side with John

Paul II and once again open the doors of paradise to animals. This can be justified in Scripture by citing the Old Testament passage Isaiah 11:6 which says in the life hereafter, "The wolf shall dwell with the lamb, and the leopard shall lie down with the young goat, and the calf and the lion and the fatted calf together," which would certainly suggest a whole lot of animals might be residing in Heaven, although the statement made by Pope Francis is really quite unambiguous. He said, "One day we will see our animals again in the eternity of Christ. Paradise is open to all God's creatures."

If the viewpoint of Pope Francis is accepted I am sure the next round of questions to be debated by ecclesiastical scholars will be, "If animals go to Heaven, can they also go to Hell?" In other words will the nasty dog who bit my grandson suffer hellfire in perdition or do all dogs have an automatic ticket to Heaven since they lack the intellect to make rational moral decisions? Where does God draw the line? Is there a hierarchy of animal life forms which separates those eligible for entry into paradise from those not sufficiently evolved, such as insects, bacteria and viruses, to benefit from the comforts of a heavenly existence? That is quite literally opening a whole new can of worms and while Catholics can draw pleasure from the fact the Pope believes they will share Heaven with their beloved pets the issue is neither simple nor clear cut.

In early Christianity the understanding of life after death and therefore Heaven was the product of both pagan and Jewish thought and custom. For them the dead were consigned to the shadowy underworld of Hades, although at times the virtuous and heroic were granted eternal life in the Elysian Fields depicted in *Gladiator*. Eventually Platonic claims that the soul was immortal but the body temporal put pagan philosophy in conflict with evolving Jewish ideas of resurrection because many 1st Century Jews were awaiting the coming of the Kingdom of Heaven which was to be brought about by a Davidian messiah who would usher in a new age for Israel and resurrect the dead. Of course later views changed and it became understood that those who believed in Jesus would be saved although those living at the time believed his return to be imminent since that is what Scripture promised, but after he failed to inaugurate the new kingdom in the lifetimes of the disciples and early apostles subsequent generations - now two millennia worth and still waiting - were left to speculate about the nature of Heaven.

Different understandings throughout history of what Heaven is like tell us more about the values of a given era than the actual nature of paradise. For Puritans it was centered on the praise and constant worship of God while in the Victorian era family became more intimately associated with views of heavenly life. The Mormon proposition that families are bonded to one another for all eternity (an understandably scary scenario for some) expanded upon the Victorian view, while for African American slaves who lived during the battle over abolition Heaven was seen as a glorious afterlife and release from their earthly bondage. In the more prosperous 20th Century Heaven morphed into a place where the redeemed were rewarded with the type of riches they had sought in life, but not surprisingly our polarized age has now produced different views of what lies beyond. Many Christians now focus on accepting Jesus as their personal savior in preparation for the world to come, or as Senior Pastor of the First Baptist Church of Atlanta Charles Stanley wrote, "Our entrance into Heaven has nothing to do with how good we are. What matters is how good Jesus is and what He did for us." He adds that by accepting Jesus' atoning sacrifice we are given "a ticket to heaven which can never be revoked." Sounds wonderful, doesn't it? Once again, in the words of Sam Harris, "Without death, the influence of faith-based religion would be unthinkable. Clearly the fact of death is intolerable to us, and faith is little more than the shadow cast by our hope for a better life beyond the grave."

You are no doubt familiar with the popular Christian version of Heaven - pearly gates, streets of gold, winged angels and the righteous eternally singing the praises of God. What's surprising is how few people have thought about what this kind of existence would actually be like. Our familiar images of Heaven come from texts written in the 1st and 2nd Centuries which were incorporated by Catholic councils into what we now call the New Testament. The Hebrew writers of the Torah had alluded to an afterlife much like the Hades of the Greeks and Romans. They imagined a hazy underworld in which the souls of the dead neither die nor fully live, but by the time the New Testament was written the concepts of Heaven and Hell had emerged in Jewish culture before entering early Christianity and subsequently Islam.

The books of the New Testament were of course written at different times and for different purposes which means they don't always agree, so although Paul says in 1 Corinthians that Heaven is beyond imagining other writers offer concrete details and as a result the popular version of Heaven we have today is a composite which comes from several texts and relies heavily on the book of Revelation.

Heaven is claimed to be a real place. The writer of John 14:2-3 put the words, "In my Father's house there are many dwelling places. If it were not so, would I have told you that I go to prepare a place for you? And if I go and prepare a place for you, I will come again and will take you to myself, so that where I am, there you may be also" in the mouth of Jesus. Some Christian leaders have even used verses from Old Testament prophets to pinpoint the location of Heaven, suggesting it is somewhere beyond the North Pole.

It is also claimed people in Heaven have bodies. While the earliest Christian texts, the epistles of Paul, suggest the eternal body is "pneuma" (spirit), later New Testament writers inclined toward the physical resurrection of both Jesus and believers with renewed, perfect bodies and this view was eventually affirmed by Church fathers and is now the predominant Christian belief. From this we get the Evangelical belief that in the "End Times" the physical bodies of believers will rise up to Heaven in a Rapture and this belief is used to explain why Christian women should keep their bodies chaste and "pure."

Many translations of the Gospel of John say the dwelling places in Heaven are mansions, which fits with other descriptions of heavenly opulence. In Revelation 21 the writer claims to glimpse Heaven for himself when he asserts, "And the foundations of the wall of the city were garnished with all manner of precious stones. The first foundation was jasper; the second, sapphire; the third, a chalcedony; the fourth, an emerald; The fifth, sardonyx; the sixth, sardius; the seventh, chrysolyte; the eighth, beryl; the ninth, a topaz; the tenth, a chrysoprasus; the eleventh, a jacinth; the twelfth, an amethyst. And the twelve gates were twelve pearls: every several gate was of one pearl: and the street of the city was pure gold, as it were transparent glass." He further states that God sits on an ornate throne and along with crowns the heavenly hosts are clothed in white, a symbol of purity and a reminder that they do not need to work.

Not surprisingly earthly treasures such as gems, mansions and streets of gold define heavenly wealth and beauty because our Iron Age ancestors yearned for the trappings of royalty and this was one way to "attain" them. They had heard rumors of the gold and jewels amassed by Pharaohs, kings and tribal warlords and wished the same for themselves. Since both greed and inequality are timeless the tale of King Midas has played out in countless variations over the millennia so the fascination of the Bible writers with gold and precious stones is understandable, but their gem-encrusted paradise is simply the product of limited imagination. It is the challenge we all face in trying to dream beyond the arts, technologies and mythologies of our own time and culture, so the

Bible's version of paradise is like a velvet painting from a tourist shop being compared to the real alpine meadow or cloud forest or coral reef it depicts.

The Christian Heaven is said to be eternal and reserved for believers with the most often quoted Bible verse, John 3:16, making the point God so loved the world he gave his only son so that everyone who believes in him may not perish but may have eternal life. The author of Revelation later assures us, "He will wipe every tear from their eyes. Death will be no more; mourning and crying and pain will be no more" and promises that in this eternity it is always light and there is no need for sleep.

According to Scripture the inhabitants of Heaven spend their "time" eternally serving and worshipping God and even though it is always light we are told the saints (i.e. the saved) will do so around the clock. Revelation 7:15 tells us, "For this reason they are before the throne of God, and worship him day and night within his temple, and the one who is seated on the throne will shelter them." Several passages also suggest the faithful will receive crowns which they can then offer up as gifts to God and as is often the case with Scripture some take this literally while others do not.

There are of course other more worldly interpretations of the foregoing passages when they are read in their original context but we now have a better understanding of where modern Christianity got the image of Heaven so often depicted in hymns, sermons, art and pop culture. Ironically to many people this biblical description is enough to make Heaven sound unappealing, especially if you then add the company of some of the people with whom you would presumably be required to spend eternity, but the problem isn't just bad company because the closer you look the more the Bible's version of paradise seems like a different version of eternal torture.

Much of what makes life worth living is the process of learning, discovery, growth and change. We delight in novelty and laugh because we are startled by the unexpected. Curiosity is one of our greatest pleasures and growth is one of our deepest values and satisfactions. In fact our whole psychological makeup is designed for tuning in to change, including our senses. When a sound is continuous we tend to stop hearing it. A static image registers as a blind spot to our eyes. Even art relies on imperfection and newness to create beauty or to trigger our aesthetic sense. In contrast timeless perfection is static and unchanging. In the book of Matthew Jesus commands, "Be ye perfect as your Father in Heaven is perfect" and we are told that in Heaven this ideal will finally be attained, but the problem is perfect means finished and complete. There is no room for improvement, change or growth. How tedious an existence that would be.

Your best qualities would also be irrelevant because if everything is perfect many of the qualities we value most in ourselves and each other become meaningless. Compassion and generosity are pointless because nobody is hurting or in need of anything. Forgiveness is not needed. Creativity, courage, resilience, decisiveness and vision are all useless. Sigmund Freud once said mental health is the ability to love and to work, but in the state of perfection both lose their meaning because with no need to create or produce there is little value in offering our affection and commitment to another person who is perfect and complete without us.

In addition to loving and creating some of life's most exhilarating experiences require risk, but that element will be gone. Think about how it feels to fly down a ski slope, jump out of an airplane, race cars, ask someone on a date or start a business. The adrenaline rushes and euphoria surges because despite our skill and preparation there was some chance we would fail, but in a perfect Heaven failure would be impossible. This is well illustrated in a 1960 episode of *The Twilight Zone* entitled *A Nice Place to Visit* in which a small-time hood named Rocky Valentine, who has been on the wrong side of the law for most of his life, is gunned down by police while robbing a pawn shop. He dies and awakens in the afterlife where he is met by a "Mr. Pip," who describes himself as a guide to his new surroundings. Rocky can't quite believe where he has ended up since he can have anything he desires, lives in a beautiful apartment, always wins at the casino, never misses a shot on the pool table and is always surrounded by beautiful women. He wonders what good deed he could have done in life to deserve this, but after a month or so the shine of having anything and everything and always winning wears off and eventually he tells Pip, "If I gotta stay here another day, I'm gonna go nuts! I don't belong in Heaven, see? I want to go to the other place." Pip replies, "Heaven? Whatever gave you the idea that you were in Heaven, Mr. Valentine? This *is* the other place!" Horrified, Rocky unsuccessfully tries to open his apartment door to escape his endless "paradise" as Pip begins to laugh at his predicament. The episode closes with host Rod Serling intoning, "A scared, angry little man who never got a break. Now he has everything he's ever wanted, and he's going to have to live with it… for eternity."

In Heaven would animal pleasures like food, drink, sleep, and sex be unknown? For example does the risen Jesus with his new and perfect body have a penis or anus? Do angels? Will you? If so, why? Eating, drinking or fornicating are physical pleasures which depend on hunger of one sort or another. Ice water tastes refreshing when you are hot and thirsty. Falling asleep is a wonderful thing when you are exhausted. The reality is our bodies and brains are made for each other and our pleasures are linked to survival but if you are never hot, thirsty or exhausted those pleasures become impossible. As Nobel Laureate George Bernard Shaw put it, "Heaven, as conventionally conceived, is a place so inane, so dull, so useless, so miserable, that nobody has ever ventured to describe a whole day in Heaven, though plenty of people have described a whole day at the seaside."

To make matters more complicated we are predators in a complex web of life. The eating of food which gives us so much sensory pleasure and sustenance simultaneously destroys the lives of the plants and animals we consume and creates bodily waste. Christians naturally disagree about whether there will be meals in Heaven, and while some point to "feasting" in the book of Revelation to reassure themselves that eating and drinking will be part of paradise none speculate on the origin of those meals or the heavenly digestive process and subsequent elimination of bodily waste.

In Heaven free will must necessarily cease to exist. Some Christians explain suffering and evil on earth as God's way of creating creatures who would love him freely by giving them the option to reject him but that is the opposite condition they expect to find in Heaven since there is no sin, no option to sin and therefore by Christianity's own definition no free will. As is discussed in another chapter secular philosophers and neuroscientists debate whether free will is real or merely an adaptive illusion, but either way in the Bible's version of Heaven even the illusion vanishes.

Another aspect which is seldom if ever discussed is the idea that ninety-eight percent of Heaven's occupants are embryos and toddlers since most fertilized eggs die before implanting, embryos and fetuses often self-abort and of course there are all the babies and young children who died untimely deaths due to accidents, SIDS, pediatric disease and so on. A statistical analysis by researcher Greg S. Paul suggests some 350 billion inhabitants of Heaven would be those who died before maturing to the point where they could voluntarily "accept the gift of salvation" so the vast majority would essentially be automatons who never had moral autonomy and did not chose to be there. Children who die before an "age of accountability" are said to go to Heaven because although Christians believe children are born bad thanks to "original sin" most assume children who die young go there because the alternative is unthinkable and to support that belief they point to two verses in the book of Matthew... "So it is not the will of your Father in Heaven that one of these little ones should be lost" and "But Jesus said, 'Let the little children come to me, and do not stop them; for it is to such as these that the kingdom of Heaven belongs.'"

The theological implications are immense because Christian theologians typically explain evil by arguing this was the best of all possible worlds since it is the only way to create free will and develop moral virtues like courage, compassion, forgiveness and so forth. The idea is to make us more "Christlike" and prepare us for Heaven, but if we stop to think for a second it appears God didn't need the whole free will/sin/redemption mechanism to fill his paradise with perfect beings because no suffering, evil or moral freedom is actually required as a prelude to glory.

The ratio of adults to embryos has social implications as well. Pastoral counselors sometimes tell women they will get to apologize in Heaven to the fetuses they aborted, which will of course be fully developed persons there, but what does that really mean since the brain and mind - i.e. our individuality and identity - and the qualities which define our personhood develop through our personal experiences. Can you imagine ninety-eight percent of the "people" around you having never made a decision or felt sorrow or experienced anything akin to an adult conversation? One of Heaven's dirty little secrets is of course that it co-exists with Hell, although some theologians have actually argued that witnessing the torment of the damned will be one of the joys of paradise. In the words of prominent Puritan theologian Jonathon Edwards, who preached an entire sermon on the topic, "When the saints in glory, therefore, shall see the doleful state of the damned, how will this heighten their sense of the blessedness of their own state, so exceedingly different from it! When they shall see how miserable others of their fellow creatures are, who were naturally in the same circumstances with themselves; when they shall see the smoke of their torment, and the raging of the flames of their burning, and hear their dolorous shrieks and cries, and consider that they in the meantime are in the most blissful state, and shall surely be in it to all eternity; how will they rejoice!"

Of course many Christians find this thought horrifying or even traumatic so some teach universal salvation or believe the unsaved are simply annihilated, but for Hell-believers the alternatives to gloating are not a whole lot better since either the faithful are blissfully indifferent to the endless suffering of the damned or their joy depends on them being unaware of the fate of their loved ones, and for that matter the bulk of mankind, meaning ignorance is necessarily a condition of their eternal bliss.

So what will the faithful do in Heaven for eternity? The same thing the angels do. Worship God and sing his praises. The writer of Revelation even offers us a sample song and in one passage twenty-four elders, "Fall before the one who is seated on the throne and worship the one who lives forever and ever; they cast their crowns before the throne, singing, 'You are worthy, our Lord and God, to receive glory and honor and power, for you created all things, and by your will they existed and were created.'" As one graduate of Evangel College (Assemblies of God) observed, "Having spent some time in North Korea, where the incessant praise music and propaganda were required and all-pervasive, I sometimes wonder if the dynastic leaders there somehow lifted a page from an older playbook." It has been said the only god worthy of worship is one who neither wants nor needs it so what are we to think of a deity who creates the earth and its inhabitants - and in fact fashions an entire universe - so that a crowd of bipedal primates, most of whom were never even born, can spend an eternity engaged in praise and adulation?

Eternity. People seem oblivious to what the concept of Heaven going on forever actually means. Most of us would naturally prefer to live longer than the time allotted to us ... but forever? Forever is infinity. It never ends. Think of the best possible experience you can imagine - your favorite symphony or rock concert, the most beautiful place you've travelled, the most intense sex ever, holding your child. Any one of them, stretched to infinity, becomes unthinkable. That is why fiction writers who explore the idea of immortality rarely treat it as something to be desired. Author Edgar Shoaff put it bluntly when he wrote, "Immortality is a fate worse than death" and the movie *Groundhog Day*, while a comedy, makes a salient point about it as well. Part of what makes the film funny is the insane suicide attempts Bill Murray makes in order to stop living the same day over and over. What could a terminally bored inhabitant of Heaven do to cease existing? Nothing.

Could an omnipotent god create an afterlife which was actually some form of paradise? Perhaps, and without a doubt some Bible believers who read this will insist their God has done exactly that. Some will fall back on the words of Paul and claim on biblical authority that we have no idea what Heaven will be like other than being eternally wonderful, but the fact is for centuries Christians have claimed they do indeed have an idea of what Heaven will be like and for almost two millennia have sought to entice small children, the desperate poor and the vulnerable to come to Jesus by promising the kind of inane, debased everlasting life just described. Crowns and white robes and streets of gold and angelic choruses and celestial mansions have long been Christianity's carrot with the threat of eternal torture as the stick, and millions of people have lived and died fearing one and anticipating the other while never realizing they are simply two different versions of the very same thing.

Up to this point the discussion has centered on the Christian view of Heaven but as previously noted there are many more versions of "paradise" out there. In Judaism the Torah says little about Heaven but the mystical writings on Kabbalah, particularly the works of disciples of the 16th Century Rabbi Isaac Luria, divided the cosmos into several spheres and layers throughout which move the sparks of souls and from the highest of these realms, known as Atziluth, the pure deity emanates.

In ancient China Heaven, known as "tian," was not a place but a god until Confucianism leached the anthropomorphic from the idea. Taoism then taught that the Jade Emperor governs the universe from Da Luo Tian, which is the highest of twenty-six heavens, by using an intricate celestial bureaucracy unsurprisingly similar to the earthly administration of Imperial China.

In Hinduism the god Vishnu reposes far above the highest heavens in "Vaikuntha," a gathering place for those who have achieved "moshka" (spiritual liberation) through him. It is also known as "Vishnupada" (Vishnu's footstep) and because the god is believed to walk the earth there are also terrestrial Vishnupada which are gateways to the sacred and eternal.

Buddhists of the Pure Land schools believe they can achieve rebirth in wonderlands which are way stations toward Nirvana, the ultimate cessation of ego and desire. For example the Buddha Amitabha vowed that all who meditate and call his name can enter his Pure Land - the Western Paradise - to be brought along to full enlightenment. In contrast Tibetan Buddhism associates Mount Kailasa in the Himalayas (which no human has ascended) with Demchog, the central deity of an archetypal mandala (a spiritual symbol representing the universe). Kailasa is also the residence of the Hindu god Shiva whose meditative power emanates from the mountain and charges the universe.

Islam believes the dead must wait until the Day of Resurrection to receive judgment but also provides many details about the rewards and pleasures awaiting the souls who are ushered into Heaven beginning with its name (which means garden in Arabic), rivers of wine and honey and the privilege of seeing Allah's face.

The religion of legendary religious teacher Zarathustra known as Zoroastrianism inspired many of the tenets of the Abrahamic religions including the dichotomy of Heaven and Hell. They believe that after death souls must try to cross a bridge with the blessed easing over into Garo Demana (House of Song) and the damned ending up in Drujo-Demana (House of the Lie).

There are/were many others including the Greek, Egyptian and Norse versions discussed elsewhere but all have much in common with the Christian Heaven, first and foremost, the comforting notion of an eternal afterlife. It is of course unlikely you believe in any of the other Heavens because naturally yours is the correct one but one needs to wonder where all of those complex ideas came from if they are not based in fact. That said, even now some Christian leaders are pointing to a completely different view of eternity. According to Executive Pastor John Blanchard of Rock Church International, "I don't believe we are going to be floating around with little wings looking like Cupid playing harps for all eternity. Heaven isn't just a place you go. Heaven is how you live your life. What's trending is a younger generation, who are motivated by causes, to make a positive difference in this world." Former Anglican bishop N.T. Wright, a leading authority on the New Testament, made an even more revealing statement when he observed, "Of course there are people who think of Heaven as a kind of pie in the sky dream of an afterlife to make the thought of dying less awful. No doubt that's a problem as old as the human race." This all points us in the direction of Humanism and to paraphrase Madalyn Murray O'Hair, "A Humanist knows that a hospital should be built instead of a church. A Humanist knows that a deed must be done instead of a prayer said. A Humanist strives for involvement in life and not escape into death. He wants disease conquered, poverty vanquished, war eliminated. A Humanist thinks heaven is something for which we should work for now - here on earth - for all men together to enjoy." What's so wrong about that?

Sure, religion teaches its followers lessons through parables about kindness and love and doing the right thing but if all that fails there's always the threat of a scary monster to drive the point home. For instance in Jewish folklore the Dybbuk is the spirit of a dead sinner who, instead of continuing on to the afterlife, decides to hide out by inhabiting the body of a living person where they can either live quietly or more frequently pester and torture the victim, but luckily they can't inhabit just anyone. The victim has to have committed some sort of sin in order for the Dybbuk to get inside so as long as you never, ever do anything bad you'll be just fine… but even if you do manage to come down with a case of Dybbuk it can be exorcised by a properly trained rabbi. Dybbuks are actually starting to get some mainstream attention with the release of two major horror movies in the last few years, 2009's *The Unborn* and *The Possession*, which both feature the demons as antagonists.

Pretas are beings unique to Eastern religions like Buddhism, Hinduism and Sikhism. While Western culture does have a tradition of spirits of the dead being punished for their sins they don't have anything on Pretas. Those who are greedy or jealous in life can become cursed by karma and returned to the world of the living, which doesn't sound so bad except they become filled with a constant, aching hunger and unquenchable thirst. No matter how much they eat or drink Pretas are never satisfied. Either they have trouble finding food or drink or they are unable to consume it when they do, as Pretas are often depicted as emaciated corpses with tiny mouths or impossibly thin necks. As if all that weren't bad enough the thing for which they hunger is typically something embarrassing such as human waste.

In Western religion and pop culture demons tend to have very specific powers which they can use to torture humans. For example maybe they can disguise themselves as others or manipulate people to their will but usually not both, however this is not the case for the Rakshasa of Hinduism and Buddhism. They're formerly evil humans said to hold a wide range of powers including shape-changing, creating illusions and working powerful magic. They tend to have toxic fingernails or claws and eat people to boot. They can appear in all kinds of forms - beautiful or ugly, massive or stunted or even with animal-like bodies. Their king Ravana was the worst of all and was said to possess ten faces, dozens of arms and exceptional cunning.

Djinni are very different from their contemporary cultural representation, the genie. Instead of granting wishes Djinni are a separate race from humans who live in a parallel reality according to Islamic texts. They're made up of flame and smoke (as humans were made up of clay) and since they are the only beings besides humans which were given free will by Allah they're also capable of being benevolent, neutral or evil just like the rest of us. In fact Satan was originally a Djinn named Iblis but when he refused to bow to Adam Allah cast him out of paradise. Naturally the most well-known Djinni are the evil ones, particularly those called Ifrits which are malevolent beings who can change shape and form, have command over fire and are immune to human weapons. As it so happens Ifrits are also currently experiencing a bit of popularity, scoring an appearance in a subplot of the television series *True Blood.*

Although traditionally used in Judaistic texts as a word simply meaning "destruction," Abaddon is later personified in Christian texts and Christianity's various offshoots as an actual being. Given titles like "Lord of the Pit," "King of the Locusts" and "The Destroyer," Abaddon has been said to have a number of attributes and also to have committed various acts. According to some texts Abaddon was originally the angel Muriel, who gathered the dust which formed Adam. Others say he was actually the angel tasked with sealing Satan into Hell. He didn't stay an angel forever however, as later writings describe him as living on a throne of maggots and commanding an army of locusts shaped like horses with human faces and scorpions' tails.

Another type of ghost from Eastern religions is the Pishacha, which is the spirit of a person who committed fraud, adultery, rape or similar criminal acts. Like other entities they can change shape or become invisible and can even possess humans and sicken them physically or mentally, but where Pishacha get really creepy is in the way they're described. According to many texts they're humanoids with a deep obsidian skin tone, red eyes and bulging veins covering their bodies.

Zoroastrianism, a once-thriving major world religion and one of the bases of Christianity, is now limited primarily to areas of Iran, Pakistan and India but still has its evil beings. Foremost among those is Azi Dahaka, who has moved into general Iranian folklore as well. He has been described as a being with six eyes, three mouths and three heads and if that sounds crazy to you I suggest you read *Revelation* in the Bible and compare notes. Azi Dahaka knows all of the sins in the world and when wounded bleeds snakes, rats and insects. He also figures heavily into the Zoroastrian apocalypse because according to prophecy he will eat all the world's livestock and one third of humanity itself. Sound nuts? Once again, read *Revelation.*

Yet another type of ghost found in Far East religions, Vetala, has one feature which distinguishes them from their brethren. Instead of bothering with the living they spend their time possessing the dead and after they successfully inhabit a corpse it stops decaying and they're free to walk the earth once more. You might already be thinking of zombies, and in fact Vetala were believed to have a form of omniscience due to their undead nature which made them desirable slaves. They also had similarities to the slave zombies of Central American legends, but unlike zombies Vetala had no interest in brains or human flesh. Their goal was simply to annoy and torment the living out of jealousy.

Chinese folk religions are much smaller than they once were with the majority of their former adherents converting to Taoism or other religions in the last few centuries, but some of their myths and legends continue on into modern Chinese folklore. One such legend is that of Hundun, a faceless deity who was the personification of chaos. Described as being either a humanoid with no orifices or even as a formless living sack (although he was sometimes also said to have useless vestigial limbs), Hundun was believed to primarily favor the wicked and eschew goodness. He was killed when two other gods named Hu and Shu, who always thought Hundun kind, decided they should drill holes in his body and give him eyes, a nose, a mouth, etc. but unfortunately despite their best intentions Hundun died from this impromptu surgery a week later.

Another god from Chinese folk religion and mythology, Xing Tian, was a giant warrior who served under the Emperor Yan. When Yan was defeated by the Yellow Emperor his pride was so wounded he challenged the Yellow Emperor to a duel, during which the Yellow Emperor decapitated Xing Tian and hid his head inside Changyang Mountain. This is where things get really bizarre. Instead of dying like a normal person Xing Tian lived on, searched in vain for his head and after an unspecified amount of time simply gave up and grew a new face on his torso using his nipples for eyes, belly button for a mouth and became a headless giant forever raging against the other gods… which brings us right back to Satan and his legion of demons,

Methodist Clergyman Pastor Robert Short wrote in the *U.S. Catholic* on April 1980, “There are in fact so many strong biblical, doctrinal, and logical arguments against the existence of a literal Hell that this question naturally arises: Why do the churches teach it, and why do people often believe it? ...The churches tend to believe that fear, rather than love, conquers all.” That is the “stick.” As for the “carrot” Mark Twain once asked, “Most people can’t bear to sit in church for an hour on Sundays. How are they supposed to live somewhere very similar to it… for eternity?” One sounds as bad as the other.

Graven Images

Or, We Can Ignore THAT One!

"Thou shalt not make unto thee any graven image, or any likeness of any thing that is in Heaven above, or that is in the earth beneath, or that is in the water under the earth. Thou shalt not bow down thyself to them, nor serve them: for I the LORD thy God am a jealous God, visiting the iniquity of the fathers upon the children unto the third and fourth generation of them that hate me." ~ *Second Commandment (Exodus 20:4-6)*

On December 17, 1996 a customer entering the Seminole Finance Corporation building in Clearwater, Florida told employees she had just seen something extraordinary on the south wall of the structure's exterior reflective-glass windows, shortly thereafter phoned a local television station with her report and that night and for days to come all Tampa Bay area newscasts lead with the story and it was not long before *AP*, *CNN*, ABC's *World News Tonight*, the *Today Show*, *American Journal* and other media had spread the word. By the New Year several hundred thousand visitors, some from other continents, would have occasion to come to witness in person what had she seen. So what was so amazing? It was an apparition of the Virgin Mary.

Dubbed the "Clearwater Virgin," the image of Mary in the glass façade of the finance building drew an estimated one million visitors over the next several years and was purchased by an Ohio Catholic revivalism group but when a local chemist examined the windows he suggested the stain was produced by water deposits which combined with weathering and yielded a chemical reaction like that often seen on old bottles, probably due to the action of the water sprinkler.

Other examples of Marian apparitions of this type which have received substantial press coverage include a fence in Coogee, Australia, a hospital in Milton, Massachusetts and a felled tree in Passaic, New Jersey. Images of the Virgin have also been reported on a rock in Ghana, an underpass in Chicago, a piece of firewood in Janesville, Wisconsin, a chocolate factory in Fountain Valley, California, a pizza pan in Houston, Texas and a grilled cheese sandwich, pretzel and pebble said to resemble the Virgin Mary have even been offered for sale on internet auction sites with the former being purchased by Internet casino GoldenPalace.com.

Another image regularly reported is that of Jesus Christ. Sightings of this type have been reported in such varied media as cloud photos, Marmite, chapattis (unleavened flatbread), shadows, Cheetos, tortillas, trees, dental x-rays, cooking utensils, windows, rocks, stones and painted and plastered walls. Again some of these items have been offered for sale on internet auction sites and a number have been bought by the Golden Palace casino because when such images receive publicity people frequently come considerable distances to see and venerate them.

One controversial incident which received considerable publicity was when the face of Mother Teresa was claimed to have been identified in a cinnamon bun at a place called Bongo Java in Nashville, Tennessee on 15 October 1996. Dubbed the "Nun Bun" by the press, it was turned into an enterprise by the company when it began selling T-shirts and mugs and that led to an exchange of letters between the company and Mother Teresa's representatives, however on 25 December 2005 the bun was stolen during a break-in at the coffee house.

On April 30, 2002 the Hubble Space Science Institute released new photographs of the Cone Nebula, also known as the Space Mountain, to showcase a new extremely high resolution camera. The Nebula, located in the constellation Monoceros, is a region which contains cones, pillars and the majestic flowing shapes which abound in stellar nurseries where natal clouds of gas and dust are buffeted by energetic winds from nurseries of newborn stars, and shortly afterwards credulous people who believed they could see Jesus' face in it began to refer to it as the "Jesus Nebula."

Such "sightings" are not exclusive to Christianity. In the Muslim community a frequently reported religious perception is the image of the word "Allah" in Arabic on natural objects and once again the discovery of such an object may attract considerable interest among believers who visit it for the purpose of prayer or veneration. Examples of this phenomenon have been reported on fish, fruit, vegetables, plants, clouds, eggs, honeycombs and on the markings on animals' coats. The Arabic script for the name of Allah is also purported to be visible in a satellite photograph of the 2004 Asian Tsunami and this was taken as evidence by some Muslims that Allah had sent the tsunami as punishment.

Several Hindu "murtis" (an image that expresses a divine spirit) are held to be "swayambhu" (self-manifested) and most are representations of Shiva. In Jurong West New Town, Singapore in September of 2007 the discovery of calluses on a tree which look like the Hanuman, the monkey deity in the Hindu pantheon, created a social phenomenon because there are two nearby trees which also resemble deities with one featuring an apparent outline of goddess of mercy Guan Yin and another resembling the Hindu elephant god Ganesh.

In some cases apparent religious images have been deliberately created from natural materials as part of an artistic endeavor or investigation into the phenomenon of perceptions of religious imagery. For example the "Pope Tart" was a hoax apparition created by Karen Stollznow in 2005 as part of an investigation into pareidolia for *The Skeptic* in Australia and in other cases these deliberate images have been commercial ventures such as the "Jesus Toaster" and "Virgin Mary Toaster" created by Galen Dively in 2010 which create images of Jesus and Mary on bread.

Getting back to Christian icons, Our Lady of Watsonville is a one-foot-high image of the Virgin Mary seen in the bark of an oak tree in Watsonville, California which was first seen by a woman named Anita Contreras. On June 17, 1993 the Virgin is claimed to have appeared while Contreras knelt to pray for her children and since then thousands of pilgrims have flocked to the site hoping for a miracle. Mary is of course venerated by many Roman Catholics as the mother of a god and Mexicans have been especially fond of her (Watsonville is about 62% Mexican-American) since her apparent apparition in 1531 to Cuauhtlatoatzin, a Nahuan peasant and Christian convert who took on the name of Juan Diego.

The story of Our Lady of Guadalupe is a bit more dramatic than that of Our Lady of Watsonville. Legend has it Juan Diego was a bit of an ascetic mystic who frequently walked the fourteen miles from his village to church in Tenochtitlan (Mexico City) while barefoot. It was on these walks that he had several visions of the Virgin Mary and he allegedly brought to the bishop his cloak on which an image of the Virgin had been painted. Legend has it the image was accompanied by roses which were out of season and which skeptics had asked Juan to have the Virgin produce as proof of his claim she had appeared to him. Many believe the painting is of heavenly origin, but quite reasonably skeptics believe the cloak was made by a human artist and passed off as being of miraculous origin in order to win more converts to Christianity.

The name "Guadalupe" is Spanish and a bit mysterious since there was no town or shrine near Juan's village of Cuauhtitlan by that name when the legend began. It is thought the word derives from the Nahuatl word “coatlaxopeuh” which supposedly sounds like Guadalupe in Spanish and means something like “one who crushes the serpent” since a serpent can be identified with Satan or the Aztec serpent-god Quetzalcoatl. It is also possible the legend has Juan saying the Virgin was to be called Our Lady of Guadalupe because the one who invented it was Spanish or the creator of the name may have been intrigued by a statue of Our Lady of Guadalupe in Estremadura, Spain. In any case it is easy to understand how a mystical Indian could become enchanted with Christianity since not only did the new religion abound in stories of the miraculous but the Spanish Christians had put an end to the Aztec empire, and remember the Aztecs had conquered the Nahuatl and perhaps even sacrificed a few of Juan’s relatives to the hungry gods.

In 1556 a formal investigation found the image had been painted by an Aztec artist named Marcos (Cipas de Aquino) and examinations have found good evidence it was painted on the cloth. For example infrared photographs show the hands have been modified and pigment has been heavily applied to the highlight areas of the face so as to obscure the texture of the cloth. There is also obvious cracking and flaking of paint all along a vertical seam and infrared photos reveal in the robe’s fold what appear to be sketch lines, suggesting an artist roughed out the figure before painting it. Portrait artist Glenn Taylor pointed out the part in the Virgin’s hair is off-center, her eyes (including the irises) have outlines as they often do in paintings but not in nature, these outlines appear to have been done with a brush and much other evidence suggests the picture was probably copied by an inexpert artist from an expertly done original. In 2002 a report on a secret study of the Image of Guadalupe was published and in it José Sol Rosales, an art restoration expert, found the cloth “appeared to be a mixture of linen and hemp or cactus fiber” which had been primed with calcium sulfate and the paint used to produce the image consisted of the rather earthly combination of pigment, water and a binding medium.

The improbability of the story of Juan Diego - some doubt his very existence in part because the name Juan Diego essentially translates as John Doe, i.e. a generic everyman whose identity is unimportant - his visions and the miraculous painting has not deterred the faithful from belief. In fact only a deep religious faith could account for the continued popularity of Virgin Mary sightings. The skeptic understands the desire to have a powerful ally in Heaven, one who will protect and guide, console and love you no matter what troubles you have here on Earth, and also understands how easy it is to find confirmation for almost any belief if one is very selective in their thinking and perception. We understand how easy it is to see things others do not see. Having visions also makes one feel special, thus it is not difficult to understand how many people "see" the Virgin Mary in the clouds, in a tortilla, in a dish of spaghetti, in patterns of light and in the bark of a tree.

The cult of the Virgin Mary probably has its roots in goddess worship, which has its roots in the desire for a Good Mother - one who loves, nourishes, protects, guides, comforts and encourages. The Virgin is pure, clean, generous with her time and infinitely patient, unlike so many people one meets. She is often the harbinger of peace. The Mother gives birth and through sympathetic magic brings fertility to the crops and the tribe. The Virgin Mary is the mother of Jesus who is believed by many to be god, making her the mother of a god even though this god is eternal and has no beginning. She is also said to have been impregnated by the holy spirit rather than by her husband Joseph. She is not divine according to the Catholic Church but her devotees certainly seem to view her as a goddess.

As for Our Lady of Watsonville, a shrine was set up near the soccer fields and playgrounds of Pinto Lake County Park and Father Roman Bunda celebrated Mass at the site on the sixth anniversary of Contreras' discovery of the image in the bark. "For those who believe no explanation is necessary," said Father Bunda, citing a well-worn apologetic, "and for those who don't believe no explanation is possible." He was right about the first part. The question is for what purpose would Jesus and Mary appear in tree bark and on grilled cheese? Even if they existed, how can anyone possibly know what they look like? Why are there so many graven images in the form of statues, icons and crucifixes?

Philosopher David Hume has observed, "There is a universal subconscious tendency among mankind to conceive all beings as being like themselves and to transfer to every object those qualities with which they are familiarly acquainted and of which they are intimately conscious. We find human faces in the moon, armies in the clouds and by a natural propensity, if not corrected by experience and reflection, ascribe malice or goodwill to everything that hurts or pleases us."

Far from being simply the opinion of Hume, this phenomenon is known as "pareidolia" and is defined as a type of illusion or misperception involving a vague or obscure stimulus being perceived as something clear and distinct. For example in the discolorations of a burnt tortilla one might see the face of Jesus or see the image of Mother Teresa or Ronald Reagan in a cinnamon bun or even a man in the moon. Under clinical circumstances some psychologists even encourage pareidolia as a means to understanding a patient, e.g. the Rorschach ink blot test.

Under ordinary circumstances pareidolia provides a psychological explanation for many delusions based upon sensory perception. For example it explains many UFO sightings as well as hearing sinister messages on records played backwards. It also explains sightings of Elvis, Bigfoot, the Loch Ness Monster, numerous religious apparitions and visions and explains why some people see a face or building in a photograph of the Cydonia region of Mars.

Astronomer Carl Sagan explained the human tendency to see faces in tortillas, clouds, cinnamon buns and the like is an evolutionary trait writing, "As soon as the infant can see it recognizes faces, and we now know that this skill is hardwired in our brains. Those infants who a million years ago were unable to recognize a face smiled back less, were less likely to win the hearts of their parents and less likely to prosper. These days, nearly every infant is quick to identify a human face and to respond with a goofy grin."

Sagan is right about the tendency to recognize faces but I don't see any reason to think there is an evolutionary advantage in seeing replicas of paintings, ghosts, demons and the like in inanimate objects. There is of course an evolutionary advantage in seeing images of dinner or predators against a varied environmental background but there would be no advantage for a hawk to be dive-bombing shadows on rocks. It seems likely the modern mind is making associations with shapes, lines, shadows and the like which are connected to current desires, interests, hopes and obsessions.

Most people recognize illusions for what they are but some become fixated on the reality of their perception and turn an illusion into a delusion. A little bit of critical thinking, however, should convince most reasonable people that a potato which looks like the Hindu god Ganesh, a cinnamon bun which looks like Mother Teresa or a burnt area on a tortilla which looks like Jesus are accidents and without significance. Employing Occam's Razor it is obviously far more likely the "Virgin Mary" someone sees in the reflection of a mirror or on the floor of an apartment complex or up in the clouds has been generated by their own imagination than it is a person who has been dead for two thousand years manifesting herself in such a mundane and useless fashion.

So why do people continue to believe in such things? According to Dr. Martina Belz-Merk, "There is currently a controversial debate concerning whether unusual experiences are symptoms of a mental disorder, if mental disorders are a consequence of such experiences or if people with mental disorders are especially susceptible to or even looking for these experiences."

Another explanation is "Aophenia" which is the spontaneous perception of connections between, and the meaningfulness of, unrelated phenomena. For example soon after his son committed suicide Episcopalian Bishop James A. Pike began seeing what he considered to be meaningful messages in such things as a stopped clock, the angle of an open safety pin and the angle formed by two postcards lying on the floor. He thought they were conveying the time his son had shot himself.

Peter Brugger of the Department of Neurology at University Hospital in Zurich gave other examples of apophenia from August Strindberg's *Occult Diary*, which is the playwright's own account of his psychotic break. In it he saw "two insignia of witches, the goat's horn and the besom" in a rock and wondered "what demon it was who had put (them)... just there and in my way on this particular morning." A building then looked like an oven and he thought of *Dante's Inferno*. He observed sticks on the ground and saw them as forming Greek letters which he interpreted to be the abbreviation of a man's name and felt he now knew this was the man persecuting him. He saw sticks on the bottom of a chest and was sure they formed a pentagram. He saw tiny hands in prayer when he looked at a walnut under a microscope and it "filled him with horror." His crumpled pillow looked "like a marble head in the style of Michelangelo." Strindberg commented that "these occurrences could not be regarded as accidental, for on some days the pillow presented the appearance of horrible monsters, of gothic gargoyles, of dragons and one night... I was greeted by the Evil One himself..."

According to Brugger, "The propensity to see connections between seemingly unrelated objects or ideas most closely links psychosis to creativity... apophenia and creativity may even be seen as two sides of the same coin." Some of the most creative people in the world must then be psychoanalysts and therapists who use projective tests like the Rorschach test or who see patterns of child abuse behind every emotional problem. Brugger noted that one analyst thought he had support for the "penis envy theory" because more females than males failed to return their pencils after a test. Another spent nine pages in a prestigious journal describing how sidewalk cracks are vaginas and feet are penises and the old saw about not stepping on cracks is actually a warning to stay away from the female sex organ.

Brugger's research indicates high levels of dopamine affect the propensity to find meaning, patterns and significance where there is none and this propensity is related to a tendency to believe in the paranormal. In statistics apophenia is called a Type I error, i.e. seeing patterns where none in fact exist. The apparent significance of many unusual experiences and phenomena are due to apophenia such as ghosts and hauntings, Electronic Voice Phenomenon, numerology, the Bible code, anomalous cognition, ganzfeld "hits," most forms of divination, the prophecies of Nostradamus, remote viewing and a host of other paranormal and supernatural experiences and phenomena including many found in Scripture. Those of us who have spent time with a person having a psychotic episode have often been asked to see the significance of such random things as automobile license plate numbers, birth dates and the arrangement of fallen twigs.

The term "apophenia" was coined by Klaus Conrad in 1958 when he published a monograph entitled *Die beginnende Schizophrenie Versuch einer Gestaltanalyse des Wahns* in which he described in groundbreaking detail the prodromal mood and earliest stages of schizophrenia. He used the word "Apophänie" to characterize the onset of delusional thinking in psychosis. This neologism is translated as "apophany" from the Greek apo [away from] and phaenein [to show] to reflect the fact the schizophrenic initially experiences delusion as revelation. In contrast to epiphany however, apophany does not provide insight into the true nature of reality or its interconnectedness but is instead a "process of repetitively and monotonously experiencing abnormal meanings in the entire surrounding experiential field" which are entirely self-referential, solipsistic and paranoid: "Being observed, spoken about, the object of eavesdropping, followed by strangers." In short "apophenia" is a misnomer that has taken on a bastardized meaning never intended by the psychiatrist who coined the neologism "apophany." In the words of British psychologist John Cohen, "Nothing is so alien to the human mind as the idea of randomness," and that view is borne out every time someone thinks they are viewing some sort of religious apparition.

Facing Reality

Or, Breaking the Spell

"For those who believe, no proof is necessary. For those who don't believe, no proof is possible." ~ Christian apologetic of unknown origin

It is hard to argue with a being which is omnipotent, omniscient, eternal, timeless, omnipresent and perfect and yet you have to wonder when something like September 11, 2001 occurs. After all if God can see everything which is happening how can something like that happen? Other examples are the Holocaust where millions died, the December 2004 tsunami where two hundred thousand people died in less than a day and the AIDS epidemic which has killed more than twenty million people in the last twenty-five years. Why doesn't God help these people?

There are smaller, more personal examples as well. For instance it is not uncommon to open the morning newspaper and find a story like one in the *Raleigh News and Observer* about a tragedy which occurred in Wake Forest, North Carolina: "They had driven together lots of times, the old man and the little girl. He picked her up every morning and took her to the brick church where she spent her days. In the afternoon, he came to the door of her classroom in the day-care center and she slipped her hand into his. Then he took her home. It all happened just that way on Monday for Tim Day and Ranika Clifton, and so it resumed on Tuesday until about 7:30 a.m., when a tragic forgetfulness seized control. Day, a quiet sixty-three-year-old retiree from Maryland, left Ranika, age two, belted into her car seat in a Ford Econoline van at the Corinth United Church of Christ near Wake Forest. Seven hours passed before anyone realized she was missing and when they found her, still in her car seat, she was dead."

Think about how this innocent little girl suffered and died in the church van which was sitting under God's sun in a church parking lot, strapped in her car seat and unable to escape. The temperature in the van rose rapidly. She screamed and cried but no one heard her. Saving Ranika should have been easy. God could have made Mr. Day less forgetful, caused someone in the day care center to notice Ranika's absence, sent clouds and rain to keep the van cool, sent an angel to roll down a window or caused Ranika's mother to stop by the school. God had a million options but he did not do any of these things. Why? Neva Rogers getting shot in the head, Steve Homel's thirty-nine neighbors losing everything they owned, the nineteen Hotshots burning to death and Jessica Lunsford being raped and buried alive didn't seem right and now a little two-year-old is baking to death in a church parking lot. It is easy to offer a platitude such as "it must be God's will" or "it is all part of God's plan" but what do those things actually mean? What if God plans to shoot you in the head tomorrow? What if he plans to bake your child to death or allow her to be raped and murdered? What if he plans to burn your home to the ground? What good is it to pray if that is what will happen anyway? The paradox of God can be perplexing because when we look at these cases only a blind person cannot see the reality but as Thomas Paine once wrote, "To argue with a person who has renounced the use of reason is like administering medicine to the dead." If the truth is so obvious why do so many people continue to profess belief? The answers are fear, indoctrination and our hard wired herd mentality. The human psyche is a fragile thing indeed and as a species we are not yet as advanced as we would like to believe.

It's truly amazing there are as many atheists in the world as there are when you consider the brainwashing process our children undergo. Baptism, church on Sundays, Catechism, Bible camps, televangelists, etc. Religion is everywhere you look. Atheists, on the other hand, are not subjected to a constant bombardment of dogma and societal pressure. Instead they tend to think for themselves and arrive at their own conclusions.

Several thinkers have offered reasons why people are believers. Marx argued religion is a numbing drug which the rich and powerful use to manipulate the common person. Freud reasoned that people believe because of a longing desire for a heavenly father figure. Nietzsche contended religion is for weak people who feel the need for purpose. These are psychologically based reasons for why someone may believe, since the mind is impressionable and we have a tendency to believe what we are first taught and will often continue to think that it's correct for life, so even smart people can find reasons to continue believing when the evidence is counter to what they believe.

From my own experience and that of nearly every believer I know this is the case. Someone you liked, cared for and/or trusted told you about Jesus and his resurrection or the process of reincarnation or the five Pillars of Islam. After all nobody would develop such ideas in a vacuum.

In my case I had never heard anything different. Everyone who ever talked to me about such things believed or at least said they did. The people who told you about Jesus or Allah or Vishnu were believable and/or in a position of authority and pointed you to some books which confirmed what they were telling you. In the case of Christians, and I am primarily addressing them now because that is the prevalent belief system in the United States, the Bible tells the story of a God who loves you so much he became a man and "died" so you could be forgiven. The gospel offers you hope, forgiveness, peace and a relationship and things happen which appear to confirm God answers your prayers, although people who regularly read their daily Horoscopes claim they are accurate too. Then you got involved in a community of believers who encouraged you and suggested other books to read which further confirmed your faith and by this point you had adopted a set of control beliefs which subsequently filtered all of the evidence you were presented. On top of that you want it to be true, you want to be immortal and you are comforted by the belief you will be spared from Hell when you die.

You believed prior to examining any evidence because someone you trusted told you that story, but they neglected to tell you of the ugliness to be found elsewhere in Scripture. In fact there is an excellent chance they were unaware of it themselves since most people only have a cursory and sanitized knowledge of the Bible. You believe based upon what someone you trusted told you and that probably explains why you are in the denomination you are presently in although it is possible you might be in one because of something you read on your own, but this is merely changing rooms in the same house. The person who introduced you to your religion most likely came to believe for the very same reasons. This chain of one person passing on a story to the next generation stretches back to the 1st Century and is the root of the enculturation process discussed at the beginning of this book, and as we go back into the superstitious past we find people have long believed in lots of divinities and miracles based upon no evidence at all.

You're afraid to doubt so you look for ways to confirm your beliefs are true and can be historically verified, and even though history cannot verify such things you read books which seem to confirm them and find they can be justified if you look at them in just the right way - but how many times when you doubt will you read what a skeptic writes? Not many Christians have sufficient faith to do this. Instead, if they are having doubts, they'll turn to the trusted writings of a Christian apologist. Few will bother to read books like this one because they "know" in advance what I'm arguing is false or "of the devil" or willfully in denial of the "gospel truth." Christians don't trust themselves to learn about such things. When they read what people like me say they usually only do so to prove us wrong because they have decided in advance that we are. As James Burnham wrote in *Suicide Of The West,* "An ideologue - one who thinks ideologically - cannot lose because his answer, his interpretation and his attitude have been determined in advance of the particular experience or observation. They are derived from the ideology, and not subject to the facts."

For example when it comes to the resurrection Christians think the evidence shows Jesus arose because they are predisposed to believe it. They likewise overlook the logical and empirical evidence against religion in general and the Christian faith in particular and are just the latest to do so since human beings have been worshipping a wide variety of gods for thousands of years. As I mentioned at the beginning it is not coincidental that religions happen to dominate certain geographic locations and cultures and it seems reasonable to assume people adopt a religion because it is part of the culture of the geographic region they are from. In India most people are Hindu and in the Middle East most are Muslim, although some Christians claim Islam is a state-imposed religion but it is a stretch to assume most Muslims only believe what they do as a result of coercion. In South America most people are Roman Catholic and in the U.S. there is a close split between Roman Catholics and Protestants but even these are largely geographical in nature. Christians might even agree with this to some degree except of course in regard to their own beliefs. It doesn't seem unreasonable to assume a person is Hindu simply because they grew up in a country filled with Hindus but I'm sure many true believers will say these people have rejected the Christian god because they have been deceived or love their sin and have adopted that religion to justify their rebellion or for some other reason, but it is more reasonable to conclude they adopted a particular belief because it is or was the popular religion of that geographic location. This is obvious to the objective observer.

Religion is divisive in many ways, but what if the human race was to begin *uniting* in an effort to make our world a better place? There would be many benefits to our society becoming more rational rather than religious, but how do we make the transition? It is no simple task to change something which has been the status quo for thousands of years. Slaves were once common but the practice of slavery has all but disappeared in the civilized world. There once was a time in America when no woman could vote and yet they all have that right today. A large majority of Americans once smoked cigarettes and it was allowed virtually everywhere and yet today smoking is banned in most public spaces. Gays have traditionally found it necessary to hide in the closet but that is no longer the case. Those changes marked tectonic shifts in public thinking and all had to start somewhere. There came a point where a group of people in the minority said "this is wrong and we need to fix it" and began openly talking about the problem. Then the minority coalesced, began to influence those on the outer edges of the majority and once that process began and gained sufficient momentum people came to their senses and the majority lost its dominance.

Can we have the same sort of effect on religion? The idea of unseating something so deeply embedded in society sounds ridiculous at first blush but when women first started talking about gaining the right to vote that sounded ridiculous too. We have to start somewhere. The way to change the world is to change people's minds through education. As more and more people openly discuss the facts the world becomes a better place. Many people are closet atheists and you would be shocked by how many there are. The key is to encourage discussion and help each other think rationally. It is amazing how much of an effect discussion can have and if we keep publicly debating the issue we will coalesce the minority, begin changing the majority and religion will eventually fall to rationality due to the immense weight of the evidence.

One of the biggest hurdles is defining what atheism is. As Sam Harris has said, "'Atheism' is a term that should not even exist. No one ever needs to identify himself as a 'non-astrologer' or a 'non-alchemist.' We do not have words for people who doubt Elvis is still alive or aliens have traversed the galaxy only to molest ranchers and their cattle. Atheism is nothing more than the noises reasonable people make in the presence of unjustified religious beliefs." That is quite true but even so the term does exist so we are forced to examine what an atheist or agnostic is within the context of our society. Stanford University computer and cognitive scientist John McCarthy put a somewhat humorous spin on that question when he said, "Put simply, an atheist doesn't have to be someone who thinks he has a proof there can't be a God. He only has to be someone who believes the evidence on the God question is at a similar level to the evidence on the werewolf question." Previous research and studies focusing on the diverse landscape of belief in America have continually placed those who profess no belief in a God or gods into one unified category known as the "religious nones." It is assumed all non-believers are the same but this "religious none" category fails to accurately capture and reflect the diversity of beliefs or unbelief and even the terms of atheism and agnosticism suffered from a similar lack of description. Many non-believers are concerned with stigmatization from their local community. Others provide quantitative indications of varied outsider perception, much of which is related to issues of equal rights, personal or familial security and the perceptions of loved ones and friends. The following classifications are derived from a dissertation entitled *Atheism, Agnosticism, and Nonbelief: A Qualitative and Quantitative Study of Type and Narrative* by Christopher F. Silver and Thomas J. Coleman III under the auspices of the University of Tennessee.

The first and most frequently discussed type is what could be termed the Intellectual Atheist/Agnostic. It includes individuals who proactively seek to educate themselves through intellectual association and acquire knowledge on various topics relating to ontology (the search for truth) and non-belief. They enjoy dialectic enterprises such as healthy democratic debate and discussions and are intrinsically motivated to do so. These individuals are typically well-versed in a variety of writings on belief and non-belief and are prone to cite these authors in discussions. They associate with fellow intellectuals regardless of the other's ontological position as long as the associate is versed and educated on various issues of science, philosophy, "rational" theology and common socio-political religious dialogue. They may enjoy discussing the epistemological positions related to the existence or non-existence of a deity and typically engage in electronic forms of intellectualism but oftentimes also belong to groups which meet face to face offline such as various skeptic, rationalist and freethinking groups for similar mentally stimulating discussions and interaction.

The next typology relates to being socially active and these individuals are termed the Activist Atheist/Agnostic. These individuals are not content with the placidity of simply holding a non-belief position and seek to be both vocal and proactive regarding current issues in the atheist and/or agnostic socio-political sphere. Their activism can be as minimal as the education of friends or others to much larger manifestations of social activities such as boycotting products, promoting legal action or marching in public demonstrations to raise awareness. Activist Atheists/Agnostics are commonly naturalistic or humanistic minded individuals but are not limited to these types of ethical concerns. They are not idle and effectuate their interests and beliefs.

The third typological characteristic is the Seeker-Agnostic who is an individual attuned to the metaphysical possibilities precluding abstract existence or at least who recognizes the philosophical difficulties and complexities in making personal affirmations regarding ideological beliefs. They may call themselves agnostic or agnostic-atheist as they simply cannot be sure of the existence of God or the divine and keep an open mind in relation to the debate between the religious, spiritual and antitheist elements within society. Seeker-Agnostics recognize the limitation of human knowledge and experience and actively search for and respond to knowledge and evidence supporting or disconfirming truth claims. Seeker-Agnostics do not hold a firm ideological position but always search for the scientifically wondrous and experientially profound confirmation of life's meaning. The diversity of others is accepted and co-existence is not only possible but welcomed. Their worldly outlook may be mediated by science, however they recognize current scientific limitations and embrace scientific uncertainty. They are comfortable with this uncertainty and even enjoy discussing it. Some Intellectual Atheist/Agnostics or Anti-Theists may accuse the Seeker-Agnostic of avoiding responsibility or commitment to a more solid affirmation of atheism while in other cases outsiders may see it as an ontological transitional state from religion or spirituality to atheism. In some cases Seeker-Agnostics may generally miss being a believer either because of the social benefits or the emotional connection they have with others such as friends or family. At times their intellectual disagreement with their former theology causes some cognitive dissonance and it is possible they may continue to identity as a religious or spiritual individual.

The fourth typology and one of the more assertive is the Anti-Theist. While the Anti-Theists may be considered atheist or in some cases labeled as "new atheists" they are diametrically opposed to religious ideology and as such the assertive Anti-Theist both proactively and aggressively asserts their views towards others when appropriate in an effort to educate theists in the passé nature of belief and theology. In other words Anti-Theists view religion as ignorance and see any individual or institution associated with it as backward and socially detrimental. They view the logical fallacies of religion as an outdated worldview which is not only detrimental to social cohesion and peace but also to technological advancement and civilized evolution as a whole and are compelled to share their view and try to educate others into their ideological position whenever the opportunity arises. Some Anti-Theist individuals feel compelled to work against the institution of religion in its various forms including social, political and ideological aspects while others may assert their view with religious persons on an individual basis. The Anti-Theist believes the obvious fallacies in religion and belief should be aggressively addressed in some form or another.

The fifth typology is termed the Non-Theist and not many individuals self-identify as this type. For the Non-Theist the alignment of oneself with religion, or conversely an epistemological position against religion, can appear quite unconventional from their perspective however a couple of terms which may best capture their sentiments are apathetic and disinterested. The Non-Theist is non-active in terms of involving themselves in social or intellectual pursuits having to do with religion or anti-religion because religion plays no role or issue in their consciousness or worldview and that includes the atheist/agnostic movement. They are not interested in any type of secularist agenda and simply do not care. Simply put Non-Theist's are apathetic non-believers. They simply do not believe and their absence of faith means the absence of anything having to do with religion in any form.

The sixth and final type, one of the most interesting and unexpected, is termed the Ritual Atheist/Agnostic. They hold no belief in God or the divine or at least tend to believe it is unlikely there is an afterlife or a God. They are open about their lack of belief and may educate themselves on the various aspects of belief by others. One of the defining characteristics is they may find utility in the teachings of some religious traditions but see these as more or less philosophical lessons of how to live life and achieve happiness rather than a path to transcendental liberation. Ritual Atheist/Agnostics find value in tradition and ritual, for example these individuals may participate in specific ceremonies, musical opportunities, meditation, yoga classes or holiday traditions and such participation may be related to an ethnic identity (i.e. Jewish) or the perceived utility of such practices in making the individual a better person. Many times the Ritual Atheist/Agnostic may be misidentified as spiritual but not religious but they are quick to point out they are atheist or agnostic in relation to their own ontological view although they may have respect for the profound symbolism inherent within various rites.

As discrimination and prejudice against non-believers is rampant the world over and throughout America in particular there is little doubt many atheists reading this have experienced those things on a personal level. They may have had to dispel stereotypical assumptions from friends, family and acquaintances ranging from "all atheists are angry and argumentative" to "all you heathens are just as dogmatic as religious people." So are all atheists angry, argumentative and dogmatic? Absolutely not, however if any subset fits that stereotype it is the Anti-Theist. If prejudice continues to exist towards atheists in general one reason may be the perceived negative experiences by religious people interacting with a very small sub-segment of the overall population of non-believers, once again mainly the Anti-Theists. In other words research has showed over eighty-five percent of non-believers sampled to be more or less your average Joe when it came to being angry, argumentative and dogmatic which falls right in line with current societal norms. It is also important to recognize this vignette does not mean some Anti-Theists don't have a right to be any of these things or they are not proper psychological responses when recontextualized in light of their life experiences to date. For example many have recently deconverted from religious belief or are socially displeased with the status quo which stigmatizes non-believers, especially in tension-based geographies such as the Southeastern United States. If you can imagine being a recent deconvert from a religious tradition, many times a very conservative one, to atheism it may be easy to see how and why this small segment is and perhaps deserves to be angry and argumentative after having previously accepted a worldview at odds with their current beliefs or lack thereof.

Religion is more than anything a matter of psychology and what better qualified and respected source of analysis is there than the father of psychoanalysis himself, Sigmund Freud? Freud was born to Jewish parents in the heavily Roman Catholic town of Freiburg, Moravia, throughout his life endeavored to understand religion and spirituality and in fact wrote several books devoted to the subject including *Totem and Taboo* (1913), *The Future of an Illusion* (1927), *Civilization and Its Discontents* (1930) and *Moses and Monotheism* (1938). He believed religion was an expression of underlying psychological neuroses and distress and at various points in his writings suggested it was an attempt to control the Oedipal complex, in other words it is a means of giving structure to social groups as well as of wish fulfillment, an infantile delusion and an attempt to control the outside world.

In *New Introductory Lectures on Psychoanalysis* he made the very succinct and insightful statement, "Religion is an illusion and it derives its strength from the fact that it falls in with our instinctual desires," and in *Moses and Monotheism* wrote, "Religion is an attempt to get control over the sensory world, in which we are placed, by means of the wish-world, which we have developed inside us as a result of biological and psychological necessities... if one attempts to assign to religion its place in man's evolution, it seems not so much to be a lasting acquisition, as a parallel to the neurosis which the civilized individual must pass through on his way from childhood to maturity."

Freud asserted dogmatic religious training contributes to a weakness of intellect by foreclosing lines of inquiry. In *Civilization and Its Discontents* he wrote, "The whole thing is so patently infantile, so foreign to reality, that to anyone with a friendly attitude to humanity it is painful to think that the great majority of mortals will never be able to rise above this view of life. It is still more humiliating to discover how a large number of people living today, who cannot but see that this religion is not tenable, nevertheless try to defend it piece by piece in a series of pitiful rearguard actions," but he concluded hopefully, "in the long run nothing can withstand reason and experience, and the contradiction which religion offers to both is all too palpable." The book further expressed Freud's "...hope that in the future science will go beyond religion, and reason will replace faith in God." Of course that is not easy for many people, for in many ways it is much like kicking a drug habit.

This book began with a discussion about how believers of every stripe co-opt the word "truth." Atheism is not a choice between either accepting or rejecting God as so many theists argue, it is a decision about what is most likely real and what is not. Truth be told many atheists wish theists were right and there were such things as eternal life and a perfect Heaven to look forward to but wishing for something does not make it true. One of the most difficult things for people to do in any aspect of life is argue against something they desire so unbelievers are to be applauded for their intellectual honesty rather than vilified for their lack of credulity. Pulitzer Prize winning astronomer Carl Sagan summed this up quite well when he said, "I would love to believe that when I die I will live again, that some thinking, feeling, remembering part of me will continue. But as much as I want to believe that, I know of nothing to suggest it is more than wishful thinking." I too would love to believe I'll see my parents again and we can all spend eternity in a perfect place filled with love and angels and believe me if there were any proof I'd be happy to accept it, but wanting something doesn't make it so. The reason people are so easily taken in by faith healers and miracle diets and get rich quick schemes is simple psychology. People want these things to be true so badly they allow themselves to be duped, but just because millions of people share the same delusion doesn't make it true.

For a very long time non-believers held their collective tongues out of fear, first of torture and execution and more recently of vilification and ostracization, but we are now in the throes of a major philosophical shift. For example in 2002 an Eagle Scout named Darrell Lambert was threatened with expulsion from the Boy Scouts despite his having earned dozens of merit badges and having held literally every leadership position in his troop. His crime? He was an outspoken atheist. When the news of his beliefs, or rather lack of them, reached scouting officials they demanded he change his mind. He was given a week to think it over and all he had to do was lie but he reasoned if he did that, "I wouldn't be a good Scout then, would I?" So for his honesty he was kicked out of the organization he'd devoted his young life to.

In New Jersey in 2006 a public high school teacher named David Paskiewicz was openly preaching Christianity in the classroom, advocating creationism and telling a Muslim student she would burn in Hell if she didn't convert, so a junior named Matt LaClair reported this illegal government preaching to the school administration. In a subsequent meeting with the principal Paskiewicz denied everything, whereupon LaClair produced audio recordings of him saying the things he had specifically denied having said. Apparently he had no problem with lying, unlike Darrell Lambert.

In Indiana in 2009 the senior class at a public school was asked to vote on whether to have a prayer as part of their graduation ceremony. A senior named Eric Workman, knowing full well school-sponsored prayer is illegal even if a majority votes for it, filed a lawsuit and won an injunction. The school administration responded by announcing it would not review graduation speeches in advance, clearly in the hope some student would use the opportunity to say the very same prayer, but the class valedictorian happened to be none other than the aforementioned Eric Workman and he used his graduation speech to explain why the school's actions were unconstitutional along with the importance of the First Amendment.

In South Carolina a graduating senior named Harrison Hopkins put a stop to school prayer with help from the Freedom From Religion Foundation, in Louisiana a senior named Damon Fowler fought against similar school-sponsored prayers at his graduation and in Rhode Island a sophomore named Jessica Ahlquist led the fight to have an illegal school prayer banner removed from her school's auditorium. The opinion of the Wisconsin Supreme Court in Weiss vs. District Board, which unanimously determined Bible reading in public schools to be unconstitutional, read in part "...there is no such source and cause of strife, quarrel, fights, malignant opposition, persecution and war, and all evil in the state, as religion. Let it once enter into our civil affairs, our government would soon be destroyed... those who made our Constitution saw this, and used the most apt and comprehensive language in it to prevent such a catastrophe."

Despite this growing trend there is unfortunately still a hostile, prejudiced religious majority which has tried to silence those who advocate the separation of church and state with bullying, persecution and harassment. For instance when Ellery Schempp prevailed in a landmark First Amendment case against school-sponsored Bible reading his principal wrote to the colleges he had applied to and asked them not to admit him out of pure spite, but fortunately it didn't work and Schempp was accepted to Tufts University, graduated with honors and became a scientist. Likewise when Jim McCollum and his mother Vashti challenged their school over a "released-time program" way back in 1945 raving bigots assaulted him, got her fired from her job, pelted their home with rotten fruit and killed their cat - but the McCollums didn't relent and won a precedent setting Supreme Court decision striking down religious instruction on public school time. Despite that ruling sixty years later a young man named Damon Fowler was demeaned by a teacher and disowned by his own parents for opposing prayer at his graduation but fortunately wasn't left to face the mob alone as had been the case with Jim McCollum because today there is a thriving, growing secular community which is capable of looking out for its own - so when Fowler was kicked out of his house a fundraiser netted enough money to pay his living expenses and college tuition. In fact the Secular Student Alliance, a national organization which supports student atheist and free-thought clubs, is growing by leaps and bounds in colleges and high schools and this is important because it's much easier to resist peer pressure if you have likeminded people standing with you.

All of these individual stories add up to a much larger picture which is confirmed by statistical evidence, namely Americans are becoming less religious with rates of atheism and secularism increasing exponentially in each new generation. This demographic transformation has been in progress ever since World War II but in recent years it has begun to seriously pick up steam. In the generation born since 1982 - variously referred to as Generation Y, the Millennials or Generation Next - one in five people identify as nonreligious, atheist or agnostic. In the youngest cohort the trend is even more dramatic with as many as thirty percent of those born since 1990 being nonbelievers and a study by a Christian polling firm found people are leaving Christianity at four times the rate new members are joining. What could be causing this generational shift? There are multiple reasons such as a changing moral landscape in the areas of homosexuality, birth control, women's rights and interracial relationships but in a society which is becoming increasingly tolerant and enlightened the big churches remain stubbornly entrenched in the past, clinging to medieval dogmas about gay people and women, presuming to lecture their members about how they should vote, whom they should love and how they should live. It's no surprise people who've grown up in this tolerant age find it absurd when they are told their family and friends don't deserve civil rights and it's even less of a surprise that when they're told they must believe such things in order to be good Christians they simply walk away. This trend is reflected in the steadily rising percentages of Americans who say religion is "old-fashioned and out of date" and can't speak to today's social problems.

The Roman Catholic Church in particular has been hit hard. According to a 2009 Pew study called *Faith in Flux* one in ten American adults is a former Catholic and a majority of ex-Catholics cite unhappiness with the church's archaic stances on abortion, homosexuality, birth control and/or the treatment of women as major factors in their departure. Evangelical and other Protestant denominations are feeling the same sting. According to a survey by sociologists Robert Putnam and David Campbell moderates and progressives are heading for the exits as the churches increasingly become the domain of conservatives. From the early 1970s to the late 1980s the fraction of Americans age eighteen to twenty-nine who identified with evangelical Protestantism rose to twenty-five percent from twenty percent but since 1990 that fraction has fallen back to about seventeen percent. Today an unprecedented seventeen percent of Americans say they have no religion and are heavily concentrated among Americans who have come of age since 1990 with between twenty-five and thirty percent of twenty-somethings saying they have no religious affiliation. That is roughly four times higher than any previous generation.

What all this means is the rise of atheism as a political force is an effect rather than a cause of the churches' hard right turn towards fundamentalism. By obstinately clinging to prejudices and pseudo-sciences which the rest of society is moving beyond they're in the process of making themselves irrelevant. For instance over the last few decades society in general and young people in particular have become increasingly tolerant of gays and other minorities. For the most part this is a predictable result of familiarity as people who've grown up in an increasingly multicultural society see less of a problem with interracial relationships and same-sex marriage and when it comes to issues such as whether gays and lesbians should be protected from job discrimination or allowed to adopt the age gap in support is even more dramatic, but while American society is moving forward on all of these fronts many churches not only refuse to go along, they're actively moving backward. Most large Christian sects, both Catholic and Protestant, have made fighting against gay and women's rights their all-consuming crusade and young people have gotten this message loud and clear. Polls find the most common impressions of Christianity are that it is hostile, judgmental and hypocritical. In particular an incredible ninety-one percent of young non-Christians say Christianity is anti-homosexual and significant majorities say Christians treat being gay as a bigger sin than almost anything else. As bad as that is, Islam is even worse.

On other social issues the gap between Gen-Nexters and the Church looms increasingly wide. For example younger folks favor full access to the morning-after pill by a larger margin than older generations, reject the notion women should return to traditional roles and are by far the least likely of all age groups to say they have old-fashioned values about family and marriage.

Of course Christianity is still by far the largest religious affiliation in America and is likely to remain so for some time but numbers don't lie and the trends of the last several decades show more and more evidence of the same secularizing wave which has already overtaken most countries in Europe. The major churches, clinging to the inferior morality and pseudo-science of long-gone ages, are increasingly out of step with a world which is more enlightened, rational and tolerant than it once was and the more they dig in their heels and adopt a bunker mentality the more we can expect this process to accelerate. One very real danger is an influx of Islam to fill the void as is occurring in Europe, but the same factors should apply to that religion as to Christianity.

Like waves lapping against a sandy beach the erosion of religiosity in America is slow to be sure but the outcome is just as inevitable. The more rationalists speak out and the more visible they are the more familiar secularism will become and the more it will be seen as a viable alternative which will encourage more people to either come out of the closet and speak out or reexamine their beliefs. This is exactly what has happened in the gay-rights movement and in a relatively short time being gay has gone from being stigmatized to being accepted and in some respects even fashionable.

Atheism is gradually becoming an accepted worldview and one indicator of that is the way it has been mainstreamed by unapologetic celebrities. It was once professional suicide to admit being an atheist but times have changed. For instance Billy Joel, Jodie Foster, Woody Allen, Lance Armstrong, Kevin Bacon, Barry Manilow, Jack Nicholson, Brad Pitt, Howard Stern, Angelina Jolie, Keanu Reeves, Ray Romano, Diane Keaton, William Shatner, Keira Knightley, George Clooney, Helen Mirren, Emma Thompson and a host of other celebrities who do not believe in a deity now come right out and say so. Comedian Kathy Griffin, a self-described "militant atheist," made her position particularly clear with a controversial Emmy Award acceptance speech in 2007 when she said, "A lot of people come up here and they thank Jesus for this award, but I want you to know that no one had less to do with this award than Jesus. He didn't help me a bit." For a comprehensive list of such people I recommend the book *Celebrities in Hell* by Warren Allen Smith.

The point is not that these people are more intelligent or have more insight into the workings of the universe than the rest of us simply because they are famous but instead that in the not too distant past they would have been forced to conceal their lack of belief in order to have successful careers and their emergence shows the average person it is okay to come out of the closet and not fear being ostracized.

Religious-themed prime time television shows such as *Highway to Heaven* and *Touched by an Angel* have now given way to wildly popular shows like *House, The Mentalist, The Big Bang Theory* and *Bones* which feature uncommonly intelligent leading characters who just happen to be atheists. When you factor in science-based shows such as *Cosmos* and *Through the Wormhole* as counter balances to the archaic *700 Club* it is clear in which direction things are moving.

A list of the nations which have the largest proportion of atheists may be surprising to some. The top ten (actually eleven since four nations tied) in order of most non-believing are China, Japan, Czech Republic, France, South Korea, Germany, Netherlands, Austria, Iceland, Australia and Ireland. On the flip side, the world's most religious countries are also worth examining with Ghana, Nigeria, Armenia, Fiji, Macedonia, Romania and Iraq heading the list. Examine that list and think about which sorts of societies are religious, and why.

Many former communist nations saw their populations eagerly run back to forbidden religions as soon as they were free to do so, demonstrating the least effective way to spread atheism is by mandate. The Czech Republic hasn't seen any such return to religion however, with only twenty-one percent of its citizens considering religion an important part of their daily lives. Unlike most Eastern European nations that nation rates high on the United Nation's Human Development Report and hasn't been riddled by the corruption and authoritarian attitudes which dominate other former communist nations such as Russia. A mountain of evidence demonstrates that stable, egalitarian economies correlate strongly with higher rates of atheism and it seems the government's demonstration of faith in its people and commitment to their well-being has gone a long way towards keeping the citizens from rekindling religious faith.

In Sweden and Denmark only seventeen and eighteen percent respectively of the population consider religion important and these nations have become icons of secularist values to the rest of the world. Phil Zuckerman, a sociologist from Pitzer College, spent a little more than a year talking to citizens to find out why and discovered the average Danish or Swedish citizen simply doesn't think much about faith and in these two cultures religion has largely been relegated to a ceremonial role.

Even though France still has a heavy layer of Catholic tradition in its culture which puts the names of saints on street signs and venerates churches such as Notre Dame as some of its most important landmarks, secularism has become a strong national value there. As with the United States, erecting a separation between church and state was a central value to the revolution which created the modern democratic state in France and in 1905 France passed a strong law mandating a strict separation of church and state. Today only twenty-five percent of French citizens consider religion an important part of their daily life and the government there has laws to prevent proselytizing in schools.

There's also a strong correlation between the happiest countries in the world and the least religious and Norway rates at the top of both lists along with Sweden and Denmark. Atheism flourishes in nations where people demonstrate high levels of commitment towards a socially just government and shared economic benefits. Norway cemented its relationship with secular values in 2014 by eliminating the Lutheran church as the official state church and aligning the law with the culture with no one in Parliament resisting the change.

In politics the belief that the electorate won't support an atheist is an article of faith stronger than faith in any God, but in Australia that wisdom fell by the wayside with the 2010 election of atheist Prime Minister Julia Gillarda. She not only made it clear she doesn't believe in

God but also called out politicians who make a show of having faith in order to attract voters by saying, "For people of faith, I think the greatest compliment I could pay to them is to respect their genuinely held beliefs and not to engage in some pretense about mine." She also didn't hide the fact her atheism is a result of thinking over the issue as she grew up Christian and even won prizes for Catechism, so the voters in Australia chose a woman who not only doesn't believe in God but came to that conclusion by actively rejecting religion for herself. Secularists even have their own political party there, the Secular Party, which is dedicated to maintaining and strengthening the separation between church and state in Australia.

Like many countries in East Asia, in Japan religion seems to be more a matter of tradition for the Japanese than a true faith which is why only twenty-five percent of Japanese believe religion is an important part of daily life. In a recently released Global Index of Religiosity and Atheism Japan ranked only below China in percentage of committed atheists with thirty-one percent convinced there are no gods of any kind. Unlike China however, Japan's atheism has nothing to do with government policy and Japanese culture has a strong, flexible approach to religious tolerance, with a diversity of religious beliefs.

In Iceland exactly zero percent of respondents in a recent survey said they believe God created the Earth. Only twenty years ago nearly ninety percent of all Icelanders were religious believers but today less than fifty percent are and even among those who are still religious, theories of science are broadly accepted among both young and old. "Secularization has occurred very quickly, especially among younger people," said Bjarni Jonsson, the managing director of the Icelandic Ethical Humanist Association. "With increased education and broad-mindedness, change can occur quickly." As of last year about seventy-five percent of Iceland's inhabitants were registered members of the Evangelical Lutheran Church but that is misleading because a significant number consider themselves to be non-believers or atheists. This is because until 2013 newborn babies were automatically registered with their mother's church and moreover all Icelanders, even atheists, have to pay a tax that is distributed among forty religious institutions including the Evangelical Lutheran Church and that is why until recently there was little reason to bother to officially drop out of the Church - but last year thousands of Icelanders suddenly joined the ancient Zuist movement, which is a religion centered on worshiping Sumerian gods. Within two weeks almost one percent of the country's population had signed up, but some of the new Zuist members might have been less interested in the movement's spiritual goals than the fact the church will pay back to its members the amount of money they were being taxed each year.

In the United States the non-religious now account for more than twenty-two percent of the population and upwards of twelve percent of the electorate and yet "atheist" is still the third rail of American politics. Some groups even refuse to recognize that atheists are American and deserve consideration from the lawmakers elected to represent all constituents, and virtually all of the lawmakers themselves present themselves as believers even though as a matter of demographics that is clearly not the case.

The number of Americans who do not identify with any religion continues to grow at a rapid pace. One-fifth of the U.S. public and a third of adults under thirty are religiously unaffiliated today, the highest percentages ever in Pew Research Center polling. In the last five years alone the unaffiliated have increased from just over fifteen to just under twenty percent of U.S. adults. Their ranks now include more than twenty-two million self-described atheists and agnostics as well as nearly thirty-three million people who say they have no particular religious affiliation.

The growth in the number of religiously unaffiliated Americans, sometimes called the rise of the "nones," is largely driven by generational replacement - the gradual supplanting of older generations by newer ones - since a third of adults under thirty have no religious affiliation compared with just one-in-ten who are sixty-five and older. Young adults today are much more likely to be unaffiliated than previous generations were at a similar stage in their lives. These generational differences are consistent with other signs of a gradual softening of religious commitment among some though by no means all Americans in recent decades. Pew Research Center surveys conducted over the last ten years, for example, find modest growth in the number of people who say they seldom or never attend religious services as well as a declining number who say they never doubt the existence of God.

This report also contains capsule summaries of some leading theories put forward by scholars in an attempt to explain the root causes of the rise of the "nones." These theories run the gamut from a backlash against the entanglement of religion and politics to a global relationship between economic development and secularization. While Pew Research Center surveys are unlikely to settle the debate they may help to rule out some misconceptions about the unaffiliated. For example the surveys show religious affiliation is declining among Americans who do not have college degrees as well as among college graduates which suggests the trend is not solely a result of attitudes toward religion on college campuses. Nor, as the new *Pew Research Center/Religion & Ethics NewsWeekly* survey shows, are the unaffiliated composed largely of religious "seekers" who are looking for a spiritual home and have not found it yet.

Similarly, the percentage of Americans who say they never doubt the existence of God has fallen modestly but noticeably over the past twenty-five years. In 1987 eighty-eight percent of adults surveyed said they never doubted the existence of God but as of 2012 this figure was down eight percentage points to eighty percent. In addition the percentage of Americans who say the Bible should be taken literally has fallen in Gallup polls from thirty-eight percent in the late 1970s and early 1980s to an average of thirty-one percent since.

Even men of the cloth are having their doubts. The Clergy Project, for instance, is a confidential online community for current and former religious leaders in vocational ministry who no longer hold supernatural beliefs and are struggling with issues such as finding a way out of the ministry, looking for new careers, telling their families and friends about their lack of faith and living as a nonbeliever with religious spouses and family. It originated from a growing awareness of the presence of these professional clergy and a concern about their dilemma as they moved beyond faith and currently there are over six hundred Forum participants. The Forum is an online meeting place where former and active professional clergy can talk freely among themselves with participants having been personally screened to verify they are active or former professional clergy/religious leaders who do not hold supernatural beliefs. One such participant is John Compere, a fifth-generation Baptist minister who was ordained at age eighteen while in college and served until age thirty-two when he left the ministry to get a PhD in Clinical Psychology. In his own words, "I had already completed a three-year seminary degree following college, which only increased my doubts about the authenticity of the theology I had learned from childhood. Leaving the ministry was not an easy decision to make since all my friends and family were in the church, but it was a decision I ultimately had to make if I didn't want to risk being publicly phony and privately cynical. I became an agnostic, then an atheist, not because I hadn't read the Bible, but because I had."

News stories about the Clergy Project began appearing in outlets from *MSNBC* to *NPR* to the *Religious News Service* to *CNN* and as a result applications to join have been going up at an even more dramatic rate. The cascade of news stories began when Methodist minister Teresa MacBain came to the American Atheists convention and made a dramatic unscheduled appearance at the podium to announce she was an atheist saying, "Being in a group of people with whom I could share openly without fear of persecution gave me the courage to come out. The opportunity to stand before the crowd, come out as an atheist and share about the Clergy Project was too good to pass up. I was at the end of my rope and I knew it. It was now or never for me. As I walked up on that stage, I felt fear like no other." MacBain had been questioning her faith since her early teens when she came across contradictions in the Bible. "I went to my dad for answers," she said. "He simply shared that God's ways are so much higher than our ways that we cannot understand everything in the Bible. Our response should be faith, not doubting. He then told me doubting was a sin. I left that day and suppressed those questions. This practice followed me for decades." Eventually the questions became too much and she let go of her biblical literalism which at first helped resolve her doubts about biblical contradictions, but this soon made room for other questions. "Things such as theodicy (the problem of suffering and evil), the question of Hell, God's omnipotence yet lack of intervention in heinous events, the historicity of Jesus... all these bubbled to the surface and demanded to be answered. My work to answer these questions began with the thought that as I discovered the truth it would create a stronger faith and give me comforting answers to those in my church who were dealing with the same issues. Instead, the truth I found led me away from faith."

Even Pope Francis sparked a debate when he said at morning Mass on May 22, 2013 that God redeems everyone, even atheists. "Just do good, and we'll find a meeting point," he said. Fair enough. So then what exactly is the point of continuing on with all the dogma, tithing and evangelizing? After all "just do good" is the Humanist mantra. The Pope seems to be channeling pagan Roman Emperor Marcus Aurelius who is attributed with saying, "Live a good life. If there are gods and they are just, then they will not care how devout you have been, but will welcome you based on the virtues you have lived by. If there are gods, but unjust, then you should not want to worship them. If there are no gods, then you will be gone, but will have lived a noble life that will live on in the memories of your loved ones." Amen.

A modern take on that rationale is the Atheist's Wager, a response to Pascal's Wager regarding the existence of God which was formulated in

1990 by Michael Martin in his book *Atheism: A Philosophical Justification* and has received some traction in religious and atheist literature since. It suggests one should live a good life without religion since a loving and kind god would reward good deeds and if no gods exist a good person will leave behind a positive legacy. If you were to analyze your options in regard to how to live your life you would come out with the following possibilities: If you live a good life and believe in god and a benevolent god exists you go to Heaven and your gain is infinite. If you live a good life without believing in god and a benevolent god exists you go to Heaven and your gain is infinite. If you live a good life and believe in god but no benevolent god exists you leave a positive legacy to the world and your gain is finite. If you live a good life without believing in god and no benevolent god exists you leave a positive legacy to the world and your gain is finite.

Conversely if you live an evil life and believe in god and a benevolent god exists you go to Hell and your loss is infinite. If you live an evil life without believing in god and a benevolent god exists you go to Hell and your loss is infinite. If you live an evil life and believe in god but no benevolent god exists you leave a negative legacy to the world and your loss is finite. If you live an evil life without believing in god and no benevolent god exists you leave a negative legacy to the world and your loss is finite. In other words, just be nice.

Clearly the option to live a good life dominates the option of living an evil life regardless of belief in a god. The real question is should we believe an invisible being is monitoring the every action, and even the thoughts, of seven billion people, keeping score, answering (some) prayers and sending some people to eternal paradise and others to eternal torture based on whether or not those people believe in something for which there is no evidence? Wouldn't it make more sense if there is another "astral plane" to which our consciousness simply goes when our physical bodies die? I am not suggesting that is the case mind you, but it makes a lot more sense than the dogmatic religious beliefs which people have long held.

Charles Bradlaugh has said, "No religion is suddenly rejected by any people. It is rather gradually outgrown. No one sees a religion die. Dead religions are like dead languages and obsolete customs: the decay is long and - like the glacier march - perceptible only to the careful watcher by comparisons extending over long periods." While still true, this phenomenon is accelerating in the modern world due to the rapid spread of scientific and philosophical information through books, the internet and television. The handwriting is on the wall. Naturally some fundamentalist Christians consider the Internet to be a "tool of the devil" because it facilitates the dissemination of information and provides a forum for debate while conveniently forgetting the hundreds of pro-Christian websites which litter the online landscape, but such protests are futile. In *Humanity's Gain From Unbelief* Chapman Cohen wrote, "The defenders of Godism are now shrieking against the growing number of Atheists, and there is a call to the religious world to enter upon a crusade against Atheism. The stage in which heresy meant little more than an exchange of one God for another has passed. It has become a case of acceptance or rejection of the idea of God, and the growth is with those who reject."

Another factor is the growing move towards Humanism, which is a philosophy based in altruism and compassion. This system of thought attaches prime importance to human rather than divine or supernatural matters and Humanist beliefs stress the potential value and goodness of human beings, emphasize common human needs and seek solely rational ways of solving human problems. In short human self-worth trumps self-loathing and the idea we are sinners. What is wrong with that worldview?

Bill Maher, when chastised for going after religion because people say it gives people comfort and doesn't hurt anything, replied by saying, "Okay, well, other than most wars, the Crusades, the Inquisition, 9/11, arranged marriages to minors, blowing up girls schools, the suppression of women and homosexuals, fatwas, ethnic cleansing, honor rape, human sacrifice, burning witches, suicide bombings, condoning slavery and the systematic f*cking of children… there's a few little things that I have a problem with. What I'm mad at him (the Pope) for is going to the continent most ravaged by AIDS and telling them they couldn't use condoms. So don't tell me religion doesn't do any actual harm." If that sounds harsh let's flip the script and consider the words of Christian anti-abortion activist Randall Terry who said, "I want you to just let a wave of intolerance wash over you. I want you to let a wave of hatred wash over you. Yes, hate is good.... our goal is a Christian nation. We have a biblical duty, we are called by God, to conquer this country. We don't want equal time. We don't want pluralism."

One way to keep the sheep in the fold was by making it a crime to question. Consider that on May 24, 1842 George Holyoake was arrested in London and charged with the crime of blasphemy. For more than nine hours he addressed the jury in an eloquent and learned appeal that freedom of speech was a priceless heritage of mankind, that liberty of opinion was essential to the progress and happiness of man and that blasphemy was an imaginary offense saying, "Morality I regard, but I do not believe there is such a thing as God." The jury found him guilty anyway and he was sentenced to six months in prison.

Abner Kneeland was an American evangelist and theologian who advocated many views, religious and social, which were considered extremely radical for his day and due to his very public stance on these issues became the last man jailed in the United States for blasphemy. He served as minister of various churches for a time, helped organize hymnals and made his own translation of the New Testament but he also debated other theologians of the day and as time went on became more and more skeptical of revealed religion, causing schisms in the churches he administered. Eventually he and the Universalist Church parted ways after his views became too far removed from Christianity. Kneeland became a freethinker and pantheist, saying the Universalists' Christian God was "nothing more than a chimera of their own imagination." He also believed in equal treatment for all people, both under the law as well as by society, and applied this even when religious Scripture would seem to indicate different roles. This included support of such controversial ideas as divorce rights for women, married women keeping their own names and property, birth control and refusal to condemn miscegenation (now known as interracial marriage). He even allowed fiery abolitionist William Lloyd Garrison the use of his lecture hall when the churches in Boston had turned him away. Under the colonial charter of Massachusetts blasphemy was still a crime, albeit one rarely punished, and perhaps because his views inflamed the judiciary Kneeland was charged with having violated the law and tried in 1838 five years after he had published the statements which had caused the upset, described by the judge as "a cantankerous and inflexible heretic." He was convicted and served sixty days in prison.

We have come a long way since that time, as a species are growing in our disbelief and as a result the social stigma which has traditionally accompanied that position had gradually dissipated. Like the child in *The Emperor's New Clothes* humanity is beginning to come to terms with reality. As Phil Slattery has observed, "To have an invisible friend at the age of eight is charming and not a cause for concern. To have an invisible friend in adulthood is however a cause for concern and could be considered psychotic. So how exactly does giving them the name of a deity change that opinion?"

The Bible is proof of God and the Quran proof of Allah in the same way lightning is proof of Thor, waves are proof of Neptune, rainbows are proof of leprechauns, Christmas presents are proof of Santa, colored eggs are proof of the Easter Bunny and comic books are proof of Spiderman. It is time for mankind to grow up and finally heed the words of Plato who a very long time ago said, “We can easily forgive a child who is afraid of the dark, (but) the real tragedy of life is when men are afraid of the light.” Open your eyes and step into the light

Epilogue

☥☯⛩ॐ✋☸✡✝☪☬

"If you have to lie to prove what you believe, then what you believe is a lie." ~ Frater Ravus

Many people are surprised by my worldview, especially once they learn I am a career Marine and was raised as a Christian by a Christian family in a Christian community. Like many people I once accepted faith without question but then one day everything began to change. One Saturday morning I was sleeping in when I heard the phone ring. My Mother answered it, I heard part of the conversation and my heart sank. My Father, who was working at his weekend job (he had three in total) had suffered a heart attack and had been taken to the hospital. As my Mother left the house I prayed harder than I ever had for my Dad to be okay. He was the best man I knew. He was a hard worker and a good provider. He was a patriot who had landed at Normandy in the first wave and fought in the Battle of the Bulge. Most importantly he was a loving Father to both myself and my two younger sisters. My Dad had never been sick or missed a day of work that I could recall and I just knew his strength, coupled with medical treatment and the power of my prayers, would see him home safely. I knew that because John 14:13-14 says, "And whatever you ask in my name, that will I do, that the Father may be glorified in the Son. If you ask me anything in my name, I will do it." I was also aware of the admonition found in James 4:3, "You ask and do not receive, because you ask with wrong motives, so that you may spend it on your pleasures," but that clearly did not apply so I awaited good news with total confidence as I continued my heartfelt prayers. It didn't come. My Father had suffered a massive heart attack and had been DOA at the hospital. He was only forty-nine years old. He would never see us grow up or marry, never see his as yet unborn grandchildren and wouldn't be around to offer the guidance only a Father can provide as we went out into the world. As the eldest at sixteen and the only son (I had a half brother and sister but they were grown and lived far away) it fell to me to make the funeral arrangements because my Mother was totally devastated and incapable of making any decisions. I chose the casket, picked out the suit my Dad would wear and even planned the funeral. Over the coming months and years I lost count of the times my Mom would break down in tears because of a song on the radio or a memory which came to mind and each time she sobbed on my shoulder and asked the same question over and over... why? I had no answer of course, but at the wake I had tried my best to make sense of it for her. I said, "God needed Dad in Heaven" because in my eyes my Father was great and who wouldn't need him, but I was quickly corrected by a family friend who was a priest and would be doing the eulogy. He said, "God needs no man. He *wanted* him." It was at that moment I questioned the goodness of God for the first time. "He has an entire universe and can do anything he wants, so why take a good man away from his loving family?" I wondered. It seemed quite selfish, unnecessary and unreasonable. Naturally people offered the usual clichés well-meaning friends use in an attempt to offer comfort such as, "God moves in mysterious ways" and "God has purposes we can't understand" and even "Some good will come of this, you'll see," but what ended up happening in reality was I had to drop out of high school to work at menial jobs and support the family and that meant I would not be able to go to college. My Mother, for her part, was never the same and was miserable for the rest of her days. As I discussed earlier in this book my Mother and older sister were later stricken with cancer and died horrible deaths, and my middle sister lost two babies in the womb. In each case I wondered why God had not answered our prayers, so I began to think about the possible reasons. I had at this point in my life never heard the "Riddle of Epicurus" but arrived at similar conclusions on my own. Was God not powerful enough to do anything? But I was taught he is omnipotent. Did God not hear our prayers or know about our suffering? But I was taught he is omniscient. Was God evil, and did he enjoy watching people suffer? But I was taught he was the embodiment of all that is good. Was God indifferent to suffering? But if all the other qualities of God were true how could he know about suffering, be good and loving, have the power to do something about it... and not do it? That left just one more possibility - there was *no* God. In a way that made me feel much better. I could accept that death and disease are part of life and have natural causes and consequences which we can understand, but believing in a God who either doesn't care or lacks the power to help us is pointless and worshipping one who is evil is just wrong. I did leave open the door to faith, don't get me wrong, but at this point would no longer accept it blindly and without question. As time went on I went from someone who simply questioned the existence of God to someone who saw the harm religious beliefs and practices could cause and it soon dawned on me there were many ways in which religion causes harm and suffering. Aside from the obvious ones such as religious wars and conflicts I thought about children being denied medical care in favor of prayer, homosexuals being persecuted to the point of suicide, people taking the law into their own hands and executing abortion doctors, the denial of contraception which contributes to overpopulation and the spread of disease, the stifling of scientific research and the injection of religious dogma into public schools and on and on and on. I do of course realize churches do some good charitable work and can lend a sense of community but those same things can and are being accomplished in secular environments as well.

As I thought back one other thing occurred to me. Like most children my religious beliefs had been inculcated since the moment of birth - from my "covenant with God" circumcision to my Baptism and other dogmatic rites and practices. There was a crucifix hanging over my bed and it was so familiar I never thought twice about the bizarre image of a man nailed to two pieces of wood. I had (and still have) a Bible presented to me by my parents. Most of all I had belief because my parents said it was so, my church said it was so, my friends said it was so and who was I to argue with all that authority? So I imagine if my Dad had come home from the hospital that day and lived a full life and my Mother and sister had gone into remission and shared the ensuing years with me I would have given thanks to God and had my belief in the power of prayer reinforced, but that is not what happened. I realize some of the faithful will claim I am simply "mad at God" due to those events but that is not the case. The painful, and as it turns out liberating, message to me was the things which happen in our lives can be explained by natural causes, statistical probabilities which dictate good outcomes vs. bad (which gives the illusion of answered prayers) and our own actions. Eventually this led me to study religion - not just the one I was raised in, but all religion - and I now have a greater understanding of the universe and life than I could ever have gotten through the faith I had once practiced. As a result I am today embarrassed by the apologetics I once regurgitated to make excuses for God and explain why he did X or didn't do Y because in retrospect they are illogical and indefensible. In other words I decided it is better to care about my beliefs being true than it is to find comfort in a cozy cocoon of willful ignorance. God had his chance, he didn't show up, and I consider this book of logic, rational thought and common sense to be my liberating gift to mankind.